Sicily

Aeolian Islands
p141

Palermo
p54

Tyrrhenian Coast
p122

Western Sicily
p91

Ionian Coast
p168

Central Sicily
p239

Mediterranean Coast
p255

Syracuse & the Southeast
p200

Gregor Clark, Brett Atkinson,
Cristian Bonetto, Nicola Williams

Contents

STALLHOLDER AT MERCATO DELLA VUCCIRIA P59

ANDREW MONTGOMERY/LONELY PLANET ©

GELATO P310

IOANA CIUSH/SHUTTERSTOCK ©

ON THE ROAD

MASTER2/GETTY IMAGES ©

BEACH AT MONDELLO P79

Contents

SOLOSERGIO/SHUTTERSTOCK ©

CARNEVALE AT ACIREALE P192

Welcome to Sicily

Eternal crossroads of the Mediterranean, the gorgeous island of Sicily continues to lure travellers with its dazzling diversity of landscapes and cultural treasures.

Classical Crossroads

Seductively beautiful and perfectly placed in the heart of the Mediterranean, Sicily has been luring passersby since the time of legends. The land of the Cyclops has been praised by poets from Homer to Virgil and prized by the Phoenicians, Carthaginians, Elymians, Romans and Greeks, whose bones lie buried here. Whether in the classical perfection of Agrigento's Concordia temple, the monumental rubble of Selinunte's columns or the rare grace of a dancing satyr statue rescued from Mazara del Vallo, reminders of bygone civilisations are everywhere.

Mediterranean Flavours

A delectable layer-cake of culinary influences, Sicily's ancient cuisine continues to rely on key island-grown ingredients: shellfish and citrus, tuna and swordfish, pistachios, almonds and ricotta. Talk to the septuagenarian chef at a Catania restaurant and she'll confide that she still uses her grandmother's recipe for *pasta alla Norma*, joyfully sharing the poetic imagery that links it to Mt Etna: the tomatoes are lava; the eggplant, cinders; the basil, leafy greenery; the ricotta, snow. Modern chefs may play with the details, but Sicily's timeless recipes – from the simplest *cannolo* to the most exquisite fish couscous – live on.

Seas & Restless Mountains

Sicily's varied landscape makes a dramatic first impression. Fly into Catania and the smoking hulk of Etna greets you; arrive in Palermo and it's the sparkling Golfo di Castellammare. This juxtaposition of sea, volcano and mountain scenery makes a stunning backdrop for outdoor activities. Hikers can wind along precipitous coastlines, climb erupting volcanoes and traipse through flowery mountain meadows; birders benefit from the plethora of species on the Africa–Europe migration route; and divers and swimmers enjoy some of the Mediterranean's most pristine waters.

Byzantine to Baroque

As if its classical heritage weren't formidable enough, Sicily is bursting at the seams with later artistic and architectural gems. In a short walk around Palermo you'll see Arab domes and arches, Byzantine mosaics and Norman palace walls. Circle around to southeast Sicily and you'll find a stunning array of baroque architectural masterpieces, from the golden-hued domes of Noto to the multi-tiered cathedral facades of Ragusa and Modica. Meanwhile, throughout the island you'll find yourself stumbling upon the evocative remains of Arab and Norman castles.

Why I Love Sicily

By Gregor Clark, Writer

Decades after my first visit, I still find Sicily one of the world's most captivating places. Among the island's innumerable charms, here are a few personal favourites: the ever-present scent of lemon trees, the purity of dawn light on terracotta walls, the colourful decrepitude of Palermo's markets, the drama of Stromboli erupting against a darkening sky, the sense that history lurks always just around the next corner, the reflective marble glow of late-night Ortygia and Marsala streets, the lonely majesty of Segesta, the exotic flavours of Sicilian food and the island's endless cultural complexities.

For more about our writers, see p352.

Above: Ragusa Ibla (p233)

Sicily

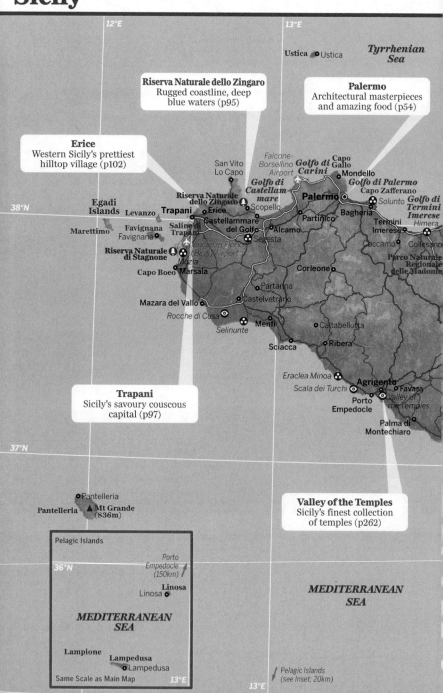

Ustica ○ Ustica

Tyrrhenian Sea

Riserva Naturale dello Zingaro
Rugged coastline, deep blue waters (p95)

Palermo
Architectural masterpieces and amazing food (p54)

Erice
Western Sicily's prettiest hilltop village (p102)

Falcone-Borsellino Airport · San Vito Lo Capo · **Capo Gallo** · **Mondello** · *Golfo di Carini*

Golfo di Castellammare · **Palermo** · *Golfo di Palermo* · Capo Zafferano · **Soluto** · *Golfo di Termini Imerese*

Egadi Islands · Levanzo · **Trapani** · **Riserva Naturale dello Zingaro** · Erice · Scopello

Marettimo · **Favignana** · Favignana · Saline di Trapani · Castellammare del Golfo · Alcamo · Partinico · Bagheria · Termini Imerese · Himera · Caccamo · Collesano

Riserva Naturale di Stagnone · Mozia · *Vincenzo Florio (Birgi) Airport* · Segesta · Corleone · **Parco Naturale Regionale delle Madonie**

Capo Boeo · Marsala · Partanna · Castelvetrano

Mazara del Vallo · *Rocche di Cusa* · Menfi · Cattabellotta

Selinunte · Sciacca · Ribera

Eraclea Minoa · **Agrigento** · Favara · *Scala dei Turchi* · Porto Empedocle · *Valley of the Temples* · Palma di Montechiaro

Trapani
Sicily's savoury couscous capital (p97)

Valley of the Temples
Sicily's finest collection of temples (p262)

38°N · 37°N · 12°E · 13°E

Pelagic Islands

○ Pantelleria

Pantelleria · ▲ **Mt Grande** (836m)

Porto Empedocle (150km)

Linosa · Linosa ○

36°N

MEDITERRANEAN SEA

MEDITERRANEAN SEA

Lampione · **Lampedusa** · ○ Lampedusa

Same Scale as Main Map · 13°E · 13°E

Pelagic Islands (see Inset; 20km)

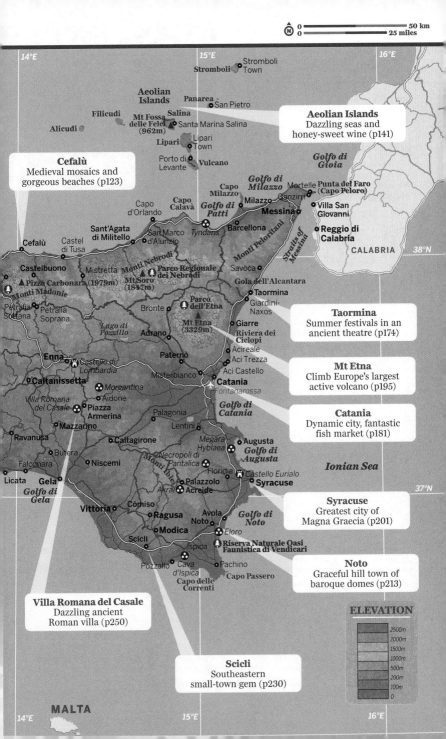

Sicily's
Top
14

Syracuse

1 Alight from the train or bus station into Syracuse's sterile modern centre, and you just might wonder what the fuss is all about. But enter the labyrinthine alleyways of the ancient island of Ortygia or the vast archaeological park north of town and layers of history will soon have you swooning. Suddenly you're standing in a vast field of Greek ruins (p206), gazing down over delicate papyrus plants in an ancient pool or wandering through a glimmering marble-paved square where ancient temple columns peek out from under a cathedral's baroque facade. Fontana Aretusa (p207)

Valley of the Temples

2 The magnificent temples of Agrigento's Valley of the Temples (p262) make an impression like no other ruins in Sicily. Strung out along the long rocky promontory where the ancient Greeks erected them 2500 years ago, their magical aura is enhanced at night, when they're brilliantly floodlit. On summer evenings, don't miss the chance to walk among the temples of the Eastern Zone after dark, an experience unparalleled at any other Sicilian ancient site. A short way up the hill, Agrigento's Museo Archeologico is one of the island's finest museums. Tempio dei Dioscuri (p264)

Cefalù

3 With its long sandy beach hugging the sparkling Tyrrhenian Sea, and its twin cathedral towers juxtaposed against La Rocca's rugged heights, Cefalù (p123) provokes many a 'love at first sight' reaction. The dazzling Byzantine mosaics of the cathedral's apse, the golden-hued towers (newly opened to the public in 2019) and the carved columns of its cloister will keep you busy on a rainy day, but once summer rolls around it's hard to resist the waterfront's allure. You won't find a better blend of beach resort and medieval town centre anywhere in Italy.

Aeolian Islands

4 Extraordinarily beautiful and surprisingly diverse, the seven volcanic islands of the Aeolian archipelago (p141) are packed with standout attractions – Vulcano's smoking crater, Salina's verdant vineyards, Panarea's whitewashed luxury hotels – yet their greatest appeal may lie in their slower rhythm. With very few cars and zero stress, this place feels a world apart from the Sicilian 'mainland'. You might just want to adopt the same mindset, lingering here your whole trip and saving 'Sicily' for later. View from Vulcano (p151)

Palermo

5 Sicily's endlessly fascinating capital (p56) is a full-on urban adventure. Recent initiatives including street art projects, expanded pedestrian zones and revamped cultural venues have brought new vibrancy to this ancient city. Meanwhile, the age-old attractions endure: the exquisite carved ceilings and mosaic-covered arches of the Cappella Palatina, the cacophonous singing of vendors at Mercato di Ballarò, the harmonic perfection of an opera performance at Teatro Massimo, or poring through millennia of well-catalogued treasures at the Museo Archeologico Regionale. Quattro Canti (p56)

Open-Air Performances

6 Aeschylus himself would doubtless be pleased to see Greek drama still flourishing in Syracuse's great amphitheatre, two-and-a-half millennia later. Every spring, the Festival of Greek Theatre brings a month's worth of live performances to the very venue where the playwright once sat. Come summer, the action moves up the coast to Taormina's Teatro Greco (p174; pictured), where you can watch everything from international film premieres to famous rockers, dancers and divas performing under balmy evening skies, all with Mt Etna as the scenic backdrop.

JONATHON STOKES/LONELY PLANET ©

MARCO OSSINO/SHUTTERSTOCK ©

Markets

7 A feast for the senses, Palermo's markets offer a heady mix of experiences. Mercato di Ballarò (p59) is as much akin to a North African bazaar as to a mainland Italian market: fruit vendors raucously hawk their wares in Sicilian dialect, with the irresistible perfume of lemons and oranges and the crackle of chickpea fritters emerging from the deep-fryer. Across the island, Catania's La Pescheria (p182) offers an equally evocative slice of Sicilian life. Mercato del Capo (p59), Palermo

Villa Romana del Casale

8 Located in a forested valley near Piazza Armerina, this Unesco-listed site (p250) – originally a lavish 4th-century villa – showcases the world's finest examples of ancient Roman floor mosaics. Highlights include the Ambulacro della Grande Caccia, an astonishing 64m-long corridor studded with mosaics featuring exotic animals including tigers, leopards and elephants, while the Sala delle Dieci Ragazze (Room of the Ten Girls) presents striking female athletes in surprisingly contemporary style.

Smouldering Volcanoes

9 Never content to sit still, Sicily's great volcanoes keep belching sulphurous steam and sending fireworks into the night sky. Three and a half centuries after burying Catania in volcanic ash, Mt Etna (p195; pictured) still broods over the city, while Stromboli continues lighting the way for passing ships as it did in ancient times. Climbing either of these fiery beauties is easily done in a day, or you can just admire them from afar. Either way, they're an unforgettable part of the Sicilian experience.

Erice

10 With every hairpin curve on the long climb to Erice, it seems that the views can't possibly get any better. But they do. Save your camera battery for the top of the hill, where the Norman Castello di Venere (p102; pictured) affords 360-degree perspectives clear out to San Vito Lo Capo, the Egadi Islands and the salt pools and windmills of the Saline di Trapani. It's small wonder that earlier cultures considered this a sacred site, building a temple to Venus that even earned a mention in Virgil's *Aeneid*.

Baroque Scicli

11 Southeastern Sicily's baroque towns, from Noto to Modica to Ragusa, form one of the island's most captivating itineraries. The most authentic of the lot, Scicli (p230) has long been something of a sleeper, but these days it's attracting world-famous photographers, designers and entrepreneurs. The baroque architecture is breathtaking, many of its aristocratic palaces have been recently restored, and it is famous for being one of the main shooting locations for the TV series *Inspector Montalbano*. Chiesa di San Bartolomeo (p231)

Hill Towns

12 Sicily's interior is a rugged place, full of rocky outcrops, precipitous hillsides and fields parched by the summer sun. It can sometimes look downright uninhabitable, but scan the horizon and you'll quickly find evidence of the island's long centuries of human settlement. Picturesquely perched hill towns such as Enna, Caltabellotta, Caccamo, Gangi, Noto (p213) and San Marco d'Alunzio are sprinkled throughout the island, most of them clinging to vertigo-inducing heights and crowned by crumbling Norman castles or traces of other long-past civilisations. Castello di Caccamo (p128)

MATT MUNRO/LONELY PLANET ©

LUCKY TEAM STUDIO/SHUTTERSTOCK ©

BRENT HOFACKER/SHUTTERSTOCK ©

WESTEND61/GETTY IMAGES ©

Sicilian Cuisine

13 Sicilian cuisine (p306) will alter your concept of Italian food. Ingredients that repeatedly appear include citrus, wild fennel and mint, pistachios and almonds, cherry tomatoes, capers and olives, tuna and sardines, swordfish and shrimp. In Catania, you'll find uniquely Sicilian treats such as *pasta alla Norma*, made with local eggplants and ricotta. In Trapani, tuck into saffron-scented couscous. In Palermo, try *pasta con le sarde* (pasta with sardines, pine nuts, raisins, fennel and breadcrumbs). Remember to save room for dessert such as *cannoli* and *cassata*. Cannoli (p309)

Riserva Naturale dello Zingaro

14 Straddling the grand sweep of the Golfo di Castellammare, Sicily's oldest nature reserve (p95) is a thing of beauty. Back in the 1980s, highway engineers were poised to build a highway through this rugged stretch of coastline, but conservationists prevailed. The result is one of Sicily's unique gems, a traffic-free coastal park scalloped with pristine coves, threaded with hiking trails, and dotted with museums that celebrate local flora, fauna, tuna fishing and agricultural traditions.

Need to Know

For more information, see Survival Guide (p327).

Currency

euro (€)

Language

Italian

Visas

Generally not required for stays of up to three months.

Money

ATMs widely available. Credit cards accepted in most hotels and restaurants.

Mobile Phones

Italian mobile phones operate on the GSM 900/1800 network. If you have an unlocked phone that supports these frequencies, you can purchase a *pre-pagato* (pre-paid) SIM card in Italy for as little as €10.

Time

Central European Time (GMT/UTC plus one hour)

When to Go

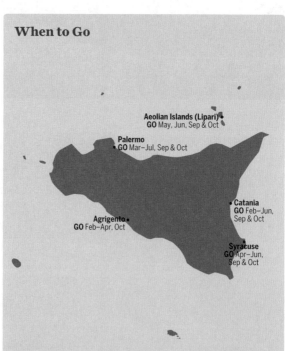

Aeolian Islands (Lipari)
GO May, Jun, Sep & Oct

Palermo
GO Mar–Jul, Sep & Oct

Catania
GO Feb–Jun, Sep & Oct

Agrigento
GO Feb–Apr, Oct

Syracuse
GO Apr–Jun, Sep & Oct

High Season (Jul–Aug)

➡ Prices skyrocket, especially around Ferragosto (15 August), and roads and beaches are jam-packed.

➡ Festival season in Taormina, Palermo and Piazza Armerina.

➡ Good time to escape to the cooler climate of Sicily's mountains.

Shoulder (Apr–Jun & Sep–Oct)

➡ Best period for good weather and reasonable prices.

➡ Spring is ideal for coastal hiking, wildflowers and local produce.

➡ June and September are best for diving.

➡ Easter is marked by colourful religious festivities.

Low Season (Nov–Mar)

➡ Accommodation prices drop by 30% or more.

➡ Offshore islands and coastal resorts largely shut down.

➡ Experience local culture without the crowds.

Useful Websites

Best of Sicily (www.bestofsicily.com) Comprehensive coverage of the island.

Lonely Planet (www.lonelyplanet.com/italy/sicily) Destination information, hotel bookings, traveller forum and more.

Visit Sicily (www.visitsicily.info) Sicily's official online tourism portal.

Important Numbers

Italy's country code	☑39
General emergency	☑112
Police	☑113
Fire	☑115
Ambulance	☑118

Exchange Rates

Australia	A$1	€0.61
Brazil	R$1	€0.23
Canada	C$1	€0.67
China	¥1	€0.13
Japan	¥100	€0.82
New Zealand	NZ$1	€0.58
Switzerland	Sfr1	€0.89
UK	UK£1	€1.12
US	US$1	€0.89

For current exchange rates, see www.xe.com.

Daily Costs
Budget: Less than €100

➡ Double room in a B&B or budget hotel: €60–80

➡ Pizza or pasta: €15–20

➡ Bus or train tickets: €5–10

Midrange: €100–200

➡ Double room in a hotel: €80–150

➡ Lunch and dinner in local restaurants: €30–60

Top end: More than €200

➡ Double room in a four- or five-star hotel: from €150

➡ Lunch and dinner in top restaurants €60–120

Opening Hours

Banks 8.30am to 1.30pm and 2.45pm to 4pm Monday to Friday.

Cafes 7am to 8pm (or later if offering bar service at night).

Museums Hours vary, but many close on Monday.

Restaurants Noon to 2.30pm and 7.30pm to 11pm; many close one day per week.

Shops 9.30am to 1.30pm and 4pm to 7.30pm Monday to Saturday.

Arriving in Sicily

Palermo Falcone-Borsellino Airport Trains (€6) and buses (€6.50) run to the city centre every 30 to 60 minutes from 5am to 12.30am. Taxis cost €35 to €45. The journey takes from 30 minutes to an hour.

Catania Fontanarossa Airport AMT's Alibus (€4, 20 to 30 minutes) runs from the airport to the train station every 25 minutes. Taxis cost €18 to €22.

Trapani-Birgi Vincenzo Florio Airport (Trapani) Buses (€4.90, 20 minutes) run hourly to Trapani's bus station and port. Taxis cost €30.

Dangers & Annoyances

➡ Despite Mafia notoriety, Sicily is not a dangerous place. The likelihood of your trip being affected by crime is low, especially if you follow a few common sense precautions, just as you would in your home country:

➡ Be aware of your surroundings, and don't flaunt your valuables.

➡ Avoid carrying large amounts of cash in unsecured pockets.

➡ Don't carelessly leave phones, purses or cameras lying about in plain view in a street-side cafe or parked vehicle.

➡ Your general attitude should be one of prevention, not paranoia. In the unlikely event that you are the victim of petty theft or other crime, always report it to the police within 24 hours, and ask for a statement (your travel insurance company will require this of you).

➡ Sicilian traffic can be a daunting prospect, especially in Palermo and Catania. Outside the main urban centres, the situation calms down and the main concerns become curvy roads, potholes and iffy signposting. As a general rule, traffic is at its quietest around lunchtime, especially on Sunday, when few people are out and about.

First Time Sicily

For more information, see Survival Guide (p327).

Checklist

➡ Check your passport: it should be valid for six months beyond your return date from Italy.

➡ Organise travel insurance.

➡ Pre-book popular festivals, opera and theatre performances, rental cars and accommodation.

➡ Inform your credit-card company of your travel plans.

➡ Check if you can use your mobile (cell) phone in Sicily.

What to Pack

➡ Sturdy shoes for walking/hiking, sandals for the beach

➡ Round two-pin electrical adapter (to fit Italian sockets)

➡ Picnic-friendly pocket knife with corkscrew

➡ Sunglasses, sunscreen and a hat

➡ Driver's licence and map if hiring a car

➡ Mobile (cell) phone charger

Top Tips for Your Trip

➡ Late spring and early autumn are ideal times to visit Sicily; temperatures are more moderate, prices are lower and crowds are smaller than in July and August.

➡ Most accommodation prices in Sicily include a simple breakfast.

➡ Sicilians dine late, especially in bigger cities, where restaurants don't typically start filling until after 9pm.

➡ Low-cost Italian SIM cards offering generous text and data plans are readily available for unlocked mobile (cell) phones.

➡ *Cannoli* pastries are meant to be eaten with your fingers!

What to Wear

Appearances matter in Italy. The concept of *la bella figura* (literally 'making a good impression') encapsulates the Italian obsession with beauty, gallantry and looking good. In cities, suitable wear for men is generally trousers and shirts or polo shirts, and for women skirts, trousers or dresses. Shorts, T-shirts and sandals are fine for summer and at the beach. For evening wear, smart casual is the norm. A light long-sleeved top or waterproof jacket is useful in spring and autumn, and sturdy shoes are advisable at archaeological sites.

Sleeping

Booking is recommended during Pasqua (Easter Week) and in the busy summer months, especially along the coast.

➡ Agriturismi – working farms or country houses that offer rooms and often delicious home-cooked meals.

➡ B&Bs – range from basic to luxurious. Most have five rooms or fewer, sometimes with a shared bathroom outside the room.

➡ Pensioni – family-run guesthouses – facilities tend to be more basic (and prices lower) than at hotels.

➡ *Alberghi* (hotels) – ranked on a star system (one to five) based on amenities.

➡ *Rifugi* – offer simple accommodation for outdoors enthusiasts.

➡ *Affittacamere* – low-cost rooms rented out by private owners.

Driving

Always carry your driving licence, the vehicle's registration papers and proof of third-party (liability) insurance. All EU member states' driving licences are recognised in Sicily. Licences from the United States and most other major countries are valid in Sicily (including for rental vehicles), but drivers are technically required to provide an International Driving Licence or a certified translation of their home country license if stopped by police.

Bargaining

Gentle haggling is common in outdoor markets; in all other instances you're expected to pay the stated price.

Tipping

➡ Restaurants – Most have a cover charge (*coperto*, around €2), and some also levy a service charge (*servizio*, 10% to 15%). If there is no service charge, consider rounding the bill up.

➡ Bars – In cafes people often place a €0.10 or €0.20 coin on the bar when ordering coffee. Consider leaving small change when ordering drinks.

➡ Taxis – Optional, but most people round up to the nearest euro.

Language

English is not as widely spoken in Sicily as in northern Europe. In the main tourist centres you can get by, but in the countryside it will be helpful to master a few basic phrases. This will improve your experience no end, especially when ordering in restaurants, some of which have no written menu.

 What's the local speciality?
Qual'è la specialità di questa regione?
kwa·le la spe·cha·lee·ta dee kwes·ta re·jo·ne

A bit like the rivalry between medieval Italian city-states, these days the country's regions compete in speciality foods and wines.

 Which combined tickets do you have?
Quali biglietti cumulativi avete?
kwa·lee bee·lye·tee koo·moo·la·tee·vee a·ve·te

Make the most of your euro by getting combined tickets to various sights; they are available in all major Italian cities.

 Where can I buy discount designer items?
C'è un outlet in zona? che oon owt·let in zo·na

Discount fashion outlets are big business in major cities – get bargain-priced seconds, samples and cast-offs for *la bella figura*.

 I'm here with my husband/boyfriend.
Sono qui con il mio marito/ragazzo.
so·no kwee kon eel mee·o ma·ree·to/ra·ga·tso

Solo women travellers may receive unwanted attention in some parts of Italy; if ignoring fails have a polite rejection ready.

 Let's meet at 6pm for pre-dinner drinks.
Ci vediamo alle sei per un aperitivo.
chee ve·dya·mo a·le say per oon a·pe·ree·tee·vo

At dusk, watch the main piazza get crowded with people sipping colourful cocktails and snacking the evening away: join your new friends for this authentic Italian ritual!

Etiquette

➡ Greetings – Shake hands and say '*buongiorno*' (good day) or '*buona sera*' (good evening) to strangers; kiss both cheeks and say '*come stai?*' (how are you?) to friends. Use '*lei*' (formal 'you') in polite company; use '*tu*' (informal 'you') with friends and children. Only use first names if invited.

➡ Asking for help – Say '*mi scusi*' (excuse me) to get someone's attention; say '*permesso*' (permission) when you want to pass someone in a crowded space.

➡ Religious etiquette – Dress modestly (cover shoulders, torsos and thighs) and be quiet and respectful when visiting religious sites. Never intrude on a church service.

➡ Eating and drinking – At restaurants, summon the waiter by saying '*per favore*' (please). When dining in an Italian home, bring a small gift of sweets (*dolci*) or wine, and dress well.

➡ Avoid – Discussing the Mafia can be a touchy subject.

Getting Around Sicily

For more information, see Transport (p333).

Travelling by Car

Nothing beats the freedom of having your own car in Sicily, especially if you fancy exploring the island's wealth of rural villages, beaches and back roads. You'll do best to walk or use public transport in larger cities such as Palermo and Catania, where a car is more of a hindrance than a help – but once you leave the city behind, you'll appreciate Sicily's mix of efficient motorways and scenic back roads. Major toll routes, such as the A18 from Messina to Catania and the A20 between Messina and Palermo, are modern, well-signposted and fast, thanks to impressively engineered tunnels and bridges. With speed limits topping out at 130km/h, these motorways allow you to zip between Sicily's major cities. At the other end of the spectrum, Sicilian back roads can be slow, narrow, meandering and poorly maintained, but often offer fabulous scenery by way of compensation.

Car Hire

International rental agencies are well-represented in Sicily, with offices at the island's three main airports (Palermo, Catania and Trapani) and in several city centres. Advance reservations made through travel booking websites usually offer the best deals.

Parking

Metered street parking is widely available in Sicily's cities and towns, often supplemented by free parking in peripheral streets or at car parks outside the

RESOURCES

Automobile Club d'Italia (ACI; www.aci.it). Round-the-clock emergency breakdown services (☑80 31 16 or 800 11 68 00).

Autostrade per l'Italia (www.autostrade.it) Information about Sicily's *autostrade* (motorways), including road closures, traffic conditions and toll booth locations.

Touring Club Italiano (www.touringclubstore.com) Publishes high-quality regional and city maps, including a 1:200,000 map of Sicily and a 1:12,500 map of Palermo.

city centre. Paying spaces are marked by blue painted lines, while free spaces are marked with white lines. Rates for metered parking are reasonable (typically €1 or less per hour) – pay at the machine or at a local tobacconist and leave the ticket under your windscreen. More expensive garage parking is also an option in places like Palermo, Catania, Trapani and Milazzo.

Driving Conditions

Sicily's *autostrade* (motorways such as the A18, A19, A20 and A29) are generally well-maintained, as is the network of smaller national highways such as the SS113 along the Tyrrhenian Coast and the SS115 along the southern coast. As you head into Sicily's interior, conditions can deteriorate, with impediments such as broken pavements and poor signage becoming more frequent.

Tolls

Tolls are charged on the A18 and A20 motorways – pay at the booth when exiting. It's advisable to carry some small change with you, as a few toll booths are automated and will not accept credit cards. To calculate toll rates for your itinerary, see www.auto stradesiciliane.it/pedaggio.

No Car?

Air

Regularly scheduled commercial air travel within Sicily is limited to infrequent short-hop flights from Palermo, Catania and Trapani to Pantelleria and Lampedusa.

Boat

Ferries and hydrofoils run regularly to Sicily's offshore islands. Key ports include Milazzo for the Aeolian Islands, Palermo for Ustica, Trapani for Pantelleria

and the Egadi Islands, and Porto Empedocle for Lampedusa and the Pelagic Islands.

Bus

Several regional bus companies offer service throughout Sicily, including Interbus, SAIS and AST. Buses offer better service than trains on certain routes, including Palermo to Syracuse, Catania to Taormina and Trapani to Palermo.

Train

Sicily's rail network, operated by Trenitalia (www. trenitalia.com), is less extensive and less efficient than in many other parts of Italy, but train travel still offers an enjoyable, practical alternative to driving, especially along the main routes connecting Palermo, Messina and Catania. Other key destinations easily reached by train include Agrigento, Syracuse, Noto, Modica and Ragusa.

DRIVING FAST FACTS

➡ Drive on the left.

➡ All vehicle occupants must wear a seatbelt.

➡ Minimum age for a full licence is 18 years.

➡ Maximum speed 130 km/h on *autostrade,* 90km/h on secondary highways, 50km/h in built-up areas.

➡ Blood alcohol limit 50mg per 100ml (0.05%).

ROAD DISTANCES (KM)

	Agrigento	Catania	Messina	Palermo
Catania	165			
Messina	255	100		
Palermo	130	210	215	
Trapani	175	315	315	105

If You Like...

Ancient Sites

Teatro Greco, Taormina Divine architecture and dreamy setting converge at this splendid Greek theatre with front-row views of Mt Etna. (p174)

Segesta Crowning an isolated, windswept hillside, this perfect Doric temple is among Sicily's most magical spots. (p97)

Villa Romana del Casale This Roman villa's ancient floor mosaics are among the most extensive and best-preserved anywhere. (p250)

Valley of the Temples Agrigento's five splendidly arrayed temples and superb archaeological museum constitute Sicily's pre-eminent classical site. (p262)

Parco Archeologico della Neapolis Syracuse's vast complex of amphitheatres and altars is backed by citrus groves and limestone caves. (p206)

Selinunte One of western Sicily's top draws, Selinunte blends an idyllic coastal setting and a magnificent diversity of ruins. (p117)

Necropoli di Pantalica This honeycomb of Iron and Bronze Age tombs may have once been the capital of the ancient Siculian culture. (p212)

Coastal Walks

Stromboli Crater Nothing in Sicily compares to climbing Europe's most active volcano and watching the sun set over the Tyrrhenian Sea. (p160)

Riserva di Vendicari Flamingos migrate through this peaceful southeastern coastal reserve, a prime birdwatching spot. (p217)

Riserva Naturale dello Zingaro In Sicily's oldest nature reserve, a spectacular coastal trail zigzags past secluded coves and museums of local culture. (p95)

Punta Troia Follow the rugged coastline from Marettimo's whitewashed main village to a dramatically perched seaside castle. (p111)

Punta Spadillo Lighthouse-Cala Cottone Loop Jet-black volcanic rock, deep blue seas and a lonely white lighthouse greet you on this Pantelleria classic. (p121)

Beaches

Cefalù The Tyrrhenian's prettiest stretch of sand is backed by medieval streets and a palm-fringed cathedral. (p123)

Spiaggia dei Conigli Lampedusa's legendary white sands and turquoise waters welcome sunbathers by day and sea turtles by night. (p274)

Lido Mazzarò Sparkling far below Taormina, this idyllic cove's crystal-clear waters cradle the islet of Isola Bella. (p181)

Spiaggia Marianelli This tranquil sweep of sand and turquoise waves form part of the beautiful Riserva di Vendicari in Sicily's southeast. (p217)

Cala Rossa Slip into the electric-blue waters of this untamed sandless cove on Favignana's north shore. (p109)

Riserva Naturale Torre Salsa This remote beach is protected within a nature reserve administered by the World Wildlife Fund. (p266)

Performing Arts

Festival del Teatro Greco Watch classic Greek dramas in the same Syracusan theatre where Aeschylus once sat. (p207)

Teatro Massimo Palermo's great opera house makes for an elegant night out. (p65)

Teatro Massimo Bellini Classical concerts in classy surrounds are the hallmark of this opera house named for Catania's native son. (p190)

Taormina Arte Brings Taormina's ancient theatre back to life with world-class opera, dance, theatre and music performances. (p177)

Teatro dei Pupi di Mimmo Cuticchio Sword-wielding knights

Top: Temple ruins in Segesta (p97)

Bottom: Piscina di Venere (p139)

and damsels in distress delight multi-aged crowds at Palermo's traditional puppet theatre. (p75)

Dessert

I Segreti del Chiostro *Fedde del cancelliere* – made-to-order shell-shaped marzipan oozing with fresh apricot jam and almond pudding. (p74)

Minotauro *Cannoli* – crispy pastry tubes hand-filled on the spot with silky ricotta and dressed with pistachio, cinnamon and candied orange. (p177)

Da Alfredo *Granita alla mandorla* – a refreshing blend of crushed ice, local almonds and sugar – the perfect summertime treat. (p156)

Caffè Adamo *Gelati* – extraordinary flavour combos, including the highly addictive raspberry-pistachio, concocted by gelato maestro Antonio Adamo using the freshest seasonal ingredients. (p219)

Dolceria Bonajuto *Xocoatl* – hot peppers add an Aztec-inspired kick at Modica's famous chocolate factory. (p230)

Pasticceria di Maria Grammatico *Frutta martorana* – Marzipan fruit from Erice's famous confectioner. (p104)

Pasticceria Cappello *Delizia al pistacchio* – possibly the world's tastiest pistachio dessert, with an exquisite mix of creaminess and granular crunch. (p74)

Panoramic Vistas

Castello di Venere Fairy-tale coastal views extend from Erice's castle to the distant point of San Vito Lo Capo. (p102)

Quattrocchi Arched sea-rocks, precipitous cliffs and a smoking volcano on the horizon make this one of the Aeolians' unmissable viewpoints. (p147)

La Rocca A long-abandoned hilltop castle provides the moody backdrop for perfect views of Cefalù and the Tyrrhenian Sea beyond. (p126)

Piazza IX Aprile On a clear day, Taormina's main square offers mesmerising perspectives of Mt Etna and the Ionian Sea. (p175)

Chiesa di Santa Maria delle Scale Stunning views of Ragusa's lower town from this church astride a panoramic staircase. (p234)

Getting off the Beaten Track

CIDMA Learn about Sicilian resistance to the Mafia in Corleone. (p81)

Cave di Cusa This olive-shaded ancient quarry near Selinunte makes a prime picnic spot. (p120)

Filo dell'Arpa Climb to the top of Alicudi, the Aeolians' least-visited island. (p167)

Cala Pulcino The most remote beach on Lampedusa, Italy's southernmost island, reachable only by foot or boat. (p275)

Cretto di Burri Stroll the surreal streets of this village destroyed by a 1968 earthquake, then artistically encased in cement. (p118)

Parco Minerario Floristella Grottacalda Explore the poignant history of Sicily's sulphur-mining industry at this reserve south of Piazza Armerina. (p249)

Regional Cuisine

Trattoria di De Fiore *Pasta alla Norma* – Catania's signature pasta dish, made with

eggplants, ricotta, basil and tomatoes. (p188)

Relais Villa Miraglia *Grigliata mista di suino nero dei Nebrodi e castrato* – mixed grill of Nebrodi black pork and kid goat. (p135)

La Bettolaccia *Couscous alla trapanese* – Trapani's North African–inspired fish couscous, seasoned with saffron, garlic, tomatoes and parsley. (p99)

A Cannata *Caponata* – Sicily's classic appetiser of eggplant, tomatoes, olives and capers, at its best in the Aeolian Islands. (p156)

Francu U Vastiddaru *Pane e panelle*, chickpea fritters, fried eggplant and potato croquettes with a touch of mint, served on a sesame roll. (p72)

Cappero *Pasta che paddunedda* – a traditional broth of noodle-like pasta and small veal meatballs. (p219)

Punta Lena *Pesce spada alla ghiotta* – fish fillets with tomatoes, capers and olives. (p164)

Nangalarruni *Antipasto montagnolo* – cheeses, sausages and wild mushrooms of the Madonie Mountains. (p129)

Trattoria Il Veliero *Frittura mista* – heavenly fried shrimp and calamari. (p111)

Pescheria Fratelli Vittorio *Pesce crudo* – the freshest, sweetest, local raw seafood served in Catania's mighty La Pescheria fish market. (p189)

Outdoor Activities

Area Marina Protetta di Ustica This fabulous marine reserve off Ustica's western shore is one of the Mediterranean's top dive sites. (p82)

San Vito Lo Capo Backed by a rugged coastal promontory,

San Vito Lo Capo is Sicily's rock-climbing capital. (p94)

Piscina di Venere Swimmers couldn't ask for a more idyllic spot than this natural pool at the Mediterranean's edge. (p139)

Amici Del Cavallo Ride horses through the Valley of the Temples with this Agrigento-based outfit. (p258)

Sicily in Kayak Sail, kayak or stand-up paddle your way through the volcanic Aeolian Islands. (p153)

Prokite Alby Rondina Kitesurf a western Sicilian lagoon north of Marsala. (p108)

Cafeci This agency's many adventures include hiking with donkeys and exploring Mt Etna's storied slopes. (p249)

Baroque Art & Architecture

Basilica Cattedrale di San Nicolò Dominating Noto's skyline, this cathedral's golden-hued dome is one of Sicily's baroque masterpieces. (p213)

Duomo di San Giorgio (Modica) Gagliardi's three-tiered beauty of a facade is well worth the 250-step climb from lower Modica. (p218)

Oratorio di Santa Cita Search for snakes and cherubs in Giacomo Serpotta's swirling stuccowork at this 17th-century Palermitan chapel. (p64)

Duomo di San Giorgio (Ragusa) The town's pride and joy is this mid-18th-century cathedral with its magnificent dome and stained-glass windows. (p233)

Month by Month

January

Hot on the heels of the New Year comes Epiphany (6 January). On Etna and Monte Mufara in Madonie it's ski season.

February

Citrus orchards are heavy with fruit; almond blossoms begin to appear in Agrigento.

Carnevale

During the week before Ash Wednesday, many towns stage carnivals. The most flamboyant are in Sciacca (www.sciaccarnevale.it) and Acireale (www.carnevaleacireale.com).

Festa di Sant'Agata

One million Catanians follow a silver reliquary of St Agata through the city streets. This festival takes place from 3 to 5 February and is accompanied by spectacular fireworks.

Sagra del Mandorlo in Fiore

Performances of drama and music among the almond blossoms in the Valley of the Temples on the first Sunday in February.

March

Changeable weather. Easter Week marks the opening date for many seasonal businesses.

Pasqua (Easter)

Some of the most colourful Holy Week events take place in Trapani, Enna, Lipari, Scicli and Modica.

April

Markets overflow with wild strawberries, artichokes and fava beans. Weather is moody.

La Processione dei Misteri

For four days, Trapani's 20 traditional *maestranze* (guilds) parade life-sized wooden statues of the Virgin Mary and other Biblical figures through the streets.

May

Many places on outer islands are just opening for the season. It's a glorious time for walking on the Aeolians or in the Vendicari and Zingaro nature reserves.

Festival del Teatro Greco

Featuring world-class actors, the Festival of Greek Theatre, held from early May to early July, brings Syracuse's ancient amphitheatre to life (www.indafondazione.org).

Infiorata

At Noto's mid-May jamboree Via Corrada Nicolaci is decorated with works of art made entirely from flower petals.

June

Great month for walking in the mountains. Beaches are crowded on weekends.

★★ Taormina Film Fest

Hollywood big shots arrive in June or early July for a week of film screenings at the Teatro Greco.

★★ Marranzano World Fest

Catania's four-night world music festival, held at a historic monastery, brings acts from around the globe. (p187)

July

Sicilians are headed to mountains or beaches for summer holidays. Prices and temperatures rise.

★★ Ortigia Sound System

Ortygia reverberates with five summery days of electronic music, boat parties and a stellar line up.

★★ Festino Di Santa Rosalia

Palermo's biggest annual festival celebrates Santa Rosalia, the patron saint of the city.

★★ Taormina Arte

Opera, dance, theatre and live-music performances are staged at the Teatro Greco from June to September.

August

Hot, expensive and crowded. Everyone is on holiday and many businesses and restaurants close for part of the month.

★★ Ferragosto

After Christmas and Easter, Ferragosto, on 15 August, is Italy's biggest holiday. It marks the Feast of the Assumption. Beaches are jam-packed and city attractions open for limited hours only.

★★ Palio dei Normanni

Piazza Armerina's medieval pageant (between 12 and 14 August) commemorates Count Roger's taking of the town from the Moors in 1087.

September

Warm weather and sea temperatures but without the summer crowds.

★★ Cous Cous Fest

San Vito Lo Capo's famous fish couscous is celebrated annually at this 10-day event. The multicultural festivities involve musicians and chefs from around the world.

October

Businesses in the outer islands begin to curtail services, even as the chestnut harvest and wild mushroom seasons begin in earnest on Mt Etna and in the Madonie and Nebrodi Mountains.

★★ Le Vie dei Tesori

During this eight-week, island-wide 'Open House' – lasting from mid-September to early November – a vast array of venues around Sicily open their doors to celebrate its cultural heritage (www. leviedeitesori.com/festival -le-vie-dei-tesori).

★★ Funghi Fest

Fungus fans flock to Castelbuono to pick wild mushrooms, taste mushroom-based recipes from celebrity chefs, and celebrate the harvest with music and special events.

★★ Scale del Gusto

Ragusa's squares, streets and Unesco-listed buildings not usually open to the public become evocative settings for this buzzing celebration of Sicilian food and artisan food producers. (p234)

November

Chilly, rainy weather creeps in, and many places to stay in beach and island communities close for winter. Opera season in Palermo and Catania is in full swing.

December

The days of alfresco living are firmly at an end. December is chilly although impending Christmas festivities help warm things up.

★★ Festa di Santa Lucia

Syracuse's patron saint is commemorated with events such as a procession from the cathedral to Piazza Santa Lucia and fireworks. Held on 13 December.

★★ Natale

During the weeks preceding Christmas, many churches set up cribs or nativity scenes known as *presepi;* these are particularly notable in Caltagirone and Erice.

Itineraries

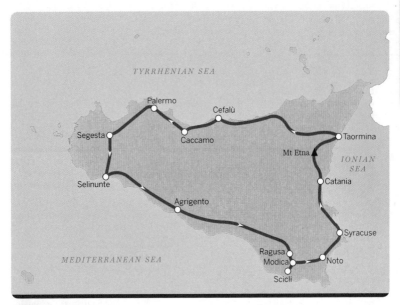

Only the Best

This two-week circle tour offers an introduction to Sicily's varied wonders – ancient archaeological sites, baroque hill towns, Arab-Norman churches and castles, volcanoes and beaches.

Begin in **Palermo**, where you can pick up a hire car for your circumnavigation of the island. After spending some time exploring the capital's diversity of architectural treasures, head southwest to the temples at **Segesta**, **Selinunte** and **Agrigento**. Next, cut east across the island to the Unesco-listed Val di Noto, where the baroque beauties of **Ragusa**, **Modica**, **Scicli** and **Noto** are all obligatory stops. From here it's on to **Syracuse**, a highlight of any trip to Sicily: split your time here between the pedestrian-friendly ancient island city of Ortygia and the vast classical ruins of the Parco Archeologico. Continue up the coast to bustling **Catania** and circle **Mt Etna** to reach **Taormina**, a town whose abundant attractions include its ancient Greek theatre and the gorgeous beaches just below. Finally, loop back to Palermo via **Cefalù** – where the beautiful beach and 12th-century cathedral will vie for your attention – and **Caccamo**, home to one of Sicily's most spectacularly sited Norman castles.

7 DAYS World Heritage Sites

Unesco has enshrined a multitude of Sicilian sites on its World Heritage list; this weeklong ramble offers a sampling, from the world-famous to the lesser-known.

Begin in **Syracuse**, one of the ancient world's great cities, where traces of Magna Graecia are omnipresent – from papyrus-fringed Fontana Aretusa to the amphitheatres, altars and caves of the Parco Archeologico. Next head west to the **Necropoli di Pantalica** – an eerie assemblage of Bronze Age tombs built into limestone cliffs – before continuing to the captivating Val di Noto. The devastating earthquake of 1693 wrought havoc on this corner of the island, but also prompted the construction of some of Sicily's greatest treasures. The late-baroque towns of **Noto**, **Modica** and **Ragusa** are the superstars here, but it's also worth seeking out the small villages of **Scicli** and **Palazzolo Acreide** and the famed ceramics centre of **Caltagirone**. Continue west to **Villa Romana del Casale**, with its dazzling Roman mosaic floors. Finish at Sicily's most magnificent archaeological site: the Valley of the Temples at **Agrigento**.

7 DAYS Wining & Dining from West to East

This culinary sampler covers the full spectrum of Sicilian cuisine and its fine wines.

Start off in elegant **Marsala**, taste-testing the town's famous sweet wine on a cellar tour at Cantine Florio, then lingering into the evening at the many *enoteche* (wine bars) and restaurants. Next morning, stop in at the **Saline di Trapani**, which have supplied salt to Sicilian tables for centuries, before lunching on legendary fish couscous in **Trapani** and enjoying dessert with a breathtaking view in **Erice**, renowned for its marzipan fruit and nougat. Next stop is **Palermo**, whose colourful markets, street food, irresistible bakeries and countless fine eateries are highlights of any Sicilian food trip. Head south for a cooking course at the 400-hectare **Tenuta Regaleali**, one of Sicily's leading wine producers, then skirt the southern edge of the Madonie and Nebrodi Mountains, sampling the local black pork, ricotta, pecorino, mushrooms and hazelnuts in pretty hill towns like **Petralia Sottana** and **Nicosia**. Last, stop in for tastings of local honey, pistachios and Etna DOC wine on the flanks of **Mt Etna** before enjoying a final evening in cosmopolitan **Catania**.

Top: Panarea (p158)

Bottom: Monte dei
Porri, Salina (p155)

ADRIENNE PITTS/LONELY PLANET ©

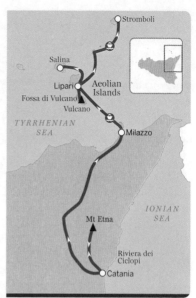

4 DAYS Mountain Retreats

Discover Sicily's more traditional side along the beautiful back roads of the Madonie and Nebrodi Mountains.

Relax into your journey in picture-perfect **Cefalù**, where you can lounge on the beach and enjoy panoramic coastal views from the ruined Norman citadel. Follow the coast east to **Castel di Tusa**, famous for its collection of open-air sculptures, then turn inland and climb towards the mountain town of **Mistretta**. Here, grand views of the little-visited Nebrodi Mountains and a distant Mt Etna begin to unfold. After detouring to explore the medieval village of **Nicosia**, continue south to **Enna**, a handsome hill town that marks Sicily's geographic centre. Snake back north through Gangi into the heart of the **Parco Naturale Regionale delle Madonie**, a magnificent natural landscape dotted with hazelnut orchards, ash forests and photogenic hilltop towns. Linger a couple of days along the mountains' western edge to explore the old stone churches of **Petralia Soprana** and **Petralia Sottana**, the Targa Florio automobile race museum at **Collesano** and the castle at **Castelbuono** before rejoining the coast at Cefalù.

7 DAYS Smoke & Fire: Volcanic Sicily

Sicily's trio of active volcanoes – Mt Etna, Vulcano and Stromboli – form the dramatic backdrop for this tour of northeastern Sicily.

Start in **Catania**, a city built of lava from the devastating volcanic eruption of 1669. First, climb the volcano that did all the damage, **Mt Etna**. As legend would have it, it was from Etna's lofty heights that the Cyclops hurled his stones at the fleeing Odysseus – you can still see their jagged forms along the dramatic **Riviera Dei Ciclopi** coastline, where traditional fishing villages have been reinvented as summer resorts. From here, circumnavigate Etna's western flank via Paternò, Biancavilla, Bronte and Randazzo and continue north to **Milazzo**, where you can catch a ferry to **Lipari**, the largest of the Aeolian Islands. Read up on the archipelago's fiery past at Lipari's Museo Archeologico, then island-hop across to **Salina**, whose twin extinct cones are one of Sicily's most harmonious sights. The more adventurous can climb smoking **Fossa di Vulcano**, with its sulphur-belching crater and gloopy mudbaths, or scale the 'lighthouse of the Mediterranean', **Stromboli**, an eternal lava-lamp whose eruptions continually light up the night sky.

10 DAYS Beach-Hopping

This tour takes in the prettiest beaches of western Sicily, from family-friendly coastal resorts to wild stretches of shoreline protected in two of the island's loveliest nature preserves.

Unpack your beach towel at **Mondello**, a summer playground just north of Palermo, whose deep roots as a coastal resort are reflected in its showy Liberty-era pier and summer villas. From here, it's an easy trip west to the Golfo di Castellammare, where the scenic walking trails and secluded coves of **Riserva Naturale dello Zingaro** are complemented by the idyllic white sands and buzzing seafood eateries of **San Vito Lo Capo**. Next, hop the 30-minute ferry from Trapani to the Egadi Islands, and relax for a day or two beside the aquamarine waters of **Favignana**'s eastern beaches before resuming your journey along Sicily's Mediterranean coast. The last leg east towards Agrigento includes stopovers to ogle ancient Greek temples from the beach at **Marinella di Selinunte**, to stroll the vast, untrammelled sands of **Riserva Naturale Torre Salsa** and to sunbathe or dive off the blindingly chalk-white outcrops at **Scala dei Turchi**.

10 DAYS Island-Hopping

Leave the car behind and settle into a slower rhythm on this island-hopping adventure through the Aeolian Islands – seven volcanic beauties with seven distinct personalities, all connected by ferry and hydrofoil to Sicily's north coast.

Begin by cruising across the Tyrrhenian from **Milazzo** to **Lipari**, home to the Aeolians' only sizeable town. Here you can split your time between urban attractions and excursions to the beaches and walking trails that lie just beyond town.

From Lipari, frequent hydrofoils fan out to all the remaining islands. **Vulcano** is a mere 10 minutes from Lipari. Here you can explore black-sand beaches, soak in mud baths and climb the island's smoking crater. Next, head north for lush green **Salina**, home to Malvasia vineyards, Sicily's most famous capers and some window-shopping in the low-key villages of Malfa and Santa Marina Salina. Eventually you'll feel called to explore the outer islands: remote **Filicudi** with its hilltop ruin of a Bronze Age village; *way* off-the-beaten-track **Alicudi**; chic, whitewashed **Panarea**; and the most spectacular of all, actively erupting **Stromboli**.

Sicily: Off the Beaten Track

Ustica

Tyrrhenian Sea

WESTERN SICILY: CRETTO DI BURRI

Stroll the surreal streets of this village destroyed by a 1968 earthquake, then encased in cement by artist Alberto Burri to create one of Europe's largest and most emotive pieces of 'land art.' (p118)

Mondello

Palermo

Castellammare del Golfo

Termini Imerese

Cefalù

Levanzo **Trapani** Erice

Partinico Bagheria

Castelbuono

Marettimo

Alcamo

Caccamo

Favignana

Pizzo Carbonara (1979m)

Marsala

Cretto di Burri

Corleone

Parco Naturale Regionale delle Madonie

Castelvetrano Partanna

Mazara del Vallo

Cave di Cusa

Menfi

Caltanissetta

Selinunte

Sciacca

Ribera

WESTERN SICILY: CAVE DI CUSA

Picnic among half-finished Greek columns in this olive-shaded ancient quarry, which provided much of the buttery yellow stone used to build the great temples of nearby Selinunte. (p120)

Agrigento

Favara

Ravanusa

Porto Empedocle

Palma di Montechiaro

Falconara

Licata

Pantelleria

Mediterranean Sea

MEDITERRANEAN COAST: CALA PULCINO

Hike or boat in to the most remote beach on Lampedusa, Italy's southernmost island. (p275)

Lampedusa
Same Scale as Main Map

Linosa (20km) (see main map)

Lampedusa

Cala Pulcino

Lampedusa (40km) (see inset)

Linosa

N 0 ——————— 50 km
0 ——————— 25 miles

AEOLIAN ISLANDS: STROMBOLI'S SLEEPIER SIDE

For an enticing glimpse of end-of-the-line island life, hop off the ferry in tiny Ginostra (pop 30) and follow the pack mules up the smoking slopes of Stromboli, Sicily's most spectacularly active volcano. (p164)

TYRRHENIAN COAST: NEBRODI & MADONIE MOUNTAINS

Wind through dazzling flower-carpeted hillsides on the forgotten back roads between Mistretta, Nicosia, Sperlinga and Gangi. (p128)

CENTRAL SICILY: PARCO MINERARIO FLORISTELLA GROTTACALDA

Explore the poignant history of Sicily's sulphur-mining industry at this reserve north of Piazza Armerina. (p249)

SOUTHEASTERN SICILY: CAVA D'ISPICA

Walk through Cava d'Ispica, a 13km-long gorge long used as a neolithic burial site, then transformed into cave dwellings in the Middle Ages. (p231)

MEDITERRANEAN COAST: BUTERA

For dizzying panoramas over the fields and hillsides of central Sicily, climb to the precipitously perched Norman castle in this sleepy off-the-beaten-track village. (p275)

Stromboli

Panarea

Filicudi
Salina

Alicudi

Lipari

Vulcano

Milazzo

Capo d'Orlando

Sant'Agata di Militello

Messina

Barcellona

Reggio di Calabria

Castel di Tusa

Mistretta

Mt Soro (1847m)
Monti Nebrodi

Monti Madonie

Parco Regionale dei Nebrodi

Taormina

Bronte

Giardini-Naxos

Adrano
Mt Etna (3329m)

Giarre

Enna
Parco Minerario Floristella Grottacalda

Paternò

Acireale

Misterbianco
Catania

Piazza Armerina

Aidone

Lentini

Mazzarino

Caltagirone

Augusta

Butera

Niscemi

Palazzolo Acreide
Floridia

Gela

Cómiso

Syracuse

Vittòria

Ragusa

Modica
Noto
Avola

Scicli
Cava d'Ispica

Pozzallo

Pachino

Ionian Sea

Parmigiana di melanzane (eggplant parmigiana)

Plan Your Trip

Eat & Drink Like a Local

If food isn't already one of your prime motivations for visiting Sicily, it should be! Over the centuries Sicilian chefs have drawn culinary inspiration from mainland Italy, North Africa and countless other sources, adding tasty and unexpected indigenous twists to create one of the world's most unique and magnificent cuisines.

The Year in Food

While *sagre* (local food festivals) go into overdrive in autumn, there's never a bad time to raise your fork in Sicily.

Spring (March–May)

Asparagus, artichokes and little wild strawberries flood the local market stalls, and Easter specialities fill bakery windows. Tuna and swordfish both come into season.

Summer (June–August)

Time for eggplants, peppers, berries and seafood by the sea. Beat the heat Sicilian style with gelato on a brioche, or fresh mulberry *granita* (crushed ice made with fresh fruit).

Autumn (September– November)

Food festivals galore, wine-harvest season and a perfect time to visit the mountains for gems such as chestnuts, hazelnuts, mushrooms and wild game.

Winter (December–February)

Time for Christmas treats such as *buccellati* – dough rings stuffed with minced figs, raisins, almonds, candied fruit and/or orange peel.

Food Experiences

Meals of a Lifetime

Osteria Nero D'Avola (p178) Owner Turi Siligato regales guests with tales of personally fishing and foraging for his ever-changing menu.

La Bettolaccia (p99) Sample Trapani's inimitable couscous, served with a delectable seafood broth, steps from the fish market.

Ristorante La Madia (p272) Every dish on Michelin-starred Madia's multi-course tasting menu is an exquisite work of art.

Ornato (p219) It might not be on the coast, but this side-street Modican restaurant serves some of the freshest, most beautiful seafood in Sicily's southeast.

Nangalarruni (p129) Lovingly sourced mountain mushrooms form the backbone of the menu at this intimate brick-and-beam dining room in Castelbuono.

Da Vittorio (p119) Fabulous seafood with a sunset view, perfect after a day of temple-gazing at Selinunte.

Cooking Classes

Serious epicureans can learn their way around the Sicilian kitchen at one of the island's cooking schools.

Cooking with the Duchess (p73) Gregarious, multilingual duchess Nicoletta Polo Lanza opens the tiled kitchen of her 18th-century seaside *palazzo* (mansion) for half-day Sicilian cooking courses. After taking students to shop in Palermo's markets and pick herbs in her backyard garden, she shares secrets of the island's multi-faceted cuisine, from street food to classic main courses to gorgeous desserts.

Anna Tasca Lanza Cooking School (p246) Affiliated with one of Sicily's leading wine producers, this fabulous school in the middle of the Sicilian countryside has been around since 1989. Classes are taught at an agricultural estate, with all ingredients sourced from the family garden or surrounding farms. Courses run from one to five days, with the option of overnight stays and additional food-related excursions to vineyards, permaculture gardens or the famous Pasticceria di Maria Grammatico in Erice.

La Corte del Sole Cooking Lessons (p208) These half-day lessons are offered by the chefs at the pretty Corte del Sole *agriturismo* (farm stay accommodation), tucked between the baroque town of Noto and the beautiful coastline of the Wildlife Oasis at the Riserva di Vendicari.

Cheap Treats

➡ *Panelle* – fried chickpea-flour fritters, often served in a sesame roll with *crocché* (fried potato dumplings made with cheese, parsley and eggs): find this classic Sicilian street food at Palermo's Friggitoria Chiluzzo (p72) or Mercato di Ballarò (p59).

➡ *Sfincione* – a spongy pizza-like Sicilian treat made with tomatoes, onions and (sometimes) anchovies; try it at I Banchi (p236) in Ragusa or Francu U Vastiddaru (p72) in Palermo.

THE ARK OF TASTE

The Ark of Taste is an international catalogue of endangered food products drawn up by the Slow Food Foundation for Biodiversity. It aims to protect indigenous edibles threatened with extinction by industrialisation, globalisation, hygiene laws and environmental dangers, and it actively encourages their cultivation for consumption. Foods included in the list must be culturally or historically linked to a specific region, locality, ethnicity or traditional production practice, and must also be rare. There are nearly 100 Sicilian foods on the list, ranging from Pantelleria capers and Zibibbo grapes to Favignana tuna roe, Iblei Mountains thyme honey and the Etna silver goat. For a full list, go to www.slowfoodfounda tion.com.

➡ *Arancini* – rice balls stuffed with meat or cheese, coated with breadcrumbs and fried; bite into a blissfully big one at Scicli's Don Tabaré (p232).

Dare to Try

➡ *Pani ca muesa* – a roll filled with calf's spleen, *caciocavallo* cheese, a drizzle of hot lard and a squeeze of lemon juice; track it down at Francu U Vastiddaru (p72) in Palermo.

➡ *Stigghiola* –seasoned and barbecued skewers of lamb or kid intestines, served from street-food stalls in Mercato di Ballarò (p59).

➡ *Spaghetti ai ricci* – pasta in an orange-tinted sauce made from the reproductive organs of sea urchins; Ristorante del Golfo (p96) in Castellammare del Golfo is a good place to try this.

➡ *'Mpanatigghi* – sweet biscuits filled with chocolate, spices and – wait for it – minced beef! Taste them if you dare at Dolceria Bonajuto (p230) in Modica.

Local Specialities

Palermo

Favourite local snacks include *pane e panelle* (a chickpea fritter sandwich with optional potato croquettes, fried eggplant and lemon), and the delicious *iris*, a fried pastry filled with sweet ricotta. At restaurants, don't miss *pasta con le sarde* (pasta with sardines, pine nuts, raisins and wild fennel) and *involtini di pesce spada* (thinly sliced swordfish fillets rolled up and filled with breadcrumbs, capers, tomatoes and olives).

Western Sicily

Savour this region's marked North African influence with a plate of *couscous di pesce alla trapanese* (fish couscous in a broth spiced with saffron, parsley and garlic) or a *bric* (savoury Tunisian pastry filled with tuna or shrimp). Top your pasta with *pesto alla trapanese* (made with fresh tomatoes, basil, garlic and almonds), and be sure to tour Marsala's world-renowned wine cellars.

Tyrrhenian Coast

Seafood is king along the coast, but some of the region's most interesting cuisine lies inland. The Madonie and Nebrodi Mountains are recognised throughout Sicily for their delicious hazelnuts, chestnuts, wild mushrooms, fresh sheep's milk ricotta, *provola* (provolone) cheese and *suino nero* (pork from local black pigs).

Aeolian Islands

With seven islands to choose from, you'll never run out of seafood. You'll also want to try *pasta all'eoliana,* with a sauce that incorporates the islands' renowned capers and olives, and sip the smooth and sweet Malvasia dessert wine grown on verdant Salina island. Other local treats include *pane cunzato* (sandwiches piled high with tuna, ricotta, eggplant, capers and olives) and delicious *granite* (crushed ice flavoured with fresh fruit or nuts).

Ionian Coast

Hit Catania for one of Sicily's most beloved first courses, *pasta alla Norma* (pasta topped with eggplant, basil, fresh ricotta and tomatoes), and if you're passing through Messina, don't miss *agghiotta di pesce spada* (swordfish with pine nuts, sultanas, capers, olives and tomatoes). Several other regional specialities are grown on Mt Etna's volcanic slopes, including Bronte pistachios, Zafferana Etnea honey and Etna DOC wine.

Caponata – a vegetable mix in a sweet-and-sour sauce

Syracuse & the Southeast

Celebrate the Southeast's earthy flavours with *macco di fave* (fava bean puree with wild fennel), *lolli con le fave* (hand-rolled pasta with fava beans), *ravioli di ricotta al sugo di maiale* (ricotta ravioli with a pork-meat *ragù*) and *cassatella di Montevago* (fried, ravioli-like pastries filled with sweetened ricotta, honey and lemon zest). The Syracuse region is famous for its lemons, blood oranges and tomatoes. Cheeses worth seeking out include the excellent Ragusano DOP, *tumazzo modicano* (a rare Modican cave-aged blue cheese) and *provola con limone Verdello* (provolone cheese embedded with a whole lemon, which imparts a distinctly citrusy flavour). Local desserts include Modica's spiced chocolate creations and Noto's fine gelati.

Central Sicily

The only place in Sicily without a coastline: the interior hill towns around Enna build their menus around meat, sausages and wild game, accompanied by mushrooms and fresh vegetables such as fava

beans and wild asparagus. If you're here in September or October, don't miss the region's delicious yellow-and-red-streaked Leonforte peaches.

LOOK OUT FOR

➡ Interdonato lemons – natural hybrid of lemon and citron with a slightly bitter taste.

➡ Almonds from Noto – intense and aromatic nuts from ancient trees.

➡ Pistachios from Bronte – emerald-green nuts with an unctuous texture and intense flavour.

➡ Black pork from the Nebrodi Mountains – can be enjoyed in succulent ham, sausages and bacon.

➡ Capers from Salina – known for their firmness, perfume and uniform size.

➡ Ricotta infornata – ricotta cheese baked in a stone oven, eaten fresh or used for grating.

SICILIAN SWEET TREATS

Most traditional Sicilian dishes fall into the category of *cucina povera* (cooking of the poor), featuring cheap and plentiful ingredients such as pulses, vegetables and bread. Supplemented by fish (locally caught and still relatively inexpensive), this diet is still widely embraced today, but differs in one major respect to that of previous generations – the inclusion of decadent desserts.

The two most beloved are *cassata siciliana* (a mix of ricotta, sugar, candied fruit and chocolate that is flavoured with vanilla and maraschino liqueur, encased by sponge cake and topped with green icing) and *cannoli* (crisp tubes of fried pastry dough filled with creamy ricotta and sometimes decorated with a maraschino cherry, candied fruit, grated chocolate or ground nuts). You'll find both on restaurant menus throughout the island.

Mediterranean Coast

Seafood takes centre stage along Sicily's southwestern shoreline, most notably in the busy fishing port of Sciacca. Inland, the region's sun-baked fields and orchards produce excellent almonds, Canicatti grapes, Ribera oranges and Nocellara del Belice olives.

How to Eat & Drink
When to Eat

Sicilians love to eat at virtually any time of day. The three set meals are interspersed with breaks for coffee, street snacks and early-evening *aperitivi*.

➡ *Colazione* (breakfast) – Many Sicilians eat the standard Italian breakfast of coffee with *cornetti* (croissants filled with cream or marmalade), *brioche* or *fette bicottate* (packaged dry toast), but they also enjoy a couple of sweet alternatives in summertime: *brioche con gelato* (a sweet roll filled with ice cream) and *granita con panna* (flavoured crushed ice, often topped with whipped cream).

➡ *Pranzo* (lunch) – Traditionally the biggest meal of the day, especially on Sundays. A full *pranzo* typically lasts at least two hours, with antipasti, a *primo* (first course), *secondo* (second course), *contorni* (side dishes), fruit, wine, water and dessert. Standard restaurant hours are from noon to 2.30pm, though most Sicilians eat after 1pm.

➡ *Aperitivi* (pre-dinner drinks) – Sicilians enjoy post-work drinks between 5pm and 8pm, often at outdoor tables when weather permits. At many places, the price of your drink includes an offering of snacks.

➡ *Cena* (dinner) – The courses available at dinnertime are the same as at lunch, though you'll be hard-pressed to finish two meals of this size in a single day. In restaurants it's always perfectly permissible to order just a *primo* or *secondo*. Another less-substantial alternative is pizza, which is widely served in the evenings throughout Sicily. Standard restaurant hours are from 7.30pm to 11pm, though locals don't arrive in earnest until 9pm or later.

Where to Eat

Sicilian eateries range from the humblest of street-side stalls to top-of-the-line gourmet restaurants, with plenty of options in-between. Here's a breakdown of the most common places to eat. Menus for most places are posted by the door.

➡ Trattoria – often family-run, this is a less formal restaurant serving regional specialities, with a focus on traditional pasta, fish and meat dishes. Many of Sicily's best eateries fall into this category.

➡ Ristorante (restaurant) – can be anything from a conservative hotel-based establishment with crisp white linen and formal service to a trendy up-and-coming eatery. Restaurants tend to serve a wider selection of dishes and charge higher prices than trattorias.

➡ Osteria – historically a tavern focused on wine, the modern version is usually an intimate, relaxed trattoria or wine bar offering a handful of dishes from a verbal menu.

➡ Pizzeria – a top place for a cheap feed, a cold beer and a buzzing, convivial vibe. Most open only at night.

➡ Enoteca (wine bar) – wines are the clear focus, but most places also serve a limited menu of deli-style snacks or simple meals.

Top: *Pasta con le sarde* – sardine pasta

Bottom: Sweets in Palermo

COFFEE, SICILIAN STYLE

Sicilians take their coffee seriously and order it in the following ways.

➡ *Espresso* – a tiny cup of very strong black coffee; usually called a *caffè* or *caffè normale*.

➡ *Caffè macchiato* – an espresso with a dash of milk.

➡ *Cappuccino* – espresso topped with hot foaming milk; only drunk at breakfast or in the mid-morning.

➡ *Caffè latte* – coffee with milk that is steamed but not frothed; an extremely milky version is called a *latte macchiato* (stained milk); again, only drunk in the morning.

➡ *Caffè freddo* – the local version of an iced coffee.

Granita di caffè – coffee-flavoured *granita*

➡ *Agriturismo* – in rural areas, this is an eatery on a country estate or working farm where much of the produce is cultivated on-site.

➡ *Friggitoria* – these street-food venues range from portable carts pushed through local markets to hole-in-the-wall eateries with small kitchens and limited, informal seating. The common denominator is the emphasis on simple fried snacks and the ultra-low prices, usually no more than a euro or two.

➡ *Tavola calda* – a simple canteen-style eatery serving pre-prepared pasta, meat and vegetable dishes, along with snacks and *panini* (bread rolls with simple fillings).

➡ *Bar-caffè* – typically varying its functions depending on the time of day, a bar-*caffè* will serve coffee and *cornetti* (Italian croissants) in the morning, drinks in the afternoon and evening, and sweet and savoury snacks all day long. Many also serve ice cream.

➡ *Pasticceria* (pastry shop) – typically serves a wide selection of pastries and cakes, including classic Sicilian treats such as *cannoli* and *cassata*. Some have a *caffè* attached, others do not.

➡ *Gelateria* (ice-cream shop) – one of the best reasons to come to Sicily, generally with a vast rainbow of flavours. Don't miss *brioche con gelato* (ice cream served on a roll), a common Sicilian treat.

Menu Decoder

Here are a few key terms that will help you decipher Sicilian menus.

➡ *Menu a la carte* – choose whatever you like from the menu.

➡ *Menu di degustazione* – tasting menu, usually consisting of six to eight 'tasting size' courses.

➡ *Menu turistico* – the dreaded 'tourist menu', a fixed-price, multicourse affair that often signals mediocre fare aimed at gullible tourists.

➡ *Piatto del giorno* – dish of the day.

➡ *Nostra produzione* or *fatta in casa* – made in-house, used to describe anything from pasta to olive oil to *liquori* (liqueurs).

➡ *Surgelato* – frozen, usually used to denote fish or seafood that has not been freshly caught.

➡ *Antipasti* – hot or cold appetisers; for a tasting plate of mixed appetisers, request an *antipasto misto*.

➡ *Primi* – first courses of pasta, rice, couscous or soup.

➡ *Secondi* – second courses of *pesce* (fish) or *carne* (meat).

➡ *Contorni* – side dishes of *verdura* (vegetables) or *insalata* (salad) intended to accompany your main course.

➡ *Dolci* – sweets (many Sicilian menus also use the English word dessert).

➡ *Frutta* – fresh fruit, served in more traditional eateries as the epilogue to your meal.

Sciara del Fuoco, Stromboli (p160)

Plan Your Trip
Activities

With its favourable climate and gorgeous mix of landscapes, Sicily offers an appealing setting for outdoor activities. Whatever is on your personal wish list for a Mediterranean vacation – hiking, swimming, boating, diving, snorkelling, birdwatching, rock climbing – Sicily has what you're after.

Diving & Snorkelling

Discover the underwater wonders of Lipari, Filicudi, Ustica, Isola Bella, Lampedusa or Pantelleria.

Volcano Viewing

Watch Stromboli's nocturnal fireworks from the summit or a boat, or teeter on the edges of Etna.

Birdwatching

Witness the annual passage of flamingos, herons and other migratory birds through the marshlands of Vendicari.

Sailing and Kayaking

Explore the coastlines, beaches, sea stacks and grottoes of the Aeolian Islands.

Guided Nature Walks

Climb into the Madonie Mountains above Cefalù to see traditional ricotta-making over an open wood fire.

Hiking

Sicily is a dream destination for walkers, with superb coastal and mountain trails and three iconic volcano treks. Top destinations include the Aeolian Islands, Mt Etna, the Madonie Mountains, the Nebrodi Mountains and the region's many nature reserves. Spring (April to June) and autumn (September to October) offer the best conditions.

Aeolian Islands

The enchantment of the Aeolian Islands lies in the archipelago's strikingly diverse yet interconnected landscapes. Each of the seven volcanic islands has its own personality, with beautiful trails and tantalising views to its sister islands across the sea. Motorised traffic is limited everywhere (virtually nonexistent on some islands), making for some of Italy's most tranquil walking.

Highlights include the following:

Stromboli One of the world's classic volcano hikes, the guided trek up 924m Stromboli (p160) at sunset is a magical experience, with the crater's fireworks juxtaposed against the darkening sky.

Lipari Wildflower-strewn coastal bluffs drop abruptly into the Mediterranean on the spectacular Pianoconte to Quattropani hike (p148).

Vulcano As much an olfactory as a visual experience, the climb to 391m Fossa di Vulcano (p153) brings you face-to-face with sulphurous fumes from the steaming crater, complemented by beautiful views of the other Aeolians lined up to the north.

Salina Climb through ferns and verdant pine forest to the Aeolians' highest point, Monte Fossa delle Felci (p156) (962m), enjoying magnificent views of vineyards, the Lingua salt lagoon, and the symmetrically arrayed cones of Filicudi and Alicudi.

Panarea Loop walks of varying length converge on Punta del Corvo (p159), Panarea's 421m summit.

Filicudi Take the easy 10-minute hike from the port to Filicudi's Bronze Age settlement, Villaggio Preistorico (p158), or the longer jaunt to the abandoned village of Zucco Grande (p166).

Alicudi For end-of-the-world tranquillity, jump ship at the Aeolians' westernmost island and follow the donkeys up stone staircases to Filo dell'Arpa (p167), where unbroken Mediterranean views stretch clear to the horizon.

Mount Etna

From Piano Provenzano (p198) on Etna's northern slopes, trails lead to Pizzi Deneri and the Volcanic Observatory at 2800m, or up to the main crater at 3200m. Both offer spectacular views of the Peloritani, Nebrodi and Madonie mountain ranges and the Valle del Bove. Further down, there's lovely walking in the pine, birch and larch trees of the Pineta Ragabo.

The ascent of the southern slopes begins at the lodging Rifugio Sapienza (1923m), from where you can take the Funivia dell'Etna (p195) cable car and walk 2km up to the volcano's four craters.

Madonie & Nebrodi Mountains

Revolving around the hulking mass of Pizzo Carbonara (1979m), the Parco Naturale Regionale delle Madonie (p128) (Madonie Mountains Natural Park) is threaded with an extensive trail network. Walkers here enjoy remarkable solitude as they pass through oak-chestnut forests, stone-walled mountain villages and montane meadows where shepherds still make *ricotta infornata* over wood fires. Highlights include the climb from Piano Battaglia to the summit of Pizzo Carbonara (p133), the flower-strewn mountain meadows around Pizzo Caterineci (p133), the trail through the Vallone Madonna degli Angeli (p133), which showcases the last 30 surviving examples of the critically endangered Nebrodi fir, and the **Sentiero degli Agrifogli Giganti** with its centuries-old oaks and maples and giant (15m-high) holly bushes.

East of the Madonie lie the **Monti Nebrodi** (Nebrodi Mountains), another sparsely populated landscape that is home to the *cavallo sanfratellano* (a horse once used by medieval Lombard knights, introduced to Sicily under the Normans). Centres of activity for hikers include the **Rocche del Crasto**, dramatic limestone peaks that rise steeply above the towns of Alcara Li Fusi and Longi, and the **Dorsale dei Nebrodi**, a 70km section of the **Sentiero Italia** (Italy's 6166km national hiking trail) that runs through the heart of the Parco Regionale dei Nebrodi (p135).

Mud bathing on Vulcano (p153)

Other Hiking

Prime spots for walking range from the Valle dell'Anapo (p212) and the Vendicari wetlands (p217) in southeastern Sicily to the nature reserves of Zingaro (p95) and Monte Cofano (www.parks.it/riserva.monte.cofano), and the island of Marettimo (p111) in western Sicily.

Organised Walks

Two companies offering guided walks with a strong Sicilian cultural component are Carmelina Ricciardello's Sicilian Experience (p133) and Anita Iaconangelo's Italian Connection (www.italian-connection.com). Other excellent Sicilian-run agencies that organise walks include Vai Col Trekking Sicilia (p135) in the Nebrodi Mountains and Cafeci (p249) near Piazza Armerina. For guided walks on Mt Etna, check with Gruppo Guide Alpine Etna Nord (p198) or Gruppo Guide Alpine Etna Sud (p198) – depending on which side of the volcano you want to tackle.

TOP TREKS

Pizzo Carbonara (p133) Walk among wildflowers to the Madonie's highest peak.

Mt Etna (p195) Hike the hulking slopes of Europe's most famous volcano.

Riserva Naturale dello Zingaro (p95) Visit museums of local culture as you hike the 7km coastal path north of Scopello.

Valle dell'Anapo (p212) Explore this dramatic limestone gorge pock-marked with Bronze Age and Iron Age necropolises.

Castello Punta Troia, Marettimo (p111) Zigzag along coastal bluffs from a whitewashed island village to a lonely castle dramatically perched atop a rocky outcrop.

Riserva di Vendicari (p217) Scan for flamingos and roseate spoonbills as you navigate boardwalks through these gorgeous coastal wetlands.

Punta Troia (p111), Marettimo

OTHER ACTIVITIES

Beyond the obvious attractions of swimming, boating and walking along Sicily's gorgeous coastlines, you'll find countless other activities on offer.

➡ Birdwatching – Given its prime position on the migratory flight path between Africa and Europe, Sicily is a prime birdwatching destination. Spring (April) and autumn (September) are the best seasons. Popular spots include the Riserva Naturale di Vendicari (p217), the Riserva Naturale dello Zingaro (p95) and the Parco Regionale dei Nebrodi (p135).

➡ Rock climbing – San Vito Lo Capo lures climbers with its variety of challenging crags and the San Vito Climbing Festival (p95), held annually in October or November. Other leading destinations include Mt Etna, the limestone pinnacles of Rocche del Crasto (p135) in the Nebrodi Mountains, and multiple sites in the Madonie Mountains including **Monte D'Oro** (outside Collesano), **Rocca di Sant'Otiero** (near Petralia Sottana) and **Passo Scuro** (near Castelbuono).

➡ Skiing – Sicily will never compete with the Alps or even the Appenines as a ski destination, but for curiosity value, there's nothing like hitting the slopes at the island's two ski mountains, Mt Etna (p198) and Piano Battaglia (p133) in the Madonie Mountains.

➡ Cycling – Cycling is a great way of getting around offshore islands like Favignana, Salina and Lampedusa, where distances are relatively short and rental bikes are readily available. Alternatively, take an organised tour with cycling specialists such as Etna Touring (p198), **Coast2Coast** (www.coast2coast.it), **Backroads** (www.backroads.com), **VBT** (www.vbt.com) or **Butterfield & Robinson** (www.butterfield.com).

➡ Mud bathing – For a low-cost beauty treatment, slather yourself in natural mud from the beach at **Eraclea Minoa**, the Pozza dei Fanghi (p153) on Vulcano or Lago Specchio di Venere (p120) on Pantelleria.

Aeolian Islands

There are good dives off most of the Aeolians, with some of the best surrounding the main island of Lipari (p148). Another highlight is the **Museo Archeologico Sottomarino** area off Filicudi, where the sunken wrecks of nine ancient Greek and Roman ships provide fabulous diving opportunities.

Diving operators in the Aeolians include La Gorgonia (p148) on Lipari, Saracen (p153) on Vulcano, **Amphibia** (☑335 6138529; www.amphibia.it; Via San Pietro) on Panarea, La Sirenetta (p163) on Stromboli and I Delfini (p166) on Filicudi.

Other Diving & Snorkelling

About an hour west of Palermo, the Riserva Naturale dello Zingaro (p95) is great for diving. Cetaria Diving Centre (p94) in Scopello organises guided dives in the waters off the nature reserve between April and October, visiting underwater caves

Flamingos at Riserva di Vendicari (p217)

Diving & Snorkelling

Diving and snorkelling opportunities abound in Sicily, most notably in the waters surrounding its offshore islands. Ustica and the Aeolian Islands are the region's leading dive destinations. The best months to dive are May through October.

Ustica

Divers from around the world come to explore the magnificent underwater sites of Ustica (p81). The island's western shores are home to a protected marine reserve, which is divided into three zones. Highlights include the underwater archaeological trail off **Punta Cavazzi**, where artefacts including anchors and Roman amphorae can be admired. Other popular dive sites are the **Scoglio del Medico**, an outcrop of basalt riddled with caves and gorges that plunge to great depths; and **Secca di Colombara**, a magnificent rainbow-coloured display of sponges and gorgonias.

The island's many dive centres organise itineraries and hire out equipment.

BEST BEACHES

San Vito Lo Capo (p94) Join the sun worshippers by the electric turquoise waters of this perennial summer holiday destination.

Spiaggia dei Conigli (p274) This sandy beauty on remote Lampedusa island regularly wins awards as one of Europe's finest beaches.

Scala dei Turchi (p266) A dazzling white outcropping shaped like a staircase, with beaches on either side, perfect for wading or diving off the rocks.

Spiaggia Marianelli (p217) Wild, gorgeous beach popular with the LGBT+ crowd, set in the Riserva Naturale di Vendicari, southeast of Noto.

Spiaggia di Cefalù (p123) A lovely, family-friendly expanse of sand backed by a dramatic promontory and one of Sicily's prettiest medieval towns.

Torre Salsa (p266) Perfect for fans of wild, unspoiled coastlines, this off-the-beaten-track gem is part of a WWF-administered nature reserve.

Beach near Taormina (p174)

and shipwrecks; it also offers boat excursions with snorkelling.

Near Taormina, the WWF-protected reserve of Isola Bella (p181) also has some good diving. Nike Diving Centre (p181) offers diving equipment and lessons, along with snorkelling excursions and stand-up paddleboarding.

Other diving hotspots include the offshore islands of Pantelleria (p120) and Lampedusa (p274).

Beaches & Swimming

Boasting nearly 1500km of coastline on the Ionian, Tyrrhenian and Mediterranean Seas, and 15 offshore islands including Ustica and Pantelleria along with the Aeolian, Pelagic and Egadi Islands, Sicily has beaches for every taste. The deep blue, turquoise and emerald-green waters that lap the shoreline are clean and warm throughout the summer and autumn months, with swimming conditions at their best from June through early October. Beaches range

from pebbly to sandy, and from crowded bathing *lidos* where you can rent sun loungers and umbrellas to long, nearly deserted expanses of sand.

Sailing, Kayaking & Other Water Sports

Boat trips of all kinds can be organised along Sicily's coast and in the outer islands.

Sicily in Kayak (p153) offers kayaking, sailing and stand-up paddleboard tours around Vulcano and the other Aeolians, ranging from half a day to an entire week. A number of other operators on the Aeolians and Sicily's other offshore islands organise round-the-island and inter-island boat trips exploring sea grottoes and secluded swimming spots.

There's some great kite-surfing in western Sicily between Marsala and Trapani; grab your board and head for the Laguna dello Stagnone with Prokite Alby Rondina (p108).

Plan Your Trip
Family Travel

Few places are as friendly to children as Sicily. Families are welcomed at restaurants, cafes and hotels, and staff are generally diligent in accommodating your needs. Family-friendly attractions abound – beaches, *gelaterie* (ice-cream shops), puppet theatres – and you'll benefit from family discounts on transport along with free children's admission at many sites.

Children Will Love...
Desserts

Gelateria Ciccio Adelfio (p74), **Palermo** Everyone loves gelato, especially for breakfast, when it's served in a sweet bun at a classic gelateria like this one!

Da Alfredo (p156), **Salina, Aeolian Islands** On a hot day, there's nothing more refreshing than a *granita* (flavoured crushed ice made with coffee or fresh fruit), topped with a dollop of whipped cream.

La Rinascente (p99), **Trapani** Meet the *cannoli*-maker and watch him fill yours on the spot as you anticipate that first crunchy, creamy bite.

In & On the Water

Spiaggia di Cefalù (p123) For sheer family fun in the sun, this long sandy beach east of Palermo is hard to beat.

Ustica (p45) Water-loving families and older kids and teenagers can snorkel and dive to their heart's desire on this island off Palermo.

Scala dei Turchi (p266) Young kids can frolic in the shallow water near Agrigento.

Grotta del Bue Marino (p165), **Filicudi** Boat to this spectacular Aeolian Islands sea grotto.

The Outdoors

Stromboli Crater (p160), **Aeolian Islands** A glimpse of Stromboli's glowing innards on a night

Practical Tips
When to Go

Spring, early summer and autumn are generally best for families with small children. High summer temperatures can make life miserable for little ones – although good beaches and the occasional gelato should make this more bearable.

Before You Go

➡ Car seats for infants and children are available from most car-rental firms, but you should always book them in advance.

➡ Stock up on sun cream even in spring and autumn, when it can still be quite warm in Sicily.

➡ Insect repellent (especially for mosquitoes) is highly recommended.

➡ For all-round information and advice, check out Lonely Planet's *Travel with Children* book.

Sicilian puppet theatre (p75)

climb is any teen's fairy-tale vision of a volcano come true.

Fossa di Vulcano (p153), **Aeolian Islands** Follow the pongy path to this steaming, sulphur-spewing crater, known to the Romans as Vulcan's forge.

Castello di Caccamo (p128) Storm the ramparts of this and other Norman castles across the island.

Ruins of Selinunte (p117) This sprawling ruined city has temples, piles of ancient rubble and wide

open spaces for kids to explore, plus a beach just below.

Azienda Agrituristica Bergi (p282), **Castelbuono** Enjoy animals, swimming pools and lots of space while overnighting at this and other *agriturismi* (farmstays) around the island.

Arts & Sicilian Culture

Piccolo Teatro dei Pupi (p206), **Syracuse** Watch brave knights defeat evil monsters in a traditional puppet play.

Farm Cultural Park (p263), **Favara** Creative teens will appreciate the edgy installations at this unique artists' community.

Villa Romana del Casale (p250), **Piazza Armerina** At this ancient Roman hunting villa, mosaics of lions, tigers and youthful gymnasts will capture many young imaginations.

Passeggiata Search out carousels, cafes and convivial company of every age during the evening stroll.

WHAT TO EXPECT

➡ Admission to many cultural sites is free for under-10s or under-18s (particularly EU citizens).

➡ On trains, the *offerta Bimbi Gratis* allows children under 15 to travel free when accompanied by at least one parent in a family group of two to five people (see www.trenitalia. com for conditions).

➡ You can stock up on nappies, baby formula and sterilising solutions at pharmacies and supermarkets.

Region by Region

Aeolian Islands

Island-hopping by boat will appeal to any kid explorer – as will climbing to Vulcano's rim and peeking inside the smoking crater.

Southeastern Sicily

Flamingos along the Vendicari coast and puppet shows with funny battle scenes will captivate kids of all ages, while open spaces like Syracuse's Piazza del Duomo help squirmy toddlers get the wiggles out.

Tyrrhenian Coast

Long sandy beaches at Cefalù make for happy family times, and the steeply perched Norman castle at Caccamo is perfect for medieval role-playing.

Western Sicily

Enjoy beach days swimming and cycling on Favignana, discover ancient cave art on Levanzo, play hide-and-seek in the abandoned streets of Cretto di Burri, or ride the funicular to Erice to sample sugary almond sweets.

Ionian Coast

Whether you're splashing on the beach below Taormina, climbing Europe's tallest volcano or getting grossed out by giant fish heads in Catania's market, the Ionian Coast creates lasting memories.

Good to Know

Dining Out

Eating in Sicily should be a breeze. In restaurants, high chairs are usually available and it's perfectly acceptable to order a *mezza porzione* (half portion) off the normal menu for little ones. Even the fussiest kids will enjoy the island's abundant fresh fruit, savoury snacks like *arancine* (fried, stuffed rice balls) or basics like pizza and pasta with a tomato sauce – while more adventurous eaters will be able to 'expand' their palate with varied seafood, fish, meat and veggie dishes. Gelati, *granite* (crushed ice with various flavours) and the many

> ### ACCOMMODATION
>
> Generally, apartment rental is easy to find and works best for families who want to self-cater. Many hotels and *pensioni* (guesthouses) offer reduced rates for children or will add an extra bed or cot on request (usually for an extra 30% or so). *Agriturismi* (farm-stays) are excellent for children, and usually have an animal or two on site.

fantastic Sicilian *dolci* (desserts) will be fought over by the entire family.

Attractions

Sicily and its smaller offshore islands offer plenty of ways to keep the family engaged, be it the mix of history and nature at the Valley of the Temples in Agrigento, the many beaches and islands, vibrant street markets at Palermo and Catania, or a simple *passeggiata* (evening stroll) with the locals, ice cream in hand. Teenagers will be able to break up lazy days with swimming and organised boat trips, while activity-seeking families have three volcanoes to climb and lots of snorkelling and diving options. Norman castles and ancient ruins are scattered around the island and are ripe for exploration.

Entertainment

Away from the beaches, smaller kids can be kept entertained at the local main square – the piazzas are usually equipped with fun rides and, well, other kids! Traditional puppet shows are a great way to introduce your children to local culture – it helps if they're into battles!

Safety

While it's generally safe for kids to run around small town squares, keep an eye on the scooters that sometimes zip in and out – pedestrian areas are something of a relative concept in Sicily.

Family-Friendliness

Family life is highly valued in Sicily. Babies will be cooed over, and children of all ages will generally be welcomed. Breastfeeding is common, and attitudes are relaxed.

Regions at a Glance

Palermo

Art & Architecture
Food
Nightlife

Cultural Treasure Chest

Palermo has everything from Byzantine mosaics to Arab-Norman palaces to exuberant rococo chapels. This city is full of surprises: verses from the Koran scrawled on church columns, Arabic marble inlay beside glimmering images of an all-powerful Christ, and baroque domes atop medieval foundations.

Culinary Capital

From appetisers such as *sarde in beccafico* (pine-nut-and-raisin-stuffed sardines rolled in breadcrumbs) to the world's most scrumptious *cannoli*, every menu page is worth lingering over. Don't limit yourself to restaurants – stroll through the city's bustling markets and discover its superb street food.

Puppets & Prima Donnas

Nights out in Palermo can mean many things: live music at one of Italy's great opera houses, medieval tales performed by exquisite hand-crafted puppets, an evening soak in a Moorish steam bath, or bar-hopping the buzzing late-night streets.

p54

Western Sicily

History
Outdoors
Food & Wine

Ancient Eyries

For an idyllic natural setting, few ruins can match Segesta and Selinunte, where temples sit in splendid, moody isolation, peeking through fields of tall grass and wildflowers. Erice's Norman castle comes close, though, perched on a spectacular hilltop that's been coveted by everyone from the Phoenicians to the ancient Greeks.

Fun in the Sun

Whether you're climbing San Vito's crags, hiking the trails of Marettimo and the Zingaro, or cycling and sunbathing on Favignana, western Sicily offers endless supplies of outdoorsy fun.

Saracen Seasonings

North African influences have always been close at hand in western Sicily, as reflected in the seductively spiced fish couscous that appears on every menu. Some of Sicily's finest wines are also produced here, most notably around Marsala.

p91

Tyrrhenian Coast

Beaches
Hill Towns
Food

Sea & Sand

Dotted with pretty resort towns such as Cefalù and Castel di Tusa, the Tyrrhenian Coast becomes a jam-packed beach playground every summer.

Mountain Retreats

Old stone villages like Castelbuono, Mistretta and Petralia Sottana hunker down against the high slopes of the Nebrodi and Madonie Mountains, offering a welcome home base to outdoors enthusiasts who are increasingly discovering the region's charms.

Fabulous Fungi

Kiss seafood goodbye and prepare to be impressed by the entirely different cuisine of the Nebrodi and Madonie Mountains. Wild mushrooms and roast meats, notably from the indigenous *suino nero* (pork from local black pigs), are mainstays of the menu, as are local hazelnuts, chestnuts, ricotta and *provola* (provolone) cheese.

p122

Aeolian Islands

Outdoors
Food & Wine
Volcanoes

Natural Paradise

If stunning coastal beauty is your idea of paradise, you've come to the right place. Each of the seven Aeolians has its own natural charms, with enough diving, swimming, kayaking, walking and climbing to satisfy outdoors enthusiasts of all stripes.

Island Flavours

Fresh seafood figures prominently in the Aeolians' divine cuisine, along with local capers and olives. The island of Salina is famous for its honey-sweet Malvasia wine, available at shops and restaurants throughout the archipelago.

Smoke & Fire

Yes, most of the Aeolians' volcanoes are now extinct. But Vulcano and Stromboli just keep on smoking, the former luring visitors with its therapeutic mud baths, the latter with its awe-inspiring fiery eruptions.

p141

Ionian Coast

Volcanoes
Festivals
Food & Wine

Volcano Views

Mt Etna's spellbinding form dominates this stretch of coast from every imaginable angle, looming on the horizon at the end of Catania's busy boulevards, peeking through the stage at Taormina's Greek theatre, providing year-round outdoor recreation and enriching local agriculture with its fertile volcanic soil.

Fabulous Festivals

This place really knows how to throw a party. Taormina buzzes all summer long with world-class festivals of film, theatre, music and dance, while winter revellers are lured into the streets by Acireale's Carnevale and Catania's massive Festa di Sant'Agata.

Markets

Foodies will find plenty to love in this corner of Sicily, from the acclaimed Etna DOC wine to Catania's colourful fish and produce markets.

p168

Syracuse & the Southeast

Architecture
History
Food

Baroque Beauty

Devastated by a 1693 earthquake, southeastern Sicily's hill towns rose like a phoenix from the ashes, adopting the appealing baroque aesthetic you see today in the Unesco-listed towns of Noto, Modica, Ragusa and their smaller sister villages throughout the southeast.

Echoes of Ancient Greece

Modern-day Syracuse still glows with the glory of its Greek past, in the repurposed temple columns of Ortygia's cathedral, the papyrus-fringed pool at the heart of town and the cycle of Greek dramas that still draws crowds to the city's ancient amphitheatre each summer.

Sweet Temptations

From Modica's chocolates to Noto's *granite* (crushed ice made with various flavours) to the wine-flavoured gelati of Ragusa, this is a region that any sweet tooth will love.

p200

Central Sicily

Hill Towns
History
Shopping

Norman Strongholds

Bearing traces of their Norman past, Central Sicily's hill towns float like islands in the sky above the surrounding landscape. The regional capital of Enna lords over them all from its prime position at Sicily's geographic centre.

Roman Splendour

The world's most extensive and best-preserved late-Roman mosaic floors are shining brighter than ever thanks to recent renovations. Look for them in the ancient Villa Romana del Casale outside Piazza Armerina.

Ceramics Central

Ceramics lovers beware! Caltagirone's dozens of artisans' shops, ceramics museum, and whimsical 142-step staircase covered top to bottom in hand-painted tiles may seduce you into an acquisitive frenzy.

p239

Mediterranean Coast

History
Beaches
Food

Transcendent Temples

Agrigento's unparalleled lineup of ancient temples, coupled with the superb collection of artefacts at the nearby archaeological museum, constitutes Sicily's greatest classical legacy.

White Cliffs, Wild Sands

Stellar beach-going spots dot the coast west of Agrigento, including the long, unspoiled shoreline of Riserva Naturale Torre Salsa, the golden sands of Eraclea Minoa and the stunning white rock formation called Scala dei Turchi, at its best when illuminated by the setting sun.

Superb Seafood

You can eat well all along Sicily's Mediterranean coast, but at no place better than Sciacca, where seafood is delivered straight from the boat into the kitchens of the many portside restaurants.

p255

On the Road

Palermo

Best Places to Eat

➡ Gagini (p71)

➡ Ristorante Ferro (p71)

➡ Trattoria al Vecchio Club Rosanero (p69)

➡ Archestrato di Gela (p69)

➡ I Segreti del Chiostro (p74)

Best Art & Architecture

➡ Palazzo dei Normanni (p57)

➡ Pinacoteca Villa Zito (p65)

➡ Cattedrale di Monreale (p80)

➡ Cattedrale di Palermo (p60)

➡ Galleria Regionale della Sicilia (p62)

Why Go?

Flamboyant, guarded, feisty yet staunchly aristocratic, Palermo is a seething mass of contradictions. Pock-marked buildings, broken pavements and decrepit infrastructure reveal deep political and economic cracks, and yet all are easy to overlook when you enter a church full of luminous Byzantine mosaics, wander along a street of stately baroque *palazzi* (palaces) or eavesdrop on the genial banter between canny stall owners and bargain hunters at a street market. Palermo is a cryptic creature, a city where nefarious neglect and soul-stirring beauty have always linked arms, where preconceptions are concurrently affirmed and subverted, where light and shade stir impressions that bury deep under your skin.

Beyond Palermo is a string of worthy day-trip destinations including the mosaicked magnificence of Monreale Cathedral, beach-loving Mondello, the pristine marine reserve of Ustica island, and the inland town of Corleone, home to a defiant anti-mafia museum.

When to Go
Palermo

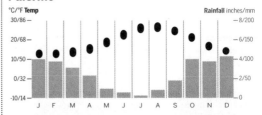

| **Apr & May** Lower prices and generally pleasant weather. | **Jul** Hot, but also time for the city's biggest celebration. Crowds peak on Mondello beach. | **Sep & Oct** Optimal diving conditions off Ustica; new opera season at the Teatro Massimo. |

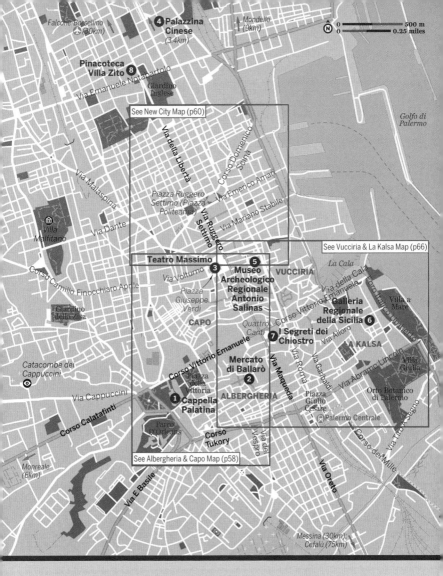

Palermo Region Highlights

1 **Cappella Palatina** (p57) Basking in Palermo's multicultural past.

2 **Mercato di Ballarò** (p59) Diving into a souk-like torrent of fresh produce.

3 **Teatro Massimo** (p73) Demanding an encore at one of Europe's grandest opera houses.

4 **Palazzina Cinese** (p65) Channelling China in a quirky royal hunting lodge.

5 **Museo Archeologico Regionale Antonio Salinas** (p64) Admiring Palermo's archaeological museum.

6 **Galleria Regionale della Sicilia** (p62) Catching up on centuries of Sicilian art.

7 **I Segreti del Chiostro** (p74) Savouring once-secret recipes.

8 **Pinacoteca Villa Zito** (p65) Admiring Sicilian brushstrokes in an elegant 18th-century villa.

PALERMO

📱091 / POP 668,400

Having been the crossroads of civilisations for millennia, Palermo delivers a heady, heavily spiced mix of Byzantine mosaics, Arabesque domes and frescoed cupolas. This is a city at the edge of Europe and at the centre of the ancient world, a place where souk-like markets rub up against baroque churches, where date palms frame Gothic palaces and where the blue-eyed and fair have bronze-skinned cousins.

Centuries of dizzying highs and crushing lows have formed a complex metropolis. Here, crumbling staircases lead to gilded ballrooms, and guarded locals harbour hearts of gold. Just don't be fooled. Despite its noisy streets, Sicily's largest city is a shy beast, rewarding the inquisitive with citrus-filled cloisters, stucco-laced chapels and crooked side streets dotted with youthful artisan studios.

Add to this Italy's biggest opera house and an ever-growing number of vibrant, new-school eateries and bars and you might find yourself falling unexpectedly in love.

◎ Sights

Palermo has its share of engaging museums, historic palaces and richly decorated churches, most of which lie in the historic neighbourhoods of La Kalsa, Vucciria, Il Capo and Albergheria. This said, Palermo's most uplifting and engaging experiences come from simply walking through the streets of these neighbourhoods and their jumble of patchwork architecture, unexpected piazzas and street markets.

Most museums offer a discounted entry price for EU citizens under the age of 18.

◎ Around the Quattro Canti

The busy intersection of Corso Vittorio Emanuele and Via Maqueda marks the charming **Quattro Canti** (Four Corners), the centre of the old city. Just off it are a handful of must-see sights, in particular the 16th-century Fontana Pretoria, the 14th-century Chiesa e Monastero di Santa Caterina d'Alessandria and the 12th-century church of La Martorana.

Quattro Canti   MONUMENT

(Map p66) Officially titled Piazza Vigliena, the elegant intersection of Corso Vittorio Emanuele and Via Maqueda is better known as the Quattro Canti. Marking the epicentre of the old city, the junction is framed by a perfect circle of curvilinear facades that dis-

appear up to the blue vault of the sky in a clever display of perspective. Each facade lights up in turn throughout the course of the day, landing it the nickname *Il Teatro del Sole* (Theatre of the Sun).

Echoing the style of late-Renaissance Rome and constructed in the early 17th century, the Quattro Canti's four symmetrical facades are the work of royal architect Giulio Lasso. Each corner is divided in three classical orders: Doric at the bottom, Ionic in the middle and Composite at the top. The decorative elements were left in the capable hands of architect Mariano Smiriglio. Statues adorn each of the three tiers, representing the seasons at the bottom, Spanish sovereigns in the middle, and female Palermitan saints at the top.

★ Chiesa e Monastero di Santa Caterina d'Alessandria   CONVENT

(Map p66; 📱091 271 38 37; Piazza Bellini; church, convent & rooftop adult/reduced €10/9, church only adult/reduced €3/2; ☉church 9am-7pm, convent & rooftop 10am-7pm) Built as a hospice in the early 14th century and transformed into a Dominican convent the following century, this monastic complex wows with its magnificent maiolica cloister, surrounded by unique balconied cells and punctuated by an 18th-century fountain by Sicilian sculptor Ignazio Marabitti. The convent's rooftop terraces offer spectacular views of the surrounding piazzas and city, while the church's baroque interior harbours works by prolific artists, among them Filippo Randazzo, Vito D'Anna and Antonello Gagini.

La Martorana   CHURCH

(Chiesa di Santa Maria dell'Ammiraglio; Map p66; 📱345 8288231; Piazza Bellini 3; adult/reduced €2/1; ☉9.30am-1pm & 3.30-5.30pm Mon-Sat, 9-10.30am Sun) On the southern side of Piazza Bellini, this luminously beautiful 12th-century church was endowed by King Roger's Syrian emir, George of Antioch, and was originally planned as a mosque. Delicate Fatimid pillars support a domed cupola depicting Christ enthroned amid his archangels. The interior is best appreciated in the morning, when sunlight illuminates the magnificent Byzantine mosaics.

Chiesa di San Giuseppe dei Teatini   CHURCH

(Map p66; Corso Vittorio Emanuele; ☉7am-noon & 4-8pm Mon-Sat, 7am-1pm & 5-8.30pm Sun) In the southwestern corner of the Quattro Canti is this 17th-century church, topped by an elegant cupola designed by Giuseppe Mariani and flanked by the two lower orders of Paolo Amato's unfinished *campanile* (bell tower). Significantly restored after suffering damage in WWII, its monumental baroque interior includes Filippo Tancredi's scenes from the life of St Gaetano capping the nave and Flemish painter Guglielmo Borremans' *Triumph of St Andrea Avellino* gracing the dome.

Fontana Pretoria   FOUNTAIN
(Map p66) Fringed by imposing churches and buildings, Piazza Pretoria is dominated by the over-the-top Fontana Pretoria, one of Palermo's major landmarks. The fountain's tiered basins ripple out in concentric circles, crowded with nude nymphs, tritons and leaping river gods. Such flagrant nudity proved a bit much for Sicilian churchgoers, who prudishly dubbed it the Fontana della Vergogna (Fountain of Shame).

Chiesa Capitolare di San Cataldo   CHURCH
(Map p66; Piazza Bellini 3; adult/reduced €2.50/1.50; ⊗9am-6.30pm summer, to 5.30pm winter) This 12th-century church in Arab-Norman style is one of Palermo's most striking buildings. With its dusky-pink bijou domes, solid square shape, blind arcading and delicate tracery, it illustrates perfectly the synthesis of Arab and Norman architectural styles. The interior, while more austere, is still beautiful, with its inlaid floor and lovely stone and brick work in the arches and domes.

Piazza Bellini   SQUARE
(Map p66) The disparate architectural styles and eras of the buildings adorning this magnificent piazza should by rights be visually discordant, but in fact contribute to a wonderfully harmonious public space. The piazza's eastern edge is adorned by the delightful **Teatro Bellini** (Bellini Theatre).

Museo Regionale d'Arte Moderna e Contemporanea della Sicilia (Riso)   MUSEUM
(Map p58; ✍ 091 58 77 17; www.poloartecontemporanea.it; Palazzo Riso, Corso Vittorio Emanuele 365; adult/reduced €6/3; ⊗10am-7.30pm Tue-Sun) In a restored 18th-century neoclassical *palazzo*, this two-level bastion of modern and contemporary art includes an extraordinary installation by Greek-born artist Jannis Kounellis in which 19 wardrobes seemingly 'float' above visitors. The museum's curators work with other city and regional institutions to provide challenging international survey shows, as well as alternative interpretations of Sicily's artistic heritage.

◉ Albergheria

Once inhabited by Norman court officials, Albergheria has been a poor and ramshackle quarter since the end of WWII – indeed, you can still see wartime bomb damage scarring some buildings. The area is now home to a growing immigrant population that has revitalised the streets with its aspirations. Albergheria's east side is home to Palermo's busiest street market, the Mercato di Ballarò, as well as the beautiful Chiesa del Gesù. However, by far the biggest tourist draws are the Palazzo dei Normanni and its exquisite chapel, Cappella Palatina, both at the far western edge of the neighbourhood, a manageable 1km walk away.

★ Palazzo dei Normanni   PALACE
(Palazzo Reale; Map p58; ✍091 705 56 11; www.federicosecondo.org; Piazza del Parlamento; adult/reduced incl exhibition Fri-Mon €12/10, Tue-Thu €10/8; ⊗8.15am-5.40pm Mon-Sat, to 1pm Sun) Home to Sicily's regional parliament, this venerable palace dates back to the 9th century. However, it owes its current look (and name) to a major Norman makeover, during which spectacular mosaics were added to its royal apartments and magnificent chapel, the Cappella Palatina. Visits to the apartments, which are off-limits from Tuesday to Thursday, take in the mosaic-lined **Sala dei Venti** and King Roger's 12th-century bedroom, **Sala di Ruggero II**.

★ Cappella Palatina   CHAPEL
(Palatine Chapel; Map p58; ✍ 091 705 56 11; www.federicosecondo.org; Piazza del Parlamento; adult/reduced incl exhibition Fri-Mon €12/10, Tue-Thu €10/8; ⊗8.15am-5.40pm Mon-Sat, to 1pm Sun) Designed by Roger II in 1130, this extraordinary chapel is Palermo's top tourist attraction. Located on the middle level of Palazzo dei Normanni's three-tiered loggia, its glittering gold mosaics are complemented by inlaid marble floors and a wooden *muqarnas* ceiling, the latter a masterpiece of Arabic-style honeycomb carving reflecting Norman Sicily's cultural complexity.

Note that queues are likely, and you'll be refused entry if you're wearing shorts, a short skirt or a low-cut top.

The chapel's well-lit interior is simply breathtaking. Every inch is inlaid with precious stones, giving the space a lustrous quality. These exquisite mosaics were mainly the work of Byzantine Greek artisans brought to Palermo by Roger II in 1140 especially for

Albergheria & Capo

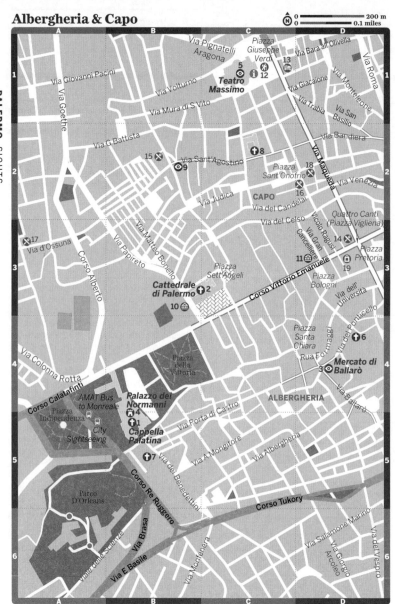

this project. They capture expressions, detail and movement with extraordinary grace and delicacy, and sometimes with enormous power – most notably in the depiction of Cristo Pantocratore (Christ All Powerful) and angels on the dome. The bulk of the mosaics recount the tales of the Old Testament,

though other scenes recall Palermo's pivotal role in the Crusades. Some of the mosaics are later and less-assured additions, for instance the Virgin and Saints in the main apse under Cristo Pantocratore. Fortunately, these don't detract too much from the overall achievement.

Albergheria & Capo

PALERMO SIGHTS

It's not only the mosaics you should be gazing at – don't miss the painted wooden ceiling featuring *muqarnas,* a decorative device resembling stalactites that is unique in a Christian church (and, many speculate, a sign of Roger II's secret identity as a Muslim). The walls are decorated with handsome marble inlay that displays a clear Islamic aesthetic, and the carved marble in the floor is stunning: marble was as precious as any gemstone in the 12th century, so the floor's value at the time of its construction is almost immeasurable by today's standards.

In case of special events, the chapel may close early or for part of the day; always check the website before heading in.

Chiesa di San Giovanni degli Eremiti CHURCH

(Map p58; ☑091 651 50 19; Via dei Benedettini 20; adult/reduced €6/3; ⊙9am-6.30pm Mon-Sat, to 1pm Sun) One of Palermo's finest examples of Arab-Norman architecture, this five-domed, 12th-century church is named for Sicilian hermit-monk and miraculous wolf tamer St William of Montervergine. Surrounded by a garden of citrus trees, palms, cacti and rosemary bushes, the church is

---

DON'T MISS

STREET MARKETS

Palermo's historical ties with the Arab world and its proximity to North Africa reverberate in the noisy street life of the city's ancient centre, and nowhere is this stronger than in its markets.

Each of the city's four historic quarters claims its own street market, but the Vucciria, Ballarò and Capo are the 'Big Three' in terms of popularity and history.

The **Mercato della Vucciria** (Map p66; Piazza Caracciolo; ⊙7am-8pm Mon, Tue, Thu-Sat, to 1pm Wed) is the most dishevelled and underwhelming of the three, with rough-edged customers, a small number of stalls selling produce and old junk, and often-grumpy stallholders. Infinitely more vibrant is the **Mercato di Ballarò** (Map p58; Via Ballaro 1; ⊙7.30am-8.30pm), filled with stalls peddling household goods, clothes and foodstuffs of every possible description – this is where many Palermitans do their daily shop. The **Mercato del Capo** (Map p58; Via Sant'Agostino; ⊙7am-8pm Mon, Tue & Thu-Sat, to 1pm Wed & Sun), which extends through the tangle of lanes and alleyways of the Albergheria and Capo quarters respectively, is the most atmospheric of all. Here, meat carcasses sway from huge metal hooks, glistening tuna and swordfish are expertly dismembered, and anchovies are filleted. Long and orderly lines of stalls display pungent cheeses, tubs of plump olives and a huge array of luscious fruits and voluptuous vegetables.

The markets are busiest in the morning. Remember: keep an eye on your belongings while exploring.

New City

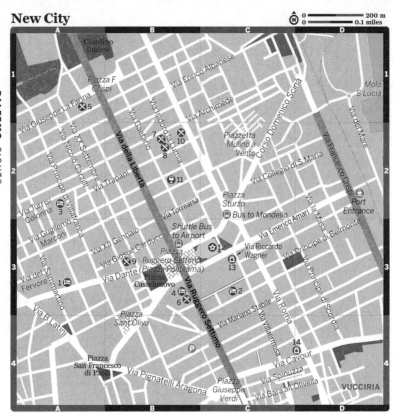

built atop a mosque that itself was super-imposed on a 6th-century Benedictine chapel. The tranquil grounds also house the ruins of the monastery's Norman-era cloister.

Chiesa del Gesù
CHURCH

(Map p58; Via del Ponticello; requested dona-tion €2; ⊙8am-7pm summer, to 3.30pm winter) Also known as Casa Professa, this is one of Palermo's most breathtaking church-es. The Jesuits first built a church on this site between 1564 and 1578. Incorporated into a larger church in 1633, the building was significantly restored after suffering major bomb damage in WWII. While the church's facade displays relative restraint typical of the late 16th century, its transept, apses and dome burst with 17th-century baroque extravagance. The dome's vault is decorated with a fresco attributed to Pietro Novelli.

◉ Il Capo

Directly north of the Albergheria quarter, Il Capo is another web of interconnected streets and blind alleys. As impoverished as its neighbour, it too has a popular street market, the Mercato del Capo (p59), which runs the length of Via Sant'Agostino and terminates at Porta Carini, one of Palermo's oldest town gates. The centrepiece of the quarter is the imposing monastery of **Chie-sa di Sant'Agostino** (Church of Saint Augus-tine; Map p58; ☑091 58 46 32; Via Sant'Agostino; ⊙7.30am-noon & 4-6.45pm Tue-Sat, to noon Mon & Sun), which ran the region in medieval times.

★Cattedrale di Palermo
CATHEDRAL

(Map p58; ☑329 3977513; www.cattedrale.paler mo.it; Corso Vittorio Emanuele; cathedral free, royal tombs €1.50, treasury & crypt €3, roof €5, all-incl ticket adult/reduced €8/4; ⊙7am-7pm Mon-Sat, 8am-1pm & 4-7pm Sun; royal tombs, treasury, crypt

New City

PALERMO SIGHTS

& roof 9am-1.30pm Mon-Sat, royal tombs & roof also 9am-12.30pm Sun) A feast of geometric patterns, ziggurat crenellations, maiolica cupolas and blind arches, Palermo's cathedral has suffered aesthetically from multiple reworkings over the centuries, but remains a prime example of Sicily's unique Arab-Norman architectural style. The interior, while impressive in scale, is essentially a marble shell whose most interesting features are the **royal Norman tombs** (to the left as you enter), the **treasury** (home to Constance of Aragon's gem-encrusted 13th-century crown) and the panoramic views from the **roof**.

Construction began in 1184 at the behest of Palermo's archbishop, Walter of the Mill (Gualtiero Offamiglio), an Englishman who was tutor to William II. Walter held great power and had unlimited funds at his disposal, but with the building of the magnificent cathedral at Monreale he felt his power diminishing. His solution was to order construction of an equally magnificent cathedral in Palermo. This was erected on the location of a 9th-century mosque (itself built on a former chapel), a detail from the mosque's original decor is visible at the southern porch, where a column is inscribed with a passage from the Koran. The cathedral's proportions and the grandeur of its exterior became a statement of the power struggle between Church and throne occurring at the time, a potentially dangerous situation that was tempered by Walter's death (in 1191), which prevented him from seeing (and boasting about) the finished building.

Since then the cathedral has been much altered, sometimes with great success (as in Antonio Gambara's 15th-century three-arched portico that took 200 years to complete and became a masterpiece of Catalan Gothic architecture), and sometimes with less fortunate results (as in Ferdinando Fu-

ga's clumsy dome, added between 1781 and 1801). Thankfully Fuga's handiwork did not extend to the eastern exterior, which is still adorned with the exotic interlacing designs of Walter's original cathedral. The southwestern facade was laid in the 13th and 14th centuries, and is a beautiful example of local craftsmanship in the Gothic style. The cathedral's entrance – through Gambara's three magnificent arches – is fronted by gardens and a statue of Santa Rosalia, one of Palermo's patron saints. A beautiful painted intarsia decoration above the arches depicts the tree of life in a complex Islamic-style geometric composition of 12 roundels that show fruit, humans and all kinds of animals. It's thought to date back to 1296.

To the left as you enter the cathedral, the Monumental Area harbours several royal Norman tombs, which contain the remains of two of Sicily's greatest rulers: Roger II (rear left) and Frederick II of Hohenstaufen (front left), as well as Henry VI and William II. The cathedral's treasury houses a small collection of Norman-era jewels and religious relics. Most extraordinary is the fabulous 13th-century crown of Constance of Aragon (wife of Frederick II), made by local craftsmen in fine gold filigree and encrusted with gems. More bizarre treasures include the tooth and ashes of Santa Rosalia, kept here in silver reliquaries.

Museo Diocesano di Palermo   MUSEUM
(Map p58; ☎091 607 72 15; www.museodiocesanopa.it; Via Matteo Bonello 2; adult/reduced €4.50/3; ☉9.30am-1.30pm Tue-Sun) Palermo's Diocesan Museum is home to an important collection of artworks. The basement hosts a medley of sculptures from the 15th to 18th centuries, including works by Renaissance artists Francesco Laurana and Antonello Gagini. The 1st floor occupies 12 halls of the old Archbishop's Palace, furnished with

Italian and Flemish paintings from the 16th to 19th centuries. Don't miss the Sala Beccadelli, capped by a mid-15th-century ceiling and the Cappella Borremans, lavished with 18th-century frescoes by Flemish painter Guglielmo Borremans.

◉ La Kalsa

Plagued by poverty, La Kalsa has long been one of the city's most notorious neighbourhoods. A recent program of urban regeneration, however, has seen many of its long-derelict *palazzos* being restored and long-abandoned streets speckled with petite bohemian bars, trendy eateries, artisan studios and street art. It's also here that you'll find some of Palermo's top cultural sights, including art repositories Galleria Regionale della Sicilia, Galleria d'Arte Moderna and the time-warped luxury of Palazzo Mirto.

★ **Galleria Regionale della Sicilia**   MUSEUM
(Map p66; ☑ 091 623 00 11; www.regione.sicilia.it/beniculturali/palazzoabatellis; Via Alloro 4; adult/reduced €8/4; ⊙ 9am-6.30pm Tue-Fri, to 1pm Sat & Sun) Housed in the stately 15th-century Palazzo Abatellis, this art museum – widely regarded as Palermo's best – showcases works by Sicilian artists dating from the Middle Ages to the 18th century. One of its greatest treasures is *Trionfo della morte* (Triumph

of Death), a magnificent fresco (artist unknown) in which Death is represented as a demonic skeleton mounted on a wasted horse, brandishing a wicked-looking scythe while leaping over his hapless victims.

Represented at the heart of the painting, under Death's horse, are the vain and pampered aristocrats of Palermo, while the poor and hungry look on from the side. The huge image, carefully restored, has been given its own space on the ground level to maximise its visual impact.

The gallery is full of countless other treasures, which collectively offer great insight into the evolution of Sicilian art. Among these is Antonello da Messina's enigmatic 15th-century masterpiece *L'Annunciata* (Virgin Annunciate), with its refined balance of Italian and Flemish influences.

The exhibition space itself was designed to fill this gorgeous Catalan Gothic *palazzo* in 1957 by Carlo Scarpa, one of Italy's leading architects.

Museo dell'Inquisizione   MUSEUM
(Map p66; ☑ 091 2389 3788; Piazza Marina 61; adult/reduced €8/5; ⊙ 10am-6pm Tue-Sun) Housed in the lower floors and basements of 14th-century Palazzo Chiaromonte Steri, this fascinating museum explores the legacy of the Inquisition in Palermo. Thousands of 'heretics' were detained here between 1601

DON'T MISS

STREET ART IN PALERMO

The side streets of Palermo's *centro storico* (historic centre) pop with bold, Insta-ready street art such as playful depictions of fantastical creatures and bold, politically sensitive murals about immigration and the mafia. You'll find works in all four of the city's old quarters, including on and around Via Carrettieri in Il Capo, the streets around the Mercato di Ballarò (p59) in Albergheria, the intersection of Via Cassari and Via Materassai in La Vucciria, and Via della Cannella in La Kalsa.

La Kalsa is home to an especially impressive trio of **large-scale murals** (Map p66; Via Dello Spasimo), commissioned as part of an urban-renewal project and occupying the multi-storey walls of a row of apartment blocks on Via Dello Spasimo. The mural on the left is by Rome-based artist Camilla Falsini, whose geometric protagonist is a young Frederick II, Sicily's famously cosmopolitan ruler. To the right, Sicilian duo Rosk e Loste (Maurizio Giulio 'Rosk' Gebbia and Mirko 'Loste' Cavalletto) celebrate cultural diversity with their vibrant depiction of a young woman of African descent. Next to it soars Gorizia-born Mbre Fats' contemporary reinterpretation of the city's famous 15th-century fresco *Trionfo della morte* (Triumph of Death), on display at nearby Galleria Regionale della Sicilia (p62). Rosk e Loste are also responsible for the **giant mural** (Map p66; cnr Via della Cala & Via Mura della Lupa) of slain anti-mafia magistrates Giovanni Falcone and Paolo Borsellino, located on the corner of Via della Cala and Via Mura della Lupa, an 800m walk north along nearby Via Butera.

For more insight into the city's ever-changing, ever-expanding street-art offerings, check out Street Art Palermo (@streetartpalermo) on Instagram.

and 1782; the honeycomb of former cells has been painstakingly restored to reveal multiple layers of their graffiti and artwork (religious and otherwise). Visits are by one-hour guided tour only, conducted in English and Italian and departing roughly every 40 to 60 minutes from the ticket desk.

Religiously themed graffiti includes a depiction of Christ being tortured by Spanish soldiers and images of local protector saints San Rocco and Santa Rosalia. Works of a more profane nature include hearts pierced with arrows or instruments of torture, elaborate maps of Sicily where other prisoners were invited to add missing details, an inquisitor holding the scales of justice, and a caricature of another inquisitor astride a defecating horse adjacent to the latrine.

The tour also takes in two works by noted Sicilian modern artist Renato Guttuso: first, a copy of his graphic depiction of the strangulation murder of inquisitor De Cisneros by the handcuffed 22-year-old prisoner Diego La Mattina; and Guttuso's original, masterful 1974 painting of the Vucciria market. Figures depicted in the latter work include the artist, his wife and Guttuso's much younger lover. The painting can be visited without touring the museum (€4).

Museo delle Maioliche   MUSEUM
(Stanze al Genio; Map p66; ☑340 0971561, 380 3673773; www.stanzealgenio.it; Via Garibaldi 11; adult/reduced €9/8; ☺ guided tours in English 3pm Tue-Fri, 10am Sat, 11am Sun, in Italian 4pm Tue-Fri, 11am Sat & Sun) Lovers of hand-painted Italian maiolica should make a beeline for this unique museum, which contains a superlative private collection of almost 6000 tiles, most from Sicily and Naples, and spanning the 15th to 20th centuries. Amassed over three decades by founder Pio Mellina, the tiles fill the walls and floors of the lovingly restored 16th-century Palazzo Torre-Piraino, itself a work of art with vaulted and frescoed ceilings. The museum also houses a small collection of vintage Italian toys.

Oratorio di San Lorenzo   CHAPEL
(Map p66; Via dell'Immacolatella 5; adult/reduced €3/2; ☺10am-6pm) The late-16th-century Oratory of St Lawrence features glorious stuccowork by master rococo sculptor Giacomo Serpotta. Capturing scenes from the lives of St Lawrence and St Francis, the work is kept in fine company by an Antonino Grano–designed marble floor and exquisite side benches with ivory and mother-of-pearl in-

laying. Above the altar is a reproduction of Caravaggio's *The Nativity with St Francis and St Lawrence*, stolen from here in 1969 and still one of the FBI's top 10 unsolved art crimes.

Galleria d'Arte Moderna   MUSEUM
(Map p66; ☑091 843 16 05; www.gampalermo.it; Via Sant'Anna 21; adult/reduced €7/5; ☺9.30am-6.30pm Tue-Sun) This lovely, wheelchair-accessible museum is housed in a 15th-century *palazzo*, which metamorphosed into a convent in the 17th century. Divided over three floors, the wide-ranging collection of 19th- and 20th-century art focuses on Sicilian works and include everything from 19th-century monumental historical genre paintings to futuristic romps from the early 20th century. There's a regular program of modern-art exhibitions, as well as a decent museum shop. English-language audioguides cost €4.

Palazzo Mirto   PALACE
(Map p66; ☑091 616 75 41; www.regione.sicilia.it/beniculturali/palazzomirto; Via Merlo 2; adult/reduced €6/3; ☺9am-6pm Tue-Sat, to 1pm Sun) Just off Piazza Marina, this *palazzo* is one of the few in Palermo open to the public. Dating back to the 17th century, the building served as the Palermo residence of the Filangeri family for four centuries, and offers visitors a glimpse of the lavish, lost world of the Sicilian nobility. English-language booklets provide information for visitors.

Chiesa di San Francesco d'Assisi   CHURCH
(Map p66; Piazza San Francesco d'Assisi; ☺4-5.30pm Mon, 9-11am & 4-5.30pm Tue-Sun) On a picture-perfect piazza, the much-amended Chiesa di San Francesco d'Assisi dates back to the 13th century. Remnants from its early history include the Romanesque facade, striking portal and left apse. The church's most interesting feature is the rare arch of the Cappella Mastrantonio, carved in 1468 by Francesco Laurana and his protégé Pietro da Bonitate, and one of the only true examples of Renaissance art in Palermo.

Orto Botanico   GARDENS
(Map p66; ☑091 2389 1236; www.ortobotanico.unipa.it; Via Abramo Lincoln 2; adult/reduced €6/3; ☺9am-8pm May-Aug, to 7pm Apr & Sep, to 6pm Mar & Oct, to 5pm Nov-Feb) Laid out by Léon Dufourny and Venanzio Marvuglia, this raffish, subtropical paradise shelters massive fig trees, tall palms and dazzling hibiscus bushes, an avenue of bizarre-looking bottle

THE GENIUS OF GIACOMO SERPOTTA

Giacomo Serpotta (1656–1732) is widely considered the greatest Sicilian artist of the late baroque and rococo period, catapulting stuccowork in Italy from a mere craft to a dizzying high art. Born to a sculptor in Palermo's La Kalsa district, the artist would establish an international reputation for his bewitching, lifelike figures, often positioned in unorthodox and asymmetrical ways to create a striking sense of realism and perspective. Complimenting his imaginative approach was a technical brilliance that saw Serpotta develop a polishing technique able to grace his stuccowork with a marble-like lustre.

To view his artistic evolution, pay a visit to the oratories of Santa Cita, San Lorenzo (p63) and San Domenico in chronological order. Santa Cita's interior bursts with the freshness of Serpotta's creativity, which includes cherubs stretching out a stucco canvas depicting the battle of Lepanto. The artist's growing prowess sizzles in the Oratorio di San Lorenzo, whose meticulous details include an extraordinary statue of a breastfeeding *Carità* (Charity) and a sea of playful *putti* (cherubs) adorning the walls. Serpotta reaches his artistic maturity in the Oratorio di San Domenico. Here, confident statements include the depiction of allegorical figures as dames dressed in lace and ostrich feathers, a representation considered highly innovative at the time.

and soap trees, as well as coffee trees, papaya plants and sycamores. It's a soothing haven of silence and fascinating botany, with shaded pathways and a large herb garden focused on Mediterranean plants.

⊙ Vucciria

The Vucciria neighbourhood is known throughout Sicily for its Mercato della Vucciria, the inspiration for Sicilian painter Renato Guttuso's most important work, *La Vucciria* (1974).

Once the heart of poverty-stricken Palermo and a den of crime and filth, the Vucciria illustrated the almost medieval chasm that existed between rich and poor in Sicily up until the 1950s. Though it's still quite shabby, the winds of change are blowing, no stronger that at the lovingly restored Palazzo Branciforte. It's one of the neighbourhood's many fascinating historic buildings, many of which are in the vicinity of the commanding 17th-century **Chiesa di San Domenico** (Church of Saint Domenic; Map p66; ☑ 091 774 64 45; www.domenicani-palermo.it; Piazza San Domenico; church free, cloister & sacristy €3; ⊙ church 8am-5pm Tue-Fri, to 7pm Sat, 9am-1pm & 5-7pm Sun, cloister 9.30am-4pm Tue-Sat).

Museo Archeologico
Regionale Antonio Salinas   MUSEUM
(Map p66; ☑091 611 68 07; www.regione.sicilia.it/bbccaa/salinas; Piazza Olivella 24; adult/reduced €6/3; ⊙9am-6pm Tue-Sat, to 1.30pm Sun) Situated in a Renaissance monastery, this splendid, wheelchair-accessible museum houses some of Sicily's most valuable Greek and Roman ar-

tefacts, including the museum's crown jewel: a series of original decorative friezes from the temples at Selinunte. Other important finds in the museum's collection include Phoenician sarcophagi from the 5th century BC, Greek carvings from Himera, the Hellenistic *Ariete di bronzo di Siracusa* (Bronze Ram of Syracuse), Etruscan mirrors and the largest collection of ancient anchors in the world.

Oratorio di Santa Cita   CHAPEL
(Map p66; www.ilgeniodipalermo.com; Via Valverde; €4, incl Oratorio di San Domenico €6; ⊙9am-6pm) This 17th-century chapel showcases the breathtaking stuccowork of Giacomo Serpotta, who famously introduced rococo to Sicilian churches. Note the elaborate *Battle of Lepanto* on the entrance wall. Depicting the Christian victory over the Turks, it's framed by stucco drapes held by a cast of cheeky cherubs modelled on Palermo's street urchins. Serpotta's virtuosity also dominates the side walls, where sculpted white stucco figures hold gilded swords, shields and a lute, and a golden snake (Serpotta's symbol) curls around a picture frame.

This chapel is associated with four other nearby churches, collectively known as the Tesori della Loggia (Treasures of the Loggia). Three of the churches – **Santa Cita** (Map p66; Via Valverde; ⊙hours vary), **San Giorgio dei Genovesi** (Map p66; Via Squarcialupo; ⊙hours vary) and **Santa Maria di Valverde** (Map p66; Largo Cavalieri di Malta; ⊙9am-12.30pm Sat) – are free, though opening times are sporadic. A combined ticket (available here) offers a small discount on admission to the remaining chapel, the Oratorio di San Domenico.

Oratorio di San Domenico CHAPEL
(Map p66; www.ilgeniodipalermo.com; Via dei
Bambinai 2; €4, incl Oratorio di Santa Cita €6;
⊙9am-6pm) Dominating this small chapel is
Anthony Van Dyck's fantastic blue-and-red
altarpiece, *The Virgin of the Rosary with St
Dominic and the Patronesses of Palermo.*
Van Dyck completed the work in Genoa in
1628, after leaving Palermo in fear of the
plague. Also gracing the chapel are Giacomo Serpotta's amazingly elaborate stuccoes
(1710–17), vivacious and whirling with figures. Serpotta's name meant 'lizard' or 'small
snake', and he often included these signature
reptiles in his work; see if you can find one!

★**Palazzo Branciforte** MUSEUM
(Map p66; ✆091 765 76 21; www.palazzobranci
forte.it; Largo Gae Aulenti 2; adult/reduced €7/5;
⊙9am-5pm Mon-Fri) One of Palermo's grandest aristocratic palaces is now an impressive, multi-faceted cultural centre. One-hour
guided tours (email ahead for English-
language tours) depart every 30 minutes
and take in the **Fondazione Sicilia Library**,
crowned by Ignazio Moncada di Paternò's
bold contemporary fresco, as well as the
Monte di Santa Rosalia, a spectacular, tim-
ber-framed exhibition space that houses an
important collection of traditional Sicilian
pupi (puppets). The ground-floor **archaeological collection** claims over 4750 objects,
many unearthed at the ruins of Selinunte.

⊙ **New City**

North of Piazza Giuseppe Verdi, Palermo's
streets widen, the buildings lengthen, and the
shops, restaurants and cafes become more
elegant (and more expensive). Glorious neoclassical and Liberty examples from the last
golden age in Sicilian architecture give the
city an exuberant, belle époque feel in stark
contrast to the narrow, introspective vibe of
the historic quarter. Head here for beautifully
curated art at Pinacoteca Villa Zito, trendy
aperitivo (pre-dinner drinks) sessions, high-
end retail therapy and rousing symphonies at
the Teatro Politeama Garibaldi.

★**Teatro Massimo** THEATRE
(Map p58; ✆box office 091 605 35 80; www.teatro
massimo.it; Piazza Giuseppe Verdi; guided tours
adult/reduced €8/5; ⊙9.30am-6pm) Taking over
20 years to complete, Palermo's neoclassical
opera house is the largest in Italy and the
second-largest in Europe. The closing scene
of *The Godfather: Part III,* with its visually

arresting juxtaposition of high culture, crime,
drama and death, was filmed here and the
building's richly decorated interiors are nothing short of spectacular. Guided 30-minute
tours are offered throughout the day in English, Italian, French, Spanish and German.

⊙ **Outside the City Centre**

★**Pinacoteca Villa Zito** GALLERY
(✆091 778 21 80; www.villazito.it; Via della Libertà
52; adult/reduced €5/3; ⊙9.30am-7.30pm Tue-
Sun) Elegant 18th-century Villa Zito houses a sharply curated collection of mainly
Sicilian-themed art spanning the 17th to
20th centuries. You'll find a number of fascinating historical depictions of Palermo,
numerous paintings by Ettore De Maria
Bergler (considered the foremost Italian
painter of the Liberty era), as well as works
by 20th-century heavyweights Ugo Attardi,
Fausto Pirandello, Filippo De Pisis, Carlo
Carrà and Renato Guttuso.

★**Palazzina Cinese
& Parco della Favorita** PALACE
(✆091 707 14 03; Via Duca degli Abruzzi 1; ⊙9am-
6pm Tue-Sat, plus 9am-1pm 1st Sun of month) Once
a retreat for King Ferdinand IV and his wife
Maria Carolina, this pagoda-inspired pavilion
exemplifies the popularity of 'Oriental exot-
ica' in 18th-century Europe. Chinese, Egyptian, Islamic and Pompeiian motifs decorate
its many rooms, with particular highlights
including a trompe l'oeil 'collapsed' ceiling by
Giuseppe Velazquez and a nifty dining table
connected to the kitchen below via a lift. To
get here, catch bus 107 to Piazza Giovanni
Paolo II and then bus 615 or 645 to Duca degli
Abruzzi – Palazzina Cinese.

Villa Malfitano HISTORIC BUILDING
(✆091 682 05 22; www.fondazionewhitaker.it/villa.
html; Via Dante 167; adult/reduced €9/6; ⊙9am-
3pm Mon-Sat) A showcase of Liberty architecture, set in a 9-hectare (22-acre) formal
garden planted with rare and exotic species,
this villa is most notable for its whimsical
interior decoration, which includes a 'Summer Room' with walls painted to resemble a
conservatory, and a music room draped with
15th-century tapestries illustrating the *Aeneid*. It's a 20-minute walk west from Piazza
Castelnuovo.

Catacombe dei Cappuccini CATACOMB
(www.catacombepalermo.it; Piazza Cappuccini;
adult/child under 8yr €3/free; ⊙9am-1pm & 3-6pm,
closed Sun afternoon Nov-Mar) These catacombs

Vucciria & La Kalsa

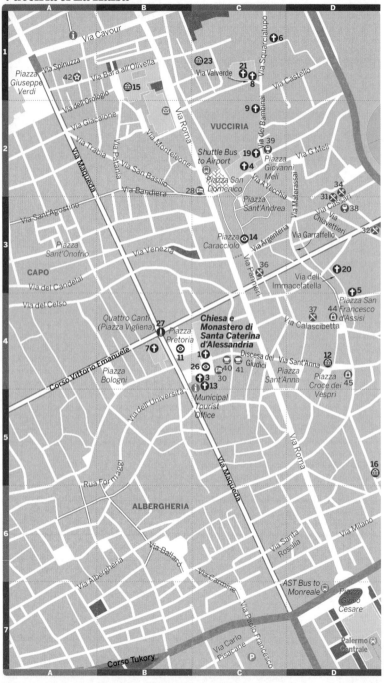

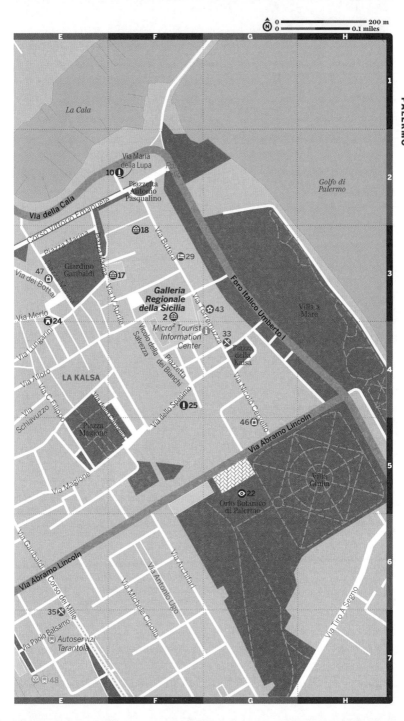

Vucciria & La Kalsa

house the mummified bodies and skeletons of some 8000 Palermitans who died between the 17th and 19th centuries. Earthly power, gender, religion and professional status are still rigidly distinguished, with men and women occupying separate corridors, and a first-class section set aside for virgins. From Piazza Indipendenza, it's a 1.2km walk west along Via Cappuccini.

Tours

Addiopizzo Travel WALKING
(Map p58; ☑ 091 861 61 17; www.addiopizzo travel. it) Runs a series of interesting mafia-themed guided tours in the region, including a three-hour Palermo No Mafia walking tour (€30). Departing from Piazza Verdi, the morning saunter offers fascinating insights into the history of Sicily's homegrown mafia, the Cosa Nostra, as well as the brave efforts of those opposed to its nefarious influence. See the website for details.

Sicilia Letteraria WALKING
(☑ 091 625 40 11, 327 6844052; www.parcotomasi.it) This organisation runs literary walks and excursions, among them regular walking tours focused on Sicilian novelist Giuseppe Tomasi di Lampedusa and his literary masterpiece *Il Gattopardo* (The Leopard). These include an English-language tour (per person €30) called 'Walking with the Leopard' every Monday morning and a monthly all-day excursion (per person €80) exploring Palermo's historic centre, Villa Nemsci and Palazzo Mirto.

 Festivals & Events

Le Vie dei Tesori
CULTURAL

(📞091 842 01 04; http://leviedeitesori.com/festival-le-vie-dei-tesori; 🕐Fri-Sun Oct & Nov; 🚇) Held over five weekends in October and November, this family-friendly 'Open House' festival sees over one hundred sites – including chapels, churches, palaces, fortifications, gardens and historic factories – open their doors to the public. Among them are places that are usually inaccessible. Special events include guided tours, concerts and tastings.

Festino di Santa Rosalia
RELIGIOUS

(U Fistinu; 🕐Jul) Palermo's biggest annual festival celebrates patron saint Santa Rosalia, beloved for having saved the city from a 17th-century plague. The most colourful festivities take place on the evening of 14 July, when the saint's relics are paraded aboard a grand chariot from the Palazzo dei Normanni through the Quattro Canti to the waterfront, with fireworks and general merriment.

✕ Eating

While Palermo's restaurant scene may not rival that of Sicily's Michelin-star-studded southeast, expect to find plenty of variety, such as heirloom trattorias serving faithful classics like *bucatini con le sarde* (pasta mixed with sardines, wild fennel, raisins, pine nuts and breadcrumbs) and next-gen hotspots tweaking nonna's recipes. Hit the markets and street-food stalls for delicious bargain bites and the *pasticcerie* (pastry shops) for staples including *frutta martorana* (fruit-shaped marzipan).

★ Trattoria al Vecchio Club Rosanero
SICILIAN €

(Map p58; 📞349 4096880; Vicolo Caldomai 18; mains €3-12; 🕐1-3.30pm Mon-Sat & 8-11pm Thu-Sat; 🕐) A veritable shrine to the city's football team (*rosa nero* refers to the team's colours, pink and black), cavernous Vecchio Club scores goals with its generous, bargain-priced grub. Fish and seafood are the real fortes here; if it's on the menu, order the *caponata e pesce spada* (*caponata* with swordfish), a sweet-and-sour victory. Head in early to avoid a wait.

Archestrato di Gela
PIZZA €

(📞091 625 89 83; www.facebook.com/archestrato digelapalermo; Via Emanuele Notarbartolo 2f; pizzas €6.50-14; 🕐7.45pm-midnight Tue-Sun; 🕐📷) If you're serious about wood-fired pie, book at least two days ahead at what many consid-

er to be the best pizzeria in town. The puffy, Neapolitan-style crusts are charred to perfection and topped with speciality, artisan ingredients from across Italy. Standouts include the Priolo, a turf-meets-surf smash of Bronte pistachio pesto, aged *prosciutto crudo, burratina* cheese (made from mozarella and cream) and Cetara tuna. Libations include cocktails.

Pan X Focaccia
SANDWICHES €

(Map p60; 📞091 507 90 24; https://panxfocaccia.it; Via Isidoro la Lumia 74; panini €4-10; 🕐noon-4pm & 7.30-midnight; 🕐📷) Panini go glam at Pan X, a contemporary, sit-down sandwich joint with a dizzying list of eat-and-go options. It offers a wide choice of breads, including gluten-free and ancient-grain varieties, plus no shortage of vegetarian and vegan bites. Hamburgers (€4 to €9.50) are available, along with craft, gluten-free and non-alcoholic beers.

Bisso Bistrot
BISTRO €

(Map p58; 📞328 1314595; http://bissobistrot.it; Via Maqueda 172; mains €5-9; 🕐9am-11pm Mon-Sat) Frescoed walls, exposed ceiling beams and reasonably priced appetisers, *primi* (first courses) and *secondi* (main courses) greet diners at this swinging, smart-casual bistro. Located beside the Quattro Canti, its edible offerings cover all meals, from morning *cornetti* (croissants) to lunch and dinner meat, fish and pasta dishes (the latter are especially good). Solo diners will appreciate the front bar seating.

Trattoria Ai Cascinari
SICILIAN €

(Map p58; 📞091 651 98 04; Via d'Ossuna 43/45; meals €20-25; 🕐12.30-2.30pm Tue-Sun, plus 8-10.30pm Wed-Sat) Yes, it's a bit out of the way, but Ai Cascinari, 1km north of the Cappella Palatina, is a long-standing Palermitan favourite. It's especially enjoyable on Sunday afternoons, when locals pack the labyrinth of back rooms and waiters perambulate nonstop with plates of scrumptious seasonal antipasti. Dishes include *primi* of ravioli with broccoli, anchovies and *caciocavallo* cheese, and mains of succulent, stuffed calamari.

★ Aja Mola
SEAFOOD €€

(Map p66; 📞091 611 91 59, 334 1508335; www.ajamolapalermo.it; Via Cassari 39; meals €35-40; 🕐12.30-3pm & 7.30-11pm Tue-Sun; 🕐) On-point Aja Mola is among Palermo's top seafood eateries. The interior's smart, subtle take on a nautical theme is reflected in the open kitchen, which eschews stock-standard cliches for modern, creative dishes. The result:

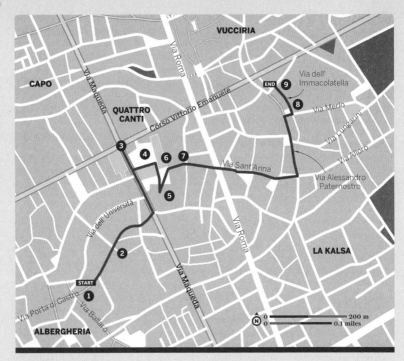

🏃 City Walk
Historic Palermo

START MERCATO DI BALLARÒ
END ORATORIO DI SAN LORENZO
LENGTH 1.3KM; THREE TO FOUR HOURS

Dense but compact, central Palermo is best explored on foot. This tour covers some of the city's most enticing assets.

Pique your appetite with an early morning trundle through the ❶ **Mercato di Ballarò** (p59), its stalls groaning under the weight of fresh produce, pungent cheeses and glistening local fish. Then head northeast on Via Casa Professa to Jesuit showstopper ❷ **Chiesa del Gesù** (p60), its rich interiors decorated in part by baroque master Pietro Novelli. Continuing northeast on Via del Ponticello, you'll hit Via Maqueda. Turn left into it to reach the ❸ **Quattro Canti** (p56), Palermo's most beautiful junction, which divides the city's four historic neighbourhoods. Backtrack to Piazza Pretoria, whose own showpiece is ❹ **Fontana Pretoria** (p57). Moved here from Tuscany in 1573, its naked nymphs led to its nickname, the Fountain of Shame.

Exit the square from its southeast corner to reach Piazza Bellini. Make time for the Byzantine mosaics inside the 12th-century ❺ **La Martorana** (p56), admire the exterior of the adjoining Chiesa Capitolare di San Cataldo, then cross the piazza to explore the ❻ **Chiesa e Monastero di Santa Caterina d'Alessandria** (p56), a former convent with a bombastically baroque church, majolica-decorated cloister, rooftop city views and superb in-house bakery. Done, relax over a well-earned coffee at neighbouring ❼ **Ideal Caffè Stagnitta** (p73).

Once refreshed, cross busy Via Roma, continue east on Via Sant'Anna, turning left into Via Paternostro, an atmospheric street dotted with independent boutiques and artisan studios. The street passes pretty Piazza San Francesco d'Assisi, whose 13th-century ❽ **church** (p63) sports a handsome Romanesque facade and celebrated Renaissance chapel. Adjoining Via dell'Immacolatella is your final stop, the 16th-century ❾ **Oratorio di San Lorenzo** (p63), home to remarkable rococo stuccowork by Giacomo Serpotta.

appetite-piquing options like teriyaki-style tartare with caperberries, or surf-turf *tagliolini* pasta with succulent shrimps and pork jowl. Bar seating available; ideal for solo diners. Book ahead.

★ Ristorante Ferro SICILIAN €€

(Map p58; ☑ 347 1618373, 091 58 60 49; www. facebook.com/ristoranteferropalermo; Piazza Sant' Onofrio 42; meals €30-40; ⊙ 8-11pm Mon-Sat) All clean lines, timber panels and tinted mirrors, intimate, family-run Ferro wouldn't look out of place in London or Sydney. Whether you're savouring a soup of squid and mussels, earthy ravioli stuffed with porcini mushrooms, or a flawless steak, the food here is superb in its simplicity, favouring prime produce cooked beautifully and without fuss. Alas, wines by the glass are limited.

Ristorante Palazzo Branciforte SICILIAN €€

(Map p66; ☑ 091 32 17 48; www.ristorantepala zzobranciforte.it; Via Bara all'Olivella 2; brunch €30; ⊙ noon-3pm & 7-11pm) Located in a blue-blooded *palazzo*, this restaurant is popular for its Sunday brunch. Book ahead for a table in the elegant courtyard, the best spot to savour buffet offerings like *parmigiana di melanzana* (aubergine parmigiana), tuna *ragù* pasta and octopus salad. Just leave room for the desserts, a tempting spread of freshly baked cakes, tarts, fruit and, if you're lucky, ricotta-stuffed *sfinci* (doughnuts).

Mo' Avast PUGLIAN, GREEK €€

(Map p60; ☑ 339 3212467; www.facebook.com/ moavastpalermo; Via Isidora la Lumia 82; meals €25-35; ⊙ 6.30-11pm Tue-Thu, to midnight Fri & Sat, noon-3pm & 6.30-11pm Sun; 🐟🖉) When your *papà* is Puglian and your *mamá* Greek, it makes sense to open a restaurant dedicated to Puglian-Greek cuisine. That's exactly what siblings Barbara and Emanuela have done, their cross-cultural eatery serving delicacies such as fried zucchini flowers stuffed with feta, and octopus balls served on creamy hummus. If you're in a group, call ahead and request the private mezzanine table.

Le Angeliche SICILIAN €€

(Map p58; ☑ 091 615 70 95; www.leangeliche.it; Vicolo Abbadia 10; meals €25-35; ⊙ 9am-3pm Mon-Thu, to midnight Fri & Sat; 🐟) An oasis of potted plants and pastel hues, Le Angeliche is run by four women passionate about honouring and refreshing Sicily's rich, sometime obscure culinary traditions. Scan the menu and you might find a soup of cannellini beans, endive, chestnuts and pasta, or perhaps *cassatella di*

Montevago – fried, ravioli-like pastries filled with sweetened sheep's milk ricotta, honey and lemon zest. Book ahead.

Bioesserì HEALTH FOOD €€

(Map p60; ☑ 091 765 71 42; www.bioesseri.it; Via Giuseppe La Farina 4; pizza €7.50-14, meals €30-35; ⊙ 7.30am-11pm Mon-Thu, to 11.30pm Fri, 8.30am-11.30pm Sat, to 11pm Sun; 🐟) Organic fare awaits at this stylish Milanese import. Part cafe, part upmarket grocery store, its virtuous bites tap all bases, including vegan *cornetti* (croissants), smoothies and soy-milk *budini* (puddings), spelt-flour pizzas and well-executed, bistro-style dishes like *fregola* pasta in a fish-and-crustacean soup, or stuffed calamari paired with herbed potato purée.

Osteria Ballarò SICILIAN €€

(Map p66; ☑ 091 32 64 88; www.osteriaballaro. it; Via Calascibetta 25; meals €35-45; ⊙ noon-3pm & 7-11pm) Bare stone columns, exposed brick walls and vaulted ceilings set an atmospheric, evocative scene at this buzzing restaurant-wine bar. Approved by the Slow Food movement, its graze-friendly menu celebrates island produce and cooking, such as artisan cheeses, *salumi* (charcuterie), *crudite di pesce* (local sashimi), seafood *primi* and memorable Sicilian *dolci* (sweets). Quality local wines top it off. Reservations recommended.

Il Maestro del Brodo TRATTORIA €€

(Map p66; ☑ 091 32 95 23; Via Pannieri 7; meals €25-35; ⊙ 12.30-3.30pm Tue-Sun, plus 7.30-11pm Fri & Sat) A homely, historic trattoria in the Vucciria, Il Maestro del Brodo revels in Italian soul-food classics, whether it be tortellini in broth, zucchini-and-prawn risotto, or grilled fresh fish. Top billing goes to the sensational antipasto buffet, a sweep of homemade delicacies such as *sarde a beccafico* (stuffed sardines), eggplant *involtini* (roulades), fried zucchini, artichokes with parsley, and sweet-and-sour *caponata*.

Gagini ITALIAN €€€

(Map p66; ☑ 091 58 99 18; www.gaginirestaurant. com; Via Cassari 35; meals €45, 4-/5-/8-course degustation menu €70/85/110; ⊙ 12.30-3pm & 7.30-11.30pm; 🐟) Expect sharp professionals and serious gastronomes at Gagini's rustic, candlelit tables. In the kitchen are Massimiliano Mandozzi and Elnava De Rosa, whose passion for season, region and fresh thinking might offer a Sicilian twist on the kebab, a playful take on classic *pasta con le sarde* (pasta with sardines), or seafood

PALERMO EATING

unexpectedly paired with cracked wheat and hazelnuts. Book ahead.

Drinking & Nightlife

Popular drinking spots include bohemian Via Paternostro, Piazza della Rivoluzione and Discesa dei Giudici, as well as cheap, gritty Via Maccherronai. Further north, lively bars line Via Isidora la Lumia. You'll also find bars in the Champagneria district due east of Teatro Massimo, centred on Piazza Olivella, Via Spinuzza and Via Patania. Higher-end drinking spots are concentrated in Palermo's new city.

★ Ferramenta   WINE BAR

(Map p66; ☑091 672 70 61; Piazza G Meli 8; ⊙6.30pm-1am Tue-Sun) Once a hardware store, this genuinely cool, piazza-side bar-eatery now fixes long days with well-mixed cocktails and clued-in vino. Rotating wines by the glass might include a natural white from western Sicily or an organic red from Etna, best paired with a *tagliere* (board) of top-notch charcuterie, seafood or vegetables (€10 to €18). More substantial dishes are also available, including pasta.

★ Hic! La Folie du Vin   WINE BAR

(Map p60; ☑349 2693038; www.facebook.com/hiclafolieduvin; Via G Mazzini 46; ⊙6.30-11.30pm, closed Sun mid-Jun—Jul & Sep, closed Mon Oct—mid-Jun, closed Aug) Hugely popular with 30- and 40-plus locals, Hic! is never short of a fun crowd, spilling out onto the footpath in a sea of banter and reasonably priced vino. The latter includes lots of Italian, French and German drops, each one approved by owner Giuseppe. Edibles include quality cheeses and cured meats, and the bar hosts live acoustic sets on Sunday evenings.

★ Bocum Mixology   COCKTAIL BAR

(Map p66; ☑091 33 20 09; www.bocum.it; Via Cassari 6; ⊙6pm-2am Wed-Mon; ☎) Decked out in contemporary art and eclectic objets, bohemian Bocum was Palermo's first proper cocktail bar and remains one of its best. While the ground-floor cantina is a fine spot for cognoscenti wines and DOP *salumi*, the

---

STREET FOOD, PALERMO STYLE

Bangkok, Mexico City, Marrakesh and Palermo: worldly gluttons know that Sicily's capital is a street-food heavyweight. Palermitans are obsessed with eating (and eating well), and almost any time is a good time to feast. What they're devouring is *buffitieri* – little hot snacks prepared at stalls and designed for eating on the spot.

Kick off the morning with *pane e panelle*, Palermo's famous chickpea fritters – great for vegetarians and a welcome change from a sweet custard-filled croissant. You might also want to go for some *crocchè* (potato croquettes, sometimes flavoured with fresh mint) or *quaglie* (literally translated as quails, they're actually aubergines/eggplants cut lengthwise and fanned out to resemble a bird's feathers, then fried). Other options include *sfincione* (a spongy, oily pizza topped with onions and *caciocavallo* cheese) and *scaccie* (discs of bread dough spread with a filling and rolled up into a pancake). In the warmer months, locals find it difficult to refuse a freshly baked brioche jammed with ice cream or *granita* (crushed ice mixed with fresh fruit, almonds, pistachios or coffee).

From 4pm onwards the snacks become decidedly more carnivorous, and you may just wish you hadn't read the following translations: how about some barbecued *stigghiola* (goat intestines filled with onions, cheese and parsley), for example? Or a couple of *pani ca meusa* (breadroll stuffed with sautéed beef spleen). You'll be asked if you want it '*schietta*' (single) or '*maritata*' (married). If you choose *schietta*, the roll will only have ricotta in it before being dipped into boiling lard; choose *maritata* and you'll get the beef spleen as well.

You'll find stalls and kiosks selling street food all over town, especially in Palermo's street markets. Top choices include **Francu U Vastiddaru** (Map p66; Corso Vittorio Emanuele 102; sandwiches €1.50-4; ⊙9am-1am), **Friggitoria Chiluzzo** (Map p66; ☑329 0615929; Piazza della Kalsa; sandwiches €1-2.50; ⊙8am-5pm Mon-Sat, to 4pm Sun) and tiny **I Cuochini** (Map p60; Via Ruggero Settimo 68; snacks from €0.70; ⊙8.30am-2.30pm Mon-Sat, plus 4.30-7.30pm Sat). For a deeper cultural perspective on Palermo and its street food scene, check out the guided tours offered by **Streaty** (www.streaty.com; 3hr tours per person adult/child €39/15) or **Palermo Street Food** (www.palermostreetfood.com; 3hr tours per person €30).

real magic happens upstairs, where skilled hands shake and stir seamless, seasonal libations. Creative, seafood-centric bites fuse Sicilian and Asian influences, from snacks to mains.

Ideal Caffè Stagnitta   CAFE

(Map p66; ☎091 617 25 13; www.casastagnitta. it; Discesa dei Giudici 42-44; ⊙6am-7pm Mon-Sat) This historic coffee roaster is now also a cafe, with tables dotting one of Palermo's most picturesque cobbled streets. People-watch over a single-origin coffee or, better still, a *gelato affogato al caffè*, a cheeky combo of ice cream, espresso and cream. For a fortifying souvenir, grab a bag or two of Stagnitta's own blends; it even makes Nespresso-compatible coffee pods.

St'orto   CAFE

(Map p66; ☎091 274 85 49; www.facebook.com/ stortopalermo; Discesa dei Giudici 40; ⊙9am-1am Tue-Thu & Sun, to 2am Fri & Sat) In the evenings, arty, indie types spill onto the cobbled street at this tiny, much-loved cafe-bar. Cocktails start at a reasonable €5, with other libations including craft beers, thoughtfully chosen Sicilian wines and organic juices. Daytime bites include *panini* stuffed with local cheeses and cured meats, while the evening *aperitivo* might see you grazing on complimentary *bruschette*.

☆ Entertainment

Palermo's cultural offerings include world-class opera, ballet, symphonies and world music. More unusual concert venues include churches and historic villas. In summer, outdoor music and ballet concerts are held at the Teatro di Verdura. Numerous bars across the city offer a variety of live music, including rock, blues, jazz and funk. For something truly unique, catch a Sicilian puppet show.

★ Teatro Massimo   OPERA

(Map p58; ☎box office 091 605 35 80; www.teatro massimo.it; Piazza Giuseppe Verdi) Ernesto Basile's six-tiered art-nouveau masterpiece is Europe's second-largest opera house and one of Italy's most prestigious, right up there with La Scala in Milan, San Carlo in Naples and La Fenice in Venice. It stages opera, ballet and music concerts from September to June.

Teatro Ditirammu   WORLD MUSIC

(Map p66; ☎391 3064887; www.teatroditiram mu.it; Via Torremuzza 6; ⊛) Tucked away in a crumbling baroque courtyard, this intimate, family-run theatre hosts wonderful concerts

---

> ### COOKING WITH THE DUCHESS
>
> Food, history and literature simmer together at **Cooking with the Duchess** (Map p66; www.butera28.it/cooking-with-the-duchess.php; Via Butera 28; day course per person €150), an out-of-the-ordinary cooking course. It's conducted by Duchess Nicoletta Polo Lanza Tomasi in a seafront palace once home to writer Giuseppe Tomasi de Lampedusa. The course includes a morning shopping trip to the market and the creation of a four-course lunch, devoured with matching wines. The day concludes with a tour of the *palazzo*.

of world and folk music, as well as theatrical performance. Performers have included renowned Sicilian folk singer Mario Incudine and actor Leo Gullotta. The venue includes a charming little bar. See the website for upcoming shows.

Teatro Politeama Garibaldi   CLASSICAL MUSIC

(Map p60; ☎box office 091 607 25 32; https://or chestrasinfonicasiciliana.it/it; Via Turati 2; ⊙box office 9.30am-4.30pm Mon-Sat, to 1.30pm Sun) This grandiose 19th-century theatre is a popular venue for classical music, staging year-round concerts of works from composers such Beethoven, Strauss, Schubert and Phillip Glass. It's home to Palermo's symphony orchestra, the Orchestra Sinfonica Siciliana.

🛍 Shopping

In the new city, Via della Libertà is lined with high-end fashion stores. More atmospheric is Palermo's historic centre, where crumbly streets harbour artisan workshops selling everything from ceramics to leather goods. Many belong to ALAB (www.alab palermo.it), an association of artisans helping to revitalise the area. For fresh edibles, hit Mercato di Ballarò (p59) or Mercato del Capo (p59). Come Sunday morning, trawl the **Mercatino Antiquariato Piazza Marina** (Map p66; Piazza Marina; ⊙7am-1pm Sun) for antiques and decorative objects.

★ Lurù Maison d'Artiste   ART

(Map p66; Via Nicolò Cervello 39; ⊙10am-7.30pm Tue-Sun May-Sep, closed Sun Oct-Apr) After years living abroad, Loredana Lo Verde returned to her native Palermo, opening this little studio-gallery in La Kalsa. Inspired by Sicilian icons, from saints and

THE SWEET LIFE

Palermo is justly famous for its sweet treats, from the delicate crunch of freshly filled *cannoli* (pastry shells with a sweet filling) to the velvety comfort of *cassata* (a concoction of sponge cake, cream, marzipan, chocolate and candied fruit). For a calorific revelation, loosen your belt and head straight to one of these cult-status pit-stops.

I Segreti del Chiostro (Map p66; ☑ 327 5882302; www.isegretidelchiostro.com; Monastero di Santa Caterina d'Alessandria, Piazza Bellini; sweets from €1; ⊘ 10am-7pm summer, to 6pm winter; ☑ ⏺) For centuries, Sicilian nuns tempted mortals with their freshly baked *biscotti* (biscuits) and pastries, prepared behind closed convent doors using closely guarded recipes. While many of the island's convents have closed, their hard-to-find specialities live on at this superlative bakery-cum-*pasticceria,* tucked away in one of Palermo's former holy houses.

Pasticceria Fratelli Magrì (Map p60; ☑ 091 58 47 88; www.pasticceriamagri.com; Via Isidoro Carini 42; pastries from €2; ⊘ 7am-9pm Mon-Sun) Yes, the made-from-scratch *cannollo* and *cassata* are just gorgeous, but this third-generation *pasticceria* (pastry shop) in the new city also peddles lesser-known classics, including the *patata* (sponge pastry with custard, marzipan and almond paste) and *torta savoia,* a multi-layered chocolate and hazelnut cake.

Pasticceria Cappello (Map p60; ☑ 091 611 37 69; www.pasticceriacappello.it; Via Nicolò Garzilli 19; desserts from €2; ⊘ 7.30am-9.30pm Thu-Tue) The *setteveli* (seven-layer chocolate cake) was invented at this bakery-cafe and has long since been copied all over Palermo. Order a serve but leave room for the dreamy *delizia di pistacchio,* a granular pistachio cake topped with creamy icing and a chocolate medallion. The *cornetti* (croissants) here are glossy, fresh and perfect for a lighter start to the day.

Gelateria Ciccio Adelfio (Map p66; ☑ 091 616 15 37; Corso dei Mille 73; gelato from €1; ⊘ 7am-midnight, closed Thu Nov-Mar) A quick walk from the train station, this old-school gelateria lures tongues from across town. Go local and have your ice cream sandwiched in a brioche (€2.20). From classic flavours like pistachio, *torrone* (nougat) or *cannolo* to more daring concoctions like Mars (an icy take on the chocolate bar), the gelato here is fabulously fresh, consistent and an utter bargain.

pupi (marionettes) to prickly pears, the talented artist creates beautiful, affordable illustrations and watercolours, as well as oil and acrylic paintings. Items range from small cards to larger pieces and even wood-framed lamps with hand-painted cotton-linen panels.

InsimuLab   ARTS & CRAFTS
(Map p66; ☑ 388 6918296; www.alabpalermo.it/laboratorio/insimulab; Piazza Aragona 19-20; ⊘ 10.30am-8.30pm Tue-Sun) InsimuLab is home to jewellery designers Valeria and Simona and ceramicists Giulia and Davide. The former make highly creative, geometric rings, earrings, necklaces and more using silver, copper, brass and aluminium, while the latter create raku-technique objects ranging from espresso cups to teapots with organic, driftwood handles. Necklaces are priced from around €15, while espresso cups start from around €8 each.

Tre Erre Ceramiche   CERAMICS
(Map p60; ☑ 091 32 77 57; www.treerreceramiche.com; Via Roma 358; ⊘ 9am-1pm & 4-8pm Tue-Sat, 10am-1pm & 5-8pm Sun) Colours pop at this family-owned ceramics showroom. There's an extensive range of vibrant, handmade items, from egg cups, platters and vases to chic house numbers and commanding *teste di Moro* (Moors' heads). Prices aren't cheap, but the quality is exceptional, and there are sale items. International shipping is available.

Siculamente   GIFTS & SOUVENIRS
(Map p60; ☑ 091 508 44 26; www.siculamente.it; Via Emerico Amari 136; ⊘ 9.30am-8pm Apr-Oct, to 1.30pm & 4-8pm Nov-Mar) Wear a little Sicilian slang with one of the T-shirts, sweat tops, hats or bags sold at this cool little shop. All bear captions in local dialect, from pithy Sicilian proverbs to cheeky, humorous or political statements. The store's online catalogue provides translations into English and Italian to help your friends decipher exactly what kind of statement you're trying to make.

Naná Aristova Jewels   FASHION & ACCESSORIES
(Map p58; ☑091 58 18 04; https://nana-aristova.
com; Corso Vittorio Emanuele 314; ⊙10am-8pm)
World travels and a Siberian childhood
inspire Naná Aristova's unique jewellery
designs, which include necklaces, earrings,
bracelets and rings. Using traditional techniques, each is handcrafted in materials
such as gold vermeil and natural stones. The
result: bold, chic, contemporary pieces that
echo ancient traditions and sensibilities.
You'll find a second branch further up the
street at number 359.

Borsa del Pellegrino   FASHION & ACCESSORIES
(Map p66; ☑366 1013512; www.borsadelpelle
grino.com; Via Calascibetta 9; ⊙10.30am-8pm
Mon-Sat) Using traditional techniques and
Tuscan leather (including vegetable-tanned
leather), self-taught leather craftsman
Francesco Pellegrino and his partner Lau-
ra D'Orso create beautiful bags and shoes
in their little side-street workshop. The
simple, stylish creations include totes and
messenger bags, with totes starting at
around €100 and wallets priced from €27
to around €55.

ⓘ Orientation

Palermo is large but easily walkable. Lively,
revitalised Via Maqueda is its central street,
extending from the train station in the south and
then changing name to Via Ruggero Settimo at
Piazza Giuseppe Verdi, the gateway to the new
city. At Piazza Castelnuovo (also commonly
known as Piazza Politeama), it continues into
Via della Libertà, a grand boulevard lined with
19th-century apartment blocks.

Via Maqueda is bisected by Corso Vittorio
Emanuele (also known as Via Vittorio Emanuele),
running east to west from the port of La Cala to
the cathedral and Palazzo dei Normanni. The
intersection of Via Maqueda and Corso Vittorio
Emanuele is the Quattro Canti (Four Corners),
which divides historic Palermo into four traditional quarters: La Kalsa (southeast), Vucciria
(northeast), Il Capo (northwest) and Albergheria
(southwest). These quarters contain the majority of Palermo's sights.

Parallel to Via Maqueda is another major
thoroughfare, Via Roma, with one-way traffic
north up Via Roma from the train station and
south down Via Maqueda. The stretch of Via
Maqueda from Corso Vittorio Emanuele to Piazza Giuseppe Verdi is pedestrian-only from 10am
to 7am (from 8am on Sundays). From 10am to
10.30pm on Saturdays and Sundays, the stretch

PALERMO ORIENTATION

DON'T MISS

SICILIAN MARIONETTE THEATRE

Sicily's most popular form of traditional entertainment is the *opera dei pupi* (rod-
marionette theatre), and the best place to attend a performance is in Palermo.

Marionettes were first introduced to the island by the Spanish in the 18th century and
the art form was swiftly embraced by locals, enthralled with the re-enacted tales of Charlemagne and his heroic knights Orlando and Rinaldo. Effectively the soap operas of their
day, these puppet shows expounded the deepest sentiments of life – unrequited love,
treachery, thirst for justice and the anger and frustration of the oppressed. Back then, a
puppet could speak volumes where a person could not.

There are traditionally two types of *opera dei pupi* in Sicily: Palermitan (practised in
Palermo, Agrigento and Trapani) and Catanese (Catania, Messina and Syracuse). Palermitan marionettes are generally smaller and more flexible than their Catanese cousins,
though the latter are known for having more elaborate costumes and larger stages. Both
are carved from beech, olive or lemon-tree wood, with the knights clad in metal suits of
armour that make them shine and resonate when they engage in swordfights with bloodthirsty Saracen warriors or mythical monsters.

Good puppeteers are judged on the dramatic effect they can create – lots of stamping
feet, thundering and a gripping running commentary – and on their speed and skill in
directing the battle scenes. Nowadays the *opera dei pupi* has been relegated to folklore
status, maintained by a few companies largely for the benefit of tourists and children.
The best places to attend a performance are at the **Museo Internazionale delle Marionette** (Map p66; ☑091 32 80 60; www.museomarionettepalermo.it; Piazzetta Antonio Pas-
qualino 5; adult/reduced €5/3; ⊙10am-2pm Mon & Sun, to 6pm Tue-Sat) or at the **Teatro dei
Pupi di Mimmo Cuticchio** (Map p66; ☑091 32 34 00; www.facebook.com/TeatroDellOp-
eraDeiPupi; Via Bara all'Olivella 95), a theatre run by the Associazione Figli d'Arte Cuticchio
(check its Facebook page for performance times).

of Corso Vittorio Emanuele between the Quattro Canti and Via Roma is also pedestrian-only.

ℹ Information

DANGERS & ANNOYANCES

Contrary to stereotypes, Palermo is a relatively safe city with low rates of violent crime. That said, it pays to follow a few basic rules.

➡ Wear handbags across your body and away from the street to avoid moped-riding thieves from snatching it.

➡ Be aware of your possessions in crowded areas, especially city buses and markets.

➡ Avoid poorly lit and deserted streets at night, especially those around the train station and the Kalsa district.

EMERGENCY

Ambulance	☑ 118
International access code	☑ 00
Italy's country code	☑ 39
Police	☑ 112

Police (Questura; ☑ 091 21 01 11; Piazza della Vittoria 8) Palermo's main station, located between Via Maqueda and Palazzo dei Normanni.

INTERNET ACCESS

Free wi-fi is available at many restaurants, cafes and bars in Palermo, and most hotels and B&Bs offer guests free, reliable wi-fi. The city also hosts numerous free wi-fi hotspots, including at Piazza Pretoria, Piazza Bellini, Piazza Bologni and Piazza San Domenico.

MEDICAL SERVICES

Hospital (Ospedale Civico; ☑ 091 666 55 17; www.arnas civico.it; Via Tricomi; ⊙ 24hr) Major hospital with 24-hour emergency department.

POST

Main Post Office (Map p66; ☑ 091 753·53 92; www.poste.it; Via Roma 320; ⊙ 8.20am-7pm Mon-Fri, to 12.30pm Sat) Smaller branch offices include one at Palermo's **main train station** (Map p66; ☑ 091 623 07 53; www.poste.it; ⊙ 8.20am-7pm Mon & Wed-Fri, from 9.30am Tue, 8.20am-12.30pm Sat).

TOURIST INFORMATION

Municipal Tourist Office (Map p66; ☑ 091 740 80 21; http://turismo.comune.palermo.it; Piazza Bellini; ⊙ 8.45am-6.15pm Mon-Fri, from 9.45am Sat) Main branch of Palermo's city-run information booths. Other locations include **Via Cavour** (Map p66; ⊙ 8.30am-1.30pm Mon-Fri), **Teatro Massimo** (Map p58; Piazza Giuseppe Verdi; ⊙ 9.30am-1.30pm Mon-Fri), the Port of Palermo and Mondello, though these are only intermittently staffed, with unpredictable hours.

Micro² Tourist Information Centre (Map p66; ☑ 091 732 02 48; www.visitpalermo.it; Via Torremuzza 15; ⊙ 10am-1pm & 2.30-5.30pm Mon-Sat, 10.30am-2pm Sun) Enthusiastic, privately run tourist-information office open seven days a week and able to book tours, transfers and accommodation.

Tourist Information Office, Falcone-Borsellino Airport (☑ 091 59 16 98; www.gesap.it/en/aeroporto/services/tourist-information-office; ⊙ 8.30am-7.30pm Mon-Fri, to 6pm Sat) Downstairs in the arrivals hall, run by Palermo Metropolitan City.

ℹ Getting There & Away

AIR

Palermo Falcone-Borsellino Airport (☑ 800 541880, 091 702 02 73; www.gesap.it) is at Punta Raisi, 35km northwest of Palermo on the A29 motorway.

Regular nonstop flights travel to mainland Italian airports and several major European cities.

BOAT

Numerous ferry companies operate from Palermo's **port** (Map p60; ☑ 091 604 31 11; cnr Via Francesco Crispi & Via Emerico Amari), just east of the New City.

Grandi Navi Veloci (☑ 010 209 45 91, 091 6072 6162; www.gnv.it; Molo Piave, Porto Stazione Marittima) Runs ferries to Civitavecchia (from €43), Genoa (from €51), Naples (from €43) and Tunis (from €44).

Grimaldi Lines (☑ 081 49 65 55, 091 611 36 91; www.grimaldi-lines.com; Molo Piave, Porto Stazione Marittima) Operates twice-weekly ferries from Palermo to Salerno (from €25, 9½ to 11 hours) and Tunis (from €38, 10 to 13½ hours). Ferries run thrice weekly to Livorno (from €32, 18½ to 19½ hours).

Liberty Lines (☑ 091 32 42 55; www.liberty lines.it; Calata Marinai d'Italia) Operates one to five daily hydrofoil services (€26, 1½ hours) between Ustica and Palermo.

Siremar (p82) Runs one daily car ferry (passenger including car from €95, three hours) between Ustica and Palermo.

Tirrenia (☑ 800 804020, 091 611 65 18; www.tirrenia.it; Calata Marinai d'Italia) Sails to Cagliari (from €45, 13 hours, once or twice weekly) and Naples (from €55, 10½ hours, daily).

BUS

Offices for all bus companies are located within a block or two of Palermo Centrale train station. The two main departure points are the **Piazzetta Cairoli Bus Terminal** (Map p66; Piazzetta Cairoli), just south of the train station's eastern entrance, and the newer **Via Tommaso Fazello Bus Terminal** (Via Tommaso Fazello), beside the station's western entrance. Check locally with your bus company to make sure you're boarding at the appropriate stop.

AST (Azienda Siciliana Trasporti; Map p66; ☑ 091 620 81 11; www.aziendasicilianatrasporti. it; Piazzetta Cairoli Bus Terminal), **Salemi** (Map p66; ☑ 0923 98 11 20; www.autoservizisalemi. it; Piazzetta Cairoli Bus Station), **Segesta** (Map p66; ☑ 0924 310 20; www.facebook.com/ groups/calecavin cenzo; Via Paolo Balsamo), **SAIS** (Map p66; ☑ 091 617 11 41; www.sais trasporti.it; Piazzetta Cairoli Bus Terminal), **SAIS Autolinee** (Map p66; ☑ 800 211020, 091 616 60 28; www.saisautolinee.it; Piazzetta Cairoli Bus Terminal) and **Interbus** (Map p66; ☑ 091 616 79 19; www.interbus.it; Piazzetta Cairoli Bus Terminal) tickets are sold at the bus terminal building at Piazzetta Cairoli. **Cuffaro** (Map p66; ☑ 091 616 15 10; www.facebook.com/ cuffaro.info; Via Paolo Balsamo 13) tickets can be purchased from the Cuffaro ticket office at Via Paolo Balsamo 13, just east of the train station, or onboard. Prestia e Comandè airport buses depart from the Via Tommaso Fazello bus terminal and tickets can be purchased onboard. **Flixbus** (https://global.flixbus.com) has daily buses to Taranto, Lecce and Rome.

CAR & MOTORCYCLE

Palermo is accessible on the A20–E90 toll road from Messina, and from Catania (A19–E932) via Enna. Trapani and Marsala are also easily accessible from Palermo by motorway (A29), while Agrigento and Palermo are linked by the SS121, a good state road through the interior of the island.

TRAIN

Regular services leave from **Palermo Centrale train station** (Piazza Giulio Cesare) to Messina (€12.80, 2¾ to three hours, six to nine daily), Catania (€13.50, three hours, five to six Monday to Saturday, transfers required Sunday) and Agrigento (€9, two hours, six to 13 daily), as well as to nearby towns such as Cefalù (from €5.60, 45 minutes to one hour, eight to 17 daily). There are also Intercity trains to Reggio di Calabria, Naples and Rome.

Inside the station are ATMs, toilets and left-luggage facilities (first five hours €6 flat fee, next

BUSES FROM PALERMO

COMPANY	DESTINATION	PRICE (€)	DURATION (HR)	FREQUENCY
AST	Ragusa	13.50	4	4 daily Mon-Fri, 3 Sat, 2 Sun
AST	Modica	13.50	4½	4 daily Mon-Fri, 3 Sat, 2 Sun
Autoservizi Tarantola	Segesta	7	1¼	3 daily Mon-Sat Apr-Oct
Cuffaro	Agrigento	9	2	7 daily Mon-Fri, 6 Sat, 3 Sun
Flixbus	Taranto	from €10	10	1 daily
Flixbus	Lecce	from €10	11½	1 daily
Flixbus	Rome	from €10	12¼	1 daily
Interbus	Syracuse	13.50	3½	2-3 daily
SAIS Autolinee	Enna	10.50	2	6 daily Mon-Fri, 2 Sat, 4 Sun
SAIS Autolinee	Messina	14	2¾	7 daily Mon-Fri, 5 Sat, 4 Sun
SAIS Autolinee	Catania	14	2¾	14 daily Mon-Fri, 12 Sat, 10 Sun
SAIS Trasporti	Petralia Soprana	10.50	2	3 daily Mon-Sat, 2 Sun
SAIS Trasporti	Petralia Sottana	10.50	1¾	3 daily Mon-Sat, 2 Sun
SAIS Trasporti	Polizzi Generosa	9.50	1¼	3 daily Mon-Sat, 2 Sun
SAIS Trasporti	Cefalù	5.50	1	4-6 daily Mon-Sat, 1 Sun
SAIS Trasporti	Rome	36	12	1 daily (overnight service)
Salemi	Mazara del Vallo	9	2	10-12 daily Mon-Fri, 9 Sat, 4 Sun
Salemi	Marsala	9.50	2¼	4-6 daily
Salemi	Trapani's Birgi airport	11	1¾	4-6 daily
Salemi	Rome	from €40	12¼	1 daily

seven hours €1 per hour, all subsequent hours €0.50 per hour; office staffed 8am to 8pm).

ⓘ Getting Around

Walking is the best way to experience central Palermo's atmosphere and architecture. Traffic and limited parking make driving challenging. There's excellent public transport into town from the airport, and Palermo's port is a 10-minute walk from Piazza Politeama, in the heart of the new city. From here, local buses whizz down Via Roma to Palermo Centrale, where trains serve destinations in Sicily and on the mainland.

TO/FROM THE AIRPORT

Prestia e Comandè (☑ 091 58 63 51; www.prestiaecomande.it; Via Tommaso Fazello Bus Terminal; 1-way/return €6.50/11) runs efficient, half-hourly buses between Palermo and the airport. From the airport, buses run from 5am to 12.30am (1am May to October; 50 minutes). From Palermo, airport-bound buses run from 4am to 10.30pm, departing from the Via Tommaso Fazello Bus Terminal (p77) beside Palermo Centrale train station and stopping at numerous points in central Palermo, including outside the Rinascente department store on **Via Roma** (Map p66; Via Roma 289) and on **Piazza Ruggero II** (Map p60; Piazza Ruggero 18). Purchase tickets onboard or, for a small discount, online.

Trinacria Express (☑ 091 704 40 07; www.trenitalia.com) trains run between the airport (Punta Raisi station) and Palermo Centrale (€5.90, around one hour). Trains run every 15 to 60 minutes and tickets can be purchased online or at the station.

Societá Autolinee Licata (SAL; ☑ 0922 40 13 60; www.autolineesal.it) runs between the airport and Agrigento (€12.60, 2¾ hours, three daily Monday to Saturday).

There is a taxi rank outside the arrivals hall and the fare to/from Palermo is between €35 and €45, depending on your destination in the city.

All the major car-hire companies are represented at the airport.

BICYCLE

Exploring the city on two wheels is becoming increasingly popular. Centrally located **Social Bike Palermo** (☑ 328 2843734; www.socialbikepalermo.com; Discesa dei Giudici 21; standard/electric bike half-day €8/15, guided bike tours €40-55; ☺ 9.30am-6.30pm) rents out numerous types of bicycles, including folding, standard, electric and tandem versions. The outfit also runs a trio of interesting bike tours.

CAR & MOTORCYCLE

In central Palermo, the area bordered by Piazza Giulio Cesare, Via Cavour, Porta Nuova and Porta Felice is a ZTL area (*Zona Traffico Limitato*,

or Limited Traffic Zone). This means that from 8am to 8pm Monday to Friday (to 1pm Saturday), non-resident vehicles need to buy a pass (one day €5) to access the area. Vehicles must meet emissions standards (currently petrol Euro standard 3 and diesel Euro 4). More information, including purchase points, is available at https://urbanaccessregulations.eu. The website is also useful for keeping abreast of any ZTL changes; there has recently been talk of extending the ZTL times overnight.

Even with a pass, however, Palermo's one-way streets, limited parking and general disregard for road rules make driving in the city highly inadvisable.

Parking

When making a booking, ask your hotel about parking; many hotels have a *garage convenzionato*, a local garage that offers special rates to their guests (typically between €12 and €20 per day).

Alternatively, you'll need to find a legal space on the city's streets or piazzas. For spaces marked by blue lines, you must obtain a ticket from a machine or a *tabaccheria* (tobacconist), usually every day except Sunday; see the hours of operation posted at the machine nearest your vehicle.

Parking spaces marked by white lines are free, although you may encounter a *parcheggiatore abusivo* (illegal parking attendant), who will expect a 'tip' (€1 should do). Sadly, it's better to pay than to risk returning to a damaged vehicle. Spaces marked by yellow lines are reserved for those with limited mobility.

PUBLIC TRANSPORT

AMAT (☑ 091 35 01 11, 848 800817; http://amat.pa.it) runs both city buses and trams. Tickets, valid for 90 minutes, cost €1.40 and can be pre-purchased from *tabaccherie* (tobacconists) or from AMAT information kiosks. Kiosk locations include **Piazza Giulio Cesare**, right outside Palermo Centrale train station, and **Via della Libertà**, just off Piazza Ruggero. Kiosk opening times can be sporadic.

Tickets can also be purchased on board buses (€1.80). A day pass costs €3.50. Once you board a bus or tram, ensure to validate your ticket in the machine.

Bus

Palermo's orange, white and blue city buses, operated by AMAT, are frequent but often overcrowded and slow. The free map handed out at Palermo tourist offices details the major bus lines; most stop at Palermo Centrale train station. One useful line is the 806, which departs from Piazza Sturzo (180m northeast of Teatro Politeama Garibaldi) and runs north along Via della Libertà to the popular beachside neighbourhood of Mondello.

Tram

Palermo's tram network currently consists of four lines, operating from 6am to 9pm. L1 runs from outside Palermo Centrale train station to suburban Rocella, home to a major shopping mall. L2, L3 and L4 run from Notarbartolo train station in the city's northwest to Borgo Nuovo, CEP and Corso Calatafimi respectively. None of the lines are particularly useful for tourists.

TAXI

Official taxis should have a *tassametro* (meter), which records the fare; check for this before embarking. The minimum starting fare is €3.81, with a range of additional charges, all of which are listed at www.taxi.it/palermo.

Hailing a passing taxi on the street is not customary; rather, you'll need to phone ahead for a taxi or wait at one of the taxi ranks at major travel hubs such as the train station, Piazza Ruggero Settimo, Teatro Massimo and Piazza Indipendenza.

For a taxi, call **Autoradio Taxi Palermo** (☑091 8481; www.autoradiotaxi.it). Taxis can also be ordered using the appTaxi (www.apptaxi.it), available on the App Store and Google Play.

PALERMO REGION

Beyond Palermo is a string of worthy daytrip destinations. Among these is the mosaicked magnificence of Monreale Cathedral, beach-loving Mondello, the pristine marine reserve of Ustica island, and the inland town of Corleone, home to a defiant anti-mafia museum.

Mondello

☑091

In the summer months, it sometimes seems as if the entire population of Palermo has packed a beach towel and a pair of D&G shades and decamped to this popular beach resort, 11km north of the city centre.

Originally a muddy, malaria-ridden port, Mondello only really became fashionable in the 19th century, when the city's elite flocked here in their carriages, thus warranting the huge Liberty-style pier that dominates the seafront and kicking off a craze for building opulent summer villas.

One can hardly blame them. Mondello's sandy coastline is gorgeous, with crystal-clear turquoise waters that are difficult to resist (and family friendly). Most of the beaches are private (two loungers and

an umbrella cost around €15 to €22 per day), but there is also a wide swath of public beach crammed with swimmers, pedalos and noisy jet skis.

Of all of Mondello's fabulous Liberty (art nouveau) buildings, none endear themselves as much as the turreted **Antico Stabilimento Balneare di Mondello** (☑091 626 29 03; www.facebook.com/stabilimento; Viale Regina Elena 17). Built as a bathing establishment in 1913, it was originally designed by architect Rudolf Stualke for the Belgian city of Ostend. Despite its whimsical storybook appearance, the building was used as a headquarters by both the Italian Fascists and German troops in WWII, before being plucked by the Allied Forces. These days it enjoys a less tense existence hosting an elegant restaurant and piano bar, Ristorante alle Terrazze (www.alleterrazze.it).

Seafood restaurants and snack stalls have colonised the *lido* (beach; Viale Regina Elena) and the main piazza hosts numerous cafes with outdoor seating. Mondello is also home to one of Sicily's Michelin-starred restaurants, **Bye Bye Blues** (☑091 684 14 15; www.byebyeblues.it; Via del Garofalo 23; 5-/6-course tasting menu €65/75; ⏱1-2.30pm & 8-10.30pm Tue-Sun), located a few streets back from the beach.

❶ Getting There & Away

AMAT bus (Map p60) 806 (€1.40, 20 to 30 minutes, every 10 to 20 minutes between 6.15am and 10.30pm, fewer services on Sunday) runs to Mondello from Piazza Sturzo in central Palermo. The last bus back to Palermo departs Mondello at 11pm.

Monreale

☑091 / POP 39,000 / ELEV 310M

According to an old Sicilian proverb, whoever visits Palermo without visiting Monreale arrives a donkey and leaves an ass. The reason: this humble hillside town claims one of Sicily's greatest cultural treasures, the World Heritage listed Cattedrale di Monreale. It is one of the greatest examples of Norman architecture in Europe, and its mosaic-encrusted interiors are pure medieval majesty. Architectural wonders aside, the town also offers commanding views over Palermo, the Conca d'Oro (Golden Valley) and the Tyrrhenian Sea. Together, they make a side trip to Monreale – 7km southwest of central Palermo – practically non-negotiable.

Around Palermo

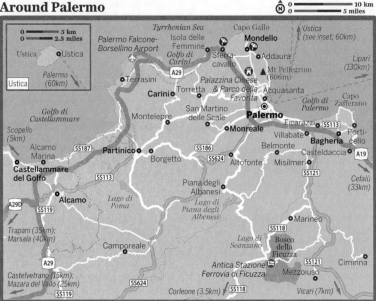

⊙ Sights

★ Cattedrale di Monreale

CATHEDRAL

(☏091 640 44 03; www.monrealeduomo.it; Piazza del Duomo; cathedral free, Roano chapel, terrace & cloister adult/reduced €10/7; ⊙cathedral 8.30am-12.30pm & 2.30-5pm Mon-Sat, 8-9.30am & 2.30-5pm Sun, cloisters 9am-7pm Mon-Sat, to 1.30pm Sun) Inspired by a vision of the Virgin and determined to outdo his grandfather Roger II, who was responsible for the cathedral in Cefalù and the Cappella Palatina in Palermo, William II set about building the Cattedrale di Monreale. Incorporating Norman, Arab, Byzantine and classical elements, the cathedral is considered the finest example of Norman architecture in Sicily. It's also one of the most impressive architectural legacies of the Italian Middle Ages.

Although the cathedral's mosaicists hailed from Sicily and Venice, Byzantine influence pervades their work. Completed in 1184 after only 10 years' work, their shimmering masterpieces depict biblical tales, from the creation of man to the Assumption, in 42 different episodes. The beauty of the mosaics cannot be overstated – you have to see for yourself Noah's ark perched atop the waves or Christ healing a leper infected with large leopard-sized spots. The story of Adam and Eve is wonderfully portrayed, with a grumpy-looking Eve sitting on a rock while Adam labours in the background. The large mosaic of Christ, dominating the central apse, is stunning. Binoculars make viewing the mosaics easier, although they are still impressive to the naked eye. Print out the handy key and map at www.seepalermo.com/monrealekeyprint.htm.

Adjacent to the cathedral is the entrance to the **cloister**, which illustrates William's love of Arab artistry. This tranquil courtyard is an ode to Orientalism, with elegant Romanesque arches supported by an array of slender columns alternately decorated with shimmering mosaic patterns. Each capital is unique, and taken together they represent a sculptural record of medieval Sicily. Especially interesting is the capital of the 19th column on the west aisle, depicting William II offering the cathedral to the Madonna.

For a bird's-eye view of the cloister, its geometric garden and the cathedral's mountainous surrounds, climb the stairs to the cathedral's **terrace**, accessed from inside the cathedral.

✗ Eating

You'll find numerous trattorias and restaurants of varying quality in the vicinity of the cathedral. As a general rule, avoid places offering a *menu turistico* (tourist menu), which usually signals mediocre meals. Two conveniently located restaurants popular with locals and clued-in foodies are meat-geared **Bricco & Bacco** (☑091 641 77 73; www.briccoebacco.it; Via d'Acquisto 13; meals €25-40; ☺12.30-3.30pm & 7.45pm-midnight Tue-Sun) and seafood-focused **Ciambra** (☑091 640 67 17; Via d'Acquisto 18; meals €30-45; ☺12.30-3pm & 7-11pm Thu-Tue; ☏).

❶ Getting There & Away

AMAT (Map p58; Piazza Indipendenza) City bus 389 (€1.40, 30 to 40 minutes, roughly every 75 minutes) runs from Piazza Indipendenza in Palermo to Monreale. In Monreale, the bus terminates in Via Fontana del Drago, from where the cathedral is a 450m uphill walk along either Via Palermo or Via d'Acquisto.

AST (Map p66) Runs buses to Monreale from in front of Palermo Centrale train station (€2.40, 40 minutes, every 60 to 90 minutes Monday to Saturday).

City Sightseeing (Map p58; ☑091 58 94 29; www.city-sightseeing.it/en/palermo/; ☏) Operates hop-on, hop-off tour buses from Palermo's Piazza Indipendenza to Monreale (adult/child €25/10, 30 minutes, every 30 minutes). Services are significantly reduced from November to March. Tickets include access to City Sightseeing's other two sightseeing bus tours of Palermo. Children aged four and under travel free.

Always ignore touts at bus stops offering lifts to Monreale in their car.

Corleone

☑091 / POP 11,130 / ELEV 550M

Having suffered centuries of poverty and possessing a well-documented history as a Mafia stronghold, the town of Corleone – 60km from Palermo and best known through Francis Ford Coppola's classic *Godfather* trilogy – has been trying to reinvent itself over the last decade. For travellers, the one reason to head here is for **CIDMA** (Centro Internazionale di Documentazione sulla Mafia e Movimento Antimafia; ☑091 8452 4295, 340 4025601; www.cidmacorleone.it; Via G Valenti 7; €8; ☺10am-5pm Mon-Fri), Corleone's small anti-Mafia museum which recounts the terrifying history of Sicily's Cosa Nostra crime syndicate. It focuses on the brave efforts of the anti-Mafia campaigners and judges who spoke out against organised crime rather than succumbing to the Mafia-promoted culture of *omertà* (silence). Visits are by guided tour only (English tours available) and should be booked in advance via the centre's website.

A huge 'No Mafia' sign greets visitors at the entrance, as does a poignant quote from murdered anti-Mafia judge Giovanni Falcone about the unbearable but necessary sacrifice demanded in order to fight this just cause. Three rooms are visited: the first holds the very documents from the groundbreaking maxi-trials of 1986–87; the second exhibits pictures by photojournalist Letizia Battaglia, who documented Mafia crimes in the 1970s and 1980s; and the third displays photos of Mafia bosses, the men of justice who fought them and people who have lost loved ones.

The museum is in a cobbled street just off Piazza Garibaldi, 450m up Via Francesco Bentivegna from Piazza Falcone e Borsellino.

❶ Getting There & Away

AST (p77) buses travel between Palermo and Corleone (€5.40, 1¾ hours, five daily) Monday to Saturday. In Corleone, passengers are dropped off at Piazza Falcone e Borsellino. Check return bus times as services are infrequent. Also, be back at the bus stop 15 minutes before the official departure time as buses sometimes leave early.

Ustica

☑091 / POP 1305

Tiny Ustica floats alone almost 60km north of Palermo in the Tyrrhenian Sea. Part of the Aeolian volcanic chain, the island is actually the tip of a submerged volcano. Blazing pink-and-red hibiscus flowers and prickly green cacti punctuate the island's black, volcanic rock and dramatic grottoes litter its shoreline.

Ustica's surrounding waters – protected within Area Marina Protetta Isola di Ustica (Island of Ustica Protected Marine Area) – are kept sparkling and clean by an Atlantic current, resulting in an underwater wonderland of fish and coral. In fact, the reserve is host to half of the marine species present in Mediterranean waters.

Palermitans flock here in July and August, so consider visiting in June and September to enjoy its natural assets without the crowds. Note that between October and Easter most of the island's services close down during the week and ferry services from the mainland can be cancelled in bad weather.

🏊 Activities

Diving & Snorkelling
Divers from all over the world come to Ustica between May and October to explore its magnificent underwater sites. Highlights

include the **underwater archaeological trail** off Punta Cavazzi, with artefacts such as Roman amphorae. Other popular dive sites are the **Scoglio del Medico**, an outcrop of basalt riddled with caves and gorges that plunge to great depths; and **Secca di Colombara**, a magnificent rainbow-coloured display of sponges and gorgonias.

Numerous dive centres offer dive itineraries and hire equipment. Among them, **Orca Diving Ustica** (☑ 334 2161588; www.usticadiving.it; Via C Colombo 39; 1 dive incl equipment €60) is the lone operator managed by local residents born and raised on Ustica.

Area Marina Protetta Isola di Ustica is divided into three zones. Zone A extends along the west flank of the island from the promontory north of Punta Spalmatore to Punta Megna and as far as 350m offshore. You can swim within its boundaries at designated spots, but fishing, boating and diving are prohibited. Two of the island's most beautiful natural grottoes – the **Grotta Segreta (Secret Grotto)** and the **Grotta Rosata (Pink Grotto)** – are located here.

Zone B extends beyond Zone A from Punta Gavazzi to Punta Omo Morto and as far as 4.8km offshore; swimming and underwater photography are permitted within its boundaries, as is hook-and-line fishing. Zone C applies to the rest of the coast; swimming and boating are allowed and national fishing regulations apply. Always check your itinerary with a dive centre or the marine national park headquarters before you dive.

Hiking

Ustica's compact size makes it ideal for walking, with a number of trails available.

For a grand four-hour walking tour of the coastline, follow the signposted **Sentiero del Mezzogiorno** south from town towards Ustica's western lighthouse (simply called **Faro** on maps), then continue north on foot or by bus to the 18th-century **Cappella della Madonna della Croce**. Here another footpath follows the northern coastal bluffs to the **Villaggio Preistorico**, the remnant of a Bronze Age village. Loop back to town along the main road.

Another scenic trail passes through pine woods to the summit of **Guardia di Mezzo** (248m), then descends to the coast at **Spalmatore**, where you can swim in natural rock pools.

Closer to town, shorter walking paths lead to the **Rocca della Falconiera**, a defensive tower above the church; to the lookout point above the lighthouse at **Punta Omo Morto**; and to the **Torre Santa Maria**, a Bourbon-era tower just south of the town centre. Ask at the tourist office for directions.

✖ Eating

Ustica is famous for its tiny, dark *lenticchie di Ustica* (Ustica lentils). The smallest variety grown in Italy, they're revered by top-tier chefs across the country. Other specialities include capers and fresh seafood. The island's fruits and vegetables are renowned for their intense flavour, attributed to Ustica's rich volcanic soil. Between October and Easter, most restaurants close during the week. Two of the best options in town, both featuring locally sourced seafood and produce, are the family-run **Da Umberto** (☑ 091 844 95 42; Via della Vittoria 7; meals €25-35; ☺ noon-2pm & 7-11pm) and **Ristorante Giulia** (☑ 091 844 90 07; Via San Francesco 16; meals €25-35; ☺ 8pm-midnight Jun–mid-Sep).

ℹ Information

Area Marina Protetta di Ustica (☑ 338 6431505; www.parks.it/riserva.marina.isola.ustica; Piazza Umberto I 4-6; ☺ 9am-noon & 5-7pm Mon-Sat, 9am-1pm Sun) The Marine Reserve Visitors Centre is in the centre of the village and can advise on activities, boat trips and dive centres.

ℹ Getting There & Away

Liberty Lines (☑ Ustica office 091 844 90 02, customer service 0923 87 38 13; www.libertylines.it; ☺ ticket office 9.30am-1pm & 3-6.15pm) Runs one to five daily hydrofoil services (€26 one way, 1½ hours) between Ustica and Palermo.

Siremar (☑ 090 57 37; https://carontetourist.it/it/siremar; ☺ ticket office 9.30am-1pm & 3-6.15pm) Operates one daily car-ferry service between Ustica and Palermo (from €97 one way, three hours).

ℹ Getting Around

A local bus (€1.20) makes regular circuits of the island, leaving every 45 to 60 minutes in each direction. If you're after your own wheels, **Ricarica ARA** (☑ 338 1100972, 091 844 96 05; www.ustica-ara.it; Banchina Barresi; ☺ hours vary) rents out 50cc and 125cc scooters.

Sicilian Architecture

Architecture lovers will find themselves in heaven in Sicily. There is hardly a town that isn't graced with at least one mini-masterpiece. The unique style of Sicilian baroque is a feast for the senses, and there are Classical temples, shimmering mosaics, Byzantine churches and Norman forts to explore.

Contents

→ Baroque Cathedrals
→ Classical Masterpieces
→ Inspiring Mosaics
→ Captivating Castles

Above Duomo di Cefalù (p123)

Baroque Cathedrals

The sight of Sicily's baroque cathedrals is one of the foremost reasons for visiting the island. Ranging from reformed ancient temples to whirling mixtures of baroque and neoclassical, each of these churches gives its city centre a unique lushness and grandeur.

Duomo

Syracuse's flamboyant cathedral (p201) lords it over the city's beautiful showpiece square. Its sumptuous facade is typically baroque, but the columns that run down the sides tell of a former life as a temple to the Greek goddess Athena.

Cattedrale di San Nicolò

In Noto, a town noted for its sublime baroque buildings, the spectacular Cattedrale di San Nicolò (p218) trumps the lot. Standing in monumental pomp at the top of a grandiose staircase, it stylishly fuses the best of baroque and neoclassical architecture.

Duomo di San Giorgio (Ragusa)

Fans of the TV series *Inspector Montalbano* might recognise Ragusa's towering baroque cathedral (p233), often used as a backdrop. The work of Sicily's grand baroque maestro Rosario Gagliardi, it's a masterclass in overstated style and unrestrained passion.

1. Duomo (p201), Syracuse 2. Cattedrale di Sant'Agata (p183), Catania 3. Duomo di San Giorgio (p233), Ragusa

Duomo di San Giorgio (Modica)

A commanding presence, Modica's great church (p218) looms over the town's serpentine streets and bustling medieval centre. Its monumental facade is a stunning example of baroque on a grand scale while the echoing interior drips with silver and gold.

Cattedrale di Sant'Agata

The highlight of Catania's centre is its wedding-cake cathedral (p183). Dedicated to the city's patron saint, Agata, it's unique among Sicily's baroque churches for its black-and-white tones, a reflection of the volcanic stone used in its construction.

SICILIAN BAROQUE

After being devastated by an earthquake in 1693, Sicily was presented with an opportunity to redesign many of its cities and experiment with a new architectural style that was taking Europe by storm: baroque. A backlash against the pared-down classical aesthetic of the Renaissance, this new style was dramatic, curvaceous and downright sexy – a perfect match for Sicily's unorthodox and exuberant character. Aristocrats in towns such as Noto, Modica, Ragusa, Catania and Syracuse rushed to build baroque *palazzi* (palaces), many decorated with the grotesque masks and *putti* (cherubs) that had long been a hallmark of the island's architecture. Even the church got into it, commissioning ostentatious churches and oratories aplenty.

1. Tempio della Concordia (p262), Valley of the Temples 2. Parco Archeologico della Neapolis (p206), Syracuse 3. Teatro Greco (p174), Taormina 4. Acropolis, Selinunte (p117)

Classical Masterpieces

Sicily is renowned for its classical masterpieces, from the perfectly preserved temples at Agrigento, Segesta and Selinunte to the ancient Greek theatres of Syracuse and Taormina.

Valley of the Temples

The model for Unesco's logo and one of the world's best-preserved Greek temples, Tempio della Concordia is the star turn of stunning Agrigento. The ruins (p262) are what's left of Akragas, once the fourth-largest city in the ancient world.

Parco Archeologico della Neapolis

A major power in ancient times, Syracuse boasts one of Sicily's great classical monuments – Teatro Greco (p206), a supremely well-preserved Greek amphitheatre. In the theatre's shadow, you can explore caves where slaves once laboured.

Selinunte

You don't have to be an archaeologist to be bowled over by the Greek temples at Selinunte (p117). They are beautifully set against a sunny seaside backdrop that looks particularly fabulous in spring, when wildflowers set the scene ablaze with colour.

Segesta

Standing in proud isolation amid rugged, green hills, the ruins of ancient Segesta (p97) are an unforgettable sight. Pride of place goes to the stately 5th-century-BC temple – but don't miss the amphitheatre, dramatically gouged out of the hillside.

Taormina

Enjoying spectacular views of snowcapped Mt Etna and the Ionian Sea, Taormina's Teatro Greco (p174) makes the perfect venue for the town's summer film and arts festivals.

1

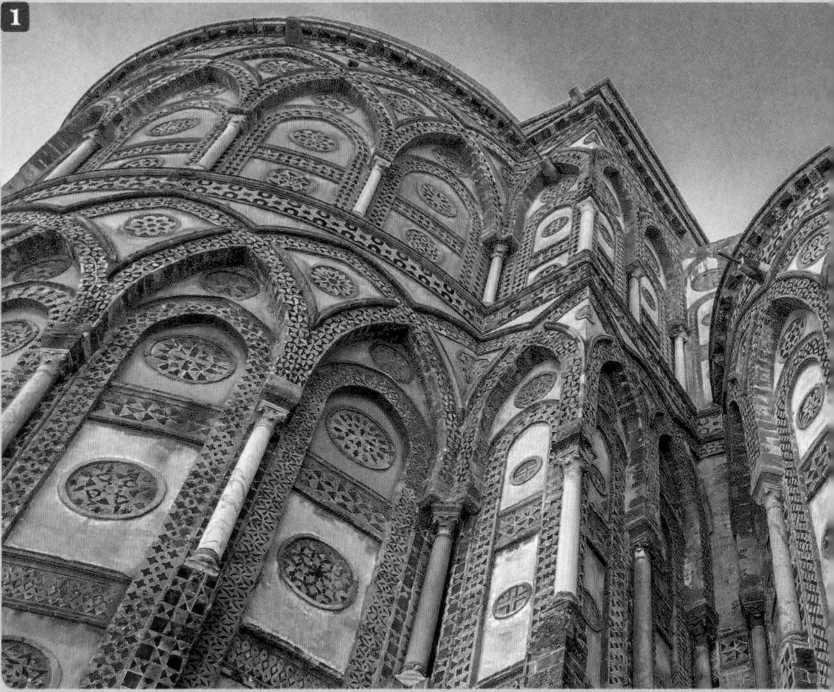

2

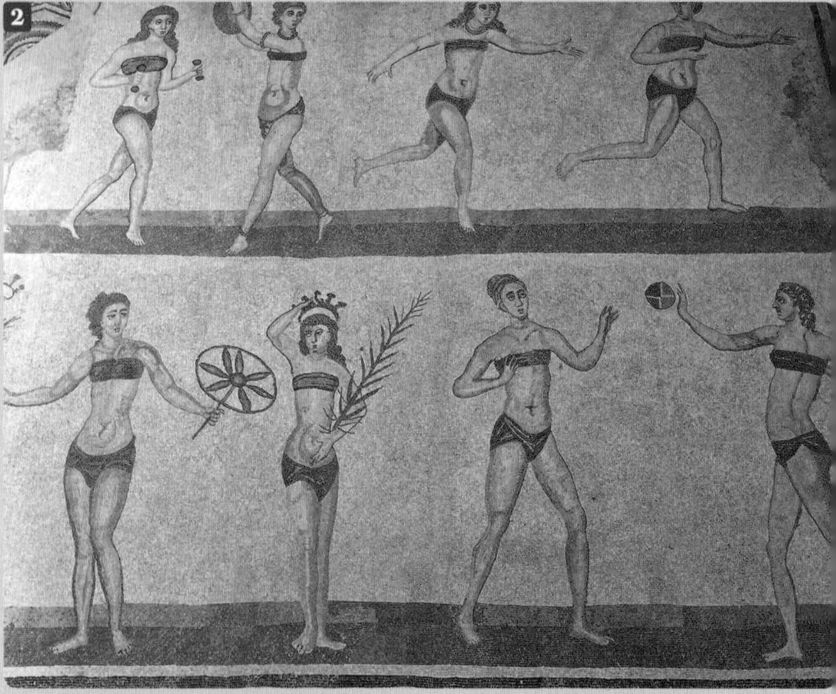

ELESI/SHUTTERSTOCK ©

1. Cattedrale di Monreale (p80) 2. Mosaic in Villa Romana del Casale (p250) 3. Cappella Palatina (p57)

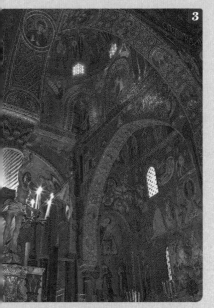

Inspiring Mosaics

Among the treasures left behind by Sicily's many invaders is the island's wealth of exquisite mosaics. Representing everything from biblical themes to wild African animals, these date to the Roman, Byzantine and Arab-Norman periods.

Cappella Palatina

Sicily's greatest work of Arab-Norman art is this sparkling mosaic-encrusted chapel (p57) in the Palazzo dei Normanni in Palermo. Every inch of the arched interior is emblazoned with golden mosaics and biblical figures. Precious inlaid marble and an Arabic-style carved wooden ceiling complete the picture.

Villa Romana del Casale

This villa (p250) in Piazza Armerina is home to some of the world's finest Roman mosaics. Buried for centuries under a layer of mud, they stand out for their scale, use of colour, and scenes of mythological monsters and bikini-clad girls working out with weights.

Duomo di Cefalù

The robust, fortress-like exterior of Cefalù's hulking Norman cathedral (p123) guards one of Sicily's most celebrated mosaics: the depiction of Cristo Pantocratore (Christ All Powerful) in the apse. Dating to the mid-12th century, it's a remarkably lifelike depiction of a severe man with drawn cheeks and a dark beard.

La Martorana

A favourite venue for local weddings, Palermo's most popular medieval church (p56) is a treasure trove of Byzantine mosaics.

Cattedrale di Monreale

An outstanding example of Norman architecture, Monreale's famous cathedral (p80) harbours a dazzling interior of Byzantine-influenced mosaics depicting stories from the Old Testament.

Palazzo dei Normanni (p57)

Captivating Castles

Sicily's castles have played a vital role in the island's history, serving as forts during the Norman era, when most of them were built. They continue to tower over landscapes and cities, and are some of the island's most impressive sights. Some are even said to be still holding ancient ghosts captive!

Palazzo dei Normanni

This palace (p57) in Palermo has long been the nerve centre of island power. It housed one of Europe's most glittering courts and is now the seat of Sicily's regional government.

Castello di Lombardia

As impressive as this formidable 14th-century castle (p241) in Enna is, the real highlight is the sweeping panorama that unfolds from the top of Torre Pisana,

the tallest of the castle's six remaining towers. As far as the eye can see, great swaths of rolling green countryside stretch off in all directions.

Castello di Caccamo

One of Italy's largest castles, Caccamo's impregnable fort (p128) served as a Norman stronghold and then a base for the powerful 14th-century Chiaramonte family. Protected by a series of forbidding walls and ingenious fortifications, it commands magnificent views.

Castello dei Ventimiglia

An evocative sight, the enormous castle (p129) that gives Castelbuono its name is said to be haunted. Every month the ghost of a long-dead queen runs the lengths of its corridors, which now host a small museum and art gallery.

Western Sicily

Best Places to Eat

➡ La Bettolaccia (p99)

➡ Osteria del Sotto Sale (p109)

➡ Da Vittorio (p119)

➡ I Sapori (p88)

➡ La Cambusa (p111)

Best Historic & Cultural Attractions

➡ Ruins of Segesta (p97)

➡ Grotta del Genovese (p110)

➡ Parco Archeologico di Selinunte (p117)

➡ Castello di Venere (p102)

➡ Cantine Florio (p113)

Why Go?

Sicily's windswept western coast has beckoned invaders for millennia. Its richly stocked fishing grounds, hilltop vineyards and coastal saltpans were coveted by the Phoenicians, Greeks, Romans and Normans, all of whom influenced the region's landscape and culture. Even the English left their mark, with 18th-century entrepreneurs lured here and made rich by one of the world's most famous sweet wines, marsala.

Today this part of the island is very much an off-the-beaten-track destination, perfect for those who savour slow travel. There's an amazingly diverse range of experiences to be had here. Standout attractions include the ancient ruins of Segesta and Selinunte, the hilltop village of Erice, the Golfo di Castellammare, with its stunning juxtaposition of sea and mountain scenery, and the beautiful offshore islands of Favignana, Levanzo, Marettimo and Pantelleria. Adding to western Sicily's appeal are its unique local cuisine and proximity to Palermo and Trapani international airports.

Road Distances (km)

	Marsala	Scopello	Segesta	Selinunte
Scopello	75			
Segesta	50	30		
Selinunte	45	70	60	
Trapani	30	35	30	95

Cagliari (140km)

Ustica (90km)

Tyrrhenian Sea

Mt Eryx (750m)

Valderice

Erice **2**

Trapani

Capo Grosso

Grotta del Genovese

Levanzo

Riserva Naturale Saline di Trapani e Paceco

Levanzo 3

Nubia

Paceco

Marettimo

Egadi Islands

Marettimo

SS187

SS115

Favignana

Vincenzo Florio (Birgi) Airport

Favignana

Stagnone Islands

Riserva Naturale di Stagnone

Mozia

San Pantaleo

Marsala 5

SS188

Capo Boeo

Mediterranean Sea

SS115

Mazara del Vallo 4

Pantelleria (85km)

Pantelleria (90km)

Western Sicily Highlights

1 Segesta (p97)
Contemplating a near-perfect classical temple atop a grassy, wild flower-peppered hillside.

2 Castello di Venere (p102)
Gorging on stunning views from this Norman castle in hilltop Erice.

3 Grotta del Genovese (p110) Exploring ancient cave art on the nature-wild island of Levanzo.

4 La Casbah (p115)
Admiring hand-painted wall tiles and savouring fish couscous in Mazara del Vallo's ancient Saracen quarter.

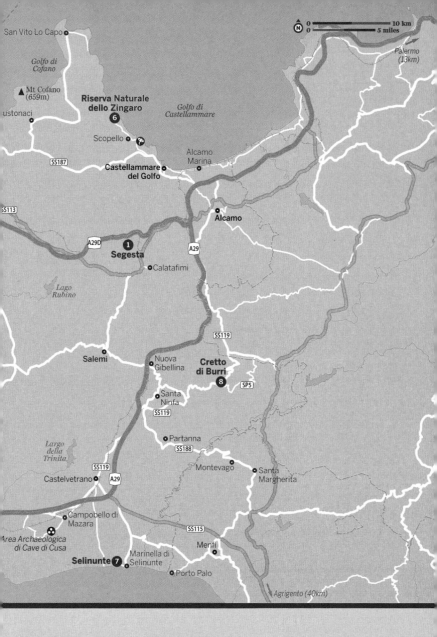

GOLFO DI CASTELLAMMARE

The stunning promontory between Castellammare del Golfo and Monte Cofano (659m) is perhaps the most beautiful in all of Sicily. The small coastal city of Castallammare is the most accessible destination on this stretch of coast, but those prepared to be a bit more adventurous will discover the unspoiled Riserva Naturale dello Zingaro a short distance to the northwest; here the wild coastal landscape is dotted with tempting swimming coves and quaint settlements built around historic *baglios* (manor houses) and *tonnare* (tuna fisheries). Added to all this are the ancient ruins of Segesta, only a short drive inland, and the popular beach town of San Vito Lo Capo at the promontory's northwestern tip.

Scopello

POP 380

The seaside hamlet of Scopello couldn't be any more charming if it tried. Built around an 18th-century *baglio* fortified with a high wall and huge gates, its white houses and smooth-stone streets are straight out of a 1950s Italian movie. The historic *tonnara* crowning the shoreline is a popular film location.

Favourite pastimes include lazily lounging over a coffee watching the Scopello world go by on the main piazza, learning about the region's fascinating tuna-fishing heritage at the former fishery, and hiking, swimming, snorkelling and frolicking on rocks in the neighbouring Riserva Naturale dello Zingaro.

If possible avoid visiting in August when the hamlet can be unpleasantly crowded.

Traditional tuna fishing is explored at **La Tonnara di Scopello** (☎388 8299472; www.latonnaradiscopello.it; Largo Tonnara Scopello; adult/child €5/free; ⊙10am-7pm summer, shorter hours rest of year), an unusual seafront museum located in a vintage *tonnara* (tuna 'factory'), in operation from the 13th century until its closure in 1984. The complex was greatly developed in the 15th and 16th centuries, and in 1874 the wealthy owners had the elegant, salmon-pink **Palazzina Florio** built right on the water. The setting alone – overlooking fluorescent blue waters, at the foot of dramatic rock formations capped by a medieval tower – makes it a visit worthwhile.

The **Cetaria Diving Centre** (☎368 3864808, 338 5445761; www.cetaria.it; Via Ciro Menotti 4; ⊙Apr-Oct) offers equipment hire, guided dives around underwater caves and shipwrecks in the Riserva Naturale dello Zingaro, snorkelling expeditions and boat excursions, and is a recommended diving school.

You'll find a good mix of eateries within 200m of the grand cobbled courtyard at the town centre – including bakeries, pizzerias and a terrace restaurant serving pricier Sicilian fare with spectacular views.

If you're staying at Pensione Tranchina (p279), be sure to take advantage of its fabulous home-cooked meals. Unfortunately, it doesn't cater for outsiders unless one of its own guests opts to skip dinner; interested non-guests are welcome to check at around 5pm to see if a table has opened up.

ℹ Getting There & Away

Scopello is 10km northwest of Castellammare del Golfo via the SS187 and the SP63.

Autoservizi Russo (www.russoautoservizi.it) runs buses between Scopello and Castellammare del Golfo (€2.70, 20 minutes, four daily except Sunday).

San Vito Lo Capo

POP 4700

Occupying the tip of Capo San Vito is the seaside town of San Vito Lo Capo, full of beachcombers and sun worshippers in summer. San Vito is renowned for its crescent-shaped sandy beach, one of the prettiest in Sicily, where limpid turquoise and ultramarine waters are juxtaposed against the dramatic mountain backdrop of Monte Monaco, a popular hiking destination. Come September, the town is invaded by couscous aficionados during the annual Cous Cous Fest.

San Vito is a tiny seaside town with no real sights beyond its sandy beach and fortress-like **church** (Piazza Santuario; ⊙hours vary) FREE looming large above its central square, halfway down the main street, Via Savoia.

Excellent local hiking opportunities include the 3km ascent of **Monte Monaco** (about 2½ hours round trip; look for the trailhead just southeast of San Vito) and the splendid coastal trails of Riserva Naturale dello Zingaro (p95), whose northern entrance lies about 10km southeast of San Vito. San Vito has also blossomed as a climbing destination in recent years, with a variety of challenging crags just outside town and an autumn climbing festival drawing enthusiasts from throughout the Mediterranean.

Constantly celebrated as one of Sicily's most beautiful beaches, **Spiaggia di San Vito** translates as a wonderfully long swathe of fine golden sand. There are plenty of spots to rent umbrellas and sunloungers (around €15 per day), showers and dozens of cafes with terraces facing the water. The beach is generously rammed in July and August, but blissfully empty most other times of the year.

The ubercool **YMCA Climbing House** (☑ 333 7075707; www.ymcaclimbingsanvito.it; Via Savoia 195-197; ⊙ hours vary) – run by a passionate bunch of young, fun outdoor enthusiasts – should be your first port of call for every imaginable outdoor activity in and around San Vito: climbing, mountain biking, trekking, Nordic walking, paragliding or sea kayaking in the nearby Zingaro nature reserve. Be it equipment, maps and/or itineraries, lessons or a qualified guide you are seeking, this is *the* address.

🎉 Festivals & Events

Cous Cous Fest FOOD & DRINK
(www.couscousfest.it; ⊙ last week Sep) Trapani's beloved local dish couscous is the fun focus of this colourful six-day food fest, celebrated with gusto in San Vito Lo Capo during the last week in September. Highlights include cooking shows, workshops, concerts, live music and – roll drum – the Couscous World Championships, in which couscous chefs from 10 countries compete.

To be part of the popular tasting jury in the semi-finals or finals, buy a ticket (€15 to €25). Otherwise, a 'tasting ticket' (€10) gives you access to dozens of different tasting stands on the beach and around town; buy in advance online or at kiosks in situ during the festival.

San Vito Climbing Festival SPORTS
(www.sanvitoclimbingfestival.it; ⊙ Oct/early Nov) This four-day festival bill celebrates the region's strong outdoor heritage with a bonanza of outdoor sporting events, with a strong focus on climbing, mountain biking, kayaking and trail running.

🍴 Eating

★ Syrah Ristorante MODERN SICILIAN €€
(☑ 0923 97 20 28, 347 1367315; Via Savoia 86; meals €30-45; ⊙ 12.30-2pm & 7.30-10pm) San Vito's refined choice, Syrah is a chic ode to contemporary ceramic wall art and modern Sicilian cuisine. Its parasol-shaded courtyard garden is a more intimate, peaceful alternative to the wooden-deck street terrace

– perfect for people-watching. Audacious appetisers (octopus with artichoke and fennel carpaccio, red shrimps with fruit, cuttlefish and smoked pumpkin) share the menu with couscous, pasta and delicious mains like garlic-spiked roast squid.

★ Hotel-Ristorante Pocho SEAFOOD €€
(☑ 0923 97 25 25; www.pocho.it; Località Isulidda Macari; meals €30-40; ⊙ 7.30-10pm Mon-Sat, noon-2pm & 7.30-10pm Sun Apr-Oct; P❄️🍴) Dinner is an unforgettable feast for the eyes and palate at this sensational hotel-restaurant, dramatically perched on a cliff edge overlooking Isulidda beach, 2km south of San Vito in the hamlet of Macari. Summer dining cooks up fish and seafood from the local market and panoramic views of the Golfo di Cofano, while Sunday is chef Marilù's couscous day.

❶ Getting There & Away

BUS
AST runs buses between San Vito Lo Capo and Trapani port (one-way/return €4/7.50, 1½ hours, eight to 10 daily) and Autoservizi Russo (www.russo autoservizi.it) travels to/from Palermo (€9.40, two to three hours, one or two daily). Buses in San Vito arrive at/depart from Via Piersanti Mattarella, near the beach and parallel to Via Savoia – look for street signs marking the stops.

San Vito Lo Capo Bus (☑ 348 2242085, 0923 36 04 31; www.sanvitolocapobus.com; Via del Mulino 96; ⊙ 9am-8pm summer, shorter hours winter) offers convenient direct van transfers to San Vito from the airports at Palermo (€24) and Trapani (€17). Reserve in advance online or in town at **San Vito Tour** (☑ 0923 3 60 43; www. sanvitotour.com; Via del Mulino 92; ⊙ 9am-8pm summer, shorter hours winter) where buses arrive/depart.

CAR & MOTORCYCLE
San Vito is roughly 45 minutes from either Castellammare del Golfo (43km via the SS187 and SP16) or Trapani (37km via the SP20 and SP16).

Riserva Naturale dello Zingaro

Saved from development by local protests in 1980, the tranquil **Riserva Naturale dello Zingaro** (☑ 0924 3 51 08; www.riservazingaro. it; adult/child €5/3; ⊙ 7am-7.30pm Apr-Sep, 8am-4pm Oct-Mar) was established in 1981 as Sicily's first nature preserve. It has become the star attraction on the gulf, drawing an ever-growing number of nature lovers and outdoors enthusiasts.

The reserve is a hiker's paradise and a haven for wildlife, including the rare Bonelli's eagle, majestic buzzard, kestrel and some 40 other bird species. Wild carob and bright-yellow euphorbia dust the hillsides, along with 700 other species of Mediterranean flora – some unique to this stretch of coast – while hidden coves provide tranquil swimming and snorkelling spots.

The park has two entrances with ticket offices: the main entrance is 2km north of Scopello and the other is 12km south of San Vito Lo Capo. The informative **visitor centre** (Centro Visitatori; www.riservanaturalezingaro. com; ◷7.10am-7.10pm summer, shorter hours in winter) is an easy 10-minute walk from the southern Scopello entrance.

◉ Sights & Activities

A stunning 7km walking trail north along the coast from the reserve's main entrance passes by the visitor centre and a series of museums focusing on local culture, crafts and heritage. The reserve's northern (San Vito) entrance is not served by public transport, making backtracking south to Scopello the most practical option for hikers. The main coastal walk takes about two hours each way, not counting stops. There are also several trails inland, detailed on park maps.

Not far from the visitor centre, a 10-minute walk from the southern Scopello entrance, don't miss the huge cavernous **gallery** that was hacked out of rock in 1980 as the start of the controversial coastal road project, scuppered after protests.

Various guided walks are organised in the reserve – a monthly schedule is posted on the park's enormously informative website. For guided sea-kayaking expeditions and treks contact the excellent YMCA Climbing House in San Vito Lo Capo.

◉ Beaches

From the main coastal path, well-signposted gravel tracks cut through aromatic scrub and broom, almond trees and orchid-dotted grassy meadows to picturesque coves laced with pretty shingle or pebble beaches. Only accessible by boat or on foot, these beaches are naturally beautiful – and invariably idyllically empty outside of July and August. Favourites include **Cala Capreria**, with bright turquoise water and ample rocks to laze on, a 1.5km downhill walk from the park's southern Scopello entrance; and **Cala della Disa**, another 2km north and popular with families for its shady fine-shingle beach and notably shallow water. The park's largest beach is smooth pebbly **Cala dell'Uzzo**, named after the neighbouring prehistoric cave Grotta dell'Uzzo, and an easy 2km walk south from the northern San Vito entrance.

Snorkellers favour **Cala Marinella** for its piercing emerald-green waters, accessed from rocks (there is no beach as such). Find it midway along the coastal path, roughly 3.5km from either entrance. For guided snorkelling expeditions, dives and underwater tours in the reserve, contact Cetaria Diving Centre in Scopello.

❶ Getting There & Away

The closest towns to the reserve are Scopello (2km to the south) and San Vito Lo Capo (12km to the north). From either town, take the SP63 until it dead-ends at the park entrance. There is no public transport to the park.

Castellammare del Golfo

POP 15,300

Founded by the Elymians as the port for nearby Segesta, the small coastal city of Castellammare del Golfo has a pleasant harbour overlooked by the remains of a much-modified Saracen castle and surrounded by sandy beaches, making it a popular summer holiday destination for Sicilians. Beyond the harbour itself, however, the city is rather sprawling and lacking in charm, making nearby Scopello and San Vito Lo Capo more appealing for an extended stay.

Paradise for meat lovers, **I Saporo** (☑0924 3 13 52; Via Giuseppe Saragat 25; meals €30-40; ◷7.30-11pm Thu-Tue) is a Sicilian grill that cooks up top-quality cuts from the adjoining butcher's shop. Be it Tuscan Chianina beef, marinated chicken wings, unbelievably tender pork ribs or one of 14 types of homemade burger, everything is cooked to perfection over the wood-fired grill. Much of the produce is fresh from the butcher's own farm near Segesta.

Formally dressed waiters roll out the day's catch on a vintage wooden trolley for diners to inspect and select before cooking at **Ristorante del Golfo** (☑0924 3 02 57, 338 774 2825; www.ristorantedel golfo.it; Via Segesta 153; meals €35-55; ◷noon-3pm & 7-11pm, closed Tue Oct-May), a perennial seafood favourite. Signature dishes include king prawns baked in an almond crust, ricci (sea urchins) and shoals of pesce in crosta di sale alla griglia (grilled fish encrusted with Trapani's famous salt).

End with *cassatelle* – deep-fried pastries filled with sweet ricotta, lemon rind and chocolate.

❶ Getting There & Away

BUS
Buses depart from Via della Repubblica. Autoservizi Russo (www.russoautoservizi.it) runs services to Palermo (€6.40, 1½ hours, six daily Monday to Saturday, one on Sunday), Scopello (€2.70, 20 minutes, four daily except Sunday) and San Vito Lo Capo (€6.40, 1¼ hours, three daily Monday to Saturday, one Sunday). Extra buses operate in July and August.

CAR & MOTORCYCLE
Castellammare del Golfo is only 44km from Palermo's Falcone-Borsellino Airport via the A29 *autostrada*.

TRAIN
The train station, 3km out of town, is linked by shuttle bus (€1.50) to downtown. Trains run up to four times daily to Trapani (€8.70, 1¾ to two hours).

SEGESTA

Set on the edge of a deep canyon amid desolate mountains, the 5th-century BC ruins of **Segesta** (⏲ 0924 95 23 56; adult/child €6/free; ⊙ 9am-7.30pm Apr-Sep, to 6.30pm Mar & Oct, to 5pm Nov-Feb) are among the world's most magical ancient sites.

Long before the arrival of the Greeks, Segesta was the principal city of the Elymians, an ancient civilisation claiming descent from the Trojans that settled in Sicily in the Bronze Age. The Elymians were in constant conflict with Greek Selinunte, whose destruction (in 409 BC) they pursued with bloodthirsty determination. More than 100 years later the Greek tyrant Agathocles slaughtered over 10,000 Elymians and re-populated Segesta with Greeks.

Little remains of ancient Segesta today, save its hilltop theatre and never-completed Doric temple, yet the ruins' remarkable state of preservation and the majesty of their rural setting combine to make this one of Sicily's enduring highlights. Occasional music concerts and cultural events held beneath the stars in the theatre on hot summer nights are nothing short of magical.

Segesta's centrepiece is its remarkably well-preserved **Doric temple**, dating from around 430 BC. Standing in splendid isolation amid fields of wildflowers and grasses, it has retained all of its columns, topped by a perfectly intact entablature and pediment – though the missing roof and lack of fluting on the columns indicate that it was never completed. On windy days the 36 giant columns are said to act like an organ, producing mysterious notes. It's a five-minute walk (250m) uphill from the ticket office.

Crowning the summit of Monte Bàrbaro, the 3rd-century BC **Greek theatre** is Segesta's most prominent ruin after its famous Doric temple. The theatre commands sweeping views north to the Golfo di Castellammare (with a rather incongruous-looking modern *autostrada* snaking its way across the valley in the foreground). A shuttle bus (€1.50, half-hourly) climbs to the theatre along the 1.25km access road from Segesta's ticket booth. Return via a lovely 30-minute downhill footpath with wonderful temple views.

❶ Getting There & Away

BUS
Tarantola (www.tarantolabus.com) operates a limited service to/from Trapani bus station and Segesta (single/return €4/6.60 return, 40 to 50 minutes). From April to October only, it also operates services to/from Palermo (single/return €7/11.20, 80 minutes, three daily Monday to Saturday). For both routes check schedules carefully as times posted are not necessarily reliable; avoid Sunday and bank holidays when there are no buses.

CAR & MOTORCYCLE
The Segesta exit is clearly marked off the A29D *autostrada* between Trapani (32km to the west) and Palermo (76km to the east). Visitors must use the sizeable, purpose-built **car park** (⏲ 389 9659764; www.segestaparking.com; Contrada Pispisa, SP 68; car/motorcycle €5/3; ⊙ 9am-7.30pm), 1.5km from the hilltop ruins and continue to the temple ruins on foot or by shuttle bus (€1.50, every 15 minutes). A second bus (€1.50) shuttles visitors between the temple and the theatre, another 1.25km uphill again. Shuttles run until 6.30pm in summer and 4pm in winter.

TRAPANI

POP 67,900

Hugging the harbour where Peter of Aragon landed in 1282 to begin the Spanish occupation of Sicily, the sickle-shaped spit of land occupied by Trapani's old town once sat at the heart of a powerful trading network that stretched from Carthage to Venice. Traditionally the town thrived on coral and tuna fishing, with some salt and wine production.

These days, Trapani's small port buzzes with ferry traffic zipping to and from the remote Egadi Islands and the mysterious volcanic rock island of Pantelleria, not far from Tunisia. Trapani's adjacent historic centre, with its small but compelling maze of ancient churches and gold-stone *palazzi* (mansions), is a mellow place to stroll, for both locals and travellers awaiting their next boat. From late afternoon onwards, car-free main street Via Garibaldi buzzes with what feels like the entire town out in force enjoying their lazy, absolute sacrosanct *passeggiata* (early evening stroll). Join them.

◉ Sights

Although the narrow network of streets in Trapani's historic centre is Moorish, the city takes most of its character from the fabulous 17th- and 18th-century baroque of the Spanish period. Prime examples include **Cattedrale di San Lorenzo** (✆0923 2 33 62; http://cattedraletrapani.it; ⊙8am-4pm) on pedestrianised Corso Vittorio Emanuele, and the striking **Palazzo Senatorio** (Palazzo Cavaretta; cnr Corso Vittorio Emanuele & Via Torrearsa) at the eastern end of the same street, along with the nearby **Palazzo Riccio di Morana** (Via Garibaldi 89-91) and **Palazzo Fardella Fontana** (Via Garibaldi 93-101).

★ Chiesa Anime
Sante del Purgatorio   CHURCH
(✆0923 56 28 82; Via San Francesco d'Assisi; by donation; ⊙7.30am-noon & 4-7pm Mon-Sat, 10am-noon & 4-7pm Sun) Just off the *corso* in the heart of the city, this church houses the impressive 18th-century m*isteri*, 20 life-sized wooden effigies depicting the story of Christ's Passion, which take centre stage during the city's dramatic Easter Week processions every year. Explanatory panels in English, Italian, French and German help visitors to understand the story behind each figure.

Some of the statues are originals; others are copies of statues that were destroyed by WWII Allied bombings or damaged after being dropped by their bearers during a procession (the statues are heavy and unwieldy, and mishaps sometimes occur).

Each statue was commissioned and is now carried by members of a particular profession. For example, *Jesus Before Herod* was commissioned by the Millers and Bakers Guild; *Jesus Entombed,* by the Pasta-Makers

Guild; and *The Whipping,* by the Bricklayers and Stonemasons Guild. One of the figures, *The Ascent of Calvary,* isn't claimed by a particular guild, but is instead accompanied by the Trapanese people at large.

Villa Margherita   PARK
(Viale Regina Margherita; ⊙hours vary) Trapani's majestic central park, first laid out in 1878, is a relaxing spot to lounge in the shade of centurion trees, admire and learn about dozens of unusual tree species (dragon trees, Chinese fan palms, ornamental cycads), and bring the children to see the resident peacock and ducks swanning around at the pond.

Museo Nazionale Pepoli   MUSEUM
(✆0923 55 32 69; www.comune.trapani.it/turismo/pepoli.htm; Via Conte Pepoli 180; adult/child €6/free; ⊙9am-5.30pm Tue-Sat, to 12.30pm Sun) Tucked away in the atmospheric cloister of a 14th-century Carmelite monastery, this wonderful decorative-arts museum dating from 1906–08 houses the collection of Agostino Pepoli (1848–1910), a local count who devoted his life to salvaging Trapani's local arts and crafts, most notably 17th- and 18th-century coral carvings, all the rage in Europe before Trapani's offshore coral banks were decimated.

🏃 Activities

Sun Club   BEACH
(✆320 4653774; www.sunclubtrapani.it; Lungomare Dante Alighieri; ⊙6pm-2am summer, 6pm-2am Thu-Sun winter; ⊛) With chic, white-washed or natural-wood furniture and the catchy background buzz of euro-pop, Sun Club is a hot summer address with Trapani's cool crowd. Its hybrid restaurant-bar cooks up breakfast, lunch and dinner, not to mention memorable cocktails at sundown, dancing on the sand and occasional live bands at weekends. By day, rent parasol-shaded sun-loungers to beach-lounge in style.

Blue Beach   BEACH
(✆393 8289289; www.facebook.com/blue beachtrapani; Lungomare Dante Alighieri 18; ⊙Mar-Oct; ⊛) The trendy beach of choice, a 3km (40-minute) walk north along the seafront from central Piazza Vittoria Emanuele, Blue Beach has it all: golden sand, comfy sun-loungers and white parasols, chic terrace with sofa seating, a hipster bar serving great cocktails, DJ sets and themed party evenings sprinkled throughout the season.

Eating

Tramura
INTERNATIONAL €

(☑ 338 8687002; www.facebook.com/tramura; Via Mura di Tramontana Ovest; meals €15-25; ⊙ 11am-3am summer, shorter hours in winter; 🛜) Grandly set on the coastal walkway atop the old city walls, this casual eatery sports brilliant sea views with not a car in sight. Potted plants suspended above each table add a Zen vibe to the nautical-styled interior and covered terrace, and the kitchen cooks up everything from quintessential pasta dishes to burgers (including a fresh tuna burger in tuna season), *bruschette* and salads.

Carni e Delizi
DELI €

(☑ 0923 2 64 08; www.facebook.com/francescoaccar; Via Virgilio 35; meals €10-20; ⊙ 9am-3pm Mon, 9am-3pm & 5-9pm Tue-Thu, 9am-3pm & 5-11pm Fri & Sat) It doesn't get more local than this neighbourhood *macelleria* (butcher's shop) and deli, with a street cart selling *panini con mezza* (burgers) and a handful of tables inside. Select from a feast of cured salami, cold cuts and lavish pre-prepared deli dishes to eat in or take away. On Friday and Saturday evenings, locals linger over a lavish *apericena* (a combination of *apertivo* and *cena,* or dinner).

La Rinascente
PASTRIES €

(☑ 0923 2 37 67; Via Gatti 3; cakes €2; ⊙ 9am-1pm & 4-7pm Mon, Tue, Thu & Fri, 7.30am-2pm Sat & Sun) Push your way through the beaded fly screen to enter this old-school bakery, unchanged since 1969. But, then, admiring the vintage white-marble work top and bakers of a certain age in their chef whites is all part of the charm. Jovial owner Giovanni Costadura is pleasantry personified and his lavish weekend displays of homemade *cannoli* and other one-bite cakes are a local legend.

⭐ La Bettolaccia
SICILIAN €€

(☑ 0923 2 59 32; www.labettolaccia.it; Via Enrico Fardella 25; meals €35-45; ⊙ 12.45-3pm & 7.45-11pm Mon-Fri, 7.45-11pm Sat) Unwaveringly authentic, this on-trend Slow Food favourite, squirrelled away down a sleepy side street, is the hotspot to feast on spicy couscous with fried fish or mixed seafood, *caponata* (eggplant and sun-dried tomatoes with capers in a sweet-and-sour sauce), the catch of the day, and other traditional Trapanese dishes in a sharp, minimalist white space. Reservations essential.

Caupona Taverna di Sicilia
SEAFOOD €€

(☑ 0923 54 66 18, 340 3421335; Piazza Purgatorio 32; meals €25-35; ⊙ 1-2.15pm & 8-11.30pm Wed-Mon) Fresh fish rules the menu at this fabulous family-run spot two blocks from the port, which markets itself very much as *'la casa del cuscus trapanese'* (the House of Trapani Couscous). Needless to say the couscous and seafood classics such as *pesce spada alla pantesca* (swordfish in a sauce of tomatoes, garlic, parsley, olives and capers) are all superb.

Save room for the monster-sized *cannoli* – big enough for two, easily.

Tentazioni di Gusto
SICILIAN €€

(☑ 0923 54 81 65; www.tentazionidigusto.it; Via Badia Nuova 27; meals €45; ⊙ 12.30-3pm & 7.30-

---

LA PROCESSIONE DEI MISTERI

Since the 18th century, the citizens of Trapani – represented by 20 traditional *maestranze* (guilds) – have begun a four-day celebration of the Passion of Christ on the Tuesday before Easter Sunday by parading a remarkable, life-sized wooden statue of the Virgin Mary through the town's streets. Over the course of the following three days, nightly processions of the remaining *misteri* (life-sized wooden statues) make their way through the old quarter and port to a specially erected chapel in Piazza Lucatelli, where the icons are stored overnight. Each procession is accompanied by crowds of locals and a Trapanese band, which plays dirges to the slow, steady beat of a drum.

The high point of the celebration is on Friday afternoon, when the 20 guilds emerge from the Chiesa del Purgatorio and descend the steps of the church, carrying each of the statues, to begin the 1km-long procession up to Via Giovanni Battista Fardella; the procession then returns to the church the following morning. The massive crowds that gather to witness the slow march often reach a peak of delirious fervour that is matched only by that of the Semana Santa parades in Seville, Spain.

To witness the procession, you'll need to book your accommodation well in advance. At other times, the figures are on display in the Chiesa Anime Sante del Purgatorio (p98). For more information, check out www.processionemisteritp.it.

Trapani

Tyrrhenian
Sea

Funicular to Erice (3km);
Erice (15km)

Via Giovanni
Battista Fardella

Via Marino Torre
Via Vespri
Via Vespri
Via Scontrino
Piazza
Umberto I
Via Mazzini
Bus
Station
Piazza
Montalto
Via Malta

AST (100m);
Carni e Delizi (150m)

Vincenzo Florio (Birgi) (15km);
Marsala (33km)

Via Spalti
Piazza
Vittorio
Emanuele
Via Osorio
Via Marinella
Via Trento
Via Ilio

Via Abate Palmerio

Via XXX Gennaio

Via Giudecca

Piazza
Vittorio
Veneto
Via Ortani
Via Merce
Via Gatti

Lungomare Dante Alighieri

Via Poeta Calvino
Via Garibaldi
Via Badia Grande
Via B Sieri Pepoli
Via Badiella
Via San Michele
Corso Italia
Via San Pietro
Via della Luce

Piazza
Mercato
del Pesce
Via Badia Nuova
Via delle Belle Arti
Via Cuba
Via degli Argentieri
Via Sant'Agostino
Port Bus
Stop

Via Torrearsa
Via Turretta
Piazzetta
Saturno
Piazza
Scarlatti
Liberty
Lines

Favignana (17km);
Levanzo (17km);
Marettimo (38km)

Via Libertà
Via Tenente Genovese
Via Tinton
Piazza
Lucatelli
Piazza
Garibaldi
Via Ammiraglio Staiti

Corso Vittorio Emanuele
Historic
Centre
Via e Verdi
Ferry
Terminal

Via Enrico Fardella
Via Generale Dom Giglio
Siremar

Via Nunzio Nasi
Via San Francesco D'Assisi
Via Cassaretto
Via Regina Elena
Via Tartaglia

Pantelleria (110km)

Trapani

11pm, closed Wed Oct-May; 🛜 'Tentazioni' (temptation) is the buzzword at Gusto, a contemporary-styled space with street lounge made for romantic *aperitivo*-quaffing and a creative kitchen mixing Trapani classics with fishy house specialties. The thyme-spiced risotto with prawns and wild fennel (paired with a Marsala white) is noteworthy, as is the cuttlefish ravioli with creamed peas and the fish soup served in a square bowl.

ⓘ Information

Hospital (Ospedale Sant'Antonio Abate; ☑ 0923 80 91 11; www.asptrapani.it; Via Cosenza 80) Five kilometres east of the centre; its emergency unit is open 24 hours.

Police Station (☑ 0923 59 81 11; http://questure.poliziadistato.it/trapani; Piazza Vittoria Veneto 1) Trapani's main police station.

Post Office (☑ 0923 43 43 82; Piazza Vittoria Veneto 11; ⊙ 8.30am-7pm Mon-Fri, to 12.30pm Sat)

Tourist Office (☑ 0923 54 45 33; Piazzetta Saturno 3bis; ⊙ 9am-1pm Mon-Fri summer, 9am-2pm & 3-5pm Mon & Thu, 9am-2pm Tue, Wed & Fri winter) Just north of the port, Trapani's tourist office distributes city maps and has information on activities, including diving and wine tasting, around Trapani. Grab maps of the Egadi Islands marked up with walking trails here, too.

ⓘ Getting There & Away

Trapani's busy port is the main departure point for the Egadi Islands and the remote Moorish island of Pantelleria. Nearby Trapani-Birgi Vincenzo Florio Airport is served by budget flights from mainland Italy and the rest of Europe.

AIR

Sicily's third-busiest airport, **Trapani-Birgi Vincenzo Florio Airport** (☑ 0923 61 01 11; www.airgest.it), is 16km south of Trapani at Birgi and is commonly known as Birgi airport.

BOAT

Trapani's **ferry terminal** (Stazione Marittima, Porto Trapani) is opposite Piazza Garibaldi. **Siremar** (☑ 090 57 37; https://carontetourist.it/en/siremar; Stazione Marittima, Porto Trapani) and **Traghetti delle Isole** (☑ 0923 2 24 67; www.traghettidelleisole.it) both operate year-round car ferries to Pantelleria (€33, six to 7¼ hours, three to five times weekly). Siremar also runs year-round ferries to the Egadi Islands of Favignana (€10.70, one to 1½ hours, three daily), Levanzo (€9.70, one to 1½ hours, three daily) and Marettimo (€14.10, three hours, one daily).

Speedy hydrofoils operated by Liberty Lines dock a few blocks east at the fast-ferry terminal on Via Ammiraglio Staiti – look for the sharp contemporary terminal building scheduled for completion by late 2019. Until then buy tickets at its temporary **Liberty Lines kiosk** (☑ 0923 87 38 13; https://eng.libertylines.it; Via Ammiraglio Staiti), next to the hydrofoil dock.

There are more than a dozen hydrofoils daily to Favignana (€11.80, 20 to 40 minutes) and Levanzo (€10.80, 25 to 50 minutes), with at least four of these continuing to Marettimo (€17.80, one to 1½ hours). Liberty Lines also has fast boats to Pantelleria (€42.50, two hours, one daily). Children aged four to 11 years pay half-fare and those aged under three sail for free.

Liberty Lines also sails year-round to/from Marsala (€17.80, one to 1½ hours).

Passengers can take one piece of luggage on board for free; subsequent bags require a ticket (€6.70).

BUS

Segesta Autolinee (www.segesta.it) buses connecting Trapani with Palermo airport (€8, 65 minutes, at least hourly between 5.30am and 8pm) and **AST** (Azienda Siciliana Trasporti; ☑ 0923 2 10 21; www.astsicilia.it; Via Virgilio 20) buses to/from Vincenzo Florio (Birgi) airport (€2.90, 55 minutes) use the bus stop in front of the hydrofoil docks. Buy tickets at **Egatour** (☑ 0923 2 17 54; www.egatourviaggi.it; Via Ammiraglio Staiti 13), located directly opposite.

The same bus stop is used by Big Bus (www.bigbus.it) buses heading to/from Palermo train station (two hours), Marsala (50 minutes) and an overnight bus to/from Naples (13¾ hours, one daily) and Rome (14¼, one daily).

Other intercity buses – scant few as they are – use Trapani's **bus station** (☑ 0923 2 00 66; Piazza Montalto). Buy tickets at the nearby tobacco shop, **Tabaccheria Barraco** (Via Virgilio 6; ☺ 9am-1pm & 4-7pm Thu-Tue), just across the street from the station.

From the bus station, Tarantola (www. tarantolabus.com) operates a limited service to Segesta (€6.60 round trip, 40 to 50 minutes each way, two to three Monday to Saturday). AST serves Erice (€2.90, 40 minutes to one hour, four to six daily), San Vito Lo Capo (€4.60, 1½ hours, eight to 10 daily), Marsala (€3.60, 1¼ hours, four daily Monday to Saturday) and Mazara del Vallo (€5.30, 1¾ hours, three daily Monday to Saturday).

TRAIN

From Trapani's train station, 1km east of the centre on Piazza Umberto, ten daily trains (five on Sunday) run to Marsala (€3.80, 25 to 40 minutes) and Mazara del Vallo (€5.10, 55 minutes). For Palermo, the bus is a much faster and more direct option.

ⓘ Getting Around

TO/FROM THE AIRPORT

Bus From the arrivals hall at Trapani-Birgi Vincenzo Florio Airport, hourly AST buses (€4.90, 20 minutes, hourly) run to/from Trapani's port. Marsala-based Salemi (https://autoservizi salemi.it) operates buses between the Birgi airport and Palermo (€11, 1¾ to two hours, five to six daily); buy tickets online or on the bus.

Taxi A taxi between Birgi airport and Trapani costs a fixed €30.

BICYCLE

Cycling is an easy and pleasant way to explore the Saline di Trapani, the flat landscape of salt pools and windmills just south of town. Rent wheels in town from **Trapani Rent Point** (☑ 388 2518505; www.trapanirentpoint.it; Via Convento San Francesco di Paola 71; city/electric bike per day from €8/20; ☺ 9am-4pm).

BUS

Tickets for city buses operated by local-bus company ATM (www.atmtrapani.it) are valid for 90 minutes and cost €1.20 at *tabaccheria* (tobacco shops) or €1.40 on board.

CAR & MOTORCYCLE

There are plenty of parking spaces at the port and near the train station. Purchase tickets from the machines on the street (prices range from €0.50 to €0.80 per hour, with rates increasing as you get closer to the city centre).

In July and August visitors to the Egadi Islands can leave their car at **Parcheggio Egadi** (Egadi Parking; ☑ 348 5952158; per hour/day €0.70/7;

☺ 24hr Jul & Aug), a fenced lot off Via dei Grandi Eventi, about 1km east of the port. Free shuttle buses (ATM lines 2A and 2B) link the car park with the port from 7am and 8.30pm Monday to Saturday, but posted hours are unreliable. An easier option – available year-round – is the covered multi-storey car park **Parcheggio Multipiano** (Multi-Storey Car Park; ☑ 0923 58 24 39; www.atmtrapani.it; Via Ilio; per hour/day/ week summer €1.20/12/60, winter €1/10/40; ☺ 24hr), a 10-minute walk from the port on Via Ilio.

TAXI

Taxi ranks are located at the ferry terminal and on Piazza Umberto I, in front of the train station.

AROUND TRAPANI

Erice

POP 27,900 / ELEV 751M

Medieval Erice watches over the port of Trapani from its giddy mountain perch atop the legendary peak of Eryx, spectacularly set 750m above sea level. It's a mesmerising, walled 12th-century village whose peculiar history, mountain charm and sensational sea-and-valley views are only enhanced by frequent unpredictable changes in weather that take you from brilliant sunshine to thick fog in the space of minutes.

Allow ample time for losing yourself in the atmospheric maze of stone-paved streets – all the more cinematic when the piercing sun plays peekaboo with swirling mist – and savouring a sweet old-world moment at Sicily's most famous pastry shop.

Virgil once compared Eryx to Mt Athos for its altitude and spiritual pre-eminence. Not that the town resembles a sanctuary today – temples and convents have given way to carpet shops selling the town's famous *frazzate* (bright rugs made from colourful rags) and innumerable souvenir stalls. Still, Erice is about wall-hugging alleys, votive niches and secret courtyards, all of which are best appreciated in low season or, in summer, early morning or in the evening after the battalions of visitors have left for the day.

The 12th- to 13th-century **Castello di Venere** (Castle of Venus; ☑ 320 8672957; www. fondazioneericearte.org/castellodivenere.php; Via Castello di Venere; adult/reduced €4/2; ☺ 10am-8pm Aug, to 7pm Jul & Sep, to 6pm Apr-Jun & Oct,

Erice

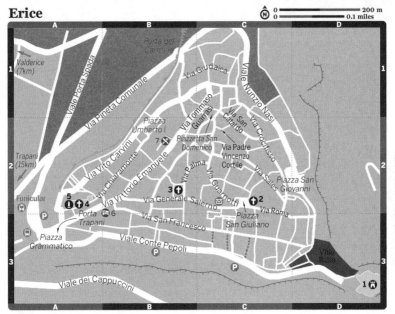

10am-1pm Sat & Sun Nov-Mar) is a Norman cas-tle built over the Temple of Venus, long a site of worship for the ancient Elymians, Phoe-nicians, Greeks and Romans. Nowadays the castle's rooms are off-limits, but visitors can explore the grassy interior courtyard, filled with ruined foundations and flanked by an impressive stone wall allegedly built by Daedalus. Stealing the show are the spectac-ular panoramic vistas extending to San Vito Lo Capo on one side and the Saline di Tra-pani on the other.

Erice's **Real Duomo** (Royal Cathedral; Via Chiaramonte; €2.50; ⊙10am-8pm Aug, to 7pm Jul & Sep, shorter hours rest of year) – a golden

mirage of sculpted buttermilk stone and Carrara marble – was built in 1314 by order of a grateful Frederick III who sheltered in Erice during the Sicilian Vespers uprising (1282–1314). Its interior was remodelled in neo-Gothic style in 1865, but the 15th-century side chapels were conserved. In the former sacristy, the **Museo di Erice La Montagna del Signore** displays sacred art-works, chalices, candlesticks and other 15th-and 16th-century silverware.

Tickets for the cathedral are sold in the neighbouring **Torre di Federico**, the cathedral's freestanding campanile with mullioned windows, crenellated tower, six bells and 108 steps spiralling to the top of its 28m height – rooftop views from the top are naturally impressive. A combined Passepartout ticket (€6) covers admission to the cathedral, bell tower and two other Erice churches: **San Martino** (Via Pietro Salerno 8; €2.50; ⊙10am-8pm Aug, to 7pm Jul & Sep, shorter hours rest of year) and **San Giuliano** (Via Roma; €2.50; ⊙10am-8pm Aug, to 7pm Jul & Sep, shorter hours rest of year).

🍴 Eating & Drinking

Erice is famous throughout Sicily for its *dol-ci ericini* (almond sweets); as a result, you'll find as many pastry shops as restaurants in the historic centre. Given the town's status

DON'T MISS

MARIA GRAMMATICO

Nothing beats a cappuccino and sweet *lingua di suocera* (lemon-laced, 'mother-in-law tongue' cake) or knobbly, almond-rich *belli e brutti* ('beautiful and ugly') in the wood-panelled tearoom or leafy courtyard of old-world **Pasticceria di Maria Grammatico** (☑ 0923 86 93 90; www.mariagrammatico.it; Via Vittorio Emanuele 14; pastries from €2; ⊗ 9am-10pm May, Jun & Sep, to 1am Jul & Aug, to 7pm Oct-Apr). The world-famous cake shop has been the heart and soul of Sicily's renowned pastry chef Maria Grammatico (b 1941), subject of Mary Taylor Simeti's book *Bitter Almonds,* since the early 1960s and is a memorable spot to lap up local life – especially on Sunday when villagers pile into the tiny old-fashioned space after church for coffee, cake and chat, as they've done for decades.

In the early 1950s, Maria's father died suddenly of a heart attack. Her impoverished mother, pregnant with a sixth child, decided to send Maria, aged 11, and her younger sister to the cloistered San Carlo orphanage in Erice to learn the art of pastry-making from the nuns. There, the children toiled in brutally hard conditions – beating sugar mixtures for six hours at a time, rising before dawn to prime the ovens, shelling kilos of almonds and surviving on an unrelenting diet of meatless pasta and vegetable gruel. At 22, Maria left the orphanage after having a nervous breakdown and started making sweets and pastries to survive.

Traditional Sicilian treats to try include quintessential *cannoli* filled with fresh ricotta; green *cassata* cakes made of almonds, sugar, vanilla, buttermilk curd and candied fruit; perfectly formed marzipan fruits; lemon-flavoured *cuscinetti* (small fried pastries); and *buccellati* (hard, fig biscuits) twisted around fig, cinnamon and clove comfit. At Easter, the shop is filled with almond-citron baby lambs, lovingly crafted to celebrate Erice's I Misteri celebrations on Good Friday.

as a tourist magnet, price-to-quality ratio is not always the greatest.

ℹ Information

Police Station (☑ 0923 55 50 00; Piazza Grammatico; ⊗ 24hr)

Post Office (Via Guarnotti 7; ⊗ 8.15am-1.30pm Mon-Fri)

ℹ Getting There & Away

BUS

There is a regular AST (p101) bus service to/from Trapani (one-way/return €2.90/4.80, 40 minutes to one hour, four to six daily). Buses use the 'Porta Trapani' bus stop in front of Trapani's hydrofoil dock at the port and at the foot of Erice's old town, near the funicular.

CAR & MOTORCYCLE

Paid parking is available in Erice next to Porta Trapani and along Viale Conte Pepoli. Down below in Trapani, there's a sizeable car park next to the funicular station. Pay €1.50 per hour for up to three hours, then €1 per hour, or €10 a day.

FUNICULAR

The best way to travel between Erice and Trapani is on the **funicular** (Cabinovia di Erice; ☑ 0923 56 93 06, 0923 86 97 20; www.funiviaerice.it; one way/return €5.50/9; ⊗ 1-8pm Mon, 8.30am-8pm Tue-Fri, 9am-9pm Sat, 9.30am-8.30pm Sun), which is also popular with local walkers and mountain bikers. The funicular station in Erice is at the foot of the village, across the street from Porta Trapani. To reach the funicular station in Trapani, catch bus 21 or 23 from Via GB Fardella down to the eastern end of Via Alessandro Manzoni (where Trapani ends and Erice begins); bus schedules and route maps are on the Funivia website.

Saline di Trapani

Along the coast between Trapani and Marsala lies this evocative landscape of *saline* (shallow salt pools) and decommissioned *mulini* (windmills). The salt from these marshes is considered Italy's finest and has been big business for centuries; today, only a cottage industry remains, providing for Italy's more discerning dinner tables. The best time to visit is summer, when the sun turns the saltpans rosy pink and makes the salt heaps shimmer. In winter, the heaps – covered with tiles and plastic tarpaulins to keep out the rain – are considerably less picturesque.

The most attractive stretches of coast are protected within two wetland preserves: Riserva Naturale Saline di Trapani e Paceco (p105) to the north near Trapani, and **Riserva Naturale di Stagnone** to the south near Marsala. The latter encompasses San Pantaleo island – home to the noted archaeological site of Mozia – and the larger Isola Lunga, which protects the shallow waters of Stagnone lagoon.

◎ Sights

★ Mulino della Saline Infersa   MUSEUM

(☑348 380 4301, 0923 73 30 03; www.salinedellala guna.it; Contrada Ettore e Infersa 55; adult/reduced €7/2.50; ⊙9am-8.30pm Apr-Sep, to 3pm Oct-Jan & Mar) The southernmost of the region's two salt museums is housed in a beautifully restored 16th-century windmill opposite the Mozia boat dock, 10km north of Marsala. It has multimedia displays about the history of salt production in the area and offers visitors a variety of fascinating hands-on experiences (all with advance online reservation) including thematic salt tastings (€20) and guided salt-pan walks (adult/reduced €15/5).

Between May and August it is possible to try your hand at being a salt worker for a half-day and even harvest salt (boots provided; adult/reduced €25/10). Summer visitors can also enjoy witnessing the windmill in action on Wednesday and Saturday from 4pm to 6pm.

Mozia   ARCHAEOLOGICAL SITE

(San Pantaleo) Located on the tiny island of San Pantaleo, ancient Mozia (also known as Motya or Mothia) was one of the Mediterranean's most important Phoenician settlements. Established in the 8th century BC and coveted for its strategic position, Mozia is today the world's best-preserved Phoenician site.

The entire island was bought by the ornithologist and amateur archaeologist Joseph Whitaker (1850–1936) in the early 20th century and bequeathed to the Joseph Whitaker Foundation by his daughter Delia on her death in 1971. Joseph, who was a member of an English family that gained great wealth from the Marsala trade, built a villa here and spent decades excavating the island and assembling a unique collection of Phoenician artefacts, many of which are now on display in the Museo Whitaker that bears his name.

The fields around the museum are strewn with ruins from the ancient Phoenician settlement. Visitors can wander around the island to explore these, following a network of trails punctuated with helpful maps and information displays. Excavations include the ancient port and dry dock, where you can see the start of a Phoenician road – now approximately 1m underwater – that once linked San Pantaleo with the mainland. There's also a bar-cafe serving drinks and snacks.

To get to the island, hop aboard a Mozia Line ferry boat (p108) from the Imbarcadero Salina Infersa next to the **Mamma Caura** (☑388 8772499, 0923 96 60 36; www.mamma caura.eu; Contrada Ettore e Infersa, Salina Ettore; ⊙9am-10pm summer, to 6pm winter) cafe-bar.

Museo Whitaker   MUSEUM

(☑0923 71 25 98; San Pantaleo; adult/reduced €9/5; ⊙9.30am-1.30pm & 2.30-6.30pm Apr-Oct, 9am-3pm Nov-Mar) This museum on San Pantaleo island, 10km north of Marsala, houses a unique collection of Phoenician artefacts assembled over decades by amateur archaeologist Joseph Whitaker. Its greatest treasure is *Il Giovinetto di Mozia,* a 5th-century-BC Carthaginian-influenced marble statue of a young man. To get here, drive or bike to the Mozia dock 10km north of Marsala and catch one of the half-hourly, 10-minute ferries operated by Mozia Line (p108).

Riserva Naturale
Saline di Trapani e Paceco   PARK

(☑327 5621529, 0923 86 77 00; www.salinedi trapani.it; SP21) Administered by the World Wildlife Fund, this nature reserve protects 1000 hectares of *saline* (salt pans), divided into two zones, extending from Trapani's southern outskirts to the hamlet of Saline Grande, south of Nubia. Look for a small hut, a few kilometres south of Trapani, on your left along the SP21.

With advance notice, WWF guides can sometimes offer free two-hour tours of the reserve, focusing on migratory waterfowl, on Wednesday, Friday and Saturday from February to May and from September to November, or accompanying visitors to observe the salt harvest from July to September. Phone or email at least two weeks ahead to check availability.

Museo del Sale   MUSEUM

(Salt Museum; ☑320 6575455, 320 6635818; www. museodelsale.it; Via Chiusa, Nubia; adult/reduced €3/2; ⊙9.30am-7pm summer, 10am-5pm winter, closed Jan & Feb) Set amid the salt pools 9km south of Trapani, this simple family-run museum in a historic windmill offers a wonderful perspective on Trapani's salt-producing industry. Historic photos of salt workers are labeled to show the division of labour, from the skilled elders who maintained the

WESTERN SICILY SALINE DI TRAPANI

ROAD TRIP>
BEST OF THE WEST

• •

This tour weaves together two ancient archaeological sites, a coastal nature reserve, a medieval hilltop town and one of Sicily's prime wine-growing regions. While the route can be driven as a one-day rental-car loop (the starting point is only 30 minutes from either Palermo or Trapani airport), it's far more rewarding to spread the journey over two or three days.

❶ Segesta

Begin in Segesta (p97), just off the A29D *autostrada*. One of Sicily's most evocative ancient sites, Segesta consists of a perfectly preserved, hauntingly beautiful Doric temple at the edge of a precipitous gorge and a hilltop amphitheatre with views clear out to the Mediterranean.

The Drive > From Segesta, meander 30km north to Scopello, stopping en route for a dip in the dazzling blue-green waters of Spiaggia di Guidaloca.

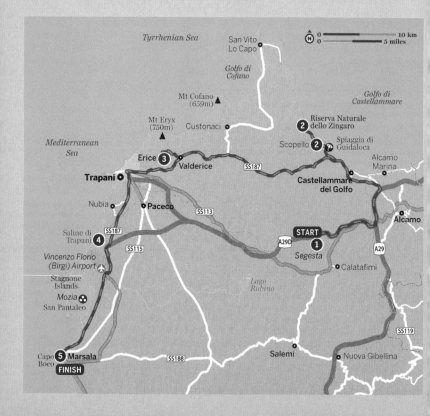

One to Three Days 109km

Great for... History & Culture, Outdoors

Best Time to Go Spring and autumn

Saline di Trapani (p104)

STEFANO_VALERI/SHUTTERSTOCK ©

❷ Scopello & Riserva Naturale dello Zingaro

Your next stop is the delightful end-of-the-road village of Scopello (pop 380), with its collection of stone houses surrounding a grand 18th-century manor house and courtyard perched above the Golfo di Castellammare. Several scenic attractions lie nearby. Don't miss the supremely photogenic *faraglioni* (rock spires) flanking the historic tuna factory on the shoreline below town, and save time for a day hike into the Riserva Naturale dello Zingaro, Sicily's oldest nature reserve, just 2km further north.

The Drive > Double back to the SS187, which winds lazily through vineyards before climbing a dizzying set of switchbacks to Erice.

❸ Erice

Perched high above a fairy-tale coastal landscape, this hilltop has been prized by every civilisation that's passed through, from the Elymians to the Normans to the day-trippers who come now to sample its fabulous views and addictive sweets. After admiring the surrounding countryside from the Norman Castello di Venere, stop in for coffee, cannoli and marzipan sweets at Maria Grammatico, Erice's most renowned pastry shop.

The Drive > Descend from Erice's heights to Trapani's coastal flatlands, zigzagging 18km down the SS187 and SP21 to the Saline di Trapani.

❹ Saline di Trapani

With their landscape of salt pools and windmills, the Saline di Trapani have been a centre for salt production since ancient times. From here take a short boat ride to the island of Mozia, home to one of Europe's finest Phoenician archaeological sites.

The Drive > Ferry back across from Mozia and follow the SP21 9km south to Marsala.

❺ Marsala

Renowned for its fortified wines both sweet and dry, Marsala is the capital of one of Sicily's great viticultural regions. Tour the Marsala cellars at Florio, then settle in for *aperitivi* and dinner among the glimmering stone-paved streets of the historic centre.

KITE-SURFING THE STAGNONE LAGOON

North of Marsala, the grassy banks of huge shallow lagoon Lo Stagnone lure kite-surfers like bees to a honeypot. The water here is shallow and flat, making it a safe and easier place to learn the exhilarating sport. Dozens of schools pepper the shoreline around **Baia dei Fenici**, most of which rent gear as well as offering tuition. The season runs from March to October.

Prokite Alby Rondina (☑ 347 5373881; www.prokitealbyrondina.com; Via Passalacqua; 2/6hr lesson €150/370, 2hr lesson plus 1/2/5 days of equipment rental €200/330/440; ☺ Mar-Oct; ⊛) is handily located just 10 minutes from Trapani's Birgi airport and 14km north of Marsala. This highly professional kitesurfing resort combining school, hotel and villa accommodation is a world-class spot to kite on a lagoon.

Rental alone (kite, bar, board, harness) is €75/205/370 per day/three days/week, plus €15/5 per day for wetsuit/helmet. On days when there is no wind – a rarity – the kite school has stand-up paddleboards to rent (€15 per two hours).

windmills to the young boys who hauled water as apprentices.

ℹ Getting There & Away

Access to the Saline di Trapani is via the SP21 (the Via del Sale or Salt Road) between Trapani and Marsala.

To reach Mozia (adult/reduced €5/2.50 return, 10 minutes, half-hourly) on San Pantaleo island, take a boat operated by **Mozia Line** (☑ 0923 98 92 49, 338 7860474; www.mozia line.com; Imbarcadero Salina Infersa; round-trip adult/reduced €5/2.50; ☺ 9.15am-6.30pm) from the Salina Infersadock, about 20km south of Trapani and 10km north of Marsala.

EGADI ISLANDS

Easily accessible by hydrofoil from Trapani or Marsala, the Egadi Islands (Isole Egadi) are popular destinations for swimming, diving, eating and general relaxation.

For centuries, the Egadi islanders have lived from the sea, as the prehistoric cave paintings on Levanzo illustrate. In 241 BC, when the islands were a key Carthaginian stronghold, one of the Punic Wars' most critical battles was fought at Cala Rossa (Red Cove; so named for the amount of Carthaginian blood spilt). When the Arabs took Sicily, they used the islands as a stepping-stone, fortifying them heavily to prevent anyone else following suit.

In 1874, Genovese bankers sold the islands to the Florio family, who established a branch of their lucrative tuna industry here, bringing great prosperity to the islands. Unfortunately, the surrounding waters have been terribly overfished, causing a dent in the local economy. The islands only became part of the Italian state in 1937.

Favignana

POP 4350

The largest of the Egadi Islands is butterfly-shaped Favignana, dominated by the fort-crowned peak of Monte Santa Caterina (287m) to the west. You can easily explore the island's eastern half on a bicycle, as the terrain here is almost completely flat. Around the coast, deep gouges in the cliffs are reminders of tufa quarrying that occurred in the past; many of these have now been reclaimed by the crystal-clear waters and are atmospheric swimming spots.

◉ Sights

★ **Giardino dell'Impossibile**   GARDENS
(Villa Margharita; ☑ 0923 92 15 01, 389 8048028; www.villamargherita.it; Strada Comunale Corso 10; guided tour €20; ☺ 10am-1pm & 6.30-7.30pm May-Oct) To get under the skin – quite literally – of the island of Favignana, take an eye-opening stroll around these unusual botanical gardens, created by owner and visionary Maria Gabriella Campo from 2005. Some 300 different species of Mediterranean flora sprout and bloom in a surreal landscape of tunnels, caves, grottos and galleries, hewn out of the island's soft tufa stone during intense quarrying in the 1950s and 1960s. Visits are strictly by guided tour (2½ hours), by advance reservation only.

In July and August bus line 1 stops 300m from the gardens; otherwise, it is a scenic 3km bike ride from Favignana town centre.

★ Castello di Santa Caterina   VIEWPOINT

No visit to Favignana is complete without a hike or run up to this hilltop fort, built atop an ancient Saracen fort in the 15th century and today ruined and abandoned. During WWII it was used as a military observation station and it is easy to see why – the 360-degree panorama of the Egadi Islands that it rewards with from its perch atop Monte Santa Caterina (287m) is sensational. Count about one hour to reach the castle on foot; the footpath begins immediately behind the main entrance to the Ex-Stabilimento Florio delle Tonnare di Favignana e Formica.

★ Ex-Stabilimento Florio delle Tonnare di Favignana e Formica   MUSEUM

(☑324 5631991; www.facebook.com/exstabilimento floriofavignana; Via Amendola 29; adult/reduced €6/3; ☺10am-2pm) Favignana's 19th-century tuna cannery – a vast, elegant, waterfront complex overlooking the port and built from the local tufa stone – is now a fascinating museum focusing on the local tuna fishing industry. The rambling maze, in operation until 1977, includes boat sheds with vintage boats ready to roll out to sea; the terrace where the tuna were hung; *la batteria de cottura,* with a trio of huge red-brick chimneys, where the tuna were cooked; and the cavernous hall with the original assembly tables where the cans were filled.

Various short films document different aspects of the cannery's history and tuna fishing traditions in the seas around Favignana. One film focuses on Favignana's famous Flavio family: Vincenzo Florio Sr (1799–1886), a brilliant Palermitan businessman who had made his name in the sulphur, shipping and Marsala industries, also invented a way of steam-cooking and preserving canned tuna that revolutionised the fish-packing industry and cemented the success of his family's business empire. This *tonnara,* constructed in 1859 and massively expanded from 1878, was one of many in Sicily to be owned by the wealthy Florio family.

Temporary contemporary-art exhibitions, always with a fishing heritage or environment theme, complement the permanent displays. Optional one-hour guided tours (in English) are included in the ticket price.

⚓ Activities

There's good diving and snorkelling in the waters around Favignana; local operators offering guided excursions include **Egadi**

Scuba Diving (☑327 3527712, 349 7420106; http://egadiscubadiving.it; Molo Barraco, Porto di Favignana; baptism/night dives €60/40, full equipment hire €25) and **Posidonia Blu Center** (☑339 8620116, 340 9650119; www.posidoniablu. com; Porticcioli di Punta Lunga).

★ Cala Rossa   BEACH

As untamed as they come, this Instagram-hot rocky cove on the island's northern shore is an exhilarating spot for a seafaring dip in clear, bright turquoise water. Flop out afterwards on the rocks to dry – there is no beach as such. The final approach to the well-signposted cove is a dirt track, followed by a fairly steep scramble down.

Scalo Cavallo   BEACH

A bicycle ride to this much-loved rocky cove – a cluster of rocks interspersed with concrete sun decks to set up camp on for the day – is a fascinating lesson in island geology. Houses with sunken gardens, at home in former tufa quarries, line the back roads leading to the cove. Find it 2km east of Favignana town centre, on the island's rocky northern coast.

Lido Burrone   BEACH

This popular beach on the island's southern coast is about the only long, graceful stretch of sand on the entire island, meaning it gets rammed in season with holiday-makers lounging on the sand and swimming in the shallow aquamarine waters. Several seasonal beach cafes and snack bars pepper the sand, and from Easter to September you can rent a parasol and deck-chair twinset (€5).

✕ Eating & Drinking

★ Osteria del Sotto Sale   OSTERIA €€

(☑329 7726127; www.sottosale.com; Via Vittorio Emanuele 19; meals €30-45; ☺12.30-4pm & 7.30pm-midnight summer, shorter hours winter) The atmosphere is casual-chic at this welcoming *osteria* (tavern) with indoor and outdoor seating on Favignana's main pedestrian street. An offshoot of the more upscale **Sotto Sale restaurant** (☑320 8432916; www.sottosale.com; Via Garibaldi 9; meals €50-60; ☺7.30pm-midnight summer, shorter hours winter) around the corner, it specialises in creative cuisine made with classic Sicilian ingredients: *busiate* (corkscrew-shaped pasta) with a tasty squid *ragù,* tuna burgers and desserts like silky crème brûlée with local pistachios.

Trattoria da Papù   SICILIAN €€

(☑324 5321497; Via Nocotera 7; meals €25-35; ☺noon-3pm & 7-11pm summer, shorter hours winter) Dodge the tourist crowds and duck into this traditional eatery, complete with fish-net-strung walls and B&W action shots of island fishermen working their trade. Fresh fish is brought to the table on metal platters for diners to size up and select, and the short menu features all the typical fishy *primi* and *secondi* alongside a dozen variations of *busiate*.

Spaghetteria Pakkaro SEAFOOD €€

(⚲ 328 061 3380; Piazza Madrice 26; meals €25-30; ⊙ noon-3pm & 7-11pm) The chef cooks up tasty, unpretentious pasta and seafood dishes at this down-to-earth, atmospheric trattoria on Favignana's central piazza. Try *busiate* with shrimp, pistachios and fish roe, or sample Pepe's island twist on *pasta alla carbonara* (with tuna instead of pancetta), followed by a grilled tuna, yellowtail or calamari.

Monique Concept Bar BAR

(⚲ 0923 178 19 20; www.facebook.com/monique barfavignana; Via Vittorio Emanuele 22; ⊙ 7am-2pm & 6pm-3am) The closest Favignana gets to 'on trend', Monique is an attractive lounge bar with a couple of tiny tables squatting on the pavement outside. Several more languish in the fashionable interior, decked out with a long bar, solitary armchair and – as you do – a buttermilk Vespa parked up for good measure. Pick from a select choice of cocktails, craft beers and other classic drinks.

❶ Information

Guardia Medica (⚲ 0923 92 12 83; Via delle Fosse) Round-the-clock medical assistance.

Police Station (⚲ 0923 92 16 70; Piazza Europa 1)

Tourist Office (⚲ 0923 92 54 43; www. welcometoegadi.it; Via Florio, Palazzo Florio; ⊙ 9.30am-1.30pm & 3-6pm Jun-Sep, 9.30am-1.30pm Apr, May & Oct) Helpful office on the ground floor of Palazzo Florio, one block from the hydrofoil dock. Has information on diving and boating operators, accommodation and excursions.

❶ Getting There & Away

Liberty Lines (p101) runs year-round hydrofoils to Favignana from Trapani (€11.80, 20 to 40 minutes) and Marsala (€11.10, 30 minutes, three daily). Inter-island hydrofoils to Levanzo (€5.80, 10 minutes) and Marettimo (€9.80, 30 to 40 minutes) also operate year-round.

❶ Getting Around

BICYCLE & SCOOTER

Bike or scooter is the best way to get around Favignana, giving you access to all the little coves and beaches dotting the island; the port area swarms with rental outlets. Bicycle hire ranges from €5 to €10 per day, depending on season; scooters run €20 to €50. No deposit is generally required but you'll need to show your ID and also pay in advance. **Infopoint Favignana** (⚲ 327 884 6915, 346 106 9124; http://info pointfavignana.it; Largo San Leonardo; bike per day €5-10; ⊙ 8am-7pm, shorter hours winter) is one of several rental outlets opposite the hydrofoil dock.

BUS

In July and August only, Tarantola Bus (www. tarantolabus.com) operates three bus lines linking the port with the eastern part of the island. Timetables are posted at the stop by the port Lungomare Dulio. Count on €1.10/3 for a one-way/one-day ticket.

Levanzo

There are two main reasons to visit tiny, essentially wild Levanzo: to admire prehistoric cave paintings at Grotta del Genovese, and to spend time swimming in sparkling turquoise waters off the island's pebbly beaches.

◉ Sights & Activities

Three spots on the island offer great swimming. To get to **Faraglione**, signposted left from the port, walk 1km along the road west of town until you see a couple of rocks sticking out of the water just offshore. For something quieter and more remote, take the 4km cross-island trail to **Capo Grosso** on the far northern shore, where there is also a lighthouse. Alternatively, take a right out of town and walk along the dirt road. The road forks 300m past the first bend; take the rocky path down towards the sea and keep going until you get to **Cala Minnola**, a small bay with crystal-clear water where, outside the month of August, you can swim in peace and tranquillity.

★ **Grotta del Genovese** CAVE

(⚲ 0923 92 40 32, 339 7418800; www.grotta delgenovese.it; guided cave tour €10, incl transport one-way/round trip €18/25; ⊙ tours 10.30am daily, extra tour 2.30pm or 3pm Jul & Aug) Between 6000 and 10,000 years old, the Upper Palaeolithic wall paintings and Neolithic incised drawings at the Genovese Cave were discovered in 1949 by Francesca Minellono, a painter from Florence who was holidaying on Levanzo. Mostly featuring bulls and horses, the later ones also include men and tuna. Visits to the grotto are by guided tour only, and reservations are required.

The all-inclusive tour takes two hours; transport is by boat if weather conditions are favourable – otherwise, it's a 10-minute drive by 4WD, then a steep but staggeringly scenic 700m descent on foot from the end of the rough gravel road to the cave. Views of the rocky coastline, wild flora and helicoptering sea gulls here are all breathtaking. You can also reach the grotto by foot from the port (1½ hours each way), or walk one way and take a 4WD or boat the other. Advance booking of the cave visit is imperative, regardless of how you get there.

🍴 Eating

Bar Arcobaleno SEAFOOD €
(☑ 329 6173445, 320 1468245; Via Calvario 8; meals €20-30; ⊘ 7am-2am summer, shorter hours in winter) Perched directly above the tiny port, Gino's no-frills village cafe cooks up a bird's-eye view of the big blue sea and ferries sailing to the island. Predictably, the day's catch dominates the menu: *ricci* (sea urchins), shrimps, squid and red tuna served with sweet onion jam. Pasta fiends will enjoy the *spaghetti alla Norma* with tomato, eggplant and ricotta.

ℹ️ Getting There & Away

Liberty Lines (p101) runs year-round hydrofoils to Levanzo from Trapani (€10.80, 25 to 50 minutes) and inter-island hydrofoils to Favignana (€5.80, 10 minutes) and Marettimo (€9.80, 25 minutes). The only boat service to/from Marsala is with a change of boat in Favignana.

Marettimo

The wildest, westernmost and least developed of the Egadi Islands, Marettimo is a collection of green mountain peaks and whitewashed houses dipping into a little harbour packed with bobbing fishing boats. With the overfishing of tuna affecting fishermen's incomes, villagers are increasingly focusing on the economic potential of tourism. While more accommodation options have cropped up in recent years, this doesn't mean you'll ever find Marettimo packed with tourists – indeed, the island still virtually shuts down in winter and remains

sleepier than its neighbours even in peak summer season.

There's only one road on the island, and the main mode of motorised transport is electric carts, making this a prime destination for walkers. Fanning out in all directions from the town centre, a well-marked trail network leads quickly into unspoilt nature, climbing through fragrant pine forests to dramatic coastal lookouts, then descending again to remote beaches.

🏃 Activities

Three of the most popular trails are the hike north from town to the crumbling Norman castle perched on the lonely promontory of **Punta Troia;** the short climb west to **Case Romane**, where the remains of Roman houses share the stage with a spare, whitewashed Byzantine church; and the longer hike following the island's southwestern shores to the secluded beach at **Cala Nera**. At various points along the trail, well-placed picnic benches invite hikers to take a shady break.

Marettimo is also a perfect place for relaxation and swimming – other good beaches include **Cala Sarda** on the south coast and stunning **Cala Bianca** at the island's northwestern corner.

🍴 Eating

★**La Cambusa** DELI €
(☑ 0923 92 34 41; Via Giuseppe Garibaldi 5b; meals €20; ⊘ 9am-1.30pm & 4.30-9pm) The finest Sicilian cheeses and artisan sauces, cured, roasted and marinated meats, veg dishes and breads tempt at this gastronomic butcher's shop and gourmet deli – an utterly fabulous ode to Slow Food and Sicilian culinary culture. Take away or enjoy in situ as a 12-course *apericena* feast (€20 with a glass of wine), served around tables in the alley outside. Reservations recommended.

Trattoria Il Veliero SEAFOOD €€
(☑ 0923 92 32 74; Via Umberto 22; meals €30; ⊘ noon-2pm & 7-10pm Mar-Oct) Just north of the hydrofoil dock, this family-run waterfront eatery is a seafood-lover's fantasy. Chef-owner Peppe Bevilacqua goes to the market daily, picking out the freshest catches. Superbly prepared Sicilian classics like *pasta con le sarde* (pasta with sardines) and *fritto misto* (fried shrimp and calamari) share the menu with octopus salad, tuna carpaccio, perfectly grilled fish and countless other delights.

ℹ Getting There & Away

Liberty Lines (p101) runs year-round hydrofoils to Marettimo from Trapani (€17.80, 1¼ hours, four or five daily), Levanzo (€9.80, 25 minutes, four daily) and Favignana (€9.80, 30 to 40 minutes, four to seven daily). Seasonal boats also sail to Marsala (€15.80, 1¼ hours, twice daily).

MARSALA

POP 82,800

Many people know about its sweet dessert wines, but few people realise what a charmer the town of Marsala is. Though its streets are paved in gleaming marble, lined with stately baroque buildings and peppered with graceful piazzas, Marsala has pleasures that are simple – a friendly *passeggiata* most nights, plenty of *aperitivo* options and family-friendly restaurants aplenty.

History

Marsala was founded by the Phoenicians who escaped from Mozia after it was defeated in 397 BC by an army led by Dionysius I of Syracuse. They settled here on Capo Lilibeo, calling their city Lilybaeum and fortifying it with 7m-thick walls that ensured it was the last Punic settlement to fall to the Romans. In AD 830 it was conquered by the Arabs, who gave it its current name Marsa Allah (Port of God).

⦿ Sights

Museo Archeologico
Baglio Anselmi   MUSEUM

(☑0923 95 25 35; Via Lungomare Boeo 30; adult/reduced €4/2; ⊙9am-6.30pm Wed-Sat, to 1.30pm Tue & Sun) Marsala's finest treasure is the partially reconstructed remains of a Carthaginian *liburna* (warship) sunk off the Egadi Islands during the First Punic War. Displayed alongside objects from its cargo, the ship's bare bones provide the only remaining physical evidence of the Phoenicians' seafaring superiority in the 3rd century BC, offering a glimpse of a civilisation extinguished by the Romans.

Among the objects found on board the ship and displayed here are ropes, cooking pots, corks from amphorae, a brush, olive stones, a sailor's wooden button and even a stash of cannabis. In an adjacent room, the impressive wreck of a Roman merchant vessel dating to the 3rd or 4th century AD is displayed. A third room displays other regional archaeological artefacts including a marble statue known as *La venere di lilybaeum* (The Venus of Lilybaeum) and some mosaics from the 3rd and 5th centuries AD.

Post-museum, don't miss an explorative stroll in the museum gardens, aka the **Insula Romana**, a vast archaeological site encompassing the remains of a 3rd-century Roman villa and a well-preserved Decumanus Maximus (Roman ceremonial road) paved with giant stones.

Piazza della Repubblica   PIAZZA

Marsala's most elegant piazza is dominated by the imposing Chiesa Madre. Just across

---

THE SWEET SMELL OF SUCCESS

Fresh out of sherry country in southern Spain, John Woodhouse's 'sweet nose' knew a business opportunity when he smelled it. The English soap merchant swiftly based himself in Marsala aiming to market its wine to the seemingly insatiable sweet palate of 18th-century England, but had to grapple with one problem: how was he to get the wine to England without it going bad? He added a dash of pure alcohol and, *voilà*, Marsala's fortified wine was born.

The real success of the wine came when the British Navy used it as an alternative to port in order to supply the sailors' ration of one glass of wine per day. Lord Nelson placed a huge order in 1800, and soon other entrepreneurs wanted to get in on the action. Benjamin Ingham and his nephew, Joseph Whitaker, set up the first rival winery, exporting to the US and Australia in 1806. The third big producer was canny Vincenzo Florio, who already owned the Egadi Islands and their lucrative tuna plants. All of the wineries were eventually bought by Cinzano in the 1920s, which merged them under the Florio label. In 1988, Cinzano sold the company to Illva Saronno, which now operates three labels: Florio, Duca di Salaparuta and Corvo.

For more information on Marsala and the wineries that produce it today, see www.marsaladoc.it.

the way, on the eastern side of the square, is the arcaded **Palazzo VII Aprile**, formerly known as the Palazzo Senatorio (Senatorial Palace) and now the town hall.

Chiesa del Purgatorio CHURCH
(Chiesa Madre; Via Cammareri Scurti 24; ⊙hours vary) This beautiful 18th-century church (1771), with showy, heavily sculpted facade, is a fine example of Sicilian baroque architecture – as is the ornate fountain piercing the cobbled square, Piazzetta Lombardo detta Purgatorio, that the church overlooks.

Complesso Monumentale San Pietro MUSEUM
(☑0923 71 87 41; Via Ludovico Anselmi Correale; adult/reduced €2/1; ⊙9am-1pm & 4-8pm Tue-Sun) Housed in a beautifully restored 15th-century convent, this arts centre is home to an intriguing complex of small museums. Most noteworthy is the upstairs space devoted to Giuseppe Garibaldi, who landed in Marsala on 11 May 1860 with his army of 1000 redshirts in the first stage of their successful campaign to conquer the kingdom of the Two Sicilies. The Garibaldi collection includes weapons, documents, uniforms and portraits but unfortunately lacks interpretive labels in English.

🏃 **Activities**

★**Cantine Florio** WINE
(☑0923 78 13 05; www.duca.it/en/florio/ospitalita; Via Vincenzo Florio 1; standard tour adult/reduced €13/5; ⊙9am-6pm Mon-Fri, to 1pm Sat, English-language tour 10am & 4pm Mon-Fri, 10am Sat) These venerable wine cellars, in a huge walled complex east of the centre and on the seafront since 1833, open their vintage doors to visitors to explain the Marsala-making process and the fascinating history of local viticulture. Afterwards, visitors can sample the goods in the sharp tasting room: tasting of four wines, accompanied by hors d'oeuvres, are included in the standard 1½-long tour.

More complete options include a 'Cioccoflorio' tour pairing three wines with Modica chocolate (in Italian only; €15/5), and 2½-long, adults-only tasting lunch (€40). All tours must be booked in advance by telephone or email. Take bus 16 from Piazza del Popolo.

🍴 **Eating & Drinking**

The historic centre between Via Garibaldi and Porta Nuova is packed with classy restaurants, interspersed with more casual eat-

---

WINE TASTING IN MARSALA
....
Prestigious Marsala wine producers include Florio, Pellegrino, Donnafugata, Rallo, Mavis and Intorcia. Some *cantine* (wine cellars) open their doors to visitors, but strictly by advance appointment only; organised tours advertised must also be booked in advance. The tourist office (p115) has a complete list of cellars.

In town, several *enoteche* (wine bars) such as the fantastic, Slow Food–endorsed Ciacco Putia Gourmet (p114), offer some lovely tastings paired with gourmet nibbles.

---

eries serving *panini* (sandwiches) and *taglieri* (meat and cheese boards) accompanied by glasses of local wine.

As one of Sicily's viticultural capitals, Marsala is naturally teeming with *enoteche* (wine bars), most of them concentrated near Via XI Maggio in the historic centre.

★**Quimera** SANDWICHES €
(☑349 0765524; www.facebook.com/quimerapub; Via Sarzana 34-36; sandwiches & salads from €5; ⊙noon-3pm & 6.30pm-2am Mon-Sat, 6.30pm-2am Sun) Smack in the heart of Marsala's pedestrianised centre, this buzzy eating-drinking hybrid is the local hotspot for artisanal craft beers, gourmet sandwiches and meal-sized salads – all served with a big smile and bags of charm by the friendly young owners. Linger over a shared cutting board of cheeses or salami, or agonise over the choice of creatively filled *panini* and *piadine* (wraps).

Vegetarians and vegans are equally well catered for.

Assud MODERN SICILIAN €€
(☑0923 71 66 52; www.facebook.com/ASSUDCucinaMeridionale; Via Armando Diaz 66; meals €25-35; ⊙noon-3pm & 6.30-11pm Tue-Sun) Mackerel and pistachio *caponata,* ravioli with beetroot and artichokes, or swordfish patties studded with squid chunks are among the classics with an inventive twist cooked up at this small *osteria* straddling Marsala's historic walls. Everything here is staunchly traditional: the decor, the local crowd, the short but excellent wine list. Coffee comes with a complimentary shot of sweet Marsala.

Il Gallo e l'Innamorata SICILIAN €€
(☑0923 195 44 46; www.osteriailgalloelinnamorata.com; Via Stefano Bilardello 18; meals €25-

Marsala

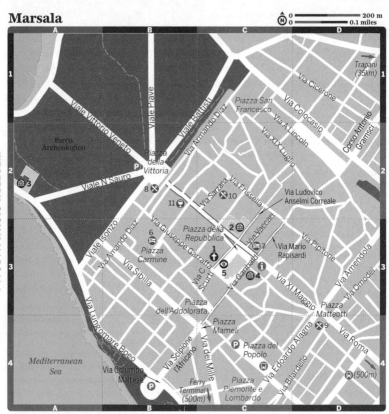

35; ⏱12.30-2.30pm & 7.30-10.30pm Tue-Sun) Warm-orange walls and arched stone doorways lend an artsy, convivial atmosphere to this Slow Food–acclaimed eatery whose wonderfully evocative name translates as 'The Rooster and the Innocent'. The à la carte menu is short and sweet, featuring a few well-chosen dishes each day, such as the classic *scaloppine al Marsala* (veal cooked with Marsala wine and lemon).

★ Ciacco Putia Gourmet   WINE BAR
(☑347 6315684; www.ciaccoputia.it; Via Cammareri Scurti 3; ⏱noon-3pm & 7-11pm Mon-Sat; 🛜) Run by Tuscan-Sicilian couple Anna and Francesco, this irresistible *enoteca* is a gorgeous spot to quaff Marsala wines with locally sourced *salumi* (cold cuts), *panini* with *burrata* (cheese made from mozzarella and cream), anchovies and other snacks. The icing on the cake is the beautiful summertime terrace on a cobbled fountain-pierced

square overlooking the showy baroque facade of 18th-century Chiesa del Purgatorio.

Enoteca della Strada
del Vino di Marsala   WINE BAR
(Palazzo Fici; ☑0923 71 34 89; www.facebook.com/enoteca.stradavinomarsala; Via XI Maggio 32; ⏱11am-3.30pm & 5.30-11.30pm) The elegant, cornice-framed facade of late 17th-century Palazzo Fici provides a magnificent prelude to the wine served at Marsala's municipal wine bar, run by local wine merchants. From shopping street Via XI Maggio, duck beneath the majestic balcony-crowned archway to enter the *palazzo's* interior courtyard, a cinematic sweep of gold-stone porticoes. Local vintages start at €3.50 a glass.

ℹ Information

Police Station (☑0923 71 88 11; Via Giuseppe Verdi 1; ⏱24hr)
Post Office (Via Roma 167; ⏱8am-6.30pm Mon-Sat)

Marsala

Tourist Office (☑ 0923 71 40 97, 0923 99 33 38; Via XI Maggio 100; ⊘ 8.30am-1.30pm & 3-8pm Mon-Fri, to 1.30pm Sat) Provides a limited range of maps and brochures, plus a list of wine cellars open by guided tour (but staff cannot make bookings for you).

❶ Getting There & Away

BOAT
Liberty Lines (p101) sails to/from Trapani (€17.80, one to 1½ hours) year-round, and operates seasonal summer hydrofoils (two to five daily) to/from Favignana (€11.10, 30 minutes) and Marettimo (€15.80, 1¼ hours).

BUS
From Marsala's **bus station** (Piazza del Popolo), AST (www.aziendasicilianatrasporti.it) buses travels to Mazara del Vallo (€2.90, 25 to 45 minutes, up to three daily except Sunday) and Trapani (€3.60, one hour, four daily except Sunday) via Birgi airport (€2.70).

Lumia (www.autolineelumia.it) operates buses to/from Agrigento (€10.10, 2¾ hours) and Sciacca (€7, 1½ hours) three times daily Monday to Friday, twice on Saturday and once on Sunday from its stop in Piazza Caprera.

Salemi (www.autoservizisalemi.it) runs buses to Palermo (€11, 2¼ to 2½ hours, up to six daily) from its stop on Viale Fazio near the train station; tickets can be bought in advance online.

TRAIN
The best way to travel along this stretch of coast is by train. There are 10 trains daily (four on Sunday) to Trapani (€3.80, 35 minutes) and Mazara del Vallo (€3.10, 20 minutes). To reach Marsala's historic centre from the train station, walk 800m up Via Roma, which meets Via XI Maggio at Piazza Matteotti.

MAZARA DEL VALLO
POP 51,500

Vaguely redolent of a North African *kasbah* (and still bearing the Casbah name), Mazara's historic quarter is a labyrinth of narrow streets, sprinkled with magnificent baroque and Norman-period buildings. It's small enough that you won't ever really get lost, and the dilapidated old buildings give it a rugged charm.

Mazara was one of the key cities of Saracen Sicily and the North African influence is still strongly felt here – the town has one of the highest percentages of immigrants in Italy, with hundreds of people from Tunisia and Maghreb arriving annually to work on Mazara's fishing fleet.

In summer, Mazara is inundated with holidaymakers who head straight to Spiaggia di Tonnarella, the city's biggest and best, white-sand beach west of the centre.

⊙ Sights

Mazara's streets and alleys are decorated with colourful hand-painted tiles, a subtle touch that adds to the pleasure of randomly strolling through town.

At the northwest corner of the historic centre, the multicultural maze of narrow streets known as **La Casbah** was once the heart of the Saracen city. The main thoroughfare was Via Bagno, which still has its *hammam* (public baths). Today the area is rundown but interesting, in large part because it retains a strong Arab connection through the Tunisian immigrants who now live here.

Mazara's central piazza, **Piazza della Repubblica**, is an attractive space edged by elegant buildings, including the **Cattedrale del San Salvatore**, the two-storey **Seminario dei Chierici** (dating from 1710) and, on the opposite side of the square, the 18th-century **Seminario Vescovile**, with its impressive 11-arched portico. Unfortunately, the 1970s office tower on the western side of the square is a visual affront of the highest order.

Mazara is Sicily's largest fishing centre, with many restaurants specialising in seafood. Be sure to try the local *gambero rosso di Mazara* (Mazara red shrimp), a delicacy renowned throughout Sicily. In the back streets of La Casbah, you'll also find a number of places serving excellent fish couscous.

For a taste of Tunisia, try the delightful hole-in-the-wall **Eyem Zemen** (⏾347 3869921; Via Porta Palermo 36; meals €20-25; ⏾12.30am-3pm & 7pm-midnight) in the heart of La Casbah, marked by a bilingual Italian-Arabic sign. Tunisian owner Fatiha serves grilled Mazara prawns, kebabs, roast mutton, multiple varieties of couscous (with vegetables, seafood, meat or wild fennel) and *brik* (savoury tuna- or shrimp-filled pastries). In warm weather, dine al fresco at tables on the adjacent piazza. Sweet Tunisian pastries with toasted pine nuts and mint tea are a deliciously sacrosanct end to any meal here.

Over the past few decades, chef Pietro Sardo has established a reputation as one of Sicily's top chefs. At his fine-dining seafood restaurant, **La Bettola** (⏾0923 94 64 22; www.ristorantelabettola.it; Via Maccagnone 32; meals €30-45; ⏾1-3pm & 7.30-11pm Thu-Tue), just around the corner from Mazara's train station, he continues to create sensational and often unexpected flavour combinations such as citrus-scented lobster or red mullet and ricotta-filled tortellini in a refined, white tablecloth-elegant dining room.

Begin with a heady mix of *cotto e crudo* (cooked and raw) seafood and end with the chef's justly famous *cassata* (traditional Sicilian, liqueur-soaked sponge cake with candied fruit and ricotta) and an obligatory glass of sweet Marsala for dessert. Reservations essential.

ⓘ Information

Hospital (Ospedale Civico A Ajello; ⏾0923 65 79 41; Via Salemi 175; ⏾24hr)

Police Station (⏾0923 93 44 11; Via Sansone 56)

ⓘ Getting There & Away

BUS

From Mazara's **bus station** (Via Salemi), next to the train station, Salemi (www.autoservizisalemi.it) buses go to/from Palermo (€9, two hours, up to five daily); Lumia (www.autolineelumia.it) buses serve Agrigento (€9.20, 2¼ hours) and Sciacca (€5.80, one hour) one to three times daily; and AST (www.aziendasiciliana trasporti.it) operates daily services to/from Marsala (€2.90, 25 to 45 minutes) and Trapani (€5.30, 1¾ to 2¼ hours).

CAR & MOTORCYCLE

Mazara is an easy, 1½-hour drive down the A29 *autostrada* from Palermo. Coming from Agrigento (116km, 1½ hours) or Sciacca (56km, 45 minutes), take the SS115 west and join the A29 at Castelvetrano. The SS115 from Marsala (23km, 35 minutes) is slower and more congested.

DON'T MISS

THE SATYR THAT ROSE FROM THE SEA

The jewel in Mazara's crown, the **Museo del Satiro Danzante** (Dancing Satyr Museum; ⏾0923 93 39 17; Piazza Plebiscito; adult/reduced €6/3; ⏾9am-7.45pm) revolves around its central exhibit, a bronze statue known as the *Satiro danzante* (Dancing Satyr), hauled from the watery depths by local fishermen in the late 1990s. The sculpture depicts a bacchanalian satyr dancing wildly like a whirling dervish, arms outstretched, head flung back, the centrifugal force evident in his flowing hair. Originally, the statue would have been used in Dionysian processions; today it commands its own form of no-less-passionate worship here.

The museum is located in the deconsecrated shell of the Chiesa di Sant'Egidio. Don't miss the 25-minute film (in Italian, with English subtitles) relaying the story of the group of fishermen who were working their nets 40km off the shores of Tunisia in 1997 when they pulled up the bronze leg of a statue. Time elapsed and they continued to fish in the same area, wondering if they would ever find the rest of the statue. Extraordinarily, they did so the next year – a rare original casting from the Hellenistic era (3rd and 2nd centuries BC). In the film the boat's captain, overcome by romanticism, recounts the dramatic rescue. What followed was a 4½-year period of painstaking restoration, during which time Mazara strenuously tussled with the powers in Rome to ensure the return of the satyr, which only came home in 2003.

A combined ticket covering admission to the Museo Nazionale Pepoli (p98) in Trapani is available for €9/4.50.

TRAIN

There are 10 daily trains (four on Sunday) from Mazara to Marsala (€3.10, 20 minutes) and Trapani (€5.10, one hour).

SELINUNTE

The ruins of **Parco Archeologico di Selinunte** (Selinunte Archaeological Park; ☑334 6040459, 0924 4 62 77; https://en.visitselinunte. com/archaeological-park/; Via Selinunte, Castelvetrano; adult/reduced €6/3; ☺9am-6pm Mar-Oct, to 5pm Nov-Feb) rank among the most impressive and captivating archaeological sites in Sicily.

Selinos (as it was known to the Greeks) was once one of the richest and most powerful cities in the world, with over 100,000 inhabitants and an unrivalled temple-building program. The most westerly of the Greek colonies, it was established by a group of settlers from nearby Megara Hyblaea in 628 BC who had been attracted by its wonderful location atop a promontory between two major rivers (now silted up), the Modione and Cottone, the latter forming a secure natural harbour. The plains surrounding the site were overgrown with celery (*selinon* in Greek), which served as inspiration for the new colony's name.

Today this vast complex of fields and ruined temples beside the Mediterranean is a delightful place to wander, especially in springtime, when the wildflowers are in full bloom.

History

Originally allied with Carthage, Selinunte switched allegiance after the Carthaginian defeat by Gelon of Syracuse at Himera in 480 BC. Under Syracusan protection it grew in power and prestige. The city's growth resulted in a litany of territorial disputes with its northern neighbour, Segesta, which ended abruptly in 409 BC when the latter called for Carthaginian help. Selinunte's former ally happily obliged and arrived to take revenge.

Troops commanded by Hannibal utterly destroyed the city after a nine-day siege, leaving only those who had taken shelter in the temples as survivors; they were spared not out of a sense of humanity but because of the fear that they might set fire to the temples and prevent their looting. In a famous retort to the Agrigentan ambassadors who sought to negotiate for the survivors' lives, Hannibal replied that as they hadn't been able to defend their freedom, they deserved

to be slaves. One year later, Hermocrates of Syracuse took over the city and initiated its recovery, though it soon fell back under Carthaginian control. Around 250 BC, with the Romans about to conquer the city, its citizens were relocated to Lilybaeum (Marsala), the Carthaginian capital in Sicily, but not before they destroyed as much as they could. What they left standing, mainly temples, was finished off by an earthquake in the Middle Ages.

The city was forgotten until the middle of the 16th century, when a Dominican monk identified its location. Excavations began in 1823, courtesy of two English archaeologists, William Harris and Samuel Angell, who uncovered the first metopes.

◉ Sights

Selinunte's ruins are spread out over a vast area dominated by the hill of Manuzza – the location of the ancient city proper. The site deserves a visit of at least three hours to do it justice.

The **entrance and ticket office** (☑0924 4 62 77; https://en.visitselinunte.com/archaeological -park/; Via Selinunte, Castelvetrano; adult/reduced €6/3; ☺9am-6pm Mar-Oct, to 5pm Nov-Feb) are near the eastern temples, adjacent to a large car park about 200m off the SP115dir. Once inside the complex, immediately to your left, you'll find a kiosk selling tickets for electric carts (one/two/three stops adult €3/6/12, children €1.50/3/6) that cut out the legwork by driving visitors around the temples.

★**Acropolis**   ARCHAEOLOGICAL SITE
(Strada dei Templi) The Acropolis, the heart of Selinunte's political and social life, occupies a slanted plateau overlooking the now-silted-up Gorgo di Cottone. Huddled in the southeastern part are five temples (A, B, C, D and O). Virtually the symbol of Selinunte, **Temple C** is the oldest temple on the site, built in the middle of the 6th century BC.

The stunning metopes found by Harris and Angell were once a part of this formidable structure, as was the enormous Gorgon's mask that once adorned the pediment; both of these can be viewed in the Museo Archeologico Regionale in Palermo. Experts believe that the temple was dedicated to Apollo.

Northernmost of the remaining temples is **Temple D**, built towards the end of the 6th century BC and dedicated to either Neptune or Venus.

The smaller **Temple B** dates from the Hellenistic period and could have been dedicated to the Agrigentan physiologist and philosopher Empedocles, whose water-drainage scheme saved the city from the scourge of malaria (a bitter irony for William Harris, who contracted the disease during the initial excavations and died soon after).

The two other temples, **Temple A** and **Temple O**, closest to the sea, are the most recent, built between 490 and 480 BC. They are virtually identical in both style and size, and it's been suggested that they might have been dedicated to the twins Castor and Pollux.

Eastern Temples
ARCHAEOLOGICAL SITE

The eastern temples are the most stunning of all Selinunte's ruins, crowned by the majestic **Temple E**. Built in the 5th century BC and reconstructed in 1958, Temple E stands out due to its completeness; as you walk from the ticket office, it's the first structure you'll come to.

Temple G, the northernmost temple, was built in the 6th century BC and, although never completed, was one of the largest temples in the Greek world. Today it is a massive pile of impressive rubble – as is its counterpart directly to the south, **Temple F**.

Lido di Zabbara
BEACH

No visit to Selinunte is complete without a walk along this attractive stretch of beach below the archaeological site, which affords marvellous views back up to the clifftop temples. Access it from the beachfront town of Marinella di Selinunte.

🍴 Eating

Avoid the tourist cafes around the archaeological site's car park and head for the coast at Marinella di Selinunte or Porto Palo, where you'll find some attractive seafood eateries along the beachfront.

Lido Zabbara
BUFFET €

(📞0924 4 61 94; www.facebook.com/lidozabbara; Via Pigafetta, Marinella di Selinunte; buffet per person €12; ⊙noon-3pm Mar-early Nov, plus 7.30-10.30pm Jun-Sep) For tasty, reasonably priced food near the ruins, hit this low-key beach eatery, rocking it on the sand since 1969. Affable

---

OFF THE BEATEN TRACK

CRETTO DI BURRI

Midway between the ancient ruins of Selinunte (38km south) and Segesta (45km north) lies the extraordinary **Cretto di Burri** (Ruderi di Gibellina; SS119 & SP5, Ghibellina; ⊙24hr) – a disconcerting, lunar-like sea of white cement tumbling down a green hillside in the Valle dei Belice where, in January 1968, the village of Gibellina was wiped out by a devastating earthquake. While the village was subsequently reconstructed 18km west (today, Nuova Gibellina), artist Alberto Burri (1915–95) set about creating an unforgettable piece of land art on the very spot where the original village stood.

Burri essentially buried the village ruins in cement to create a dramatic labyrinth of narrow streets said to mirror the destroyed village's original street plan. Lack of funds saw work on the monumental art piece – at around 85,000 sq m one of Europe's largest – grind to a halt in 1989 and it was only finished in 2015, to mark what would have been the Italian artist's 100th birthday. Staggering on foot up the steep, uncannily quiet passages carved out within the 1.5m-thick slab of cement is eery and unsettling. Big green views of the natural landscape surrounding the cement monstrosity only heighten the drama.

To grasp and appreciate the full horror of Gibellina's destruction and the harrowing story of displacement that ensued as villagers struggled to adapt to life in a 'new town', void of intimate village piazzas and tiny village cafes, it's worth a fleeting visit afterwards to **Nuova Gibellina**, 18km west along the corkscrew SS119. Designed as a 'utopian town' in collaboration with some of Europe's top architects of the time, the modern town is a soulless, deserted grid of streets, built for 20,000 inhabitants but home to less than 5000 today. The gargantuan theatre – never completed – stands abandoned and derelict, while many of the elderly people who do live here struggle to walk up the monumental flight of stairs leading to the Chiesa Madre (1972), a Modernist church built around a colossal 15m-diameter white globe.

To reach the Cretto di Burri by car, take the Santa Ninfa exit off the Mazara-Palermo *autostrada* (A29) and follow the brown signs for 'Ruderi di Gibellina' (Ruins of Gibellina) along the SS119. To drive directly to Nuova Gibellina, exit the A29 further north at the 'Gibellina' exit.

Selinunte

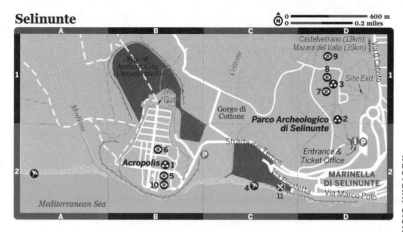

long-time owner Jòjò welcomes temple-weary travellers onto his delightful outdoor terrace for grilled fish and a varied buffet of two-dozen items, including many salads and vegetables. Afterwards, rent umbrellas and sunloungers and stick around to sunbathe.

Come dark DJs and dance parties morph Zabbara into a buzzing bar.

★ **Da Vittorio** SEAFOOD €€
(✆ 0925 7 83 81; www.ristorantevittorio.it; Via Friuli Venezia Giulia, Porto Palo; meals €30-45; ⊙ 12.30-2.30pm & 7-10pm) Travellers with their own vehicles should consider detouring 15km east of Selinunte to this venerable eatery right on the beach in Porto Palo. In business for five decades, Da Vittorio has earned a reputation as one of western Sicily's best spots for fresh seafood. The front-row view of crashing breakers is wonderful any time of day, but especially at sunset.

Hotel rooms (single/double €60/85) are available upstairs for anyone too contentedly stuffed to contemplate moving on.

La Pineta SEAFOOD €€
(✆ 0924 4 68 20; Via Punta Cantone, Marinella di Selinunte; meals €25-35; ⊙ 9am-10.30pm summer) You couldn't ask for a peachier beach setting. From the entrance of the Foce del Belice nature preserve on Marinella's far eastern edge, a gravel track leads down to the sand and this sizeable beach shack with corrugated-iron roof. Its terrace, peppered with royal-blue parasols, is particularly dreamy after dark when bamboo torches set it aglow. Grilled fish and finger-licking seafood are the specialities.

Selinunte

◎ **Top Sights**
1	Acropolis	B2
2	Parco Archeologico di Selinunte	D1

◎ **Sights**
3	Eastern Temples	D1
4	Lido di Zabbara	C2
5	Temple A	B2
	Temple B	(see 1)
	Temple C	(see 1)
6	Temple D	B2
7	Temple E	D1
8	Temple F	D1
9	Temple G	D1
10	Temple O	B2

✖ **Eating**
11	Lido Zabbara	C2

❶ Getting There & Away

BUS

Salemi (https://autoservizisalemi.it) runs regular buses between Marinella di Selinunte and Castelvetrano train station (€1.50, 25 to 35 minutes), where you can make onward rail connections to Mazara del Vallo (€3.10, 20 minutes), Marsala (€4.30, 45 minutes) and Trapani (€6.20, 1¼ hours). For eastbound travellers, Lumia (www.autolineelumia.it) runs buses from Castelvetrano to Agrigento (€8.60, two hours, one to three daily).

CAR & MOTORCYCLE

Coming from Palermo and other points north, take the Castelvetrano exit off the A29 and follow the signs (briefly east on the SS115, then south on the SS115dir). If you're driving from Agrigento, take the SS115 west for about 85km,

CAVE DI CUSA

Most of the buttery yellow stone used to construct the great temples of Selinunte was hewn at the ancient Greek quarries at **Area Archaeologica di Cave di Cusa** (☑334 6040459; http://selinunte.gov.it; ⊙9am-1hr before sunset). The setting is charming – overgrown and wild, it's dotted with olive trees and wildflowers. Huge column drums forever awaiting transport to Selinunte are scattered around, and if you look carefully you will come across two carved columns ready for extraction. When removed, the columns would have been transported to Selinunte across wooden logs by oxen or slaves.

The site is about 17km northwest of Selinunte. Head 4km north on SS115dir, then 9km west on SP56 to Campobello di Mazara; from Campobello, follow the series of signposted backroads 4km further to reach the site. From Mazara del Vallo, take the SS115 east for 11km to Campobello di Mazara, then follow the signs 4.5km south to Cave di Cusa.

then exit onto the SS115dir south. The turn-off for the ruins is clearly signposted, on the northwestern outskirts of the coastal town of Marinella di Selinunte.

PANTELLERIA

Halfway between Trapani and Tunisia, this volcanic outcrop is Sicily's largest offshore island. Originally named Bent-el-Riah ('daughter of the wind' in Arabic) for the year-round winds that buffet it, Pantelleria is characterised by jagged lava rock formations, steaming fumaroles and mud baths. The island's unique agricultural traditions, characterised by low-slung caper bushes, dwarf grapevines and olive trees laid out on terraces between dry stone walls, earned UNESCO World Heritage status in 2014. There are no true beaches, but Pantelleria's gorgeous, secluded coves are perfect for snorkelling, diving and boat excursions.

Throughout the island you'll find Pantelleria's unique *dammusi* – lava rock houses with thick, whitewashed walls, shallow cupolas, and cisterns for collecting rainwater. Near Mursia on the west coast, there are also signposted remnants of *sesi* (Bronze Age funerary monuments). The island's exotic and remote atmosphere has long made it popular with celebrities, including Truman Capote, Sting, Madonna and Giorgio Armani.

◉ Sights

★**Lago Specchio di Venere**   HOT SPRINGS
Just inland from Pantelleria's north coast, the iridescent waters of this volcanic lake are a stunning sight. Along the southern lakeshore, natural hot springs and mud baths bubble up from below the surface at temperatures ranging from 40°C to 50°C; for a natural beauty treatment, spread the volcanic mud on your skin, wait for it to dry, then rinse off in the geothermal spring water.

★**Balata dei Turchi**   BEACH
Those willing to brave the steep and treacherous 3km descent on an unpaved road will be rewarded with one of Pantelleria's most beautiful swimming spots, a gorgeous cove of sparkling blue-green waters at the island's southern tip. After parking your vehicle near the bottom, the final approach is on foot, down a smooth, wave-sculpted chute of ancient lava rock.

Arco dell'Elefante   LANDMARK
This sweeping natural arch of rugged grey stone is reputed to look like an elephant's trunk – and indeed it does! To get here, first head for the twin coves of Cala Tramontana and Cala Levante on Pantelleria's eastern shore, then turn south and follow the coast another 700m.

**Parco Archeologico
dei Sesi**   ARCHAEOLOGICAL SITE
FREE This archaeological site on Pantelleria's northwestern coast preserves the remains of several mound-shaped Megalithic stone necropolises known as *sesi*. Dating back to around the second millennium BC, and unique to Pantelleria, most of the *sesi* have been reduced to piles of rubble, but the largest (Sese Grande, or Sese del Re) remains intact and makes an evocative sight.

🏃 Activities

Pantelleria is famous for its sweet wines, especially the amber-coloured Passito di Pantelleria, made from sun-dried Zibibbo grapes. There are a number of excellent wineries on the island, including Donnafugata (p121), Maddalena (www.vinimaddalena.it), Basile (www.cantinabasile.com), Vinisola (www.vinisola.it) and Salvatore Muràna (www.vinimurana.it).

Pantelleria has some excellent signposted hiking trails along the coast and in the island's high-altitude forests and vineyard country.

★ Punta Spadillo
Lighthouse-Cala Cottone Loop   WALKING

One of Pantelleria's most enjoyable day hikes – signposted as trail No 4 – this moderate two-hour loop around the island's northeast corner takes you through a variety of land- and seascapes, from stone-walled agricultural terraces to the tortured lava-rock formations at Cala Cottone, and from the lighthouse at Punta Spadillo to the plunging flower-covered cliffs of Cala Cinque Denti.

Park just north of Gadir, near the junction of Salita Carrera and the SP 54 (Strada Perimetrale Dietro Isola), and follow the trail signs towards Cala Cottone.

★ Donnafugata   WINE

(☑ 335 6242563, 0923 91 56 49; www.donnafugata.it; Contrada Khamma; ◷ wine shop 10.30am-1.30pm & 5-8pm Mon-Fri early Jun-late Sep, plus Sat & Sun in Aug, tours noon, 4.30pm & 7pm) Pantelleria's most famous winery offers summertime tastings and tours in English or Italian at its old stucco farmhouse, surrounded by terraced century-old vineyards. Adjacent to the winery is a lovely restored *giardino pantesco* (traditional circular stone enclosure used to protect citrus trees from Pantelleria's notorious wind).

Eating

Island cuisine makes ample use of locally grown olives, capers, lemons and tomatoes along with fresh-caught seafood. Specialties include *spada alla pantesca* (Pantelleria-style swordfish with olives, capers, tomatoes, garlic and parsley) and *ravioli alla pantesca* (ravioli filled with ricotta and fresh mint).

Many places to stay have their own restaurants.

Il Principe e il Pirata   SEAFOOD €€

(☑ 0923 69 11 08; www.principeepirata.it; Località Punta Karace; meals €35-45; ◷ 12.30-2.30pm & 7.30-10.30pm mid-Apr–Oct) Enjoying sublime sea views from its turquoise-tiled terrace, the Prince and the Pirate cranks out exquisite *pantesco* (Pantelleria-style) cuisine, from antipasti of fresh-caught raw fish, to *macco*

di fave (fava bean puree with wild fennel) to traditional fish-and-veggie couscous. Whatever you do, save room for *bacio pantesco*, an addictively delicious island dessert consisting of two crunchy wheel-shaped wafers filled with lemon-scented ricotta.

Al Tramonto   SICILIAN €€

(☑ 0923 69 74 20; www.ristorantealtramonto.it; Località Penna, Contrada Scauri Basso; meals €39-45; ◷ 12.30-2.30pm & 7.30-11pm mid-May–Oct) As the name implies, this hillside-hugging restaurant is the perfect place to watch the *tramonto* (sunset) – but the food here is equally radiant, from traditional ricotta-mint ravioli to creative seafood concoctions and veggies from the garden outside. It's all served in the childhood home of Pantelleria-raised owner Oscar, whose mother used to host large dinner gatherings in these same rooms.

ⓘ Getting There & Away

AIR

The airport, **Aeroporto di Pantelleria** (☑ 0923 91 13 98; www.aeroportodipantelleria.it), is on a plateau near the island's northern tip, about 5km south of the ferry port. DAT (www.dat.dk) flies direct to Pantelleria from Palermo, Catania and Trapani. Volotea (www.volotea.com) and Alitalia (www.alitalia.com) connect Pantelleria with several cities on the Italian mainland, including Rome, Milan, Venice, Verona, Turin and Bergamo.

BOAT

Siremar (www.carontetourist.it/en/siremar) and **Traghetti delle Isole** (www.traghettidelleisole.it) both operate year-round ferries from Trapani to Pantelleria (€37, 7½ hours). Between June and September, **Liberty Lines** (www.libertylines.it) also runs hydrofoils along this same route (€40, 2¼ hours, daily except Tuesday). The ferry dock is just north of the town centre.

ⓘ Getting Around

From the ferry port, a 42km loop road circles the island, granting access to Pantelleria's many natural attractions. **Autonoleggio Policardo** (☑ 0923 91 28 44, 339 4287767; www.autonoleggiopantelleria.it; Via Messina 31; car per day/week from €35/180, scooter from €20/100), with offices at the port and the airport, rents out cars and scooters on a daily or weekly basis. Other rental agencies, including regional operator **Sicily by Car** (☑ 0923 91 29 40; www.sicilybycar.it; Contrada Margana), have counters at the airport.

Tyrrhenian Coast

Best Places to Eat

➡ A Fuoco Lento (p132)
➡ Nangalarruni (p129)
➡ Il Sarchiapone (p137)
➡ Casale Drinzi (p134)
➡ Da Salvatore (p132)

Best Outdoors Activities

➡ La Rocca (p126)
➡ Piscina di Venere (p139)
➡ Spiaggia di Cefalù (p123)
➡ Spiaggia San Gregorio (p137)
➡ Rocche del Crasto (p135)
➡ Dorsale dei Nebrodi (p135)

Why Go?

The coastal stretch between Palermo and Milazzo is packed with dramatic beach and mountain scenery, and appealing coastal towns like Cefalù and Castel di Tusa – but once summer rolls around, it's holiday central, characterised by crowded roads and beaches. Somehow neither this, nor the ever-growing proliferation of concrete buildings marring the coastline, can dissuade locals from coming here for their annual holiday and having a whale of a time.

Few sun-worshippers head inland from these sybaritic summer playgrounds to visit the nearby Madonie and Nebrodi Mountains, but those who do are swiftly seduced. These superb natural landscapes enfold hilltop villages where the lifestyle is traditional, the sense of history palpable and the mountain cuisine exceptional, featuring wild forest mushrooms, *suino nero* (pork from local black pigs) and ricotta straight from the sheep.

Road Distances (km)

	Caccamo	Castelbuono	Cefalù	Milazzo
Castelbuono	75			
Cefalù	50	20		
Milazzo	185	135	130	
Petralia Sottana	90	35	60	175

CEFALÙ

📞 0921 / POP 14.300

Beautiful Cefalù offers a rare combination of tourist attractions: one of Sicily's finest beaches side-by-side with one of its greatest Arab-Norman architectural masterpieces. The squares, streets and churches of this medieval town are so postcard-pretty that it's no wonder director Giuseppe Tornatore chose to set parts of his much-loved film *Cinema Paradiso* here.

You won't be alone in admiring Cefalù's honey-hued stone buildings, mosaic-adorned cathedral and dramatic mountain backdrop. Holidaymakers from all over Europe flock here to relax in resort hotels, stroll the narrow cobbled streets and sun themselves on the long sandy beach – and the opening of a brand-new flagship Club Med here in 2018 has only magnified the crowds.

The town is perfectly suited to slow, pedestrianised exploration. The little port is lined with fishing boats and populated with fishermen who can be observed maintaining their boats, mending their nets and discussing the day's catch.

⊙ Sights

Most of Cefalù's sights are found in the historic town centre around Corso Ruggero and Piazza del Duomo. The only exception is La Rocca – to appreciate the magnificent views from this ancient eyrie you'll need to brave a steep walk up the mountainside.

★ Duomo di Cefalù   CATHEDRAL
(📞 092 192 20 21; www.cattedraledicefalu.com; Piazza del Duomo; towers & apse or treasury & cloisters €5, combo ticket incl towers, apse, treasury & cloisters €8; ⊙ 8.30am-6.30pm Apr-Oct, 8.30am-1pm & 3.30-5pm Nov-Mar) Cefalù's cathedral is one of the jewels in Sicily's Arab-Norman crown, only equalled in magnificence by the Cattedrale di Monreale and Palermo's Cappella Palatina. Filling the central apse, a towering figure of Cristo Pantocratore (Christ All Powerful) is the focal point of the elaborate Byzantine mosaics – Sicily's oldest and best preserved, predating those of Monreale by 20 or 30 years.

In his hand, a compassionate-looking Christ holds an open Bible bearing a Latin and Greek inscription. Other mosaic groups include the Virgin with Four Archangels dressed as Byzantine officials.

The 16 interior columns with Roman capitals probably came from the Tempio di Diana on La Rocca.

Legend tells us that the cathedral was built by Roger II in the 12th century to fulfil a vow to God after his fleet was saved during a violent storm off Cefalù. In fact, it was more likely the result of Roger's tempestuous relationship with the Palermitan archbishopric. Eager to curb the growing influence of the papacy in Sicily (with whom the Palermo archbishopric had close ties), Roger thought that building a mighty church so far from Palermo would prove an effective reminder of his power across the island and pose a disincentive to any potential usurpers. It's thus hardly surprising that the cathedral's architecture is distinctly fortress-like.

You can enjoy the view of the cathedral's soaring twin pyramid towers, framed by La Rocca, over a morning coffee or evening *aperitivo* in the Piazza del Duomo. Better yet, climb the **towers** themselves for lofty perspectives over the town, the cathedral's interior and the sparkling Tyrrhenian Sea. In 2019 the towers were opened to the public for the first time; to enter, buy a special €5 ticket at the door, which also grants access to close-up views of the famous Cristo Pantocratore mosaic from a privileged position within the **apse**.

A separate €5 ticket grants access to the cathedral's treasury and cloisters. The **treasury** houses a wide array of ecclesiastical vestments and ornate metalwork, while the **cloisters** are noteworthy for their ancient columns supporting graceful Arab-Norman arches. The finely carved capitals depict a mix of religious and secular images – among the most interesting are the depictions of acrobats, a pair of crocodiles and Noah's Ark.

★ Spiaggia di Cefalù   BEACH
Cefalù's crescent-shaped beach is one of the most popular along the Sicilian coast. In summer it is packed, so be sure to arrive early to get a good spot. Though some sections require a ticket, the area closest to the old town is public and you can hire a beach umbrella and deckchair for around €15 per day.

Museo Mandralisca   MUSEUM
(📞 0921 42 15 47; www.fondazionemandralisca.it; Via Mandralisca 13; adult/reduced €6/2; ⊙ 9am-7pm, to 11pm Aug, closed Mon Nov-Feb) This small, privately owned museum showcases a collection amassed by parliamentarian, archaeologist and natural-history buff, Baron

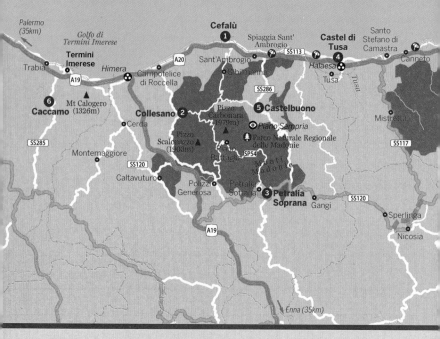

Tyrrhenian Coast Highlights

1 **Cefalù** (p123) Choosing between the glitter of the Duomo's sparkling mosaics or the nearby beach scene.

2 **Museo Targa Florio** (p134) Reliving the glory days of Italy's greatest road race in this little Collesano museum.

3 **Petralia Soprana** (p132) Whiling away a chilly mountain evening by the blazing fire in a pizzeria.

4 **Castel di Tusa** (p137) Celebrating the summer solstice at the hilltop pyramid, the newest installation in the innovative Fiumara d'Arte project.

5 **Castelbuono** (p129)
Visiting a bakery to try a sweet taste of manna, an ancient delicacy made from the sap of local ash trees.

6 **Caccamo** (p128) Enjoying bird's-eye views of rugged hills and the distant Tyrrhenian Sea from the imposing Norman castle.

7 **San Marco d'Alunzio**
(p136) Trying to count all the churches without running out of fingers and toes.

Cefalù

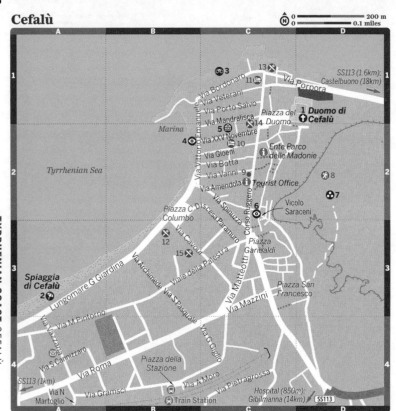

Mandralisca (1809–64). The rather faded displays of Greek ceramics and Arab pottery are of marginal interest compared to Antonello da Messina's splendid *Ritratto di un uomo ignoto* (Portrait of an Unknown Man; 1465), considered one of the most distinctive portraits of the Italian Renaissance.

Acquired by the Baron after he discovered it being used as a makeshift cupboard door in Lipari, da Messina's painting depicts a man with an enigmatic smirk, almost as captivating and thought provoking as the Mona Lisa's – albeit without the attendant hype.

Lavatoio   HISTORIC SITE
(Via Vittorio Emanuele) FREE Descend the curving stone steps to this picturesque cluster of 16th-century wash basins, built over a spring that was well known in antiquity.

Bastione Capo Marchiafava   VIEWPOINT
For fabulous sea views in the heart of Cefalù, make your way to this 17th-century fortification, off Via Bordonaro. Crowds gather here

to watch the sunset or simply catch some rays on a sunny afternoon.

🏃 Activities

⭐**La Rocca**   HIKING
(adult/reduced €4/2; ⊙8am-7pm May-Sep, 9am-4pm Oct-Apr) Looming over Cefalù, this imposing rocky crag was once the site of an Arab citadel, superseded in 1061 by the Norman castle whose ruins still crown the summit. To reach the top, follow signs for Tempio di Diana, taking Vicolo Saraceni off Corso Ruggero or Via Giuseppe Fiore off Piazza Garibaldi. The 30- to 45-minute route climbs the **Salita Saraceni**, a winding staircase, through three tiers of city walls before emerging onto rock-strewn upland slopes with spectacular coastal views.

Before the summit, a couple of signposted forks in the trail veer left to the **Tempio di Diana**, a worthwhile detour either on the ascent or the way back down. Built of massive

Cefalù

limestone blocks quarried directly from the mountainside, this megalithic structure dates back to the 4th or 5th century BC. On the same site are a sacred dolmen-type cistern dating to the 8th or 9th century BC, and the remains of a Byzantine church dedicated to St Venera. Just beyond the temple is an overlook with bird's-eye views of Cefalù's cathedral, the historic town centre and the Tyrrhenian Sea.

🧭 Tours

Visit Sicily Tours BOATING

(☑ 0921 92 50 36; www.visitsicilytours.com; Corso Ruggero 83; boat tours €30-80; ⊙ Apr–Oct) This agency offers three-hour boat tours of the coastline surrounding Cefalù, with stops for swimming and snorkelling. Fresh fruit, soft drinks and transfers to the port from any Cefalù hotel are included in the price. Full-day boat trips to the Aeolian Islands are also offered, along with excursions to Agrigento, Piazza Armerina, Taormina and other mainland Sicilian hotspots.

🍴 Eating

Despite being packed with restaurants, Cefalù does not generally offer great value for money. If all you're after is a passable meal with a beautiful view, you'll find plenty of seafront terrace restaurants along Via Bordonaro in the old town centre.

Bottega Tivitti PIZZA $

(☑ 0921 92 26 42; www.bottegativitti.com; Lungomare Giardina 7; mains €6-15; ⊙ 11am-4pm & 7pm-midnight) This casual waterfront spot serves pizzas, salads and inventive 'Sicilian burgers' made with top-of-the-line local ingredients – like the Tivitti Burger, with sheep's-milk cheese, olive tapenade, sun-dried tomatoes and roasted eggplant. It's a great spot to watch the sunset while sampling Sicilian wines and microbrews and snacking on local cheese and meat platters.

Sutt'a Ràvia SEAFOOD $$

(☑ 0921 82 02 53; www.facebook.com/suttaravia; Piazza Cristoforo Colombo; meals €20-35; ⊙ noon-2.45pm & 7-11.30pm Tue-Sun) Fresh seafood holds centre stage at this cute blue-and-white trattoria near the beachfront, an offshoot of the neighbouring fish market. Order bargain-priced pasta like *linguine alla tarantina* (with mussels, white wine, garlic, olive oil and parsley, €7) from the Classic menu, or splurge on fancier fare from the Prime menu: grilled Mazara prawns or sea bass–stuffed ravioli with citrus zest.

Mandralisca 16 Bistrot SICILIAN $$

(☑ 0921 99 22 45; www.facebook.com/mandralisca16; Via Mandralisca 16; meals €25-35; ⊙ noon-3pm & 7-11pm Tue-Sun) Picturesque setting combines with scrumptious Sicilian cuisine at this relative newcomer with sidewalk seating in an alley gazing towards the Duomo's bell towers. Start with a perfect *caponata* (eggplant, olives, capers, onions and celery in a sweet-and-sour tomato sauce), then move on to chickpea, chard and sage soup or *involtini* (roulades) of fish with citrus, bay leaves and breadcrumbs.

Locanda del Marinaio SEAFOOD $$

(☑ 0921 42 32 95; www.locandadelmarinaiocefalu.it; Via Porpora 5; meals €35-45; ⊙ noon-2.30pm & 7-11pm Wed-Sun, 7-11pm Mon) Fresh seafood rules the chalkboard menu at this upscale eatery along the old town's main waterfront thoroughfare. Depending on the season, you'll find dishes such as red tuna carpaccio with toasted pine nuts, shrimp and zucchini on a bed of velvety ricotta, or grilled octopus served with thyme-scented potatoes, all accompanied by an excellent list of Sicilian wines.

ⓘ Information

Ente Parco delle Madonie (☑ 0921 92 33 27; www.parcodellemadonie.eu; Corso Ruggero

116; ⊙ 8am-2pm Mon, to 6pm Tue-Sat) Knowledgeable staff supply information about the nearby Parco Naturale Regionale delle Madonie.

Hospital (☑ 0921 92 01 11, emergency 0921 92 05 01; www.fondazionesanraffaelegiglio.it; Contrada Pietrapollastra; ⊙ 24hr) On the main road out of town in the direction of Palermo.

Police (Questura; ☑ 0921 92 60 11; Via Roma 15)

Post Office (Via Vazzana 2; ⊙ 8.30am-7pm Mon-Fri, to 12.30pm Sat) Just in from the *lungomare* (seafront promenade).

Tourist Office (☑ 0921 42 10 50; www.turismocefalu.sicilia.it; Corso Ruggero 77; ⊙ 9am-7.30pm Mon-Fri, 8am-2pm Sat) English-speaking staff, lots of leaflets and good maps.

❶ Getting There & Away

BUS

Buses depart from the stop outside the train station regularly from Monday to Saturday, with occasional Sunday services. **SAIS** (☑ 091 617 11 41; www.saistrasporti.it) travels to Palermo (€5.70, one hour, five Monday to Saturday, one Sunday) and Castelbuono (€2.60, 40 minutes, five to seven Monday to Saturday).

CAR & MOTORCYCLE

Cefalù is situated just off the A20-E90 toll road that travels between Messina and Palermo. Finding a car park can be a nightmarish challenge in summer. The most convenient spots are next to the train station or along the *lungomare* (€1 per hour).

To hire a mountain bike, Vespa or motorbike, try **Scooter for Rent** (☑ 092 142 04 96; www.scooterforrent.it; Via Vittorio Emanuele 57; per day/week 50cc Vespa €35/175, mountain bike €10/45; ⊙ 8.30am-12.30pm & 4-6pm Mon-Sat, 9am-noon Sun).

TRAIN

Frequent trains run to/from Palermo (€5.60, 45 minutes to 1¼ hours), Milazzo (from €8.70, 1½ to 1¾ hours) and virtually every other town on the coast.

Arriving at the station, exit right down Via Gramsci to reach Via Matteotti, which leads directly into the old town centre. If heading for the beach, exit left from the station into Via Gramsci, turn right down Via N Martoglio, then take Via Vazzana, which will bring you to the western end of the *lungomare*.

CACCAMO

☑ 091 / POP 8180

Lorded over by its imposing Norman castle, this hilltop town is a popular day trip from both Cefalù and Palermo. Though the area was settled in ancient times, Caccamo was officially founded in 1093, when the Normans began building their fortress on a rocky spur of Monte San Calogero. The castle was enlarged by the noble Chiaramonte family in the 14th century and is now one of Italy's largest and most impressive, with walls and fortifications that originally included ingenious traps for any intruder who might have breached the outer perimeter.

Originally constructed by the Normans in the 11th century, Caccamo's clifftop **Castello di Caccamo** (☑ 091 814 92 52; www.comune.caccamo.palermo.it; adult/reduced €4/free; ⊙ 9am-1pm & 3-7pm) is one of the most dramatically sited in all of Sicily. Beyond the castle's first gate, a ramp leads to a broad courtyard that gives access to the prisons, a chapel, a ragtag arms museum and several monumental, sparsely decorated rooms, from which you can enjoy magnificent views of the surrounding countryside.

Located in the grain stores of the castle, the Slow Food–acclaimed **A Castellana** (☑ 091 814 86 67; www.castellana.it; Piazza dei Caduti 4; set menu €25; ⊙ 12.30-3pm & 7.30-midnight Tue-Sun) has a panoramic terrace for summer dining and is renowned for its assured treatment of classic Sicilian dishes. You can order à la carte or opt for an excellent-value set menu comprising four courses plus coffee.

❶ Getting There & Away

Caccamo is on the SS285 between Palermo and Agrigento. **Randazzo** (☑ 091 814 82 35; www.autolineerandazzo.it) offers limited service to/from Cefalù (€4.60, 70 minutes, one daily) and Palermo (€4.60, 70 minutes, two daily). There are no Sunday services.

PARCO NATURALE REGIONALE DELLE MADONIE

After jostling with armies of sun-seeking holidaymakers on the overdeveloped coast, savvy visitors abandon their deckchairs and head to the hills to savour the lovely scenery and tranquil surrounds of the 400-sq-km Madonie regional park.

An outdoorsy paradise that's well suited to slow, culturally rich travel, the Monti Madonie (Madonie Mountains) are crowned by Pizzo Carbonara (at 1979m the highest mountain in Sicily after Mt Etna), and the regional park takes in farms, hilltop towns and – yes – even a ski resort.

Spring here sees spectacular spreads of wildflowers carpeting the mountain slopes; autumn brings wild mushrooms and richly coloured foliage; winter draws snow sports enthusiasts to Piano Battaglia; and June through August offers an escape from the coastal crowds.

This is not just a nature reserve but an area where people live and work, so you can combine hiking with visits to historic hilltop towns and meals in some fine restaurants.

Castelbuono

☑ 0921 / POP 8840 / ELEV 423M

The charming capital of the Madonie is set amid ancient manna ash and chestnut forests. It owes much of its building stock and character to the Ventimiglias, a powerful noble family who ruled here between the 14th and 16th centuries and whose castle still dominates the town's skyline.

◉ Sights

Castello dei Ventimiglia   CASTLE
(☑ 0921 67 12 11; www.museocivico.eu; Piazza Castello; adult/reduced €5/3; ⊙ 9.30am-1pm & 3-6.30pm Apr-Sep, 9.30am-5pm Oct-Mar) Originally known as the Castello del Buon Aere (Castle of Good Air), the enormous castle that soars above Castelbuono's golden patchwork of houses gave the town its name and is its most distinctive landmark. Built by Francesco I Ventimiglia in 1316, it features displays on local archaeology and Castelbuono's history.

Popular legend has it that the castle is haunted by the 14th-century Queen Constance Chiaramonte, who is said to run along the corridors, regular as clockwork, on the first Tuesday of the month. At the heart of the fortress is the Cappella di Sant'Anna (Chapel of St Anne), which dates from 1683 and is decorated with marvellous stuccowork from the school of renowned Sicilian sculptor Giacomo Serpotta. It houses the supposed skull of the saint in a silver urn.

**Museo Naturalistico
Francesco Minà Palumbo**   MUSEUM
(☑ 0921 67 71 74; www.francescominapalumbo. it; Piazza San Francesco 3; adult/reduced €3/2; ⊙ 9am-1pm & 3-7pm Tue-Sun) Named after the naturalist Francesco Minà Palumbo (1814–99), this unassuming museum is housed

in the former convent of Santa Venera. Its wide-ranging collection of artefacts – painstakingly mounted insects, taxidermied animals, mineral specimens, elegantly rendered nature illustrations from Palumbo's own hand – offer an exhaustive insight into the natural history and archaeology of the Monti Madonie.

★☆ Festivals & Events

Funghi Fest   FOOD & DRINK
(www.funghifest.it; ⊙ Oct) For three days in mid- to late October, thousands of fungus fans descend on Castelbuono to pick wild mushrooms in the Parco Regionale delle Madonie, taste mushroom-based recipes from celebrity chefs, and celebrate the harvest season with music and special events.

✗ Eating

Castelbuono's rustic regional cuisine showcases fruits of the Madonie such as *funghi di bosco* (forest mushrooms) and *cinghiale* (wild boar). Castelbuono is one of the few remaining towns in Sicily that actively harvests manna, the edible sap of the local ash trees.

★ Nangalarruni   SICILIAN $$
(☑ 0921 67 12 28; www.hostariananangalarruni.it; Via delle Confraternite 7; meals €29-45; ⊙ 12.30-3pm & 7-10pm Thu-Tue) Famous throughout Sicily for its delicious dishes featuring forest mushrooms and wild boar, Giuseppe Carollo's eatery deserves equal renown for its splendid Sicilian wine selection, displayed on the shelves of the cosy wood-beamed dining room. Spike your appetite with an array of local cheeses, then move on to mains featuring fresh ricotta, locally sourced vegetables and roast meats.

🛍 Shopping

Fiasconaro   FOOD & DRINKS
(☑ 0921 67 12 31; www.fiasconaro.com; Piazza Margherita 10; ⊙ 7am-11pm Thu-Tue; 🖵) This beloved sweet shop on Castelbuono's main street is the perfect place to stock up on unique foodie gifts. Make sure to try the *cubaita*, a crunchy nut brittle made with hazelnuts, pistachios and sesame seeds, and *oro di manna*, an addictively creamy spread made with honey, almonds, hazelnuts and manna.

ℹ Information

Pro Loco (☑ 389 6893810; www.prolococastel buono.it; Piazza Margherita 5; ⊙ 10am-1pm)

ROAD TRIP >
MONTI MADONIE

• •

Winding through fields and forests at the foot of the region's highest mountain, Pizzo Carbonara (1979m), this tour takes in the most picturesque towns in the Madonie Mountains and rewards leisurely exploration. Along the way, several places offer opportunities to sample the Madonie's distinctive mountain cuisine. It's possible to see everything in one day, but it will be tiring, so linger overnight if you can.

❶ Santuario di Gibilmanna

Spectacularly perched 800m above sea level on the slopes of Pizzo Sant'Angelo (1081m) the **Santuario di Gibilmanna** (☑ 0921 42 18 35; Contrada Valle Grande, Gibilmanna; ⊘ 8am-8pm Apr-Sep, to 5pm Oct-Mar) sits 15km south of Cefalù. Here, in the 17th century, the Virgin Mary reputedly restored sight to two blind worshippers and speech to a person who

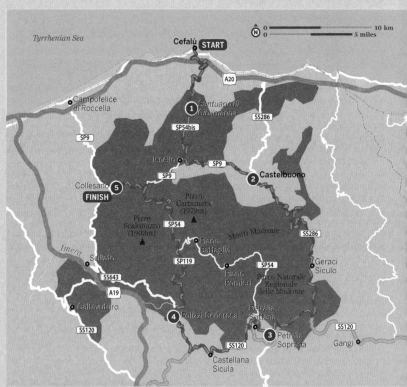

One to Three Days 113km

Great For... Food & Drink, Outdoors

Best Time to Go Spring & autumn

Castelbuono (p129)

couldn't speak. The miracle was later confirmed by the Vatican, and the church has since become one of Sicily's most important shrines. The views over the Madonie from the belvedere out front are spectacular.

The Drive > From Gibilmanna, head 18km southeast on the SP9 to Castelbuono.

❷ Castelbuono

Serving as a northern gateway to the Monti Madonie, the mountain town of Castelbuono is presided over by its magnificent 14th-century castle. Stop in at Pasticceria Fiasconaro in the heart of town for a taste of *mannetto* (manna cake), a sweet delicacy made using the sap of the local flowering ash trees.

The Drive > Follow the winding SS286 for 36km south to the picturesque mountain town of Petralia Soprana. The road, intermittently fringed by dense forest, is relentlessly curvy but offers wonderful views over the valleys.

❸ Petralia Soprana

Centered around pretty Piazza del Popolo, Petralia Soprana (1147m) is the Madonie's highest village. Wander its labyrinth of ancient stone streets, then stop to sample the generous spread of antipasti at Da Salvatore, a beloved traditional trattoria.

The Drive > Continue downhill 4km to neighbouring Petralia Sottana, where you'll pick up the SS120 for the 19km drive to Polizzi Generosa.

❹ Polizzi Generosa

Nestled at the entrance to the Imera Valley, this hilltop village was dubbed *generosa* (generous) by Frederick II in the 1230s. Polizzi Generosa is now best known as a trekking base for the Madonie, and is riddled with churches that are often shrouded in mist. It's also home to a pastry known as the *sfoglio*: sweet dough filled with artisanal sheep's milk cheese, cinnamon, chocolate and sugar.

The Drive > From Polizzi Generosa, head 26km northwest on the SP119 and SP54 to Collesano, enjoying splendid mountain views en route.

❺ Collesano

Medieval Collesano is your last stop. Don't miss the Targa Florio museum, which celebrates the history of the Madonie's storied mountain road race, and make sure you stick around town for a hearty mountain dinner at delightful Casale Drinzi.

In Castelbuono's main square, a three-minute walk from the castle; offers information on Castelbuono and the Madonie in general.

ⓘ Getting There & Away

Castelbuono is 23km southeast of Cefalù via the SS113 and SS286. If travelling along the A20 *autostrada*, take the Pollina/Castelbuono exit.

SAIS Trasporti (☑ 091 617 11 41; www.sais trasporti.it) runs buses to Castelbuono from Palermo (€8.60, 1¾ hours, two to three direct buses Monday to Saturday, one Sunday) and Cefalù (€2.60, 40 minutes, five to seven daily Monday to Saturday).

Petralia Soprana

☑ 0921 / POP 3310 / ELEV 1147M

Beautifully positioned at the top of a hill above a treeline of pines, Petralia Soprana (from the Italian word *sopra,* meaning 'above') is one of the best-preserved small towns in north-central Sicily, full of picturesque stone houses and curling wrought-iron balconies brimming with geraniums. It's also the highest village in the Madonie. There's not much for visitors to do except wander around the narrow cobbled lanes, visit the churches of **Santa Maria di Loreto** (Via Loreto; ⊗ 9am-12.30pm & 4-7pm) and **Santi Pietro e Paolo** (Piazza del Duomo; ⊗ 9am-12.30pm & 4-7pm), and soak up the sweeping views from the town's belvederes.

Salvatore Ruvutuso, his wife Maria and two children run the Slow Food–acclaimed **Da Salvatore** (☑ 0921 68 01 69; Piazza San Michele 4; pizzas €4-8, meals €16-25; ⊗ 1-3pm & 8-11pm Wed-Mon Mar-Oct, 8-11pm Fri-Sun Nov-Feb), with its summertime sidewalk seating and wonderfully cosy interior dining room. Kick off with a delicious selection of antipasti including frittata, superb *caponata* and pungent *provola delle Madonie,* then choose from a daily menu that usually features a rustic pasta, vegetable soup or fragrant stew.

Pizzas are only served in the evening. The restaurant is tucked into a little square near the Chiesa di Santa Maria di Loreto – just follow the signs. Note: no credit cards.

A Fuoco Lento (☑ 338 2890100; www.lalo candadicadi.it/afuocolento.htm; Borgo Cipampini; meals incl house wine €35) is an intimate stone-walled gem of a restaurant in Cipampini, 10km below Petralia Soprana. Chef-owners Diego and Patrizia seat only 30 people each evening for multicourse dinners that celebrate unique regional flavours: wood-fired bread with pecorino cheese and homemade rose jam, locally foraged herbs and flowers, artisanal cold cuts, ricotta-mint frittatas, Madonie pork with apples and ginger, local wine and more.

Guests are encouraged to linger and talk, or take a turn on the piano tucked into the corner of the dining room.

ⓘ Getting There & Away

BUS

SAIS Trasporti operates two to three daily buses from Palermo to Petralia Soprana (€10.30, two hours).

CAR & MOTORCYCLE

To reach Petralia Soprana from Petralia Sottana, drive up Corso Paolo Agliata to Piazza Umberto and follow the winding narrow road leading uphill through the arch at the right-hand side of the Chiesa Madre, veering right at the first fork.

There is limited free car parking in Piazza del Popolo. Alternatively, park on the side of the road leading uphill into town.

Petralia Sottana

☑ 0921 / POP 2770 / ELEV 1000M

Below Petralia Soprana, the town of Petralia Sottana (from the Italian *sotto,* meaning 'under') is the southern gateway to the Parco Naturale Regionale delle Madonie and home to the park's main headquarters. The town centre is well worth a wander for its picturesque collection of stone churches and towers.

Petralia Sottana is dominated by its main street, Corso Paolo Agliata, which is a popular shopping strip during the day and hosts the town's surprisingly busy *passeggiata* (evening stroll) in the early evening. Like Petralia Soprana, the town possesses a number of handsome churches, including the baroque **Chiesa di San Francesco** (Corso Paolo Agliata 114) and the 17th-century **Chiesa Madre** (Piazza Umberto I) at the Corso's northern end. The campanile of the latter is the town's major landmark. Just off the road leading to Petralia Soprana is the **Chiesa della Santissima Trinità alla Badia**, which has a handsome marble altarpiece carved by Giandomenico Gagini.

ⓘ Information

Ente Parco delle Madonie (Madonie Park Authority; ☑ 0921 68 40 11; www.parcodelle madonie.eu; Corso Paolo Agliata 16) The park's official website has detailed information.

HIKING IN THE MADONIE MOUNTAINS

The Parco delle Madonie offers some fine hiking opportunities. Unfortunately, trails are often poorly marked, and access can be difficult without your own vehicle. The most enjoyable way to get out and explore the park without getting lost or frustrated is with a certified guide. Two recommended English-speaking guides with a thorough knowledge of the park are Carmelina Ricciardello and Marian Watson at **Sicilian Experience** (📞 388 9729174; www.sicilianexperience.com; Sant'Ambrogio). Other useful resources include Sunflower Books' *Sicily Car Tours and Walks*, Cicerone's *Walking in Sicily* and the 1:50,000 *Madonie/Carta dei Sentieri e del Paesaggi* map sold at park offices, though none of these offer foolproof information on locating trailheads.

A few of our favourite walks in the park:

Pizzo Carbonara The classic ascent of Pizzo Carbonara (1979m), the Monti Madonie's highest peak, is one of the park's most popular hikes. It can be done as a three-hour, 6km loop from Piano Battaglia, but should only be undertaken in clear weather, both for safety reasons – it's easy to get lost in the fog – and for the amazing views that unfold up top.

The trail begins as a dirt track off the main road at Piano Battaglia, a few hundred metres northeast of Rifugio Marini. Park near the informational display labeled 'Sentiero Battaglietta–Piano Sempria' (but note that this refers to a different, longer trail into the high country).

Pizzo Caterineci This gorgeous four- to five-hour loop hike climbs into the high country above Petralia Soprana, offering expansive views across forested slopes and rolling pastures towards Pizzo Carbonara and (on a clear day) Mt Etna. The trailhead is at Portella Ferrone, 3km north of Petralia Soprana or 4.5km northeast of Petralia Sottana. You'll need a guide, as signage is nearly nonexistent.

Vallone Madonna degli Angeli This 8km, 2.5-hour hike loops through a river valley on the park's western edge, climbing initially past spectacular views of jagged rocky promontories and distant rolling countryside, then branching onto a narrower path along forested slopes, where you'll encounter examples of the rare Nebrodi fir (*Abies nebrodensis*). Look for the signposted trailhead along the SP119, 7km southwest of Piano Battaglia.

TYRRHENIAN COAST PIANO BATTAGLIA

Tourist Office (📞 0921 64 18 11; www.petralia visit.it; Corso Paolo Agliata 100; ☺ 8am-2pm & 3-6.30pm Mon-Fri, 9.30am-12.30pm & 3.30-6.30pm Sat & Sun) In the foyer of the Museo Civico Antonio Collisani. Supplies a good collection of maps and books about natural history, wildlife and walking in the Madonie, along with information about Petralia Sottana itself.

❶ Getting There & Away

BUS
SAIS Trasporti operates two to three daily buses from Palermo to Petralia Sottana (€10.30, 1¾ hours).

CAR & MOTORCYCLE
Petralia Sottana is on the SS120. If coming from Palermo via the A19 *autostrada,* exit at Tremonzelli.

There is a car park overlooking the valley directly opposite the junction of the SS120 and Corso Paolo Agliata (Petralia's main street). You'll find a second free car park around the

back side of the Chiesa Madre – drive through the arch just above the church, take the first left-hand fork and look for it on the left-hand side.

Piano Battaglia

📞 0921 / ELEV 1572M

More Swiss than Sicilian, the high mountain plateau of Piano Battaglia is a year-round recreation destination, dotted with chalets that play host to an ever-growing number of winter visitors seeking fun in the snow. With the advent of spring, Piano Battaglia becomes an equally popular walking, climbing and mountain-biking destination, with sign-posted paths and a profusion of wildflowers.

Activities

Piano Battaglia Ski Area SKIING
(📞 0921 68 81 30; www.pianobattaglia.it; SP54; lift ticket €30; ☺ 9am-4pm winter, 10am-6pm summer) Who says you can't ski in Sicily? Piano

DON'T MISS

REMEMBERING THE MADONIE'S LEGENDARY CAR RACE

Vintage sports car enthusiasts will be in seventh heaven at a pair of museums commemorating the legendary Targa Florio road race, which for more than 70 years lured drivers from around the world to test their mettle against the twists and turns of the Madonie Mountains' narrow back roads.

Museo Targa Florio (☑ 0921 66 46 84; www.museotargaflorio.it; Corso Vittorio Emanuele 3; adult/reduced €2.50/1.50; ⊙ 9.30am-12.30pm Mon & Thu, 9.30am-12.30pm & 3.30-7pm Tue, Wed & Fri-Sun) This unique little museum in Collesano displays photographs and memorabilia documenting the Targa Florio, the world's oldest sports-car racing event. Established by wealthy automobile enthusiast Vincenzo Florio in 1906, then discontinued in 1977 due to safety concerns, the 72km race along the Monti Madonie's treacherous narrow roads was intensely challenging, with countless hairpin bends testing both the driver's skill and the car's performance.

A plaque here chronicles the names and car models of all the winners throughout the event's seven-decade history (in case you're wondering, Porsche won the most times, followed closely by Alfa Romeo).

Museo del Motorismo Siciliano (☑ 335 8026361; www.asimusei.it/museo/museo-del-motorismo-siciliano-e-della-targa-florio; Località Mulinelli, Termini Imerese; ⊙ 8.30am-1pm & 3-8pm) FREE This unique museum, 33km northwest of Collesano on the outskirts of Termini Imerese, is a labour of love for owner-founder Nuccio Salemi, whose amazing collection of original sports cars from the Targa Florio race fills this converted slaughterhouse. Salemi caught the car racing bug as a young boy, watching famed Targa Florio drivers land their helicopters on his grandfather's field in the nearby Madonie Mountains. His Italian-English displays pay tribute to the race's history, while visitors are invited to roam the floor and discover the cars at close range.

Admission is free, though you'll be gently cajoled to take home some merchandise (hats, stickers and the like).

Battaglia's northern slopes reach heights of 1840m, with 3.5km of ski runs, while the Mufaretta (southwest slope) reaches 1680m, with a run about 500m long. A pair of ski lifts whisks skiers to the top. Cross-country skiing, sledding and snowboarding are also popular here.

In summer, the same lifts carry hikers and mountain bikers to the summit of Monte Mufara (1865m), a perfect jumping-off point for several high-altitude trails. The ski area also rents out e-mountain bikes and organises guided small group excursions.

✗ Eating

Ristoro dello Scoiattolo   SICILIAN $
(☑ 349 6439987; meals €20-25; ⊙ 9am-5pm) Perched at 1600m, near the base of the Mufara ski slope, this rustic year-round restaurant is Piano Battaglia's perennial favourite spot to indulge in reasonably priced dishes of pasta with mushrooms or wild boar ragù, roast pork loin and other hearty mountain fare. Cosy up by the fireplace or enjoy panoramic vistas from the outdoor deck.

❶ Getting There & Away

From Petralia Sottana it's a twisty 19km climb along the SP54 to Piano Battaglia. To get here from Collesano (22km) or Castelbuono (36km), take the SP9 to the SP54 south.

Collesano

☑ 0921 / POP 4030 / ELEV 468M

The upper reaches of this charming medieval town are dominated by the pink-and-cream Basilica San Pietro on Corso Vittorio Emanuele and the weathered remains of a nearby Norman castle. Like Castelbuono, the town was once governed by the Ventimiglias and retains an aristocratic air.

There are a number of churches worthy of a visit, including the frescoed 15th-century **Duomo** (aka Santa Maria la Nuova), the 12th-century **Chiesa di St Maria la Vecchia**, the 17th-century **Chiesa di St Maria del Gesù** and the early-16th-century **Chiesa di St Giacomo**.

Casale Drinzi (☑ 0921 66 40 27; www.casale drinzi.it; SP9, Contrada Drinzi; pizzas €4-8, meals €20-25; ⊙ noon-3pm & 7-11pm Mar-Jan), a wooden chalet in the hills immediately above Collesano, is one of the Madonie's gems – one whiff of the delicious aromas emanating from the kitchen and you'll know you've come to the right place. The menu features hearty mountain specialities like stewed pork with artichokes and smoked ham, alongside other rustic favourites featuring Slow Food–recognised regional ingredients.

Items not to be missed when available include the *degustazione di antipasti* (a plate of stuffed zucchini flowers, deep-fried ricotta, lardo-topped bruschetta and chargrilled local onions), *pappardelle al sugo di selvaggina* (homemade pasta ribbons with a game sauce) and *fagiolo Badda Nera* (beans grown in the area around Polizzi Generosa). Pizzas are added to the menu at night – a good reason to book into the on-site B&B (singles/doubles €40/60).

🛈 Getting There & Away

Collesano is 23km west of Castelbuono via the SP9. **AST** (Azienda Siciliana Trasporti; 🖰 091 620 81 11; www.aziendasicilianatrasporti.it) runs three to five buses from Palermo to Collesano (€6, 1¼ to 1¾ hours) Monday through Saturday.

PARCO REGIONALE DEI NEBRODI

Encompassing the Monti Nebrodi (Nebrodi Mountains) of northeastern Sicily, the Nebrodi Regional Park (www.parcodeinebrodi.it) was established in 1993 and constitutes the single largest forested area in Sicily, dotted with remote and traditional villages that host few visitors. The forest here ranges in altitude from 1200m to 1500m; the park's highest peak is Monte Soro (1847m), and the Lago di Biviere is a lovely natural lake supporting herons and stilts.

The lovely, off-the-beaten-track park encompasses an undulating landscape of beech, oak, elm, ash, cork, maple and yew trees that shelter the remnants of Sicily's wildlife: porcupines, San Fratello horses and wildcats, as well as a healthy population of birds of prey including golden eagles, lanner and peregrine falcons and griffon vultures. The high pastures have always been home to hard-working agricultural communities that harvest mushrooms and hazelnuts, churn out creamy ricotta and graze cows, sheep, horses, goats and pigs.

🏃 Activities

★ Dorsale dei Nebrodi   OUTDOORS

Popular with hikers, mountain bikers and equestrians, the Parco dei Nebrodi's most iconic trail is the Dorsale dei Nebrodi (Nebrodi Backbone), running 70km across the entire breadth of the park. The best section for a day trip runs from Portella Calacudera (about 1.5km east of the SS289) to Lago Biviere, a remote backcountry lake with excellent birdwatching opportunities.

To reach the trailhead for Lago Biviere, turn off the SS289 at Portella Femmina Morta, 0.5km north of Relais Villa Miraglia (p282). From the car park at Portella Calacudera, it's a 15.6km out-and-back trip (about six hours on foot).

★ Rocche del Crasto   HIKING

Jutting dramatically out of the high mountain pastures at the northern edge of the Nebrodi park, these pinnacles of rock are a favourite hiking destination. Park your car at the mountain saddle between Alcara Li Fusi and Longi, and take the three-hour out-and-back trail to the summit, where views stretch far out over the Tyrrhenian Sea to the Aeolian Islands.

Vai Col Trekking Sicilia   HIKING

(🖰 349 7362863; www.vaicoltrekkingsicilia.com) Certified environmental guide Attilio Caldarera runs this recommended agency, which organises day trips and multiday walking excursions in the Parco Regionale dei Nebrodi.

🍴 Eating

★ Relais Villa Miraglia   SICILIAN $$

(🖰 095 883 48 98; www.relaisvillamiraglia.it/ristorante; SS289; meals €27-35) *Suino nero dei Nebrodi* (the park's DOC black pork) is the star attraction at the Relais Villa Miraglia's excellent restaurant, where big picture windows overlook a forest-backed lawn strewn with picnic tables for warm-weather dining. Beyond the *suino nero*, enjoy hearty portions of ravioli stuffed with truffles, potato and pumpkin, delicious grilled sausages and lamb or veal with sautéed local mushrooms.

🛈 Information

The main **park office** (🖰 0941 79 39 04; Via Ugo Foscolo 1; ⊗ hours vary) is in the small town of Alcara Li Fusi, with a peripheral office in **Cesarò** (🖰 095 773 20 61; Via Bellini 79; ⊗ hours vary). Both keep irregular hours, and most staff speak

TYRRHENIAN COAST PARCO REGIONALE DEI NEBRODI

Italian only. For more information about the park, see www.parcodeinebrodi.it.

ℹ️ Getting There & Away

The best way to explore the park is with your own wheels, as bus services are few and far between. **Interbus** (☑ 091 34 20 55; www.interbus.it) operates very limited weekday service into the park from Messina, with one bus daily to Cesarò (€9.20, three hours) and another to Mistretta (€9.60, 2¼ hours).

San Marco d'Alunzio

☑ 0941 / POP 1960 / ELEV 548M

This spectacularly situated hilltop town, 9km from the coast, was founded by the Greeks in the 5th century BC and then occupied by the Romans, who named it Aluntium and built structures such as the Tempio di Ercole (Temple of Hercules) at the town's entrance. A Norman church, now roofless, was subsequently built on the temple's red marble base.

Southeast of the town is the trekking base, Longi, and southwest is Alcara Li Fusi, a small village situated beneath the impressive Rocche del Crasto (1315m), a nesting site of the golden eagle.

🔘 Sights

Virtually all of San Marco d'Alunzio's older buildings and its 22 churches (grab a map at the tourist office) were made using locally quarried marble. At the top of the hill are the scant remains of the first **castle** built by the Normans in Sicily. The town's small **mu-**seum (Museum of Byzantine & Norman Culture & Figurative Art; ☑ 0941 79 73 39; Badia Nica, Via Ferraloro; adult/reduced €2.50/1.50; ⊙ 9am-1pm & 3-7pm) has a hodgepodge of local archaeological finds dating to the Greek, Roman, Byzantine and Norman periods.

ℹ️ Information

Tourist Office (☑ 0941 79 73 39; www.face book.com/SanMarcoTurismo; Via Aluntina 53; ⊙ 9am-1pm year-round, plus 3-7pm Oct-Apr, 3.30-7.30pm May, Jun & Sep, 4-8pm Jul & Aug) Opposite the Chiesa Madre.

ℹ️ Getting There & Away

From the coastal SS113 just east of Sant'Agata di Militello, turn onto the squiggly SP160, which makes the steep 7km ascent to San Marco d'Alunzio.

Mistretta

☑ 0921 / POP 4640 / ELEV 970M

Located on the western border of Nebrodi Regional Park, and accessed via the SS117 from Santo Stefano di Camastra, is the charming hilltop time capsule of Mistretta. The streets here have hardly changed over the past 300 years, and most of the locals look as if they've been around for almost as long. Little disturbs the mountain quietude, making this a pleasant retreat for nature lovers.

Perched north of town at a height of nearly 1000m, the ruins of Mistretta's 11th-century Norman castle. **Castello Arabo-Normanno**, make an atmospheric spot to survey the old town's huddle of stone houses

---

OFF THE BEATEN TRACK

CROSSING THE NEBRODI MOUNTAINS

Several charming routes wind across the Nebrodi ranges, weaving through tiny mountain hamlets and steep, forested slopes. The SS116 starts at Capo d'Orlando on the coast and climbs to Floresta (1275m), the highest village in the park, where you can stop for local olives, cheeses and meats at Alimentari Giuseppe Calabrese on the main square. From here, the road makes a spectacular descent to Randazzo, with unforgettable views of Mt Etna.

Cutting through the heart of the park is the enchanting SS289, which links Sant'Agata di Militello with Cesarò in the interior. Along the route is San Fratello, a typical Nebrodi town originally founded by Roger I's third wife, Adelaide di Monferrato, for her Lombard cousins (hence the strange local dialect).

If you're coming from the Monti Madonie, a pretty highland route into the Nebrodi is the SS120. Starting from Petralia Sottana, head east through the gorgeous hill towns of Gangi, Sperlinga and Nicosia, then turn north on the SS117 to Mistretta. The landscape is especially picturesque in springtime, when the high rolling hills are covered in wildflowers. On clear days, there are good distant views of Mt Etna to the southeast.

and the surrounding patchwork of fields and rolling hills. First mentioned in historical accounts dating to 1083, the castle nowadays is a crumbling shell of its former self, but the views are lovely, and the evocative approach through Mistretta's narrow stone streets is reason enough to make the climb.

ℹ️ Information

Tourist Office (Pro Loco Mistretta; ☎334 9355522; www.prolocomistretta.it; Via Libertà 267)

ℹ️ Getting There & Away

Mistretta is 17km south of the coastal town of Santo Stefano di Camastra. Coming off the A20 motorway, it's about a 25-minute drive, once you've navigated the insanely circuitous exit ramp!

CASTEL DI TUSA

☎0921 / POP 2860

Named after the castle that now lies in ruins 600m above it, this small coastal resort about 25km east of Cefalù is best known for the controversial Fiumara d'Arte, an open-air sculpture park featuring a collection of contemporary artworks scattered along the *fiumara* (riverbed) of the Tusa River. The most recent, and most impressive, installation is the Piramide 38° Parallelo, a gleaming rust-coloured steel pyramid high on a hilltop above the sea, now a regular gathering point for solstice celebrations.

From Castel di Tusa's beach, a small road leads inland to the parent village of Tusa. Between the coastal resort and the village, about 3km up from the coast, you'll see a signpost for the ancient Greek ruins of Halaesa Arconidea.

Perched on a hillside 4km south of Castel di Tusa, and accessed through a small olive grove, the scant remnants of a 5th-century-BC Greek city at **Halaesa Arconidea** (☎0921 33 45 31; SP177; adult/reduced €2/1; ⊙9am-1hr before sunset) command fine views of the surrounding countryside and the Aeolian Islands. The most conspicuous ruins are those of its agora and its massive, rusticated walls. A small archaeological museum displays finds from the site. Downhill near the entrance are the remains of a Colombarium, a 2nd-century Roman necropolis with some well-preserved stonework.

ℹ️ Getting There & Away

Just 800m east of the town centre, Castel di Tusa station (labeled Tusa on the Trenitalia website) is serviced by trains from Milazzo (€7.90, 1¼ hours, two direct trains daily), Cefalù (€3.10, 25 minutes, eight daily) and Palermo (€6.90, 1¼ to 1½ hours, eight daily).

CAPO D'ORLANDO

☎0941 / POP 13,300

The busiest resort town on the coast after Cefalù, Capo d'Orlando was founded – legend tells us – when one of Charlemagne's generals, a chap called Orlando, stood on the *capo* (headland) and declared it a fine place to build a castle. The ruins of this structure are still visible. In 1299 Frederick II of Aragon was defeated here by the rebellious baron Roger of Lauria, backed up by the joint forces of Catalonia and Anjou. More-recent rebels include the town's shopkeepers and traders, who made a name for themselves in the 1990s with their stand against the Mafia's demands for *pizzo* (protection money).

Visitors come here for the beaches, both sandy and rocky, that are on either side of town. The best swimming is to the east.

Turquoise waters lap the gorgeous **Spiaggia San Gregorio** to the east of the point at Capo d'Orlando. Framed by rocky outcrops, with a mix of sand and pebbles and gorgeous full-on views of the Aeolian Islands, it's among the most charmed spots on the entire Tyrrhenian Coast.

Local families and tourists alike flock to **Il Sarchiapone** (☎0941 91 27 13; Via Cairoli 6; meals €27-33; ⊙noon-2.30pm & 7.30-11.30pm Thu-Tue) for its phenomenal fresh seafood, served with good cheer in an unpretentious mustard-yellow dining room accented with exposed stone. The chalkboard menu always features bargain-priced daily specials (from €3.50) alongside pricier maritime delights: from raw fish antipasti, to ravioli stuffed with scallops, shrimp and swordfish roe, to seafood mixed grills.

ℹ️ Information

Tourist Office (☎0941 95 52 25; www.turismo capodorlando.it; Lungomare Andrea Doria; ⊙9am-1pm & 3-7pm Sep-Jun, 9am-1pm & 5-9pm Jul & Aug) On the waterfront, just west of the point.

CAPO TINDARI

At Capo Tindari, just off the *autostrada* between Milazzo and Cefalù, a historic church, Santuario della Madonna del Tindari, and an ancient Greco-Roman site, Tyndaris, make an interesting detour. Coming from the east, turn off the *autostrada* at Oliveri and follow signs for Tindari/Tyndaris. If you're coming from the west, the site is 12km from Marina di Patti on the SS113. Drivers must park in the paid car park at the foot of the hill, then walk (15 minutes) or take the shuttle bus (€1 return, five minutes) up to the sanctuary and the ruins.

The enormous **Santuario della Madonna del Tindari** (Sanctuary of the Madonna of Tindari; ☑0941 36 90 03; www.santuariotindari.it; ⊙6.45am-12.30pm & 2.30-7pm Mon-Sat, to 8pm Sun) can be seen from miles around: it sits right on Capo Tindari, its dome glistening in the sun. A sanctuary was built here in the 16th century to house the icon of the Bruna Madonnina del Tindari (Black Madonna of Tindari), but the current garishly decorated building mainly dates from the 20th century. The inscription underneath the icon reads *Nigra sum, sed formosa* (I am black, but beautiful).

From the church's *belvedere* (panoramic terrace) there's a spectacular view down to the Laghetti di Marinello, a series of small lakes punctuating a long sandbar, surrounded by the sparkling blue Tyrrhenian Sea.

The ancient Greek holy place of **Tyndaris** (☑0941 36 90 23; Via del Teatro Greco, Tindari; adult/reduced €6/3; ⊙9am-1hr before sunset) was founded by Dionysis of Syracuse after his victory over the Carthaginians in 396 BC. The secluded ruins (a basilica, an agora, a Roman house and a Greek theatre) are set on the cliff edge amid prickly pears, olives and cypress trees. In summer you can clearly see the Aeolian Islands and the lovely Oliveri lagoon in the bay below. There's also a small museum displaying artefacts excavated at the site.

Spiaggia di Oliveri in the town of Oliveri, just below the ancient settlement of Tyndaris, is a sandy stretch of beach that makes a good place for a swim, with a series of lidos renting sun loungers and beach umbrellas.

❶ Getting There & Away

Capo d'Orlando sits on the SS113, the Tyrrhenian Coast's main waterfront highway. Without your own wheels, the easiest access is by train from Milazzo (€5.10, 45 minutes), Cefalù (€6.20, one hour) or Palermo (€9, two hours).

MILAZZO

☑090 / POP 31,500

For many, the prime reason for setting foot in this town is to head for the hydrofoil docks and set sail for the Aeolian Islands. But, away from its refineries and industrial port development, Milazzo boasts an impressive hilltop castle and a pretty Borgo Antico (Old Town), and the isthmus that juts out to the north is an area of great natural beauty dotted with rocky coves – well worth a visit for those with time to spare.

◎ Sights & Activities

★ Capo Milazzo
WATERFRONT

If you have a car, don't miss the scenic drive north along Strada Panoramica to see the gorgeous, rugged coastline of Capo Milazzo. At the end of the isthmus is a lighthouse; park in the nearby lot, from where short walks lead to the atmospheric ruins of the 13th-century **Santuario Rupestre di San Antonio da Padova** (Capo Milazzo) and the Piscina di Venere, an idyllic natural pool that's perfect for a dip on a hot day.

Alternatively, you can arrange a boat trip (ask at the tourist office) around the rocky cape to Baia del Tonno on the western side of the isthmus.

Castello di Milazzo
CASTLE

(☑090 922 12 91, guided tours 328 8316110; www.compagniadelcastellomilazzo.it; Salita Castello; adult/reduced €5/3.50, Sun guided tour adult/reduced €5/2; ⊙9am-1.30pm & 4.30-8.30pm May-Sep, 9am-6.30pm Oct-Apr, closed Mon year-round) Originally the site of a Greek acropolis, then an Arab-Norman citadel, Milazzo's enormous castle was built by Frederick II in 1239, expanded by Charles V of Aragon and stormed by Garibaldi's troops in 1860. The whole of Milazzo once fitted within its massive walls. Nowadays it's a lovely site to clamber around, full of flowers and crumbling fortifications, with dreamy views of the bay and the Aeolians from atop the Torre Normanna, the castle's oldest and highest part.

The castle grounds, enclosed within late-15th-century Aragonese outer walls, contain the city's Duomo Vecchio (old cathedral) and the ruins of the Palazzo dei Giurati (the old town hall). To get here, climb the Salita Castello, which rises up through the atmospheric old town. Guided tours (available in English with advance notice) are offered at 4.30pm on Sunday afternoons throughout the summer.

★ **Piscina di Venere**   SWIMMING
(Venus' Pool) Out at the very tip of Capo Milazzo, this gorgeous rock-fringed pool makes an idyllic spot for swimming and sunbathing. Accessed by a 15-minute walk from the Capo Milazzo car park through a landscape of olive groves, cactus and stone walls, its tranquil turquoise waters are separated by a small ring of rocks from the ultramarine Mediterranean just beyond.

✖ Eating

There's a good mix of eateries, from sidewalk pizzerias to fancy fish restaurants, along the waterfront just north of the port – convenient even for those just grabbing a quick bite between ferries.

★ **Al Bagatto**   SICILIAN $$
(☑ 090 922 42 12; www.locandadelbagatto.com/restaurant.php; Via Massimiliano Regis 11; meals €25-40; ☺ 7.30pm-midnight Mon-Sat) Three decades after opening as one of the region's first wine bars, this place is still thriving under affable chef-owner Chiara Surdo. Mellow music and lighting and a fabulous wine list complement a Slow Food–celebrated menu of dishes made fresh on the spot with local ingredients, from divine beef carpaccio to tube-shaped *paccheri* pasta with Nebrodi black pork ragù.

Toto Passami L'Olio   OSTERIA $$
(☑ 090 240 30 18; www.totopassamilolio.it; Via Cumbo Borgia 29; meals €35-38; ☺ 11.30am-4pm & 7.30-11pm Thu-Tue; ☑) Specialising in locally sourced 'km0' cuisine, this intriguing restaurant serves up creative dishes built around sometimes obscure ingredients, with vegan and vegetarian options always in the mix. Everything is beautifully presented, from lentil soup with mussels and seaweed, to vegetarian pasta with fennel, Corinthian raisins, saffron and toasted breadcrumbs, to Nebrodi 'black pork' chops with tomatoes, capers and onions.

Doppio Gusto   SEAFOOD $$$
(☑ 090 924 00 45; www.facebook.com/Ristorante DoppioGusto; Via Luigi Rizzo 44; meals €45-55; ☺ noon-3pm & 8-11.45pm Wed-Mon) For stellar seafood that paces from the port, this upscale eatery with a devoted local following is the obvious choice. Service can be a bit stiff and formal, but food quality is exceptional, with everything fresh off the boat. Stay cool in the air-conditioned interior or watch the world go by under the awning out front.

❶ Information

Hospital (Ospedale Giuseppe Fogliani; ☑ 090 9 29 01; Villaggio Grazia; ☺ 24hr)

Police (Questura; ☑ 090 923 03 11; Via Municipio 1)

Tourist Office (☑ 090 922 28 65; strmilazzo@regione.sicilia.it; Piazza Caio Duilio 20; ☺ 8am-2pm Mon-Fri, plus 3.30-6.30pm Tue & Thu) Milazzo's tourist office is just a short walk north of the hydrofoil dock.

❶ Getting There & Away

BOAT

Milazzo is the primary point of departure for ferries and hydrofoils to the Aeolian Islands, with three companies providing year-round service. The main operators – Liberty Lines (p143), Siremar (p143) and NGI (p143) – have ticket offices along Via dei Mille near the port.

BUS

From its stop immediately south of the hydrofoil port, **Giuntabus** (☑ 090 67 37 82; www.giuntabus.com) runs direct seasonal buses to Catania's Fontanarossa Airport (€15, 1¾ hours, two daily April and May, five daily June through September). Its affiliate **Giuntabus Trasporti** (☑ 090 67 57 49; www.giuntabustrasporti.com) offers frequent year-round service to Messina (€4.20, 50 minutes, 18 daily Monday to Friday, 15 on Saturday, three on Sunday), where you can make onward connections to Taormina and other points along the Ionian Coast.

CAR & MOTORCYCLE

Milazzo is situated just off the A20-E90 toll road that travels between Messina and Palermo.

If you want to leave your car in Milazzo while you island-hop, private garages charge around €12 per day. A less expensive alternative is to

TYRRHENIAN COAST MILAZZO

park on the street in spaces marked with blue lines; buy scratch-off parking tickets (€5 per 24hr, available at tobacconists) for as many days as you'll be gone and place them all visibly on your car's dashboard. Short-term street parking (€0.70 per hour) is also available in the same spaces.

TRAIN

Milazzo's **train station** is 3.5km southeast of the port. Trains travel roughly hourly to Messina (€3.80, 20 to 45 minutes) and Capo d'Orlando (€5.10, 35 minutes to one hour). Six to nine daily services also continue west to Cefalù (€8.70, 1¾ to two hours) and Palermo (€11.30, 2½ to 2¾ hours).

 Getting Around

BUS

From AST's **local bus stop** just north of the hydrofoil port, bus 5 runs to Milazzo's train station (€1.50, 10 minutes) half-hourly between 6am and 9pm. Bus 6 runs between the port and Capo Milazzo (€1.50, 15 minutes) every 90 minutes or so between 7.50am and 5.10pm. Note that there is no Sunday service on either route. Tickets (valid for two hours) can be bought from the driver, at local tobacconists (including the shop with the AST sign opposite the quayside bus stop) or inside the train station.

TAXI

A taxi from the station to the port will cost between €10 and €15.

Aeolian Islands

Best Places to Eat

➡ Ristorante La Canna (p166)

➡ Trattoria da Pina (p154)

➡ A Quadara (p156)

➡ Punta Lena (p164)

➡ Sangre Rojo (p150)

➡ Da Alfredo (p156)

Best Hikes

➡ Stromboli Crater (p160)

➡ Pianoconte to Quattropani (p148)

➡ Fossa di Vulcano (p153)

➡ Zucco Grande (p166)

➡ Filo dell'Arpa (p167)

➡ Punta del Corvo (p159)

Why Go?

Rising out of the cobalt-blue seas off Sicily's northeastern coast, the Unesco-protected Aeolian Islands (Vulcano, Lipari, Salina, Panarea, Stromboli, Filicudi and Alicudi) are a little piece of paradise, a seven-island archipelago offering a wealth of opportunities for relaxation and outdoor fun. Stunning waters provide sport for swimmers, sailors, kayakers and divers, while trekkers can climb hissing volcanoes and gourmets can sip honey-sweet Malvasia wine.

The obvious base is Lipari, the largest and liveliest of the seven islands, but it's by no means the only option. Salina boasts excellent accommodation and good transport links, while Stromboli and Vulcano entertain nature lovers with awe-inspiring volcanic shenanigans and black-sand beaches. Chic Panarea offers luxurious living at lower prices in low season, while Filicudi and Alicudi have an end-of-the-line appeal that's irresistible for fans of off-the-beaten-track adventure.

Road Distances (km)

Messina	50			
Milazzo	35	40		
Santa Maria Salina	20	80	65	
Stromboli	45	75	70	45
	Lipari	Messina	Milazzo	Reykjahlið (Mývatn)

Aeolian Islands Highlights

1 Lipari (p144) Digging through five millennia of history at the archaeological museum.

2 Salina (p155) Savouring local wine in the tranquil interior of the Aeolians' lushest island.

3 Stromboli (p160) Watching the volcano erupt at sunset, then hiking back with the moonlit Tyrrhenian Sea glowing far below.

4 Panarea (p158) Lounging poolside on a sunny whitewashed terrace, or exploring the island's five offshore islets.

5 Filicudi (p165) Diving in search of sunken Greek and Roman ships off Capo Graziano.

6 Vulcano (p153) Covering your body with sulphurous ooze in the island's otherworldly mud baths.

7 Alicudi (p166) Escaping to this isolated outpost, where donkeys sometimes outnumber tourists.

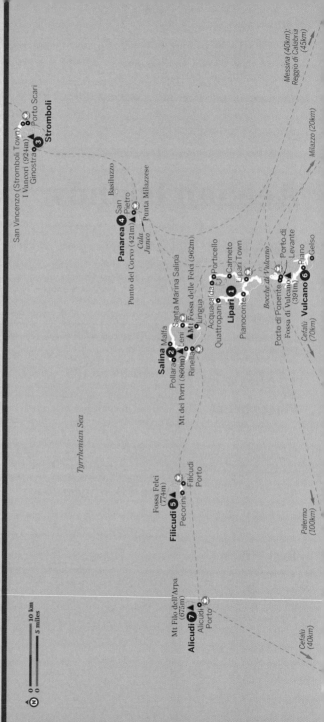

➊ Getting There & Away

Almost all visitors to the Aeolians come by sea. The main point of departure is Milazzo on the Sicilian 'mainland', from where there are regular year-round car ferries and hydrofoils. Lipari is the Aeolians' main point of arrival and its transport hub, with connections to all the other islands. Services are most frequent between June and September and much reduced in winter, when heavy seas can affect schedules. Ferries are cheaper, less frequent and much slower than hydrofoils, although they are less vulnerable to bad weather.

AIR

The only way to reach the Aeolians by air is to take a helicopter. Panarea-based **Air Panarea** (📞 340 3667214; www.airpanarea.com) operates transfers to the Aeolians year-round from Catania, Taormina and other points in Sicily and the Italian mainland. Prices cover the entire six-seat helicopter and vary according to departure point and destination; for details, contact Air Panarea via its online form.

BOAT

Liberty Lines (📞 0923 87 38 13; www.liberty lines.it) operates the lion's share of hydrofoils to the islands, including summer-only services from Palermo that make stops on all seven islands. Check the Liberty Lines website for up-to-the-minute schedules.

Ferry services from Milazzo (cheaper but slower and less frequent than hydrofoil service) are provided by **Siremar** (📞 090 57 37; www. carontetourist.it/en/siremar) and **NGI Traghetti** (📞 090 928 40 91; www.ngi-spa.it).

From Naples, Siremar runs twice-weekly car ferries to the islands (Tuesdays and Fridays southbound, Mondays and Thursdays northbound), while **SNAV** (📞 081 428 55 55; www. snav.it) operates summer-only hydrofoils (Friday through Sunday in June, daily July and August).

BUS

Travellers arriving at Catania's Fontanarossa Airport can reach the Aeolians fairly easily, thanks to regular shuttle bus services. **Eoliebooking** (📞 090 981 42 57; www.eoliebooking.com/navetta) runs direct shuttles to Milazzo's hydrofoil dock (€25 per person, minimum two people, 1¾ hours, up to seven departures daily). **Giuntabus** (📞 090 67 37 82; www.giuntabus.com/milazzo-aeroporto-catania) runs similar direct shuttles in spring and summer (€15, 1¾ hours, two to five daily), along with a slower year-round bus service requiring a transfer in Messina (2½ to 3¾ hours, five to seven departures Monday to Friday, fewer on weekends).

CAR & MOTORCYCLE

Only Lipari, Vulcano, Salina and Filicudi have roads suitable for vehicle traffic. Bringing your own car over to the islands is expensive: from Milazzo to Lipari or Vulcano, the minimum cost is €55 each way; to Salina or Filicudi, it's €72 each way. If you're only visiting the islands for a

AEOLIAN ISLANDS

THREE PERFECT DAYS

Pamper Yourself on Salina

The Aeolians' greenest island struts its stuff at meal times with garden-fresh produce, abundant seafood and locally grown Malvasia wine. Hotels here are among the islands' cushiest. Wake up late to cappuccino with a sea view, indulge in a *ciclo benessere* (spa treatment) at Signum Spa (p156) in Malfa, pack a picnic to photogenic Pollara (p155) or visit one of the local vineyards, then dine at A Cannata (p156), A Quadara (p156), Porto Bello (p157), La Pinnata del Monsù (p157) or any of the island's other standout restaurants.

Scale a Pair of Active Volcanoes

It's not every day you can climb two active volcanoes in less than 24 hours. Here's how: catch an early morning hydrofoil from Lipari to Vulcano, and reach the island's steam-belching summit (p153) by midmorning, before the heat and hordes of day-trippers arrive. Return to Lipari's Marina Corta (p145) for lunch, then hop on a tour boat to Stromboli in time to join your trekking party in the late afternoon. By sunset, you'll be oohing and aahing over the stunning fireworks of Europe's most active volcano (p160). Trek back down for pizza in the piazza, then ride a boat home to your familiar Lipari bed.

Island-Hop Till You Drop

No matter what island you wake up on, a boat tour can expand your horizons in a hurry. Local operators typically offer tours to multiple islands in a single day, offering a taste of the Aeolians' varied personalities even to those with limited time.

HYDROFOILS TO THE AEOLIAN ISLANDS

FROM	TO	COST (€)	DURATION	FREQUENCY
Messina	Lipari	31.10	1½-3½hr	5 daily in summer, 1 daily in winter
Milazzo	Alicudi	32.70	3hr	2-3 daily
Milazzo	Filicudi	27.25	2½hr	2-3 daily
Milazzo	Lipari	20.80	1hr	12-17 daily
Milazzo	Panarea	22.80	1½-2½hr	3-7 daily
Milazzo	Salina	22.55	1½hr	12 daily
Milazzo	Stromboli	25.95	1¼-3hr	3-7 daily
Milazzo	Vulcano	20	45min	12-16 daily

couple of days, you're generally better off leaving your car in a garage in Milazzo (from €12 per day). For longer trips, bringing your own vehicle can still work out cheaper than hiring one, but note that restrictions apply – between July and September you can only take a car if you have booked accommodation for at least seven days. Meanwhile, local buses and scooter- and car-rental outlets are readily available on Lipari, Salina and Vulcano, so leaving your car behind may still be the most convenient option.

LIPARI

✔ 090 / POP 12,800

Lipari is the largest, busiest and most accessible of the Aeolian Islands. Visitors arriving from the mainland will likely experience it as a relaxing introduction to island life; on the other hand, if you've just come from the outer Aeolians, it may feel a bit like a big city!

The main focus is Lipari Town, the archipelago's principal transport hub and the nearest thing that islanders have to a capital city. A busy little port with a pretty, pastel-coloured seafront and plenty of accommodation, it makes the most convenient base for island-hopping. Away from the town, Lipari reveals a rugged and typically Mediterranean landscape of low-lying *macchia* (dense Mediterranean shrubbery), silent, windswept highlands, precipitous cliffs and dreamy blue waters.

History

Named after Liparus, the father-in-law of Aeolus (the Greek god of the winds), Lipari was settled in the 4th millennium BC by the Stentinellians, a middle Neolithic culture with roots in Sicily and Calabria. These early islanders developed a flourishing economy based on obsidian, a glassy volcanic rock used to make primitive tools.

Commerce continued under the Greeks, but the arrival of the Romans in the 3rd century BC signalled the end of the islanders' good fortunes. The Roman authorities were in a vengeful mood after the islanders had sided against them in the First Punic War, and reduced the island to a state of poverty through punitive taxation.

Over the ensuing centuries, volcanic eruptions and pirate attacks – most famously in 1544, when Barbarossa burnt Lipari Town to the ground and took off with most of its female population – kept the islanders in a state of constant fear.

Unremitting poverty ensured large-scale emigration, which continued until well into the 20th century, leaving the island remote and unwanted. During Italy's fascist period in the 1930s, Mussolini used Lipari Town's castle to imprison his political opponents. Things gradually started to improve with the onset of tourism in the 1950s, and now Lipari sits at the heart of one of Sicily's most revered holiday destinations.

◉ Sights

◉ Lipari Town

Although it's the main tourist centre in the Aeolians, Lipari Town hasn't yet sold its soul, and it retains a charming, laid-back island vibe. There are few sights beyond the soaring clifftop citadel and archaeological museum, but it's lovely to stroll the labyrinthine alleyways with the sun on your face and nothing to do but enjoy the relaxed atmosphere. The best approach to the citadel is Via del Concordato, a stairway that leads up from Via Garibaldi to the Cattedrale di San Bartolomeo.

★ Museo Archeologico Regionale Eoliano   MUSEUM

(☏090 988 01 74; www.regione.sicilia.it/benicultur ali/museolipari; Via Castello 2; adult/reduced €6/3; ☺9am-7.30pm Mon-Sat, to 1.30pm Sun) A must-see for Mediterranean history buffs, Lipari's archaeological museum has one of Europe's finest collections of ancient finds. Especially worthwhile are the **Sezione Preistorica**, devoted to locally discovered artefacts from the Neolithic and Bronze Ages to the Graeco-Roman era, and the **Sezione Classica**, the highlights of which include ancient shipwreck cargoes and the world's largest collection of miniature Greek theatrical masks. Pay admission fees at the **ticket office**, about 100m north of the Sezione Classica.

The museum is divided into several sections, each housed in a separate building. Start in the Sezione Preistorica in the Palazzo Vescovile (Bishop's Palace) next to the Cattedrale. A plethora of artefacts displayed in chronological order provides a fascinating insight into the development of the island's earliest cultures. Among the first items on display are finely sculpted tools made from the obsidian on which Lipari's early economy was based – telling evidence of the relative sophistication of the island's prehistoric civilisation. Prehistoric finds from the other islands are housed in a small pavilion directly in front of the Palazzo Vescovile.

On the other side of the cathedral is the Sezione Classica. Highlights here include finds from Lipari's 11th-century BC necropolis, including a sizeable collection of burial urns. There's also a staggering array of amphorae salvaged from shipwrecks off the coasts of Panarea, Filicudi and Lipari itself. Upstairs are impressive displays of decorated vases and the museum's treasured collection of Greek theatrical masks. On this same floor you'll find a number of statuettes – the one of *Andromeda con bambino* (Andromeda with Child) is particularly beautiful – along with some elegant jewellery and a collection of polychromatic vases decorated by an artist simply known as Il Pittore Liparoto (the Lipari Painter; 300–270 BC).

Other sections worth a quick look are the **Sezione Epigrafica** (Epigraphic Section), across the road from the Sezione Preistorica, which has a small garden littered with engraved stones and a room of Greek and Roman tombs; and the **Sezione Vulcano-**

Lipari Island

logica (Vulcanology Section), which illustrates the Aeolians' volcanic geology.

Town Centre   AREA

One of Lipari Town's great pleasures is simply wandering its streets, lapping up the laid-back island atmosphere. Lipari's liveliest street is **Corso Vittorio Emanuele**, a cheerful thoroughfare lined with bars, cafes and restaurants. The street really comes into its own in early evening, when it's closed to traffic and the locals come out for their *passeggiata* (evening stroll). Equally atmospheric is **Marina Corta**, down at the end of Via Garibaldi, a pretty little marina ringed by popular bars and restaurants.

Citadel   FORTRESS

After the pirate Barbarossa rampaged through in 1544, murdering most of Lipari's men and enslaving the women, the island's Spanish overlords fortified Lipari by constructing a citadel (also known as the castle) around the town centre. The town has since moved downhill, but much of the citadel's impregnable wall structure survives; it's an impressive sight, especially when seen from below.

Cattedrale di San Bartolomeo   CHURCH

A fine example of 17th-century baroque architecture, the Aeolians' 'mother church' was built to replace the 11th-century Norman

Lipari Town

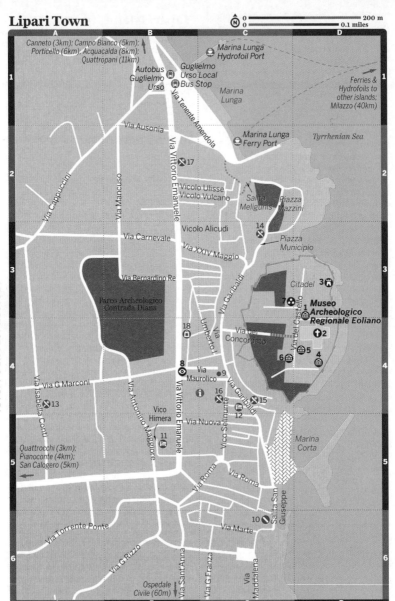

Canneto (3km); Campo Bianco (5km);
Porticello (6km); Acquacalda (8km);
Quattropani (11km)

Marina Lunga
Hydrofoil Port

Autobus
Guglielmo
Urso

Guglielmo
Urso Local
Bus Stop

Ferries &
Hydrofoils to
other islands;
Milazzo (40km)

Marina
Lunga

Via Ausonia

Marina Lunga
Ferry Port

Tyrrhenian Sea

Via Tenente Amendola

Via Vittorio Emanuele

17

Vicolo Ulisse
Vicolo Vulcano

Salita
Meligunìs

Piazza
Mazzini

Via Cappuccini

Via Mancuso

Vicolo Alicudi

Via Carnevale

14

Via XXIV Maggio

Piazza
Municipio

Via Bernardino Re

Parco Archeologico
Contrada Diana

Citadel

3

7

Museo
Archeologico
Regionale Eoliano

Via Garibaldi

Via del Castello

18

Via
Umberto I

Via del
Concordato

1

2

6

5

4

8

Via
Maurolico

9

Via G Marconi

Via Isabella Conti

13

Via Antonino Maggiore

Vico
Himera

16

Via Garibaldi

15

Vico Selinunte

12

11

Via Nuova

Marina
Corta

Quattrocchi (3km);
Pianoconte (4km);
San Calogero (5km)

Via Vittorio Emanuele

Via Roma

Via Roma

Salita San
Giuseppe

Via Torrente Ponte

10

Via Marte

Via G Rizzo

Via Sant'Anna

Via G Franza

Via
Maddalena

Ospedale
Civile (60m)

cathedral destroyed by Barbarossa. Little remains of the original except a section of Benedictine cloister to the right of the entrance. The interior features a silver statue of St Bartholomew (1728), Lipari's patron saint, with his flayed skin tucked under his arm.

Parco Archeologico

RUINS

In the sunken area opposite Lipari's cathedral, you can see the remains of a series of circular huts, the oldest of which date to the 17th century BC. Nearby, at the southern end of the citadel, you'll find some Greek

Lipari Town

sarcophagi adjacent to an open-air amphitheatre that was built in 1978.

◉ Around Lipari

Lipari's main sights, most notably the archaeological museum, are in Lipari Town, and there's enough going on that you could conceivably never leave the city limits. However, to find the best swimming and hiking spots and enjoy some sensational views, it's well worth exploring the island's rugged hinterland.

★ Quattrocchi VIEWPOINT
Lipari's best coastal views are from a celebrated viewpoint known as Quattrocchi (Four Eyes), 3km west of town. Follow the road for Pianoconte and look on your left as you approach a big hairpin bend about 300m beyond the turnoff for Spiaggia Valle Muria. Stretching off to the south, great cliffs plunge into the sea, while in the distance plumes of sinister smoke rise from the dark heights of neighbouring Vulcano.

★ Spiaggia Valle Muria BEACH
Lapped by clean waters and surrounded by sheer cliffs, this dark, pebbly beach on Lipari's southwestern shore is a dramatically beautiful swimming and sunbathing spot. From the signposted turnoff, 3km west of Lipari town towards Pianoconte, it's a steep 25-minute downhill walk; come prepared with water and sunscreen. In good weather, Lipari resident **Barni** (☑ 339 8221583, 349 1839555) sells refreshments from his rustic cave-like beach bar, and provides memorably scenic boat transfers to and from Lipari's Marina Corta (€5/10 one-way/return).

The turn-off is easily reached by car, scooter or local bus from Lipari Town. The path down to the beach starts as a paved road, but eventually narrows to a dirt trail, passing through a rugged landscape of long grass, flowers and cacti. Slogging back up the hill is a real workout, so it's preferable to arrange return boat transit with Barni beforehand. Navigating through the *faraglione* (rock towers) of Lipari's western shore at sunset, with Vulcano's crater smoking on the horizon, is an unforgettable experience, and the perfect way to return home after a long day on the beach.

L'Osservatorio VIEWPOINT
Down near Lipari's southwesternmost tip, this high perch commands unparalleled views south to Vulcano (backed by Mt Etna on a clear day), and west into a dizzyingly steep ravine (stay away from the edge!) backed by the islands of Alicudi and Filicudi at sunset. You'll need your own vehicle or strong lungs and legs to get up here. Park at the end of the road and follow the dirt path out onto the headland for the best views.

Spiaggia di Canneto BEACH
The nearest beach to Lipari Town, and the most popular swimming spot on the island, is the long, pebbly strip at Canneto, 3km north of town on the other side of a jutting headland.

Campo Bianco MINE
A few kilometres north of the beach at Canneto lies the Campo Bianco quarry, where huge gashes of white rock streak down the green hillside. These are the result of extensive pumice quarrying, which was an

AEOLIAN ISLANDS LIPARI

important local industry until 2000, when Unesco called for curtailment of mining operations as a condition for granting World Heritage status to the Aeolians.

Spiaggia della Papesca   BEACH
Below Campo Bianco and the abandoned pumice mines at Porticello, this pebble beach is nicknamed Spiaggia Bianca in reference to the layers of white pumice dust that once covered it. These have been slowly washed away by the rough winter seas, leaving it a dark shade of grey. However, residual pumice still gives the sea a limpid turquoise colour here.

🏃 Activities

Hiking
Away from the more obvious coastal pleasures, there's some lovely hiking on Lipari, especially along the rugged northern and western coastlines. Most walks involve fairly steep slopes, although the summer heat is as likely to wear you down as the terrain. Take all the usual precautions: a hat, sunscreen, plenty of water, and try to avoid the midday sun.

★ Pianoconte to Quattropani   HIKING
This three- to four-hour hike starts from Pianoconte's school (5km west of Lipari Town), descending toward the sea along a paved road, which eventually narrows to a trail. Levelling out along the coastal bluffs, a relatively flat section skirts Lipari's western shoreline, affording fabulous views of Salina, Vulcano, Filicudi and Alicudi, before climbing steeply to the town of Quattropani.

As you descend from Pianoconte, you'll pass the old Roman baths of **San Calogero**, famous in antiquity for the thermal spring that flowed at a constant temperature of 60°C. Climbing back to Quattropani, you'll also pass the **Old Kaolin Mine**, where the hillside is still visibly scarred. The trail can just as easily be hiked in the opposite direction, starting just south of the town of Quattropani. Either way, the strenuous climbs and steep descents are rewarded with spectacular coastal scenery. Both ends of the trail can be reached by local bus – on the way there, ask the driver to let you off at the trailhead; returning, look for the official bus stop in either Pianoconte or Quattropani.

Quattropani to Acquacalda   WALKING
The pleasant hour-long downhill stroll from Quattropani to Acquacalda follows a paved but lightly travelled road hugging Lipari's north shore, affording spectacular views of Salina and a distant Stromboli. Take the bus to Quattropani (€2.40), then simply proceed downhill on the main road 5km to Acquacalda, where you can catch the bus (€1.55) back to Lipari Town.

Diving
Lipari's crystalline waters provide plenty of sport for snorkellers and scuba divers.

Diving Center La Gorgonia   DIVING
(☑ 090 981 26 16; www.lagorgoniadiving.it; Salita San Giuseppe; per dive with own/rented equipment €40/60, courses €70-750) This outfit offers courses, boat transport, equipment hire and general information about scuba diving and snorkelling around Lipari. See the website for a complete price list.

DON'T MISS

DIVING SPOTS AROUND LIPARI

Lipari's got some spectacular spots for divers to explore. The folks at Diving Center La Gorgonia can point you to the following spots and many more:

Punta Castagna (difficult; depth 10m to 40m) A spectacular dive with a 10m white pumice platform interrupted by multicoloured channels.

Secca del Bagno (difficult; depth 40m to 45m) A breathtaking collection of colourful walls that are swathed with schools of technicolour fish.

Pietra Menalda (medium; depth 18m to 40m) See the homes of octopuses, eels, groupers and other sea critters on the southern side of the island.

Pietra del Bagno (all levels; 20m to 40m) Circumnavigate the Bagno rock, while witnessing colourful rock surfaces and sea life.

La Parete dei Gabbiani (medium; 20m to 45m) A black-and-white dive: black lava rock streaked with white pumice stone, hiding cracks that are home to lobsters.

☞ Tours

A boat tour around Lipari is a good way of seeing the island, and the only way of getting to some of the more inaccessible swimming spots. Lipari's high concentration of tour operators also makes it a great base for day trips to the outer Aeolian islands.

Numerous agencies in town offer tours. Prices vary depending on the season, but as a rough guide allow €20 for a tour of Lipari and Vulcano, €45 to visit Filicudi and Alicudi, €45 for a day trip to Panarea and Stromboli, or €80 for a late-afternoon trip to Stromboli with a guided walk up the mountain at sunset and a late-night return to Lipari. Tour companies generally operate from March to October.

Da Massimo/Dolce Vita　　　BOATING
(☑090 601 98 41; www.damassimo.it; Via Maurolico 2) One of Lipari's best-established agencies, down a side street between Corso Vittorio Emanuele and Via Garibaldi. Specialises in sunset hikes to the top of Stromboli, returning by boat to Lipari the same evening. Also hires boats and dinghies.

✸ Festivals & Events

Easter　　　RELIGIOUS
Heartfelt and theatrical, Lipari's traditional Easter (Pasqua) celebrations begin on Palm Sunday with the **Via Crucis**, a candle-lit procession from Piazza Mazzini to the citadel, culminating in a re-enactment of the crucifixion. On Good Friday, groups of barefoot penitents accompany statues of Christ around town in an atmosphere of funereal silence.

Easter Day is more light-hearted, with two processions, one headed by the resurrected Jesus and the other by the Virgin Mary, meeting in Marina Corta to fireworks and noisy rejoicing.

✗ Eating

✗ Lipari Town

Lipari's town centre is packed with restaurants, bars, cafes and gelaterie; many line the edges of Corso Vittorio Emanuele and Via Garibaldi, the twin thoroughfares running north–south between Marina Lunga and Marina Corta, while others are tucked enticingly into side alleys along the way.

Gilberto e Vera　　　SANDWICHES €
(☑090 981 27 56; www.gilbertoevera.it; Via Garibaldi 22; half/full sandwiches €3.50/5; ☉7.30am-11pm

mid-Mar–mid-Nov) Still run by the friendly couple who founded it four decades ago (ably assisted by daughter Alessia), this beloved shop sells two dozen varieties of *panini,* many named for now-grown locals who once stopped by here on their way to school. It's the perfect stop for morning hiking and beach-hopping provisions, or afternoon glasses of wine on the street-side terrace.

L'Officina del Cannolo　　　SEAFOOD €€
(☑090 981 34 70; www.officinadelcannolo.com; Corso Vittorio Emanuele 214; meals €30-45; ☉noon-2.30pm & 7.30-10pm Tue-Sun) On Lipari's main pedestrian thoroughfare, just down from the ferry port, L'Officina incorporates fresh-caught seafood into appetisers (mussel soup, squid salad), *primi* (homemade pasta with swordfish, capers, tomatoes, olives and basil) and *secondi* (seared tuna in a pistachio crust); but the real show-stopper is its namesake *cannoli,* made with creamy ricotta from Vulcano and a light crunchy shell.

E Pulera　　　MODERN SICILIAN €€
(☑090 981 11 58; www.pulera.it; Via Isabella Conti; meals €35-45; ☉7.30-11.30pm late Apr–mid-Oct) With its serene garden setting, low lighting, tile-topped tables and exquisite food – from tuna carpaccio with blood oranges and capers for dinner to *cassata* (sponge cake, ricotta, marzipan, chocolate and candied fruit) served with sweet Malvasia wine for dessert – E Pulera makes an upscale but relaxed choice for a romantic dinner.

Filippino　　　SICILIAN €€
(☑090 981 10 02; www.filippino.it; Piazza Mazzini; meals €33-45; ☉noon-3pm & 7-11pm, closed Mon Oct-Mar) Going strong for over a century, Filippino is a mainstay of Lipari's culinary scene, widely considered the island's finest restaurant. Housed in a glass pavilion adjacent to the citadel, its army of white-coated waitstaff serves a dizzying array of Sicilian classics and home-grown innovations, from savoury fish stews to jasmine mousse for dessert. Smart-casual attire and advance bookings recommended.

Kasbah　　　MEDITERRANEAN €€
(☑090 921 37 42; www.kasbahlipari.it; Vico Selinunte 43; pizzas €10-12, meals €35, tasting menu €45; ☉7-10.30pm Apr-Oct) Tucked down narrow Vico Selinunte, with a window where you can watch the chefs at work, this place serves everything from fancy pasta, fish and meat dishes to simple wood-fired pizzas (try the Kasbah, with smoked swordfish, rocket,

lemon and black pepper). The stylish dining room with its grey linen tablecloths is complemented by a more casual outdoor terrace.

✖ Around Lipari

The lion's share of restaurants are concentrated in Lipari Town, but you'll also find eating options in outlying communities such as Canneto, Quattropani, Pianoconte and Acquacalda. Many restaurants close during the winter season between late October and Easter.

★ Sangre Rojo   SICILIAN €€
(📋338 2909524; www.facebook.com/ristorante sangrerojo; meals €34-39; ◔noon-2.30pm & 7pm-midnight Wed-Mon Easter–mid-Oct) Dazzling vistas of Salina, Filicudi and Alicudi floating in the Tyrrhenian are reason enough to visit this hilltop restaurant near Lipari's northern tip. But the cuisine, based on fresh fish and classic Aeolian ingredients like wild fennel, capers, olives and mint, is the real clincher. Enjoy lunch on the sun-drenched terrace or linger over dinner with a sunset view.

Le Macine   SICILIAN €€
(📋090 982 23 87; www.lemacine.org; SP 179, Pianoconte; meals €30-45, pizzas €5-8.50; ◔noon-2.30pm & 7-10pm daily May-Sep, Sat & Sun Oct-Apr) This country restaurant in Pianoconte, 4.5km from Lipari Town, comes into its own in summer, when meals are served on the terrace. Seafood and fresh vegetables star in dishes such as swordfish cakes with artichokes, shrimp-filled ravioli or fish in *ghiotta* sauce (with olive oil, capers, tomatoes, garlic and basil). Call ahead to request its free shuttle service from Lipari Town.

☖ Drinking & Nightlife

Marina Corta is the most scenic spot to people-watch while chilling out over a cool drink; grab an outdoor seat at one of the touristy bars lining the waterfront square. Corso Vittorio Emanuele is the other big hot spot for early-evening *aperitivi*.

🔒 Shopping

Fratelli Laise   FOOD & DRINKS
(📋090 981 27 31; www.fratellilaise.com; Corso Vittorio Emanuele 118; ◔7am-1pm & 4-8.30pm) About two-thirds of the way down from Marina Lunga to Marina Corta, a lush, technicolour fruit display announces the presence of this traditional greengrocer, piled high with wines, sweets, *anis* (aniseed) biscuits, pâtés, capers and olive oils. It's an excellent place to find gifts to bring home – or simply to stock up on picnic provisions.

❶ Information

Farmacia Sparacino (📋090 981 13 92; Corso Vittorio Emanuele 176; ◔8.30am-1pm & 4-8pm Mon-Fri)

Hospital (Ospedale Civile; 📋090 988 51 11; Via Sant'Anna) First-aid and emergency services.

Police Station (📋090 981 13 33; Via Madre Florenzia Profilio)

Tourist Office (📋090 988 00 95; Via Maurolico 17; ◔9am-1pm Mon-Fri, plus 4-6pm Wed & Fri) Lipari's sporadically staffed office provides information covering all of the Aeolian Islands.

❶ Getting There & Away

Lipari's main port is Marina Lunga, at the north edge of Lipari Town. Here you'll find the **ticket office** (📋090 981 24 48; ◔5am-8.40pm) for hydrofoil operator Liberty Lines and ferry operators NGI and Siremar. Hydrofoils run frequently to the mainland port of Milazzo (€15.80, one hour) and to the other Aeolian islands: Vulcano (€5.80, 10 minutes), Santa Marina Salina (€8.80, 20 minutes), Panarea (€10.40, one hour), Stromboli (€17.80, 1½ to 1¾ hours), Filicudi (€15.80, one to 1¼ hours) and Alicudi (€18.85, 1½ to two hours). There's also hydrofoil services to Messina (€26.10, 1½ to 3¼ hours, five daily in summer, one daily in winter). Ferry services are less expensive but much slower and less frequent.

In summer (late May through early September), SNAV (p143) also offers daily hydrofoil services from Naples to Lipari (from €62, 6½ hours).

Schedules for all companies are posted prominently outside the Marina Lunga ticket office.

Lipari's other port, Marina Corta, on the southern side of the clifftop citadel, is used exclusively by tour boats.

❶ Getting Around

BUS

Autobus Guglielmo Urso (📋090 981 10 26; www.ursobus.com/Orario-ita.htm) runs buses all over the island from its bus stop opposite the Marina Lunga hydrofoil dock. One main route serves the island's eastern shore, from Lipari Town to Canneto (five minutes) and Acquacalda (20 minutes); another runs from Lipari Town to the Quattrocchi viewpoint and the western highland settlements of Pianoconte and Quattropani. Individual tickets range in price from €1.30 to €2.40. If you're making multiple trips, you'll save money by buying a round-trip ticket (discounted roughly 20%) or a ticket booklet (six/10/20 tickets for €10/14/28). Service is limited to nonexistent on Sundays.

CAR & MOTORCYCLE

Lipari is not big – only 38 sq km – but to explore it in depth it can be helpful to have your own wheels. The seafront road circles the entire island, a journey of about 30km. Various outfits opposite the Marina Lunga hydrofoil dock rent out bikes, scooters and cars, including **Da Marcello** (☑ 090 981 12 34; www.noleggiodamarcello.com; Via Amendola). Allow about €10 per day for a bike, between €15 and €40 per day for a scooter, and from €30 to €70 per day for a small car.

VULCANO

POP 720

With its visibly smoking crater and vile sulphurous fumes, Vulcano makes an indelible first impression. The island's volcanic nature has long been impressing visitors: the ancient Romans believed it to be the chimney of the fire god Vulcan's workshop, and today it remains famous for its therapeutic mud baths and hot springs. The main drawcard, however, remains the Fossa di Vulcano (Gran Cratere), the steaming volcano that towers over the island's northeastern shores.

Vulcano's most obvious attractions – climbing the crater, strolling over to the mud baths and the black beaches at Porto di Ponente – are easily managed on a day trip from Lipari. Visitors who linger and explore beyond touristy Porto di Levante will discover a whole different island, swimming off Gelso's volcanic beaches, kayaking the wild coast or enjoying the rural tranquillity of the central plateau, filled with vegetable gardens, birdsong and a surprising amount of greenery.

◎ Sights

★ Capo Grillo   VIEWPOINT

For spectacular sea and island views without the physical exertion of climbing Fossa di Vulcano, follow the signposted road to Capo Grillo, about 7km southeast of Vulcano port, near the mid-island settlement of Piano. From here you'll get breathtaking perspectives on Lipari and Salina, with Panarea, Stromboli and Filicudi floating off in the distance.

Spiaggia Sabbie Nere   BEACH

Vulcano's beach scene is centred on this smooth strip of black sand at Porto di Po-

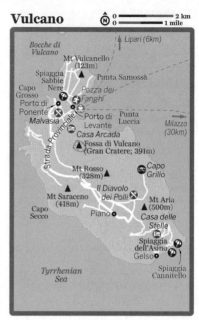

Vulcano

nente, about 10 minutes' walk beyond the mud pools on the western side of the peninsula. One of the few sandy beaches in the Aeolians, it's a scenic spot, curving around a bay of limpid, glassy waters out of which rise jutting *faraglioni* (rock towers).

From the beach, a road traverses a small isthmus to **Vulcanello** (123m), a bulb of land that was spewed out by a volcanic eruption in 183 BC. Here you'll find the famous **Valle dei Mostri** (Valley of the Monsters), a group of wind-eroded dark rocks that have formed grotesque shapes.

Gelso   AREA

On the island's southern coast, down a sinuous, narrow paved road, Gelso is a minuscule but picturesque port with a pair of family-run restaurants and a couple of black-sand beaches that rarely get very crowded. In summer there's a bus service to get there, but you'll be much better off hiring a car or scooter, as services are limited and it's a 15km walk back if you get stranded.

West of the port a trail runs a few hundred metres to the 18th-century church of **Santa Maria delle Grazie** and an abandoned **lighthouse**. Just uphill (north) from the port, a steep dirt track (pedestrians only) branches off to **Spiaggia dell'Asino** (Donkey Beach), a crescent of black sand giving onto

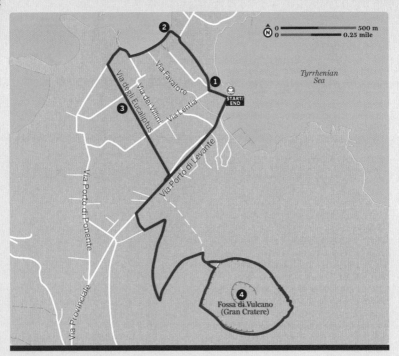

Tyrrhenian Sea

Fossa di Vulcano
(Gran Cratere)

Walking Tour
From the Mud Baths to the Crater

START PORTO DI LEVANTE
END PORTO DI LEVANTE
LENGTH 9KM; FOUR HOURS

This walk brings you face to face with all of Vulcano's best-known sights in one exhilarating afternoon. Starting from the hydrofoil dock, walk 100m due west past the dramatic *faraglione* (rock spire) that towers above the port, and brace yourself for the stench of rotten eggs as you approach the ❶ **Pozza dei Fanghi**. Long the island's favourite beauty spot, this pool of thick, coffee-coloured mud is usually filled with curious swimsuit-clad tourists.

Continue less than 10 minutes northwest across the isthmus to reach Vulcano's famous black-sand beach, ❷ **Spiaggia Sabbie Nere** (p151). Cradled in a graceful curve of the shoreline, it's one of the Aeolians' few sandy beaches and a favourite swimming spot.

Next, stop in for lunch at ❸ **Malvasia** (p154), maker of what many consider to be the best *pane cunzatu* (traditional Aeolian open-faced sandwich) in the entire archipela-

go. The homemade bread here, brushed with extra virgin olive oil to create a delightfully light crunch, is topped with insane quantities of the islands' finest ingredients: tuna, ricotta, olives, capers, cherry tomatoes, basil and more. Unless you're ravenous, share one with a friend – accompanied by a glass of the Aeolians' renowned Malvasia wine.

Thus fortified, you're ready for the afternoon's main event: an ascent of Vulcano's smoking ❹ **crater**. Splendid views of the island unfold as the wide zigzag path takes you gently up the volcano's ruddy, sulphur-streaked slopes. A climb of less than 300m brings you to the rim, where you can peer down into the crater's otherworldly depths, a spot long mythologised by the Romans as Vulcan's forge.

For even more spectacular views, continue counterclockwise around the crater's rim. From the volcano's southern edge, you can see all six other Aeolian islands lined up on the northern horizon, with the gaping crater in the foreground. End the walk by retracing your steps downhill to the port.

inviting waters. A second beach, **Spiaggia Cannitello**, is surrounded by lush, almost tropical greenery. Both beaches have rudimentary bar-cafes in summer, where you can hire sun loungers and umbrellas.

🏃 Activities

⭐ Fossa di Vulcano
HIKING

Vulcano's star attraction is the straightforward trek up its 391m volcano (no guide required). Start early if possible and bring a hat, sunscreen and water. Follow the signs south along Strada Provinciale, then turn left onto the zigzag gravel track that leads to the summit. It's a 30- to 60-minute climb to the lowest point of the volcano's rim (290m), where you'll be rewarded with fine views of the steaming crater encrusted with red and yellow crystals.

It's well worth lingering up top and climbing another 15 minutes around to the southern rim for stunning views of the other Aeolian islands lined up on the northern horizon, with the gaping crater in the foreground. The truly ambitious can descend steeply to the crater floor (but beware of hot steam vents and the accompanying toxic fumes).

Pozza dei Fanghi
HOT SPRINGS

(Mud Baths; 📞 338 8335514; www.geoterme.it; admission €3, shower/towel €1/2.60; ⊙ 7am-10pm Jul & Aug, 8am-7.45pm late Mar-Jun & Sep-early Nov) Backed by a *faraglione* (rock tower) and stinking of rotten eggs, Vulcano's harbourside pool of thick, coffee-coloured sulphurous gloop isn't exactly a five-star beauty farm. But the warm (29°C) mud is considered an excellent treatment for rheumatic pains and skin diseases, and rolling around in it can be fun if you don't mind smelling funny for a few days. Keep the mud away from your eyes (as the sulphur is acidic and can damage the cornea) and hair.

Once you have had time to relax in the muddy water, get some soft clay from the bottom of the pool and apply it to your body and face. Wait for the clay mask to dry, wash it off in the pool, then run to the natural spa around the corner, where there are hot, bubbling springs in a small natural seawater pool.

⭐ Sprint da Luigi
CYCLING

(📞 347 7600275; www.nolosprintdaluigi.com; Porto di Levante; bike/electric bike/scooter/car rental per day from €7/20/25/50) Long-time residents and wonderful all-around human beings Luigi and Nidra rent out high-quality bicy-

---

ℹ️ MUD BATH TIPS

➡ Don't stay in longer than 10 or 15 minutes – the water and mud is slightly radioactive. Pregnant women should avoid it altogether.

➡ Keep the mud away from your hair and eyes (the sulphur is acidic).

➡ Don't use your favourite fluffy towel or one you've 'borrowed' from a hotel – most hotels will provide a special *fanghi* towel on request.

➡ If you have a sulphite allergy, stay away.

➡ Remember to remove watches and jewellery.

➡ Take flip-flops or sandals – there are hot air vents that can scald your feet.

➡ Wear a swimsuit you don't mind destroying: once the smell gets in, it's easier to buy a new one than to get rid of the pong.

---

cles (both traditional and electric) and trekking gear, and offer top-notch, multilingual advice about exploring the island. If you're feeling less energetic, they can also set you up with a car or a scooter. Ask about their rental apartment (€40 to €70) in Vulcano's tranquil interior.

Diving Center Saraceno
DIVING

(📞 347 7283341; www.scuolasubpalermo.it; Resort Mari del Sud, Via Porto Ponente; snorkelling €35, dives incl equipment from €50; ⊙ Easter-Oct) This local dive centre offers a range of dives, plus snorkelling excursions that focus on Vulcano's many marine caves and subterranean hot springs. It also sponsors the **Vulcano Dive Festival** (www.vulcanodivefestival.it) in late June.

Centro Nautica Baia di Levante
BOATING

(📞 339 3372795; www.baialevante.it; ⊙ Apr-Oct) To explore Vulcano's waters on your own, rent boats from this agency 200m south of the hydrofoil dock.

👉 Tours

Sicily in Kayak
BOATING

(📞 329 5381229; www.sicilyinkayak.com; excursions from €55) Kayaking enthusiast Eugenio Viviani heads this home-grown outfit offering everything from half-day explorations of Vulcano's sea caves to multiday paddling excursions visiting multiple islands in the Aeolian archipelago. Recent new initiatives include sailing tours and stand-up paddleboard excursions down Lipari's dramatic west coast. See the website or contact Eugenio directly for full details.

Eating

★ Malvasia
SANDWICHES €

(☑346 6039439; www.ristorantemalvasiavulcano.it; Via degli Eucaliptus; sandwiches from €12; ⊙11.30am-2.30pm & 7.30-11pm late Apr-early Oct) After years selling open-faced sandwiches from a cart near Vulcano's port, jovial owner Maurizio Pagano opened this popular restaurant and wine bar in 2015. Bask on the sunny front patio and enjoy his trademark *pane cunzatu eoliano* (tuna, olives, capers, tomatoes and buffalo-milk mozzarella on delectable toasted homemade bread drenched in extra-virgin olive oil), or go for salads and daily specials.

★ Trattoria da Pina
SEAFOOD €€

(☑368 668555; Gelso; meals €29-32; ⊙12.30-2.30pm & 8-9.45pm Apr–mid-Oct) With sea-blue tablecloths and an intimate outdoor porch overlooking the black-sand beach at Vulcano's southern tip, this down-to-earth trattoria serves up delicious pasta and fresh-caught fish in a wonderful end-of-the-line setting. Two local men do the fishing, and their families do the cooking. Save room for scrumptious desserts such as pistachio *semifreddo*, or homemade biscotti and sweet Malvasia wine.

La Forgia Maurizio
SICILIAN €€

(☑334 7660069; www.laforgiamaurizio.it; Strada Provinciale 45, Porto di Levante; meals €30-45; ⊙12.30-3pm & 7-11pm; ☑) Maurizio, owner of this devilishly good restaurant between the port and the volcano, spent 20 winters in Goa, India. Eastern influences sneak into his menu of Sicilian specialities, and several items are vegan- or vegetarian-friendly. Check out the multicourse tasting menu (€30 including wine, water and dessert), finished off with *liquore di kumquat e cardamom*, Maurizio's homemade answer to *limoncello* (lemon liqueur).

Maria Tindara
SICILIAN €€

(☑090 985 30 04; www.mariatindaravulcano.it; Strada Provinciale 37, Piano; meals €25-35; ⊙12.30-2.30pm & 8-10pm) On Vulcano's fertile central plateau, 7km south of the port, this family-run restaurant serves delicious *caponata* (sweet-and-sour vegetable salad) and homemade pasta alongside mountain specialities such as grilled lamb. With locals hanging out at the bar up front, it's a pleasant antidote to Porto di Levante's tourist-thronged eateries. Snacks of local cheese and capers (€7) are also offered to refuel hungry hikers and cyclists.

ℹ Information

Emergency Doctor (Guardia Medica; ☑090 985 22 20, 335 7662988; Via Favaloro, Porto di Levante; ⊙24hr)

Farmacia Bonarrigo (☑090 985 22 44; Via Favaloro 1, Porto di Levante; ⊙9am-1pm & 4-8pm Mon-Fri, 9am-1pm Sat)

Police (☑090 985 21 10; Strada Provinciale)

ℹ Getting There & Around

Of the seven Aeolian islands, Vulcano is closest to the mainland, meaning that hydrofoil services here are especially frequent, with departures every hour or so; all Lipari-bound boats from Milazzo or Messina stop here first.

BIKE

Bikes can be hired from Sprint da Luigi (p153), who can also organise island tours.

BOAT

Vulcano is an intermediate stop between Milazzo (ferry/hydrofoil €12.30/€15, 1¼ hours/50 minutes) and Lipari (ferry/hydrofoil €6.20/€5.80, 25 minutes/10 minutes), with frequent service in both directions. Liberty Lines (p143) and Siremar (p143) are the main hydrofoil and ferry operators, respectively. Beyond Lipari, most boats continue to the outer Aeolian Islands.

Alternatively, you can travel from Naples to Vulcano aboard Siremar's biweekly ferry (from €58, 14½ to 16½ hours), or catch the daily, summer-only hydrofoil (from €62, 6¼ hours) operated by SNAV (p143).

Ticket offices (☑090 985 22 30; ⊙6.15am-8pm Mon-Sat, from 6.40am Sun) for all companies are just south of the **dock** at Porto di Levante.

BUS

Scaffidi Bus (Vulcania Tour; ☑338 6961723, 090 985 30 73) runs buses around the island. There's year-round service from Porto di Levante to Porto di Ponente (€2), Piano (€2.50) and Capo Grillo (€2.50, 20 minutes, five Monday to Saturday, two Sunday). From mid-June to mid-September, buses also run to Gelso (€2.80, 40 minutes, around three daily). There's a timetable posted at the main bus stop, at the beginning of Strada Provinciale near the hydrofoil dock. Buy tickets on the bus.

If you're going to the beaches at Gelso, ask the driver to let you off at the dirt track.

CAR & MOTORCYCLE

Sprint da Luigi (p153) Rent some wheels from this well-signposted outfit just south of the port.

TAXI

Santi (📞366 3028712; www.taxivulcanosanti tour.com) Provides taxi service as well as guided trips around the island. Call ahead to negotiate rates.

SALINA

POP 4000

In delightful contrast to the exposed volcanic terrain of the other Aeolians, Salina – the archipelago's second largest island – boasts a lush, verdant landscape thanks to its natural freshwater springs. Woodlands, wildflowers, thick yellow gorse bushes and serried ranks of grape vines carpet its hillsides, while high coastal cliffs plunge into the breaking waters below.

Named for the *saline* (salt works) of Lingua at the island's southeastern edge, Salina is shaped by two extinct volcanoes, Monte dei Porri (860m) and Monte Fossa delle Felci (962m), two of the Aeolians' highest peaks. These form a natural barrier in the centre of the island, ensuring that the sleepy villages around the perimeter retain their own individual character. Tourism is most evident in the main port of Santa Marina Salina; elsewhere there's a distinct sense that the rest of the world is a long way away. If that sounds good, you'll love Salina.

☉ Sights

Some of the best swimming spots in the area are only accessible by sea, so you'll need to sign up for a boat tour or hire a boat for yourself. **Salina Relax Boats** (📞345 2162308; www.salinarelaxboats.com; Piazza Santa Marina 4, Santa Marina Salina; tours per person €60-70) offers various tours of Salina and the other islands; it also hires out boats and runs a water-taxi service.

Santa Marina Salina   VILLAGE

Salina's main port, Santa Marina is a typical island settlement with steeply stacked whitewashed houses rising up the hillside. The principal street is Via Risorgimento, a lively pedestrian-only strip lined with cafes

and boutiques. It's not a big place, and there are no specific sights, but it makes an ideal base for exploring the rest of the island.

Malfa   VILLAGE

Tumbling down the hillside to a small shingle beach, this settlement on Salina's north coast is the island's largest, though you'd never guess it from the tranquil atmosphere. About halfway between the town entrance and the sea is the main church square, the focal point of Malfa's laid-back social life, from which sloping lanes fan up and down the hillsides.

Pollara   VILLAGE

Don't miss a trip to sleepy Pollara, sandwiched dramatically between the sea and the steep slopes of an extinct volcanic crater on Salina's western edge. The gorgeous **beach** here was used as a location in the 1994 film *Il Postino,* although the land access route to the beach has since been closed due to landslide danger.

You can still descend the steep stone steps at the northwest end of town and swim across to the beach, or simply admire the spectacular view, with its backdrop of volcanic cliffs.

Lingua   VILLAGE

Three kilometres south of Santa Marina Salina, the tiny village of Lingua is a popular summer hang-out, with a couple of hotels, a few trattorias and a small beach. Its main feature is the **salt lagoon**, which sits under an old lighthouse at the end of the village. The centre of the summer scene is seafront Piazza Marina Garibaldi.

Until quite recently the salt works were an important local employer, but now the lagoon only provides sustenance for the migrating birds that pass through in spring and autumn en route to and from Africa. Lingua's most famous business venture these days is Da Alfredo (p156), a bar-gelateria famous across Sicily for its flavourful *granite.*

Rinella   VILLAGE

This tiny hamlet on the south coast is Salina's second port, regularly served by hydrofoils and ferries. Pastel-coloured houses huddle around the waterfront, and there are a couple of decent swimming spots nearby. If the sandy beach by the village centre gets too cramped, follow the path to Punta Megna, from where you can access the pebbly **Spiaggia Pra Venezia**.

AEOLIAN ISLANDS SALINA

Salina

Spiaggia di Pollara
Malfa
Capofaro
Pollara
Panarea (20km); Stromboli (40km)
Monte dei Porri (860m)▲
Fenech
Santa Marina Salina
Valdichiesa
Leni
Monte Fossa delle Felci (962m) ▲
Lipari (10km)
Spiaggia Pra Venezia
Rinella
Lingua
Filicudi (22km); Alicudi (40km)
Tyrrhenian Sea
Lipari (10km)

🏃 Activities

★ Monte Fossa delle Felci   HIKING

For jaw-dropping views, climb to the Aeolians' highest point, Monte Fossa delle Felci (962m). The two-hour ascent starts from the **Santuario della Madonna del Terzito**, an imposing 19th-century church at Valdichiesa, in the valley separating the island's two volcanoes. Up top, gorgeous perspectives unfold on the symmetrically arrayed volcanic cones of Monte dei Porri, Filicudi and a distant Alicudi.

From the sanctuary – an important place of pilgrimage for islanders, particularly around the Feast of the Assumption on 15 August – you can follow a signposted track up through pine and chestnut woodlands and fields of ferns, all the way to the top. Along the way you'll see plenty of colourful flora, including wild violets, asparagus and a plant known locally as *cipudazza* (Latin *Urginea marittima*), which was sold to the Calabrians to make soap, but is used locally as mouse poison!

Once you've reached the summit (the last 100m are particularly tough), the views are breathtaking, particularly looking west towards Filicudi and Alicudi and also from the southeast ridge where you can look down over the Lingua salt lagoon and over to Lipari and Vulcano.

To get to the trailhead by public transport, take the bus from Santa Marina Salina to Malfa, then change for a Rinella-bound bus and ask the driver to let you off at Valdichiesa (look for the church on the left side of the bus as you crest the hill between Malfa and Rinella).

★ Signum Spa   SPA

(Salus Per Aquam; ☑ 090 984 42 22; www.hotel signum.it; Via Scalo 15, Malfa; €30, treatments extra; ⊙10am-8pm Apr-Sep) Enjoy a revitalising hot spring soak or a cleansing sweat in a traditional adobe-walled steam house at Hotel Signum's fabulous spa. The complex includes several stylish Jacuzzis on a pretty flagstoned patio, and blissful spaces where you can immerse your body in salt crystals, get a massage or pamper yourself with natural essences of citrus, Malvasia and capers.

✖ Eating

Malvasia wine and fat, juicy capers are Salina's twin specialities, which you'll find on virtually every menu. Island cuisine also benefits from the widespread availability of fresh produce from local gardens. Eating venues range from bars, cafes and sandwich shops to *trattorie* and seafood restaurants; most are concentrated in Santa Marina and Malfa, though you'll also find a few options in Lingua, Pollara and Rinella.

★ Da Alfredo   SANDWICHES, GELATERIA €

(Piazza Marina Garibaldi; granite €3, sandwiches €10-14; ⊙8am-11pm Jun-Sep, reduced hours Oct-May) Straddling a sunny waterfront terrace in Lingua, Alfredo's place is renowned Sicily-wide for its *granite:* ices made with coffee, fruit or locally grown pistachios, hazelnuts and almonds. For an affordable lunch, try its *pane cunzato,* open-faced sandwiches loaded with smoked tuna carpaccio, citrus, wild fennel, almond-caper pesto, ricotta, tomatoes, capers, olives and more; split one with a friend – they're huge!

★ A Quadara   TRATTORIA €€

(☑ 389 1519650; www.aquadaratrattoria.it; Via Roma 88; meals €25-39; ⊙6.30-11pm) Since opening in 2018, Malfa's newest restaurant has won a loyal following for its delicious, authentic Aeolian cuisine. The menu abounds in seasonal specials and enticing local recipes, from pasta with chickpeas and fennel, to rabbit stewed with veggies, pine nuts, almonds, lemon, cinnamon and capers. Scrumptious homemade *cannoli* and an excellent local wine selection are icing on the cake.

★ A Cannata   SICILIAN €€

(☑ 090 984 31 61; www.acannata.it; Lingua; meals €35; ⊙12.30-2.30pm & 7.30-10pm) Meals are built around locally sourced produce and seafood caught fresh daily by owner Santino at this unassuming but excellent restaurant, run by the same family for four decades. Expect dishes such as squid-ink risotto, *maccheroni* (macaroni) with eggplant, pine nuts, mozzarella and ricotta, fresh grilled fish, sautéed wild fennel, almond *semifreddi* (light frozen desserts) and local Malvasia wine.

La Pinnata del Monsù
TRATTORIA €€

(☑ 327 7971853; www.lapinnatadelmonsu.it; Via Sorgente 1a; meals €30-40; ⊙ noon-2pm & 7.30-10pm mid-Apr–Oct) With a sunny terrace overlooking the vineyards and the sea at Malfa's southern edge, this relaxed trattoria serves up superbly rendered Sicilian classics such as *caponata, busiate* (corkscrew-shaped tube pasta) with squid and wild fennel, and *cannoli* filled on the spot with fresh ricotta from nearby Vulcano.

Porto Bello
SEAFOOD €€

(☑ 090 984 31 25; www.portobellosalina.com; Via Lungomare 2, Santa Marina Salina; meals €25-45; ⊙ noon-2.30pm & 7.15-11pm Easter-Oct, by reservation Nov-Easter) For some of Santa Marina's best seafood head for this restaurant with a terrace overlooking the harbour, run by the same family since 1978. In low season, the €25 daily special offers great value, featuring the house speciality *pasta al fuoco* (fiery pasta with hot peppers) and *secondi* of grilled fish or squid stewed in Malvasia wine.

Al Cappero
SICILIAN €€

(☑ 090 984 39 68; www.alcappero.it; Via Chiesa 38; meals €25-30; ⊙ noon-2pm & 7.30-10pm Jun–mid-Sep; ☑) This family-run place in Pollara, with a sprawling outdoor terrace, specialises in old-fashioned Sicilian home-cooking, including several vegetarian options. It also sells home-grown capers and rents out simple rooms down the street (€350 to €550 per week).

Trattoria Cucinotta
SICILIAN €€

(☑ 090 984 34 75; Via Risorgimento 66, Santa Marina Salina; meals €30-45; ⊙ 12.30-2.30pm & 7-10.30pm Mar-Oct) Homemade pasta and fresh-caught fish predominate on the menus posted daily outside this cheerful yellow house, tucked just back from Via Risorgimento, Santa Marina's busy pedestrian thoroughfare. The atmosphere is simple and

AEOLIAN ISLANDS SALINA

MALVASIA: SAMPLING SALINA'S HONEY-SWEET WINE

Salina's good fortune is its freshwater springs. It is the only island of the Aeolians with significant natural water sources, the result of which is the startling greenery. The islanders have put this to good use, producing their own style of wine, Malvasia. It is thought that the Greeks brought the grapes to the islands in 588 BC, and the name is derived from Monemvasìa, a Greek city.

The wine is still produced according to traditional techniques using the Malvasia grape and the now-rare red Corinthian grape. The harvest generally occurs in the second week of September when the grapes are picked and laid out to dry on woven cane mats. The drying process is crucial: the grapes must dry out enough to concentrate the sweet flavour but not too much, which would caramelise them.

The result is a dark-golden or light-amber wine that tastes, some say, of honey. It is usually drunk in very small glasses and goes well with cheese, sweet biscuits and almond pastries. In recent years Salina's wineries have also started producing some excellent dry Malvasia whites that go nicely with seafood.

Sampling the island's famous Malvasia is one of the great pleasures of travelling here. You'll find the largest concentration of producers in and around Malfa, where the **Caravaglio** (☑ 339 8115953; www.caravaglio.it; Via Provinciale 33), **Colosi** (☑ 090 938 55 49; www.cantinecolosi.it; Via Nazionale 80), **Fenech** (☑ 090 984 40 41; www.fenech.it; Via Fratelli Mirabito 41), **Marchetta** (☑ 090 984 40 48; www.vinidisalina.it; Via Umberto I, No 9) and **Virgona** (☑ 090 984 44 30; www.malvasiadellelipari.it; Via Bandiera 2) wineries are all signposted off the main road. Other important Malvasias are produced in Salina's interior at **Azienda Agrobiologica d'Amico** (☑ 335 7878795; www.cantinedamico.it; Via Libertà 27) in Leni, and at **Hauner** (☑ 090 984 31 41; www.hauner.it; Via Umberto I, Lingua), near the town of Lingua at Salina's southeast corner. All of these wineries will generally let you stop in for a taste if you call ahead. Alternatively, you'll find local Malvasias well represented on restaurant wine lists around the island and elsewhere in the Aeolian archipelago.

unpretentious, with an elevated front porch that makes for good people-watching.

Drinking & Nightlife

★ Maracaibo
BAR

(📞331 6244981; Punta Scario; ⊘8am-11pm late May-Sep) This palm-thatched beach bar on the rocky shoreline of Punta Scario (just below Malfa town) makes for a dreamy spot for a sunset drink. The friendly owners also rent out loungers, beach umbrellas and kayaks.

ℹ️ Information

Emergency Doctor (Guardia Medica; 📞090 984 40 05; Via Risorgimento; ⊘24hr)

Farmacia Comunale (📞090 984 30 98; Via Risorgimento 112, Santa Marina Salina; ⊘5-8pm Mon, 9am-1pm & 5-8pm Tue-Fri, 9am-1pm Sat)

Police Station (📞090 984 30 19; Via Lungomare, Santa Marina Salina)

ℹ️ Getting There & Around

Salina has two ferry ports: Santa Marina on the island's east shore, and tiny Rinella on the south shore. Most boats from Lipari will stop at Rinella en route to Filicudi and Alicudi, while those bound for Panarea and Stromboli will typically stop at Santa Marina Salina. Some stop at both ports.

BIKE

Hire mountain bikes from **Antonio Bongiorno** (📞338 3791209; Via Risorgimento 222, Santa Marina Salina; ⊘8am-8pm), one block uphill from Santa Marina's hydrofoil dock.

BOAT

Liberty Lines (📞090 984 30 03; www.liberty lines.it; ⊘5.20am-8.05pm Mon-Fri, 5.20am-8.55pm Sat, 6am-8.05pm Sun) runs frequent hydrofoils to Santa Marina Salina from Lipari (€8.80, 20 to 45 minutes), Vulcano (€10.40, 35 to 50 minutes) and Milazzo (€17.55, 1½ to 1¾ hours). Less frequent services connect Santa Marina with Stromboli, Panarea, Filicudi and Alicudi. Liberty Lines also offers daily sailings to/from Messina (€28.85, 2¼ to 2¾ hours, three daily in summer, one in winter). Some of these services call at Rinella en route. The ticket office is just above the hydrofoil dock.

Alternatively, you can travel from Naples to Santa Marina Salina aboard the weekly ferry (from €57, 12¾ hours) operated by Siremar (p143), or the summer-only hydrofoil (from €62, 5¾ hours, daily) operated by SNAV (p143).

BUS

CITIS (📞090 984 41 50; www.trasportisalina. it) provides dependable local bus service year-round. There are bus stops near the ports in Santa Marina and Rinella, and timetables are posted around the island.

Direct buses run from Santa Marina to Lingua (€2, five to 10 minutes), Malfa (€2, 15 to 20 minutes), Valdichiesa (€2.50, 25 minutes), Leni (€2.80, 30 minutes) and Rinella (€2.80, 40 minutes). From Santa Marina to Pollara (€2.50, 25 minutes to 1½ hours), a change of bus in Malfa is always required. Service to all destinations is more frequent in July and August; see schedules online.

CAR & MOTORCYCLE

Antonio Bongiorno hires scooters (from €20 per day) and cars (from €50 per day).

PANAREA

POP 280

Exclusive and expensive, Panarea is the smallest and most fashionable of the Aeolians, attracting international jet-setters and Milanese fashionistas for a taste of *dolce far niente* (sweet nothing). In summer, luxury yachts fill the tiny harbour and flocks of day-trippers traipse around the car-free whitewashed streets of San Pietro, the port and principal settlement. Panarea is a strictly summer-only destination with very little going on outside the tourist season – in fact, arrive between November and Easter and you'll find most places closed.

◉ Sights

All of the island's main sights are within easy striking distance of the San Pietro boat docks. North of town lie the tiny community of **Ditella** and the rocky beach at Spiaggia Fumarola. South is the village of **Drautto**, followed by sandy Spiaggetta Zimmari, the prehistoric village, and the crystal-clear waters of Cala Junco.

★ Cala Junco
BEACH

Directly below Panarea's prehistoric village, about 45 minutes south of San Pietro, steps lead down to this gorgeous little cove with a rock-strewn beach and dreamy aquamarine waters.

Villaggio Preistorico
ARCHAEOLOGICAL SITE

Dramatically sited on Punta Milazzese, an elevated headland surrounded by the sea, these round foundations of 22 stone huts are the only vestiges of a prehistoric village dating back to the 15th century BC. Pottery found here shows distinctly Minoan influences, lending credence to the theory that the islanders maintained trading ties with the Cretans. The village is about a 45-minute walk south of San Pietro; from Spiaggetta Zimmari, climb the steep stone-paved steps, then follow signs along the coast.

Spiaggia della Calcara
BEACH
At Panarea's northeastern corner, this pebbly beach with full-on Stromboli views and jets of hot water escaping from undersea fumaroles is reached via a steep, winding dirt path descending off the main road north of Ditella. Outside peak months it's an isolated spot ideal for a quiet swim, but in July and August the sun-seekers move in en masse and the ringing of mobile phones becomes incessant.

Spiaggetta Zimmari
BEACH
This small stretch of brown sand backed by a steep overgrown dune, about 25 minutes on foot south of San Pietro, is Panarea's only sandy beach and gets packed in summer.

 ## Activities

Panarea offers a nice mix of activities, both on the mainland and offshore. Its largely traffic-free streets and small network of trails make it an appealing walking destination, especially in spring and autumn.

Punta del Corvo
HIKING
At 421m, this rocky outcropping is Panarea's highest point and a popular day-hiking destination. Two trails (marked 1 and 2 on local maps) converge here, and can be combined into a scenic full-island circuit. Allow about four hours for the full round trip, and be ready for some steep, rocky climbs and descents. From up top, there are spectacular views of all six of the neighbouring Aeolian islands.

Eating

Panarea has a plethora of seafood restaurants near the port, including many with nice views across the water to Stromboli. A few additional eateries are scattered along the narrow lanes leading north to Ditella and south to Drautto.

Da Francesco
SICILIAN €€
(☑090 98 30 23; www.dafrancescopanarea.com; Via San Pietro; meals €28-33; ⊙noon-2.30pm

& 7-10pm Mar-Nov) Up a short flight of stairs from the port (follow the signs), Da Francesco is a laid-back trattoria with a straightforward fish-focused menu and fine sea views toward Stromboli from its upstairs terrace. Try the speciality: *spaghetti alla disgraziata* (with tomatoes, aubergines, chilli, capers, olives and ricotta). Simple rooms are also available (singles €35 to €70, doubles €70 to €140).

Trattoria da Paolino
SICILIAN €€
(☑090 98 30 08; Via Iditella 75; meals €29-35; ⊙12.30-3pm & 7.30-10pm Easter–mid-Oct) For four and a half decades, Paolino has been serving top-quality, home-style Aeolian specialities on his breezy blue-and-white terrace overlooking the sea, a 10-minute walk north from the harbour. Tuna figures prominently on the menu (smoked, *sott'olio,* or mixed with pine nuts and wild fennel in *pasta magna magna*) alongside plenty of other fish, pasta and vegetable dishes.

Cusiritati
SICILIAN €€€
(☑090 98 30 22; Via San Pietro; meals €55; ⊙noon-3pm & 7pm-midnight Apr-Oct) Since 1970, three generations of women from the same family have run this classy, white-linen-clothed spot above the port. Federica, whose grandmother Amelia founded the place, greets everyone with a smile, while her mother Marilena cooks up phenomenally tasty Aeolian seafood specialities that evolve with the seasons; for dessert, linger over homemade *sesamini* (sesame cookies) and sweet Malvasia wine.

ⓘ Getting There & Away

Hydrofoils and ferries dock in the main settlement of San Pietro.

In summer Liberty Lines (p143) runs up to seven hydrofoils daily to/from Stromboli (€11.10, 30 to 45 minutes), Santa Marina Salina (€9.60, 30 minutes), Lipari (€10.40, 25 minutes to one hour) and Milazzo (€17.80, 1¼ to 2¼ hours). In winter, there are fewer services.

Siremar (p143) also runs ferries to all these destinations; ferries cost less than the hydrofoil, but take about twice as long.

The quickest way to reach Panarea from the Italian mainland is via the summer-only hydrofoil from Naples operated by SNAV (p143) (from €62, five hours, late May through early September).

The **ticket office** (☑090 98 33 44; ⊙7.15am-12.30pm & 2.20-7.30pm) for all companies is at the foot of the dock in San Pietro.

❶ Getting Around

Cars are not allowed on Panarea, but you won't need one as the island is small enough to get around on foot. The other preferred mode of transport is golf carts; to arrange a lift, call **Pantaxi** (☑ 333 3138610).

STROMBOLI

POP 500

For many the most captivating of the Aeolians, Stromboli conforms perfectly to one's childhood idea of a volcano, with its symmetrical, smoking silhouette rising dramatically from the sea. It's a hugely popular day-trip destination, but to best appreciate its primordial beauty, languid pace and the romance that lured Roberto Rossellini and Ingrid Bergman here in 1949, you'll need to give it at least a couple of days.

Volcanic activity has scarred and blackened much of the island, but the northeastern corner is inhabited, and it's here that you'll find the island's famous black beaches and the main settlement sprawled attractively along the volcano's lower slopes. Despite the picture-postcard appearance, life here is tough: food and drinking water have to be ferried in, there are no roads across the island, and until relatively recently there was no electricity in Ginostra, the diminutive second settlement on Stromboli's west coast.

◎ Sights

★ **Stromboli Crater**   VOLCANO

For nature lovers, climbing Stromboli is one of Sicily's not-to-be-missed experiences. Since 2005 access has been strictly regulated: you can walk freely to 400m, but need a guide to continue any higher. Organised treks depart daily (between 3.30pm and 6pm, depending on the season), timed to reach the summit (924m) at sunset and to allow 45 minutes to an hour to observe the crater's fireworks.

The climb itself takes 2½ to three hours, while the descent back to Piazza San Vincenzo is shorter (1½ to two hours). All told, it's a demanding five- to six-hour trek up to the top and back; you'll need to have proper walking shoes, a backpack that allows free movement of both arms, clothing for cold and wet weather, a change of T-shirt, a handkerchief to protect against dust (wear glasses not contact lenses), a torch

(flashlight), 1L to 2L of water and some food. If you haven't got any of these, Totem Trekking (p163) hires out all the necessary equipment, including boots (€6), backpacks (€5), hiking poles (€4), torches (€3) and windbreakers (€5).

★ **Sciara del Fuoco Viewpoint**   VIEWPOINT
(Path of Fire) An alternative to scaling Stromboli's summit is the hour-long climb to this viewpoint (400m, no guide required), which directly overlooks the Sciara del Fuoco (the blackened laval scar running down Stromboli's northern flank) and offers fabulous if more distant views of the crater's explosions. Bring plenty of water, and a torch if walking at night. The trail (initially a switchbacking road) starts in Piscità, 2km west of Stromboli's port; halfway up, you can stop for pizza at L'Osservatorio (p164).

During active periods, explosions occur every 20 minutes or so and are preceded by a loud belly-roar as gases force hot magma into the air. After particularly strong eruptions, you can watch as red-hot rocks tumble down the seemingly endless slope, creating visible splashes as they plop into the sea. For best viewing, come on a still night, when the livid red Sciara and exploding cone are dramatically visible.

Arriving here around sunset will allow you to hike one direction in daylight, then stop for dinner and more volcano-gawking at L'Osservatorio on the way back down. Making the trek just before dawn is also a memorable experience, as you'll likely have the whole mountain to yourself. From Piscità it takes about 30 minutes to get to L'Osservatorio, and another half-hour to reach the viewpoint. Be prepared – the trail narrows and gets steeper as you climb; the end is marked by a multilingual sign reading 'Beware! Do not trespass this limit'.

Red House   HISTORIC BUILDING
(Via Vittorio Emanuele 22) Ingrid Bergman and Roberto Rossellini lived together in this rusty-red house while filming *Stromboli, Terra di Dio* in 1949. Their liaison provoked a scandal in the film world, as both were married to other people at the time. Descending from San Vincenzo church on Stromboli's main square, look for a white marble plaque marking the house on the right-hand side.

You can't actually go inside, but it's interesting to see the scene of such a famous romance.

Stromboli

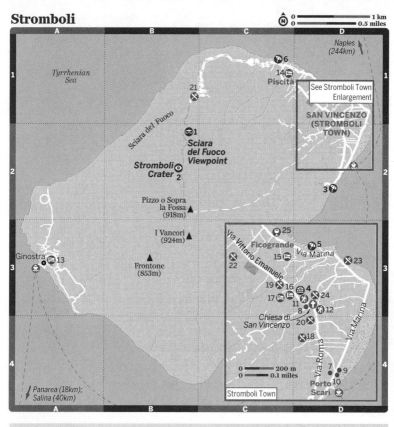

Stromboli

Spiaggia di Ficogrande   BEACH
Stromboli's black sandy beaches are the best in the Aeolian archipelago. The most accessible and popular swimming and sunbathing is at Ficogrande, a strip of rocks and black volcanic sand about a 10-minute walk northwest of the hydrofoil dock.

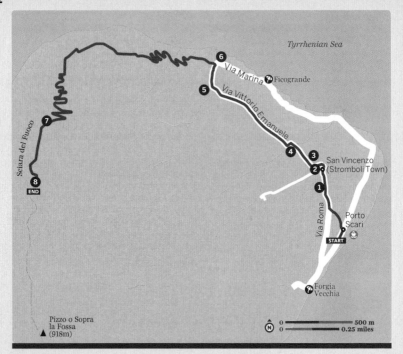

🏃 Walking Tour
Stromboli & the Sciara del Fuoco

START STROMBOLI HYDROFOIL PORT
END SCIARA DEL FUOCO
LENGTH 4KM; 1½ TO TWO HOURS ONE WAY

This self-guided jaunt takes you through the whitewashed streets of Stromboli town before climbing halfway up the mountain for dramatic perspectives on the volcano's eruptions from below. You're allowed to hike this trail unaccompanied, as the viewpoint sits below the 400m 'restricted' level.

Leave the port two to three hours before sundownso that you arrive at the viewpoint in time to watch the volcano's fireworks juxtaposed against the darkening sky. Make sure to bring a torch (flashlight); it's absolutely essential for the return hike.

From the port, walk up Via Roma toward Stromboli's main square, stopping in for homemade gelati at ❶ **Lapillo Gelato**. After passing Stromboli's main church, ❷ **Chiesa di San Vincenzo**, continue downhill to the ❸ **Red House** (p160), site of Ingrid Bergman and Roberto Rossellini's torrid love affair

while filming *Stromboli: Terra di Dio* in 1949. A few hundred metres further on, as the main road jogs briefly left, look for ❹ **La Bottega del Marano**, a neighbourhood grocery where you can pick up trail snacks and water.

About 2km from your starting point, pass ❺ **Chiesa di Piscità** on your left. Here you can take an optional five-minute detour down to the black sand beach of ❻ **Piscità**, tucked into a rocky cove, before retracing your steps back up to the church. Continue northwest along the main road to a side street branching west with signs for L'Osservatorio. Start climbing gradually, paralleling the sea at first, then following a series of switchbacks to ❼ **L'Osservatorio** (p164) pizzeria.

The climb to the viewpoint is much steeper. Arriving at the ❽ **Sciara del Fuoco viewpoint** (p160), prepare to be amazed! In clear weather, the sight of the volcano's explosive eruptions, followed by cascades of red-hot rock crashing down the mountainside into the sea, is stunning. Linger past nightfall, when the orange glow becomes more dramatic.

Spiaggia di Piscità   BEACH
Backed by rugged bluffs, this moderate-sized stretch of black-sand beach lies 2km west of Stromboli's port, at the edge of the small whitewashed settlement of Piscità.

Forgia Vecchia   BEACH
About 300m south of the port, Forgia Vecchia is a long stretch of black pebbles curving around a tranquil bay and backed by the volcano's green slopes.

Chiesa di San Vincenzo   CHURCH
(Piazza San Vincenzo) A major Stromboli landmark, San Vincenzo is the island's main church. In mid- to late afternoon, the square out front becomes a gathering point for trekkers preparing to climb the volcano.

🏃 Activities

Volcano Climbs
To climb to the top of Stromboli you'll need to go on an organised trek. Maximum group size is 20 people, and although there are usually multiple groups on the mountain, spaces can still fill up. To avoid disappointment, book early – if possible a week or more before you want to climb. The standard fee for group climbs is €28 per person. Local agencies include Magmatrek, **Stromboli Adventures** (☑090 98 60 95, 339 5327277; www.stromboliadventures.it; Via Vittorio Emanuele 17), **Stromboli Fire Trekking** (☑090 98 62 64; www.strombolifiretrekking.com; Via Vittorio Emanuele) and **Il Vulcano a Piedi** (☑090 98 61 44; www.ilvulcanoapiedi.it; Via Pizzillo).

★ Magmatrek   HIKING
(☑090 986 57 68; www.magmatrek.it; Via Vittorio Emanuele) Magmatrek is one of Stromboli's longest-established and most professional agencies, with experienced, multilingual (English-, German- and French-speaking) guides. In addition to regular daily treks up the volcano (maximum group size 20 people), it can also put together tailor-made excursions for individuals or groups.

Totem Trekking   HIKING
(☑090 986 57 52; www.totemtrekkingstromboli.com; Piazza San Vincenzo 4; ◷9.30am-1pm & 3.30-7pm Mar-Nov) Friendly proprietors Gabriella, Domenico and Naomi hire out hiking equipment, including boots (€6), backpacks (€5), hiking poles (€4), torches (€3), fleece jackets (€5) and windbreakers (€5).

Boat Tours
One of the most popular ways of viewing Stromboli's nocturnal fireworks is to take a boat tour of the island. **Società Navigazione Pippo** (☑090 98 61 35, 348 0559296; www.facebook.com/pipponavigazionestromboli; Porto Scari) and **Antonio Caccetta** (☑339 5818200; Vico Salina 10) are among the numerous outfits running boat tours out of Porto Scari. The two most popular itineraries are a three-hour round-the-island daytime cruise (€25), including an hour of free time to explore Ginostra and a swimming break at Strombolicchio (the rock islet jutting out of the water off the north coast), and a 1½-hour sunset excursion (€20) to watch the Sciara del Fuoco explosions from the sea. Extended evening excursions, with a stop in Ginostra for *aperitivi* or dinner, are another popular alternative.

Diving
La Sirenetta Diving   DIVING
(☑331 2545288; Via Mons di Mattina 33; ◷late May–mid-Sep) Offers diving courses and accompanied dives; opposite the beach at La Sirenetta Park Hotel.

🍴 Eating

Eating out in Stromboli can be pricey, as many food items have to be shipped in. Seafood is ubiquitous, while pizza provides a more wallet-friendly alternative.

★ Lapillo Gelato   GELATO €
(Via Roma; gelato €3-5; ◷10am-1pm & 3.30pm-midnight Jun-Aug, 10.30am-12.45pm & 3.30-8pm Sep-May) On the main street between the port and the church, this artisanal gelateria is a great place to fuel up with homemade gelato before making the big climb. The pistachio flavour is pure creamy bliss.

La Bottega del Marano   DELI €
(Via Vittorio Emanuele; snacks from €2; ◷8.30am-1pm & 4.30-7.30pm Mon-Sat) The perfect source for volcano-climbing provisions or a self-catering lunch, this reasonably priced neighbourhood grocery – at a bend in the road five minutes west of the trekking agency offices – has a well-stocked deli case full of meats, cheeses, olives, artichokes and sun-dried tomatoes, plus shelves full of wine and awesomely tasty fresh-baked focaccias.

AEOLIAN ISLANDS STROMBOLI

L'Osservatorio
PIZZA €

(☑ 090 958 69 91; www.facebook.com/osservatorio stromboli; pizzas €8-11; ⊙10am-10pm Apr-Jun & Sep–mid-Nov, to 2am Jul & Aug) Sure, you could eat a pizza in town, but come on – you're on Stromboli! On clear evenings, nothing compares to the full-on views of the volcano's eruptions from l'Osservatorio's panoramic outdoor terrace. From Piscità, 2km west of Stromboli's port, it's a 30-minute uphill trek or a bumpy ride on the free included shuttle (call ahead to be met at Piscità).

Ritrovo Ingrid
CAFE €

(☑ 090 98 63 85; Piazza San Vincenzo; pizza €6.50-12; ⊙8am-3am Jul & Aug, to 1.30am Sep-Jun) A Stromboli institution, the panoramic terrace of this all-purpose cafe-gelateria-pizzeria is busy throughout the day as islanders come for their morning cappuccino, tourists pop in for a gelato and trekkers compare notes over an evening pizza.

★ Punta Lena
SICILIAN €€

(☑ 090 98 62 04; http://ristorantepuntalena.business.site; Via Marina 8; meals €36-45; ⊙12.15-2.30pm & 7-10.30pm Thu-Tue, 7-10.30pm Wed May-Sep) For a romantic outing, head to this upscale waterfront restaurant with cheerful blue decor, lovely sea views and the soothing sound of waves lapping in the background. The food is among the island's finest, with signature dishes including fresh seafood, fish stewed with local olives and capers, and *spaghetti alla stromboliana* (with wild fennel, mint, anchovies, cherry tomatoes and breadcrumbs).

Pardès
SICILIAN €€

(☑ 377 1505194; www.facebook.com/pardes. stromboli; Via Vittorio Emanuele 81; meals €30-42; ⊙noon-2.30pm & 6-10pm late May-Oct; 🛜) West of town on the main road to Piscità, this wine bar–cafe dishes up small but delicious portions of homemade lentil soup, pasta and local fish, accompanied by veggies from the adjacent garden. There's pleasant seating on a back terrace with direct views up to the volcano, plus Sicilian wines, and beer on tap.

Ai Gechi
SEAFOOD €€

(☑ 338 3577559; www.facebook.com/trattoria gechistromboli; Vico Salina 12, Porto Scari; meals €30-45; ⊙noon-3pm & 6.30-11pm Easter–mid-Oct) Follow the trail of painted lizards to the shady verandah of this whitewashed Aeolian house, hidden down an alley off Via Roma. Eclectically decorated with ship lamps, a towering cactus and a whale skeleton discovered nearby, Ai Gechi serves traditional seafood with a slightly modern twist, backed by an excellent local wine list.

🍷 Drinking & Nightlife

La Tartana Club
BAR

(☑ 090 98 60 25; Via Regina Elena, Ficogrande; ⊙9.30am-2am late Jun-early Sep) Rub elbows with the likes of Dolce and Gabbana and the president of Italy at this chic resto-bar, a long-standing favourite of Stromboli's beautiful people. La Tartana hits its stride every

---

OFF THE BEATEN TRACK

STROMBOLI'S SLEEPIER SIDE

To see Stromboli's less touristy side, hop off the ferry at **Ginostra**, a tiny village on the island's western shore. There are only 30 year-round residents here, but you can sleep overnight at **B&B Luna Rossa** (☑ 090 988 00 49; www.ginostra-stromboli.it/bed-breakfast. php; Via Piano 3; d €40-100; ⊙Apr-Oct) or ask around about the several other local *affittacamere* (rental rooms) in town. Foodwise, Ginostra has a couple of small grocery stores and two restaurants serving local seafood.

It's possible to climb from Ginostra to Stromboli's crater, but this is a physically demanding approach due to the steeper ascent and constant exposure to sunlight coming in from the west. Experienced guide Mario Pruiti, who lives in Ginostra, arranges trips according to demand and weather conditions; contact Magmatrek (p163) to see if he's got anything planned during your visit. If there's a big enough group, prices per person (€28 to €35) are comparable to those for the classic ascent from Stromboli Town.

Liberty Lines runs occasional hydrofoils from Stromboli's main port to Ginostra (€7.80, 10 minutes, three daily in summer, one daily in winter). Hydrofoils from Lipari (€17.60, 50 minutes to 1½ hours), Santa Marina Salina (€16.30, 55 minutes) and Panarea (€10.90, 20 to 45 minutes) also stop here.

evening when a refined crowd gathers for *aperitivi* at the piano bar and couples romance each other over cocktails at candlelit tables on the seafront terrace.

Regulars also flock here to read the morning paper over coffee at breakfast time, graze at the casual lunch buffet or indulge in La Tartana's trademark dessert, *coppa Stromboli*, a volcano-shaped mass of chocolate, sweet cream and hazelnut ice cream studded with candied cherries and doused in a lava flow of strawberry syrup.

ⓘ Information

Emergency Doctor (☑ 090 98 60 97; Via Vittorio Emanuele; ⊘ 24hr)

Police Station (☑ 090 98 60 21) On the left as you walk up Via Picone toward Via Roma.

ⓘ Getting There & Away

Stromboli is the easternmost of the Aeolians, meaning that ferry and hydrofoil services are less frequent than to islands in the centre of the archipelago, and stormy weather is more likely to disrupt service. If you're only coming here to climb the volcano, note that many private boat operators in Lipari offer day-trip packages including a guided excursion to the craters followed by return transport to Lipari the same evening.

Liberty Lines (p143) offers daily hydrofoil services to Panarea (€11.10, 25 minutes), Santa Marina Salina (€16.30, one to 1¼ hours), Lipari (€19.30, one to two hours) and Milazzo (€20.95, 2¼ to three hours). There are up to eight daily services in high season, but this falls to two or three a day in winter.

Siremar (p143) also runs car ferries from Stromboli to Naples (from €48.40, 10 hours) and Milazzo (from €16.75, six hours), as well as to Lipari (€13.90, 3½ hours) and the other Aeolians. In bad weather the service is often disrupted or cancelled altogether, as Stromboli's dock is smaller than others on the Aeolians.

The quickest way to reach Stromboli from the Italian mainland is via the summer-only hydrofoil from Naples operated by SNAV (p143; from €62, 4½ hours, late May through early September).

The **ticket office** (☑ 090 98 60 03; ⊘ 6-8am, 9.30am-12.30pm & 3-5.30pm) for these three companies is 150m north of Stromboli's ferry dock.

ⓘ Getting Around

There are no cars on Stromboli, just scooters, electric carts and three-wheeler vehicles known locally as *ape*. Many hotels provide free shuttle service from the boat dock to your accommodation. Taxi operators around town, including **Paolo Taxi** (☑ 327 0916421, 339 3253419), offer transport on golf-cart-style vehicles. Walking on the island is also easy and pleasant.

You can hire scooters from **Giovanni 'Il Catanese'** (☑ 090 98 63 37; Lungomare; scooter per day €20); look for him about 800m north of the hydrofoil dock (150m north of the ENEL building), on the waterfront road toward Ficogrande.

FILICUDI

POP 235

Among the prettiest and least developed of the Aeolian Islands, Filicudi is also one of the oldest, dating back to tectonic activity 700,000 years ago. Shaped like a snail when seen from some angles, the island entices visitors with its rugged coastline lapped by crystal clear waters and pitted with deep grottoes. The island has just a few small villages.

◉ Sights

Villaggio Preistorico di Capo Graziano
ARCHAEOLOGICAL SITE

FREE Follow the main road 10 minutes southeast of the port toward Capo Graziano, where a marked trail branches off and climbs 10 minutes further to the lichen-covered stone foundations of 27 Bronze Age huts on a terraced hillside. Discovered in 1952, they date to 1700 BC, 300 years before Panarea's Punta Milazzese. It's an extremely evocative spot, with dramatic sea and island views and bilingual signs providing historical context.

From the village you can descend to Filicudi's only real beach, a stony affair that offers the easiest swimming on the island – if you want to take a dip elsewhere, you'll have to clamber down some jagged rocks or rent a boat.

Grotta del Bue Marino
CAVE

Boat tours often visit this beautiful sea cave lapped by brilliant turquoise waters on Filicudi's western shore. Measuring roughly 30m wide, 20m high and 20m deep, it's large enough for small boats to enter.

Scoglio della Canna
LANDMARK

(Cane Reef) Rising off Filicudi's northwestern shore is this dramatic 71m *faraglione* (rock tower); boat trips around the island will take you to see it up close.

⚡ Activities

Offshore from Capo Graziano lies the **Museo Archeologico Sottomarino** area,

AEOLIAN ISLANDS FILICUDI

where the sunken wrecks of nine ancient Greek and Roman ships provide fabulous diving opportunities. The island also boasts a small network of hiking trails, including the multihour climb to **Fossa Felci** (774m) at the centre of the island.

★ Zucco Grande   HIKING

A beautiful 60- to 75-minute uphill hike from the port leads to Zucco Grande, a largely abandoned village on Filicudi's northeast flank. Branching north from the hillside community of Valle di Chiesa, the trail winds along cactus- and flower-draped hillsides high above the sea, with spectacular views back to Capo Graziano and the port.

Filicudi Wildlife Conservation   OUTDOORS

(☑349 4402021; www.filicudiconservation.com; Pecorini Mare) Run by Monica Francesca Blasi and her team of professional biologists, this outfit organises nature-focused day hikes and boat excursions around Filicudi. Proceeds help support the organisation's efforts to protect turtles, dolphins and other local marine life.

Lido La Sirena   BEACH

(☑349 3617577; Pecorini Mare; ⊘9.30am-midnight mid-Jun–early Sep) This dreamy spot at the far end of Pecorini Mare's waterfront rents out loungers and umbrellas (per person €15) so you can soak up the sun between dips all afternoon, snacking on skewers of grilled lamb or pork from Sicily's Nebrodi Mountains, sampling Aeolian classics such as *caponata* and *granite* or sipping *aperitivi* at sundown.

I Delfini   OUTDOORS

(☑090 988 90 77, 340 1484645; www.idelfinifilicudi.com; Via Pecorini Mare) At this all-purpose agency, Nino Terrano organises dives, rents out diving equipment and scooters, and offers boat trips around the island, pointing out local attractions along the way. He can usually be found at Pecorini's small marina.

✖ Eating

Most accommodation options have their own restaurants serving fresh seafood. There are also a couple of low-key eateries down by the port.

★ Ristorante La Canna   SEAFOOD €€

(☑090 988 99 56, 336 926560; www.lacannahotel.it; via Rosa 43; meals €28; ⊘12.30-1.30pm & 7-9.30pm) Delicious traditional Sicilian seafood is accompanied by fresh produce from the surrounding gardens at this hillside restaurant, adjacent to the hotel of the same name. It's a 10- to 15-minute walk up a steep series of steps from the harbour. Non-hotel guests must reserve ahead.

La Sirena Restaurant   SEAFOOD €€

(☑090 988 99 97; www.pensionelasirena.it; meals €35-55; ⊘1-3pm & 8pm-midnight late Apr-Sep) Facing the waterfront in tiny seaside Pecorini Mare, La Sirena's colourful open-air terrace is an atmospheric place to dine. Pull up a straw-seated chair, admire the front-row view of multi-hued boats, rocky beach and sparkling Mediterranean and feast on fresh local seafood preceded by appetisers such as tuna and *neonata* fritters or *carbonara di pesce* (spaghetti with fish-based carbonara sauce).

⊙ Getting There & Away

Liberty Lines (☑0923 02 20 22; www.libertylines.it) runs hydrofoils from Filicudi to Alicudi (€11.10, 25 minutes), Rinella (€10.40, 25 minutes), Santa Marina Salina (€12.70, 40 minutes), Lipari (€15.80, 1¼ hours) and Vulcano (€15, 1½ hours). Service is considerably less frequent than elsewhere in the archipelago. Siremar (p143) and NGI (p143) also run occasional car ferries to/from Filicudi. **Ticket offices** (☑327 8827777; ⊘5.55am-5.05pm) for all companies are at the foot of the **ferry dock**.

⊙ Getting Around

Friendly taxi driver **Guido** (☑346 0255905) gives tours of the island, with visits to off-the-beaten-track viewpoints and lesser known sights such as Le Macine (19th-century grinding wheels carved from Filicudi's stratified stone, now littering the rocky shores of Capo Graziano).

ALICUDI

POP 120

If your goal is to really get away from it all, Alicudi just might be your dream destination. As isolated a place as you'll find in the entire Mediterranean basin, its main settlement has minimal facilities and no roads. Transportation here means boats and mules – you'll see the latter hauling goods up and down the steep stone steps from the port the minute you disembark.

Outside summer season, Alicudi is the kind of place where you have to ask around for rooms, and where the evening's chief entertainment may be watching fishermen unload and clean fish. By day it offers prime opportunities for off-the-beaten-track hiking or peaceful sunbathing – the best spots are south of the port, where you'll have to clamber over boulders to reach the sea. The waters are crystal clear and there's nothing to disturb you save the occasional hum of a fishing boat.

Activities

Filo dell'Arpa   HIKING
A two-hour trek up a relentlessly steep but pretty series of stone staircases leads to Alicudi's central peak (675m); simply follow the blue arrows painted on the walls. A pretty church, **Chiesa di San Bartolo**, marks the hike's midpoint. At the T-intersection up top where the trail dead ends at a stone wall, turn left to circle the crater of the extinct volcano or right to continue on the main trail to the dramatic cliffs at Alicudi's western edge.

Near the summit you'll also find the **Timpone delle Femmine**, huge fissures where women are said to have taken refuge during pirate raids.

Make sure you wear sturdy shoes and bring plenty of water as there is virtually no shade along the way.

Eating

There are a couple of bars and a pizzeria down by the port, supplemented by Hotel Ericusa's restaurant during its short opening season. During the rest of the year your accommodation can arrange meals with local fishing families; ask when booking your room.

Silvio & Gabriella Taranto   SEAFOOD €
(☑ 090 988 99 22; meals €25) Numbering among Alicudi's few year-round residents are this local fisherman and his wife, who can arrange simple but tasty home-cooked meals any time of year. Call at least a day ahead to reserve. They're just a block south and a block uphill from the boat dock, next door to the *affittacamere* (rental rooms) of **Marcella & Isabella** (☑ 090 988 99 17; r without bathroom per person €25-30).

ⓘ Getting There & Away

Liberty Lines runs two to four daily hydrofoils from Alicudi to Filicudi (€11.10, 25 minutes), Rinella (€15.80, 55 minutes), Santa Marina Salina (€17.80, 1¼ hours), Lipari (€18.85, 1¾ hours) and Vulcano (€18.35, two hours). The **ticket office** (⊙ 8.30-11.30am & 1-6pm) is at the foot of the dock.

AEOLIAN ISLANDS ALICUDI

Ionian Coast

Best Places to Eat

➡ Il Barcaiolo (p177)

➡ Osteria Nero D'Avola (p178)

➡ Mè Cumpari Turiddu (p188)

➡ Cave Ox (p198)

➡ I Dolci di Nonna Vincenza (p187)

Best Festivals

➡ Carnevale (p193)

➡ Taormina Arte (p177)

➡ Festa di Sant'Agata (p187)

➡ Alkantara Fest (p198)

➡ Marranzano World Fest (p187)

Why Go?

The Ionian Coast is studded with enough Sicilian icons to fill a souvenir tea towel. It's here that you'll find the skinny Strait of Messina, mighty Mt Etna and the world's most spectacularly located ancient Greek theatre. Catania is the region's centre, a gritty, vibrant city packed with students, bars and nightlife. Its black-and-white baroque piazza is World Heritage–listed, while its hyperactive fish market is one of Sicily's most appetising sights. Halfway up a rocky mountainside, regal Taormina is sophisticated and exclusive, a favourite of holidaying VIPs and day-tripping tourists. Brooding menacingly on the city's doorstep, Mt Etna offers unforgettable hiking, both to the summit craters and around the woods that carpet its lower slopes. Etna is also a vino-making hotspot, dotted with vines and celebrated wineries. With a car and a little planning, the mountain sets a stunning scene for hunting out the perfect vintage.

Road Distances (km)

	Acireale	Catania	Messina	Nicolosi
Catania	15			
Messina	85	95		
Nicolosi	20	15	100	
Taormina	40	50	50	60

MESSINA

🎵 090 / POP 234,300

Underrated Messina sits on a curved harbour at the northernmost point of Sicily's Ionian Coast, a few kilometres from the Italian mainland. A major transport hub for centuries, it remains an important gateway to and from the island.

While a devastating earthquake in 1908 razed many of Messina's historic monuments, it allowed the city to re-emerge with a distinctly belle époque air. Wide boulevards and lower-rise, turn-of-the-century buildings exude a sense of space and calm missing from other major Sicilian cities. And though the city's cultural cachet doesn't quite match that of its more coveted rivals, it does claim one of Sicily's finest cathedrals and an outstanding regional museum, not to mention swordfish and *granita* celebrated by connoisseurs across the island.

◎ Sights

★ Museo Regionale Interdisciplinare   MUSEUM

(🎵090 36 12 92; Viale della Libertà 465; adult/reduced €8/4; ⊙9am-7pm Mon-Sat, to 1pm Sun) Messina's redeveloped regional museum is one of Sicily's lesser-known highlights, with an extensive collection of fascinating art and archaeology, including the ram bow of an ancient Roman warship, the wonderfully figurative *San Gregorio* (St Gregory) polyptych by local boy Antonello da Messina (1430–79), and two splendid works by Caravaggio (1571–1610): *L'Adorazione dei pastori* (Adoration of the Shepherds) and *Risurrezione di Lazzaro* (Resurrection of Lazarus).

Other standout paintings include an early-16th-century depiction of *Cristo alla colonna* (Christ at the Pillar) and the striking *Deposizione dalla croce* (Deposition from the Cross) by Colijn de Coter (1474–1536). The collection also includes the original Neptune from Messina's 16th-century **Fontana del Nettuno** and a fascinating navigational map of the Mediterranean created by Placido Caloiro e Oliva in 1646. You'll also find the excavated ruins of a monastery's *putridarium,* a crypt in which corpses were left to decompose on masonry chairs before the remaining bones were collected, cleaned and stored in an ossuary.

To reach the museum, catch a tram at Piazza Cairoli and take a ride up the sickle-shaped harbour. Halfway along, you'll see the 16th-century Fontana del Nettuno in the middle of two busy roads, and the colossal golden statue, the **Madonna della Lettera**, towering over the port. Alight at the Ringo tram stop, from where the museum is a short walk.

Duomo di Messina   CATHEDRAL

(Messina Cathedral; Piazza del Duomo; ⊙cathedral 7am-12.30pm & 3.30-7.30pm Mon-Sat, 8am-1pm & 3.30-7.30pm Sun, cathedral museum 11am-1pm Tue-Sat) Messina's one great sight is the Norman Duomo (or at least a faithful replica of it). One of Sicily's finest cathedrals, its treasures include an impressive carved altar and a grand inlaid organ, the second-largest in Italy. Originally built in the 12th century and accidentally burnt to the ground in 1254, the cathedral was destroyed again in the earthquakes of 1783 and 1908, as well as by an incendiary WWII bomb in 1943.

Very little remains of the original structure, except for the striped marble inlay, the tracery of the facade and the arresting Catalan Gothic portal. Treasures such as the famous Manta d'Oro (Golden Mantle), used to 'cloak' holy pictures during religious celebrations, are kept in the Museo della Cattedrale, accessed from inside the cathedral.

Piazza del Duomo   SQUARE

Piazza del Duomo is home to Messina's cathedral and its curious *campanile* (bell tower). Soaring 60m into the sky, the tower incorporates an astronomical clock, said to be the world's largest. Built in Strasbourg in 1733, it strikes at noon, setting in motion a procession of bronze automata that sets off a comical roaring lion and crowing cockerel. Facing the tower is the 1553 marble **Fontana di Orione**. Created by Florentine sculptor Giovanni Angelo Montorsoli (pupil to Michelangelo), it commemorates Orion, the mythical founder of Messina.

Nearby, just off Piazza Catalani, the 12th-century **Chiesa della Santissima Annunziata dei Catalani** (Via G Garibaldi 111) is a fine example of Arab-Norman construction.

✖ Eating

Messina is famous for its quality *pesce spada* (swordfish), which is typically served *agghiotta,* with pine nuts, sultanas, garlic, basil and tomatoes. It's also lauded for its *granita con panna* (granita served with cream), considered by many to be the best in Sicily. One of the best spots to savour the latter is at the historic *pasticceria* and cafe Irrera 1910 (p172).

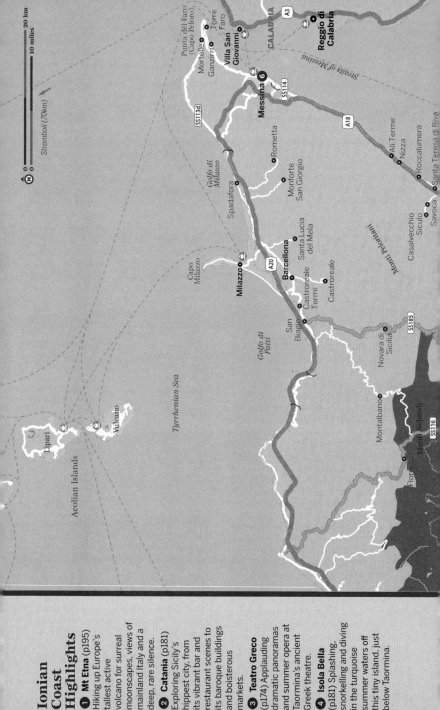

Ionian Coast Highlights

1 Mt Etna (p195) Hiking up Europe's tallest active volcano for surreal moonscapes, views of mainland Italy and a deep, rare silence.

2 Catania (p181) Exploring Sicily's hippest city, from its vibrant bar and restaurant scenes to its baroque buildings and boisterous markets.

3 Teatro Greco (p174) Applauding dramatic panoramas and summer opera at Taormina's ancient Greek theatre.

4 Isola Bella (p181) Splashing, snorkelling and diving in the turquoise summer waters off this tiny island, just below Taormina.

5 Planeta Feudo di Mezzo
(p199) Sampling extraordinary *vino* at one of Etna's most revered wineries, just outside Passopisciaro.

6 Museo Regionale Interdisciplinare
(p169) Soaking up a wealth of art and archaeology at Messina's underrated regional museum.

7 Trattoria La Grotta (p193)
Feasting at a much-loved seaside trattoria, set snugly in the tiny coastal village of Santa Maria la Scala.

Messina

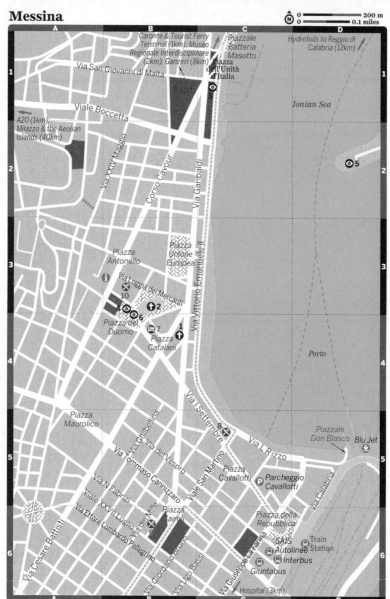

Ionian Sea

Porto

Irrera 1910

CAFE, PASTRIES €

(☎ 090 71 21 48; www.irrera.it; Piazza Cairoli 12; granita with brioche €4, pastries/cakes from €2.50; ⊙ 8am-8.30pm Mon-Fri, to 9pm Sat & Sun; ☎ 🚻) Messina is renowned for its *granita,* and you'll devour one of the very best at this polished cafe-pasticceria. To order like a lo-

cal, ask for a *mezza con panna e brioche,* which will get you a glass of coffee-flavoured *granita* topped with cream and served with a brioche bun for dipping. Other *granita* flavours are available, and it also sells decent cakes and pastries.

Messina

⊙ Sights
1 Chiesa della Santissima
  Annunziata dei Catalani B4
2 Duomo di Messina B3
3 Fontana del Nettuno C1
4 Fontana di Orione............................... B3
5 Madonna della Lettera D2
6 Piazza del Duomo B4

⊖ Sleeping
7 B&B del Duomo B4

⊗ Eating
8 Fratelli La Bufala................................ C5
9 Irrera 1910 .... B6
10 Osteria del Campanile B3

Fratelli La Bufala   PIZZA €

(☏090 66 25 13; www.fratellilabufala.com; cnr Via
Vittorio Emanuele II & Viale San Martino; pizzas
€4-9, dishes €6-19; ⊙12.30-3.30pm & 7.30pm-
12.30am Sun-Fri, to 1am Sat; 🛜🍴🐾) Contemporary, light-filled and bustling, this successful
Naples chain churns out bubbling, doughy,
Neapolitan-style pizzas to famished suits, couples and the odd nun. The menu's star-turn
is buffalo mozzarella and buffalo meat, available in numerous other dishes, from antipasto
platters and pasta dishes to grilled meats. Beyond these are fresh, satisfying salads and a
decent number of flesh-free options.

Osteria del Campanile   SICILIAN €€

(☏090 71 14 18; www.osteriadelcampanile.com; Via
Loggia dei Mercanti 7-13; meals €20-30; ⊙noon-
3pm & 7pm-midnight; 🛜) With its prime location – just behind the *duomo* – this cosy,
retro hostelry is a handy spot for classic
Sicilian homecooking. The menu features
all the usual suspects – pasta with seafood,
grilled meat and fish – as well as some less
ubiquitous offerings. Among these is Friday
special *stocco alla ghiotta,* a local speciality
of dried cod fish cooked with olives, capers
and a tomato *sugo.*

ⓘ Information

Police Station (☏090 36 61; Via Placida 2)
One block west of the Fontana del Nettuno.

Policlinico G Martino (☏090 22 11; www.
polime.it; Via Consolare Valeria 1) Major hospital with a 24-hour casualty ward.

Tourist Office (☏090 67 29 44; Corso Cavour;
⊙8am-1pm & 2.30-4.30pm Mon-Fri) Friendly
English-speaking staff with good information
about Messina. Located on Corso Cavour, just
off Piazza del Duomo.

ⓘ Getting There & Away

BOAT
Messina is the main point of arrival for ferries
and hydrofoils from the Italian mainland.

Blu Jet (Bluferries; ☏340 9848540, 340
1545091; www.blujetlines.it) Runs hydrofoils
from Messina to Reggio di Calabria (€3.50, 30
minutes, 16 daily Monday to Friday, six daily
Saturday and Sunday) and Villa San Giovanni
(€2.50, 20 minutes, 10 daily Monday to Friday,
seven daily Saturday and Sunday).

Caronte & Tourist (☏090 5737; www.caronte
tourist.it; Viale della Libertà) Runs frequent car
ferries to/from Villa San Giovanni (passenger/
car including up to five passengers €2.50/38,
25 minutes). It also runs a daily service from
Salerno to Messina (passenger/with car from
€29/79, nine hours). Ferries from Messina to
Salerno sail once daily Tuesday to Saturday
and twice daily on Sunday. Car ferries depart
from Rada San Francesco ferry terminal on Via
della Libertà, around 1.3km north of Piazza
dell'Unità d'Italia.

BUS
All long-distance bus companies run services
from Piazza della Repubblica, right outside the
train station.

Flixbus (https://global.flixbus.com) Runs two
direct daily services to Rome (from €38, nine
to 10 hours), one in the afternoon and one
overnight.

Giuntabus (☏090 67 57 49; www.giuntabus
trasporti.com; Piazza della Repubblica) Has
a service to Milazzo (€4, 50 minutes, 15 to 18
daily Monday to Saturday, three Sunday) for
connections to the Aeolian Islands.

Interbus (☏090 66 17 54; www.interbus.it;
Piazza della Repubblica 16) Runs to Taormina
(€4.30, 1½ to 1¾ hours, five daily Monday to
Friday, four Saturday, one Sunday).

SAIS Autolinee (☏090 77 19 14, 800 211020;
www.saisautolinee.it; Piazza della Repubblica
11) Operates buses to Palermo (€14, 2¾ hours,
seven daily Monday to Friday, five Saturday,
four Sunday), Catania (€8.40, 1½ hours, 22
daily Monday to Friday, 13 Saturday, 10 Sunday)
and Catania airport (€9.30, 1¾ hours, 17 Monday to Friday, 13 Saturday, 11 Sunday).

CAR & MOTORCYCLE
For Palermo, Milazzo (connections to the Aeolian
Islands), Taormina, Catania and Syracuse, turn
right from the docks and follow Via Vittorio
Emanuele II along the waterfront up to Piazza
dell'Unità d'Italia. Here, double back on Corso
Cavour and turn right into Viale Boccetta, follow-
ing the green A20 *autostrada* (motorway) signs.

Car hire is available at **Hertz** (☏090 34 44
24; www.hertz.it; Via Garibaldi 128) and **Sicilcar**

IONIAN COAST MESSINA

(☑ 339 4484484, 090 4 69 42; www.sicilcar. net; Via Garibaldi 187).

TRAIN

As a rule, buses are a better bet than trains, particularly to Milazzo and Taormina, but there are several trains daily to Catania (€7.60, 1½ to two hours), Syracuse (€10.50, 2½ to three hours) and Palermo (€12.80, three hours). Services are significantly reduced on Sunday.

🛈 Getting Around

CAR & MOTORCYCLE

If you have no luck parking on the street (blue lines denote pay-and-display meter parking), there's a useful multistorey car park, **Parcheggio Cavallotti** (Via I Settembre; per hr €0.50; ☺ 4.30am-11pm), near the train station and port. Pay at the automated ticket machine before leaving.

TRAM

An electric tram runs from Piazza Cairoli via the train station up to the Museo Regionale Interdisciplinare. Buy tickets (€1.70 return) from *tabacchi* (tobacco shops). All-day tickets (€2.60) are also available.

PUNTA DEL FARO

From Messina the coast curves around to Sicily's most northeasterly point, Punta del Faro (also called Capo Peloro), just 3km across the water from the Italian mainland. South of the cape is the lakeside town of **Ganzirri**, a popular summer hang-out and a pretty setting for a fish dinner. On the other side of the cape, **Mortelle** is the area's most popular summer resort, where the Messinese go to sunbathe and hang out.

🍴 Eating

Mussels *(cozze)* are the local speciality on Punta del Faro and the molluscs are cultivated in the peninsula's salty lake waters. The area is also a good spot to tuck into fresh *vongole* (clams), *pesce spada* and *stoccafisso* (stockfish).

Trattoria La Sirena di Mancuso   SEAFOOD €€
(☑ 090 39 12 68; https://mancusolasirenaganzirri.oneminutesite.it; Via Lago Grande 96, Ganzirri; meals €25-35; ☺ 12.15-3pm & 8-11.30pm Thu-Tue; ☜) Among the numerous eateries flanking Lago di Ganzirri, La Sirena stands out for its affable nature and well-executed, surf-centric homecooking. Celebrate coastal flavours in dishes like zesty marinated

prawns, octopus salad and crunchy *alici fritte* (fried anchovies). To sample Punta del Faro's famous mussels, opt for a simple, classic *impepata di cozze* (steamed peppered mussels). Book ahead, especially later in the week.

🛈 Getting There & Away

The easiest way to explore Punta del Faro is by car. From Messina, take the SP43, a picturesque coastal road that leads to Ganzirri and, beyond it, Mortelle. From Ganzirri, local streets lead to the adjacent neighbourhood of Torre Faro and the very tip of the peninsula.

TAORMINA

☑ 0942 / POP 10,900 / ELEV 204M

Spectacularly perched on the side of a mountain, Taormina is one of Sicily's most popular summer destinations, a chic resort town popular with holidaying high-rollers and those wanting a taste of Sicilian *dolce vita*.

Although unashamedly touristy and expensive, the town merits a couple of days for its stunning ancient theatre, people-watching and breathtaking vistas.

Founded in the 4th century BC, Taormina enjoyed great prosperity under the Greek ruler Gelon II and later under the Romans, but fell into quiet obscurity after being conquered by the Normans in 1087. Its reincarnation as a tourist destination dates to the 18th century, when northern Europeans discovered it on the Grand Tour. Among its fans was DH Lawrence, who lived here between 1920 and 1923.

Taormina gets extremely busy in July and August and virtually shuts down between November and Easter. Ideally, head up in April, May, September or October.

◉ Sights

★ **Teatro Greco**   RUINS
(☑ 0942 2 32 20; Via Teatro Greco; adult/reduced €10/5; ☺ 9am-1hr before sunset) Taormina's premier sight is this perfect horseshoe-shaped theatre, suspended between sea and sky, with Mt Etna looming on the southern horizon. Built in the 3rd century BC, it's the most dramatically situated Greek theatre in the world and the second largest in Sicily (after Syracuse). In summer, it's used to stage concerts and festival events. To avoid the high-season crowds, try to visit early in the morning.

Corso Umberto I STREET

Taormina's chief delight is wandering this pedestrian-friendly, boutique-lined thoroughfare. Start at the tourist office in **Palazzo Corvaja** (Piazza Santa Caterina; ⊙hours vary), which dates back to the 10th century, before heading southwest for spectacular panoramic views from **Piazza IX Aprile**. Facing the square is the early-18th-century **Chiesa di San Giuseppe** (📞0942 2 31 23; ⊙8.30am-8pm). Continue west through the **Torre dell'Orologio**, the 12th-century clock tower, into **Piazza del Duomo**, home to an ornate baroque fountain (1635) that sports Taormina's symbol, a two-legged centaur with the bust of an angel.

You're now in the Borgo Medievale, the oldest quarter of town. On the eastern side of Piazza del Duomo is the 13th-century **cathedral**. It survived much of the Renaissance-style remodelling undertaken throughout the town by the Spanish aristocracy in the 15th century. Just north of the Corso is the 14th-century **Palazzo Ciampoli** (Salita Ciampoli 9), adjacent to the Hotel El Jebel. Just to the south (and near Porta Catania) stands the **Palazzo Duca di Santo Stefano** (Vicolo De Spuches), a 13th-century palace once home to the De Spuches, a noble family of Spanish origin. It's now used as a functions space, but its Norman Gothic windows and Arab accents make it one of Taormina's architectural pin-ups.

Villa Comunale PARK

(Parco Duchi di Cesarò; Via Bagnoli Croce; ⊙8am-midnight summer, to 6pm winter; 📶) Created by Englishwoman Florence Trevelyan in the late 19th century, these stunningly sited public gardens offer breathtaking views of the coast and Mt Etna. They're a wonderful place to escape the crowds, with tropical plants and delicate flowers punctuated by whimsical follies. You'll also find a children's play area.

Castelmola VILLAGE

For eye-popping views of the coastline and Mt Etna, head for this cute hilltop village above Taormina, crowned by a ruined castle. If you're reasonably fit, head up on foot (one hour) for a good workout and sweeping panoramas. Alternatively, take the hourly Interbus service (one-way/return €1.90/3, 15 minutes). While you're up here, stop in for almond wine at Bar Turrisi (p179), a multi-level bar with some rather cheeky decor.

For information on the Sentiero dei Saraceni and Sentiero Madonna della Grazie, the two walking trails that lead up to Castelmola, visit the tourist office (p180) in Taormina.

Monte Tauro VIEWPOINT

The short climb to the top of Monte Tauro (378m) is not exactly Himalayan, but it is steep and the final steps are quite hard work. Your reward is a breathtaking panoramic view over Taormina's rooftops, the Teatro Greco and, beyond, to the coast.

From Via Circonvallazione, a signposted path leads up past the tiny **Santuario Madonna della Rocca** (📞338 8033448; ⊙hours vary). Founded by the abbot Francesco Raineri in around 1640, the church is built inside a grotto. According to legend, the Virgin Mary and baby Jesus appeared to a young shepherd who had taken refuge in the grotto during a sudden storm. The lofty panorama from the church's terrace is almost as heavenly, taking in Taormina and the deep-blue Ionian Sea beyond. Further up the mountain lie the windswept ruins of a Saracen **castello** (castle), once the site of Taormina's ancient Greek acropolis. You can't actually get to the castle – a locked gate blocks the path – but it's the views, rather than the sights, that are the real attraction.

👉 Tours

SAT BUS

(📞0942 2 46 53; www.satexcursions.it; Corso Umberto I 73; ⊙8.30am-1pm & 4-7.30pm) One of a

LOCAL SPECIALITIES

Swordfish (Messina) You'll find *pesce spada* (swordfish) on menus across Sicily, but the best are caught in the Strait of Messina between May and July.

Pasta alla Norma (Catania) Named after a Bellini opera, this is a rich, classic Catania dish of fried aubergine (eggplant), tomato and salted ricotta.

Wine (Mt Etna) Grapes grown on Etna go into Etna DOC, one of Sicily's best-known wines.

Honey (Zafferana Etnea) This small town on Etna's eastern slopes is celebrated for its honey, made from a range of local flowers.

Mussels (Ganzirri) Diners head up here from Messina to dine on *cozze* (mussels) cultivated in a salt lake.

Taormina

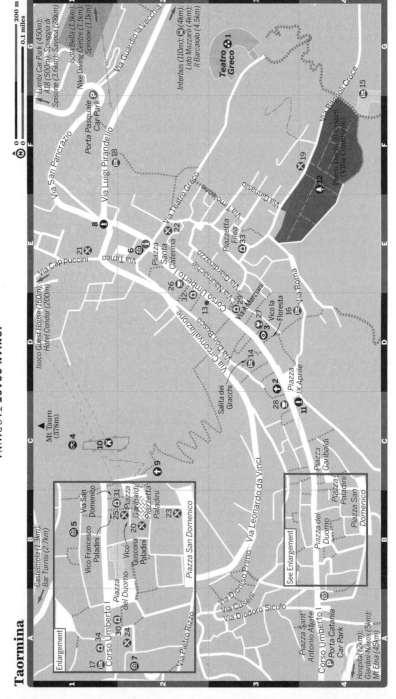

Castelmola (1.3km);
Bar Turrisi (2.7km)

Isoco Guest House (160m);
Hotel Condor (200m)

Lumbi Car Park (450m);
A18 (500m); Spiaggia di
Spisone (3.6km); Savoca (28km)

Isola Bella (1.1km);
Nike Diving Centre (1.1km);
Spisone (1.1km)

Interbus (110m); ✈ (4km);
Lido Mazzarò (4km);
Il Barcaiolo (4.5km)

Teatro
Greco 1

Parco Duchi di Cesarò
(Villa Comunale)

Via Bagnoli Croce 15

19

12

Porta Pasquale
Car Park

Via San Pancrazio

Via Guardia la Vecchia

Via Luigi Pirandello

18

8 1

21

6

Piazza
Santa
Caterina

22

Via Timoleone

Via Teatro Greco

Via Ginnasio

Piazzetta
Filea

33

Via Cappuccini

Via Timeo

26

32

13

Corso Umberto I

Via Naumachie

Via Giardinazzo

Via A Marzani

29

27

Vico la
Floresta

3

16

Via Roma

Mt Tauro
(378m)

4

10

Via Circonvallazione

Via Don Bosco

14

Piazza
IX Aprile

2

28

11

Salita dei
Gracchi

Via Pietro Rizzo

9

Piazza
San Domenico

Via Leonardo da Vinci

Piazza
Garibaldi

Piazza del
Duomo

Piazza
Paladini

Piazza San
Domenico

See Enlargement

Via Dionisio Primo

Via Cuseni

Via Diodoro Siculo

Piazza Sant'
Antonio Abate

Corso Umberto I

Porta Catania
Car Park

Hospital (2km);
Giardini-Naxos (5km);
Mt Etna (45km)

Enlargement

17

34

30

24

7

Corso Umberto I

Piazza del
Duomo

Via Pietro Rizzo

5

Via San
Domenico

25 31

Piazza
Garibaldi

Piazzetta
Paladini

23

Vico Francesco
Paladini

Vico
Cuscona

20

Piazza
Paladini

0   200 m
0   0.1 miles

Taormina

number of agencies that organises day trips to Mt Etna (from €35), Syracuse (€45), Noto (€50), Palermo and Cefalu (€55), as well as Agrigento (€55).

⚜ Festivals & Events

Italian Opera Taormina MUSIC
(☑ 340 6426230; www.italianoperataormina.com; Teatro San Giorgio, Via Don Bosco; ☺ Apr–Nov) Opera stars sing famous arias and duets at Taormina's Teatro San Giorgio on Monday, Wednesday and Saturday evenings at 9.15pm from May through October, with performances on Saturday evenings only in April. The glass of prosecco is on the house.

Taormina Arte PERFORMING ARTS
(☑ 391 7462146; www.taoarte.it; ☺ Jun–Sep) Taormina Arte oversees a plethora of cultural events in town, including the annual **Taormina Film Fest** (http://taofilmfest.it; ☺ Jun or Jul). The peak season for offerings is summer, when the Teatro Greco becomes a hub for world-class opera, dance, theatre and music concerts, with no shortage of internationally renowned acts. See the website for what's on.

✗ Eating

Eating in Taormina is expensive. Prices are higher here than in the rest of Sicily, and service can be lacklustre. That said, there are some excellent restaurants serving quality local produce and wines that are popular with locals and discerning visitors. Avoid touts and tourist menus and make reservations at the more exclusive and popular places. Reserve up to a week ahead in the summer.

★**Minotauro** PASTRIES €
(☑ 0942 2 47 67; Via di Giovanni 15; pastries from €1, cannoli €2.50; ☺ 9am-8.30pm, to midnight mid-Jun-Aug, closed Dec–mid-Mar) Tiny Minotauro has an epic reputation for its calorific, made-from-scratch treats. Scan the counters for old-school tempters such as artful marzipan, sticky *torrone* (nougat) and *paste di mandorla* (almond biscuits) with fillings like orange or pumpkin. Top billing goes to the silky ricotta *cannoli,* filled fresh to order and pimped with pistachio, cinnamon and candied orange.

★**Il Barcaiolo** SICILIAN €€
(☑ 0942 62 56 33; www.barcaiolo.altervista. org; Via Castellucci 43, Spiaggia Mazzarò; meals €33-45; ☺ 1-2.30pm & 7-10.45pm Wed-Mon Jun-Aug, to 10pm Wed-Mon Apr, May, Sep-early Jan) Book five days ahead come summer, when every *buongustaio* (foodie) and hopeless romantic longs for a table at this fabulous trattoria. Set snugly in a boat-fringed cove at Mazzarò beach, it's celebrated for its sublimely fresh seafood, such as sweet *gamberi*

rossi marinati agli agrumi (raw Mazzara shrimps served with citrus fruits) and *sarde a beccaficu* (stuffed sardines).

Leave room for the homemade *cassata* or deliciously naughty chocolate-and-orange mousse.

★Osteria Nero D'Avola
SICILIAN €€

(☑0942 62 88 74; Piazza San Domenico 2b; meals €40-50; ☉7-11pm daily mid-Jun–mid-Sep, noon-2.30pm & 7-11pm Tue-Sun rest of year; ☎) Owner Turi Siligato fishes, hunts and forages for his smart *osteria*, and if he's in, he'll probably share anecdotes about the day's bounty and play a few tunes on the piano. This is one of Taormina's top eateries, where seasonality, local producers and passion underpin outstanding dishes, such as grilled meatballs in lemon leaves, and fresh fish with Sicilian pesto.

L'Arco dei Cappuccini
SICILIAN €€

(☑0942 2 48 93; www.facebook.com/arcodei cappuccini; Via Cappuccini 5; meals €30-45; ☉6pm-midnight Mon & Wed-Sat, 12.30-3.30pm Sun, closed Nov–mid-Dec & early Jan–mid-Mar) If you demand your seafood ridiculously fresh, reserve a table at this superlative local favourite. The *crudo* antipasto makes for a showstopping prologue, followed by beautifully balanced dishes like *fettuccine cernia* (pasta with grouper) and an earthy *pasta con le sarde* (spaghetti with sardines, raisins, pine nuts and fennel) in which every ingredient sings. Service is kind and gracious.

Tischi Toschi
SICILIAN €€

(☑339 3642088; www.tischitoschitaormina.com; Vico Paladini 3; meals €35-45; ☉12.30-2.30pm Wed-Sun & 7-10.30pm daily summer, 12.30-2.30pm & 7-10.30pm Wed-Sun winter) With only a handful of tables (book ahead), this generous, Slow Food–acclaimed trattoria offers a level of creativity and attention to detail generally lacking in touristy Taormina. The limited menu changes regularly based on what's in season, and is filled with less-common regional specialities, from a chocolatey *caponata* (a cooked, sweet-and-sour salad of aubergines, peppers and onion) to heavenly wild-fennel 'meatballs'.

La Piazzetta
SICILIAN €€

(☑0942 62 63 17; www.ristorantelapiazzettatormi na.it; Via Paladini 5; meals €30-45; ☉7.30pm-midnight daily, plus 12.30-2.30pm Fri-Sun Jul-Sep, 12.30-2.30pm & 7.30-10.30pm Tue-Sun Oct-Jun; ☎) Tucked into the corner of picturesque Piazza Paladini, seafood-focused La Piazzetta is an agreeable place to enjoy homestyle Sicilian

cooking. Staples like *pasta alla Norma* (pasta with basil, eggplant, ricotta and tomato) and grilled fish are accompanied by daily specials that might include a risotto of shrimps and sweet lemon peel. Service is gracious and the alfresco area intimate and lush.

Osteria RossoDivino
SICILIAN €€€

(☑0942 62 86 53; www.osteria-rosso-divino.com; Vico De Spuches 8; meals €45-65; ☉7pm-midnight Jul-early Sep, noon-3pm & 7-11pm Wed-Mon Mar-Jun & mid-Sep–Dec; ☎) With seating on an intimate, candlelit courtyard, this coveted nosh spot (book ahead!) is the passion project of siblings Jacqueline and Sara Ragusa. The day's offerings are dictated by the season, the local fishers' catch, and the siblings' own morning market trawl. Expect anything from heavenly anchovy tempura (the secret: mineral water in the batter) to *paccheri* pasta with gorgonzola crema and dehydrated pears.

Andreas
SICILIAN €€€

(☑0942 2 40 11; Via Bagnoli Croce 88; meals €35-55, 4-course set menu €55-60; ☉12.30-2.30pm Wed-Sun, plus 7.30-10.30pm Tue-Sun; ☎) Subdued and sophisticated (if slightly clinical), Andreas is home to chef Andreas Zangerl, a long-time fixture on Taormina's fine-dining scene. While the menu can be a little hit and miss, the seafood antipasti and *primi* are often highlights. These might include local shrimps and vegetables served tempura-style, or a sultry dish of *paccheri* pasta with tuna and spicy '*nduja* (spreadable Calabrian salami).

🍸 Drinking & Nightlife

Taormina's nightlife revolves around the town's fashionable bars and cafes, mostly located on or just off the main pedestrian strip of Corso Umberto I. Most venues have outdoor seating for alfresco posing.

★Morgana
COCKTAIL BAR

(☑0942 62 00 56; www.morganataormina.it; Scesa Morgana 4; ☉7.30pm-late daily Apr-Oct & mid-Dec–early Jan, 7.30pm-late Fri & Sat Nov–mid-Dec; ☎) This so-svelte cocktail-lounge sports a new look every year, with each concept inspired by Sicilian culture, artisans and landscape. It's the place to be seen, whether on the petite dance floor or among the prickly pears and orange trees in the dreamy, chi-chi courtyard. Fuelling the fun are gorgeous libations, made with local island ingredients, from wild fennel and orange to sage.

Consider booking ahead to ensure entry.

Médousa
COCKTAIL BAR

(✆0942 38 87 33; www.facebook.com/medousa taormina; Via Sesto Pompeo 1; ⊙8am-1am; 🛜) Médousa's enchanting garden does more than set a romantic scene for *aperitivo* (3pm to 9pm), the best time to hit this all-day cafe-bar-bistro. It also provides fresh fruits and aromatic herbs for its impeccable cocktails. Tapas-style bites include Sicilian-inspired sushi and French oysters, and while there is a full restaurant menu, the place shines brightest as a place to drink and graze.

Ape Nera
CAFE

(✆0942 2 39 38; www.facebook.com/ApeNera Taormina; Corso Umberto I 65; ⊙9am-late summer, reduced hours rest of year; 🛜 ♿) In hues of dusty pink, blue and gold, new-school Ape Nera is a good allrounder: drop in for an almond-milk cappuccino, a smoothie or perhaps a made-from-scratch infusion of ginger, lemon, lime, orange, mint, apple and honey. Quality wines and cocktails are on offer, as well as edibles ranging from breakfast *cornetti* (croissants), scrambled eggs and pancakes, to *panini,* salads and luscious cakes.

Wunderbar Caffè
CAFE

(✆0942 62 50 32; www.wunderbarcaffe.com; Piazza IX Aprile 7; ⊙9am-late; 🛜) A Taormina landmark since the *dolce vita* 1960s, this achingly expensive see-and-be-seen cafe has served them all – Tennessee Williams, who liked to watch 'the squares go by', Greta Garbo, Richard Burton and Elizabeth Taylor. With tables spread over the vibrant piazza and jacketed waiters taking the orders, it is still very much the quintessential Taormina watering hole.

Bar Turrisi
BAR

(✆0942 2 81 81; www.barturrisi.com; Piazza Duomo, Castelmola; ⊙10am-late; 🛜) A few kilometres outside Taormina, in the hilltop community of Castelmola, lies this chuckle-inducing bar. It's famous for its unconventional decor, which includes a giant *minchia* (you'll need no translation once you see it). Sip a glass of almond wine, enjoy the view – and keep your mind out of the gutter!

🛍 Shopping

Shopping is a popular pastime in Taormina, particularly on pedestrianised Corso Umberto I. Lining the street is a mix of high-end fashion, shoes and accessories, quality ceramic goods, lace and linen tableware and antique furniture, as well as local culinary deli treats and wine. Make sure to explore the side streets, which harbour some interesting boutiques and artisan studios.

Dieffe
FASHION & ACCESSORIES

(✆0942 62 86 79; Corso Umberto I 226; ⊙10am-10pm Apr-Nov, 11am-7pm Thu-Tue Dec-Feb) A bastion of 'Made in Italy', Dieffe offers sharp edits of men's threads, shoes and accessories from unique local and mainland artisans. Expect to find – among other items – silk ties, hand-stitched shirts and hand-painted leather belts. Footwear includes casually chic moccasins and bold, contemporary sneakers. A must for lovers of idiosyncratic Italian style.

Majolica
CERAMICS

(✆327 4075883; Via Bagnoli Croci 6; ⊙9.30am-9.30pm Mon-Sat, from 5pm Sun summer, reduced hours rest of year) Siblings Maria and Elvira

IONIAN COAST TAORMINA

WORTH A TRIP

GOLE ALCANTARA

Located 15km inland from Giardini-Naxos, **Gole Alcantara** (✆0942 98 50 10; www.gole alcantara.com; €1.50; ⊙8am-sunset; ♿) is a vertiginous 25m-high natural gorge bisected by the freezing waters of the Alcantara river (the name is derived from the Arabic *al qantara*, meaning bridge). Characterised by its weirdly symmetrical rock formations – created when a red-hot lava flow hit the water and splintered the basalt into lava prisms – it's a spectacular sight well worth searching out.

The gorge is now part of the Gole Alcantara Parco Botanico e Geologico, which is within the Parco Fluviale dell'Alcantara regional park. It's out of bounds between November and March due to the risk of flash flooding, but is open during the rest of the year. To get to the bottom, there's a lift near the car park or a 224-step staircase some 200m or so uphill from the lift. Once down by the river, you can hire waders to splash around in the icy waters or simply sunbathe on the surrounding banks. Note that heavy crowds in summer can make this spot feel somewhat less wild and serene, though the 3.5km of nature trails in the area provide the opportunity to explore further afield.

Interbus runs here from Taormina (€3.20, one hour, up to eight daily).

handcraft upbeat, contemporary ceramics in their workshop-cum-store, hidden away on a Taormina side street. Bright, vibrant colours underscore everything from espresso cups and mugs, to condiment bottles, serving plates, jewellery, even little ceramic scooters. Products are lead-free, dishwasher and microwave safe, and can be shipped worldwide.

Pafumi JEWELLERY

(📞 0942 62 50 35; Corso Umberto I 251; ⊙ 9.30am-11.30pm Mon-Sat, 9.30am-1.30pm & 3-11.30pm Sun summer, to 7.30pm winter) Made in Sicily and not sold anywhere off the island, the colourful earrings, bracelets and pendants of the Isola Bella jewellery line are reason enough to browse at this shop near Porta Catania. Other Italian lines are also well represented.

Kerameion CERAMICS

(📞 339 2079032; www.kerameion.com; Corso Umberto I 198; ⊙ 9am-1pm & 2.30-8.30pm Mon-Sat, 9am-1pm Sun) Local artist Marco Monforte runs this shop specialising in colourful Sicilian tiles featuring hand-painted scenes. Made-to-order ceramics are available, as are ready-made objects such as colourful plates, platters, jugs and super-cute espresso cups.

Carlo Mirella Panarello GIFTS & SOUVENIRS

(Corso Umberto I 122; ⊙ 10am-10pm summer, reduced hours rest of year) This eclectic shop is a fun place to browse for striking Italian jewellery, as well as ceramics, paintings, local fragrances and curiosities that might see you fawning over a miniature merry-go-round.

La Torinese FOOD & DRINKS

(📞 0942 2 31 43; Corso Umberto I 59; ⊙ 9.30am-1pm & 4-8.30pm) Apothecary-like La Torinese stocks mouthwatering local edibles such as olive oil, capers, marmalade, honey, cheese, cured meats, old-fashioned sweets and wines. Smash-proof bubble wrapping helps to bring everything home in one piece.

❶ Information

Hospital (Ospedale San Vincenzo; 📞 0942 57 91; Contrada Sirina) Hospital with an emergency department, located 2km downhill from the centre.

Police Station (📞 0942 61 11; Piazza San Domenico de Guzman 1) A 100m walk south of Piazza del Duomo.

Post Office (📞 0942 21 30 52; Piazza Sant'Antonio Abate; ⊙ 8.20am-7pm Mon-Fri, to 12.30pm Sat) Located just outside the Porta Catania city gate.

Tourist Office (📞 0942 2 32 43; Palazzo Corvaja, Piazza Santa Caterina; ⊙ 8.30am-2.15pm & 3.30-6.45pm Mon-Fri Jan-Dec, 9am-1pm & 4-6.30pm Sat summer) Handy for information, including transport timetables and town maps.

❶ Getting There & Away

BUS

Bus is the easiest way to reach Taormina. The bus station is on Via Luigi Pirandello, 400m east of Porta Messina, the northeastern entrance to the old town. **Interbus** (📞 0942 62 53 01; www.interbus.it; Via Luigi Pirandello) services leave daily for Messina (€4.30, 55 minutes to 1¾ hours, one to five daily), Catania (€5.10, 1¼ to two hours, once or twice hourly) and Catania airport (€8.20, 1½ hours, once or twice hourly). It also runs services to Castelmola (€1.90, 15 minutes), roughly every one to two hours from around 9.40am to 5.40pm.

CAR & MOTORCYCLE

Taormina is on the A18 *autostrada* and the SS114. The historic centre is closed to nonresident traffic and Corso Umberto I is closed to all traffic. You can hire cars and scooters at **California Car Rental** (📞 0942 2 37 69; www.californiarentcar.com; Via Bagnoli Croce 86; scooter per day/week €40/250, Fiat Panda €70/333) near Villa Comunale.

Some top-end hotels offer limited parking; otherwise, you'll have to leave your car in one of three car parks outside the historic centre: **Porta Catania** (per 24hr Jul & Aug €16, Sep-Jun €14), **Porta Pasquale** (per 24hr Jul & Aug €16, Sep-Jun €14) or **Lumbi** (per 24hr €16 Jul & Aug, Sep-Jun €14). All three are within walking distance of Corso Umberto I, though Lumbi (the furthest) runs a free shuttle bus up to the centre.

TRAIN

There are frequent trains to and from Messina (from €4.30, 45 minutes to 1¼ hours) and Catania (€4.30, 35 minutes to one hour), but the awkward location of Taormina's station (a steep 4km below town) is a strong disincentive. If you do arrive this way, catch a taxi (€15) or an Interbus coach (€1.90, 10 minutes, roughly one to three an hour) up to town. Note that train frequency is reduced on Sunday.

SAVOCA

📞 0942 / POP 1720 / ELEV 303M

Hidden away in the hills above Santa Teresa di Riva, Savoca is a tiny village with Hollywood credentials. Francis Ford Coppola filmed part of *The Godfather* here, the village standing in for Corleone. One of the locations used was **Bar Vitelli** (📞 334 9227227; Piazza

Fossia 7; ⊘ 9am-midnight summer, to 5pm rest of year), a rickety cafe near the village entrance. It was here that a love-struck Michael Corleone (Al Pacino) asks the wrong man about Apollonia Vitelli, the beautiful woman who had caught his eye. Order a *granita* (with a side of *biscotti* for dipping) and devour it on the bar's front patio. From here you can see the 14th-century Chiesa di Santa Lucia, where Michael marries Apollonia.

Time stands pleasantly still here. Indeed, with its gated walls, rustic stone cottages and haunting churches, the village seems unchanged since medieval times.

◉ Sights

Catacomb   CATACOMB
(⊋ 380 6948408; www.conventocappuccinisavoca.com; Via Cappuccini 10; admission by donation; ⊘ 9.30am-7.30pm Apr-Oct, to 3.30pm Wed-Sun Nov-Mar) Located beneath a 17th-century Capuchin monastery, Savoca's small catacomb is considered one of Sicily's most significant. Its mummified corpses date back to the 17th and 18th centuries and represent some of the town's bigwigs. Among them is monk Bernardo della Limina, located second from left in the middle row facing the stairs. Considered a miracle-performing, quasi-saint, his patchwork garment was sewn using fabric donated by the faithful.

Other original garments include beautiful silks, a testament to Savoca's once-thriving silk production industry.

❶ Information

Tourist Office (⊋ 0942 76 11 25; www.comunesavoca.gov.it/turismo; Via Pineta; ⊘ 9am-2pm Mon-Fri, to 6pm Sat & Sun) For more information about the village, ask at this small office.

❶ Getting There & Away

You will need a car to reach Savoca. From Taormina, take the A18/E45 towards Messina and exit for Roccalumera. Follow the signs for Catania/Savoca, which lead you southbound through Santa Teresa di Riva on the SS114 before leading you inland and uphill on the SP19 for 4km to Savoca.

CATANIA

⊋ 095 / POP 311,600

For all the noise, chaos and scruffiness that hit the visitor at first glance, Catania has a strong magnetic pull. This is Sicily at its most youthful, a city packed with cool and gritty bars, abundant energy and an earthy spirit in sharp contrast to Palermo's aristocratic airs.

Catania's historic core is a Unesco-listed wonder, where black-and-white *palazzi* tower over sweeping baroque piazzas. One minute you're scanning the skyline from a dizzying dome, the next perusing contemporary art in an 18th-century convent. Beneath it all are the ancient ruins of a town with over 2700 candles on its birthday cake. Indeed, food is another local forte. This is the home of Sicily's iconic *pasta alla Norma* and the extraordinary La Pescheria market.

Keeping an eye on it all is Catania's skyscraping frenemy, Mt Etna, a powerful presence that adds another layer of intensity and beauty to Sicily's second-biggest city.

IONIAN COAST CATANIA

DON'T MISS

BEACHES NEAR TAORMINA

The nearest beach to Taormina is **Lido Mazzarò**, accessible by **funivia** (Cable Car; Via Luigi Pirandello; 1-way/day pass €3/10; ⊘ every 15min 9am-1am Mon, from 8am Tue-Sun summer, reduced hours rest of year). It's a popular pebbly beach, well serviced with umbrellas and deck chairs for hire (around €20 to €25 for one umbrella and two deck chairs).

To the south of Mazzarò, and an easy walk past the Sant'Andrea hotel, is **Isola Bella** (www.parconaxostaormina.com; adult/reduced €4/2; ⊘ 9am-7pm May-Aug, to 6.30pm Apr & early–mid-Sep, reduced hours rest of year), a tiny island set in a stunning cove, which was once home to Florence Trevelyan; it's her house that sits in silent solitude on top of the rocky islet. There's wonderful snorkelling in the crystalline waters or you can hire a boat and pootle around the rocky bays. If you prefer your adventures underwater, **Nike Diving Centre** (⊋ 339 1961559; www.diveniketaormina.com; Spiaggia dell'Isola Bella) offers a range of packages from its base at the northern end of the beach.

For a real sandy beach you will have to go to **Spisone**, just beneath the *autostrada* exit. It's about a 2km walk north from the Mazzarò cable-car station.

⊙ Sights

Piazza del Duomo SQUARE

A Unesco World Heritage Site, Catania's central piazza is a set piece of contrasting lava and limestone, surrounded by buildings in the unique local baroque style and crowned by the grand Cattedrale di Sant'Agata. At its centre stands **Fontana dell'Elefante** (1736), a naive, smiling black-lava elephant dating from Roman times and surmounted by an improbable Egyptian obelisk. Another fountain at the piazza's southwest corner, **Fontana dell'Amenano**, marks the entrance to Catania's fish market.

Legend has it that the elephant belonged to the 8th-century magician Eliodorus, who reputedly made his living by turning people into animals. The obelisk itself is said to possess magical powers that help ease Mt Etna's volatile temperament. Much younger is the 19th-century Amenano fountain. Created by Neapolitan sculptor Tito Angelini, the splash-happy piece commemorates the Amenano river, which once ran above ground and on whose banks the Greeks first founded the city of Catania, which they named Katáne.

★**La Pescheria** MARKET

(Via Pardo; ⊙ 7am-2pm Mon-Sat) Catania's raucous fish market, which takes over the streets behind Piazza del Duomo every workday morning, is pure street theatre. Tables groan under the weight of decapitated swordfish, ruby-pink prawns and trays full of clams, mussels, sea urchins and all manner of mysterious sea life. Fishmongers gut silvery fish and high-heeled housewives step daintily over pools of blood-stained water. It's absolutely riveting. Surrounding the market are a number of good seafood restaurants.

★**Teatro Massimo Bellini** THEATRE

(☑095 730 61 35, guided tours 344 2249701; www.teatromassimobellini.it; Via Perrotta 12; guided tour adult/child €6/4) Completed in 1890 and made for homegrown composer Vincenzo Bellini, Catania's opera house is suitably lavish, from the stucco-and-marble extravagance of the foyer (dubbed the *ridotto*) to the glory of the theatre itself, wrapped in four tiers of gilded boxes. Its painted ceiling, by Ernesto Bellandi, depicts scenes from four of Bellini's best-known operas. The **Associazione Guide Turistiche Catania** (www.guidecatania.it; info@guidecatania.it) runs 45-minute guided tours;

email to book a tour and call ahead to confirm times as the theatre isn't always open.

Monastero dei Benedettini di San Nicolò l'Arena MONASTERY

(☑095 710 27 67; www.monasterodeibenedettini.it; Piazza Dante 32; grounds free, guided tours adult/reduced €8/5; ⊙ 8.30am-8pm Mon-Fri, to 2pm Sat, guided tours hourly 9am-5pm Mon-Sun, 11am-6pm daily Aug) This is one of Europe's largest monasteries and an example of the wealth enjoyed by the Benedictine order. Built in 1703 and now part of the city university, it's home to two grand internal cloisters and one of Sicily's most important libraries. Engaging daily guided tours visit the cloisters and library, as well as other areas usually closed to the public. Alternatively, you can view the cloisters on your own from the surrounding corridors. Not all the tours are in English, so call ahead to confirm English-language tour times.

Two tickets are available: the first (adult/reduced €9/3.50) includes entry to the Monastero dei Benedettini, while the second (adult/reduced €14/4.50) also includes access to the **Museo Diocesano** (☑095 28 16 35; www.museodiocesanocatania.com; Piazza del Duomo; adult/reduced €7/4, incl baths €10/6; ⊙ 9am-2pm Mon, Wed & Fri, to 2pm & 3-6pm Tue & Thu, to 1pm Sat) and its subterranean Roman baths.

★**Monastero delle Benedettine** CHURCH

(www.officineculturali.net/benedettine.htm; cnr Via Teatro Greco & Via Crociferi; adult/reduced €5/3; ⊙ 10am-5pm Tue, Fri & Sat, plus 11am-5pm 1st Sun of the month) The Monastero delle Benedettine covers two adjacent sites: a Benedictine convent and the **Chiesa di San Benedetto**. Top billing goes to the church, built between 1704 and 1713 and adorned with splendid stucco, marble and a late-18th-century altar made of Sicilian jasper. Standout artworks include Giovanni Tuccari's glorious ceiling frescoes and a graphic depiction of St Agatha being tortured in front of a curious sultan.

Via Crociferi STREET

A lovely, tranquil spot for a morning stroll, Via Crociferi is one of Catania's most attractive streets, famous for its exuberant baroque churches and imposing 18th-century *palazzi*.

Arco di San Benedetto (Via Crociferi), built by the Benedictines in 1704, marks the beginning of Via Crociferi. According to legend, the arch was built in a single night to defy a city ordinance against its construction on the grounds that it was a seismic liability.

TOP TOURS & TRAILS

Etna Guided Tours (p198) You can explore Mt Etna on your own, but going with an expert guide offers a much richer experience. Consider opting for a smaller, less-touristy operator for a more intimate encounter with Sicily's fiery giant.

Gole Alcantara (p179) A renowned beauty spot, this deep rocky canyon is bisected by the freezing Alcantara river. In summer you can wade through the waters, sunbathe or walk along the surrounding nature trails.

Riviera dei Ciclopi (p192) Take a boat tour to explore the caves and black volcanic rocks along the popular stretch of coastline north of Catania. Inquire at Catania's tourist office (p191) for more information.

Castelmola (p175) There are two panoramic walking trails leading from Taormina to the pretty village of Castelmola, including the especially beautiful Sentiero dei Saraceni. Drop into Taormina's tourist office (p180) for route details.

Isola Bella (p181) The picture-perfect bay flanking this tiny island offers some of the best swimming near Taormina, not to mention excellent diving courtesy of beachside outfit Nike Diving Centre.

Ferrovia Circumetnea (p199) If you prefer to keep some distance between yourself and Etna's volatile craters, jump on a train and tour the small towns that circle the volcano's base.

Parco Archeologico Greco Romano RUINS
(☑095 715 05 08; Via Vittorio Emanuele II 262; adult/reduced incl Casa Liberti €6/3; ☉9am-7pm) West of Piazza del Duomo lie Catania's most impressive ancient ruins: the remains of a 2nd-century Roman Theatre and its small rehearsal theatre, the Odeon. The ruins are evocatively sited in the thick of a crumbling residential neighbourhood, with vine-covered buildings that appear to have sprouted organically from the half-submerged stage. Adjacent to the main theatre is the **Casa Liberti** (closed Sundays), an elegantly restored 19th-century apartment now home to two millennia worth of artefacts discovered during the excavation of the site.

Via Etnea STREET
It's not difficult to see how Catania's main shopping street got its name – on a clear day you can see Mt Etna rising majestically at the end of it. Via Etnea runs straight from Piazza del Duomo up to the foothills below Etna. Lined with stores, bars and pavement cafes, it's busy at most times but heaves on Saturday afternoons, when shoppers pile in from the suburbs to strut, schmooze and update their wardrobes.

At its southern end, Piazza dell'Università is an atmospheric spot to take stock over a coffee and cake. On the other side of the square is **Palazzo dell'Università**, the Vaccarini-designed building that houses the city university. On the eastern flank is another Vaccarini edifice, **Palazzo Sangiuliano**.

To escape the madding crowds, continue up to the **Giardino Bellini** (☉6am-11pm summer, to 10pm spring & autumn, to 9pm winter; ⊞) where you can relax on a bench in the shady gardens and admire views up to that volcano.

Chiesa Badia di Sant'Agata CHURCH
(☑340   4238663;   www.badiasantagata.word press.com; Via Vittorio Emanuele II 182; dome €5; ☉9.30am-12.30pm daily, plus 3.30-5.30pm Tue-Sat & 4-8.30pm Sun) With an elegant concave-convex facade reminiscent of Borromini, this 18th-century church was designed by Palermitan architect Giovanni Battista Vaccarini. The architect's death in 1768 saw Nicolò Daniele take over completion of the interior, his own contributions including the dramatic Carrara marble floor and amber-coloured altars in Castronovo marble. The pièce de résistance, however, is the spectacular, 360-degree panorama from the dome, which takes in the city's rooftops and domes, and a brooding Mt Etna to the north.

Cattedrale di Sant'Agata CATHEDRAL
(☑095 32 00 44; Piazza del Duomo; ☉7am-noon & 4-7pm Mon-Sat, 7.30am-12.30pm & 4.30-7.30pm Sun) Inside the vaulted interior of this cathedral, beyond its impressive marble facade sporting two orders of columns taken from the Roman amphitheatre, lie the relics of the city's patron saint. Its other famous resident is the world-famous Catanian composer Vincenzo Bellini, his remains transferred here

Catania

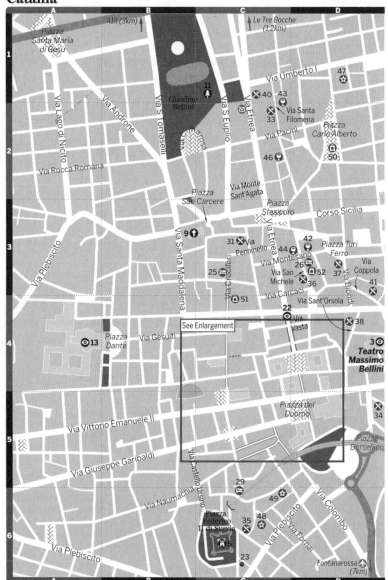

in 1876, 41 years after his death in France. Consider visiting the Museo Diocesano (p182) next door for access to the Roman baths directly underneath the church.

The young virgin Agata resisted the advances of the nefarious Quintian (AD 250) and was horribly mutilated (her breasts were hacked off and her body rolled in hot coals). You can actually visit the dungeons where these atrocities were committed under the **Chiesa di Sant'Agata al Carcere** (☑ 338 1441760; Piazza San Carcere; ☉ 10am-noon Wed & Sat Jun & Jul, Sat & Sun Sep-May, closed Aug) behind the Roman amphitheatre on Piazza

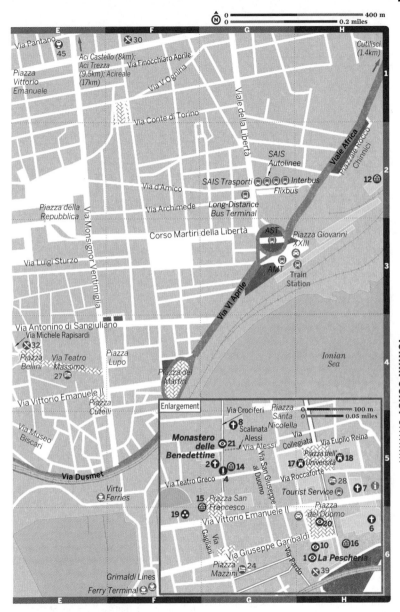

Stesicoro. The saint's jewel-drenched effigy is ecstatically venerated on 5 February in one of Sicily's largest festivals.

Castello Ursino CASTLE
(Piazza Federico II di Svevia) Catania's forbidding 13th-century castle once guarded the city from atop a seafront cliff. However, the 1669 eruption of Mt Etna changed the landscape and the whole area to the south was reclaimed by the lava, leaving the castle completely landlocked. The castle now houses the **Museo Civico** (☑ 095 34 58 30; Castello Ursino, Piazza Federico II di Svevia; adult/

Catania

reduced €6/3; ⊙ 9am-7pm), home to the valuable archaeological collection of the Biscaris, Catania's most important aristocratic family. Exhibits include colossal classical sculpture, Greek vases and some fine mosaics.

Museo Arte Contemporanea Sicilia GALLERY
(MACS; ☑ 095 617 20 35; www.museomacs.it; Via San Francesco 30; adult/reduced €5/3.50; ⊙ 10.30am-5.30pm Tue-Sun) Old and new conspire at MACS, a compact, contemporary-art museum inside an 18th-century abbey of the Monastery of St Benedict. Occupying two floors, the collection includes over 70 works, from painting and sculpture to photography and mixed-media pieces. Artists hail from Sicily, mainland Italy and other corners of Europe, as well as countries as far-flung as Cuba, Argentina and Singapore.

Chiesa di San Giuliano CHURCH
(☑ 351 9301007; Via Crociferi; guided tour €4; ⊙ 10am-1pm Thu-Sat) Attributed to Sicilian baroque maestro Vaccarini and built between 1739 and 1751, the Chiesa di San Giuliano features an elegant convex facade and, above the portal, a broken pediment graced by two allegorical female figures. Capping the church is a polygonal porch, from which the convent's cloistered nuns (often hailing from noble families) could view the passing procession on the feast day of St Agatha. Tours of the church include access to the dome loggia, which offers sweeping city views.

Museo Belliniano MUSEUM
(☑ 095 715 05 35; Piazza San Francesco 3; adult/reduced €5/2; ⊙ 9am-7pm Mon-Sat, to 1pm Sun)

One of Italy's great opera composers, Vincenzo Bellini was born in Catania in 1801. The house he grew up in has since been converted into this museum, which houses an interesting collection of memorabilia, including original scores, photographs, pianos once played by Bellini, and the maestro's death mask.

In his short life (he died aged 34), Bellini composed 10 operas, including the famous trio: *La sonnambula* (The Sleepwalker), *I puritani* (The Puritans) and *Norma,* which has since been immortalised as the name of Sicily's most famous pasta dish – *pasta alla Norma.*

Le Ciminiere MUSEUM

(Viale Africa 12) Le Ciminiere is a modern museum complex housed in a converted sulphur refinery. The most interesting of its museums is the **Museo Storico dello Sbarco in Sicilia** (☑095 401 19 29; www.facebook. com/museostoricodellosbarco1943; adult/reduced €4/2; ⊙10am-6pm, last entry 4pm Tue-Sun Jul & Aug, 9am-5pm Tue-Sun, last entry 3pm Sep-Jun), which illustrates the history of the WWII Allied landings in Sicily. Also noteworthy is the **Museo del Cinema** (☑095 401 19 28; adult/reduced €4/2; ⊙10am-5pm Tue-Sun Jul & Aug, 9am-4pm Tue-Sun Sep-Jun), which explores the evolution of movie making and features movie posters, memorabilia and vintage cinema equipment. Museums aside, Le Ciminiere is also home to performance space **Zo** (☑095 816 89 12; www.zoculture.it; Piazzale Rocco Chinnici 6; 🛜).

✸ Festivals & Events

Festa di Sant'Agata RELIGIOUS

(www.festadisantagata.it; ⊙3-5 Feb) In Catania's biggest religious festival one million people follow the Fercolo (a silver reliquary bust of St Agatha) along the main street of the city. On the evening of 3 February, spectacular fireworks are set to music, with some folk heading into the square early in the afternoon to secure a good vantage point.

Marranzano World Fest MUSIC

(www.mondodimusica.it; Monastero dei Benedettini di San Nicolò l'Arena, Piazza Dante 32; ⊙Jun) A four-night festival of world music, evocatively held at the historic Monastero dei Benedettini di San Nicolò l'Arena. Expect anything and everything from traditional Sicilian song to desert blues and electro-shamanic sounds, performed by acts from across the island and the globe.

✕ Eating

Eating in Catania is a pleasure, whether by market stalls at La Pescheria or on trendy Via Santa Filomena. Snack bars, trattorias and restaurants are plentiful, including vegetarian and vegan-friendly options, and the street food is superb. Classic bites include *arancini* (fried rice balls), *cartocciate* (bread stuffed with ham, mozzarella, olives and tomato) and *pasta alla Norma,* all invented right here.

★ I Dolci di Nonna Vincenza SWEETS €

(☑095 715 18 44; www.dolcinonnavincenza.it; Piazza San Placido 7; cannoli & arancini from €2.30; ⊙8.30am-8pm Mon-Sat, 9am-1.30pm Sun; 🛦) Nuns taught a young Nonna Vincenza the art of baking. Today, her fragrant sweets are the stuff of glutinous dreams. Under huge chandeliers, counters gleam with irresistible treats, among them cinnamon- and lemon-flavoured *geli* (jellies) and crisp *cannoli* filled with combos like ricotta and hazelnut. Take-home treats include cult-status *cassatella di Agira,* shortcrust biscuits filled with cocoa, cinnamon, almond and citrus zest.

Savoury edibles include golden arancini; ask if the *arancino al pistachio* is on offer. Come summer, the shop-cum-cafe also serves gelato.

La Deliziosa SICILIAN €

(☑095 668 18 06; www.deliziosacatania.it; Via Crociferi 77; meals €20-25; ⊙12.30-4pm & 5.30pm-midnight Tue-Sun; 🛜✕) Affable Aurora and Carminia run this adorable little eatery, with alfresco tables on atmospheric Via Crociferi. The weekly-changing menu celebrates regional produce and modern takes on Sicilian cooking, with staples including *facciazza,* a pizza-style concoction topped with uncooked ingredients like tomatoes, cheese and prosciutto. Those wanting to graze can drop in for an afternoon *aperitivo* of Sicilian nibbles, vino, beer and *spritz.*

Al Vicolo ITALIAN €

(☑095 836 07 30; www.alvicolopizzaevino.it; Via del Colosseo 5; panini €5-7, cheese & charcuterie boards from €12, pizzas €6-16; ⊙noon-12.30am Sun-Fri, to 1am Sat; 🛜) 🌿 Clued-in Al Vicolo wears several hats well: bustling pizzeria, gourmet deli and designer bistro. The competent pizzas are huge, with a signature *bordo* pizza (not available Saturday) that sees the crust stuffed with cream cheese, pistachio and cherry tomatoes. The deli counter furnishes everything from take-away *panini* to graze-friendly *taglieri* laden with artisan charcuterie and cheeses. Gluten-free options are available.

Agricolab SICILIAN €

(☑ 095 1693 2878; www.agricolab.it; Via F Crispi 258; meals €20-27; ⊙ 12.30-3pm & 6-10.30pm Mon, Wed & Thu, to midnight Fri & Sat, winter times vary; ☏ ☑ ♠) ♪ Small Sicilian farms and producers are showcased at this hip, up-beat cafe-bistro, run by Singaporean Fawn and her Sicilian partner Giuseppe. Tuck into anything from sourdough bread with homemade spreads, to Agricolab's signature *pasta aglio e olio* (pasta with olive oil and garlic). Service is friendly, and the option of bar seating makes it perfect for solo diners. Book ahead on weekends.

La Cucina dei Colori VEGETARIAN €

(☑ 095 715 98 93; Via San Michele 9; mixed plates €10-14, meals €20; ⊙ 12.30-3pm & 7.30-11pm, closed Sun mid-Jun–Sep; ☑ ♠) Take away or dine in at communal tables at this contemporary ode to seasonal, organic, meat-free nosh. Scan the counters for the daily-changing options, which might include wholewheat pasta with artichokes, sautéed seitan (wheat gluten) with vegetables, or an egg, vegetable and *caciocavallo* cheese flan. Vegan and gluten-free options are available and drinks include organic wines.

Comis Ice Cafè GELATO €

(☑ 095 715 24 99; Piazza Vincenzo Bellini 8; granita €3; ⊙ 7am-8.30pm Mon, to 1.30am Tue-Sun summer, to 8.30pm Mon-Thu, to 1.30am Fri-Sun winter; ☏ ♠) Siblings Santino and Sergio make the finest *granita* in town, known for its especially smooth, creamy consistency. Their house-made brioche is wonderfully soft, and the brothers even churn their own gelato; the pistachio and ricotta are particularly popular. Libations include decent coffee and *spritzes*, the perfect prop while sitting at a table, gazing out at one of Catania's most beautiful squares.

Millefoglie VEGETARIAN €

(☑ 331 2505331; Via Sant'Orsola 12; dishes €6.50-12; ⊙ 12.45-3pm Mon-Sat Nov-Apr, Mon-Fri May-Oct; ☏ ☑) Delicious, flesh-free grub awaits at little Millefoglie, a shabby-chic, whitewashed eatery with concrete floor, communal tables and an open kitchen. The morning's market produce dictates the menu, which might feature vibrant wholewheat *casarecce* (twisted pasta) with zucchini, fava beans, peas, *pecorino*, lemon zest and basil, or chocolate

mousse with chilli and strawberries. A few vegan dishes usually dot the menu.

FUD Bottega Sicula BURGERS €

(☑ 095 715 35 18; www.fud.it; Via Santa Filomena 35; burgers €7-12.50, salads €9.50-11.50, pizza €6.50-10; ⊙ 12.30pm-1am; ☏ ♠) With sharp service and pavement seating on trendy Via Santa Filomena, this hip, back-alley eatery epitomises youthful Catania's embrace of 'Sicilian fast food', made with high-quality, locally sourced ingredients, from Sicilian cheeses to Nebrodi black pork. With wry humour, every burger and *panino* on the menu is spelled using Italian phonetics, from the 'cis burgher' (cheeseburger) to the rustic 'cauntri' (country) sandwich.

Neapolitan-style pizzas are available nightly, as well as at lunch on weekends.

Trattoria di De Fiore TRATTORIA €

(☑ 095 31 62 83; Via Coppola 24/26; meals €20-27; ⊙ 7pm-12.30am Mon, 1pm-12.30am Tue-Sun) For over 50 years, chef Rosanna (yes, that's her in Jamie Oliver's TV series *Jamie Cooks Italy*) has been recreating her great-grandmother's recipes, including the best *pasta alla Norma* you'll taste anywhere in Sicily. Service can be slow, but for patient souls this is a rare chance to experience classic Catanian cooking from a bygone era. Closed Mondays from October to April.

Rosanna says her grandmother referred to *pasta alla Norma* as *pasta Mungibeddu* in honour of Mt Etna (Mungibeddu being the traditional Sicilian name for Catania's famous volcano): tomatoes represented Etna's red lava, aubergine the black cinders, ricotta the snow and basil leaves the mountain vegetation.

★ Mè Cumpari Turiddu SICILIAN €€

(☑ 095 715 01 42; www.mecumparituriddu.it; Piazza Turi Ferro 36-38; meals €26-40; ⊙ 11.30am-12.30am; ☏) Old chandeliers, recycled furniture and vintage mirrors exude a nostalgic air at this quirky bistro-restaurant-providore, where tradition and modernity meet to impressive effect. Small producers and Slow Food sensibilities underline sophisticated, classically inspired dishes like ricotta-and-marjoram ravioli in a pork sauce, soothing Ustica lentil stew or a playful 'deconstructed' *cannolo*. There's a fabulous selection of Sicilian cheeses, lighter bistro grub and cakes.

Consider booking ahead for dinner and Sunday lunch.

Pescheria Fratelli Vittorio
SEAFOOD €€

(☑339 7733890; Via Dusmet 1; meals €25-40; ⊙11.30am-3.30pm & 7pm-midnight Tue-Sun, closed Sun dinner Nov–mid-May) Cats would kill for a table at Fratelli Vittorio, a cult-status eatery whose counter glistens with Catania's freshest fish and seafood. It's not surprising given that co-owner Giovanni is a fishmonger, handpicking the best ingredients from the nearby market. For an overview, order the *degustazione di antipasti del giorno,* or feel the love in the generous *zuppa di pesce* (seafood soup).

If there's still room, finish with a serve of *fedora,* a sweet concoction of ricotta, chocolate chips and toasted almonds.

Le Tre Bocche
SEAFOOD €€

(☑095 53 87 38; Via Ingegnere 11; meals €35-45; ⊙8.30-11.45pm, plus 1-3.30pm Sun) Reservations are essential at this Slow Food–recommended restaurant, which even has its own stand at La Pescheria market. The tasting of antipasti is a non-negotiable feast of fresh, vibrant coastal flavours. If you still have room, opt for a standout *primo* (first course), whether it be spaghetti soaked in sea urchins or squid ink, or perhaps a risotto of courgette and prawns.

Il Gambero Pazzo
SICILIAN €€

(☑333 4616819; Via Vela 1; meals €25-35; ⊙6.45-11pm Wed-Mon, plus 12.45-2.30pm Sun Oct-May; ⓓ) Weathered stairs lead up to 'The Crazy Prawn', a humble, family-run eatery loved for its fresh, affordable seafood and homestyle cooking. Don't miss the *carrellata di antipasti,* a mini tsunami of appetisers that are almost a meal in themselves. Unsurprisingly, both the *primi* (first courses) and *secondi* (mains) favour surf, from garlicky spaghetti with clams to golden, fried calamari. Book ahead.

Cutilisci
SICILIAN €€

(☑095 37 25 58; www.cutilisci.it; Via San Giovanni li Cuti 67-69; pizzas €6.50-14, meals €28-35; ⊙12.30-3pm & 7.30pm-midnight Wed-Mon, 7.30pm-midnight Tue; ⓡⓓ) When the weather's fine, the tables are out on the pavement terrace at Cutilisci, a much-loved waterfront restaurant in the harbour of San Giovanni li Cuti. Wholesome ingredients and global influences define the menu, whose offerings might include swordfish steak with orange and fennel salad and a barley, spelt and vegetable tabbouleh. A taxi from the city centre will cost around €15 one-way.

🍷 Drinking & Nightlife

★Mercati Generali
CLUB

(☑334 9197095, 095 57 14 58; www.mercatigen erali.org; Strada Statale 417, Contrada Lungetto; 9pm-4am Sat; ⓡ) The 11km drive southwest of central Catania is worth it: this is one of Sicily's finest clubs, with top-tier Italian and international DJs and live-music acts, plus edgy exhibitions and other cultural events. Then there's the enchanting setting, in a converted 19th-century wine-pressing warehouse, complete with summertime courtyard. Attention to detail extends to the drinks and food, which include decent wood-fired pizzas.

Admission varies according to what's on, but expect to pay between €10 to €20; check the website for upcoming events.

★Fud Off
COCKTAIL BAR

(☑347 1360586; www.fudoff.it; Via Santa Filomena 28; ⊙6pm-2am; ⓡ) From the quality of the cocktails to the attentive staff, Fud Off just gets it. This is one of Catania's top bars, a slinky, cavernous space of tinted glass, pink neon, and the odd velvet armchair. Drinks include a small, interesting selection of wines by the glass, while the excellent bites include tapas-style morsels and a standout smoked, grilled octopus with potato purée.

Bohéme Mixology Bar
COCKTAIL BAR

(☑095 250 33 40; www.bohememixologybar.com; Via Montesano 27-29; ⊙7pm-3am; ⓡ) There's no drinks list at this intimate cocktail den, decked out in mismatched furniture, gilded mirrors and the odd gramophone. Simply state your flavour and spirit preferences and let the barkeeps work their magic. While the cocktails aren't cheap (€8 to €12), they're better than most local offerings, with everything from the syrups to the grilled pineapple marmalade made from scratch.

Live jazz or blues hits the place several times a week, usually kicking off around 10pm.

Vermut
BAR

(☑347 6001978; Via Gemmellaro 37-39; ⊙11am-2am; ⓡ) Vermouth, vino and *salumi* (charcuterie) keep this budget-friendly hotspot pumping. Scattered with vintage liquor posters and old wooden tables, its ample drinks list includes numerous takes on the martini cocktail, not to mention over 20 versions of the ubiquitous *spritz* on Tuesday nights. Served on deli paper, the rustic, tapas-style bites (€1 to €7.50) include both meaty and vegetarian options.

If you'd rather sit than stand, book ahead in the evenings.

Rix COCKTAIL BAR

(www.facebook.com/ritzcatania; Via Pantano 54; ⊙7pm-1.30am Mon-Sat summer, Tue-Sun winter; 🕾) Svelte, convivial, urbane Rix takes its cocktails seriously. Each is made with passion and precision, from punchy Aviations to a very local Etna Kir (spumante Brut rosé, Etna cherry-liqueur, hazelnut crust). The bar harbours some lesser-known local craft spirits, and almost half of the wines are natural. Food options are seasonal and top notch, with some especially memorable desserts.

Razmataz BAR

(📞095 31 18 93; Via Montesano 17; ⊙9am-late Mon-Sat, 5pm-late Sun, from 9am Sun winter; 🕾) The wines by the glass might be average, but this corner institution is a fabulous spot to while away an hour or two, with tables invitingly spread out across the tree-shaded flagstones of a backstreet square. The bar gets packed from *aperitivo* time onward, and there's a blackboard of decent meals (from €7), from earthy soups and pasta to meat and seafood.

☆ Entertainment

★ Teatro Massimo Bellini THEATRE

(📞095 730 61 11; www.teatromassimobellini. it; Via Perrotta 12) Catania's premier theatre is named after the city's most famous son, composer Vincenzo Bellini. It's one of Italy's most glorious old theatres, staging annual seasons of world-class opera and classical music, as well as dance performances. Tickets, which are available online, start at around €20 and can rise to over €100 for a seat in the stalls.

MA Catania LIVE MUSIC

(📞095 34 11 53; www.macatania.com; Via Vela 6-8; ⊙8pm-2am Thu & Sun, to 4pm Fri & Sat) Queues are the norm at MA, a stylish, high-profile club serving up quality DJ sets, live bands and jam sessions. The space comes with its own restaurant, and the Sunday evening *aperitivo* (dubbed 'No Ordinary Sunday') is a particular hit with locals. Check the club's Facebook page for upcoming events.

Monk Jazz Club JAZZ

(📞340 1223606; www.facebook.com/MonkClub Catania; Via Scuto 19; ⊙hours vary) Monk hosts top-notch Italian and international jazz talent, with past acts including saxophonist Pietro Tonolo and world-renowned pianist Dado Moroni. It's also a good spot to catch emerging acts. Check the club's Facebook page for upcoming events, which also include jam sessions.

Arena Argentina CINEMA

(📞095 32 20 30; www.cinestudio.eu; Via Vanasco 10; adult/reduced €3.50/3; ⊙Jun-Sep) For local cinephiles, summer means sultry outdoor film nights at Arena Argentina. Head up for mainly cult and art-house flicks, from *Purple Rain* and *Labyrinth* to more recent features like *Capernaum* and *Three Billboards Outside Ebbing, Missouri*. Warning: films are usually dubbed in Italian. On Fridays, admission is a bargain €1.50 for those aged under 26.

🛍 Shopping

★ Nelson Sicily FOOD & DRINKS

(📞095 836 16 34; www.nelsonsicily.com; Via Crociferi 50; ⊙10am-2pm & 4-9pm Mon-Sat, to 8pm Sun) Nirvana for gourmands, Nelson is a one-stop shop for all things artisanal and Sicilian. Stock the pantry with everything from single-origin olive oils from Mt Etna to luggage-friendly jars of pistachio pesto, peperoncino, tuna, organic tomato sugo, marinated red garlic from Nubia and more. There's also a well-curated choice of liquor, including natural wines from smaller producers and niche *amari* digestifs.

Boudoir 36 COSMETICS

(📞095 715 23 58; www.boudoir36.it; Via Santa Filomena 36; ⊙6-10pm Tue-Sat) Engineer by day, fragrance maestro by night, Antonio Alessandria indulges his passion for scents at his lavish little perfumery. You won't find mainstream brands here, just cognoscenti wonders from Europe and beyond. You'll also find Antonio's own fragrances, inspired by different aspects of Sicilian culture and geography. Niche soaps, shaving creams, hair care, as well as room and linen sprays are also available.

Tabaré ART

(📞338 7509597; Via San Michele 24; ⊙4.30-8pm Mon, 10am-1pm & 4.30-8pm Tue-Sat) Tabaré sells the wares of five Catanian artisans. Marisa Casaburi creates whimsical models and sculptures in papier maché, Carla Marletta turns recyclables into photo frames, while Ljubiza Mezzatesta paints and prints. Then there's Lina Lizzio's funky jewellery and Giovanna Cacciola's graphic tees. The small upstairs gallery hosts rotating exhibitions of local artists and weekly art workshops for children (€15); English spoken.

La Fiera MARKET

(Piazza Carlo Alberto; ⊙ 8am-1pm Mon-Fri, to 7pm Sat) Every morning except Sunday, Piazza Carlo Alberto (just off Via Etnea) is flooded by the chaos of La Fiera. Not dissimilar to a Middle Eastern kasbah, the market peddles, among other things, curvaceous eggplants, oranges, fresh fish and meats, CDs, handbags and dirt-cheap jeans, tops, bras and underwear.

ℹ️ Information

Airport Tourist Office (☑ 095 723 96 82; www.comune.catania.it/la-citta/turismo; ⊙ 8am-7pm, 8.30am-1.30pm Sun) In the arrivals hall.

Catania Pass (www.cataniapass.it) Offers free or reduced admission to a selection of museums and unlimited use of public transport. One- or multi-day passes are available for individuals (one-/three-/five-day pass €12.50/16.50/20) and families (€23/30.50/38), with passes available for purchase at numerous outlets. These include the tourist information office at Catania Airport, the main tourist office off Piazza del Duomo and participating museums, including the Museo Civico, Museo Belliniano, Museo Diocesano and Monastero dei Benedettini di San Nicolò l'Arena.

Hospital (Presidio Ospedaliero Garibaldi-Centro; ☑ 095 759 11 11; www.ao-garibaldi.catania.it/presidio-osp-garibaldi; Piazza Santa Maria di Gesù 5) Major hospital with a 24-hour emergency department.

Police (Questura; ☑ 095 736 71 11; Piazza Santa Nicolella 8) Just off Via Etnea.

Post Office (☑ 095 715 50 71; www.poste.it; Via Etnea 215; ⊙ 8.20am-7pm Mon-Fri, to 12.30pm Sat) Handy branch on one of Catania's main thoroughfares.

Tourist Office (☑ 095 742 55 73; www.comune.catania.it/la-citta/turismo; Via Vittorio Emanuele II 172; ⊙ 8am-7pm Mon-Sat, 8.30am-1.30pm Sun) City-run tourist office just off Piazza del Duomo.

ℹ️ Getting There & Away

AIR

Catania Fontanarossa Airport (☑ 095 723 91 11; www.aeroporto.catania.it; 🛜) is located 7km southwest of the city centre. It's Sicily's busiest airport, with regular non-stop connections to major Italian cities and numerous destinations in Europe, as well as to Dubai.

Shuttle-bus service **Alibus** (www.amt.ct.it; 🛜) runs to the airport from numerous stops in central Catania, including the train station (€4, 20 to 30 minutes, every 25 minutes). Tickets can be purchased on board using cash (carry the correct change) or credit card.

A **taxi** (☑ 095 33 09 66; www.radiotaxicatania.org) will cost around €20 to €26.

BOAT

Catania's **ferry terminal** (Via Dusmet) lies at the southeast edge of the historic centre. From here **Grimaldi Lines** (☑ 095 586 22 30; www.grimaldi-lines.com; Via Dusmet) operates overnight car ferries between Catania and Salerno (passenger/with car from €23/57, 13 hours, one nightly Monday to Saturday).

From May through September, **Virtu Ferries** (☑ 095 703 12 11; www.virtuferries.com) runs daily catamarans from Pozzallo (south of Catania) to Malta (1¾ hours). Fares vary depending on length of stay in Malta (same-day adult return €90 to €141, open return €118 to €166 depending on the season). Coach transfer between Catania and Pozzallo (€14 each way) adds two hours to the journey. Catamaran frequency is reduced from October to April.

BUS

As a rule, buses are quicker than trains for most destinations. All long-distance buses leave from a **terminal** (Via Archimede) 300m northwest of the train station, with ticket offices across the street on Via D'Amico.

Tickets for SAIS Autolinee, Salemi and Big Bus services can also be purchased at **Nafè** (☑ 095 219 45 50; https://coffeebarnafe.business.site; Piazza Papa Giovanni XXIII 6; ⊙ 5.30am-8.30pm, closed Sun winter), a cafe-bar opposite Catania train station. Around the corner from Nafè, **TDS Service** (☑ 095 216 64 54; Via Sturzo 245; ⊙ 9am-8pm Mon-Sat) is a good-value, cash-only left-luggage office (per hour/day €2/6). It also sells bus tickets for numerous long-distance bus companies, including SAIS Autolinee.

Flixbus (https://global.flixbus.com; Via d'Amico) Operates direct long-distance buses from Catania to numerous mainland destinations, including Taranto (from €20, 7½ hours, one daily), Bari (from €23, eight to nine hours, twice daily) and Naples (from €26, 8½ to nine hours, twice daily).

Interbus (☑ 095 53 27 16; www.interbus.it; Via d'Amico 187) Runs to Syracuse (€6, 1½ hours, 20 daily Monday to Friday, 10 daily Saturday and Sunday), Taormina (€5, 1¼ to two hours, 20 daily Monday to Saturday, 15 Sunday), Ragusa (€8.50, two hours, 14 daily Monday to Friday, eight daily Saturday and Sunday) and Piazza Armerina (€9, 1¾ hours, six daily Monday to Friday, four Saturday, two Sunday).

SAIS Autolinee (☑ 800 211020, 095 53 61 68; www.saisautolinee.it; Via d'Amico 181) Serves

Palermo (€14, 2¾ hours, 14 daily Monday to Friday, 12 Saturday, 10 Sunday), Messina (€8.50, 1½ hours, 23 daily Monday to Friday, 13 Saturday, 12 Sunday) and Enna (€8, 1¼ hours, eight to nine daily Monday to Friday, six Saturday, three Sunday).

SAIS Trasporti (☑ 090 601 21 36; www.sais trasporti.it; Via d'Amico 181) Runs to numerous destinations, including Agrigento (€13.50, three hours, 14 daily Monday to Saturday, 10 Sunday) and overnight to Rome (€44, one daily, 10½ hours).

Tourist Service (☑ 095 820 42 81; www.tourist service2006.com; Via Vittorio Emanuele II 188) Operates hop-on, hop-off tourist buses from Catania to Aci Castello and Aci Trezza. Tickets cost €15 and are valid all day. The bus stop and ticket office are just off Piazza del Duomo.

CAR & MOTORCYCLE

Catania is easily reached from Messina on the A18 *autostrada* as well as from Palermo on the A19. From the *autostrada*, signs for the city centre direct you to Via Etnea.

TRAIN

Frequent trains depart from Catania Centrale station on Piazza Papa Giovanni XXIII. Destinations include Messina (€7.50, 1¼ to 2¼ hours), Syracuse (€7, one to 1½ hours) and Palermo (€13.50, three hours). Train services are significantly reduced on Sunday.

❶ Getting Around

BUS

Several useful **AMT** (☑ 800 018696, 095 751 91 11; www.amt.ct.it) city bus routes terminate in front of Catania Centrale train station, including bus 2-5, which runs every 10 to 40 minutes from the station west to Via Etnea and southwest to Piazza Borsellino (just south of the Cattedrale di Sant'Agata). Also useful is bus D, which runs every 50 minutes from Piazza Borsellino to the local beaches south of the centre. Tickets, available from *tabacchi* (tobacconists), cost €1 and last 90 minutes. A two-hour combined bus-metro ticket costs €1.20. All-day tickets are also available (€2.50).

AST (☑ 095 723 05 11; www.aziendasiciliana trasporti.it) runs to many smaller towns around Catania, including Acireale (€2.70). It also connects Catania to Rifugio Sapienza on Mt Etna. AST tickets can be purchased at AST ticket office **Ufficio Movimento** (Via Sturzo 230-232; ⊙ 6.30am-8pm Mon-Sat), located just off the piazza fronting Catania Centrale station.

CAR & MOTORCYCLE

Choosing to drive in town means you will have to deal with the city's complicated one-way system – for example, you can only drive along Via Vittorio Emanuele II from west to east, while the parallel Via Giuseppe Garibaldi runs from east to west.

Parking is extremely difficult in the city centre. If you're bringing your own car, consider staying at a hotel or B&B with parking facilities; if you're hiring a car, you're best advised to pick up the car as you leave town and return it when you re-enter.

METRO

Catania's one-line metro currently has 11 stops, all on the periphery of the city centre. For tourists, it's mainly useful as a way of getting from Catania Centrale station to the Circumetnea train that circles Mt Etna. A 90-minute metro ticket costs €1. A two-hour combined metro-bus ticket costs €1.20.

TAXI

For a taxi, call Radio Taxi Catania (p191). You'll find taxi ranks at the **train station** and at the northwest corner of **Piazza del Duomo**.

RIVIERA DEI CICLOPI

Extending north of Catania, the Riviera dei Ciclopi is an attractive stretch of coastline that draws no shortage of beach-seeking *catanesi* (Catanians). Until quite recently it was a desperately poor area of isolated fishing villages, but tourism has given it a much needed impetus and it is now a lively summer stomping ground. While many of the beaches are rocky, the swimming is excellent, and the area's booty of restaurants, bars, nightclubs and accommodation keeps punters revelling long after their last dip.

The coast owes its name to a Homeric legend, according to which the towering black rocks that rise out of the sea – actually great hunks of solidified lava – were thrown by the blinded Cyclops, Polyphemus, in a desperate attempt to stop Odysseus escaping. Volcanic activity has created dramatic coastal features, including gorgeous grottoes and dizzying cliffs smothered in thick, lush vegetation.

Acireale

☑ 095 / POP 52,300

The main town on the Riviera, Acireale is set on a series of lava terraces that drop to the sea about 17km north of Catania. Although it's not exactly undiscovered, it remains largely tourist free, a mystery given its stately baroque centre and imposing public buildings. An easy 2km walk down-hill is Santa Maria la Scala, a tiny fishing village seemingly made for perfect seafood lunches.

And while Acireale has long been known for its thermal waters, its modern claim to fame is its spectacular Carnevale festivities, which burst into life each February.

◉ Sights

To eye-up Acireale's most impressive architecture, start in Piazza Duomo, a grandiose square surrounded on three sides by monumental buildings. On the western flank is the **cathedral** (⊙8.30am-12.30pm & 4-8pm), built in the early 1600s and topped by towering conical-capped spires. Inside, the echoing vaults and chapels are richly frescoed.

Next to the cathedral, the **Basilica dei Santi Pietro e Paolo** (⊙8.30am-12.30pm & 4-8pm) displays a typically elaborate 18th-century facade. To the right of it, the **Palazzo Municipale** impresses with its wrought-iron balconies and imposing central portal.

From the piazza, Via Ruggero Settimo leads south to Piazza Lionardo Vigo and the gorgeous **Basilica di San Sebastiano** (⊙8.30am-12.30pm & 4-8pm), one of the town's finest baroque buildings. Guarded by statues of Old Testament characters, the basilica lifts the spirit with its luminous facade, whimsically lined with *putti* (cherubs). Inside, splendid frescoes recount episodes from the life of St Sebastian.

Santa Maria la Scala   VILLAGE

There are two reasons to make the 2km downhill walk to this minute fishing village. One is the walk itself, which, once you've crossed the main road, is a lovely country stroll with gorgeous coastal views. The other is to feast on super-fresh seafood at one of the delightful trattorias.

To get to the village, which consists of little more than a tiny harbour, a church, some houses and a black beach, follow Via Romeo down from Piazza Duomo, head under the bluestone railway underpass, cross the pedestrian bridge and continue down the nature trail (look for the 'La Chiazzette' sign).

Teatro-Museo dell'Opera dei Pupi   THEATRE
(🖉museum 329 1189522, show bookings 347 8061464; www.operadeipupi.com; Via Nazionale 195; adult/reduced €10/5; ⊙9am-noon & 5-8pm summer, 9am-noon & 3-6pm winter) FREE Acireale has a long tradition of puppet theatre, and you can learn all about it here. One-hour guided tours of the museum are available in English, albeit with less detail than those given in Italian. It's always a good idea to call ahead before visiting, as the museum is sometimes closed. If you don't have your own wheels, you can request a pick-up (return €5) from Acireale train station.

✸ Festivals & Events

Carnevale   CARNIVAL
(www.carnevaleacireale.it; ⊙Feb or Mar) The best time to visit Acireale is during February's Carnevale, when the town puts on one of the best spectacles in Sicily. The stars of the show are the elaborately decorated floats, some bedecked in technicolor flower displays, others carrying huge papier-mâché caricatures of local celebrities. All around bands play, costumed dancers leap about and confetti rains.

The exact dates vary each year, but you can get details on the event's comprehensive website. And if you miss it first time round, don't worry, there's a rerun, albeit on a smaller scale, in early August.

✗ Eating

★**In Un Angolo di Mondo**   PIZZA €
(🖉095 87 77 24; www.inunangolodimondo.it; Via Nazionale per Catania 180, Capomulini; pizzas €12-16; ⊙8-11pm Thu-Sun; 🖉🖢) ✐ South of Acireale, this snug, organic, family-run pizzeria creates outstanding wood-fired pie. Prices may be higher, but so is the quality. The bases are wonderfully light, and the creative toppings a showcase for wholesome, seasonal and local produce. Wines include lesser-known Sicilian winemakers, and the place includes a small, ecofriendly boutique selling everything from organic olive oil to soaps. Book ahead.

Caffè Cipriani   CAFE €
(🖉095 60 56 96; Piazza Lionardo Vigo 3; granita €2.20, cakes €3.50; ⊙3.30am-midnight Thu-Tue; 🖢) While it makes its own pastries, cakes and gelato, this 1950s veteran is famous for its *granita,* considered among the best in Sicily. If the weather is behaving, swoon away at one of the outdoor tables, which overlook the extraordinary Basilica di San Sebastiano. Look closely and you'll also spot a faded, Fascist-era sign on one of the neighbouring buildings.

Trattoria La Grotta   TRATTORIA €€
(🖉095 764 81 53; Via Scalo Grande 46, Santa Maria la Scala; meals €30-35; ⊙1-2.30pm & 8-10.30pm Wed-Mon) Book ahead for a table at what is Santa Maria la Scala's best

seafood restaurant. As you enter you'll find the fish counter, where your order is picked out and weighed before going in the pot. Your work done, feast in the tiny dining room (atmospherically set in the body of a cave) or, in the summer, at a table overlooking the harbour.

Tip: specialities include the *insalata di mare* (seafood salad), a mouth-watering medley of prawns, calamari and octopus, and the sensational grilled fish.

L'Oste Scuro   SEAFOOD €€
(☑ 095 763 40 01; Piazza Lionardo Vigo 5-6; meals €30-40; ⊗ 12.30-3.30pm & 7pm-midnight; 🛜) Plastered with old photographs, time-warped L'Oste Scuro is a solid spot for classic, homestyle seafood. The produce is fresh and cooked simply, whether it be house-made *panzotti* pasta stuffed with fish, grilled calamari, or the day's catch oven-baked in a delicate broth with cherry tomatoes and fresh parsley. You'll find it directly opposite the Basilica di San Sebastiano.

ℹ Information

Tourist Office (Piazza Lionardo Vigo; ⊗ 3-6pm Mon-Fri) Small, helpful tourist kiosk with limited hours.

ℹ Getting There & Away

BUS

AST (p192) buses run frequently between Catania and Acireale (€2.70, 80 minutes, quarter-hourly to hourly Monday to Saturday). AST buses stop at Acireale train station.

Interbus (p191) runs buses to Acireale from Catania (€2.70, 50 minutes, four daily Monday to Saturday, one Sunday) and Taormina (€4, 70 minutes, three to four daily Monday to Saturday, one Sunday). Interbus services stop on Corso Umberto I and Via Vittorio Emanuele II in the centre of Acireale.

CAR & MOTORCYCLE

If driving from Catania, head north along the SS114 coastal road. Alternatively, take the A18 tollway and exit for Acireale.

TRAIN

Trains to Acireale run one to three times hourly from Catania (€2.50, 10 to 20 minutes). From Taormina, trains to Acireale run once or twice hourly (€3.80, 25 to 45 minutes). Frequency is significantly reduced on Sunday. Acireale train station is inconveniently located 2km south of the city centre, making buses a better option.

Aci Trezza

☑ 095 / POP 4950

A few kilometres south of Acireale, the small fishing village of Aci Trezza has a lively seafront and a number of good restaurants. Offshore, a series of surreal, jagged basalt rocks, the **Scogli dei Ciclopi**, rise out of the sea. These are the mythical missiles that the blinded Cyclops, Polyphemus (who lived in Etna), is supposed to have thrown at the fleeing Odysseus. Aci Trezza is also celebrated as the setting of *I Malavoglia*, Giovanni Verga's 19th-century literary masterpiece of life in a poor, isolated fishing community.

✘ Eating & Drinking

Osteria dei Marinari   SEAFOOD €€
(☑ 095 27 79 21; http://maredeiciclopi.com/osteria-dei-marinai; Lungomare Ciclopi 185; meals €30-45; ⊗ 12.30-3pm & 7.30pm-midnight Fri-Wed) Right by the harbour, this polished stalwart is where locals come for quality fish and seafood, tucking into tried-and-tested dishes like tuna tartare, linguine pasta with clams, fish roe and lime zest, and a simply gorgeous *frittura mista del golfo* (fried local seafood). Book ahead in the summer.

Banacher   CLUB
(☑ 095 27 10 24, 389 6472466; www.banacher.com; Via Vampolieri 2; ⊗ hours vary) This is one of the Riviera's largest nightclubs, with multiple dance floors, a swimming pool and various club nights catering to the young and not so young.

ℹ Information

Pro Loco Aci Castello (☑ 347 6868900, 095 092 35 72; www.prolocoacicastello.com; Lungomare dei Ciclopi 137; ⊗ 9am-noon Mon-Fri, also 3.30-5.30pm Tue & Thu) Don't be thrown by the name, this waterfront tourist office is actually located in Aci Trezza. It provides information on the Riviera dei Ciclopi, including boat excursions.

ℹ Getting There & Away

If driving from Catania, head north on the SS114.

AMT (p192) city bus 534 (€1, hourly) runs to Aci Trezza and Aci Castello from Catania's Piazza Borsellino. A more expensive option is the Tourist Service (p192) hop-on, hop-off bus (daily ticket €15), which also runs from Catania to Aci Castello and Aci Trezza. Buses depart hourly (every 90 minutes in the winter) from Catania's Via Vittorio Emanuele, just off Piazza del Duomo.

Aci Castello

☑ 095 / POP 18,580

Marking the beginning, or end, of the Riviera dei Ciclopi, the small town of Aci Castello lies 9km from central Catania, making it an easy day trip from the city, even by public transport. Swim off and tan on the volcanic rocks; otherwise, the main attraction is the Norman *castello* set atop an immense black rock.

◉ Sights

Castello
Normanno   CASTLE

(☑320 4339691; adult/reduced €3/1.50; ◷9.30am-1pm & 4-8.30pm mid-Jun–Aug, 9am-1pm & 3-7pm late Mar-May, Sep & Oct, 9am-1pm & 3-5pm rest of year) Built in the 13th century, this dark, brooding Norman castle sits over an earlier Arab fortification. It's in surprisingly good shape considering its age, and hosts a small museum with a collection of geological rock samples and bizarre prehistoric skulls. The castle appears to be grafted atop the Rocca di Acicastello, a vast, black volcanic rock. The rock is considered a vulcanological rarity, having emerged from an underwater fissure.

✕ Eating

Pizzeria Pellegrino   PIZZA €

(☑095 27 40 12; Via Francesco Crispi 17; pizzas €3.50-10.50; ◷7pm-1am Jun-Sep, reduced hours Oct-May; 🍴) This popular joint in Aci Castello is a short walk from the town's famous castle. While the place offers salads and burgers, it's best known for its bubbling, wood-fired pizzas. The latter range from simple classics to creative concoctions like the Finocchietto, a combo of *datterino* tomatoes, bocconcini, fennel cream, breadcrumbs and extra-virgin olive oil.

ⓘ Getting There & Away

If driving from Catania, head north on the SS114. AMT (p192) city bus 534 (€1, hourly) runs to Aci Castello and Aci Trezza from Catania's Piazza Borsellino. A more expensive option is the Tourist Service (p192) hop-on, hop-off bus (daily ticket €15), which also runs from Catania to Aci Castello and Aci Trezza. Buses depart hourly (every 90 minutes in the winter) from Via Vittorio Emanuele in Catania, just off Piazza del Duomo.

MOUNT ETNA

ELEV 3326M

Dominating the landscape of eastern Sicily, Mt Etna is a massive brooding presence. At 3326m it is Italy's highest mountain south of the Alps and the largest active volcano in Europe. It's in an almost constant state of activity and eruptions occur frequently, most spectacularly from the four summit craters, but more often, and more dangerously, from the fissures and old craters on the mountain's flanks. This activity, which is closely monitored by 120 seismic activity stations and satellites, means that it is occasionally closed to visitors.

Since 1987 the volcano and its slopes have been part of a national park, the **Parco dell'Etna**. Encompassing 581 sq km and some 21 towns, the park's varied landscape ranges from the severe, snowcapped mountaintop to lunar deserts of barren black lava, beech woods and lush vineyards where the area's highly rated DOC wine is produced.

🏃 Activities

Hiking

SOUTHERN SLOPE

Mt Etna's southern slope is the most accessible and popular gateway for those wanting to ascend the volcano, and the starting point for getting up to the crater area is **Rifugio Sapienza** (1923m), a small cluster of souvenir shops and bars based around the eponymous mountain refuge (p286). From here there are various options for heading up towards the peak.

The easiest is to take the **Funivia dell'Etna** (☑095 91 41 41; www.funiviaetna.com; return adult/child €30/23, incl bus & guide adult/child €65/48; ◷9am-4pm) up to 2500m and then a minibus to the Torre del Filosfo at 2920m. Alternatively, you can forego the minibus and walk from the upper cable-car station. It's quite a steep 2km walk and you should allow yourself up to four hours to get back in time for the return cable car. Another option is to walk all the way from Rifugio Sapienza, but this is a strenuous climb that will take about four hours (less on the way down). Note that in windy weather the cable-car service is suspended and replaced by a minibus.

There are four craters at the top: Bocca di Nord-Est (northeast crater), Voragine, Bocca Nuova and Cratere Sud-Est (southeast crater). The two you're most likely to see

IONIAN COAST ACI CASTELLO

ROAD TRIP >
ETNA'S WESTERN FLANK

The five small, under-the-radar towns on the western side of the Parco dell'Etna offer a wonderful escape, each with its own unique character. On this leisurely drive, you'll have a chance to sample Sicily's most famous pistachios at the source and soak up centuries of local history at Norman castles and baroque churches, all the while enjoying dreamy views towards Mt Etna's snowy summit.

❶ Paternò

Punctuated with baroque churches and monasteries, the town of Paternò gazes up at Mt Etna's southern slopes about 20km west of Catania. A deeply historic place, its acropolis reveals traces of Graeco-Roman, Arab and Norman occupation. These include the keep of an 11th-century Norman castle, one of several castles built along the Simeto

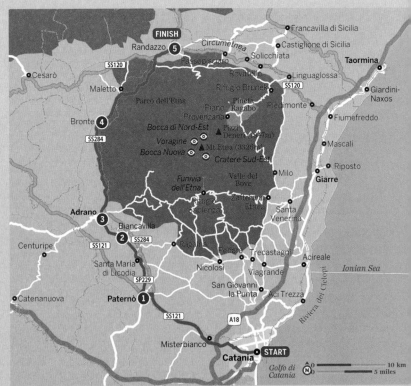

One Day 78km

Great For Food & Drink, History & Culture, Outdoors

Best Time to Go May, June, September & October

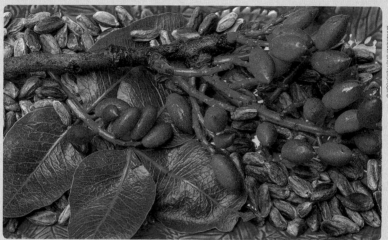

Pistachio nuts and leaves

River Valley by Roger II to control the area. The keep itself is a fine example of Norman military architecture, while the views of the valley and Etna are superb.

The Drive > Head 12km north along the SP229ii to Biancavilla.

❷ Biancavilla

Huge *fichi d'india* (prickly pears) and orange groves signal your arrival in Biancavilla, a small town founded by Albanian refugees in 1480 but now typically Sicilian with many baroque churches.

The Drive > Continue 4km northwest along the SP229ii to Adrano.

❸ Adrano

The market town of Adrano boasts a robust Norman *castello* rising from a huge fortified base, commissioned by Count Roger II in the late 11th century. It now houses a small museum. Nearby, on Via Catania, you can see the remains of Adranon, a 4th-century-BC Greek settlement.

The Drive > The SS284 heads directly north 17km to Bronte.

❹ Bronte

Acres of nut groves surround the town of Bronte, famous throughout Italy for its pistachios. Harvested every other year, the emerald green Bronte pistachio enjoys DOP protected status and is recognized as a national treasure by Italy's Slow Food Foundation for Biodiversity. Make sure to pause for a pistachio ice cream along the main strip, Corso Umberto.

The Drive > Beyond Bronte, the road leads through an increasingly rugged landscape, interspersed with chunks of lava flow, as it heads up to Randazzo, the most interesting of Etna's towns.

❺ Randazzo

Heavy bombing in WWII meant that much of Randazzo's grey medieval centre had to be reconstructed. The main sights are the three crenellated churches, Cattedrale di Santa Maria, Chiesa di San Nicolò and Chiesa di San Martino, which in the 16th century took turns serving as the town cathedral. Round off the day with dinner at San Giorgio e Il Drago, a Slow Food–recommended restaurant with outdoor seating Note that the restaurant is closed on Tuesdays.

BARMALINI/SHUTTERSTOCK ©

are Cratere Sud-Est, one of the most active, and Bocca Nuova. How close you can get will depend on the level of volcanic activity. If you're hiking without a guide, always err on the side of caution as the dangers around the craters are very real. To the east of the crater area, the Valle del Bove, a massive depression formed after a cone collapsed several thousand years ago, falls away in a precipitous 1000m drop.

NORTHERN SLOPE

The gateway to Etna's quieter and more picturesque northern slope is **Piano Provenzana** (1800m), a small ski station about 16km upslope from Linguaglossa.

Further down the volcano, there's lovely summer walking in the pine, birch and larch trees of the **Pineta Ragabo**, a vast wood accessible from the Mareneve road between Linguaglossa and Milo.

Note that you'll need your own car to get to Piano Provenzana and the Pineta Ragabo, as no public transport passes this way.

Cycling

If cycling is your thing, there are some fine (albeit tough) trails around the mountain; **Etna Touring** (☑095 791 80 00; www.etnatouring.com; Via Roma 1, Nicolosi) in Nicolosi organises guided rides on request. From 2020, it also plans to resume offering bike hire (€15 per day). Contact the outfit for updates.

Skiing

Sicily is an unlikely skiing destination, but you can do both downhill and cross-country here between late December and March. The state of the slopes and how many lifts are working depends on the latest volcanic activity – check the current situation at www.etnasci.it (in Italian). A useful English-language website with information of Mt Etna's ski slopes is www.skiresort.info.

In decent conditions there are five pistes on the southern side of the mountain and three on the northern side. A daily ski pass costs €30.

☞ Tours

There are many operators offering guided tours up to the craters and elsewhere on the mountain, and even if your natural inclination is to avoid them, they are well worth considering. The guides know the mountain inside out, and are able to direct you to the most spectacular points, as well as explain what you're looking at. They also offer a valuable safety precaution. Tours typically involve some walking and 4WD transport.

Recommended operators include **Etna Guided Tours** (☑340 5780924; www.facebook.com/EtnaGuidedTours), **Gruppo Guide Alpine Etna Nord** (☑348 0125167, 095 777 45 02; www.guidetnanord.com; Via Roma 81-83, Linguaglossa), **Gruppo Guide Alpine Etna Sud** (☑389 3496086, 095 791 47 55; www.etnaguide.eu) and **Etna Experience** (☑349 3053021, 347 6620341; www.etnaexperience.com; Piazza Federico di Svevia 32).

Prices vary depending on the tour you take, but you should bank on spending from around €45 per person for a half-day tour (usually morning or sunset) and from about €65 for a full day.

⚡ Festivals & Events

Alkantara Fest MUSIC
(☑349 5149330; www.alkantarafest.it; ☺Jul-Aug) This popular celebration of folk and world music runs over three weeks, with live acts as well as music workshops, art exhibitions, excursions, yoga sessions and no shortage of food, craft beers and Etna vino. Events are held in numerous locations around Mt Etna, including Bronte, Linguaglossa, Zafferana Etnea, Taormina and Catania.

✗ Eating

Mt Etna's slopes are dotted with trattorias, restaurants and *agriturismi* (farmstays), many serving rustic, turf-based local fare. Numerous wineries also offer local charcuterie, cheese or more substantial local fare as part of their wine and olive-oil degustations, which usually require booking at least a day ahead.

★ Cave Ox SICILIAN €€
(☑0942 98 61 71; www.caveox.it; Via Nazionale Solicchiata 159, Solicchiata; meals €25-30, pizzas €5-10; ☺noon-3.30pm & 7-11pm Wed-Mon) Modest Cave Ox is a fabulous spot to sample local produce, including *salumi* (charcuterie) made from local black pigs. Whether it's a bowl of carbonara tweaked with speck and asparagus, or spectacular pork and wild-fennel sausages, dishes burst with flavour. Pizzas are available in the evenings and owner Sandro Dibella's impressive wine cellar includes his own collaboration with maverick local winemaker Frank Cornelissen.

Antico Orto Dei Limoni SICILIAN €€
(☑095 91 08 08; www.ortolimoni.com; Via Grotte 4, Nicolosi; meals €25-30, pizzas €4-10; ☺1-4.30pm & 8pm-midnight Wed-Mon; ☏) There can be

SAVOURING ETNA: WINE & HONEY TASTING

Mt Etna's rich volcanic soils produce some of Italy's finest wines. This is the home of Etna DOC, one of 23 Sicilian wines to carry the Denominazione di Origine Controllata denomination. While there are numerous wineries offering wine degustations, many (including those listed below) require that you book at least a day ahead.

Among the area's standout wineries is **Planeta Feudo di Mezzo** (☑ 0925 195 54 60; https://planeta.it; Contrada Sciara Nuova), a highly acclaimed estate located 3.2km south-west of Passopisciaro. Wine degustations take place in a historic pressing room, with a tasting of five wines (€30 per person) including samples of typical local bites. A lunch of traditional recipes (€55 to €65) is also available.

For an especially intimate winery experience, make time for **Cantina Malopasso** (☑ 393 9728960; www.cantinamalopasso.it; Via Sguazzera 25, Zafferana Etnea). Just south of Zafferana Etnea on Etna's eastern flank, its young, talented winemakers are making waves with nuanced, small-batch wines, often blended with less-common local varietals. Degustations (€22, with a first course €27) are offered from mid-April to December.

Zafferana Etnea itself has a long tradition of apiculture, producing up to 35% of Italy's honey. For a taste, visit **Oro d'Etna** (☑ 095 708 14 11; www.orodetna.it; Via San Giacomo 135, Zafferana Etnea; ⊘ 8.30am-6.30pm), where you can try honey made from the blossoms of orange, chestnut and lemon trees.

few better ways of rounding off a day in the mountains than with a meal at this Nicolosi stalwart. Occupying a converted wine and oil press, it specialises in earthy, rustic fare. Pique the appetite with marinated vegetables, salami and cheese, then tuck into coaxing staples like *trofie* pasta with porcini mushrooms or *cotechino e lenticchie* (pork sausage and lentils).

Come dinner time, giant, wood-fired pizzas are also on the menu.

ⓘ Orientation

The two main approaches to Etna are from the north and south. The southern route, signposted as Etna Sud, is via Nicolosi and Rifugio Sapienza, 18km further up the mountain. The northern approach, Etna Nord, is through Piano Provenzana, 16km southwest of Linguaglossa.

ⓘ Information

Mountain rescue Call 118.

Nicolosi Tourist Office (☑ 095 91 44 88; Piazza Vittorio Emanuele 32; ⊘ 9am-1pm daily, plus 4-6pm Wed & Thu) In central Nicolosi on Etna's southern side.

Parco dell'Etna (☑ 095 91 44 88; www.parcoetna.ct.it; Via del Convento 45; ⊘ 9am-1.30pm Mon-Fri, also 4-6pm Wed & Thu) Offers specialist information about Mt Etna, including climbing and hiking information. About 1.3km north of the centre of Nicolosi.

Proloco Linguaglossa (☑ 095 64 30 94; Piazza Annunziata 5; ⊘ 9am-1pm & 4-7pm Mon-Sat, 9am-noon Sun) In central Linguaglossa on Etna's northern side.

ⓘ Getting There & Away

BUS

AST (☑ 095 723 05 11; www.aziendasiciliana trasporti.it) runs daily buses from Catania to Rifugio Sapienza (one-way/return €3.40/6.50, two hours). Buses leave from the car park opposite Catania's train station at 8.15am, travelling via Nicolosi. The bus back to Catania departs Rifugio Sapienza at 4.30pm, arriving in Catania at 6.30pm.

CAR & MOTORCYCLE

Nicolosi is about 17km northwest of Catania on the SP10. From Nicolosi it's a further 18km up to Rifugio Sapienza. For Linguaglossa, take the A18 *autostrada* from Catania, exit at Fiumefreddo and follow the SS120 towards Randazzo.

TRAIN

Slow train **Ferrovia Circumetnea** (FCE; ☑ 095 54 11 11; www.circumetnea.it; Via Caronda 352a, Catania) follows a 114km trail around the base of the volcano from Catania to Riposto. Affording great views, the local service stops off at a number of small towns on the way, including Bronte and Randazzo. From Catania it takes two hours to reach Randazzo (one way/return €5.50/9) in the mountain's northern reaches. Note that most trains terminate in Randazzo, with a waiting time of around 40 to 80 minutes for those wanting to continue to Riposto by train.

Syracuse & the Southeast

Best Places to Eat

➡ Ristorante Duomo (p236)

➡ Accursio (p219)

➡ Ornato (p219)

➡ Sicilia in Tavola (p208)

➡ Moon (p208)

Best Historic Sites

➡ Parco Archeologico della Neapolis (p206)

➡ Museo Archeologico Paolo Orsi (p206)

➡ Necropoli di Pantalica (p212)

➡ Basilica Cattedrale di San Nicolò (p213)

➡ Duomo di San Giorgio, Modica (p218)

Why Go?

Sicily's southeast is the island at its most seductive. This is the cinematic *Sicilia* of TV series *Inspector Montalbano*, a swirl of luminous baroque hill towns, sweeping topaz beaches and olive-laden hillsides.

The region's coastal protagonist is Syracuse (Siracusa), where Graeco-Roman ruins meet magnificent piazzas, boutique-studded side streets and crystalline waves. To the southwest lies the undulating Val di Noto, its string of late-baroque towns the most beautiful in Sicily. Noto, Modica, Ragusa and Scicli are the fairest of them all, each one a feast of architectural flourishes and gastronomic delights.

Then there is the region's countryside, a sun-bleached canvas of sleepy back roads lined with carob trees, rocky ravines pierced with prehistoric tombs, and rugged coastline dotted with crumbling *tonnare* (tuna fisheries), Mediterranean herbs and precious, migratory birdlife.

Road Distances (km)

	Modica	Noto	Pachino	Ragusa
Noto	40			
Pachino	40	25		
Ragusa	15	50	55	
Syracuse	75	40	55	85

SYRACUSE & AROUND

Syracuse

📞 0931 / POP 121,600

More than any other city, Syracuse (Siracusa) encapsulates Sicily's timeless beauty. Ancient Greek ruins rise out of lush citrus orchards, cafe tables spill onto dazzling baroque piazzas, and honey-hued medieval side streets lead down to the sparkling blue sea. It's difficult to imagine now, but in its heyday this was the largest city in the ancient world, bigger even than Athens and Corinth. Its 'once upon a time' begins in 734 BC, when Corinthian colonists landed on the island of Ortygia (Ortigia) and founded the settlement, setting up the mainland city four years later. Almost three millennia later, the ruins of that then-new city constitute the Parco Archeologico della Neapolis, one of Sicily's greatest archaeological sites. Across the water from the mainland, Ortygia remains Syracuse's most beautiful corner, a deeply atmospheric quarter with an ever-growing legion of fans enamoured with its beautiful streetscapes and attractive dining, drinking and shopping options.

◉ Sights

◉ Ortygia

A labyrinth of atmospheric alleyways and refined piazzas, Ortygia is really what Syracuse is all about. Skinny streets are lined with attractive *palazzi* (mansions), vibrant eateries and cafes, and the central square, Piazza del Duomo, is one of Sicily's most breathtaking. The entire mini-peninsula is framed by beautiful houses and walls that look out onto the sea; there is swimming off the rocks in the summer months and incredible views all year. Get away from the tourist crowds and explore the mesmerising maze of la Giudecca, Ortygia's old Jewish Quarter. The area, accessed by way of Ponte Umbertino or Ponte Santa Lucia, is best explored on foot.

★ Piazza del Duomo   PIAZZA

(Map p204) Syracuse's showpiece square is a masterpiece of baroque town planning. A long, rectangular piazza flanked by flamboyant *palazzi*, it sits on what was once Syracuse's ancient acropolis (fortified citadel). To the north of the Duomo, over Via Minerva, **Palazzo Municipale** (Map p204) (or Palazzo

Senatoriale) is home to Syracuse city council. It was built in 1629 by the Spaniard Juan Vermexio, who was nicknamed 'Il Lucertolone' (the Lizard) – you can see the architect's signature (a small lizard) carved into a stone on the left corner of the cornice. On the other side of the Duomo, the elegant, 17th-century **Palazzo Arcivescovile** (Archbishop's Palace; Map p204; 📞0931 6 65 71; http://arcidiocesi.siracusa.it/biblioteca-alagoniana; Piazza del Duomo 5) is home to the **Biblioteca Alagoniana** and some rare 13th-century manuscripts.

Over the square, in the northwestern corner, is the **Palazzo Beneventano del Bosco** (Map p204), which sports a pretty 18th-century facade, while at its southern end is the **Chiesa di Santa Lucia alla Badia** (Map p204; 📞0931 6 53 28; Via Santa Lucia alla Badia 2; by donation; ⏱11am-4pm Tue-Sun), home to Caravaggio's arresting masterpiece, *Il seppellimento di Santa Lucia* (Burial of St Lucy), painted in Syracuse between 1608 and 1609.

★ Duomo   CATHEDRAL

(Map p204; Piazza del Duomo; adult/reduced €2/1; ⏱9am-6.30pm Mon-Sat Apr-Oct, to 5.30pm Nov-Mar) Built on the skeleton of a 5th-century BC Greek temple to Athena (note the Doric columns still visible inside and out), Syracuse's 7th-century cathedral became a church when the island was evangelised by St Paul. Its most striking feature is the columned baroque facade (1728–53) added by Andrea Palma after the 1693 earthquake. A

ⓘ FLYING INTO SOUTHEASTERN SICILY

Catania Fontanarossa (p333), 62km north of Syracuse and easily reached on the E45 motorway, is the closest major airport. It's served by numerous airlines with connections to many Italian cities and destinations across Europe. Interbus (p211) runs frequent services between the airport and Syracuse (€6.20, 1¼ hours). It also runs direct services to Noto (€8.40, 1½ hours) and Ragusa (€8.60, 1¾ hours). Reduced service on weekends; check times on the Interbus website.

A small number of flights to Italian and some European cities also fly from the much smaller **Comiso Airport** (📞0932 96 14 67; www.aeroportodicomiso.eu; SP5, Comiso; 🚐), 27km northwest of Ragusa.

Southeast Sicily Highlights

❶ Syracuse (p201) Exploring ancient ruins and the cosmopolitan, labyrinthine streets of the city's island core.

❷ Noto (p213) Taking in scoops of gelato and swirls of late baroque in the Val di Noto's pin-up town.

❸ Scicli (p230) Exploring time-warped aristocratic palaces, churches and the office of Inspector Montalbano in the Val di Noto's most authentic, laid-back town.

❹ Modica (p217) Gorging on superlative chocolate and bombastic baroque in a dramatically set town.

❺ Ragusa (p232) Falling for beautiful, twisting streets and whirling baroque architecture in Ragusa's historic heart.

❻ Riserva di Vendicari (p217) Spotting feathered travellers and cooling off in turquoise waters in a protected natural wonderland.

❼ Necropoli di Pantalica (p212) Lacing up your hiking boots and exploring Sicily's foremost Iron and Bronze Age necropolis.

❽ Marzamemi (p217) Lunching, sipping and sunning in a pretty, peeling fishing village.

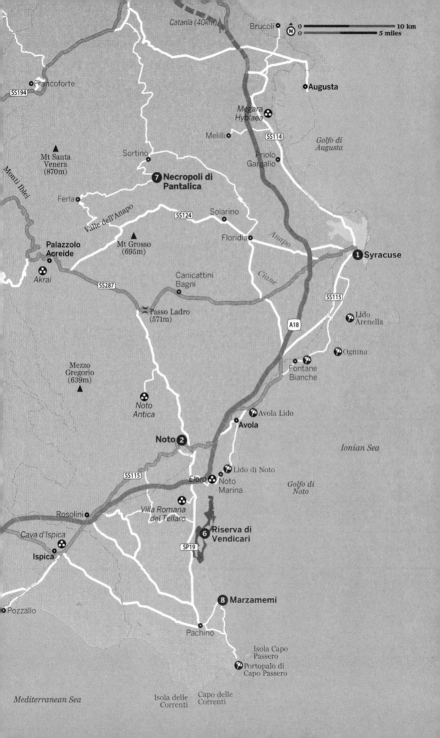

Ortygia

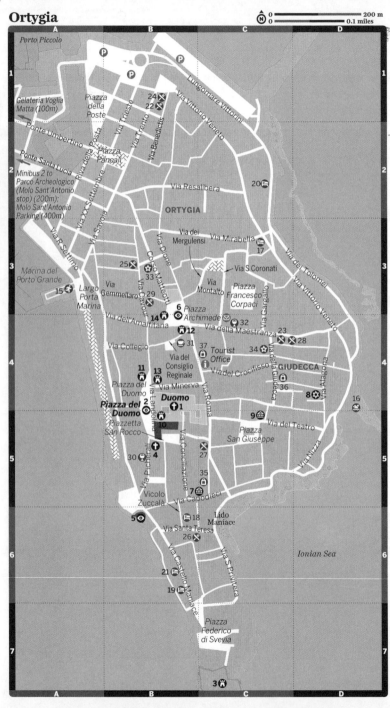

Ortygia

statue of the Virgin Mary crowns the rooftop, in the same spot where a golden statue of Athena once served as a beacon to homecoming Greek sailors.

The original temple was renowned throughout the Mediterranean, in no small part thanks to Cicero, who visited Ortygia in the 1st century BC. Note the interesting baptismal font to the right as you enter; it consists of an ancient Greek *krater* (large vase) adorned by seven 13th-century bronze lions.

Castello Maniace   CASTLE
(Map p204; Piazza Federico di Svevia; adult/reduced €4/2; ⊙2.30-6.45pm Mon, 8.30am-1pm Tue-Fri & Sun, 8.30am-6.45pm Sat Apr-Sep, reduced hours rest of year) Guarding the island's southern tip, Ortygia's 13th-century castle is an evocative place to wander, gaze out over the water and contemplate Syracuse's past glories. Built for Emperor Frederick II, it's an important example of Swabian (German) architecture, with a magnificent, vaulted central hall (Sala Ipostila). The grounds house a small antiquarium displaying archaeological objects from the site, including Norman-era ceramics and some curious-looking ceramic hand grenades from the 16th century.

**Galleria Regionale
di Palazzo Bellomo**   GALLERY
(Map p204; ☑0931 6 95 11; www.regione.sicilia.it/beniculturali/palazzobellomo; Via Capodieci 16; adult/reduced €8/4; ⊙9am-7pm Tue-Sat, to 1.30pm Sun) Housed in a 13th-century Catalan-Gothic palace, this art museum's eclectic collection ranges from early Byzantine and Norman stonework to 19th-century Caltagirone ceramics. In between there's a good range of medieval sculpture, as well as medieval, Renaissance and baroque religious paintings. Among the latter is *Annunciation* (1474), executed by Sicily's greatest 15th-century artist, Antonella da Messina. The museum also claims a couple of storybook 18th-century Sicilian carriages.

⊙ Mainland Syracuse

Although not as picturesque as Ortygia, the mainland city is home to a number of fascinating archaeological sights. The most compelling is the Parco Archeologico della Neapolis northwest of the city centre, but you'll also find plenty of interest at the city's renowned archaeological museum, the Museo Archeologico Paolo Orsi.

★**Parco Archeologico
della Neapolis** ARCHAEOLOGICAL SITE
(Map p209; ☎0931 6 62 06; Viale Paradiso 14; adult/
reduced €10/5, incl Museo Archeologico €13.50/7;
☺8.30am-1hr before sunset) For the classicist,
Syracuse's real attraction is this archaeological park, home to the pearly **Teatro Greco**.
Constructed in the 5th century BC and rebuilt in the 3rd century, the 16,000-capacity
amphitheatre staged the last tragedies of
Aeschylus (including *The Persians*), first performed here in his presence. From early May
to early July it's brought to life with an annual
season of classical theatre.

Beside the theatre is the mysterious **Latomia del Paradiso** (Garden of Paradise), a
deep, precipitous limestone quarry out of
which stone for the ancient city was extracted. Riddled with catacombs and filled with
citrus and magnolia trees, it's also where
the 7000 survivors of the war between Syracuse and Athens in 413 BC were imprisoned.
The **Orecchio di Dionisio** (Ear of Dionysius),
a 23m-high grotto extending 65m back into
the cliffside, was named by Caravaggio after
the tyrant Dionysius, who is said to have
used the almost perfect acoustics of the
quarry to eavesdrop on his prisoners.

Back outside this area you'll find the
entrance to the 2nd-century **Anfiteatro Romano**, originally used for gladiatorial combats and horse races. The Spaniards, little
interested in archaeology, largely destroyed
the site in the 16th century, using it as a
quarry to build Ortygia's city walls. West of
the amphitheatre is the 3rd-century-BC **Ara
di Gerone II** (Altar of Hieron II), a monolithic
sacrificial altar to Hieron II, where up to 450
oxen could be killed at one time.

To reach the park, take Sd'A Trasporti minibus 2 (€1, 15 minutes) from Molo
Sant'Antonio, on the west side of the main
bridge into Ortygia; purchase tickets onboard. Alternatively, walking from Ortygia
will take about 30 minutes. If driving, there
is limited free parking on Viale Augusto.

There are two ticket offices: one office
is located near the corner of Via Cavallari
and Viale Augusto, opposite the main site,
while the second outlet is located down
the path leading to the actual ruins. Those
wanting a break will find a cafe between
the second ticket office and the Anfiteatro
Romano.

★**Museo Archeologico Paolo Orsi** MUSEUM
(Map p209; ☎0931 48 95 11; www.regione.sicil
ia.it/beniculturali/museopaoloorsi; Viale Teocrito
66; adult/reduced €8/4, incl Parco Archeologico
€13.50/7; ☺9am-6pm Tue-Sat, to 1pm Sun) Located about 500m east of the archaeological park, Syracuse's archaeological museum
claims one of Sicily's largest and most interesting collections of antiquities. Allow
at least a couple of hours to investigate its
various sprawling sections, which chart the
area's prehistory, as well as the city's development from foundation to the late Roman
period.

DON'T MISS

LA GIUDECCA

Simply walking through Ortygia's tangled maze of nougat-coloured alleys is an atmospheric experience, especially down the narrow streets of **Via della Maestranza**, the
heart of the old guild quarter, and the gentrifying Jewish ghetto of Via della Giudecca. At
the Alla Giudecca hotel you can visit an ancient Jewish **miqweh** (Ritual Bath; Map p204;
☎0931 2 14 67; Via Alagona 52; tours €5; ☺tours 10am-6pm May-Oct, reduced hours rest of
year) some 20m below ground level. Blocked up in 1492 when the Jewish community was
expelled from Ortygia, the baths were rediscovered during renovation work at the hotel.

A short walk away, Syracuse's much-loved puppet theatre, the **Teatro dei Pupi** (Map
p204; ☎0931 46 55 40; www.teatrodeipupisiracusa.it; Via della Giudecca 22; ☺6 times weekly
Mar-Jul, Sep & Oct, 6 to 18 times weekly Aug, fewer Nov-Feb) stages puppet shows re-enacting
traditional tales involving magicians, love-struck princesses, knights and dragons. See
the website for a calendar of performances. Just down the road, the small **Museo dei
Pupi** (Map p204; ☎328 5326600; www.museodeipupisiracusa.it; Palazzo Midiri-Cardona,
Piazza San Giuseppe; adult/reduced €3/2; ☺11am-1pm & 2-7pm Mon-Sat Mar-Nov) chronicles
Sicily's rich history of puppet theatre. On you way you'll stumble upon a handful of interesting boutiques, among them Giudecca Trentasette (p210), a one-stop shop for all
things artisanal and Sicilian, from ceramics and chocolate, to jewellery and fashion.

FABLED FOUNTAINS

Fresh water has been bubbling up at the **Fontana Aretusa** (Map p204; Largo Aretusa) since ancient times when it was the city's main water supply. The fountain, now the place to hang out on summer evenings, is a monumental affair set around a pond full of papyrus plants and grey mullets.

Legend has it that Artemis, the mythical goddess of hunting, transformed her beautiful handmaiden Aretusa into the spring to protect her from the unwelcome attention of the river god Alpheus. In her watery guise, Aretusa fled from Arcadia under the sea, hotly pursued by Alpheus, their waters mingling as she came to the surface in Ortygia.

Artemis is the star turn of **Fontana di Artemide** (Fontana di Diana; Map p204), the 19th-century fountain that's the highlight of Piazza Archimede, a handsome square that's circled by imposing Catalan Gothic *palazzi*, including **Palazzo Lanza-Bucceri** (Map p204) and **Palazzo Platamone** (Palazzo dell'Orologio; Map p204), now home to the Banca d'Italia.

Basilica Santuario di Santa Lucia al Sepolcro   CHURCH

(Map p209; ✆0931 6 46 94; www.kairos-web.com; Piazza Santa Lucia; catacombs guided tour adult/reduced €8/5; ⊗basilica 7.30am-12.15pm & 4-7pm Mon-Sat, 8am-12.15am & 4-7pm Sun) This 17th-century basilica occupies the site where Syracuse's patron saint, Lucia, an aristocratic girl who devoted herself to saintliness after being blessed by St Agatha, was martyred in 304. The marble column to the right of the altar is believed to be the very spot where the saint's life was taken. Beneath lie early-Christian catacombs, accessible on guided tours (available in English). Tour times vary, so email or call ahead to confirm the current schedule.

Basilica & Catacombe di San Giovanni   CATACOMB

(Map p209; ✆0931 6 46 94; www.kairos-web.com; Via San Sebastiano; guided tours adult/reduced €8/5; ⊗9.30am-12.30pm & 2.30-5.30pm Apr-Jul, Sep & Oct, 10am-1pm & 2.30-6pm Aug, reduced hours rest of year) The city's most extensive catacombs lie beneath the Basilica di San Giovanni, itself a pretty, truncated church that served as the city's cathedral in the 17th century. It is dedicated to the city's first bishop, St Marcian, who was tied to one of its pillars and flogged to death in 254. The church and eerie catacombs are only accessible on 30- to 40-minute guided tours (available in English), which depart regularly from the site's ticket office.

🕴 Activities

Compagnia del Selene   BOATING

(Map p204; ✆347 1275680; www.compagnia delselene.it; Foro Vittorio Emanuele II; 50min tour per adult/under 10yr €10/free) This sailing outfit takes passengers around Ortygia on a ride that offers splendid views of the city. In the summer months, tour options include a sightseeing-and-swimming combo.

Forte Vigliena   SWIMMING

(Map p204; Via Nizza) Flanked by the crenellated walls of Forte Vigliena along Ortygia's eastern waterfront, this platform surrounded by flat rocks is a favourite local hang-out for swimming and sunbathing in the summer months.

Lido Arenella   SWIMMING

(Traversa Arenella) Serious beach bunnies make the short trip south from Ortygia to Arenella, where sandy beaches await. Be warned, though, that it gets very busy here, particularly on summer weekends. Catch bus 23 from Corso Umberto I and ask the driver to let you off at Lido Arenella.

☞ Tours

Natura Sicula   OUTDOORS

(Map p209; ✆328 8857092; www.naturasicula.it; Piazza Santa Lucia 24c) Local association Natura Sicula runs excursions and guided nature walks (around €7 to €8 per person) in the countryside surrounding Syracuse. See the website for upcoming excursions.

✹ Festivals & Events

★**Festival del Teatro Greco**   THEATRE

(Festival of Greek Theatre; www.indafondazione.org; ⊙mid-May–early Jul) Syracuse claims the only school of classical Greek drama outside Athens, and from early May to early July it hosts live performances of Greek plays (in Italian) at the Teatro Greco, attracting Italy's finest performers. Tickets (from around €29 to €55) are available online, from the **Fondazione Inda ticket office** (Map p204; ✆office 0931 48 72 48, tickets 800 542644; www.indafon

---

TOP COURSES
....

Italian cookery classes Brush up your Sicilian cooking skills with a lesson at **La Corte del Sole** (📞0931 82 02 10; www. lacortedelsole.it/en/lezioni-di-cucina-siciliana; Contrada Bucachemi, Lido di Noto; 2½-3hr lessons for hotel guests/nonguests €85/95; ⊙9.30am-12.30pm Tue-Sat, closed Aug), a *masseria* (farmhouse) turned hotel near Lido di Noto.

Learn the language In Syracuse, **Biblios Cafè** (Map p204; 📞 0931 6 16 27; www.biblioscafe.it; Via del Consiglio Reginale 11) runs Italian language courses for those wanting deeper interactions with the locals.

---

dazione.org; Corso Matteotti 29; ⊙10am-1pm Mon-Sat) in Ortygia or at the **ticket booth** (Map p209; 📞800 542644; ⊙10am-5pm Mon, to 7pm Tue-Sun) outside the theatre.

★**Ortigia Sound System**   MUSIC
(www.ortigiasoundsystem.com; ⊙ Jul) One of Sicily's top music festivals, OSS takes over Ortygia with five summery days of electronic music spanning various styles. Events take place across the island, with boat parties and a stellar lineup of top-tier Italian and international artists. Past guests have included Virgil Abloh (US), Danielle (UK) and Italy's own 'Father of Disco' Giorgio Moroder.

Festa di Santa Lucia   RELIGIOUS
(⊙13 Dec) On 13 December, the enormous silver statue of the city's patron saint wends its way from the cathedral to Piazza Santa Lucia accompanied by fireworks.

✖ Eating

Ortygia is the best place to eat. Its postcard-pretty streets heave with bustling trattorias, fashionable restaurants and cafes. While some are obvious tourist traps, many are not, and you'll have no trouble finding somewhere to suit your style. Most places specialise in surf, so expect plenty of seafood pasta and grilled catches of the day. The island is also home to exceptional vegan restaurant Moon.

★**Caseificio Borderi**   SANDWICHES €
(Map p204; 📞329 9852500; www.caseificioborderi.eu; Via Benedictis 6; sandwiches €6; ⊙7am-4pm Mon-Sat) No visit to Syracuse's market is complete without a stop at this colourful

deli near Ortygia's far northern tip. Veteran sandwich-master Andrea Borderi stands out front with a table full of cheeses, olives, greens, herbs, tomatoes and other fixings and engages in nonstop banter with customers while creating free-form sandwiches big enough to keep you fed all day.

Fratelli Burgio   SICILIAN €
(Map p204; 📞0931 6 00 69; www.fratelliburgio.com; Piazza Cesare Battisti 4; panini €3.50-7.50, platters €12-20; ⊙7am-4pm Mon-Sat; 🍴) A hybrid deli, wine shop and eatery edging Ortygia's market, trendy Fratelli Burgio is all about artisanal grazing. Consider opting for a *tagliere*, a wooden platter of artful bites, from cheese, charcuterie and smoked fish, to zesty *caponata* (sweet-and-sour vegetables). If you're euro-pinching, fill up on one of the gourmet *panini*, stuffed with a range of seasonal veggies, herbs, cured meats and cheeses.

Gelateria Voglia Matta   GELATO €
(📞0931 6 71 18; Corso Umberto 34; gelato from €2.30; ⊙8am-late, closed Thu Oct-Apr) 'Voglia Matta' means 'Mad Desire', which is exactly what you'll feel at this busy corner gelateria. The ice cream here is superlative, made fresh and with quality ingredients. Flavours range from Sicilian *cassata* and ultra-rich *nero fondente* (dark chocolate), to less ubiquitous options like *ricotta e pera* (ricotta and pear) and cheesecake.

★**Moon**   VEGAN €€
(Map p204; 📞0931 44 95 16; www.moonortigia.com; Via Roma 112; meals €22-30; ⊙6-11.30pm Wed-Mon, also open 12.30-3pm Wed-Mon Apr-Jun, Sep & Oct, closed mid-Jan–mid-Mar; 🛜🍴) This moody, boho-chic restaurant and bar makes vegan food so good even a hardcore carnivore could convert. A cast of mostly organic and biodynamic ingredients beam in balanced, intriguing dishes that might see a tower of thinly sliced pears interlayered with a rich, soy-based cashew cream cheese, or chickpea and tofu conspiring in a smokey carbonara pasta as wicked as the Roman original.

From the contemporary art and sculptural lighting, to the upcycled furniture, everything at Moon is for sale. It also doubles as a performance space, serving up live music or theatre two to three times weekly in the summer.

★**Sicilia in Tavola**   SICILIAN €€
(Map p204; 📞392 4610889; www.siciliaintavola.eu; Via Cavour 28; meals €27-40; ⊙1-2.30pm & 7.30-10.30pm Tue-Sun) One of the longest

Syracuse

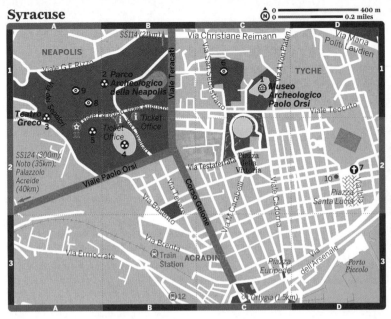

established and most popular eateries on Via Cavour, this snug, wonderfully hospitable trattoria has built its reputation on delicious homemade pasta and seafood. To savour both at once, tuck into the *fettuccine allo scoglio* (pasta ribbons with mixed seafood) before sampling *secondi* (mains) like beautifully cooked octopus with chilli, garlic, potatoes and a sublime tomato *sugo*. Reservations recommended.

Retroscena SICILIAN €€
(Map p204; ☏0931 185 42 78; www.facebook.com/retroscenaristorante; Via della Maestranza 108; meals €40; ⊙7.30-11.30pm Mon-Sat summer, to 10.30pm winter; 🛜) After running a restaurant in Greece for 18 years, Syracuse local Fabio and his Greek partner Kiri are pleasing palates at their hotspot Ortygia restaurant. Vintage mirrors, midcentury lighting and velvet in shades of blue and dusty pink set a fashionable scene for creative, rotating options like trofie pasta with pesto, ricotta, sun-dried tomatoes and crispy zucchini ribbons, or mandarin-and-honey glazed prawns.

Fabio only uses fresh fish and the all-Sicilian wine list includes some stellar smaller producers. In the warmer months, reserve a table in the courtyard.

Syracuse

Il Pesce Azzurro
SEAFOOD **€€**

(Map p204; ☑366 2445056; Via Cavour 53; meals €30-35; ⊗noon-3.30pm & 7-11pm) Seafood-loving locals swear by this easy-to-miss *osteria* (casual tavern), its white-and-blue interior somewhat reminiscent of a Greek-island taverna. The menu favours simplicity and top-notch produce, whether it's Mazara shrimps drizzled in lime juice, *vongole* (clams) paired with spaghetti and garlic, or *polpo* (octopus) served *alla luciana* (in a rich tomato and onion sauce). Honest, flavour-packed goodness.

La Medusa
SICILIAN **€€**

(Da Kamel; Map p204; ☑0931 6 14 03; Via Santa Teresa 21-23; meals €26-45; ⊗noon-3pm & 7-11pm Tue-Sun) This friendly, family-run spot made its name serving delicious couscous, but chef-owner Kamel also knows his way around a fish – the must-try *fritto misto* (mixed fish fry) is wonderfully light. If there's more than one of you, order the *pasta fibus*, an epic, plate-licking serve of *pennette* pasta with seafood, cherry tomatoes, radicchio and crunchy *pangrattato* (toasted breadcrumbs). Book ahead.

★ Don Camillo
SICILIAN **€€€**

(Map p204; ☑0931 6 71 33; www.ristorantedoncamillo.it; Via della Maestranza 96; meals €45-75; ⊗12.30-2.30pm & 8-10.30pm Mon-Sat; ☎☑) One of Ortygia's most elegant restaurants, Don Camillo specialises in sterling service and innovative Sicilian cuisine. Pique the appetite with a *crudo* of crustaceans paired with sweet-and-sour celery gelato, swoon over decadent braised-beef ravioli with butter, sage and *ragusano* cheese, or (discreetly) lick your whiskers over an outstanding *tagliata di tonno* (tuna steak) with red-pepper 'marmalade'. A must for Slow Food gourmands.

🍷 Drinking & Nightlife

A vibrant university and tourist town, Syracuse has a lively bar scene, with cafes, wine bars, pubs and cocktail hotspots spilling over the gorgeous streets of Ortygia. You'll also find a handful of popular bars and pubs just across the bridges on the mainland, including on and around Via Cairoli.

★ Cortile Verga
COCKTAIL BAR

(Map p204; ☑333 1683212; www.facebook.com/cortilevergaortigia; Via della Maestranza 33; ⊗11am-midnight summer, from 5.30pm winter, closed Jan–mid-Mar; ☎) Take an aristocratic courtyard, add an intimate interior kitted out in vintage coffee tables and a Chesterfield lounge, and you have Cortile Verga. This is one of Ortygia's top cocktail bars, crafting top-tier drinks like the Eleutheria, a blend of vermouth, mezcal, *amaro* (Italian herbal liqueur) and hibiscus tonic. While they're not cheap (€8 to €10), they're a cut above the competition.

Nibbles include great *taglieri* (tasting boards) of Sicilian cheeses and charcuterie, as well as *bruschette* and a rather decadent toast with egg, cream of white truffle, porcini mushrooms and grated black truffle.

Biblios Cafè
CAFE

(Map p204; ☑0931 6 16 27; www.biblioscafe.it; Via del Consiglio Reginale 11; ⊗5-11pm Wed-Sat) This beloved bookshop-cafe organises a whole range of cultural activities, including Italian language courses and regular literary events. It's also a great place to drop in for a restorative *caffè* (coffee), an *aperitivo* or simply to mingle.

Barcollo
BAR

(Map p204; ☑0931 2 45 80; www.facebook.com/barcollosiracusa; Via Pompeo Picherali 10; ⊗6.30pm-2am; ☎) Hidden away in a flamboyant baroque courtyard, sultry Barcollo lures with its fresh flowers, flickering tealights and chi-chi outdoor deck. *Aperitivo* is served daily between 7pm and 9pm (there's an *aperitivo* buffet on Sunday), with DJ sets on Friday and Sunday, and live music on Saturday.

Enoteca Solaria
WINE BAR

(Map p204; ☑0931 46 30 07; www.facebook.com/solariaenoteca; Via Roma 86; ⊗noon-2pm & 6pm-1am Mon-Sat; ☎) Sommeliers Elisa and Gianfilippo source wines they personally enjoy for their wonderfully old-school *enoteca*, with rows of rustic wooden tables and dark bottles lined up on floor-to-ceiling shelves. Over two-thirds of the drops are Sicilian, with numerous natural wines in the mix. A limited selection of nibbles includes *bruschette* and *taglieri* cheeses, charcuterie and olives.

🛍 Shopping

Browsing Ortygia's quirky boutiques is great fun. Good buys include papyrus paper, ceramics and handmade jewellery. While shops are peppered across the island, you'll find a concentration of interesting boutiques and galleries on Via Cavour, Via Roma and Via della Giudecca.

★ Giudecca Trentasette
GIFTS & SOUVENIRS

(Map p204; ☑349 0837461; www.facebook.com/giudeccatrentasetteortigia; Via della Giudecca 37-39;

⊙10am-1pm & 3-10pm May-Oct, 10am-12.30pm & 4-7pm Mon-Sat rest of yr) Salvatore Davì is passionate about Sicily and all things artisanal, and his petite emporium only stocks idiosyncratic, high-quality goods with Sicilian DNA. It's a fantastic one-stop shop for quality souvenirs and gifts, from contemporary takes on traditional island ceramics, to chic, handmade frocks and kaftans, graphic-style maps of Ortygia, jars of organic pistachio cream, lemon-flavoured *amaro* (herbal liqueur), and even knitted cactus fridge magnets.

Ebano
FASHION & ACCESSORIES

(Map p204; ☎331 4311553; www.ebanostore.com; Via Roma 154; ⊙noon-9pm, closes early Jan-Easter) Using Tuscan leather and recycled materials like bike tyres, inner tubes and old army tents, artisans Kal and Giuliana create durable, handmade leather goods, from wallets, totes, handbags, laptop sleeves, coin purses and shoes, to super-cool backpacks that will have everyone asking 'Where did you get that?!'. You'll even find striking industrial lamps made using car parts and oil cylinders.

Hélène Moreau
FASHION & ACCESSORIES

(Map p204; ☎333 5944518; www.silkinortigia.wordpress.com; Via Roma 27; ⊙11am-2pm & 5-8.30pm) In her island workshop, French artist Hélène Moreau channels her love of Sicily and the Mediterranean into her work, hand-painting stunning, one-of-a-kind silk scarves and canvases with patterns inspired by the region's light, colours, flora and architecture. Bespoke creations are available, taking around two to three days to complete. It's always a good idea to call ahead as opening times do vary.

Fish House Art
ARTS & CRAFTS

(Map p204; ☎339 7771364; www.fishhouseart.it; Via Cavour 29-31; ⊙10am-9pm) The theme is marine at Fish House Art, a quirky gallery and shop swimming with whimsical, beautifully crafted objects inspired by the sea. It's a showcase for both emerging and established Italian artisans, whose wares span anything from richly hued fish made of hand-blown glass, to curious, recycled-metal creatures and wearable art.

❶ Orientation

Syracuse's main sights are concentrated in two areas: Ortygia, and 2km across town at the Parco Archeologico della Neapolis. Ortygia, Syracuse's historic centre and most atmospheric neighbourhood, is an island joined to the mainland by a couple of bridges. It is well signposted and has a useful car park (Parcheggio Talete). If

coming by bus, you'll be dropped off at the bus terminal in front of the train station. From here it's about a 1km walk to Ortygia – head straight down Corso Umberto. Alternatively, catch grey minibus 1, which loops around the island every half hour or so, making stops at a number of convenient locations. Via Roma is Ortygia's main thoroughfare.

❶ Information

Hospital (Ospedale Umberto I; ☑ emergency department 0931 72 42 85, switchboard 0931 72 41 11; www.asp.sr.it/default.asp?id=424; cnr Via Testaferrata & Corso Gelone) Located just east of the Parco Archeologico.

Police Station (☑ 0931 6 51 76; Piazza San Giuseppe 6) Ortygia's police station.

Post Office (Map p204; ☑ 0931 2 17 79; www.poste.it; Via dei Santi Coronati 12; ⊙ 8.20am-1.30pm Mon-Fri, to 12.30pm Sat) Handy post office in Ortygia.

Tourist Office (Map p204; ☑800 055500; www.provincia.siracusa.it; Via Roma 31; ⊙7.30am-2pm Mon, Tue, Thu & Fri, to 4.30pm Wed) Offers a free city map and small selection of brochures.

❶ Getting There & Away

BOAT

A number of international cruise ships dock in Syracuse from spring to autumn. The **cruise-ship terminal** (Porto Grande; Largo Molo Stazione di Porto) is located 500m west of Ortygia.

BUS

Buses are generally faster and more convenient than trains, with long-distance buses arriving and departing from the **bus terminal** (Map p209; Corso Umberto I), 180m southeast of the train station.

Interbus (Map p209; ☑ 091 611 95 35; www.interbus.it) runs buses to Catania (€6.20, 1½ hours, one to two hourly) and its airport, Noto (€3.60, 55 minutes, three to seven daily) and Palermo (€13.50, 3½ hours, two to three daily). Tickets can be purchased at the bus station ticket kiosk.

AST (Map p209; ☑ 0931 46 27 11; www.aziendasicilianatrasporti.it) routes include Palazzolo Acreide (€4.30, 1¼ hours, 10 daily Monday to Saturday). Tickets are available from the *edicola* (newsagent) at the train station.

SAIS Autolinee (Map p209; ☑ 091 617 11 41; www.saistrasporti.it) runs an overnight service to Rome (€41, 12 hours, one nightly) and both daytime and overnight services to Bari (€40, 9½ to 11 hours, one to two daily). Purchase tickets from the train station *edicola* (newsagent).

Flixbus (Map p209; https://global.flixbus.com) runs direct buses from Syracuse to numerous destinations on the Italian mainland, including Taranto (from €26, nine hours, one daily), Bari (from €26, 10½ hours, one nightly) and Naples (from €28, 10¼ hours, one nightly). Buy tickets on the Flixbus website.

CAR & MOTORCYCLE

The dual-carriageway SS114 heads north from Syracuse to Catania, while the SS115 runs south to Noto and Modica. While the approach roads to Syracuse are rarely very busy, traffic gets increasingly heavy as you enter town and can be pretty bad in the city centre.

If you're staying in Ortygia, the best place to park is the **Talete parking garage** (Parcheggio Talete; Map p204; ☑ 0931 46 32 89) on Ortygia's northern tip, which charges a 24-hour maximum of €10 (payable by cash or credit card at the machine). **Molo Sant'Antonio** (Via Bengasi; car per hr €1, campervan per hr/day €1.50/30) on the mainland, just across the bridge from Ortygia, is another option.

Note that most of Ortygia is a limited traffic zone, restricted to residents and those with special permission. On-street parking is hard to find during the week, and less so on Sunday when it's often free.

TRAIN

From Syracuse's **train station** (Via Francesco Crispi), trains depart daily for Catania (€6.90, one to 1½ hours, 12 daily Monday to Saturday, six Sunday) and Messina (from €10.50, 2½ to 3¼ hours, 11 daily Monday to Saturday, five Sunday). Some go on to mainland Italy. Note that passengers travelling from Syracuse to Messina may need to interchange at Catania Centrale station.

There are also trains to Noto (€3.80, 30 to 45 minutes, seven daily Monday to Friday, six Saturday), Scicli (€6.90, 1½ to 1¾ hours, six daily Monday to Friday, five Saturday), Modica (€7.60, 1¾ to two hours, six daily Monday to Friday, five Saturday) and Ragusa (€8.30, 2¼ hours, five daily Monday to Friday, four Saturday).

❶ Getting Around

Siracusa d'Amare Trasporti (☑ 0931 175 62 32; 90min ticket €1) runs an innovative system of inexpensive electric minibuses around Syracuse and Ortygia. To reach Ortygia from the bus and train stations, catch minibus 1 (Map p209). To reach the Parco Archeologico della Neapolis, take minibus 2 from Molo Sant'Antonio (just west of the bridge to Ortygia). Buses run every 20 minutes between 8am and 8pm from March to June and every 30 minutes between 9am and 9pm from July to December. Tickets can be purchased onboard.

Be warned that during the Ciclo di Rappresentazioni Classiche (p207) festival, minibus 2 can get extremely crowded, with lengthy delays.

THE SOUTHEAST

Valle Dell'Anapo, Ferla & the Necropoli di Pantalica

Around 40km northwest of Syracuse is the World Heritage–listed Necropoli di Pantalica, a significant Iron Age and Bronze Age necropolis. Situated on a huge plateau, the site is surrounded by the wild and unspoilt landscape of the Valle dell'Anapo (Anapo Valley), a deep limestone gorge laced with walking trails (paths marked 'B' are slightly more challenging).

◉ Sights

★ **Necropoli di Pantalica** ARCHAEOLOGICAL SITE
FREE On a huge plateau above the Valle dell'Anapo is the site of Sicily's most important Iron and Bronze Age necropolis, the Necropoli di Pantalica, with more than 5000 tombs of various shapes and sizes honeycombed along the limestone cliffs. The site is terribly ancient, dating between the 13th and 8th century BC, and its origins are largely mysterious although it is thought to be the Siculi capital of Hybla, who gave the Greeks Megara Hyblaea in 664 BC.

Very little survives of the town itself other than the Anaktron or prince's palace.

Set aside half a day for the site, which is best explored with a knowledgeable guide – **Pantalica Experience** (☑ 338 4752390; p.cavarra@ tin.it) is a reputable operator. Don't forget to wear sensible hiking shoes and bring plenty of water.

❶ Getting There & Away

You will need your own wheels to explore the area. From Syracuse, the easiest way to reach the Necropoli di Pantalica is by heading north on the A18/E45 motorway and taking the exit for Sortino. From here, Sortino is 15km southwest along SP2 and SP60. In the town, road signs lead to the necropolis and the surrounding Valle dell'Anapo.

If you don't feel like hiring a car, Pantalica Experience runs tailored tours of the site and area, and is able to pick you up from your hotel in Syracuse or other towns in the area.

Palazzolo Acreide

☑ 0931 / POP 8670 / ELEV 670M

Few make it up to Palazzolo Acreide, but those who do find a charming, laid-back town with a wealth of baroque architecture and some of the area's finest (and least publicised) ancient ruins. The original medieval town was abandoned after the 1693 earthquake, after which a new Palazzolo was built in the shadow of the Greek settlement of Akrai.

◉ Sights

The town's central focus is **Piazza del Popolo**, which is a striking square dominated by the ornate bulk of the 18th-century **Chiesa di San Sebastiano** and **Palazzo Municipale**, Palazzolo's Liberty-inspired, early-20th-century town hall. From here you can take a short walk north that will bring you to **Piazza Moro** as well as two other exquisite baroque churches, the **Chiesa Madre** and **Chiesa di San Paolo**.

These two churches, the first on the square's southern flank and the second on the northern side, form a theatrical ensemble of columns, gargoyles and fleurs-de-lis. At the top of Via Annunziata (the main road leading right out of Piazza Moro) is the fourth of the town's baroque treasures, the **Chiesa dell'Annunziata**, with a richly adorned portal of twirling columns.

**Area Archeologica
di Akrai**   ARCHAEOLOGICAL SITE
(🖉0931 87 66 02; Colle dell'Acromonte; adult/reduced €4/2; ⊗8am-6pm Jun-Sep summer, to 4pm Oct-May) Accessed via a 20-minute uphill walk from Piazza del Popolo (or an easy drive up Via Teatro Greco), the archaeological park of Akrai is one of the area's best-kept secrets. The city of Akrai, Syracuse's first inland colony, was established to defend the overland trading route to other Greek settlements. Nowadays, its ruins are an evocative sight. The most impressive (and obvious) ruin is the **Greek theatre**, built at the end of the 3rd century BC but later altered by the Romans.

A perfect semicircle, the theatre once had a capacity of 600. Behind it are two *latomie* (quarries), later converted into Christian burial chambers. The larger of the two, **Intagliata**, has catacombs and altars cut into its sides, while the narrower one, **Intagliatella**, has a wonderful relief of a large banquet cut into the rock face.

South of the archaeological zone is a series of 3rd-century-BC stone sculptures known as the **Santoni** (Holy Men), closed indefinitely for restoration.

✖ Eating

The town is home to a handful of traditional *trattorie* peddling local specialities. For a sweet pick-me-up, stop by **Pasticceria Caprice** (🖉0931 88 28 46; www.pasticceriacaprice.com; Corso Vittorio Emanuele 21; snacks from €1.50; ⊗6am-11pm Tue-Fri, to 1am Sat, to midnight Sun).

❶ Information

Tourist Office (🖉 0931 87 12 60; www.palazzoloacreideturismo.it; ⊗ 9am-noon & 3-6pm Mon-Fri) Located in the Palazzo Municipale (Town Hall) on Piazza del Popolo.

❶ Getting There & Away

Palazzolo is around 42km west of Syracuse via the scenic SS124.

AST (p211) buses connect with Syracuse (€4.30, 45 minutes to 1¼ hours, nine daily Monday to Saturday).

Noto

🖉 0931 / POP 24,000 / ELEV 152M

Noto is an architectural supermodel, a baroque belle so gorgeous you might mistake it for a film set. Located less than 40km southwest of Syracuse, the town is home to one of Sicily's most beautiful historic centres. The pièce de résistance is Corso Vittorio Emanuele, an elegant walkway flanked by thrilling baroque *palazzi* and churches. Dashing at any time of the day, it's especially hypnotic in the early evening, when the red-gold buildings seem to glow with a soft inner light.

Although a town called Noto or Netum has existed here for many centuries, the Noto that you see today dates to the early 18th century, when it was almost entirely rebuilt in the wake of the devastating 1693 earthquake. Creator of many of the finest buildings was Rosario Gagliardi, a local architect whose extroverted style also graces churches in Modica and Ragusa.

◉ Sights

★Basilica Cattedrale
di San Nicolò   CATHEDRAL
(🖉 327 0162589; www.oqdany.it; Piazza Municipio; ⊗10am-2pm & 4.30-9pm Jul & Aug, 10am-6pm Sep-Jun) Pride of place in Noto goes to San Nicolò Cathedral, a baroque beauty that had to undergo extensive renovation after its dome collapsed during a 1996 thunderstorm. The ensuing decade saw the cathedral

scrubbed of centuries of dust and dirt before reopening in 2007. Today the dome, with its peachy glow, is once again the focal point of Noto's skyline.

Piazza Municipio
PIAZZA

About halfway along Corso Vittorio Emanuele is the graceful Piazza Municipio, flanked by Noto's most dramatic buildings. To the north, sitting in stately pomp at the head of Paolo Labisi's monumental staircase is the Basilica Cattedrale di San Nicolò (p213), surrounded by a series of elegant palaces. To the left (west) is **Palazzo Landolina**, once home to the powerful Sant'Alfano family. Across the street, **Palazzo Ducezio** (☑0931 83 64 62; www.comune.noto.sr.it/la-cultura/la-sala-degli-specchi; Sala degli Specchi €2, panoramic terrace €2; ☉10am-6pm) features a partly convex facade, its graceful arches supported by Ionic-capital columns.

★ Palazzo Castelluccio
PALACE

(☑0931 83 88 81; http://palazzocastelluccio.it; Via Cavour 10; adult/child €12/free; ☉11am-7pm) Abandoned for decades, this 18th-century *palazzo* found its saviour in French journalist and documentary filmmaker Jean-Louis Remilleux, who purchased the aristocratic pad and set about restoring it. Now accessible by guided tour, it offers the most complete insight into how Noto's nobility once lived, its sumptuous rooms awash with original frescoes and tiles, faithfully reproduced wallpaper, as well as Sicilian and Neapolitan baroque furniture from the owner's collection.

Palazzo Nicolaci di Villadorata
PALACE

(☑338 7427022; www.comune.noto.sr.it/palazzo-nicolaci; Via Corrado Nicolaci; admission €4; ☉10am-6pm mid-Mar–mid-Oct, 10am-1pm & 3-5pm rest of year) The fantastical facade of this 18th-century palace wows with its wrought-iron balconies, supported by a swirling pantomime of grotesque figures. Inside, the richly brocaded walls and frescoed ceilings offer an idea of the sumptuous lifestyle of Sicilian nobles, as brought to life in the Giuseppe Tomasi di Lampedusa novel *Il Gattopardo* (The Leopard).

Basilica del Santissimo Salvatore
CHURCH

(☑327 0162589; www.oqdany.it; Via Vincenzo Gioberti; ☉10am-2pm & 4.30-9pm Jul & Aug, 10am-6pm Sep-Jun) Situated towards the grand Porta Reale is the Basilica del Santissimo Salvatore. Its recently restored interior is the most impressive in Noto, crowned by a glorious vault fresco by Antonio Mazza

depicting the Holy Spirit's descent. Mazza is also responsible for the church's facade, completed in 1791 and showing influences of a more restrained neoclassical style. The adjoining Benedictine convent offers sweeping views from its bell tower.

Chiesa di San Domenico
CHURCH

(☑327 0162589; www.oqdany.it; Piazza XVI Maggio; church free, guided tour of crypt €2; ☉10am-2pm & 4.30-9pm Jul & Aug, 10am-6pm Sep-Jun) Towering over the tourist office on Piazza XVI Maggio is the 18th-century Chiesa di San Domenico. Considered one of Noto's finest baroque buildings, the church was designed to a Greek-cross plan by baroque starchitect Rosario Gagliardi, who is reputedly buried here. Inside you'll find some beautiful stuccowork, inspired by St Dominic's devotion to the Madonna of the Rosary.

Chiesa di Santa Chiara
CHURCH

(Corso Vittorio Emanuele; adult/reduced €2/1; ☉10.30am-1pm & 2.30-4pm) Commissioned by the Benedictine order, the Chiesa di Santa Chiara was built by Rosario Gagliardi between 1730 and 1758. You can still see the ornate original portal on Corso Vittorio Emanuele, made redundant after the street was lowered in the 19th century. The elliptical interior, awash with whimsical stuccowork, features one of Noto's finest baroque altars, overlooked by apostles perched on lofty columns. The main drawcard, however, is the panoramic view from the rooftop terrace.

Teatro Tina Di Lorenzo
THEATRE

(Teatro Vittorio Emanuele; ☑0931 83 50 73; www.fondazioneteatrodinoto.it; Piazza XVI Maggio; general visit €2, theatre tickets adult/reduced from €10/8; ☉general visits 10am-6pm) A swirl of boxes and stuccowork, this petite 19th-century theatre is named in honour of Italian stage and silent-film actress Tina Di Lorenzo (1872–1930), one of numerous stars to have graced its stage; the supreme Eleonora Duse (1858–1924) is another. The theatre remains in operation, serving up annual seasons of both classic and contemporary theatre in Italian.

Chiesa di San Francesco d'Assisi all'Immacolata
CHURCH

(☑0931 83 52 79; Corso Vittorio Emanuele 142; ☉9am-12.30pm & 3-8.30pm) Constructed between 1704 and 1745, this single-nave Franciscan belle is the work of architects Rosario Gagliardi and Vincenzo Sinatra. Step inside to admire Olivio Sozzi's 18th-century paintings *Rapture of St Francis* and *St An-*

Noto

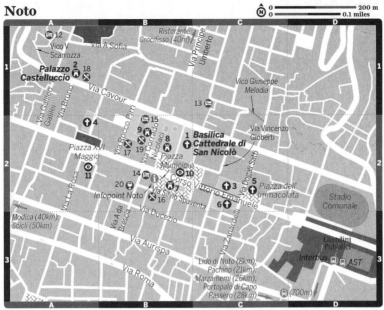

thony Preaches to the Fish, located at the first altar on the left and the first altar on the right respectively. The wooden statue of the Immaculate Conception in the apse dates from the 16th century.

🎊 Festivals & Events

Infiorata   CARNIVAL

(⊙ mid-May) Noto's big annual jamboree is the Infiorata, celebrated over three days with music concerts, parades and the breathtaking decoration of Via Corrado Nicolaci with designs made entirely of flower petals.

✖ Eating & Drinking

Like many towns in Sicily's southeast, Noto has a vibrant food scene, with a mix of innovative, sophisticated restaurants and old-school *trattorie* serving unfussy classics. The best spots are in the *centro storico* (historic centre), within walking distance of Corso Vittorio Emanuele.

★ Manna   SICILIAN €€

(☑ 0931 83 60 51; www.mannanoto.it; Via Rocco Pirri 15; meals €35-47; ⊙ noon-2.30pm & 7-10.30pm Wed-Mon Easter-Jul & Sep-Dec, 7-10.30pm daily Aug; 🛜) Divided into a hip front bar and sultry back dining rooms, Manna wows with its competent, contemporary creations. Premium produce dictates the menu, which

Noto

◉ Top Sights
1 Basilica Cattedrale di San Nicolò	B2
2 Palazzo Castelluccio	A1

◉ Sights
3 Basilica del Santissimo Salvatore	C2
4 Chiesa di San Domenico	A2
5 Chiesa di San Francesco d'Assisi all'Immacolata	C2
6 Chiesa di Santa Chiara	C2
7 Palazzo Ducezio	B2
8 Palazzo Landolina	B2
9 Palazzo Nicolaci di Villadorata	B2
10 Piazza Municipio	B2
11 Teatro Tina Di Lorenzo	A2

⊟ Sleeping
12 Nòtia Rooms	A1
13 Ostello Il Castello	C1
14 San Carlo Suites	B2
15 Seven Rooms Villadorata	B2

✖ Eating
Caffè Sicilia	(see 14)
16 Dolceria Corrado Costanzo	B2
17 Manna	B2
18 Ristorante Il Cantuccio	A1
19 Ristorante Vicari	B2

◉ Drinking & Nightlife
20 Anche gli Angeli	B2

DON'T MISS

ICE CREAM & GRANITE

According to some gelato aficionados, Noto claims two of the best *gelaterie* (ice-cream shops) in Italy: the nationally renowned **Caffè Sicilia** (☑ 0931 83 50 13; www.caffesicilia.it; Corso Vittorio Emanuele 125; pastries €2.50; ☺ 8am-10pm Tue-Sun, closed Nov & early Jan-early Mar; ⓘ) and, just around the corner, **Dolceria Corrado Costanzo** (☑ 0931 83 52 43; Via Silvio Spaventa 9; gelato from €2; ☺ 7.30am-11pm Thu-Tue). Of the two, Corrado has the better ice cream – try a lick of pistachio or *amaro* (dark liqueur) flavour – but Caffè Sicilia is famous for its *granite* (drinks made of crushed ice with fruit juice). Depending on the season, you could go for *fragolini* (tiny wild strawberries) or *gelsi* (mulberry) flavours, or stick to the classic *caffè* (coffee) or *mandorla* (almond).

Both places make superb *cassata* (made with ricotta cheese, chocolate and candied fruit), *dolci di mandorle* (almond cakes and sweets) and *torrone* (nougat). Don't know which to choose? Try them all. (Your secret is safe with us.)

might see *tagliatelle* pasta paired with duck *ragù* and Parmesan crisps, or mackerel fillet served with aromatic herbs, seaweed and a salted lemon *gelo* (Sicilian jelly). Staff are competent and friendly, and the wine list is focused on worthy drops.

Ristorante Il Cantuccio   SICILIAN €€

(☑ 0931 83 74 64; www.ristoranteilcantuccio.it; Via Cavour 12; meals €32-36; ☺ 7.45-11pm Jun-Sep, 12.30-2.30pm & 7.45-10.30pm Tue-Sun rest of year; ☎ ⓘ) Tucked into the courtyard of a former noble's palace, this inviting restaurant combines familiar Sicilian ingredients in inspired ways. Perennial favourites such as the exquisite *gnocchi al pesto del Cantuccio* (ricotta-potato dumplings with basil, parsley, mint, capers, toasted almonds and cherry tomatoes) are complemented by seasonally changing specials like lemon-stuffed bass with orange-fennel salad or white-wine-stewed rabbit with *caponata*.

★ Ristorante Vicari   SICILIAN €€€

(☑ 0931 83 93 22; www.ristorantevicari.it; Ronco Bernardo Leanti 9; meals €45-60; ☺ 12.30-2pm Mon, Tue & Thu-Sat, plus 7-10pm daily Jul-Sep, 12.30-2pm Tue-Sat, plus 7-10pm Mon-Sat Oct-Jun) Low-slung lamps spotlight linen-clad tables at Vicari, and rightfully so. In the kitchen is young-gun chef Salvatore Vicari, who thrills with his whimsical takes on Sicilian produce: succulent squid stuffed with tomato and almonds and served on a pistachio cream, or ravioli stuffed with roast chicken and paired with a carrot, lemon and spinach cream. Reservations highly recommended.

★ Anche gli Angeli   LOUNGE

(☑ 0931 57 60 23; www.anchegliangeli.it; Via A da Brescia 2; ☺ 8am-1am; ☎) Sophisticated, LG-BT-friendly and irrefutably cool, 'Even the

Angels' is *the* place to schmooze in Noto. A cafe-bar, lounge, restaurant and concept store in one, it's as fabulous for a cappuccino and house-baked pastry as it is for browsing books, *aperitivo* sessions, a modern-Sicilian dinner (meals €32 to €60) or a late-night tipple. Live music Wednesdays and Fridays, with DJ sets Fridays and Saturdays.

ⓘ Information

Infopoint Noto (☑ 339 4816218; www.notoinforma.it; Corso Vittorio Emanuele 135; ☺ 10am-7pm Apr, May & Oct, to 8pm Jun & Sep, to 9pm Jul, to 10pm Aug, to 6pm rest of year) Offers maps, brochures, free computer access and a complimentary left-luggage service. Visitors can print boarding passes or other documents (€1), and the enthusiastic, multilingual staff also organise guided tours in Italian, English and French.

Police Station (☑ 0931 83 52 02; Vico Brindisi 1) Near the Giardini Pubblici.

ⓘ Getting There & Away

BUS

Noto's bus station is conveniently located just to the southeast of Porta Reale and the Giardini Pubblici.

AST (☑ 0931 46 27 11; www.aziendasiciliana trasporti.it) Runs to various destinations, including Syracuse (€3.60, one hour, seven daily Monday to Saturday) and Catania (€7.50, 1½ hours, six daily Monday to Saturday, two Sunday). Buses to Catania stop at Catania airport on the way.

Interbus (☑ 091 611 95 35, 0935 2 24 60; www.interbus.it) Also runs to Catania (€8.40, 1½ to 2½ hours, eight to nine daily Monday to Friday, six Saturday, three Sunday) and Syracuse (€3.60, one hour, four to five daily Monday to Friday, four Saturday, three Sunday).

Buy bus tickets from **Bar Flora** (Hotel Flora, Via Pola 1), just west of the bus stop.

CAR & MOTORCYCLE
The SS115 connects Noto with Syracuse, about 36km to the northeast.

TRAIN
Trains run to Syracuse (€3.80, 30 to 40 minutes, seven daily Monday to Friday, six Saturday), Sicli (€4.30, one hour, six daily Monday to Friday, five Saturday), Modica (€5.10, 1¼ hours, six daily Monday to Friday, five Saturday) and Ragusa (€6.20, 1½ hours, five daily Monday to Friday, four Saturday). The station is inconveniently located 1km downhill from the historic centre.

The Noto Coast

While Sicily's southeastern tip lacks big-ticket cultural sights, its electric colours, Roman mosaics, rugged beaches and wineries make for a relaxing day trip from Noto. From town, the SP19 heads south towards the wonderfully atmospheric fishing village of **Marzamemi**, a popular summertime hang-out packed with buzzing bars and restaurants.

From here, the SP84 follows the coast south to **Portopalo di Capo Passero**, home to what was once one of Sicily's largest *tonnare* (tuna fisheries). The small island off the coast is **Isola Capo Passero**, home to a hulking fortress.

From Portopalo di Capo Passero, the SP8 leads southwest towards tiny **Isola delle Correnti** (Island of the Currents) and its lighthouse. This is Sicily's southernmost point, located further south than the north African city of Tunis.

◉ Sights

Riserva di Vendicari   NATURE RESERVE
(☑0931 46 88 79; www.riserva-vendicari.it; ◷7am-8pm Apr-Oct, to 5pm Nov-Mar) FREE Butting onto the ruins of Eloro is a wonderful stretch of wild coastline encompassing three separate marshes and a number of sandy beaches. The most beautiful of these is **Marianelli**, known locally as a nudist and gay-friendly beach. From the main entrance (signposted off the Noto–Pachino road), it's about a 10-minute walk to the nearest waves, where you can pick up a path along the coast.

The reserve, which claims its own Swabian tower and an abandoned tuna-processing plant, is an important marine environment, providing sanctuary to resident and migratory birds. Among these is the black-winged stilt, the stork, wild goose and flamingo. Observation posts enable you to watch in relative comfort.

Villa Romana del Tellaro   ROMAN SITE
(☑0931 57 38 83; www.villaromanadeltellaro. com; ◷8.30am-7.30pm, last entry 6pm) FREE Going south towards Pachino on the main SP19 brings you to this Roman villa, home to some fascinating mosaics. The villa was largely destroyed by fire in the 4th century, but painstaking excavation has brought to light fragments of the original floor mosaics, depicting hunting scenes and episodes from Greek mythology.

✖ Eating

One of the best places to eat in the area is the fishing village of Marzamemi, which has an abundance of *trattorie*, mostly focused on fresh fish and seafood. Worthy choices here include **Liccamúciula** (☑338 4638731; www.liccamuciula.it; Piazza Regina Margherita 2, Marzamemi; panini & salads €6-9; ◷10am-3am daily Jul & Aug, 10am-10pm Mon-Thu, to 3am Fri & Sat, to midnight Sun rest of yr, closed Jan; 🗟 ✢) and **La Cialoma** (☑0931 84 17 72; Piazza Regina Margherita 23, Marzamemi; meals €40-50; ◷1-3pm & 7.30-11pm daily Easter-early Nov, closed Nov & Tue rest of the yr; 🗟). Further south, the northern outskirts of Portopalo di Capo Passero is home to outstanding, higher-end restaurant **ViDi** (☑345 1663741; www.ristorantevidi. it; Castello Tafuri, Via Tonnara 1, Portopalo di Capo Passero; ◷7.30-9.30pm daily, also noon-2pm Sun; 🗟), serving creative Sicilian cuisine on a spectacular sea-facing terrace.

❶ Getting There & Away

You will need a car to explore the area as public transport is either very limited or nonexistent. Interbus runs between Noto and Pachino (€2.90, 25 minutes, 10 daily Monday to Friday, eight Saturday, five Sunday), but once there you will need to catch a taxi to reach Marzamemi (around €8 to €10 one-way).

Modica

☑0932 / POP 54,530 / ELEV 296M
Modica is one of southern Sicily's most distinctive towns, its steeply stacked medieval centre pierced by a towering baroque cathedral. But unlike some of the other Unesco-listed cities in the area, it doesn't package its assets into a single easy-to-see street or central piazza: rather, they're spread around the town and take some discovering. And while it can take

WINE TASTING IN SICILY'S SOUTHEAST

Sicily's southeastern tip is one of the island's lesser-known wine regions, a place where vines grow in a landscape of olive, almond and citrus trees. Grape varieties grown here include red-producing Nero d'Avola and syrah, as well as white-producing moscato bianco. The latter produces Noto's highly perfumed Moscato di Noto, as well as its Passito di Noto dessert wine.

Several *cantine* (wine cellars) in the area welcome visitors, offering guided tours of the vineyards, degustations of their wines and olive oils, even grazing plates or lunches showcasing local produce. Among these are highly regarded **Cantina Zisola** (☑ 0931 83 92 88, 392 6865741; www.mazzei.it; Contrada Zisola; winery tour & degustation per person €20), **Feudo Maccari** (☑ 346 8071173, 0931 59 68 94; www.feudomaccari.it; Strada Provinciale 19 Noto-Pachino; wine degustation per person from €15) and **Planeta Buonivini** (☑ 0925 195 54 65; https://planeta.it; Contrada Buonivini; wine degustations per person from €30), the latter one of Sicily's most prolific winemakers. Email or phone bookings are essential; a couple of days in advance is usually fine.

a little while to orientate yourself, once you've got the measure of the bustling streets and steep staircases, you'll find a warm, genuine place with a welcoming vibe, cosmopolitan air and strong sense of pride.

An important Greek and Roman city, Modica had its heyday in the 14th century when, as the personal fiefdom of the Chiaramonte family, it was one of the most powerful cities in Sicily.

◉ Sights

★ Duomo di San Giorgio   CHURCH
(☑ 0932 94 12 79; Corso San Giorgio, Modica Alta; ⊙ 8am-12.30pm & 3.30-7pm) The high point of a trip to Modica – quite literally as it's up in Modica Alta – is the Duomo di San Giorgio, one of Sicily's most extraordinary baroque churches. Considered Rosario Gagliardi's great masterpiece, it stands in isolated splendour at the top of a majestic 250-step, 19th-century staircase, its sumptuous three-tiered facade towering above the medieval alleyways of the historic centre.

The lavish interior, a sunlit kaleidoscope of silver, gold and egg-shell blue, encapsulates all the hallmarks of early-18th-century Sicilian baroque. One of the two chapels flanking the central apse houses the equestrian statue of San Giorgio, which is carried through the town during the saint's annual festival in April. The saint's earthly remains are stored in the so-called *Santa Arca* (Holy Ark), located in the right nave. Interestingly, the Duomo was also dedicated to Sant'Ippolito, whose death is depicted in Cicalesius's 17th-century canvas *Martirio di Sant'Ippolito* (Martyrdom of St Hippolytus). Also noteworthy is an early 16th-century

marble statue of the *Madonna della Neve* (Our Lady of the Snows), attributed to Giuliano Mancino and Bartolomeo Berrettaro.

Duomo di San Pietro   CATHEDRAL
(Corso Umberto I 159, Modica Bassa; ⊙ 8.30am-12.30pm & 2-7pm Mon-Sat, to 8pm Sun) In Modica, the Duomo di San Pietro plays second fiddle only to the Cattedrale di San Giorgio. The original 14th-century church was damaged in the earthquake of 1693, leading to its reconstruction in 1697. Construction continued way into the 19th century; the rippling staircase, lined with life-sized statues of the Apostles, was only completed in 1876.

Inside, the marble and pitchstone floor also dates from the 19th century. Above it, the vault is adorned with scenes from the Old Testament, executed by Gian Battista and Stefano Ragazzi in the late 18th-century. The right side of the nave harbours a 15th-century marble statue of the *Madonna di Trapani* and a group of late 19th-century wooden statues representing *San Pietro e il Paralitico* (St Peter and the Paralysed Man), the latter by sculptor Benedetto Civiletti. Also noteworthy are the pair of 17th-century paintings in the first chapel on the left side of the nave, one depicting Christ handing St Peter the keys to the Kingdom of Heaven, the other depicting St Joseph's passing.

Chiesa di San Giovanni Evangelista   CHURCH
(Piazza San Giovanni, Modica Alta; ⊙ hours vary) Attributed to Rosario Gagliardi and marking the top of Modica Alta is this grand baroque church. Prefaced by a sweeping staircase, the church underwent major restoration work in the 19th century, its current facade completed between 1893 and 1901. If the church

is open, slip inside its elliptical interior for beautiful, neoclassical stuccowork. Nearby, at the end of Via Pizzo, a viewing balcony offers arresting views over the old town.

Chiesa Rupestre
di San Nicolò Inferiore CHURCH
(☑333 1271331; www.viatourism.it; Piazzetta Grimaldi, Modica Bassa; adult/reduced €2.50/1.50; ⊘10am-1.30pm & 2.30-6pm summer, reduced hours rest of year) Carved into the rock and discovered by accident in 1987, this 12th-century church is Modica's oldest. It's worth a visit for its Byzantine frescoes; the central figure depicts Cristo Pantocratore (Christ All Powerful), holding open the Gospel with the words *Ego Sum Lux Mundi* (I am the light of the world).

🎊 Festivals & Events

Festa di San Giorgio RELIGIOUS
(⊘Apr) Drums, confetti and fireworks set a hypnotic scene as a statue of Modica's patron saint is raced through the town's streets before making a victorious entrance into the Duomo di San Giorgio.

✕ Eating

Modica merits a stop on any Sicilian foodie trail, with both Slow Food *trattorie* and creative, high-end restaurants. It's renowned for its grainy chocolate, a blend of bitter cocoa, sugar and spices worked at low temperature using an ancient method. Savoury specialities include *scacce* (flat-bread dough stuffed with various fillings and folded), *buccatureddi* (half-moon shaped rolls traditionally filled with broccoli) and *'mpanati* (durum-wheat focaccia traditionally stuffed with lamb).

★ Caffè Adamo GELATO €
(☑0932 197 25 46; www.caffeadamo.it; Via Maresa Tedeschi 15-17, Modica Bassa; cup/cone from €2/2.50; ⊘6am-1am summer, to 11pm rest of year, closed Mon Sep-Mar; ☎) There is great gelato and then there's gelato made by Antonio Adamo. The affable *modinese* makes all his confections from scratch; even the Agrigento pistachios are ground on-site. The result is ice cream packed with extraordinarily natural flavour and freshness. Gelato aside, Antonio's *cremolate* (water ices), Modica chocolate blocks and take-home jars of *babà* (rum-soaked sponge cake) are also outstanding.

★ Ornato SEAFOOD €€
(☑0932 94 24 23; http://ornato-ristorante-di-pesce.thefork.rest; Via Pozzo Barone 30, Modica Bassa; meals €35-50, tasting menu €60; ⊘noon-2pm

& 7-10.30pm Tue-Sun Sep-Jul, 7-10.30pm daily Aug; ☎) The decorative tagines at stylish Ornato reflect Luca Ornato's love of global flavours, a fact also echoed in out-of-the-box dishes like *crudo* (raw seafood) with yuzu. The talented cook marries tradition and innovation with impressive skill, his menu as likely to offer flawless *spaghetti con frutti di mare* (spaghetti with seafood) as it is a sweet interpretation of the Caprese salad.

Attention to detail extends to everything from the locally handmade glass plates to a wine list championing smaller producers. Book ahead.

★ Cappero SICILIAN €€
(☑393 9078088; www.facebook.com/Cappero Bistrot; Corso Umberto I 156, Modica Bassa; meals €25-40; ⊘noon-3pm & 7-10.30pm Fri-Wed, closed Aug; ☎✎) Small, quietly confident Cappero wows food lovers with beautiful cooking that's refined and comforting in equal parts. The house-made pasta is made using ancient grains, herbs are picked fresh from the restaurant's vertical herb garden, and the seasonal menu includes typically Modican dishes like broth with veal meatballs and noodles. If it's on the menu, sink your teeth into the succulent rabbit. Reservations recommended.

★ Accursio SICILIAN €€€
(☑0932 94 16 89; www.accursioristorante.it; Via Grimaldi 41, Modica Bassa; meals €80-90, tasting menus €90-150; ⊘12.30-2pm & 7.30-10pm Tue-Sat, 12.30-2pm Sun) Love the modernist furniture and vintage Sicilian tiles, but the food is the real thrill at this intimate Michelin-starred maverick. Head chef Accursio Craparo specialises in creative, nuanced dishes inspired by childhood memories and emblematic of new Sicilian thinking. For a well-rounded adventure, opt for a tasting menu.

A few steps away is the restaurant's simpler, more affordable sibling **Accursio Radici** (☑331 2369404; www.accursioristorante.it/en/radici; Via Grimaldi 42, Modica Bassa; meals €37-40; ⊘12.30-2.30pm & 7.30-10.30pm Wed-Mon).

🍷 Drinking & Nightlife

In the evenings, crowds flock to Corso Umberto I to stroll, hang out and eat gelato. Just behind it, skinny Via Clemente Grimaldi throngs with evening revellers of all ages, who schmooze and drink at the handful of bars dotting the street. Further uphill in Modica Alta, you'll find buzzing wine bar

(Continued on page 230)

ROAD TRIP >
SICILIAN BAROQUE

• •

Stretching from the sparkling blue of the Ionian Sea to the green hills and gorges of the interior, this trip showcases Sicily's most spectacular, Unesco-listed baroque sites. Wander among the golden-hued domes of Noto, get lost in the labyrinthine streets of Modica, and discover the charms of Ragusa, Scicli and the other southeastern Sicilian towns that were rebuilt in baroque style after the region's devastating 1693 earthquake.

❶ Catania

Though surrounded by ugly urban sprawl, Sicily's second-largest city is a thriving metropolis with a large university and a beautiful, Unesco-listed centre. Brooding on the horizon, snow-capped Mt Etna is a powerful presence.

The volcano is deeply set in Catania's DNA. Much of the city's historic core was built from lava that poured down Etna's slopes during a

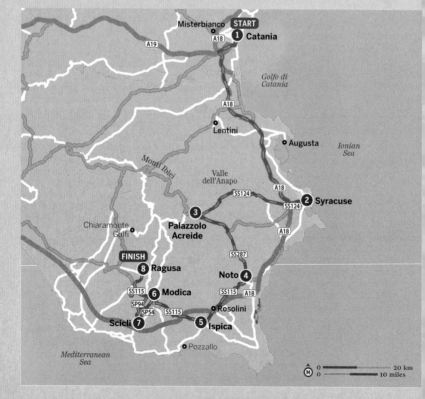

Five Days 213km

Great for... History & Culture; Food & Drink

Best Time to Go April, May, September & October

Cava d'Ispica (p231)

massive eruption in 1669. From its exuberant baroque *palazzi* to grand set-piece squares, this is a city dressed in shades of charcoal and ashen grey. At its heart is elegant **Piazza del Duomo** (p182), the city's collective living room. It's also where you'll find Catania's majestic **Cattedrale di Sant'Agata** (p183), final resting place of homegrown composer Vincenzo Bellini. Just off the square is famous fish market **La Pescheria** (p182), serving up more colour, noise and theatrics than any Bellini opera.

The Drive > From Catania to Syracuse, it is a 66km drive down the A18/E45 autostrada. This is orange-growing country and you'll see many orchards, which are gorgeously fragrant when in bloom. Exit onto the SS124 for the last 4km into central Syracuse.

➋ Syracuse

Settled by colonists from Corinth in 734 BC, Syracuse was considered the most beautiful city of the ancient world, rivalling Athens in power and prestige. You can still explore the city's ancient heart at the extraordinary **Parco Archeologico della Neapolis** (p206), the star attraction of which is the huge Greek theatre, whose origins lie in the 5th century BC.

In the wake of the 1693 earthquake, Syracuse underwent a baroque facelift. There are a number of baroque paintings at the **Galleria Regionale di Palazzo Bellomo** (p205), but the city's true period masterpiece is **Piazza del Duomo** (p201), a marvel of 17th-century town planning and the home of numerous architectural masterpieces. Top billing goes to the **Duomo** (p201), its 18th-century facade considered a masterpiece of high Sicilian baroque. Look beneath the baroque veneer, though, and you can still see traces of the city's Greek origins, including 5th-century-BC temple columns embedded in the Duomo's exterior.

The Drive > From Syracuse, head through rolling and unspoilt countryside along the SS124 for 42km to Palazzolo Acreide.

➌ Palazzolo Acreide

A charming town of baroque architecture and ancient ruins, Palazzolo Acreide's focal point is **Piazza del Popolo** (p213), a striking square dominated by the ornate bulk of the **Chiesa di San Sebastiano** and **Palazzo Municipale**, an impressive town hall. A 20-minute uphill walk from Piazza del Popolo leads to the archaeological park of **Akrai** (p213), once a thriving Greek colony and one of the area's best-kept secrets. You'll discover an ancient Greek theatre and Christian burial chambers with exquisitely carved reliefs.

FROG DARES/SHUTTERSTOCK ©

Basilica Cattedrale di San Nicolò (p213)

The Drive > Head southeast along the SS287 for a 30km drive through more beautiful countryside. The road becomes curvier as you head into Noto.

❹ Noto

Rebuilt after being flattened by the 1693 earthquake, Noto claims one of Sicily's most beautiful baroque centres. The golden-hued sandstone buildings and churches that flank **Corso Vittorio Emanuele**, many designed by local architect Rosario Gagliardi, are especially impressive in the early evening light (when they seem to glow with a soft inner light) and at night (when illuminations accentuate the beauty of their intricately carved facades).

Particularly eye-catching is the **Basilica Cattedrale di San Nicolò** (p213), a late baroque masterpiece crowned by a distinctive dome. For an elevated view of the cathedral, hit the

HITTING THE HIGH NOTE

Catania's most famous native son, Vincenzo Bellini (1801–35), was the quintessential composer of *bel canto* opera. Hugely successful in his lifetime, he was known for his inimitable ability to combine sensuality with melodic clarity and his works still woo audiences today. The **Museo Belliniano** (p186), in the composer's former Catania home, has an interesting collection of his memorabilia. Catania's lavish, 19th-century **Teatro Massimo Bellini** (p190) is the place to hear *I Puritani*, *Norma* and his other masterworks

panoramic terrace at **Palazzo Ducezio** (p214), itself worth a visit for its richly stuccoed, French-inspired Sala degli Specchi (Hall of Mirrors).

To see how the local aristocracy lived in baroque times, wander through nearby **Palazzo Nicolaci di Villadorata** (p214) or take a guided tour of the meticulously restored **Palazzo Castelluccio** (p214).

The Drive > Head southwest 22km along SS115 through more fields and orchards, passing through the town of Rosolini. Hilltop Ispica will rise up in front of you. Catch the sharply winding SP47 to the town centre.

❺ Ispica

Between Noto and Modica, this hilltop town claims a number of fine baroque buildings. However, the real reason to stop is to peer into the **Cava d'Ispica** (p231), a verdant, 13km-long gorge studded with thousands of natural caves and grottoes. Evidence of human habitation here dates to about 2000 BC, and over the millennia the caves have served as Neolithic tombs, early Christian catacombs and medieval dwellings.

The Drive > Start this 17km leg on the SS115 through relatively flat agricultural land. As you reach the suburbs of Modica, follow signs to Modica Centro and then to Corso Umberto I, the town's main thoroughfare.

❻ Modica

With its steeply stacked medieval centre and lively central strip, Modica is one of southern

JONATHON STOKES/LONELY PLANET ©

Ragusa Ibla (p233)

Sicily's most atmospheric towns. But its treasures are spread around the town and take some discovering. The highlight is the **Duomo di San Giorgio** (p218), a spectacular baroque church considered to be architect Rosario Gagliardi's great masterpiece. It stands in isolated splendour atop a majestic 250-step staircase in Modica Alta, the high part of town.

As well as impressive churches, Modica is also famous for its distinctly grainy chocolate, worked at low temperature using an ancient method. To stock up on it, hit **Antica Dolceria Bonajuto** (p230), Sicily's oldest chocolate factory, or visit award-winning **Caffè Adamo** (p219), the latter also famous for its gelato and *cremolate* (water ices).

The Drive > From Modica to Scicli, wind your way southwest along the SP54 for 10km through rugged, rocky countryside.

❼ Scicli

Compact Scicli is the most authentic of the Val di Noto towns, with an easy, salubrious vibe favoured by a growing number of VIP residents, from northern Italian entrepreneurs to international photographers and artists.

Its wealth of baroque churches include the **Chiesa di Santa Teresa** (p232), home to a 16th-century fresco featuring a rare inscription in Sicilianised Latin. Around the corner, pedestrianised Via Francesco Mormino Penna claims a number of interesting sights, including the beautifully restored **Palazzo Bonelli Patanè** (p231), charming apothecary **Antica Farmacia Cartia** (p232) and **Palazzo Mu-**

nicipio (p231), home to working sets from TV series *Inspector Montalbano.*

Overlooking everything is a rocky peak topped by an abandoned church, the **Chiesa di San Matteo**. The 10-minute walk up rewards you with fine views over the town.

The Drive > The first half of this 26km stretch winds north on SP94, passing along the rim of a pretty canyon typical of the region. Then catch the winding SS115 as it heads up to Ragusa. Across a small canyon, you will see the old, hillside historic centre of Ragusa rising grandly.

❽ Ragusa

Set amid rocky peaks, **Ragusa Ibla** – Ragusa's historic centre – is a joy to wander, with its labyrinthine lanes weaving through rock-grey *palazzi,* then opening suddenly onto beautiful, sun-drenched piazzas. After the 1693 earthquake, the aristocracy, ever optimistic, rebuilt Ragusa on exactly the same spot. It's easy to get lost but you can never go too far wrong, and sooner or later you'll end up at **Piazza Duomo**, Ragusa's sublime central space. At the top end of the sloping square is the town's pride and joy, the 1744 **Duomo di San Giorgio** (p233), set high on a grand staircase. It's one of Rosario Gagliardi's finest accomplishments; the extravagant convex facade rises like a three-tiered wedding cake supported by gradually narrowing Corinthian columns.

Up the hill from Ragusa Ibla is **Ragusa Superiore**, the town's modern and less attractive half.

ROAD TRIP > WONDERS OF ANCIENT SICILY

More than a trip around la bella Sicilia, this is also a journey through time, from spare Greek temples to a mosaic-clad ancient Roman villa, from Norman palaces decked out with Arab and Byzantine finery, to the showy baroque churches established here during Spanish rule. As you circumnavigate the island, you'll come face to face with Sicily's astonishingly rich mix of historical and cultural influences.

❶ Palermo

Palermo is a fascinating conglomeration of splendour and decay. Unlike Florence or Rome, many of its treasures are hidden rather than scrubbed up for endless streams of tourists. The city's cross-cultural history infuses its daily life, lending its dusty back-street markets a distinct Middle Eastern feel

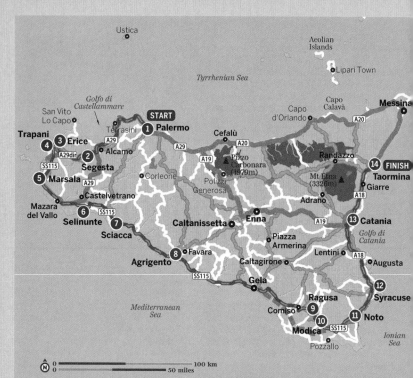

12 to 14 Days 664km

Great for... History & Culture; Food & Drink; Outdoors

Best Time to Go April, May, September & October

Piazza della Repubblica, Marsala (p112)

and its architecture a unique East-meets-West look.

A trading port since Phoenician times, the city, which is best explored **on foot** (p70), first came to prominence as the capital of Arab Sicily in the 9th century AD. When the Normans rode into town in the 11th century, they used Arab know-how to turn it into Christendom's richest and most sophisticated city. The **Cappella Palatina** (p57) is the perfect expression of this marriage, with its gold-inflected Byzantine mosaics crowned by a honeycomb *muqarnas* ceiling – a masterpiece of Arab craftsmanship.

For an insight into Sicily's long and turbulent past, the **Museo Archeologico Regionale Antonio Salinas** (p64) houses some of the island's most valuable Greek and Roman artefacts.

The Drive > From Palermo the 82km trip to Segesta starts along the fast-moving A29 as it skirts the mountains west of Palermo, then runs along agricultural plains until reaching the hills of Segesta. The Greek ruins lie just off the A29dir.

2 Segesta

Set on the edge of a deep canyon in the midst of desolate mountains, the 5th-century-BC ruins of **Segesta** (p97) are a magical site. The city, founded by the ancient Elymians, was in constant conflict with Selinunte, whose destruction it sought with dogged determination and singular success. Time, however, has done to Segesta what violence inflicted on Selinunte; little remains now, save the theatre and the never-completed Doric temple. The latter dates from around 430 BC and is remarkably well preserved. On windy days its 36 giant columns are said to act like an organ, producing mysterious notes.

The Drive > Keep heading along A29dir through a patchwork of green and ochre fields and follow signs for the 40km to Trapani. As you reach its outskirts, you'll head up the very windy SP31 to Erice, with great views of countryside and sea.

3 Erice

A spectacular hill town, Erice combines medieval charm with astounding 360-degree views from atop the legendary **Mt Eryx**

Duomo di San Giorgio, Modica (p218)

(750m) – on a clear day, you can see as far as Cape Bon in Tunisia. Wander the medieval streets interspersed with churches, forts and tiny cobbled piazzas. Little remains from its ancient past, though as a centre for the cult of Venus, it has a seductive history.

The best views can be had from the **Giardino del Balio**, which overlooks the rugged turrets and wooded hillsides down to the saltpans of Trapani and the sea. Adjacent to the gardens is the Norman **Castello di Venere** (p102), built in the 12th and 13th centuries over the ancient Temple of Venus. And while Venus may be the goddess of love, Erice's goddess of all things sweet is Maria Grammatico, whose eponymous **pasticceria** (p104) is revered around the globe. Don't leave town without savouring one of her cannoli or lemon-flavoured *cuscinetti* (small fried pastries).

The Drive > For the 12km to Trapani, it's back down the switchbacks of the SP31.

❹ Trapani

Once a key link in a powerful trading network that stretched from Carthage to Venice, Trapani occupies a sickle-shaped spit of land that hugs its ancient harbour. Although Trapani's industrial outskirts are rather bleak, its historic centre is filled with atmospheric pedestrian streets and some lovely churches and baroque buildings. The narrow network of streets remains a Moorish labyrinth, although it takes much of its character from the fabulous 18th-century baroque of the Spanish period. Make time for the **Chiesa Anime Sante del Purgatorio** (p98), home to the 18th-century *Misteri*, 20 life-sized effigies depicting the Passion of Christ.

The Drive > For the 33km trip from Trapani to Marsala, head south on the SS115. Small towns alternate with farmland until you reach Marsala on Sicily's west coast.

❺ Marsala

Best known for its eponymous sweet dessert wines, Marsala is an elegant town of stately baroque buildings within a perfect square of city walls. Founded by Phoenicians escaping Roman attacks, the city still has remnants of the 7m-thick ramparts they built, ensuring that it was the last Punic settlement to fall to the Romans.

Marsala's finest treasure is the partially reconstructed remains of a Carthaginian *liburna* (warship) – the only remaining physical evidence of the Phoenicians' seafaring superiority in the 3rd century BC. You can visit it at the **Museo Archeologico Baglio Anselmi** (p112).

The Drive > For this 52km leg, once again head down the SS115, passing through farmland and scattered towns until you reach the A29. Continue on the autostrada to Castelvetrano, then follow the SS115 and SS115dir for the last leg through orchards and fields to seaside Selinunte.

❻ Selinunte

Built on a promontory overlooking the sea, the Greek **ruins of Selinunte** (p117) are among the most impressive in Sicily, dating to around the 7th century BC. There are few historical records of the city, which was once one of the world's most powerful, and even the names of the various temples have been forgotten and are now identified by letters. The most impressive, **Temple E**, has been partially rebuilt, its columns pieced together from their fragments with part of its tympanum. Many of the carvings, which are on a par with the Parthenon marbles, particularly those from **Temple C**, are now in Palermo's archaeological museum.

THE 1693 EARTHQUAKE

On 11 January, 1693, a devastating, 7.4-magnitude earthquake hit southeastern Sicily, destroying buildings from Catania to Ragusa. The destruction was terrible, but it also created a blank palette for architects to rebuild the region's cities and towns out of whole cloth, in the latest style and according to rational urban planning – a phenomenon practically unheard of since ancient times. In fact, the earthquake ushered in an entirely new architectural style known as Sicilian baroque, defined by its seductive curves and elaborate detail, which you can see on display in Ragusa, Modica, Catania and many other cities in the region.

The Drive > Head back up to the SS115 and past a series of hills and plains for the 37km trip to Sciacca.

7 Sciacca

Seaside Sciacca was founded in the 5th century BC as a thermal resort for nearby Selinunte. Until 2015, when financial woes forced the spa to shut down indefinitely, Sciacca's healing waters continued to be the big drawcard, attracting coachloads of Italian tourists who came to wallow in its sulphurous vapours and mineral-rich mud. Spas and thermal cures apart, it remains a laid-back town with an attractive medieval core and some excellent seafood restaurants.

The Drive > Continue eastwards on the SS115 as it follows the southern coast onto Porto Empedocle and then, 10km inland, Agrigento's hilltop centre. In all, it's about 62km.

8 Agrigento

Seen from a distance, Agrigento's unsightly apartment blocks loom incongruously on the hillside, distracting attention from the splendid Valley of Temples below. In the Valley, the mesmerising **ruins** (p262) of ancient Akragras claim the best-preserved Doric temples outside of Greece.

The ruins are spread over a 13-sq-km site which is divided into eastern and western halves. Head first to the eastern zone, where you'll find the three best temples: the **Tempio di Hera**, the **Tempio di Ercole**, and, most spectacularly, the **Tempio della Concordia** (Temple of Concord). This, the only temple to survive relatively intact, was built around 440 BC and was converted into a Christian church in the 6th century.

Uphill from the ruins, Agrigento's **medieval centre** also has its charms, with a 14th-century cathedral and a number of medieval and baroque buildings.

The Drive > For this 133km leg head back to the SS115, which veers from inland farmland to brief encounters with the sea. Past the town of Gela, you will head into more hilly country, including a steep climb past Comiso, followed by a straight shot along the SP52 to Ragusa.

9 Ragusa

Set amid the rocky peaks northwest of Modica, Ragusa has two faces. Atop the hill sits **Ragusa Superiore**, a busy town with all the trappings of a modern provincial capital, while etched into the hillside is **Ragusa Ibla**. This sloping area of tangled alleyways, grey stone houses and baroque *palazzi* (mansions) is Ragusa's magnificent historic centre.

Like other towns in the region, Ragusa Ibla collapsed after the 1693 earthquake.

Colourful steps in Agrigento (p258)

DETOUR: VILLA ROMANA DEL CASALE

Start: **8** **Agrigento** (p227)

Near the town of Piazza Armerina in central Sicily, the stunning 3rd-century Roman **Villa Romana del Casale** (p250) is thought to have been the country retreat of Diocletian's co-emperor Marcus Aurelius Maximianus. Buried under mud in a 12th-century flood, the villa remained hidden for 700 years before its floor mosaics – considered some of the finest in existence – were discovered in the 1950s. Covering almost the entire villa floor, they are considered unique for their range of hues and natural, narrative style

But the aristocracy, ever impractical, rebuilt their homes on exactly the same spot. Grand baroque churches and *palazzi* line the twisting, narrow lanes, which then open suddenly onto sun-drenched piazzas. Piazza del Duomo, the centre of town, is dominated by the 18th-century baroque **Duomo di San Giorgio** (p233), with its magnificent neoclassical dome and stained-glass windows.

The Drive > Follow the SS115 for this winding, up-and-down 15km drive through rock-littered hilltops to Modica.

⑩ Modica

Atmospheric Modica recalls a *presepe* (traditional nativity crib), its medieval buildings climbing steeply up either side of a deep gorge. But unlike some of the other Unesco-listed cities in the area, its treasures aren't packaged into a single easy-to-see street or central piazza: rather, they are spread around the town and take some discovering. Its star attraction is the baroque **Duomo di San Giorgio** (p218), which stands in isolated splendour atop a majestic 250-step staircase.

The city's nerve centre is Corso Umberto. A wide avenue flanked by graceful palaces, churches, restaurants and bars, the thoroughfare is where the locals take their evening *passeggiata* (stroll). Originally a raging river flowed through town, but after major flood damage in 1902 it was dammed and Corso Umberto was built over it.

The Drive > Head back onto the SS115, which becomes quite curvy as you close in on Noto, 40km away.

⑪ Noto

Flattened in 1693 by an earthquake, Noto was rebuilt quickly and grandly, and its golden-hued sandstone buildings make it the finest baroque town in Sicily, especially impressive at night when illuminations accentuate its intricately carved facades. The *pièce de résistance* is **Corso Vittorio Emanuele**, an elegantly manicured walkway flanked by thrilling baroque *palazzi* and churches.

Just off Corso Vittorio Emanuele, the **Palazzo Castelluccio** (p214) reveals the luxury to which the local nobility were accustomed. Recently restored, its suite of lavish rooms are awash with murals, evocative paintings, gilded settees, and worn glazed floors revealing the paths of long-gone servants.

The Drive > The 39km drive to Syracuse from Noto takes you down the SP59 and then northeast on the A18/E45, past the majestic Riserva Naturale Cavagrande del Cassibile as you parallel Sicily's eastern coast.

⑫ Syracuse

It's difficult to imagine now but in its heyday Syracuse was the largest city in the ancient world, bigger even than Athens and Corinth. Your visit, like the city itself, can be split into two easy parts: one dedicated to the ancient archaeological site, the other to Ortygia, the ancient island neighbourhood connected to the modern town by bridge.

The **Parco Archeologico della Neapolis** (p206) is home to well-preserved Greek (and Roman) remains, with the remarkably intact **Teatro Greco** as the main attraction. In the grounds of Villa Landolina, about 500m east of the archaeological park, is the exceptional **Museo Archeologico Paolo Orsi** (p206).

Compact, labyrinthine **Ortygia** encompass 25 centuries of history. At its heart, the city's 7th-century **Duomo** (p201) lords it over Piazza del Duomo, one of Italy's most magnificent squares. The cathedral was built over a pre-existing 5th-century-BC Greek temple, incorporating most of the original Doric columns in its three-aisled structure. The sumptuous baroque facade was added in the 18th century.

The Drive > From Syracuse to Catania, it is a 66km drive north along the A18/E45. This is orange-growing country and you will see many orchards, which can be gorgeously fragrant when in bloom.

Parco Archeologico Greco Romano, Catania (p183)

ROMAS_PHOTO/SHUTTERSTOCK ©

⑬ Catania

Gritty, vibrant Catania is a true city of the volcano, much of it constructed from the lava that poured down on it during Mt Etna's 1669 eruption. The baroque centre is lava-black in colour, as if a fine dusting of soot permanently covers its elegant buildings, most of which are the work of Giovanni Battista Vaccarini. The 18th-century architect almost single-handedly rebuilt the civic centre into an elegant, modern city of spacious boulevards and set-piece piazzas.

Long buried under lava, the submerged stage of a 2nd-century Roman theatre and its small rehearsal theatre, part of the **Parco Archeologico Greco Romano** (p183), remind you that Catania's history goes back much further. Picturesquely sited in a crumbling residential area, the ruins are occasionally brightened by laundry flapping on the rooftops of vine-covered buildings.

The Drive > The 53km drive to Taormina along the A18/E45 is a coast-hugging northern run, taking in more orange groves as well as glimpses of the sparkling Ionian Sea.

⑭ Taormina

Over the centuries, Taormina has seduced an exhaustive line of writers and artists, from Goethe to DH Lawrence. The main reason for their infatuation? The perfect horseshoe-shaped **Teatro Greco** (p174), a lofty ancient marvel looking out towards mighty Mt Etna and the Ionian Sea. Built in the 3rd century BC, the *teatro* is the most dramatically situated Greek theatre in the world and the second largest in Sicily (after Syracuse).

The 9th-century capital of Byzantine Sicily, Taormina also boasts a well-preserved, if touristy, **medieval town**, its chi-chi streets dotted with fashionable cafes and bars perfect for a glamorous wrap-up toast to your journey.

(Continued from page 219)

Rappa Enoteca (📞328 5446285; www.face book.com/rappaenoteca; Corso Santa Teresa 97-99; ⊙5-11.30pm Mon-Sat).

🛍 Shopping

Antica Dolceria Bonajuto   CHOCOLATE
(📞0932 94 12 25; www.bonajuto.it; Corso Umberto I 159, Modica Bassa; ⊙9am-8.30pm Sep-Jul, to midnight Aug) Sicily's oldest chocolate factory is the perfect place to taste Modica's famous chocolate. Flavoured with cinnamon, vanilla, orange peel and even hot peppers, it's a legacy of the town's Spanish overlords who imported cocoa from their South American colonies. Leave room for Bonajuto's *'mpanatigghi*, sweet local biscuits filled with chocolate, spices...and minced beef!

Mercatino delle Pulci   MARKET
(Viale Medaglie d'Oro, Modica Bassa; ⊙7am-4pm last Sun of month) Modica's much-loved flea market is one of the best in the region. Held on the last Sunday of the month, its rows of stalls peddle everything from vintage jewellery, tea sets, records and postcards, to old Sicilian chests, locks, chiselled coats of arms and Caltagirone ceramics. Serious collectors head in early to score the most valuable finds.

Casa del Formaggio   CHEESE
(📞0932 94 61 92; www.casadelformaggiomodi ca.com; Via Marchesa Tedeschi 5, Modica Bassa; ⊙9.30am-2pm & 4.30-9pm Mon-Sat) Cheesemonger Giorgio Cannata peddles a mouthwatering range of *formaggi* (cheeses), including harder-to-find Sicilian varieties. If you're lucky you might stumble upon the rare *tumazzo modicano*, an ancient blue cheese produced by shepherds in local caves. Cheese aside, you'll also find artisan Sicilian *salumi* (charcuterie), from pistachio-studded and Nebrodi black-pig salami to *salsiccia al finocchietto* (pork and fennel sausage).

🛈 Orientation

Modica is divided into two parts: Modica Alta (Upper Modica) and Modica Bassa (Lower Modica). Whether driving or coming by public transport you'll arrive in Modica Bassa. The main street here, Corso Umberto I, forms the bottom of the V-shaped wedge on which the historic centre sits. Most hotels and restaurants are in Modica Bassa, within easy walking distance of Corso Umberto I, although the cathedral and a number of churches are in the high town. It's a fairly tough climb to the top.

🛈 Information

Police Station (📞0932 76 92 11; Via del Campo Sportivo 481) Located southeast of Modica Bassa's historic centre.
Tourist Office (📞0932 75 96 34, 346 6558227; www.comune.modica.rg.it; Corso Umberto I 141; ⊙8.30am-1.30pm & 3-7pm Mon-Fri, 9am-1pm & 3-7pm Sat) City-run tourist office in Modica Bassa.

🛈 Getting There & Away

BUS

Modica's bus station is at Piazzale Falcone-Borsellino at the top end of Corso Umberto I. **AST** (📞0932 76 73 01; www.aziendasicilianatraspor ti.it) bus routes include Noto (€3.90, 1½ to 1¾ hours, seven to 11 daily Monday to Saturday, one Sunday), Ragusa (€2.40, 25 to 30 minutes, 14 to 18 daily Monday to Saturday, two Sunday) and Catania (€9, 2¼ hours, seven to eight daily Monday to Saturday, four Sunday). AST buses also reach Scicli (€2.40, 40 minutes, seven daily Monday to Saturday, three Sunday), though the limited train service running between the two towns from Monday to Saturday is much faster.

CAR & MOTORCYCLE

From Noto to Modica it's about 40km along the SS115.

Parking can be a problem, particularly if you arrive mid-morning. A good place to try is Corso Garibaldi (turn right at the Duomo di San Pietro). There's a free car park opposite the train station on Viale Medaglie d'Oro.

TAXI

For a taxi, call 392 1027894 or 338 9402682. You'll find a taxi rank on Corso Umberto I, just beside the roundabout on Piazza Principe di Napoli.

TRAIN

There are trains to Ragusa (€2.50, 20 to 30 minutes, nine daily Monday to Friday, seven Saturday), Scicli (€1.70, 10 minutes, six daily Monday to Friday, five Saturday) and Syracuse (€7.60, 1¾ hours, six daily Monday to Friday, five Saturday).

Scicli

📞0932 / POP 27,050 / ELEV 106M
About 10km southwest of Modica, Scicli is the most authentic and relaxed of the Val di Noto's showpiece baroque towns. Its relatively compact, quickly gentrifying historic centre is awash with cultural sights, from beautiful churches and aristocratic *palazzi* to eclectic museums and a time-warped apothecary. The town makes regular cameos

on the hit TV series *Inspector Montalbano*, and visitors can visit two of the show's sets inside Palazzo Municipio.

Overlooking the town is a rocky peak topped by an abandoned church, the **Chiesa di San Matteo**. It's not too hard a walk up to the church to take in the sweeping views – simply follow the yellow sign up from Palazzo Beneventano and keep going for about 10 minutes.

⊙ Sights

★ Palazzo Bonelli Patanè   PALACE
(☑340 4756053; Via Francesco Mormino Penna; adult/reduced €9/5; ⊙10am-1pm & 4-7.30pm daily mid-Mar–early Nov) Never judge a book by its cover, or a *palazzo* by its facade. Take the 19th-century Palazzo Bonelli Patanè, its demure neoclassical facade tight-lipped about the Liberty-era decadence beyond. A swoon-inducing feast of silk wallpaper, stuccowork and precious antique furniture, the palace flaunts the luxury enjoyed by Scicli's upper class in the early 20th century. Among the highlights are dashing frescoes by Sicilian artist and decorator Raffaele Scalia, who spent part of his career working in New York.

Chiesa di San Bartolomeo   CHURCH
(☑333 9252365; Via San Bartolomeo; ⊙10.30am-1pm & 4-8pm Mon-Thu, 10.30am-1pm & 3.30-10.30pm Fri-Sun summer, reduced hours rest of yr) Although its origins lie in the 15th century, the luminous church standing today was built between the mid-18th and late-19th centuries. Like many of Scicli's churches, the facade consists of three orders. Here, the bottom columns are Doric, the middle columns Ionic and the top columns Corinthian. Giovanni Gianforma's rich rococo stuccowork adorns the interior, whose treasures include Francesco Pascucci's late 18th-century altarpiece *Martyrdom of St Bartholomew* and a monumental 18th-century *presepe* (nativity crib) attributed to Neapolitan craftsman Pietro Padula.

Palazzo Beneventano   ARCHITECTURE
(Via Penna 202) The Unesco-listed 18th-century Palazzo Beneventano is Sicilian baroque on steroids. Fantastical stone creatures taunt, terrorise or merely bemuse from the palace's corbels, arches and cornices. Among them are turban-wearing Moors and shaven, collar-wearing black slaves, unusual features in Sicilian baroque decoration and a sobering reminder of Europe's historic slave trade. The palace itself is named for

the Beneventano, a noble family originally from the Sicilian town of Lentini, south of Catania.

Chiesa di San Giuseppe   CHURCH
(☑338 8614973; www.tanitscicli.wix.com; Via San Marco 5; guided tour adult/reduced €2.50/2; ⊙10am-1pm Jun-Sep) Completed in 1772, the pared-back, late-baroque Chiesa di San Giuseppe claims beautiful stuccowork and a valuable marble statue of Santa Agrippina, attributed to Gabriele Di Battista and dating from 1497. Its other notable protagonist is a wooden statue of San Giuseppe, decorated with floral-motif silver plates and created by Pietro Padula and Pietro Cultraro between 1773 and 1780. In late March, the church becomes the focal point for the colourful Festa di San Giuseppe (p232).

Palazzo Municipio   FILM LOCATION
(Palazzo Iacono; ☑333 2613428; www.facebook.com/agirescicli; Via Francesco Mormino Penna; admission incl guided tour €3; ⊙10am-10pm summer, 10am-2pm & 3-6.30pm winter) To fans of the popular TV series *Commissario Montelbano* (Inspector Montalbano), Scicli's Town Hall – completed in 1906 – is better known as police headquarters of the fictional town of Vigàta. Thirty-minute guided tours of the building take in two sets used in the show: the police

OFF THE BEATEN TRACK

CAVA D'ISPICA

The town of Ispica, about 12km southeast of Modica, is located at the head of the 13km-long gorge known as **Cava d'Ispica** (☑0932 95 26 08; www.cavadispica.org; Crocevia Cava Ispica; adult/reduced €4/2; ⊙9am-6.30pm May-Oct, to 1.15pm Mon-Sat Nov & Dec). Long used as a neolithic burial site, the caves were transformed into cave dwellings in the Middle Ages. The gorge is verdant and you can follow a path along the whole length of the valley. The area includes a restored 18th-century watermill, now the fascinating **Museo Cavallo d'Ispica** (☑0932 77 10 48; https://cavallodispica.it; Via Cava Ispica 89; adult/reduced €3.50/2; ⊙10am-7pm), which offers a glimpse of rural Sicilian life as it once was.

If you do plan on exploring the gorge, make sure to wear sensible walking shoes and to bring a bottle of water.

station directed by Montalbano and the grander office of Montalbano's boss, Questore Bonetti Alderighi, the chief of police.

Taping of the series takes place in spring or summer, when you may just stumble upon the rugged inspector (played by actor Luca Zingaretti) on Scicli's photogenic streets. Combination tickets are available, including a full-tour ticket (€8) that includes guided tours of the nearby **Palazzo Spadaro** (Via Francesco Mormino Penna 34) and **Chiesa di Santa Teresa** (Via Santa Teresa 16).

Museo del Costume   MUSEUM
(☑328 9432070, 334 3658158; www.associazioneisola.it; Via Francesco Mormina Penna 65; admission €3.50; ☉10.30am-1pm & 4-8pm Apr-Jul & Sep, 10.30am-1pm & 4-11pm Aug, 10.30am-1pm Oct-Mar) Housed in a former monastery, Scicli's Museo del Costume mainly explores the costumes and fashions of the region. The collection spans several centuries and offers atmospheric insight into the living conditions, traditions and tastes of locals through the ages. One-hour guided tours are available in English but should be requested a day ahead by phone.

Antica Farmacia Cartia   HISTORIC SITE
(La Farmacia di Montalbano; ☑338 8614973; www.tanitscicli.wix.com; Via Francesco Mormina Penna 24; adult/reduced €2/1; ☉10am-1pm & 5-8pm Jul-Sep, 10am-1pm & 4-7pm Apr-Jun & Oct–mid-Nov, 10am-1pm & 3-6pm Mar & Dec, closed rest of yr) Dating from 1902, this time-warped pharmacy is a sight to behold, adorned with antique apothecary jars, scales and cash register. Fans of *Inspector Montalbano* may feel a sense of déjà vu: the place has made cameo appearances in the hit TV series, earning it the sobriquet *La Farmacia di Montalbano.*

✦ Festivals & Events

Festa di San Giuseppe   RELIGIOUS
(☉Mar) On the weekend before or after the Feast of St Joseph (March 19), Scicli commemorates the biblical Flight into Egypt with a colourful two-day festival. Events include bonfires, tastings of local products and, on the Saturday, a spectacular parade which sees locals in medieval peasant garb riding horses adorned with handwoven floral mantles.

✖ Eating

Don Tabaré   CAFE €
(☑349 2428333; www.facebook.com/dontabare; Via Aleardi 16a; arancini €3.50, schiacciate €5.50-7, gelato €3; ☉10am-11pm Tue-Sun;) A playful, contemporary cafe, *pasticceria* and prov-

idore, Don Tabaré collaborates with high-profile Sicilian chefs and food artisans to offer high-quality, light bites. Options range from excellent *arancini* (rice balls) and *schiacciate farcite* (local, stuffed focaccia), to cheese platters, *cannoli* and gelato. You'll also find top-notch coffee, *granite*, Sicilian wines and craft beers, and cocktails. Stylish alfresco tables and top-notch service seal the deal.

Baqqala   SICILIAN €€
(☑0932 93 10 28; Piazzetta Ficili 3; meals €30-40; ☉12.30-2.30pm & 7.30-10.30pm, closed lunch Mon, Wed & Sun Jul-Sep, closed Wed Oct-Jun) Peppe Mezzasalma's pretty, bohemian eatery serves Sicilian classics with thoughtful tweaks. Daily offerings are respectful of the season and market produce, whether it be *parmigiana di alici* (anchovy parmigiana) with fresh tomato foam or spaghettone with scampi and a delicate almond cream. Book ahead for a seat on the gorgeous shaded terrace, overlooking the baroque exuberance of Palazzo Beneventano.

🛈 Getting There & Away

BUS
From Largo Gramsci in the centre of town, AST buses run to Modica (€2.40, 35 to 55 minutes, eight Monday to Saturday, three Sunday). Buy bus tickets at Bar Rendo on Largo Gramsci. Note that the last bus to Modica departs Scicli at 4.50pm (5.50pm on Sunday).

CAR & MOTORCYCLE
Both the SP54 and SP42 connect Scicli to Modica, about 10km to the northeast.
For a taxi call 388 0643263.

TRAIN
From Scicli, trains run to Modica (€1.70, 10 to 14 minutes, six daily Monday to Friday, five Saturday), Ragusa (€3.10, 30 to 40 minutes, five daily Monday to Friday, four Saturday), Noto (€4.30, 50 minutes to one hour, six daily Monday to Friday, five Saturday) and Syracuse (€6.90, 1½ hours, six daily Monday to Friday, five Saturday). Trains do not run on Sunday. The train station is located about 550m southwest of Scicli's historic core.

Ragusa
☑0932 / POP 73,640 / ELEV 502M
Set amid the rocky peaks northwest of Modica, Ragusa is a town of two faces. Sitting on the top of the hill is Ragusa Superiore, a busy workaday town with sensible grid-pattern streets and all the trappings of a

modern provincial capital, while etched into the hillside further down is Ragusa Ibla. This sloping area of tangled alleyways, grey stone houses and baroque *palazzi* on handsome squares is effectively Ragusa's historic centre and it's quite magnificent.

Like every other town in the region, Ragusa Ibla (the old town) collapsed after the 1693 earthquake and a new town, Ragusa Superiore, was built on a high plateau above. But the old aristocracy was loath to leave the tottering *palazzi* and rebuilt Ragusa Ibla on exactly the same spot. The two towns were merged in 1927, becoming the provincial capital at Modica's expense.

⊙ Sights

★ Ragusa Ibla   AREA
Ragusa Ibla is a joy to wander, its labyrinthine lanes weaving through rock-grey *palazzi* to open onto beautiful, sun-drenched piazzas. It's easy to get lost but you can never go too far wrong, and sooner or later you'll end up at **Piazza Duomo**, Ragusa's sublime central square.

Facing the piazza, on Corso XXV Aprile, is **Palazzo Arezzo di Trifiletti** (☑339 4000013, 349 6487463; www.palazzoarezzo.it; Corso XXV Aprile 4; 20min tour €5, tour & aperitivo €15-40; ⊘guided tours 10.30am-7pm daily Jun-Sep, by appt rest of the year), built between the 17th and early 19th centuries. Guided tours of the aristocratic palace include its showpiece ballroom, graced with rare, late-18th-century Neapolitan majolica tiles and luminous 19th-century frescoes that have never needed touching up.

Opposite the palace, Via Novelli leads to the entrance of jewel-box **Teatro Donnafugata** (☑334 2208186; www.teatrodonnafugata.it; Via Novelli 3; guided tour €10; ⊘guided tours Apr-Oct, shows year-round), a 99-seat theatre that looks like a grand Italian opera house in miniature form. The theatre is a stop on the A Porte Aperte (p234) walking tour of Ragusa Ibla.

Via Novelli leads to Via Orfanotrofio, home to Cinabro Carrettieri, the colourful workshop of world-famous Sicilian cart craftsmen Biagio Castilletti and Damiano Rotella. The street continues south back to Corso XXV Aprile, where you're met by an eye-catching Gagliardi church, the elliptical **Chiesa di San Giuseppe** (Piazza Pola; ⊘9am-12.30pm & 3-7pm daily Jun-Sep, reduced hours rest of year), its cupola graced by Sebastiano Lo Monaco's fresco *Gloria di San Benedetto* (Glory of St Benedict, 1793).

Further downhill, the street to the right of the entrance of the Giardino Ibleo (p234) harbours the Catalan Gothic portal of what was once the large **Chiesa di San Giorgio Vecchio** (Via dei Normanni), now mostly ruined. The lunette features an interesting bas-relief of St George killing the dragon.

At the other end of Ragusa Ibla, the **Chiesa delle Santissime Anime del Purgatorio** (☑0932 62 18 55; Piazza della Repubblica; ⊘10am-7pm daily Jun-Sep, reduced hours rest of year) is one of the few churches in town to have survived the great earthquake of 1693. Step inside to admire Francesco Manno's *Anime in Purgatorio* (Souls in Purgatory; 1800) at the main altar.

★ Duomo di San Giorgio   CATHEDRAL
(Ragusa Ibla; ⊘10am-1pm & 3-6.30pm Apr-Oct & Dec, reduced hours rest of year) At the top end of the sloping Piazza Duomo is the town's pride and joy, the mid-18th-century cathedral with a magnificent neoclassical dome and stained-glass windows. One of Rosario Gagliardi's finest accomplishments, its extravagant convex facade rises like a three-tiered wedding cake, supported by gradually narrowing Corinthian columns and punctuated by jutting cornices.

Cinabro Carrettieri   WORKSHOP
(☑340 8444804; www.cinabrocarrettieri.it; Via Orfanotrofio 22, Ragusa Ibla; 15/30min guided tour €3/5; ⊘10.30am-9pm) Biagio Castilletti and Damiano Rotella are two of only a handful of master artisans still making *carretti siciliani* (traditional Sicilian carts) the traditional way. Their skill with bold Sicilian colours wasn't lost on Italian designers Dolce & Gabbana, who commissioned the pair to create the artwork for their own line of Smeg kitchen appliances. Guided tours of the workshop (in Italian) include a short historical video with English subtitles. While advanced bookings are not obligatory, they are recommended.

If you fancy trying your own hand at this traditional genre of Sicilian painting, you can participate in an on-site painting workshop (€40), also in Italian. The workshops, run for a minimum of two hours, must be booked a few days ahead, either by email or phone. Children welcome.

Ragusa Superiore   AREA
One of the best reasons for heading up to Ragusa's modern and less-attractive half is to walk down again. It takes about half an hour to descend the Salita Commendatore,

Ragusa

a winding pass of stairs and narrow archways that leads down to Ragusa Ibla past the **Chiesa di Santa Maria delle Scale** (⊙10am-1pm & 3-7pm daily Jun-Sep, reduced hours rest of year), a 15th-century church with impressive views. To reach the Salita, follow Corso Italia eastwards and then pick up Via XXIV Maggio.

The main attraction up top is the **Cattedrale di San Giovanni Battista** (📞0932 62 15 99; www.cattedralesangiovanni.it; Piazza San Giovanni, Ragusa Superiore; belltower €2; ⊙10am-8pm daily Jun-Sep, 7.30am-12.30pm & 3-7.30pm Mon-Sat, 8.30am-12.30pm & 3-7pm Sun rest of the yr, belltower 9.30am-noon & 3-6.30pm Mon-Sat), a vast 19th-century church whose highly ornate facade is set off by Mario Spada's pretty *campanile*. Nearby, below Ponte Nuovo, the somewhat forlorn **Museo Archeologico Ibleo** (📞0932 62 29 63; Via Natalelli, Ragusa Superiore; ⊙9am-6.30pm Mon-Sat) FREE houses notable finds from the 6th-century-BC Greek settlement of Kamarina on the coast.

Giardino Ibleo
GARDENS
(📞0932 65 23 74; Piazza Odierna, Ragusa Ibla) At the eastern end of the old town, this pleasant public garden laid out in the 19th century is perfect for a picnic lunch.

🏃 Activities

A Porte Aperte
WALKING
(📞366 3194177; www.facebook.com/aporte aperte; guided tour €10; 👤) Cultural association 'Iblazon' runs 50-minute walking tours of three historic sites in Ragusa Ibla: the 'Circolo di Conversazione' (a club for Ragusan aristocrats), the private garden Palazzo Arezzo-Bertini and the Teatro Donnafugata (p233), a jewel-box 19th-century theatre. Tours are offered in Italian and English and must be booked at least a day ahead, either by email, SMS or calling.

🎆 Festivals & Events

Ibla Grand Prize
MUSIC
(www.ibla.org; ⊙Jul) A week-long international musical festival and competition, with free classical, jazz and contemporary music concerts in numerous locations across town, including historic churches and theatres.

★ Scale del Gusto
FOOD & DRINK
(www.scaledelgusto.it; ⊙Oct) For three days in October, Ragusa's squares, streets and Unesco-listed buildings not usually open to the public become evocative settings for this buzzing celebration of Sicilian food and artisan food producers. The program includes masterclasses by prolific chefs, talks,

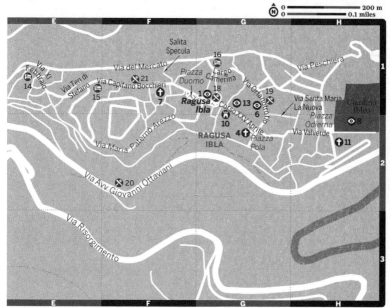

aperitivo sessions, pop-up restaurants, art exhibitions, live performances and light installations.

🍴 Eating

Ragusa's highly regarded dining scene spans Michelin-starred destination restaurants, cheerful neighbourhood trattorias and hip cafe-providores. Pork is a popular local meat, appearing in typical dishes like *cavati* (shell-shaped pasta) in pork sauce and *sfogghiu* (delicate puff pastry filled with ricotta and pork sausage). Christmas brings *mucatoli* (biscuits stuffed with dried fruit). In October, artisan food, wine and culture make for an appetising trio at the three-day Scale del Gusto festival.

Delicatessen in Drogheria MEDITERRANEAN €
(☑0932 191 05 51; Via Archimede 32, Ragusa Superiore; panini €4-8, dishes €8-10; ⊘8am-midnight Mon-Fri, from 9am Sat; 🛜🍴) DID is a hip deli-cafe-bistro in one, with communal tables, bar seating and playful '70s-style wallpaper running up the wall and ceiling. The open kitchen keeps things wholesome, whether it's breakfast-friendly yoghurt, smoothies or *ricotta calda* (warm ricotta), classic *panini* stuffed with organic and biodynamic ingredients, or more substantial dishes like couscous with seasonal vegetables. The chocolate, pear

Ragusa

LOCAL KNOWLEDGE

CITY OF MURALS

Think street art and Ragusa isn't likely to spring to mind. And yet, this baroque belle is one of southern Italy's top picks for the art form. The city is awash with spectacular, soaring murals, pimping everything from the sides of schools and apartment buildings, to the odd rooftop.

Much of it is the legacy of FestiWall, a street-art festival held annually in Ragusa from 2015 to 2019. Aimed at beautifying dreary streetscapes in Ragusa Superiore, the event drew some of the world's top creative talent. Years later, their creative output lives on, turning mundane streets into unlikely creative highlights.

Standout pieces include **The Farmer** (Via Berlinguer) by Australian artist Fintan Magee, the equally Sicilian-flavoured **Ficupala** (cnr Via G la Pira & Viale dei Platani) by Greek artist Dimitris Taxis, **Ogni bene è mobile** (cnr Via Anfuso & Viale Melilli) by Berlin-based Italian Agostino Iacurci, and the touching **Preparato** (cnr Via Canova & Via Pio La Torre) by Dutch duo Telmo Pieper and Miel Krutzmann. The FestiWall website features a handy map of all the murals, which are dispersed across the city.

One work not pinned on the map is Australian artist Guido Van Helton's tender **mural** (Via G Bruno) of a mother tending to two infants. Located 750m northeast of the train station, the imposing work was completed in 2019 to celebrate 40 years of the *Associazione Volontari Italiani del Sangue* (AVIS), Italy's major non-profit blood-donation organisation.

and ricotta cake is non-negotiable. Vegetarian, vegan and gluten-free friendly.

Gelati DiVini
GELATO €

(☏0932 22 89 89; www.gelatidivini.it; Piazza Duomo 20, Ragusa Ibla; gelato from €2; ☉10am-late, closed Mon winter) This exceptional gelateria makes wine-flavoured ice creams with Marsala, passito and muscat, plus other unconventional offerings such as pine nut, prickly pear, watermelon, ricotta, and chocolate with spicy chilli. If you're after a bottle of quality Sicilian *vino* to take home, the place doubles as an *enoteca*.

★I Banchi
ITALIAN €€

(☏0932 65 50 00; www.ibanchiragusa.it; Via Orfanotrofio 39, Ragusa Ibla; panini €6-6.50, meals €40-50, tasting menus €30-70; ☉8.30am-11pm; ⊕⊘) Michelin-star chef Ciccio Sultano is behind this contemporary, smart-casual eatery, which includes a dedicated bakery, specialist deli counter and the freedom to choose anything from *caffè* and just-baked pastries, to made-on-site gourmet *panini*, lazy wine-and-cheese sessions or more elaborate, creative dishes that put twists on Sicilian traditions, such as carob-glazed local pork with hummus and Modican chocolate salsa.

Agli Archi
SICILIAN €€

(☏0932 62 19 32; www.facebook.com/agliarchi trattoria; Piazza della Repubblica 15, Ragusa Ibla; meals €25-30; ☉12.30-3pm & 7.30-10.30pm Fri-Wed, closed Jan & Feb; ⊕⊕) With an outdoor terrace facing the pretty Chiesa delle Santissime Anime del Purgatorio, Agli Archi re-

veals a genuine passion for local ingredients and less-ubiquitous regional recipes. Rotating with the seasons, offerings might include *cavatelli* (elongated, shell-like pasta) with broccoli, anchovies and breadcrumbs, or succulent pork fillet cooked with oranges and served in a carob salsa.

★Ristorante Duomo
SICILIAN €€€

(☏0932 65 12 65; www.cicciosultano.it; Via Capitano Bocchieri 31, Ragusa Ibla; tasting menus €135-150; ☉12.30-2pm Mon, 12.30-2pm & 7.30-10.30pm Tue-Sat) Widely regarded as one of Sicily's finest restaurants, Duomo comprises a cluster of small rooms outfitted like private parlours behind its stained-glass door, ensuring a suitably romantic ambience for chef Ciccio Sultano's refined creations. The menu abounds in classic Sicilian ingredients such as pistachios, fennel, almonds and Nero d'Avola wine, combined in imaginative and unconventional ways. Reservations essential.

Locanda Don Serafino
SICILIAN €€€

(☏0932 22 00 65; www.locandadonserafino.it/ ristorante; Via Giovanni Ottaviano 13, Ragusa Ibla; 3-course lunch €55, meals €90, 6-/9-course tasting menu €120/155; ☉1-2.30pm & 8-10.30pm Wed-Mon) Powerhouse chef Vincenzo Candiano steers this softly lit, Michelin-starred darling, evocatively set in a series of rocky caves. Reserve a linen-draped table and settle in for top-shelf local produce and out-of-the-box creations like raw-scallop millefeuille with green tomato and fennel, almond milk, caviar and plankton or pumpkin gnocchi with pumpkin cream, hemp oil, lamb meatballs and foraged local vegetables. Book ahead.

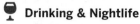 Drinking & Nightlife

Prima Classe
BAR

(📞 0932 65 23 00; www.primaclassebar.com; Via Ercolano 7, Ragusa Superiore; ⏱ 7am-1.30am Mon-Sat, 5pm-1am Sun, closed Sun Jun-Sep; 📶) Off the tourist trail, Prima Classe is where the *ragusani* play. A slick mix of concrete floors and designer Spanish lighting, it's a cafe, bar and art space in one, with rotating exhibitions, regular live music (except in summer), decent drinks and fantastic *aperitivo* bites. It's also a handy coffee or lunch spot if you're near the bus station, 400m to the south.

The bar hosts emerging and established Italian musicians, playing anything from rock to funk and reggae. As for the green-themed restroom, don't leave without a look.

🛍 Shopping

Le Formiche
GIFTS & SOUVENIRS

(📞389 4828295; www.facebook.com/LeFormicheStore; cnr Via San Massimiliano Kolbe & Via Ozanam, Ragusa Superiore; ⏱4.30-8.30pm Mon, 9am-1pm & 4.30-8.30pm Tue-Sat) Located in an up-and-coming pocket of the modern city, concept store 'The Ants' stocks products designed and crafted by artists, artisans and architects, both Italian and international. Expect to find anything from geometric jewellery, natural soaps and beautifully designed toys, to hand-stitched Sicilian bags made from recycled materials, local wines, liquors and edibles. Souvenir shopping: check.

ℹ Orientation

If you're driving, follow signs to Ragusa Ibla, where the main sights, hotels and restaurants are concentrated. Leave your car in one of the signposted car parks and walk into town. From the car park under Piazza della Repubblica it's a 10-minute walk or so to the central Piazza Duomo – follow Via Del Mercato, then Via XI Febbraio; go left up Via Ten Di Stefano then along its continuation, Via Capitano Bocchieri.

If taking public transport you will arrive in Ragusa Superiore, whose main streets are Via Roma and Corso Italia. From the upper town a local bus runs down to Giardino Ibleo in Ragusa Ibla.

ℹ Information

Police Station (📞 0932 67 31 11; Via Ispettore Giovanni Lizzio, Ragusa Superiore)

Tourist Office (📞0932 68 47 80; www.comune.ragusa.gov.it; Piazza San Giovanni, Ragusa

Superiore; ⏱9am-7pm Mon-Fri year-round, 9am-2pm Sat & Sun Easter–mid-Oct & Dec) Ragusa's main tourist office, with friendly, helpful staff. Opposite Cattedrale di San Giovanni Battista.

ℹ Getting There & Away

BUS

Long-distance and municipal buses share a terminal on Via Zama in the upper town (Ragusa Superiore). Buy tickets at the ticket kiosk at the terminal or from the bar **Tre Passi Avanti** (📞 0932 191 00 60; Via Zama 24; ⏱5am-9pm Mon-Sat), located 70m away.

AST (📞 0932 76 73 01; www.aziendasicilianatrasporti.it; Via Zama) runs direct services to numerous destinations, including Modica (€2.70, 25 minutes, 15 to 17 daily Monday to Saturday, two Sunday) and Syracuse (€7.20, 3¼ hours, three daily Monday to Saturday).

Interbus (📞 091 611 95 35; www.interbus.it; Via Zama) runs to Catania (€8.60, two hours, hourly Monday to Friday, every one to three hours Saturday, every one to two hours Sunday).

Flixbus (https://global.flixbus.com) operates direct services to the Calabrian port of Villa San Giovanni (from €14, 3¾ to five hours, three daily) on the Italian mainland.

CAR & MOTORCYCLE

If coming from Modica (15km away) or Syracuse (some 90km to the northeast) take the SS115.

Unless your hotel has parking or can advise you on where to park, your best bet is to leave your car at the car park below Piazza della Repubblica in Ragusa Ibla; much of the old town is closed to non-residential traffic.

TRAIN

Trains run to Modica (€2.50, 20 to 25 minutes, nine daily Monday to Friday, seven Saturday), Scicli (€3.10, 30 to 35 minutes, four daily Monday to Friday, three Saturday) and Syracuse (€8.30, two to 2½ hours, four daily Monday to Friday, three Saturday).

ℹ Getting Around

Monday through Saturday, AST's city buses 11 and 33 (€1.20) run hourly between Via Zama bus terminal and Giardino Ibleo in Ragusa Ibla. On Sunday, bus 1 makes a similar circuit. Daily tickets are available (€2).

For taxi service, call 0932 18 32.

Chiaramonte Gulfi

📞 0932 / POP 8125 / ELEV 668M

Nicknamed *il Balcone della Sicilia* (Sicily's balcony), this delightful hilltop town offers (on a clear day) views that stretch from

WORTH A TRIP

CASTELLO DI DONNAFUGATA

Located 18km southwest of Ragusa, the sumptuous neo-Gothic **Castello di Donnafugata** (☑ 0932 67 65 00; www.comune.ragusa.gov.it; Contrada Donnafugata; adult/reduced €6/3; ☺ 9am-1pm & 2.30-7pm Tue-Sun summer, 9am-1pm & 2-4.45pm Tue-Sun winter) houses the Collezione Gabriele Arezzo di Trifiletti, an extraordinary fashion and costume collection. The easiest way to reach the *castello* is by car. From Monday to Saturday, trains run from Ragusa to Donnafugata (three to four daily, 20 to 25 minutes, €2.50), from where it's a 600m walk to the castle. Alternatively, **Autotrasporti Tumino** (☑ 0932 62 31 84; www.tuminobus.it; Via Zama) runs a very limited bus service from Ragusa (return €4.80); see the company website for times.

Spanning the 16th to 20th centuries and considered one of Europe's finest, the collection provides a lavish overview of Sicily's once-glorious aristocratic culture. Indeed, its value led to a proposal to have it transferred to Palazzo Pitti's Costume Gallery in Florence, a suggestion swiftly quashed by the Sicilian government. The near 3000 pieces – displayed on rotation – include ball gowns, uniforms, bodices, chemises, cloaks, shawls, underwear, gloves, stockings, veils, military and ecclesiastical millinery, shoes, combs, thimbles, bags, umbrellas, cosmetic items and fans. Among the many prized possessions is a gown belonging to belle-époque fashion icon Donna Franca Florio, a rare hunting outfit from the late 17th century, 18th-century liveries worn by the servants of Sicilian nobility and the very gown that inspired Claudia Cardinale's famous frock in Luchino Visconti's film *Il Gattopardo* (The Leopard; 1963).

Originally a medieval watchtower, the building itself was expanded by nobleman Vincenzo Arezzo La Rocca, Baron of Serri, who bought the estate in 1648. This expansion would subsequently form the core of the castle's 19th-century reworking. This revamp was commissioned by Corrado Arezzo de Spuches, Baron of Donnafugata, who used the palace as a rural residence.

Gela in the south to Mt Etna in the north. Yet many visitors head here for a high of the gastronomic kind. Chiaramonte Gulfi produces a highly rated olive oil, accredited with the Denominazione d'Origine Protetta (DOP), not to mention premium pork products, from *salumi* to *salsiccie* (sausages).

To build up an appetite, wander the knot of old medieval streets in the historic centre, crow over views that steal the breath and drop by **Museo dell'Olio** (Olive Oil Museum; ☑ 338 5048476; www.comune.chiaramonte-gulfi. gov.it/musei; Palazzo Montesano, Via Montesano; €1; ☺ hours vary), the pick of the town's string of museums.

✖ Eating

It might be small, but Chiaramonte Gulfi's foodie cred is known across Italy. Seek out *salumi* made from prized black swine from the Nebrodi mountains. Some of it is flavoured with wild fennel, Bronte pistachios or carob. Salami made with local donkey meat is also common.

Ristorante Majore   SICILIAN €€
(☑ 0932 92 80 19; www.majore.it; Via dei Martiri Ungheresi 12; meals €25-30; ☺ 9am-4pm & 6-11pm Tue-Sun) The place to buy ham, and indeed to lunch on superb pork, is Ristorante Majore, a much-acclaimed trattoria just off central Piazza Duomo. It's unpretentious and old-school, and the menu is unapologetically meaty, with signature dishes *risotto alla majore* (with pork *ragù* and local cheese) and *falsomagro alla siciliana* (pork meatballs stuffed with salami, cheese, eggs and carrot).

❶ Getting There & Away

Chiaramonte Gulfi lies around 20km north of Ragusa. The shortest and most scenic drive between the two is on the SP10.

AST (p237) runs buses to Ragusa (€2.70, 50 minutes, one daily Monday to Saturday).

Central Sicily

Best
Places to Eat

➡ La Rustica (p242)

➡ Al Fogher (p249)

➡ Coria (p253)

➡ Disiu (p249)

➡ Umbriaco (p242)

Best
Festivals

➡ Holy Week (p242), Enna

➡ Festa di San Giacomo
(p253), Caltagirone

➡ Palio dei Normanni (p249),
Piazza Armerina

Why Go?

Sicily's wild, empty interior is a beautiful, uncompromising land, a timeless landscape of silent, sunburnt peaks, grey stone villages and forgotten valleys. Traditions live on and life is lived at a gentle pace. It's an area that encourages simple pleasures – long lunches of earthy country food, meanders through hilltop towns, quiet contemplation over undulating vistas. It's also an area of surprising natural diversity – one minute you're driving through rolling hills reminiscent of Tuscany, the next through pockets of eucalypt bush akin to Australia.

Scattered across these landscapes are the legacies of many cultures and countless generations – windswept Greek shrines, sunbaked Norman churches and frescoed flourishes of the baroque. It's in Villa Romana del Casale that you'll find the world's most important Roman mosaics; in tiny Morgantina, a Hellenic statue that caused a modern tug-of-war; and in Caltagirone, some of Italy's most coveted ceramics. Prepare to be pleasantly surprised.

Road Distances (km)

Caltanissetta	85			
Enna	60	30		
Nicosia	100	65	50	
Piazza Armerina	30	50	35	70
	Caltagirone	Caltanissetta	Enna	Nicosia

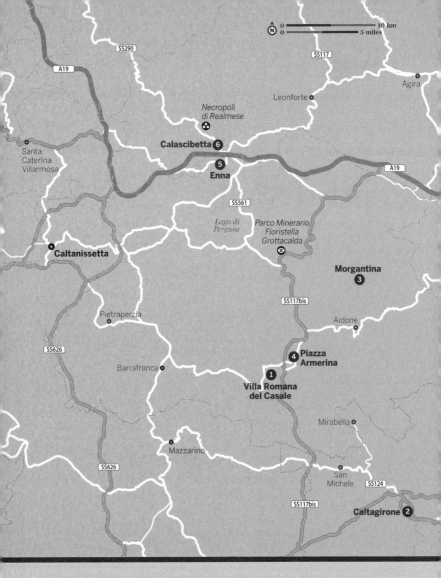

Central Sicily Highlights

1 **Villa Romana del Casale**
(p250) Admiring ancient
artistry and creativity at a
decadent Roman villa, home to
the most extraordinary Roman
tile work in existence.

2 **Caltagirone** (p252)
Tackling Sicily's most
spectacular staircase, then

stocking up on the town's
nationally renowned ceramics.

3 **Morgantina** (p250)
Sitting on the very steps where
ancient Greeks once debated,
conspired and gossiped.

4 **Piazza Armerina** (p247)
Losing yourself in a warren
of atmospheric streets and
eclectic local museums.

5 **Enna** (p241) Exploring a
whimsical cathedral, scaling a
Lombardi castle and soaking
up spectacular views in central
Sicily's busiest town.

6 **Calascibetta** (p246)
Enjoying a little downtime and
strolling through the nougat-
coloured streets of this sleepy
Sicilian hilltop village.

ENNA

📞 0935 / POP 27,240 / ELEV 931M

Italy's highest provincial capital, Enna stands above the hills and valleys of central Sicily. The town is a dramatic sight, seemingly impregnable atop a precipitous mountain. Inside you'll discover a calm working centre with a handsome medieval core and, cloud cover permitting, some mesmerising views. There's not enough to warrant an extended stay, but it is a great place to escape the tourist pack and enjoy some cool mountain air, particularly in summer when the sun bakes everything around to a yellow crisp.

The town of Enna is split in two: the hilltop historic centre, Enna Alta, and the modern town, Enna Bassa, below. Everything of interest is up in Enna Alta.

◉ Sights

Castello di Lombardia   CASTLE
(📞 0935 50 09 62; ⊘ 9am-8pm Apr-Aug, to 7pm Sep & Oct, to 5pm Nov-Mar) FREE One of Sicily's most formidable castles guards Enna's highest point, at the easternmost edge of the historic centre. The original castle was built by the Saracens and later reinforced by the Normans; Frederick II of Hohenstaufen ordered that a powerful curtain wall be built with towers on every side.

The wall is still intact, but only six of the original 20 towers remain, of which the tallest is the **Torre Pisano**. Accessible from the Cortile dei Cavalieri (one of the castle's well-preserved inner courtyards), the tower delivers spectacular views over the valley to the town of Calascibetta and to Mt Etna in the northeast.

Rocca di Cerere   VIEWPOINT
Just below the entrance to Castello di Lombardia is a huge rock, which was once home to Enna's Temple of Demeter (Ceres to the Romans), goddess of fertility and agriculture. The temple, built in 480 BC by the tyrant Gelon, is supposed to have featured a statue of King Triptolemus, the only mortal to witness the rape of Demeter's daughter Persephone.

There's not much left of the temple now, but the rocky platform, accessible by a series of steep steps, is a great place for a picnic or to take in the sunset.

Duomo   CATHEDRAL
(Via Roma; ⊘ 9am-1pm & 4-7pm) The Duomo is the most impressive of the historic buildings that line Via Roma, Enna's showpiece street. Built over 200 years after the original Gothic

cathedral burnt down in 1446, the current cathedral is topped by a muscular 17th-century *campanile* (bell tower) and graced with a sumptuous interior. Entry is usually through Jacopo Salemi's 16th-century side portal, which features a depiction of St Martin taking off his coat to cover the poor.

While the transept and polygonal apses offer traces of the original church, the interior is predominantly baroque, from the ornamental coffered wood ceiling and chandeliers, to the scene-stealing altar. Other points of interest include the bases of the grey basalt columns, decorated with grotesque carvings of snakes with human heads; the pulpit and stoup, both set on Greco-Roman remains from the Temple of Demeter; 17th-century presbytery paintings by Filippo Paladino; and the altarpieces by Guglielmo Borremans.

Piazza Crispi   PIAZZA
Just off Piazza Vittorio Emanuele is another small square, Piazza F Crispi, commanding sweeping views over the valley to Calascibetta. The piazza is home to the Fontana del Ratto di Prosperina, a monumental creation commemorating Enna's most enduring ancient legend.

Torre di Federico II   TOWER
(Viale IV Novembre; ⊘ 8am-6pm) FREE Secret passageways once led to this octagonal tower, which now stands in Enna's pine-studded public gardens. Once part of the town's old defence system, it stands nearly 24m high.

**Museo Archeologico
di Palazzo Varisano**   MUSEUM
(📞 0935 507 63 04; Piazza Mazzini 8; ⊘ 9am-7pm) FREE Enna's archaeological museum houses a good collection of local artefacts (labelled in Italian) excavated from throughout the region, as well as objects borrowed from the archaeological museums of both Syracuse and Agrigento. Of particular interest is the Attic-style red-and-black *krater* (drinking vase), found in the town itself and dating back to the 5th century BC.

Fontana del Ratto di Prosperina   FOUNTAIN
(Fountain of the Rape of Persephone) Right on Piazza Crispi is this monumental creation commemorating Enna's most enduring ancient legend.

Lago di Pergusa   LAKE
Surrounded by woodland about 9km south of town is one of Sicily's few natural lakes.

Enna

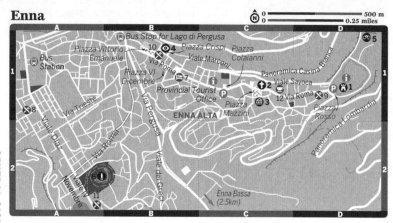

Enna

⊙ Sights

1 Castello di Lombardia	D1
2 Duomo	C1
Fontana del Ratto di Prosperina	(see 4)
3 Museo Archeologico di Palazzo Varisano	C1
4 Piazza Crispi	B1
5 Rocca di Cerere	D1
6 Torre di Federico II	A2

⊜ Sleeping

7 B&B Centro Sicilia	B1

⊗ Eating

8 La Rustica	A1
9 Meimuna	D1
10 Paccamora Bio Bar	B1
11 Umbriaco	A2

⊖ Drinking & Nightlife

12 Al Kenisa	C1

It's a popular summer hang-out with a few compact beaches, big resort-style hotels and an unlikely motor-racing circuit, but out of season it's a rather forlorn place. Alas, it also has nothing to connect it to the mythical tale of Persephone, for which it's so famous.

The lake is signposted along the SS561. On public transport, take local bus 5 (€1.20) from the bus stop on Via Pergusa. You can purchase bus tickets from Coppola travel agency, right beside the bus stop.

⭐ Festivals & Events

Holy Week   RELIGIOUS

The week building up to Easter is marked by solemn religious celebrations, during which the city's religious confraternities parade around in eerie capes and white hoods. The main events are on Palm Sunday, Good Friday and Easter Sunday.

Festa di Maria Santissima della Visitazione   CARNIVAL

(⊙2 Jul) Fireworks and scantily clad farmers mark the town's patron saint's day on 2 July.

Dressed in white sheets, the farmers drag an effigy of the Madonna of the Visitation through town on a cart called La Nave d'Oro (Golden Ship).

✕ Eating

⭐ Umbriaco   FAST FOOD €

(☎0935 37467; Viale 4 Novembre 11; snacks from €1.50; ⊘) ◉ Slow Food and organic ingredients are harnessed for some of Sicily's best *arancini* (stuffed deep-fried rice ball). Flavours often showcase what is seasonally available, but could include rice flavoured with porcini mushrooms or mortadella ham partnered with pistachios. Excellent pizza by the slice is also available, and the attached store sells interesting gourmet products from around the island, including craft Sicilian gin.

Visit around lunchtime or in the evening for the best selection of *arancini*.

⭐ La Rustica   SICILIAN €

(☎0935 2 55 22; Via Aidone 28; meals €17-22; ⊘1-3pm & 8-10.30pm Mon-Sat) Slow Food stalwart La Rustica ticks all the right boxes: off the tourist trail, popular with locals and run by a couple passionate about classic local grub. Gaetano tends to the vinyl-lined tables while Carmela whips up old family recipes such as superlative *caponata* (sweet-and-sour cooked vegetable salad) and *polpettone ripieno all'enese* (egg-stuffed meatloaf with peas and a tomato sauce).

Osteria al Canale SICILIAN €

(☑339 6155928, 0935 95 89 66; Via Mazzini 101, Valguarnera Caropepe; meals €20-28; ⊙noon-2.30pm & 8-10pm; 🐾) Enna foodies know all about this simple village eatery, a 24km drive southeast of Enna. Lorded over by head chef Lillo Serra, its shtick is honest, locally rooted dishes such as seasoned pecorino with onion marmalade, *pasta sfoglia* (puff pastry) stuffed with seasonal veggies, and spaghetti with *pesto siciliano* (tomato, salted ricotta, basil, chilli and almonds). Dinner reservations are obligatory.

That the dining-room cabinet features a photo of Australian-born singer Tina Arena is no coincidence. Her parents hail from the village and the star herself has been known to scribble down some of Lillo's recipes.

Paccamora Bio Bar SICILIAN €

(Piazza Vittorio Emanuele 21-22; sandwiches €3.50, lunch dishes €9, dinner platter from €8; ⊙7.30am-1am Mon-Sat; 🐾☑) This next-gen cafe has a focus on the fresh, wholesome and local, from great organic coffee (non-dairy milk available), juices and wholemeal *cornetti* (croissants), to lunchtime soy-bread *panini* and daily specials such as spelt lasagne with carrot and artichoke. Come dinner, nibble on a tapas platter, or refresh with a Sicilian craft beer.

Meimuna ITALIAN €€

(☑0935 2 22 36; www.meimuna.it; Via Lombardia 5; meals $30-35; ⊙7-11.30pm; ☑) Meimuna's contemporary reinterpretation of a trattoria combines stylish decor with modern versions of traditional Sicilian flavours. Hearty dishes like pasta with pistachio cream, mushrooms and bacon go well with Sicilian craft beers – try the zesty wheat beer from Bruno Ribaldi. There's also a good array of vegetarian dishes on offer. Regular fixed price menus are good value.

🍷 Drinking & Nightlife

★ Al Kenisa CAFE

(☑0935 500972; http://alkenisa.blogspot.com; Via Roma 481; ⊙6pm-midnight Tue-Sun) Housed in a former chapel of the adjacent cathedral, Al Kenisa is Enna's best spot for an *aperitivo*, glass of wine or craft beer. Books and art prints are for sale, there's occasional live music and DJ sets (usually from around 10pm on Thursday and Saturday nights), and the optional spooky adventure of descending into Al Kenisa's crypt.

ℹ Information

Hospital (Ospedale Umberto I; ☑0935 51 67 54; Contrada Ferrante, Enna Bassa) Major hospital in the lower town.

Municipal Tourist Office (Castello di Lombardia; ⊙10am-7pm) In the main courtyard of the castle. Also features interesting displays on the history of Enna and the castle and a shop selling local arts and crafts.

Police Station (☑0935 52 21 11; Via San Giovanni 4)

Provincial Tourist Office (Infopoint; ☑0935 50 23 62; www.provincia.enna.it/infopoint.htm; Via Roma 413; ⊙9am-1pm & 3-5.30pm Mon-Fri, 9am-1pm Sun) On the main street in the historic centre.

ℹ Getting There & Away

BUS

Bus is the best way to reach Enna by public transport. Enna's official **bus station** (Viale

---

THE MYTH OF PERSEPHONE

The tale of Hades' capture of Demeter's daughter Persephone (also known as Proserpina) is one of the most famous Greek myths. According to Homeric legend, Hades (god of the underworld) emerged from his lair and abducted Persephone while she was gathering flowers around Lago di Pergusa. Not knowing where her daughter had disappeared to, Demeter (goddess of the harvest) forbade the earth to bear fruit as she wandered the world looking for her. Eventually, she turned to Zeus, threatening that if he didn't return her daughter she would inflict eternal famine on the world. Zeus submitted to her threat and ordered Hades to release Persephone, though stipulating that every year she should spend six months in the underworld with Hades and six months in Sicily with her mother. Demeter still mourns during Persephone's time in the underworld, bringing winter to the world; her joy at her daughter's return is heralded by the blossoms of springtime.

ROAD TRIP >
ENNA TO ETNA

• •

This tour meanders through the rural heart of Sicily, ushering you into a landscape of rolling agricultural fields and dramatically perched hill towns, where multi-coloured houses tumble down steep slopes below ancient castles and baroque churches. The layers of history here span many millennia, from prehistory to WWII. In spring, the entire countryside is carpeted with a riot of wildflowers.

❶ Enna

Begin your trip in the imposing hill town of Enna, smack in Sicily's geographic centre. A climb to the Castello di Lombardia at the top of town affords fine views over the rolling landscape to the north, which you'll soon be travelling through.

The Drive > Snake your way down the hill and across the valley 7km to Calascibetta.

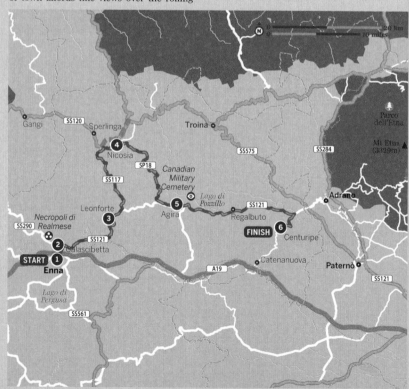

One or Two Days 115km

Great for... History & Culture, Outdoors

Best Time to Go May, September & October

Calascibetta (p246)

TRABANTOS/SHUTTERSTOCK ©

❷ Calascibetta

Calascibetta's most impressive sight is its landmark cathedral, the 14th-century Chiesa Madre. Northwest 3km is the Necropoli di Realmese, boasting some 300 rock tombs dating from 850 BC.

The Drive > From Calascibetta, the SS121 winds and weaves 20km up to Leonforte,

❸ Leonforte

An attractive baroque town once famous for horse breeding. Leonforte's most imposing building is the Palazzo Baronale, but the drawcard is the lavish Granfonte fountain. Built in 1651 by Nicolò Branciforte, it's made up of 24 separate jets against a sculpted facade.

The Drive > Continue 26km up the SS117 through dramatic scenery to Nicosia.

❹ Nicosia

Set on four hills, the town of Nicosia revolves around central Piazza Garibaldi. Check out the **Cattedrale di San Nicolò** (p247), the Franco-Lombard *palazzi* and the **Basilica di Santa Maria Maggiore** (p247). Near the entrance to town, **Baglio San Pietro** (p247) is great for a meal break or even an overnight stop.

The Drive > Push southeast 26km along the SP43 and SP18 to Agira.

❺ Agira

Lovely Agira is yet another sloping hillside village capped by a medieval Norman castle. A couple of kilometres out of town on the SS121 the well-tended Canadian Military Cemetery houses the graves of 490 soldiers killed in July 1943.

The Drive > From Agira, follow the SS121 about 9km east to Lago di Pozzillo, a scenic stretch of water surrounded by hills and almond groves, ideal for a picnic. Continue another 20km along the SS121 to Centuripe.

❻ Centuripe

Centuripe is a small town whose grandstand views of Mt Etna have earned it the nickname il Balcone di Sicilia (the Balcony of Sicily). Unfortunately, its strategic position has also brought bloodshed and the town has often been fought over. In 1943 the Allies captured the town and the Germans, realising that their foothold in Sicily had slipped, retreated to the Italian mainland.

DON'T MISS

COOKING COURSES & WINE TASTING

The area west of Caltanissetta is wild and remote. But if you want to get away from everything, head to beautiful **Tenuta Regaleali** (☑0921 54 40 11; www.tascadalmerita. it; Contrada Regaleali, Sclafani Bagni), near the village of Vallelunga. One of five wine-producing estates owned by the Tasca d'Almerita family, it's home to some 400 hectares of vineyards, a high-tech winery and, in a restored 19th-century building, the **Anna Tasca Lanza Cooking School** (☑0934 81 46 54; www.annatascalanza.com).

Visits to the winery are limited to guided tours (with optional tastings) for between eight and 25 people, which must be booked ahead. Cooking courses range from a day-long lesson and lunch (€175) to overnight and up to five-day packages (€495 to €2475 per person including accommodation). Best of all, all that kneading, mixing and nibbling is laced with gorgeous glasses of vino from the winery. Further details are available on the websites. Also scheduled throughout the year are special programmes incorporating yoga, sketching, bread-making and pasta-making.

Diaz) is in the upper town; to get to the town centre from the station turn right and follow Viale Diaz to Corso Sicilia, turn right again and follow it to Via Sant'Agata, which leads to Via Roma, Enna Alta's main street.

Service is more frequent from the stop in Enna Bassa, 3km downhill. Hourly local buses connect Enna Bassa with the upper town, except on Sundays when it's every two hours. Check when you book to establish which bus station you're arriving at. The upper town bus station is more convenient for recommended accommodation and restaurants.

SAIS Autolinee (☑0935 50 09 02; www. saisautolinee.it) runs services to Catania (€8, 1½ hours, up to nine daily Monday to Friday, six Saturday, three Sunday) and Palermo (€10.30, 1¾ hours, one daily Monday to Saturday). There are two daily services from Palermo to Enna on Sunday. Regular buses also run to Piazza Armerina (€3.60, 40 minutes, up to seven daily Monday to Friday, up to six Saturday, two Sunday) and Calascibetta (€1.90, 30 minutes, five to eight daily Monday to Saturday).

The **Coppola Viaggi & Turismo** (☑0935 50 20 11; Via Sant'Agata 86; ⊙9am-1pm & 4-7.30pm Mon-Fri, 9am-1pm Sat) travel agency sells bus tickets.

CAR & MOTORCYCLE

Enna is on the main Catania–Palermo A19 *autostrada,* about 83km from Catania, 135km from Palermo. There's handy free parking on Piazza Rosso, right beside the Castello di Lombardia. Free parking is also available on Piazza Europa, close to Torre di Federico II.

❶ Getting Around

To reach Lago Di Pergusa on public transport, take local bus 5 (€1.20) from the bus stop on Via Pergusa. You can purchase bus tickets from Coppola travel agency, right beside the bus stop.

CALASCIBETTA

☑0935 / POP 4400 / ELEV 691M

A densely packed maze of narrow streets set above a sheer precipice, 7km north of Enna, Calascibetta was originally built by the Saracens during their siege of Enna in 951 and was later strengthened by the Norman king Roger I. The most impressive sight is the 14th-century **Chiesa Madre** (☑0935 3 38 49; Piazza Matrice; ⊙9am-1pm & 3.30-7pm), Calascibetta's landmark cathedral, and meandering through the town's sleepy labyrinth is a relaxing way to spend a few hours.

The **Necropoli di Realmese** `FREE`, 3km northwest, is worth investigating, with some 300 rock tombs dating from 850 BC. To reach the site, head north out of town on Strada Statale 290, turn right into Strada Provinciale 80 and look for the sign marked 'Necropoli di Realmese' (a further 700m, on your left).

❶ Getting There & Away

Calascibetta is 7km from Enna. SAIS Autolinee runs buses from Enna to Calascibetta (€1.90, 30 minutes, five to eight daily Monday to Saturday).

NICOSIA

☑0935 / POP 13,760 / ELEV 724M

Two churches make Nicosia worthy of a visit, and the centrally located Piazza Garibaldi reinforces a handsome, heritage townscape. Set on four hills, this ancient town was once the most important of a chain of fortified Norman towns stretching from Palermo to Messina. Modern times have been tougher, and between 1950 and 1970 nearly half the town's population emigrated.

A nearby *agriturismo* with an excellent restaurant merits an overnight stop.

◎ Sights

The centre of action is Piazza Garibaldi, a handsome square dominated by the elegant 14th-century facade and Catalan-Gothic *campanile* of the **Cattedrale di San Nicolò** (⊘9am-noon & 4-7pm).

From the piazza, Via Salamone leads past crumbling Franco-Lombard *palazzi* to the **Basilica di Santa Maria Maggiore** (✐0935 64 67 16; Largo Santa Maria; ⊘9am-noon & 4-7.30pm), a 1767 reconstruction of a 13th-century church destroyed by a landslide in 1757. The terrace offers a view of the ruins of a Norman castle, perched on a rocky crag.

✖ Eating

Nicosia's most famous edible is the heavenly *nocattolo* pastry, consisting of a shortbread crust topped with cinnamon-spiced almond paste and dusted in icing sugar. Beyond a few local eateries, the best place to eat in the area is the restaurant at the *agriturismo* (farm stay), Baglio San Pietro.

Baglio San Pietro   SICILIAN €€
(✐0935 64 05 29; www.bagliosanpietro.com; Contrada San Pietro; meals €30-40, tasting menu €70; ⊘noon-2.30pm & 5.30-10pm Thu-Tue) Effortlessly blurring country and creative (think truffle caviar followed by smoked veal carpaccio), this *agriturismo* restaurant is also well known for its delicious wood-fired *porchetta* (suckling pig). Comprehensive tasting menus are good value and excellent craft beers from Nicosia's very own Birrificio 24 Baroni are a real surprise in this sleepy Sicilian hilltown. Book ahead for Friday and Saturday night.

❶ Getting There & Away

The SS117 links Nicosia to the town of Leonforte 26km to the south. From here, the SS121 continues to Enna, 21km to the southwest.

Interbus (✐0913 4 20 55, 0935 2 24 60; www.interbus.it) runs services to Catania (€8.40, two to 2¼ hours, four daily Monday to Friday, three Saturday, one Sunday). Services run from Piazza San Francesco di Paola.

PIAZZA ARMERINA

✐0935 / POP 21,800 / ELEV 697M

Piazza Armerina's hilltop medieval centre is laced with atmospheric, labyrinthine streets; the highpoint is the cathedral, a landmark for miles around, with its towering dome rising 66m. Set amid fertile farming country, this charming market town takes its name from the Colle Armerino, one of the three hills on which it is built.

Piazza Armerina is actually two towns in one: the original Piazza was founded by the Saracens in the 10th century on the slope of the Colle Armerino, while a 15th-century expansion to the southeast was redefined by an urban grid established in the 17th century.

The town makes a convenient base if visiting the extraordinary ancient mosaics at nearby Villa Romana del Casale.

◎ Sights

Off Piazza Duomo is Via Monte, the arterial road of the 13th-century city. A warren of tiny alleys fan off Via Monte like the ribs of a fishbone. This is the town's most picturesque quarter and worth an aimless wander. Alternatively, take Via Floresta, beside Palazzo Trigona, to arrive at the ruins of the 14th-century Castello Aragonese.

From the cathedral, Via Cavour hairpins down to Piazza Garibaldi, the elegant heart of the old town. Overlooking the square is the late-baroque **Palazzo di Città**, Piazza's former town hall (closed to the public), and the **Chiesa di San Rocco** (Piazza Garibaldi; ⊘hours vary), also known as the Fundrò, graced by a magnificent, tuff-stone portal.

Cathedral   CATHEDRAL
(Piazza Duomo; ⊘8.30am-noon & 3.30-6pm) You can spot the dramatically sited dome of the huge cathedral from a few kilometres away. It rises majestically from the hilltop and the terraced houses skirt its base in descending tiers. The severe facade dates from 1719, with the dome added in 1768. Inside the airy blue-and-white interior, behind the altar, is a copy of a Byzantine painting, *Madonna delle Vittorie* (Virgin of the Victories), the original of which was supposedly presented to Count Roger I by Pope Nicholas II.

In front of the cathedral is a beautiful belvedere (panoramic terrace) while to the right of it is the baronial **Palazzo Trigona** (Piazza Duomo). A **statue** of Baron Marco Trigona – who financed the cathedral's construction – stands in the square.

To the side of the main church, the 44m-high **campanile** is a leftover from an earlier 14th-century church.

CENTRAL SICILY PIAZZA ARMERINA

Piazza Armerina

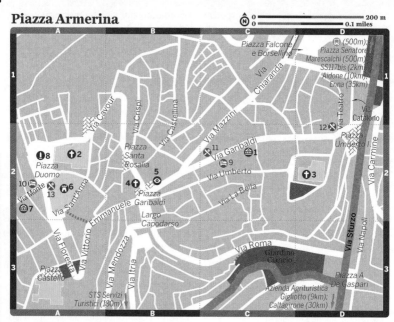

Piazza Armerina

◎ Sights

⬤ Sleeping

✴ Eating

Pinacoteca Comunale GALLERY

(☎0935 68 76 13; Via Monte 4; ⊙9am-6pm Tue-Sun) **FREE** Piazza Armerina's small, slick public art gallery showcases mostly local artwork from the 15th to 19th centuries, including altarpieces and frescoes from long-gone churches and works by renowned local painter Giuseppe Paladino (1856–1922). Seek out the portrait of 17th-century scholar and Jesuit missionary Prospero Intorcetta.

Born in Piazza Armerina and active in China, he was the first European to translate the works of Confucius into Latin.

Also of interest is the altarpiece *Sant'Andrea Avellino intercede per Piazza presso la Madonna delle Vittorie* (St Andrew Avellino intercedes for Piazza at Our Lady of Victories), which depicts Piazza Armerina as it appeared in the 17th century.

Casa Museo del Contadino MUSEUM

(☎333 9138634; Via Garibaldi 57; by donation; ⊙9am-noon & 3.30-6.30pm) A labour of love for its founder, Mario Albanese, this small but meticulously detailed ethnographic museum recreates a typical Sicilian peasant house of the 19th century. Mario's knowledge of the museum's artefacts and subject matter is impressive, and he happily offers visitors engrossing, oft-moving insight into the living conditions and sheer ingenuity of the region's rural workers (in Italian and French).

Chiesa di San
Giovanni Evangelista CHURCH

(Largo San Giovanni; ⊙hours vary) Founded in the 14th century, the current Chiesa di San Giovanni Evangelista dates back to the 18th century. Its interior is lavished with the glorious, vivid brush strokes of Dutch painter Guglielmo Borremans (1670-1744) and his students.

Parco Minerario Floristella Grottacalda HISTORIC SITE

(www.enteparcofloristella.it; ☉sunrise to sunset) FREE Around 15km north of Piazza Armerina are the historic remains of sulphur mining that was active in the region until the mid-20th century. It's now pleasantly verdant and forested, but a poignant reminder of the industry's harsh realities are the black-and-white photographs in the park's interesting museum of child miners forced to work in very dangerous conditions. To get the most out of a visit, join a hike or day trip with Cafeci based in nearby Valguarnera.

👉 Tours

Cafeci HIKING

(Officina AgroCulturale Cafeci; ☑WhatsApp/Carmen 328 1357424, WhatsApp/Michele 328 6812913; www.facebook.com/OfficinaAgroCulturaleCafeci; Valguarnera; guided hikes per day per group from €120) Based near Valguarnera, 20km south of Piazza Armerina, Cafeci offers diverse outdoor activities including hiking with donkeys, beekeeper-for-a-day experiences (€25) at its own organic hives and trips further afield to Mt Etna. Multi-night hikes incorporating overnight stays at B&Bs and *agriturismi* can also be arranged along with interesting visits to the Parco Minerario Floristella Grottacalda.

Both Carmen and Michele speak excellent English. Contact them via WhatsApp and they'll send you details on how to reach their farmhouse. They can also arrange pickups from Enna or Piazza Armerina.

🎊 Festivals & Events

Palio dei Normanni CARNIVAL

(www.paliodeinormanni.it; ☉12-14 Aug) Piazza Armerina bursts into life in August, when a medieval pageant celebrates Count Roger's capture of the town from the Moors in 1087. Events kick off with the blessing of the knights on the first day, costumed parades on the second and a great joust *(quintana)* between the town's four districts on the third day.

The winning district is presented with a standard depicting Our Lady of the Victories.

🍴 Eating

★Disìu GELATO €

(☑389 485 8865; https://disiu-gelateria-naturale.business.site; Plazza Umberto 1; gelato from €2; ☉7am-1pm & 2pm-midnight) This unassuming but modern cafe is one of Sicily's best ice-cream spots. Excellent gelati and *granite* (flavoured crushed ice with local seasonal fruits) combine with a sunny location near the Chiesa Santo Stefano. Other tasty offerings from Disìu's young and hip crew include a good range of Sicilian wines and craft beers. Secure a table outside and relax.

Da Totò TRATTORIA €

(☑0935 68 01 53; Via Mazzini 27; meals €22-26; ☉noon-3pm & 6pm-midnight Tue-Sun) Don't let the stark white lights and bland decor put you off, this popular, affable trattoria serves excellent value-for-money food. Antipasti are of the ham, cheese and grilled veg variety, while pastas are matched with earthy sauces of porcini mushrooms or ripe local vegetables. Main courses are similarly unpretentious with grilled pepper steak a menu mainstay.

La Locanda SICILIAN €€

(☑377 125 3594; https://la-locanda.business.site; Via de Assoro 2-12; meals €30-35; ☉noon-3.30pm & 7-10pm Fri-Wed) Celebrating a hilltop location near Piazza Armerina's cathedral, La Locanda combines a top Sicilian wine list with creative spins on traditional flavours. Try the pasta with wild fennel, sardines and pine nuts or the pistachio and almond–crusted swordfish. Of course we're fans of the wall-covering map of the world that's a spectacular highlight of the ground floor dining room.

★Al Fogher SICILIAN €€€

(☑0935 68 41 23; https://alfogher.sicilia.restaurant; Contrada Bellia, SS117bis; meals €50; ☉7.30-10.30pm Mon, noon-2.30pm & 7.30-10.30pm Tue-Sat, noon-2.30pm Sun) This is one of central Sicily's top restaurants, serving sophisticated modern cuisine to a demanding and appreciative clientele. It's about 3km out of town, but your journey is rewarded with dishes such as suckling pig with tuna-egg sauce and asparagus, or mullet served with yellow capsicum, wild rice and pistachio. Reservations required.

Equal attention is given to the wine list, which contains up to 400 labels.

ℹ️ Information

STS Servizi Turistici (☑0935 68 70 27; www.guardalasicilia.it) This helpful information point has English-speaking staff who can give you free town guides and maps of the Roman Villa (maps are often unavailable at the site itself).

ℹ️ Getting There & Away

BUS

Interbus (☑0913 4 20 55, 0935 2 24 60; www.interbus.it) runs a service to Catania

(€9.20, 1¾ hours, six daily Monday to Friday, four Saturday, two Sunday). **SAIS Autolinee** (☏199 244141, 800 211020; www.saisautolinee.it) buses connect Piazza Armerina with Enna (€3.60, 40 minutes, up to six daily Monday to Friday, up to five Saturday) and Palermo (€12.50, two hours, five daily Monday to Friday, three Saturday, two Sunday). Buses depart from Piazza Armerina's Piazza Senatore Marescalchi.

Between May and September **SAVIT Autolinee** (☏0934 55 66 26; www.savitautolinee.it) runs eight daily buses from Piazza Senatore Marescalchi to Villa Romana del Casale (€1, 30 minutes), departing from on the hour (9am to noon and 3pm to 6pm) and returning from the villa on the half-hour.

A **taxi** (☏329 2911435) to the villa costs around €25 return.

CAR & MOTORCYCLE

The SS117bis links Piazza Armerina with Enna 33km to the north. You'll find a large open-air car park in Piazza Europa, at the northeastern edge of the old city.

VILLA ROMANA DEL CASALE

The Unesco-listed Villa Romana del Casale is central Sicily's biggest attraction for good reason: the site, situated in a wooded valley 5km southwest of the town of Piazza Armerina, is home to the finest Roman floor mosaics in existence.

◉ Sights

★ **Villa Romana
del Casale** ARCHAEOLOGICAL SITE
(☏0935 68 00 36; www.villaromanadelcasale.it; adult/reduced €10/5, combined ticket incl Morgantina & Museo Archeologico di Aidone €14/7; ◷9am-7pm Apr-Oct, to 5pm Nov-Mar, open to 11pm Fri-Sun Jul-Aug) Villa Romana del Casale is sumptuous, even by decadent Roman standards, and is thought to have been the country retreat of Marcus Aurelius Maximianus, Rome's co-emperor during the reign of Diocletian (AD 286–305). Certainly, the size

---

WORTH A TRIP

AIDONE & MORGANTINA

For a quiet rendezvous with the ancients, hit the road and shoot northeast of Piazza Armerina. A 10km drive away lies Aidone, a sleepy hilltop village whose small **archaeological museum** (☏0935 8 73 07; www.regione.sicilia.it/beniculturali/deadimorgantina; Largo Torres Truppia 1; adult/reduced €6/3, incl Morgantina adult/reduced €10/5, incl Villa Romana del Casale & Morgantina €14/7; ◷9am-7pm Tue-Sun) is worth a stop on your way to the ancient Greek ruins of Morgantina. The museum collection includes artefacts from the Morgantina site, and has displays chronicling life in ancient times. It's also home to the long-lost *Dea di Morgantina*, an ancient statue of Venus, repatriated to Italy in 2011 from the Getty Museum in Los Angeles, California.

A short 4km downhill drive from Aidone leads you to the ruins of **Morgantina** (☏0935 8 79 55; adult/reduced €6/3, incl Museo Archeologico di Aidone €10/5, incl Villa Romana del Casale & Museo Archeologico di Aidone €14/7; ◷2-7pm Tue-Sun Jun-Aug, 10am-5pm Tue-Sun Sep-May). The ancient town's centre is the two-storey agora (marketplace), its trapezoidal stairway used as seating during public meetings. The upper level had a market; note the walls that once divided the shops. The lower level was the site of the 1000-capacity theatre, originally built in the 3rd century BC and subsequently altered by the Romans.

To the northeast are the city's residential quarters, where the town's well-off lived, as testified by the ornate wall decorations and handsome mosaics in the inner rooms. Another residential quarter has been found behind the theatre and its considerable ruins are well worth checking out. The southwest corner of the site contains the remains of a public bath complex.

The area was originally home to Morgeti, an early Sicilian settlement founded in 850 BC on Cittadella hill. This town was destroyed in 459 BC and a new one was built on a second hill, Serra Orlando. It was an important trading post during the reign of the Syracusan tyrant Hieron II (269–215 BC), but slipped into decline after defeat by the Romans in 211 BC and was eventually abandoned. In 1955 archaeologists identified the site and began its excavation, which continues to this day.

To get to the site you'll need your own transport as no buses stop nearby. .

Villa Romana del Casale

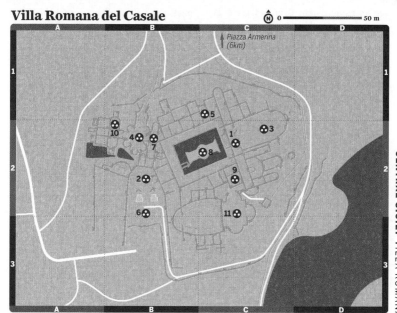

N 0 ══════════ 50 m

of the complex – four interconnected groups of buildings spread over the hillside – and the 3535 sq metres of astoundingly well-preserved multicoloured floor mosaics suggest a palace of imperial standing.

Following a landslide in the 12th century, the villa lay under 10m of mud for some 700 years, and was thus protected from the damaging effects of air, wind and rain. It was only when serious excavation work began in the 1950s that the mosaics, considered remarkable for their natural, narrative style, the range of their subject matter and the variety of their colour, were brought back to light.

The villa's recent restoration has covered almost the entire complex with a wooden roof (to protect the mosaics from the elements), while an elevated walkway allows visitors to view the tiled floors and the structure itself in its entirety. Architects report a dissatisfaction with the structure for the lack of light, and the shadows that obscure the colours and vivacity of the mosaics, but the condition of the mosaics has been much improved.

To the north of the villa's **main entrance**, which leads through the remnants of a triumphal arch into an elegant **atrium** (forecourt), is the villa's baths complex. Accessible via the **palaestra** (gymnasium), which has a splendid mosaic depicting a chariot race at the

Villa Romana del Casale

⊙ **Sights**

Circus Maximus in Rome, is the octagonal **frigidarium** (cold bath), where the radiating apses contained cold plunge pools, and a **tepidarium** (warm room), where you can now see the exposed brickwork and vents that allowed hot steam into the room.

The main part of the villa is centred on the **peristyle**, a vast covered courtyard lined with amusing animal heads. This is where guests would have been received before being taken through to the **basilica** (throne room).

Of the rooms on the northern side of the peristyle, the most interesting is a dining room featuring a hunting mosaic called the **Little Hunt** – 'little' because the big hunt is over on the eastern flank of the peristyle in the **Ambulacro della Grande Caccia** (Corridor of the Great Hunt).

On one side of the Ambulacro is a series of apartments, the floor illustrations of which reproduce scenes from Homer and other mythical episodes. Of particular interest is the **triclinium** (banquet hall), with a splendid depiction of the labours of Hercules, where the tortured monsters are ensnared by a smirking Odysseus.

Just off the southern end of the Ambulacro della Grande Caccia, in the **Sala delle Dieci Ragazze** (Room of the 10 Girls), is the villa's most famous mosaic. It depicts nine (originally there were 10) bikini-clad girls working out with weights and dinky dumbbells, in preparation for the Olympic games.

The site is equipped with enough interpretive panels (in English) for you to explore the villa autonomously. If you do want to arrange a guide, however, contact the STS Servizi Turistici in Piazza Armerina; otherwise you can organise one directly at the site.

ⓘ Getting There & Away

If driving to Villa Romana del Casale, follow signs along the SP15 from Piazza Armerina's town centre.

By public transport it's harder, but not impossible. Between May and September SAVIT Autolinee runs eight daily buses to the site from Piazza Armerina (€1, 30 minutes), departing from Piazza Senatore Marescalchi on the hour (9am to noon and 3pm to 6pm) and returning from the villa on the half-hour.

Outside summer you will have to walk – it's downhill, not too strenuous, and takes about an hour. The walk back is only steep for the last part. Another option is to prearrange a taxi, which costs around €25 return.

CALTAGIRONE

☑ 0933 / POP 38,500 / ELEV 608M

Hilltop Caltagirone is renowned throughout Sicily for its ceramics. The area's high-quality clay has supported production for more than 1000 years and still today the industry is an important money-spinner. The town's earliest settlers worked with terracotta, but it was the Arabs, arriving in the 10th century, who kick-started the industry by introducing glazed polychromatic colours, particularly the yellows and blues that have distinguished the local ceramics ever since.

Everywhere you go in Caltagirone you're reminded of its ceramic traditions, most emphatically at the Scalinata di Santa Maria del Monte, the town's ceramic-inlaid staircase.

Caltagirone's history dates to pre-Greek times, but the town's name is Arabic in origin, a derivation of the words *kalat* and *gerun*, meaning 'castle' and 'cave'. Little remains of the town's early incarnations, as it was almost entirely destroyed by the earthquake in 1693 and subsequently rebuilt in the baroque style so typical of Sicily's southeast.

◉ Sights

Caltagirone has an extraordinary number of churches, almost 30 in the historic centre alone. Most are baroque, dating to the building boom of the early 18th century, although some have earlier origins.

★ Scalinata di Santa Maria del Monte   LANDMARK

Caltagirone's most evocative sight is this monumental staircase, which rises from Piazza Municipio to **Chiesa di Santa Maria del Monte**. Built in the early 17th century to connect the old hilltop centre with newer developments around Piazza Municipio, it was originally divided into several flights of steps separated by small squares. These tiers were eventually unified in the 1880s to create the 142-step flight that stands today. The hand-painted majolica tiles were a relatively recent addition, only being added in 1956.

It's all very impressive, although by the time you get to the top, you'll probably be more interested in having a sit-down than admiring the tile-work. Fortunately, the huge views will quickly restore your will to move. Flanked by colourful ceramic shops, the steps are at their finest during Caltagirone's annual celebration, the Festa di San Giacomo (Feast of St James).

At the bottom of the staircase, **Piazza Municipio** is overshadowed by a number of grand buildings, including the **Palazzo Senatorio**, where the town senate once sat. The building is now home to a cafe.

Museo della Ceramica   MUSEUM

(Regional Ceramics Museum; ☑ 0933 5 84 18; Via Giardini Pubblici; adult/reduced €4/2; ⊙ 9am-6.30pm Tue-Sun) Down from the main historic centre, this museum is the place to learn about the Sicilian ceramics industry. Exhibits, which include Greek terracotta works, medieval kitchenware and some excessively elaborate 18th-century maiolica statuettes, chronicle developments from prehistoric times to the 19th century.

Giardino Pubblico
GARDENS

(Via Giardini Pubblici) Next to the Museo della Ceramica, the Giardino Pubblico is a lovely place to see out the late afternoon, perhaps with an ice cream or a glass of something cool at the park bar. Manicured avenues lead down to a beautiful (if unloved) pavilion, inspired by Moorish architecture and built in the early 1950s.

Look the other way for views stretching into the distance – on a clear day, as far as Mt Etna.

Activities

Ebike On
CYCLING

(☑ 347 8032681; www.facebook.com/ebikeon; Via Roma 45; bike rental from €5; ☉ 9am-1pm & 4.30-7.30pm) Rents out a variety of two-wheeled transport including mountain bikes and e-bikes and can advise on recommended cycling routes around the town.

Festivals & Events

Festa di San Giacomo
CULTURAL

(☉ 24 & 25 Jul) Caltagirone's annual celebration is the Festa di San Giacomo (Feast of St James), when the town's famous staircase – Scalinata di Santa Maria del Monte – is lit by more than 4000 oil lamps. The spectacle is repeated on 14 and 15 August.

Eating

The hilltop town's specialities are earthy and rustic. Look out for *pasta cu maccu* (with puréed fava beans), *pasta chi mirangiani* (with eggplant and salted ricotta) and *piruna* (calzoni filled with spinach and other vegetables). Come Christmas, tuck into *cuddureddi ri Natali* (shortcrust pastry filled with almonds, honey and sweet, dense *vincotto* paste made from reduced wine). Caltagirone's dining scene includes bustling pizzerias and the fine-dining savvy of Coria.

La Piazzetta
SICILIAN €

(☑ 0933 2 41 78; www.ritrovolapiazzetta.it; Via Vespri 20; pizzas from €5, meals €22-25; ☉ 1-2.30pm & 8-11pm Fri-Wed; ☎) For many locals, Saturday night means a meal at La Piazzetta. That might mean a pizza and beer or something more substantial such as fresh pasta with pistachio pesto followed by a mountainous mixed grill. It's not haute cuisine, but the food is tasty, the atmosphere is convivial and the prices are honest.

Bar Judica & Trieste
SICILIAN €

(☑ 0933 2 20 21; Via Principe Amedeo 22; calzone €2; ☉ 8am-midnight Wed-Mon) It's all about the street food at this unassuming neighbourhood bar, complete with pavement patio. Scan the counter for cheap, filling bites such as *pizza a taglio* (pizza by the slice), *arancini* and calzoni. The latter come in a variety of fillings, from sautéed spinach and pecorino cheese, to a combo of eggplant, mozzarella and tomato.

Two calzoni should satiate the hungriest of punters. Seal the deal with a postprandial gelato, granita or espresso.

Il Locandiere
SEAFOOD €€

(☑ 0933 5 82 92; Via Sturzo 55-59; meals €30-35; ☉ 12.30-2.30pm & 8-10.30pm Tue-Sun; ☎) Those in the know head to this smart little restaurant for top-quality seafood and impeccable service. What exactly you'll eat depends on the day's catch, but the fish couscous is superb and the *casarecce con ragù di tonno* (pasta fingers with tuna sauce) a sure-fire hit. *Dolci* show-stoppers include delicious *cannoli a cucchiao* (*cannoli* with fig cream).

The mostly Sicilian wine list is long enough to please most palates.

★ Coria
SICILIAN €€€

(☑ 0933 2 65 96; www.ristorantecoria.it; Via Infermeria 24; meals & tasting menus €75-90; ☉ 12.30-2pm & 7.30-10pm Tue-Sat, 7.30-10pm Mon) Caltagirone's top restaurant is an established address on the island's fine-dining circuit. Its reputation rides on innovative, visually arresting cuisine, and while not every dish on the menu truly flies, the strike rate is very good. Expect seasonal dishes that could see grilled cod paired with plum mayonnaise, or tender beef conspiring with carob. Reservations required.

Drinking & Nightlife

Gusto e Arte
CAFE

(Via Bosco; ☉ 7pm-midnight) Vintage gardening paraphernalia and retro furniture combine with a friendly welcome at this cafe tucked away in Caltagirone's historic city centre. Order a glass of Sicilian wine or beer and combine it with an overflowing plate of cheese and charcuterie from the compact kitchen. Look for the bright pink racing bike out the front and you're in the right place.

🛍 Shopping

If you're in the market for a souvenir, there are about 120 ceramics shops in town.

★ Ceramiche Alessi
Di Giacomo Alessi   CERAMICS

(☎0933 2 19 67; www.giacomoalessi.com; Corso Principe Amedeo 9; ⊙9.30am-1.30pm & 3.30-8pm) Giacomo Alessi is arguably Caltagirone's most famous ceramicist. Not only has his work been exhibited at La Biennale di Venezia, but he received a Knighthood of the Italian Republic in 2007. Inspired by classical myths, Sicilian traditions, magic, poetry and even war, he creates astounding works that masterfully balance classic and contemporary aesthetics. Also has shops at Palermo and Catania airports.

Le Maioliche di
Riccardo Varsallona   CERAMICS

(☎0933 2 61 67; www.maiolichevarsallona.com; Via Colombo 33; ⊙9am-1pm & 2.30-8pm Mon-Sat) This reliably creative and innovative local ceramicist produces some interesting designs as well as the more traditional *testa di Moro* (Moor's head).

ℹ Information

Tourist Office (☎335 5795945; www.comune.caltagirone.ct.it; Via Duomo 15; ⊙9am-7pm Mon-Sat) In the town's main square near the bottom of the Scalinata di Santa Maria del Monte.

ℹ Getting There & Away

BUS
AST (☎840 000323; www.aziendasiciliana trasporti.it) buses run to Piazza Armerina (€4.30, 1½ hours, one daily Monday to Saturday) and Syracuse (€10.50, three hours, twice daily Monday to Saturday). **SAIS Autolinee** (☎199 244141, 800 211020; www.saisauto linee.it) runs a service to Enna (€5.80, 1¼ hours, twice daily Monday to Saturday, once daily Sunday).

CAR & MOTORCYCLE
Caltagirone is just off the SS417, the road that connects Gela on the south coast with Catania in the east. From Piazza Armerina, follow the SS-117bis south and then cut across on the SS124.

If you're staying in the upper town, there's useful parking on Viale Regina Elena.

Mediterranean Coast

Best
Places to Eat

➡ Ristorante La Madia (p272)

➡ M.A.T.E.S. (p272)

➡ Kalòs (p260)

➡ Hostaria Del Vicolo (p271)

➡ Aguglia Persa (p260)

➡ Terracotta (p260)

Best
Ancient Sites

➡ Tempio della Concordia (p262)

➡ Giardino della Kolymbetra (p262)

➡ Museo Archeologico, Agrigento (p264)

➡ Museo Archeologico, Gela (p273)

Why Go?

The main attraction of Sicily's Mediterranean Coast is the magnificent ruins of the Valley of the Temples, unparalleled across the island for their significance, expanse and beauty. Nearby, Agrigento has an elegant medieval old town with good restaurants and accommodation, while just beyond the city limits, the Farm Cultural Park is an innovative and vibrant art project that has revived the neighbouring town of Favara.

West of Agrigento, the development subsides and the landscape takes on a wilder, more natural aspect. You'll find excellent sandy beaches at the Riserva Naturale Torre Salsa and Eraclea Minoa, along with the spectacular chalk cliffs of Scala dei Turchi. Further west, the spa town of Sciacca is worth a visit for its excellent seafood restaurants and handsome historic streets.

Some 200km offshore, accessible by ferry from Porto Empedocle, the remote island of Lampedusa is home to some of Sicily's most spectacular beaches.

Road Distances (km)

	Agrigento	Caltabellotta	Gela	Licata
Caltabellotta	60			
Gela	75	130		
Licata	45	100	30	
Sciacca	60	20	130	100

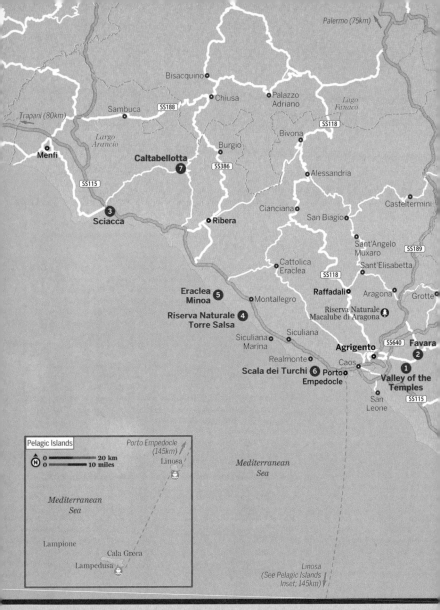

Mediterranean Coast Highlights

1 Valley of the Temples
(p262) Marvelling at the
genius of the ancient Greeks
as you wander among
Agrigento's spectacular ruins.

2 Farm Cultural Park
(p263) Getting an alternative
take on Sicilian culture at this
innovative art 'neighbourhood'
in Favara.

3 SciacCarnevale (p271)
Dancing through the streets
accompanied by giant papier-
mâché puppets at Sciacca's
flamboyant carnival.

4 Riserva Naturale Torre Salsa (p266) Experiencing the wild beauty of one of Sicily's most isolated beaches.

5 Eraclea Minoa (p267) Exploring the ancient Greek theatre, then indulging in a natural mud scrub on the beach.

6 Scala dei Turchi (p266) Contemplating sunset over the Mediterranean from the stunning white cliffs.

7 Caltabellotta (p272) Soaking up dizzying views from the ruined Norman castle atop this classic hill town.

Agrigento

🏛 0922 / POP 59.600

Running through Agrigento's medieval core is Via Atenea, an attractive strip lined with smart shops, trattorias and bars. Narrow alleyways wind upwards off the main street, past tightly packed *palazzi* (mansions) interspersed with historic churches. A good range of restaurants, cafes and accommodation make the town an excellent base to explore the nearby Valley of the Temples and good beaches further west along the coast.

Beyond the elegant old town, however, greater Agrigento is not an immediately appealing prospect. Huge elevated motorways converge on a ragged hilltop centre scarred by brutish tower blocks and riddled with choking traffic. Focus on the city's attractive old town and the proximity to the Valley of the Temples to maximise your enjoyment of an Agrigento sojourn.

◉ Sights

Cathedral
CATHEDRAL

(www.cattedraleagrigento.com; Via Duomo; ⊙10am-1.30pm & 3.30-7pm Apr-Oct, 10am-1pm Nov-Mar, closed Mon) The city's magnificent and striking 11th-century cathedral has been much altered over the centuries. It boasts a wonderful Norman ceiling and a mysterious letter from the Devil. Old Nick is reputed to have tried to seduce Sister Maria Crocifissa della Concezione, a nun in Agrigento's Benedictine convent, by writing to her promising all the treasure in the world. Sister Maria was having none of it, though, and she dobbed him in to the church, which still holds this mysterious missive.

Monastero di Santo Spirito
CONVENT

(🏛 0922 20664; www.monasterosantospirito.com; Cortile Santo Spirito 9; ⊙9am-7pm) At the top of a set of steps off Via Atenea, this convent was founded by Cistercian nuns around 1290. A handsome Gothic portal leads inside, where the nuns are still in residence, praying, meditating and baking heavenly sweets, including *cuscusu* (sweet couscous made with local pistachios), *dolci di mandorla* (almond pastries) and *conchigliette* (shell-shaped marzipan sweets filled with pistachio paste). Press the doorbell and say *'Vorrei comprare qualche dolce'* ('I'd like to buy a few sweets').

Casa Natale di Pirandello
MUSEUM

(🏛 0922 51 18 26; Piazzale Kaos; €4; ⊙9am-1pm & 3-7pm) Fans of Luigi Pirandello (1867–1936) will appreciate this small museum 5km southwest of Agrigento, set in the family villa where the author was born. One of the giants of modern Italian literature, and winner of the 1934 Nobel Prize, Pirandello started his career writing short stories and novels, but is best known as a playwright, author of masterpieces such as *Sei personaggi in cerca d'autore* (Six Characters in Search of an Author) and *Enrico IV* (Henry IV).

Pirandello left Agrigento as a young man but returned here most summers to spend time at the family villa. The museum is stacked full of first editions, photographs, reviews and theatre bills, and Pirandello's ashes are kept in an urn buried at the foot of a pine tree in the garden.

Bus 1, operated by TUA (p261), makes four runs daily from Agrigento to the museum (30 minutes). Bus tickets cost €1.20 if purchased in advance from a *tabaccheria* (tobacconist), or €1.70 on board the bus.

Chiesa di Santa Maria dei Greci
CHURCH

(www.museodiocesanoag.it; Salita Santa Maria dei Greci; ⊙10am-1.30pm & 3.30-7pm Apr-Oct, 10am-1pm Nov-Mar, closed Mon) This lovely, small church stands on the site of a 5th-century Doric temple dedicated to Athena. Inside are some badly damaged Byzantine frescoes, the remains of a Norman ceiling and traces of the original Greek columns.

🏃 Activities

Amici Del Cavallo
HORSE RIDING

(🏛 328 9615224; www.amicidelcavalloag.com) Local riding enthusiast Alessandro Salsedo runs this agency that specialises in horse-riding tours of the Valley of the Temples and other sites around Sicily, with an emphasis on off-the-beaten-track discovery.

☞ Tours

Associazione Guide Turistiche Agrigento
WALKING

(🏛 345 8815992; www.agrigentoguide.org) Agrigento's official tour-guide association offers guided visits of the Valley of the Temples, Agrigento and the surrounding area in English and eight other languages.

Temple Tour Bus
BUS

(🏛 331 8313720; www.templetourbusagrigento.com; adult/child day ticket €15/8, night ticket €10/6, combo ticket €20/10) Painted with

Agrigento

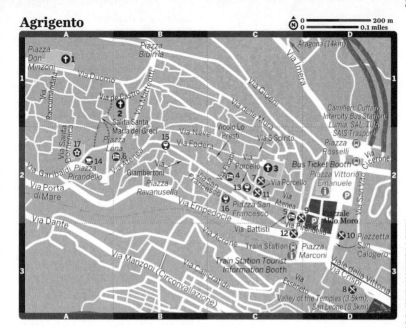

colourful designs to resemble a tradition-al Sicilian cart, this open-roofed bus offers hop-on, hop-off tours both day and night between Agrigento and the Valley of the Temples, along with optional visits to other attractions such as Scala dei Turchi and Casa Natale di Pirandello. A ticket valid for two days is €38/18.

🎉 Festivals & Events

Mandorlo in Fiore   CULTURAL
(Almond Blossom Fest) Encompassing food and wine tastings, concerts and folkloric events, this nine-day festival spans two weekends in late February or early March, when the Valley of the Temples is cloaked in almond blossoms.

🍴 Eating

Antichi Sapori Salumeria   DELI €
(✆ 0922 55 45 85; Via Cesare Battisti 20; sandwich-es €4-5; ⏰ 8.30am-11.30pm; ✈) A good option for *panini* (sandwiches) and *piadine* (Ital-ian flatbreads) crammed either with your choice of cheese, vegetables and meat, or from the concise menu of recommended variations. Partner the Giunone sandwich (smoked ham, mushroom and pistachio cream) with a fruity Sicilian wine and stock up on edible gifts and goodies like local blood orange marmalade before you leave.

A' Putia Bottega Siciliana   ITALIAN €

(☑0922 20 743; www.facebook.com/aputiasiciliana; Via Porcello 18; sandwiches €6, platters from €12; ⊙6.30pm-midnight; ☑) This wine bar fills the gap between snack bar and restaurant and is a good option for an informal lunch or dinner. Sicilian wines and craft beers are best enjoyed with good-value platters of local cheeses and cured meats, and the menu stretches to focaccia sandwiches and shared plates like grilled eggplant. Try the delicious black swine pancetta.

★ Terracotta   SICILIAN €€

(☑0922 2 97 42; www.spaziotemenos.it/terracotta; Via Pirandello 1; meals €35-40; ⊙7pm-midnight Tue-Sun) Upstairs from the popular Caffe San Pietro, Terracotta combines a Slow Food ethos with modern and stylish decor. Seasonal standout dishes could include *antipasti* of *buffala* cheese with pomegranate and pistachios or *tagliolini* pasta with *bottarga* (swordfish roe), artichokes and sundried tomatoes. Leave room for dessert of burned cinnamon and ricotta gelato.

★ Aguglia Persa   SEAFOOD €€

(☑0922 40 13 37; www.agugliapersa.it; Via Crispi 34; meals €30-40; ⊙noon-3.30pm & 7-11pm Wed-Mon) Set in a mansion with a leafy courtyard just below the train station, this place is a welcome addition to Agrigento's fine-dining scene. Opened in 2015 by the owners of Porto Empedocle's renowned Salmoriglio restaurant, it specialises in fresh-caught seafood in dishes such as citrus-scented risotto with shrimp and wild mint, or marinated salmon with sage cream and fresh fruit.

★ Kalòs   SICILIAN €€

(☑0922 2 63 89; www.ristorantekalos.it; Piazzetta San Calogero; meals €35-45; ⊙12.30-3pm & 7-11pm Tue-Sun) For fine dining, head to this restaurant just outside the historic centre. Tables on little balconies offer a delightful setting to enjoy homemade *pasta all'agrigentina* (with fresh tomatoes, basil and almonds), grilled lamb chops or *spada gratinata* (baked swordfish in breadcrumbs). Superb desserts, including homemade *cannoli* (pastry shells with a sweet filling) and almond *semifreddi* (a light frozen dessert), round out the menu.

Naif   STEAK €€

(☑0922 187 07 35; www.facebook.com/naifsteakhouse; Via Vela 8; meals €30-45; ⊙6.30-10.30pm) In warm weather, tables spill from the interior dining room into the courtyard at this sweet eatery tucked between two side streets in the medieval centre. Billing itself as a steakhouse, Naif spoils carnivores with tempting choices – wild boar stew, roast pork glazed in Nero d'Avola wine, steak with porcini mushrooms – while also serving a perfectly respectable seafood menu.

Sal8   INTERNATIONAL, VEGAN €€

(☑0922 66 19 90; Via Cesare Battisti 8; meals €30-40; ⊙noon-3pm & 6-11pm; ☑) Creative cuisine complements a good drinks list at this wine bar–restaurant near the entrance to Via Atenea. Depending on the chef's whim, expect anything from sushi to seafood tagliatelle to tapas with a Sicilian twist – think shrimp and fava-bean cakes or *panelle* (chickpea fritters) served with sparkling wine. An entire section of the menu is devoted to vegan offerings.

🍷 Drinking & Nightlife

Agrigento's medieval centre has a lively drinking scene. Pedestrianised Via Atenea is the place to be during the evening *passeggiata* (stroll), with bars up and down the street serving *aperitivi* (pre-dinner drinks) on sidewalk terraces. A couple of other good bars are tucked just off the main thoroughfare.

Enotria   WINE BAR

(☑0922 2 75 16; www.enotriashop.it; Via Atenea 223; ⊙5-11pm Mon-Tue & Thu-Sat, from 6pm Sun; 🔊) Our favourite spot for *aperitivi* features such a generous array of pre-dinner snacks that you may well be convinced to linger for a second negroni. Service is warm and friendly and the best place to enjoy the complimentary nibbles is watching the old town's pedestrian flow from Enotria's outside tables. A full menu features good salads, burgers and shared platters.

Caffè San Pietro
WINE BAR

(☑ 0922 2 97 42; www.spaziotemenos.it/sanpietro; Via Pirandello 1; ⊙ 7.30am-late Oct-Apr, from 11am May-Sep, closed Mon) This hip cafe serves excellent coffee, Sicilian wines and evening *aperitivi*, but what really sets it apart is the adjacent 18th-century San Pietro church, accessed through a doorway just beyond the bar. Beautifully restored by the bar's owners over an eight-year period, the church sometimes serves as a lively venue for concerts, films and other cultural events.

Upstairs is the affiliated restaurant Terracotta, specialising in Slow Food–inspired Sicilian cuisine.

Caffè Concordia
CAFE

(Piazza Pirandello 36; almond milk €2; ⊙ 6am-9.30pm Tue-Sat) Since 1948, this simple cafe has been a local favourite for its delicious almond milk, made with fresh-ground local almonds, sugar, water and a hint of lemon peel.

Mojo Wine Bar
WINE BAR

(☑ 339 3543211; www.facebook.com/mojowinebar. agrigento; Via San Francesco 15; ⊙ 7.30pm-3am Wed-Mon) This trendy *enoteca* (wine bar) sits in a pretty piazza just off the main thoroughfare. Enjoy a cool *aperitivo* whilst munching on olives and listening to laid-back jazz.

Café Girasole
BAR

(☑ 393 6288189; Via Atenea 68-70; ⊙ 8am-late Mon-Sat) With outdoor seating in the thick of Via Atenea, by evening this popular cafe morphs into a trendy hangout for the 30-something *aperitivi* set, who stop by for cocktails, table snacks and occasional DJ sets.

☆ Entertainment

Teatro Pirandello
THEATRE

(☑ 0922 59 02 20; www.fondazioneteatropirandello.it; Piazza Pirandello; tickets €18-23) This city-run theatre is Sicily's third largest, after Palermo's Teatro Massimo and Catania's Teatro Massimo Bellini. Works by local hero Luigi Pirandello figure prominently. The program runs from November to early May.

❶ Information

Tourist Office (☑ 0922 59 32 27; www.living agrigento.it; Piazzale Aldo Moro 1; ⊙ 8am-7pm Mon-Fri, to 1pm Sat) In the provincial government building.

Train Station Tourist Information Booth (Train station, lower level; ⊙ 9am-1pm Mon-Fri)

❶ Getting There & Away

BOAT

The industrial port of Porto Empedocle, 7km southwest of Agrigento, is the departure point for ferries and hydrofoils to Lampedusa (p276), the main beach destination in Sicily's Pelagic Islands.

BUS

From most destinations, the bus is the easiest way to get to Agrigento. The intercity bus station and ticket booth are on Piazza Rosselli, just off Piazza Vittorio Emanuele.

Buses to Palermo (€9, two hours) are operated by **Cuffaro** (☑ 091 616 15 10; www.facebook.com/cuffaro.info; 8 trips Mon-Fri, 6 Sat, 3 Sun) and **Camilleri** (☑ 0922 47 18 86; www.camilleriargentoelattuca.it; trips Mon-Fri, 4 Sat, 1 Sun), while **SAL** (Società Autolinee Licata; ☑ 0922 40 13 60; www.autolineesal.it) serves Palermo's Falcone-Borsellino Airport (€12.60, 2¾ hours, three to four Monday through Saturday). SAL also operate southeast along the coast to Gela (1¾ to 2¼ hours) and Licata (one hour).

Lumia (☑ 0922 2 04 14; www.autolineelumia.it) runs to Trapani and its Birgi airport (€11.90, three to four hours, three daily Monday to Friday, two on Saturday, one on Sunday).

SAIS Trasporti (☑ 0922 2 60 59; www.saistrasporti.it) runs 10 to 14 buses daily to Catania and its Fontanarossa airport (€13.40, three hours) via Caltanissetta (€6.40, 1¼ hours).

CAR

Agrigento is easily accessible by road from all of Sicily's main towns. The SS189 and SS121 connect with Palermo, while the SS115 runs along the coast to Sciacca and Licata. For Enna or Catania, take the SS640 via Caltanissetta.

TRAIN

Trains run regularly to/from Palermo (€9, two hours, hourly). For Catania, the bus is a better option as there are no direct trains. The train station has left-luggage lockers (per 12 hours €2.50).

❶ Getting Around

TUA (Trasporti Urbani Agrigento; ☑ 0922 41 20 24; www.trasportiurbaniagrigento.it) buses run down to the Valley of the Temples from the Intercity Bus Station, stopping in front of the train station en route.

In town, Via Atenea, the main street in the historic centre, is closed to traffic from 9am to 8pm, with a short break during lunchtime when cars can pass through the centre (for loading luggage). Parking can be a nightmare in Agrigento. There's metered parking at Piazza Vittorio Emanuele and on the streets around Piazzale Aldo Moro, although you'll have to arrive early to find a space.

Valley of the Temples

Situated about 3km below the modern city of Agrigento, the Unesco-listed **Valley of the Temples** (Valle dei Templi; ☑ 0922 62 16 11; www.parcovalledeitempli.it; adult/reduced €10/5, incl Museo Archeologico €13.50/7, incl Museo Archeologico & Giardino della Kolymbetra €15/10; ☺ 8.30am-8pm, to 11pm mid-Jul–mid-Sep) is one of the most mesmerising sites in the Mediterranean, boasting the best-preserved Doric temples outside Greece. On the travel radar since Goethe sang their praises in the 18th century, the temples now constitute Sicily's single biggest tourist site, with more than 600,000 visitors a year. As impressive as the temples are, what you see today are mere vestiges of the ancient city of Akragas, which was once the fourth-largest city in the known world.

Sights

Sicily's most enthralling archaeological site encompasses the ruined ancient city of Akragas, highlighted by a stunningly well-preserved series of ridge-top temples that once served as beacons for homecoming sailors. The 13-sq-km park, 3km south of Agrigento, is split into eastern and western zones.

Eastern Zone

★**Tempio della Concordia**   RUINS
(Temple of Concordia) One of the best-preserved ancient Greek temples in existence, this temple has survived almost entirely intact since it was constructed in 430 BC. It was converted into a Christian basilica in the 6th century and the main structure reinforced, giving it a better chance of surviving earthquakes. In 1748 the temple was restored to its original form and given the name it is now known by.

Another reason why it has survived while other temples have not, is that beneath the hard rock on which the temple stands is a layer of soft clay that acts as a kind of natural shock absorber, protecting it from earthquake tremors. Whether the Greek engineers knew this when they built the temple is the subject of debate, but modern scholars tend to think they did.

Tempio di Hera   RUINS
(Temple of Hera, aka Juno) The 5th-century-BC Temple of Hera is also known as the Tempio di Giunone (Temple of Juno). Though partly destroyed by an earthquake in the Middle Ages, much of the colonnade remains intact, as does a long altar, originally used for sacrifices. The traces of red are the result of fire damage, most likely during the Carthaginian invasion of 406 BC.

Tempio di Ercole   RUINS
(Temple of Hercules) The last of the temples in the eastern zone, the Tempio di Ercole is the oldest, dating from the end of the 6th century BC. Eight of its 38 columns have been raised and you can wander around the remains of the rest.

Tomba di Terone   RUINS
(Tomb of Theron) A little temple set on a high base, it dates to 75 BC, about 500 years after the death of Theron, Agrigento's Greek tyrant.

Western Zone

★**Giardino della Kolymbetra**   GARDENS
(☑ 335 1229042; www.visitfai.it/giardinodella kolymbethra; adult/reduced €6/2; ☺ 9.30am-7.30pm Jul & Aug, to 6.30pm May, Jun & Sep, to 5.30pm Mar, Apr & Oct, 10am-2pm Feb, Nov & Dec) In a natural cleft between walls of soft tuff (volcanic rock), the Giardino della Kolymbetra is a lush garden of olive and citrus trees interspersed with more than 300 labelled species of plants and some welcome picnic tables. Managed independently by the non-profit historical preservation organisation FAI, it's a peaceful, shady spot, perfect for escaping the heat of the valley and breaking for a picnic lunch. The climb down is steep (best avoided if you've got dicky knees).

Daily from mid-June to September and on Saturday and Sunday from March to mid-June and from October to December, one-hour guided tours (adult/reduced €16/11) of a hypogeum (underground chamber) within the gardens are available. Booking ahead is recommended at www.agrigentosotterranea.it; the tours incorporate negotiating compact tunnels and an underground river.

Tempio di Giove   RUINS
(Temple of Olympian Zeus) The main feature of the western zone is the crumbled ruin of the Tempio di Giove. Covering an area of 112m by 56m with columns 20m high, this would have been the largest Doric temple ever built had its construction not been interrupted by the Carthaginians sacking Akragas. The incomplete temple was later destroyed by an earthquake.

Lying flat on his back amid the rubble is an 8m-tall *telamon* (a sculpted figure of a

---

OFF THE BEATEN TRACK

FAVARA

The mid-sized town of Favara (population 32,900), 10km east of Agrigento, makes for an interesting off-the-beaten-track destination, thanks to the presence of its innovative artists' community, the **Farm Cultural Park** (www.farmculturalpark.com; Cortile Bentivegna; gallery €5; ⊙10am-10pm Tue-Thu, to midnight Fri-Sun) **FREE**. The Farm's gallery of provocative modern art and its ongoing series of cultural events are the main points of interest for visitors. Weekends are the best time to visit, when visitors from Agrigento and beyond enjoy the widest range of events and bar and cafe openings.

In 2010, married couple Andrea Bartoli and Favara-born Florinda Saieva bought several abandoned buildings in the town's dilapidated heart and set up this unique neighbourhood devoted to art. Since then, the Farm has become a centre for exhibitions by international and local artists, housing a gallery of thought-provoking, often politically charged, artwork, along with shops, bars and cafes, cultural events, talks, screenings, workshops and shows going on throughout the year. There's also now stylish accommodation within the area's arty streets.

The project has brought a whole new breath of life to Favara, previously known mostly for its general decrepitude and for having one of Italy's highest unemployment rates. Several elderly local women, who had clung to their homes in the semi-abandoned town centre, now live among the exhibition spaces, happy to have company and to once again reside in a neighbourhood that is safe and alive. Meanwhile, a growing number of local youth have come to volunteer at the project.

Building walls serve as giant canvases for paintings and sculptures, while courtyards are full of practical installations like plant-pot chairs and brick fountains. Everything is beautifully designed, with a pervasive sense of whimsy and innovative energy. Bartoli and Saieva have even managed to incorporate the local castle, the Castello dei Chiaramonte, a largely unused 13th-century building, into the Farm project, hosting occasional workshops there.

The adjacent town centre, focused on Piazza Cavour, has seen an influx of restaurants, bars and other new businesses, making it a pleasant spot to overnight as an alternative to Agrigento, or somewhere to while away a few relaxed hours on a day trip. Two of the best places to grab a bite are **Cosi Dunci** (☑0922 66 51 23; www.facebook.com/Cosidunci; Via Salita Madrice 10; snacks from €2; ⊙10am-6pm) for *cannoli* and **U Maccicuni Wine & Food** (☑347 8500844; Piazza Cavour 29; meals €20-25; ⊙noon-3pm & 6.30-11pm) for traditional Sicilian specialties accompanied by local beer and liqueurs.

Fans of Sicily's delicious almonds should also schedule a visit to the town's new **Museo della Mandorla Siciliana** (Marzipan; ☑0922 83 89 95, 338 6797105; https://marzipan-museo-della-mandorla-siciliana.business.site; Via Vittorio Emanuele 96/100; ⊙9am-6.30pm) **FREE**. Located in a restored Favara mansion, this interesting museum showcases the importance of the humble almond to Sicily. Exhibits are well labelled in both Italian and English, and there's an excellent onsite shop selling gourmet food products sourced from the surrounding region. Call ahead a few days prior to arrange cooking classes (per person €100) in the museum's well-equipped kitchen.

Favara is about 10km east of Agrigento via the SP80 or the SS122. Note that Farm Cultural Park is poorly signposted, and parking is nearly impossible on the narrow streets surrounding it. Your best bet is to look for parking along Via Umberto, the main street above Piazza Cavour, then ask directions and walk from there.

Cuffaro (p261) runs buses from Palermo to Favara (€9, two hours, six daily Monday through Friday, four on Saturday, two on Sunday). Most buses run via Agrigento.

Valley of the Temples

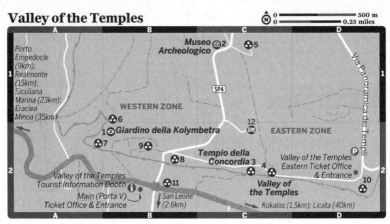

Valley of the Temples

◎ Top Sights

◎ Sights

🛏 Sleeping

man with arms raised), originally intended to support the temple's weight. It's actually a copy of the original, which is in the Museo Archeologico.

Tempio dei Dioscuri RUINS
(Temple of Castor and Pollux) Four columns mark the Tempio dei Dioscuri. Built towards the end of the 5th century, it was destroyed by the Carthaginians, later restored in Hellenistic style, and then destroyed again by an earthquake. What you see today dates from 1832, when it was rebuilt using materials from other temples.

Santuario delle Divine Chtoniche ARCHAEOLOGICAL SITE
(Sanctuary of the Chthonic Deities) Just behind the Tempio dei Dioscuri is a complex of altars and small buildings believed to be part of the Santuario di Demetra e Kore. It dates from the early 6th century BC.

⊙ Other Sites

★**Museo Archeologico** MUSEUM
(☏ 0922 40 15 65; Contrada San Nicola 12; adult/reduced €8/4, incl Valley of the Temples €13.50/7; ☺ 9am-7.30pm Tue-Sat, to 1.30pm Sun & Mon) North of the temples, this wheelchair-accessible museum is one of Sicily's finest, with a huge collection of clearly labelled artefacts from the excavated site. Noteworthy are the dazzling displays of Greek painted ceramics and the awe-inspiring reconstructed *telamon*, a colossal statue recovered from the nearby Tempio di Giove.

Quartiere Ellenistico-Romano ARCHAEOLOGICAL SITE
(Hellenistic-Roman Quarter; admission with Valley of the Temples ticket only) To the east of the Museo Archeologico is the Hellenistic-Roman Quarter, featuring a well-preserved street layout which was part of urban Akragas (and later, under the Romans, Agrigentum). The regular grid is made up of main streets *(plateiai)* intersected at right angles by secondary streets *(stenopoi)*, all of which were laid out towards the end of the 4th century BC.

🍴 Eating

Kokalos PIZZA €
(☏ 0922 60 64 27; www.ristorante-kokalos.com; Via Cavaleri Magazzeni; pizzas €6-11, meals €20-30; ☺ 12.30-2.30pm & 7-11.30pm) This eatery, resembling a Wild West ranch, is the perfect place to enjoy wood-fired pizza on the

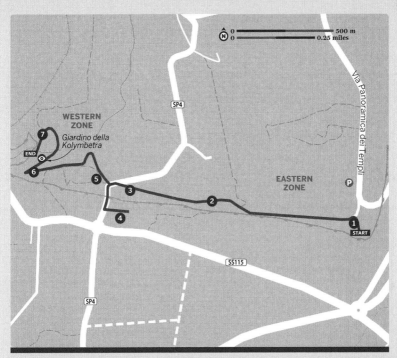

Walking Tour
Valley of the Temples

START TEMPIO DI HERA
END GIARDINO DELLA KOLYMBETRA
LENGTH 3KM; THREE HOURS

Begin your exploration in the so-called Eastern Zone, home to Agrigento's best-preserved temples. From the Eastern Ticket Office, a short walk leads to the 5th-century BC **1 Tempio di Hera** (p262), perched on the ridge top. Though partly destroyed by an earthquake, the colonnade remains largely intact, as does a long sacrificial altar.

Next, descend past a gnarled 500-year-old olive tree and a series of Byzantine tombs to the **2 Tempio della Concordia** (p262). This remarkable edifice, the model for Unesco's logo, has survived almost entirely intact since its construction in 430 BC, partly due to its conversion into a Christian basilica in the 6th century, and partly thanks to the shock-absorbing, earthquake-dampening qualities of the soft clay underlying its hard rock foundation.

Further downhill, the **3 Tempio di Ercole** (p262) is Agrigento's oldest, dating from the

end of the 6th century BC. Down from the main temples, the miniature **4 Tomba di Terone** (p262) dates to 75 BC.

Cross the pedestrian bridge into the western zone, stopping first at the **5 Tempio di Giove** (p262). This would have been the world's largest Doric temple had its construction not been interrupted by the Carthaginian sacking of Akragas. A later earthquake reduced it to the crumbled ruin you see today. Lying flat on his back amid the rubble is an 8m-tall *telamon* (a sculpted figure of a man with arms raised), originally intended to support the temple's weight. It's actually a copy; the original is in Agrigento's archaeological museum.

Take a brief look at the ruined 5th-century BC **6 Tempio dei Dioscuri** and the 6th-century BC complex of altars and small buildings known as the **7 Santuario delle Divine Chtoniche**, before ending your visit in the Giardino della Kolymbetra (p262), a lush garden in a natural cleft near the sanctuary, with more than 300 (labelled) species of plants and some welcome picnic tables.

summer terrace while gazing out over the temples. You will need a car to get here – it's up a dusty track 2km southeast of the Valley of the Temples site.

Accademia del Buon Gusto SICILIAN €€
(📋 0922 51 10 61; www.accademiadelbuongusto.it; Via Guastella 1c, Contrada Maddalusa; meals €40-45; ⏱ 7pm-midnight Mon-Fri) The restaurant of the Foresteria Baglio della Luna (p291) is an elegant fine-dining establishment offering innovative Sicilian cuisine and views over the Valley of the Temples. Fresh local seafood appears in sophisticated creations such as sea bream with pecorino cheese and aubergine tartare, or grilled tuna with mint couscous and pepper sauce. Reservations required.

ⓘ Information

There are two entrances to the archaeological site, each with its own car park. The **Main (Porta V) Ticket Office** (Piazzale dei Templi) and entrance is at the foot of the hill near the western temples, while the smaller Eastern Ticket Office and entrance sits on the ridgetop above the eastern temples. At either entrance, you can enquire about guided tours or pick up an audio guide (English and Italian only, fee payable). You'll also find a tourist information **booth** (Piazzale Porta V; ⏱ 9am-1pm Mon-Fri) at the main (Porta V) entrance, in a small wooden shack adjacent to the car park.

ⓘ Getting There & Away

BUS

City bus 1, operated by TUA (p261), runs half-hourly from Agrigento's bus and train stations to the archaeological museum (15 minutes) and the Porta V entrance to the temples (20 minutes). 'Bus 2/', as distinct from 'bus 2' (which has a different route – watch out for the hard-to-spot slash!) runs every hour or so to the temples' eastern entrance near the Tempio di Hera (10 to 15 minutes). Tickets cost €1.20 if purchased in advance from a tobacconist, or €1.70 on board the bus.

CAR & MOTORCYCLE

Starting from Piazza Marconi (in front of Agrigento's train station), take Via Francesco Crispi down the hill towards the temples. After 1.5km, bear gently left onto Via Panoramica Valle dei Templi to reach the valley's eastern entrance and car park. To reach the Main (Porta V) entrance and car park, bear right on Via Passeggiata Archeologica, then left on the SP4 and right on Viale Caduti di Marzabotto.

Scala dei Turchi, Siciliana Marina & Torre Salsa

With your own wheels, you'll find some stunning beaches and beauty spots west of Agrigento. From south to north, these include Scala dei Turchi, Siciliana Marina and Torre Salsa, all within an easy 30- to 45-minute drive of the city via the SS115.

⊙ Sights

★**Riserva Naturale Torre Salsa** PARK
(www.wwftorresalsa.com) This stunning 761-hectare natural park, administered by the World Wildlife Fund, offers plenty of scope for walkers, with well-marked trails and sweeping panoramic views of the surrounding mountains and coast. The long, deserted Torre Salsa beach is especially beautiful, although the access road is rough. The park is signposted off the SS115: exit at Siciliana Marina (with its own great sandy beach) or continue 10km north to the second Montallegro exit and follow the signs for 'WWF Riserva Naturale Torre Salsa'.

Torre Salsa beach is reached from the northern entrance. Check out the spectacular drone footage on the reserve's website to inspire a visit.

Scala dei Turchi BEACH
This blindingly white rock outcropping, shaped like a giant staircase, juts into the sea near Realmonte, 15km west of Agrigento. It's a very popular spot with local sunseekers who come to sunbathe on the milky-smooth rock and dive into the indigo sea. To escape the crowds, walk another few hundred metres north along the white rocky shelf, and descend to the long sandy beach below.

The beach was named after the Arab pirates who used to hide out from stormy weather here (known colloquially as Turchi, or 'Turks').

Siciliana Marina BEACH
Siciliana Marina's beach stretches northwest of the sleepy town of the same name.

ⓘ Getting There & Away

All beaches are signposted off the coastal SS115 highway. Coming from Agrigento, leave the SS115 for Scala dei Turchi at the signposted exit just north of Porto Empedocle (about 10km from Agrigento) and continue northwest along the coastal SP68, following the signs. The Siciuliana Marina exit off SS115 is about 20km from Agrigento, while the turnoff for Torre Salsa is at Campobianco, 34km northwest of Agrigento.

Parking can be very difficult at Scala dei Turchi during July and August. Consider visiting on the Temple Tour Bus (p258) from Agrigento.

Eraclea Minoa

✔ 0922 / POP 3810

Nowadays a small summer resort – empty most of the year, packed in July and August – Eraclea Minoa was an important Greek settlement in ancient times. It was legendarily founded by the Cretan king Minos, who came to Sicily in pursuit of Daedalus after his escape from Crete. Historical evidence suggests the city was established by Greek colonists in the 6th century BC and went on to flourish in the 5th and 4th centuries BC. The ancient city's scant remains can be seen at the **archaeological park** (✔ 0922 84 60 05; adult/reduced €4/2; ⊘ 9am-1hr before sunset) above town.

Today Eraclea Minoa's greatest attraction is its **beach**, a photogenic strip of golden sand backed by willowy eucalyptus trees, cypress groves and chalk cliffs. At the beach's western end there's a natural mud rock, which you can scrape off and massage into your skin. Dry off in the sun, then rinse in the sea and you'll have removed 10 years in 10 minutes.

ℹ Getting There & Away

Eraclea Minoa is 4km off the SS115, roughly halfway between Agrigento and Sciacca. Upon exiting the main highway, follow SP30 southwest to the beach.

Sciacca

✔ 0925 / POP 40,700

Famous for its historic spas and flamboyant carnival celebrations, Sciacca is a laid-back town with an attractive medieval core and some excellent seafood restaurants. Healing waters were its big drawcard until 2015, when financial woes forced its spa to shut down indefinitely. Sciacca was founded in the 5th century BC as a thermal resort for nearby Selinunte. It later flourished under the Saracens, who arrived in the 9th century and named it Xacca (meaning 'water' in Arabic), and the Normans.

The city retains its original layout, with neighbourhoods built on strips of rock descending towards the sea. The historic centre revolves around its main thoroughfare, Corso Vittorio Emanuele, and the vast square Piazza Scandaliato, where views (and staircases) extend to the fishing harbour below.

◉ Sights

Palazzo Steripinto   NOTABLE BUILDING
(Corso Vittorio Emanuele) This most imposing of Sciacca's *palazzi* is recognisable by its diamond-point rustication and twin-mullioned windows. It was built in the Catalan-Gothic style at the beginning of the 16th century.

To the *palazzo's* south, the **Porta San Salvatore**, a 16th-century town gate, is covered in Renaissance ornamentation.

Chiesa Madre   CHURCH
(Piazza Duomo; ⊘ 8am-noon & 4.30-7.30pm) Northeast of Piazza Scandaliato is Sciacca's cathedral, first erected in 1108 and rebuilt in 1656. Only the three apses survive from the original Norman structure. The unfinished baroque facade features a set of marble statues by Gagini.

Chiesa di Santa Margherita   CHURCH
(Via Incisa; ⊘ 8am-noon & 4-7pm) This 14th-century church features a superb Renaissance portal and a rather chipped baroque interior.

Castello Incantato   PUBLIC ART
(Enchanted Castle; ✔ 339 2340174; www.sciaccamusei.it; Via Bentivegna 16; €4; ⊘ 9am-1pm & 3.30-8pm Apr-Oct, 9am-1pm & 3.30-5.30pm Nov-Mar) About 3km east of town, the Castello Incantato is actually a large park festooned with thousands of sculpted heads. The man behind this bizarre collection was Filippo Bentivegna (1888–1967), a local artist who used sculpture to exorcise the memories of an unhappy sojourn in the USA – each head is supposed to represent one of his memories.

His eccentricities were legion and still today people enjoy recalling them. Apparently, he regarded his work as a sexual act and demanded to be addressed as 'Eccellenza' (Your Excellency).

✗ Eating

Trattoria Al Faro   SEAFOOD €
(✔ 092 52 53 49; Via Al Porto 25; meals €20-25, set menu €30; ⊘ 12.30-3pm & 7-11pm Mon-Sat) If the idea of budget seafood usually sets alarm bells ringing, think again. This welcoming

MEDITERRANEAN COAST ERACLEA MINOA

ROAD TRIP >
TEMPLES, ART & BEACHES

• •

Experience the best of Sicily's Mediterranean coast on this multi-day ramble from Sciacca to Licata. Along the way, you'll wander some of the island's prettiest beaches, gaze on Agrigento's amazing assemblage of ancient Greek temples, and visit the Farm Cultural Park, a thriving artists community in Favara. At every stop, fresh-caught seafood offers sustenance for the road ahead.

❶ Sciacca

Start in the lovely seaside town of Sciacca (p267), where you can explore the historic centre's many elegant *palazzi* or spend the morning shopping for ceramics before de-

scending to the picturesque working port for a lunch of fresh-caught fish.

The Drive > Take the SS115 southeast, following the coast 30km to Eraclea Minoa.

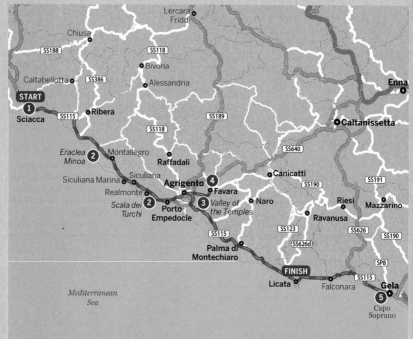

Three to Four Days 150km

Great for... History & Culture, Outdoors, Food & Drink

Best Time to Go April, May, September or October

NIKOLPETR/SHUTTERSTOCK ©

Scala dei Turchi (p266)

➋ Eraclea Minoa & Scala dei Turchi

Dip your toes into ancient history at Eraclea Minoa's archaeological park, then into seawater on the sandy strand below. Smother yourself with rejuvenating clay scraped off the rock at the beach's far end before continuing down the coast to the spectacular Scala dei Turchi, a chalky-white rock formation in the shape of a giant staircase. It's a great place to linger over dinner while watching the sun set over the Mediterranean.

The Drive > From Scala dei Turchi, continue east 16km on the SS115 to Agrigento.

➌ Valley of the Temples

The highlight of the tour is Agrigento's Valley of the Temples, Sicily's greatest archaeological site. Take an entire day to wander the expansive park and discover its magnificent Greek temples, from the splendidly preserved Tempio della Concordia to the shattered vestiges of the Tempio dei Dioscuri.

The Drive > Wind your way 10km east along the SP80 from Agrigento to Favara.

➍ Favara

In Favara, stop in at the innovative Farm Cultural Park, an artists community that has taken over an entire section of the town's historic centre and injected vibrancy into the local community. Favara's new museum showcasing the importance of almonds to the region is also well worth a look.

The Drive > Continue 73km east along the SS115 towards Gela.

➎ Beaches East of Agrigento

Spend your final afternoon taking the slow road and exploring the beaches east of Agrigento, culminating in the wild and unspoilt expanses along the Gela Riviera. At the western edge of Gela, check out Capo Soprano, where you'll find the town's ancient Greek fortifications and the ruins of Sicily's only surviving Greek baths. Double back on the SS115 to end your tour at Licata, where the double Michelin-starred Ristorante La Madia awaits – considered one of Sicily's finest, it makes a great finale for the journey.

Sciacca

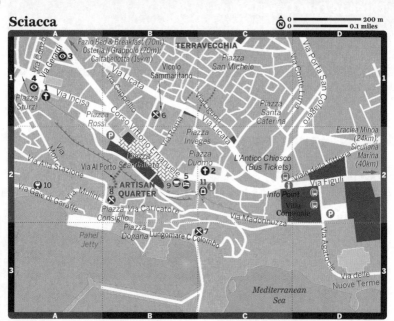

▲ 0 _____ 200 m
Ⓝ 0 _____ 0.1 miles

Sciacca

◉ Sights
1 Chiesa di Santa Margherita A1
2 Chiesa Madre C2
3 Palazzo Steripinto A1
4 Porta San Salvatore A1

⊜ Sleeping
5 Domus Maris Relais B2

⊗ Eating
6 Hostaria Del Vicolo B1
7 La Lampara C3
Otto ....(see 5)
8 Trattoria Al Faro B2

⊜ Drinking & Nightlife
9 Gran Caffè Scandaglia B2
10 Mastro Malto A2

⊕ Shopping
11 Ceramiche Gaspare Patti C2

portside trattoria is one of the few places you can feast on delicious fresh fish and still get change from €20. What's served depends on what the boats have brought in.

Tasty staples to look out for include *pasta con le sarde* (with sardines, fennel, breadcrumbs and raisins) and grilled calamari.

Don't miss the gossamer-light ricotta ravioli for dessert.

Otto SICILIAN €€
(☏0925 08 01 99; www.ottoristorante.it; Corso Vittorio Emanuele 107; meals €35-40; ⊙12.30-3pm & 7-11pm) Opened in July 2018, Otto's stylish and minimalist dining room, with just 10 tables, is the perfect showcase for modern reinterpretations of traditional Sicilian flavours. Local seafood is often the star on the seasonal menu, and dishes could include fresh red shrimp and octopus. Otto's version of *cannoli* is superb, so definitely leave room for dessert.

Osteria Il Grappolo OSTERIA €€
(☏0925 8 52 94; www.facebook.com/OsteriaIl-GrappoloSciacca; Via Conzo 9a; meals €25-35; ⊙1-3pm & 8-11pm Tue-Sun) A friendly neighborhood *osteria* (casual tavern), Salvatore Ciaccio's 'Grappolo' embraces the Slow Food aesthetic: carefully chosen local ingredients incorporated into classic Sicilian dishes like *cozze al limone* (mussels with fresh lemon), *pasta con sarde e finocchietto* (pasta with sardines, wild fennel, pine nuts, raisins and breadcrumbs) or *maltagliati pesce spada e melanzane* (rough-cut pasta with swordfish and eggplant).

Check the chalkboard outside for regular seasonal specials.

La Lampara
SEAFOOD €€

(☑0925 8 50 85; Lungomare Cristoforo Colombo 13; meals €30-45; ☺noon-2pm & 7.30-11pm Mon-Sat) In contrast to the scruffy portside streets, La Lampara is a modish, contemporary restaurant serving a modern, creative fish menu. Highly recommended is the tuna steak, cooked in sesame seeds and served with balsamic vinegar, and the chocolate cake with pistachio ice cream.

★Hostaria Del Vicolo
SICILIAN €€€

(☑0925 2 30 71; www.hostariadelvicolo.it; Vicolo Sammaritano 10; meals €45-70; ☺12.30-2pm & 7.30-10.30pm Tue-Sun; ☑) Tucked away in a tiny alley in the old town, this formal restaurant is a culinary tour de force, with heavy tablecloths, noiseless service and an ample wine list. A perennial Slow Food favourite, it serves a traditional Sicilian menu embellished with modern twists, including many gluten free and vegetarian offerings. Degustation menus (€60 to €70) are a brilliant culinary experience.

For a *primo* (first course) try the *taglioni al nero di seppia e ricotta salata* (flat strings of fresh pasta with cuttlefish ink and salted ricotta), followed by a *secondo* (main course) of *merluzzo ai fichi secchi* (cod with dried figs).

🍷 Drinking & Nightlife

Mastro Malto
CRAFT BEER

(☑389 1830958; www.facebook.com/mastro maltobeershop; Via Gaie di Garaffe 24/25; ☺6.30pm-2am Tue-Sun; 🔊) One of Sciacca's friendliest bars is also a great spot for a wide range of Italian and international craft beers. Four revolving beer taps keep things interesting, and the bar's fridge is overflowing with various tipples. Out front is a bit too close to the road so adjourn to the pleasant garden deck out the back. Always good music too.

Gran Caffè Scandaglia
CAFE

(☑334 3265648, 0925 2 10 82; Piazza Scandaliato 5-6; ☺7.30am-11.30pm) This is a good place to enjoy breakfast in the shade, or a sunset drink, overlooking the harbour. Soft pastry, *caffè latte* in tall glasses and fresh orange juice are delicious, as are the *granite* (flavoured crushed ice) and gelati. Unfortunately service can be haphazard, but the stellar views still make it a Sciacca highlight.

🛍 Shopping

Ceramiche Gaspare Patti
CERAMICS

(☑092 599 32 98; www.gasparepatti.com; Corso Vittorio Emanuele 95; ☺9am-1pm & 3.30-7pm) Sciacca has a tradition of ceramic production and there are numerous shops selling colourful crockery. For something more original, visit this Aladdin's cave of a shop in front of Chiesa Madre. Gaspare Patti prides himself on his idiosyncratic style; his shop is packed with strange and original creations, well worth a browse if not a purchase. Access via the car park.

ℹ Information

Hospital (Ospedale Giovanni Paolo II; ☑0925 96 21 11; Via Pompei; ☺24hr)

Main tourist office (☑0925 2 04 78; www. prolococosciaccaterme.com; Corso Vittorio Emanuele 87; ☺4-7pm Tue-Fri, 10am-1pm & 4-7pm Sat & Sun) On Sciacca's main strip, with an occasionally open **info point** (☑324 8720502; www.prolococosciaccaterme.com; Piazza Friscia; ☺10am-1pm & 4-7pm) just east near the Villa Comunale park.

Police Station (☑092 596 50 11; Via Ruffini 12)

ℹ Getting There & Away

BUS

Lumia (☑0925 2 11 35; www.autolineelumia. it) serves Agrigento (€6.50, 1½ hours, 11 daily

---

CARNIVAL IN SCIACCA

Sciacca's **SciacCarnevale** (Carnevale di Sciacca; www.facebook.com/sciaccar nevale; ☺Feb or Mar) carnival is famous for its flamboyance and fabulous party atmosphere. Held between the last Thursday before Lent and Shrove Tuesday, it features an amazing parade of huge papier-mâché figures mounted on floats. The festival opens with carnival king Peppe Nappa receiving the city's keys. The technicolor floats are then released into the streets with their bizarre cast of grotesque caricatures.

The figures are handmade each year using traditional methods and are modelled on political and social personalities. The floats wind through the streets of the old town, while masked revellers dance to locally composed music and satirical poetry is read aloud.

Monday to Saturday, one Sunday) and Trapani (€9, 2¼ hours, three Monday to Saturday, one Sunday). All buses arrive at the bus stop by the Villa Comunale on Via Figuli and leave nearby from Via Agatocle. Schedules and departure times are also displayed there. Buy your tickets at L'Antico Chiosco on Piazza Friscia.

CAR & MOTORCYCLE

Sciacca is about 65km from Agrigento along the SS115. There's parking on Via Agatocle near the Nuovo Stabilimento Termale, and on Piazza M Rossi, adjacent to Piazza Scandaliato.

Caltabellotta

📞 0925 / POP 3610

It's quite a drive up to Caltabellotta: the road rises almost vertically as it winds up to the hilltop village at 949m above sea level. But make it to the top and you're rewarded with some amazing panoramic views of 21 (apparently) surrounding villages. The highest vantage point is the ruined **Norman castle** at the top of the village, where a peace treaty was signed in 1302 ending the Sicilian Vespers. Viewed from here, the town's terracotta roofs and grey houses appear to cling to the cliffside like a perfect mosaic. The town was originally named Kal'at Bellut by the Arabs, meaning 'oak rock'.

On the edge of the village lies the derelict monastery of **San Pellegrino**, from where you can see caves that were used as tombs as far back as prehistoric times.

⊙ Sights

Chiesa Madre CHURCH
(⊙10.30am-1pm & 3.30-7pm) Dating to the late 11th century, this lovely hilltop church with its broad stone facade retains an original Gothic portal and pointed arches.

Eating

★M.A.T.E.S. SICILIAN €€
(📞0925 95 23 27; www.matesonline.it/ristorante.html; Vicolo Storto 3; meals €30-35; ⊙noon-2pm & 7-10pm Mon-Sat, noon-2pm Sun, closed 2 weeks in Oct) For traditional Sicilian fare in cosy, rustic surroundings, head for this family-owned and highly recommended Slow Food restaurant in Caltabellotta's historic centre. The menu is local and seasonal, and dishes could include pasta with pistachios, almonds and eggplant; roast potatoes with wild fennel; or juicy, falling-off-the-bone roast pork and lamb. Complete a brilliant meal with one of the fantastic *cannoli*.

🛈 Getting There & Away

From Sciacca, allow at least half an hour for the sinuous 20km drive up the SP37 to Caltabellotta. Upon arrival in the lower town, follow signs left up the hill and be prepared to brave some narrow streets en route to Piazzale Ruggero di Lauria, where you can park between the castle and the Chiesa Madre.

If you're without a car, Lumia (p271) runs buses to Caltabellotta from Sciacca (€2.90, 40 minutes, five daily Monday to Friday, four on Saturday).

Licata

📞 0922 / POP 37,400

One of Sicily's true destination fine-dining restaurants and a charming, if rather worn, historic centre make the workaday port of Licata worthy of a visit. The centre of action is **Piazza Progresso**, which divides the two main streets, Corso Roma, flanked by elegant baroque *palazzi*, and Corso Vittorio Emanuele. At the top of town, a 16th-century castle affords views down to the harbour.

Some 22km west of Licata, the town of **Palma di Montechiaro** is the ancestral seat of the princes of Lampedusa, made famous by Giuseppe Tomasi di Lampedusa, author of *Il Gattopardo* (The Leopard). The family's 17th-century ancestral palace has been unoccupied for some time, but the **Chiesa Matrice** still stands and can be visited.

Eating

★Ristorante La Madia SICILIAN €€€
(📞0922 77 14 43; www.ristorantelamadia.it; Via Filippo Re Capriata 22; meals €95-130; ⊙1-2pm & 8-10pm Wed-Mon) One of Sicily's finest restaurants, double Michelin-starred La Madia is a labour of love for local-born chef Pino Cuttaia. It serves modern Sicilian dishes based on authentic Mediterranean ingredients, such as *merluzzo* (cod) smoked over pine cones or cuttlefish served with fennel cream. Items on the elaborate tasting menus are presented as works of art, with exquisite flavours to match.

Hostaria L'Oste e il Sacrestano SICILIAN €€€
(📞0922 77 47 36; www.losteeilsacrestano.it; Via Sant'Andrea 19; meals €28-69; ⊙12.30-2pm Tue-Sun, 7.30-10pm Tue-Sat) Feast on local meat and freshly caught seafood at this Slow Food favourite just off Corso Vittorio Emanuele. Choose from the à la carte menu of three appetisers, three *primi*, three *secondi* and three desserts – many with fanciful names

including 'evolution of the octopus' and 'a stroll through Sicily' – or go all out with the seven-course tasting menu.

① Getting There & Away

Licata is on the coastal SS115, 50km southeast of Agrigento and 32km west of Gela.

Hourly buses operated by SAL (p261) connect Licata with Agrigento (one hour) and Gela (45 minutes).

Falconara

☑ 0934 / POP 100

The tiny settlement of Falconara consists of a few hotels, campgrounds and holiday homes on Sicily's southern coast between Licata and Gela. The prime draw for travellers is the superb sandy beach overlooked by an impressive 14th-century castle, the **Castello di Falconara**. The castle is privately owned by an aristocratic family and closed to the public for visits, but you can stay there overnight.

The road from Falconara towards Gela passes several more wild and unspoilt beaches before arriving at the so-called Gela Riviera on the outskirts of Gela. This section of Sicily's southern coast was heavily defended against the threat of an Allied invasion during WWII, and abandoned pillbox defences still litter the area.

① Getting There & Away

Falconara sits on the SS115 between Gela (21km to the east) and Licata (11km to the west).

Gela

☑ 0933 / POP 75,500

Gela offers a fascinating and well-run archaeology museum and the well-preserved remains of the city's ancient fortifications. Apart from those significant attractions – and a distinguished past as one of Sicily's great ancient cities – however, Gela is now a chaotic industrial centre with a reputation as a Mafia hotspot. Little remains of its heyday as the economic engine room of the great Greek colony that eventually founded Akragas, Eraclea Minoa and Selinunte.

The city was sacked by Carthage in 405 BC and then razed by forces from Agrigento in 282 BC. More recently it was the first Italian town to be liberated by the Allies in WWII (in July 1943), but not before it had been bombed to rubble in the build-up to the invasion. Post-war development saw the construction of the vast petrochemical refineries that still blight the city along with swathes of cheap housing blocks.

◎ Sights

★ Museo Archeologico   MUSEUM

(☑ 0933 91 26 26; Corso Vittorio Emanuele; adult/reduced incl Acropoli & Capo Soprano €4/2; ◎ 9am-6pm Mon-Sat, plus 1st Sun of month) This splendid archaeological museum offers insight into Gela's great artistic past. It contains artefacts from the city's ancient acropolis and is famed for its fine collection of red-and-black *kraters:* these terracotta vases, used to mix wine and water, were a local specialty between the 7th and 4th centuries BC, admired throughout the Greek world for their delicate designs and superb figurative work. Other treasures include a remarkable collection of 530 silver coins minted in Agrigento, Gela, Syracuse, Messina and Athens.

At one time the coin collection numbered over 1000 pieces, but it was stolen in 1976 and only about half of it was ever recovered. More recently, the museum has acquired a Greek ship dating to the 6th century BC (discovered in 1988 on the sandy sea bottom off Gela) and three unusual terracotta altars (discovered in 2003 in a 5th-century-BC warehouse that had been buried under 6m of sand).

Greek Fortifications
of Capo Soprano   RUINS

(Mura Timoleontee di Capo Soprano; adult/reduced incl Acropoli & Museo Archeologico €4/2; ◎ 9.30am-1pm & 2-6pm Mon-Sat Apr-Oct, to 4.30pm Nov-Mar) Built in 333 BC along Gela's western coastline at Capo Soprano by the tyrant of Syracuse, Timoleon, Gela's ancient Greek fortifications are remarkably well preserved, most likely the result of being covered by sand dunes for thousands of years before their discovery in 1948. The 8m-high walls were originally built to prevent huge amounts of sand being blown into the city by the blustery sea wind. Today authorities have planted trees to act as a buffer against the encroaching sand.

Planted with mimosa and eucalyptus trees, the site is perfect for a picnic. To get here from Gela's archaeological museum, follow the *lungomare* (waterfront road) 4km west.

ⓘ Getting There & Away

BUS

From Piazza Stazione, in front of the train station, SAL (p261) runs buses to Licata (45 minutes) and Agrigento (1¾ to 2¼ hours). There are also buses to Syracuse and Caltanissetta.

CAR & MOTORCYCLE

Gela is well connected by road: the SS115 leads westwards to Agrigento and east to Ragusa and Modica, while the SS117bis connects with Caltagirone (via the SS417) and Piazza Armerina.

Arriving in town, follow the signs for the city centre and museum, which is at the eastern end of Corso Vittorio Emanuele, the town's principal east–west street.

Lampedusa

Lampedusa, the largest of the three Pelagic Islands (the others are Linosa and Lampione), lies about 200km south of Sicily, closer to Tunisia than Italy. Surrounded by stunning aquamarine waters, with its south shore protected as a marine reserve, it's a popular summer holiday destination whose year-round population of 6300 more than trebles in summertime. In winter transport connections are cut back and almost every hotel and restaurant shuts down.

The island's main tourist attraction are its beaches, which are strung along the 11km south coast. The most famous, and one of the Mediterranean's most beautiful, is Spiaggia dei Conigli (aka Rabbit Beach) at Isola dei Conigli, a dreamy secluded bay lapped by shallow, turquoise waters.

Lampedusa has also made headlines in recent years as Italy's main port of entry for refugees from Africa and the Middle East, with tens of thousands of migrants arriving mostly from Libya and Tunisia.

◉ Sights

From east to west, Lampedusa's most gorgeous coves and beaches include **Mare Morto**, **Cala Pisana**, **Cala Francese**, **Cala Guitgia**, **Cala Croce**, **Cala Madonna**, **Cala Greca**, **Cala Galera**, Cala Tabaccara, Spiaggia dei Conigli and Cala Pulcino.

★ Spiaggia dei Conigli   BEACH

(Rabbit Beach) Few beaches in the world enjoy such legendary status as this long stretch of pristine white sand lapped by turquoise waters, with pretty views out to a verdant offshore island. It's managed to retain its beauty thanks in large part to its protected status as the centrepiece of the **Riserva Naturale Isola di Lampedusa**. The beach is accessible only by boat or on foot via a 15-minute trail off the main road (look for the sign of the lounging rabbit).

Spiaggia dei Conigli is one of the few places in Italy where *Caretta caretta* (loggerhead sea turtles) lay their eggs, and is strictly off-limits at night during peak nesting season (typically between May and August; watch for signs advising of current restrictions).

★ Cala Tabaccara   BAY

Reachable only by boat, the limpid electric-blue waters of this cove off Lampedusa's south shore are one of the island's most awe-inspiring sights. There's no beach, so swimming from a boat is your only option; any Lampedusa operator will take you here for around €40 per person.

Capo Ponente   VIEWPOINT

For Lampedusa's best sunset, head to this viewpoint near the island's northwestern corner, where you can gaze towards Tunisia as the sun drops directly into an unbroken expanse of sea. About 3km east of Capo Ponente on the main road, you'll pass another fine sunset-viewing spot at **Albero Sole** (133m), Lampedusa's highest point; from May to September, the mobile bar Sprizzando sets up daily in the parking lot here to ply the late-afternoon *aperitivi* set with Aperol Spritzes.

Lampedusa Turtle Group   WILDLIFE RESERVE

(🖉338 2198533; www.lampedusaturtlegroup.org; Lungomare Luigi Rizzo; ☺5-7pm Mon-Sat) **FREE** Lampedusa's pristine beaches are prime nesting habitat for sea turtles, in particular the loggerhead, and this volunteer-based organisation has been working doggedly for their protection for the past 10 years, taking in and rehabilitating injured turtles while educating local school kids and the general public about turtle conservation. Visitors can get a first-hand look at the Turtle Group's work, and meet a turtle or two, on guided afternoon tours (usually available in English with advance notice).

🏊 Activities

You'll find a plethora of operators down by the port offering *gite in barca* (boat tours), including the ever-popular *giro dell'isola* (island circuit).

Cala Pulcino Trail
HIKING

Lampedusa's prettiest hiking trail is an out-and-back affair (30 minutes each way) leading to this magnificent pebble-strewn cove sandwiched between two rocky headlands along the island's southwest shore. From the car park, the signposted trail drops immediately into shady pine forest, then slowly opens into a lovely mini-canyon, with rock walls on either side pointing the route towards the sea.

There's no sandy beach at Cala Pulcino, but the cove's dramatic beauty and magnificent isolation make it a delightful place to linger.

Marina Diving Center
DIVING

(✐ 338 5054554; www.facebook.com/MarinaDiving Lampedusa; Lungomare Luigi Rizzo 161) Lampedusa's crystalline waters are a diver's dream, and this long-established outfit can take you to all the best sites. The professional, safety-conscious guides and top-notch equipment here earn regular accolades.

🍴 Eating

The best place to browse for restaurants is along Lampedusa's main street, Via Roma, and perpendicular streets such as Via Vittorio Emanuele. Fresh seafood is at the heart of Lampedusa's cuisine, with *pesce spada* (swordfish), *sgombro* (mackerel), *cernia* (grouper) and *dentice* (snapper) all making frequent appearances. Other local specialities include *pasta alla bottarga di ricciola* (pasta with amberjack roe, local capers, lemon juice and olive oil) and fish couscous.

Bar dell'Amicizia
BAKERY €

(✐ 0922 97 04 32; Via Vittorio Emmanuele 60; desserts from €2; ⊙ 5am-8pm) Ask people where to find the best desserts in Lampedusa and they'll likely point you to the 'Bar of Friendship' – just look for the cute sign depicting two dolphin friends sharing a gelato. Yes, the gelati are good, but perhaps even better are the *cannoli*, filled on the spot with fresh ricotta and available as early as 5am when the doors open.

Gastronomia Mancino
SICILIAN €

(Via Vittorio Emanuele 39; snacks & light meals €1.50-5; ⊙ 6am-1.30am) At lunchtime, locals pour into this downtown *tavola calda* (cafeteria) with abundant outdoor seating on a central Lampedusa square. The reasonably priced offerings include *arancini* (rice balls stuffed with everything from shrimp to prosciutto and mozzarella), *panini,* pizza slices and delicious *primi* such as pasta with swordfish and eggplant or grouper-stuffed ravioli with Sicilian pesto.

★ Trattoria Terranova
GASTRONOMY €€

(✐ 0922 97 19 25; www.trattoriaterranova.it; Via Terranova 3; meals €26-41; ⊙ noon-2pm & 7-10pm Apr-Oct) Hidden away from Lampedusa's beach-loving crowds on an inland back street, Bernardo's venerable trattoria inspires confidence the minute you step through the door. Filled with tantalising aromas and the cheerful hum of conversation

---

OFF THE BEATEN TRACK

BUTERA & MAZZARINO

For anyone travelling north from Gela or Licata to Piazza Armerina, the back roads through these picturesque hilltop villages offer a scenic detour.

Prosperous, self-sufficient and content from its years under the rule of the Branciforte family, Butera lacks the down-at-heel atmosphere of many rural interior towns. Its lovely town church, the **Chiesa Madre**, boasts some modest treasures (a Renaissance triptych and a Madonna by 16th-century Tuscan painter Filippo Paladini), but the star attraction here is the dizzying panorama that unfolds from the hilltop **Norman castle**.

Mazzarino, the historic seat of the Branciforte clan, is now just a small, sleepy town, but merits a quick look for its clutch of baroque churches, decorated with the ostentatious funerary monuments of the Branciforte princes and more artworks by Paladini. Many of the churches are closed to the public, but you can request access at the helpful **tourist office** (✐ 093 438 49 84; Corso Vittorio Emanuele 410; ⊙ 9am-1pm & 4-8pm summer, 9am-1pm & 3-7pm winter) on Mazzarino's main street.

From Gela, it's an easy 18km drive along the SP8 to Butera. Continue another 18km north on the SP8 and the SS191 to reach Mazzarino. From here, a 24km jaunt northeastward along the SP26, SP169 and SP15 will bring you to Piazza Armerina.

from a multi-generational local crowd, Terranova serves splendid Slow Food specialties, from the *carrellata di antipasti* (caponata, marinated sardines, vegetable couscous) to fresh grilled seafood mains.

Cavalluccio Marino
SEAFOOD €€€

(☑0922 97 00 53; www.hotelcavallucciomarino.com/ristorante; Contrada Cala Croce 3; meals from €45, tasting menus €60-80; ☺8-9.30pm May-Oct) Lampedusa's go-to address for refined island cuisine, Cavalluccio Marino puts a modern spin on Sicilian classics, from swordfish *cannoli* to champagne risotto with red Mazara prawns. In summer, dine on white tables and chairs spread across the romantically lit sea-facing patio. Island specialties available with advance notice include *couscous di cernia* (grouper fish couscous) and *zuppa di pesce* (fish soup).

Getting There & Away

AIR
Aeroporto di Lampedusa (LMP; ☑0922 97 07 31; www.aeroportodilampedusa.com) is just 1km east of the main town and the ferry dock. **DAT** (www.dat.dk) offers direct flights from Palermo and Catania, while **Volotea** (www.volotea.com) flies direct to Bergamo, Genoa, Turin, Venice and Verona. A handful of other airlines connect Lampedusa with Rome, Milan and/or Bologna, including **Alitalia** (www.alitalia.com), **Blue Panorama** (www.blue-panorama.com), **Neos** (www.neosair.it) and **Vueling** (www.vueling.com).

BOAT
Siremar (www.carontetourist.it/en/siremar) and **Traghetti delle Isole** (www.traghettidelle isole.it) both run year-round ferries from Porto Empedocle to Lampedusa (€49, 9¾ hours). Between late June and September, **Liberty Lines** (www.libertylines.it) also runs four to five weekly hydrofoils along this same route (€61, 4¼ hours).

Getting Around

BICYCLE
The island is relatively small (20.2 sq km), and cycling is an excellent way to get around. **Noleggio Ecologico** (☑333 3246668; www.noleggioecologicolampedusa.com; Via Pellico 12; ☺8am-12.30pm & 3.30-7.30pm) rents a wide range of two-wheelers, including city bikes, mountain bikes, tandems, electric bikes and scooters.

BUS
Lampedusa's public buses run on two circular routes, both leaving from a stop on Piazza Brignone in the town centre. The **Linea Azzurra** (Blue Line) runs west of town to Spiaggia dei Conigli, with several stops en route including Cala Croce and Camping La Roccia. The **Linea Rossa** (Red Line) heads northeast from town, with stops at popular coastal spots such as Cala Creta and Mare Morto. Both lines run from around 8.30am to 8pm daily. Tickets cost €1 and can be purchased from the driver.

CAR & MOTORCYCLE
Distances are short on Lampedusa, but it can still be convenient to have your own wheels. Car and scooter rental companies abound, both at the airport and in town. In low season (May or October) weekly prices start around €90 for a 50cc scooter, €100 for a 125cc scooter, or €130 for a basic economy car. In peak summer season (August) expect to pay as much as €180, €210 or €240 for the same vehicles.

Accommodation

Where to Stay

The best place to base yourself in Sicily will depend on your interests and travel style. Cities such as Palermo, Catania, Taormina and Syracuse have the most cosmopolitan mix of higher-end and boutique hotels. If you're happier in a rural setting, the *agriturismi* (farm-stay accommodation) of Central Sicily and the Madonie and Nebrodi Mountains are some of the nicest on the island.

Budget travellers also have plenty of options to choose from: hostels in Palermo and Catania, mountain chalets in the Madonie Mountains and Mt Etna region, or excellent low- to midrange B&Bs throughout the region, in places such as Syracuse, Agrigento, Lipari and Marsala. Syracuse, Catania and Palermo make convenient bases for anyone travelling by train or other public transport, while beach-lovers benefit from an appealing mix of accommodation in Cefalù and Taormina.

Best
Places to Stay

➡ Suite d'Autore (p291)

➡ Nòtia Rooms (p288)

➡ Pensione Tranchina (p279)

➡ Domus Maris Relais (p292)

Pricing

The following price ranges refer to a double room with private bathroom (breakfast included) in high season. July, August and Christmas are generally considered high season. Low-season rates usually apply from October to Easter (with the exception of the Christmas holidays), while mid-season rates apply the remainder of the year.

Category	Cost
€	less than €110
€€	€110–200
€€€	more than €200

Best
Agriturismi

➡ Monaci delle Terre Nere (p286)

➡ Agriturismo Vultaggio (p279)

➡ Casa Migliaca (p281)

➡ Masseria Quartarella (p287)

PALERMO REGION

Palermo

★ Stanze al Genio Residenze
B&B €

(Map p66; 📞340 0971561; www.stanzealgeniobnb.it; Via Garibaldi 11; s €85-100, d €100-120; ❉⬧) Speckled with Sicilian antiques, this B&B offers four gorgeous bedrooms, three with 19th-century ceiling frescoes. All four are spacious and thoughtfully appointed, with Murano lamps, old wooden wardrobes, the odd balcony railing turned bedhead, and top-quality, orthopaedic beds. That the property features beautiful maiolica tiles is no coincidence; the B&B is affiliated with the wonderful Museo delle Maioliche (p63) downstairs.

Palazzo Pantaleo
B&B €

(Map p60; 📞091 32 54 71; www.palazzopantaleo.it; Via Ruggero Settimo 74h; s/d/ste €80/100/150; P⬧) Offering unbeatable comfort and a convenient location, Giuseppe Scaccianoce's elegant B&B occupies the top floor of an old *palazzo* (mansion) half a block from Piazza Politeama, hidden from the busy street in a quiet courtyard with free parking. Glowing with warm, earthy tones, five rooms and one spacious suite feature high ceilings, marble, tile or wooden floors, soundproof windows and modern bathrooms.

B&B Amélie
B&B €

(Map p60; 📞328 8654824, 091 33 59 20; www.bb-amelie.it; Via Prinicipe di Belmonte 94; s €40-60, d €60-80, tr €90-100; ❉@⬧) On a central, car-free street, affable, multilingual Angela has converted her grandmother's spacious 6th-floor flat into a cheery B&B. Rooms are simple, colourful and spotless. All have private bathroom (either as an ensuite or in the hallway) and two come with private terrace. Breakfast includes homemade cakes and jams, and Angela, a native Palermitan, is a font of local knowledge.

BOOK YOUR STAY ONLINE

For more accommodation reviews by Lonely Planet authors, check out hotels. lonelyplanet.com. You'll find independent reviews, as well as recommendations on the best places to stay. Best of all, you can book online.

BB22 Palace
B&B €€

(Map p66; 📞091 32 62 14; www.bb22.it; cnr Via Roma & Via Bandiera; d €140-180, whole apt €700-1000) Occupying a flouncy *palazzo* in the heart of the city, BB22 Palace offers chic, contemporary rooms, each with its own style. Top billing goes to the Stromboli room, complete with spa bath and a bedroom skylight offering a glimpse of its 15th-century neighbour. Peppered with artworks, coffee-table tomes and an honour bar, the communal lounge makes for an airy retreat.

Butera 28
APARTMENT €€

(Map p66; 📞333 3165432; www.butera28.it; Via Butera 28; apt per day €80-240, per week €520-1600; P❉⬧) Delightful multilingual owner Nicoletta rents 12 apartments in the 18th-century Palazzo Lanzi Tomasi, the last home of Giuseppe Tomasi di Lampedusa, author of *The Leopard*. Graced with family antiques, the units range from 30 to 180 sq metres, most sleeping a family of four or more. Five apartments face the sea and all feature laundry facilities, well-equipped kitchens and soundproofed windows.

Apartment nine even comes with its own grand piano. Parking costs €15 per night and Nicoletta also offers fabulous cooking classes.

Massimo Plaza Hotel
HOTEL €€

(Map p58; 📞091 32 56 57; www.massimoplazahotel.com; Via Maqueda 437; d €140-250; P❉⬧) The intimate Massimo Plaza sits in a prime location along vibrant, pedestrianised Via Maqueda. Tie-back curtains and wooden furniture give rooms a classic feel. Seven of the rooms offer a prime view of the iconic Teatro Massimo across the street. Breakfast can be delivered directly to your room at no extra charge.

★ De Bellini Apartments
APARTMENT €€€

(Map p66; 📞331 8836589; http://debellinipalermo.it; Piazza Bellini 5; apt from €200; ❉⬧) In a 17th-century *palazzo* on one of Palermo's finest squares, these 10 architect-designed apartments are spectacular. Six have their own kitchen with high-tech appliances, and while all have different configurations and looks, all feature contemporary art, striking designer furniture, contemporary bathrooms and quality bedding. Bellini's balcony apartment is so close to the 12th-century La Martorana you can almost touch it from your private terrace.

Grand Hotel Villa Igiea
HOTEL €€€

(☑ 091 631 21 11; www.villa-igiea.com; Salita Belmonte 43; d from €289; P ❄ @ 🛜 ⛱) What can you say about an art nouveau villa that was designed by Ernesto Basile for the Florio family (of tuna and Marsala-wine fame)? This is Palermo's top hotel, located around 3km north of the city centre and with its own private beach, swimming pool, tennis court, spa centre, gym and restaurants. The rooms are predictably elegant, with blissful beds and palatial bathrooms.

Hotel Principe di Villafranca
BOUTIQUE HOTEL €€€

(Map p60; ☑ 091 611 85 23; www.principedivillafranca.it; Via Giuseppina Turrisi Colonna 4; d €199-253, ste €268-363; P ❄ @ 🛜) Furnished with fine design and antiques, this sophisticated slumber pad is just west of Via della Libertà in one of Palermo's most peaceful, exclusive neighbourhoods. Public spaces include a cosy sitting area with library, fireplace and displays of local artists' work; among the comfortable rooms, junior suite 105 stands out, decorated with artwork loaned from artists and private collections.

WESTERN SICILY

Golfo di Castellammare

★ Agriturismo Vultaggio
AGRITURISMO €

(☑ 0923 86 42 61; www.agriturismovultaggio.it; Contrada Misiliscemi 4, Guarrato; d €76, tents from €80; P ⊛) 🍃 Head 15km south of Trapani, into the countryside, to find this outstanding farm retreat. Four of its 13 attractive rooms have sea views and there are safari tents for 'glampers'. Pool lounging, biking and hiking aside, dining in the sensational zero-kilometre farm restaurant and drooling over the fresh ricotta and pecorino, honey and organic fruit in the farm shop are memorable highlights.

Scopello

★ Pensione Tranchina
PENSION €

(☑ 0924 54 10 99; www.pensionetranchina.com; Via Armando Diaz 7; B&B per person €35-50, half board per person €60-75; ⊛ 🛜) Sensational home-cooked meals, predominantly organic to boot, and a prime location in downtown Scopello make this – the inviting home of welcoming host Marisin Tranchina – one of western Sicily's most beloved *pensioni*. Rooms, some with distant sea views, are modern and breakfast is a memorable feast of warm bread and sweet pastries, local honey and olive oil, sun-rich tomatoes, creamy ricotta and market-fresh beans.

Trapani

Ai Lumi
B&B €

(Map p100; ☑ 0923 54 09 22; www.ailumi.it; Corso Vittorio Emanuele 71; s €53-70, d €85-106, tr €111-132, q €138-159; ⊛ 🛜) Husband-and-wife team Francesca and Riccardo have run this atmospheric guesthouse with much TLC since 2003. In an 18th-century *palazzo* with Instagram-worthy courtyard full of potted plants, it mixes traditional B&B rooms with kitchenette-clad apartments sleeping up to five. Breakfast is served next door in Ai Lumi's **tavernetta** (Map p100; ☑ 0923 87 24 18; www.ailumi.it; Corso Vittorio Emanuele 75; meals €30-40; ⏲ 7am-3pm & 7.30-11pm, closed Tue Oct-May); guests get 15% discount on other meals there.

★ La Gancia Residence
HOTEL €€

(Map p100; ☑ 0923 43 80 60; www.lagancia.com; Piazza Mercato del Pesce; d €110-170, tr €200, q €189-280; ⏲ reception 7am-midnight; ⊛ 🛜) Spoon yourself a jelly sweet out of the huge sweetie jar at reception, admire the soaring centuries-old ceiling and chic Moorish-styled lounge, and congratulate yourself on landing a room at one of the most beautiful spots in town, practically on the water. Sea views from many rooms could not be bolder or more romantic, and the breakfast terrace is a dream.

★ Room Mate Andrea
DESIGN HOTEL €€

(Map p100; ☑ 912 179287; https://room-matehotels.com/en/andrea; Viale Regina Margherita 31; d €79-135; P ❄ @ 🛜 ⛱) Graceful Palazzo Platamone, with neoclassical caramel-coloured facade dating to the 1900s, is the grandiose setting for the Sicilian debut of Spanish urban hotel group, Room Mate. Andrea is predictably stylish, with the city's only rooftop pool. Beautifully decorated, vintage-chic rooms mix original neoclassical fittings and fixtures with modern comforts. Breakfast costs €19.90 and is served until noon; the bar serves tip-top seasonal cocktails.

Saline di Trapani

Relais Antiche Saline   BOUTIQUE HOTEL €€
(☑ 389 0611558, 0923 86 80 42; www.relaisan
tichesaline.it; Via Giuseppe Verdi, Nubia; d €80-
200; ☺ Nov-Mar; 🅿 ❄ @ 🛜 ≋) Watching
flocks of herons and flamingoes flutter
overhead, swooning over glorious sunsets
or finding out about local salt culture is
what a stay at this remote, whitewashed hotel, amid glistening salt pans in the Saline
di Trapani e Paceco nature reserve, is all
about. Comfortable four-star rooms sport
nautical blue-and-white colour schemes,
and there are an outdoor pool and Jacuzzi
April to October.

The hotel owners are born-and-
bred salt-working stock (starting with
great-grandfather Angelo Culcasi in the
1900s) and are happy to set up a salt-pan
trek or WWF tour of the nature reserve
for guests. Half-/full board costs an extra
€25/45 per person per day.

Pantelleria

Dammusi Sciuvechi   GUESTHOUSE €€
(☑ 338 9707429; www.dammusisciuvechi.it; Località Sciuvechi; 2-person dammuso per week €500-
1580; ❄ 🛜 ≋) Surrounded by olive trees,
vineyards and distant sea views, this secluded resort in Pantelleria's western highlands
is a perfect place to get away from it all.
The collection of self-contained *dammusi*
(whitewashed, shallow-domed Pantelleri-
an stone houses) includes units of varying
sizes, many equipped with kitchens, private
pools and/or verandahs. All share a Jacuzzi, a Turkish bath, a swimming pool and a
solarium.

Mazara del Vallo

★ Meliaresort   BOUTIQUE HOTEL €€
(☑ 335 1250100, 0923 90 64 97; www.meliaresort.
it; Via Bagno 2; d €130-300; ❄ 🛜) Smack in the
middle of La Casbah, this unique boutique
hotel features nine beautifully restored
rooms, suites and kitchen-equipped apartments with terrace – all in a historic *palazzo* or *dimore storiche* (historic residence).
Grandiose period features run riot throughout and one suite has its own grand piano.
Factor in ample time for the sweet feast of a
Sicilian breakfast.

Marsala

★ Il Profumo del Sale   B&B €
(Map p114; ☑ 0923 189 04 72; www.ilprofumodel
sale.it; Via Vaccari 8; s/d €40/65; 🛜) Perfectly
positioned in Marsala's historic city centre, this lovely B&B offers three attractive
rooms – including a palatial front unit with
cathedral views from its small balcony – enhanced by welcoming touches like almond
cookies, fine soaps and ample breakfasts
featuring homemade bread and jams. Sophisticated owner Celsa is full of helpful tips
about Marsala and the surrounding area.

★ ProKite Alby Rondina   HOTEL €
(☑ 347 5373881; www.prokitealbyrondina.com; Via
Passalacqua; s/d/tr from €60/85/115; ☺ Mar-Nov;
🅿 ❄ @ 🛜) Wake up to an invigorating view
of colourful kites dancing above the pretty
waters of Lo Stagnone lagoon at this bright
and modern three-star hotel run by one of
Marsala's top kite-surfing schools (p108).
Its 29 rooms, in an attractive terraced row
of whitewashed cottages footsteps from the
lagoon shore, sport a refreshingly contemporary interior design with hipster surfing
photos on the wall.

Hotel Carmine   HOTEL €€
(Map p114; ☑ 0923 71 19 07; www.hotelcarmine.
it; Piazza Carmine 16; s/d/tr €105/125/160;
🅿 ❄ @ 🛜) This lovely hotel in a converted
16th-century monastery has elegant rooms,
with original blue-and-gold maiolica tiles,
stone walls, antique furniture and lofty
beamed ceilings. Enjoy your cornflakes in
the baronial-style breakfast room with its
historic frescoes and over-the-top chande-
lier, or sip your drink by the roaring fireplace in winter. Modern perks include a
rooftop solarium.

Erice

Hotel Elimo   HOTEL €€
(Map p103; ☑ 0923 86 93 77; www.hotelelimo.it; Via
Vittorio Emanuele 75; s €72-100, d €90-160, q €120;
❄ 🛜) Communal spaces at this atmospheric historic house are filled with tiled beams,
marble fireplaces, intriguing art, knick-
knacks and antiques. The bedrooms are
more mainstream, although many (along
with the hotel terrace and restaurant) have
breathtaking vistas south and west towards
the Saline di Trapani, the Egadi Islands and
the shimmering sea.

Marettimo

★ **Marettimo Residence**   B&B €€

(⏰0923 92 32 02; www.marettimoresidence.it; Via Telegrafo 3; d €130-210, tr €160-240, q €250-320; @ 🛜 ⚊) Lovingly landscaped with bougainvillea, palms and herbs, this hillside complex south of the port is ideal for families or anyone wishing to linger a while on Marettimo. Each of the 44 apartments comes with a kitchen and porch. It has a small swimming pool, a pair of spa baths, a kids playground, cafe, barbecue area and multilingual library.

Favignana

★ **La Casa del Limoneta**   B&B €€

(⏰340 4184858, 331 3430654; www.lacasadellimoneto.it; Vicolo Cimarosa 12; d €90-170; P ❄ 🛜) An enchanting sunken garden full of centurion lemon trees frames this cosy whitewashed guesthouse, home of Gaetana and Giuseppe. Rooms open onto the lemon groves or a tiny grassy walled garden and breakfast, served beneath lemon trees in warm weather, is a sweet feast of homemade cakes, lemon curd and peachy medlar fruits fresh from the garden.

★ **Villa Margherita**   RESORT €€

(⏰331 4601817; www.villamargherita.it; Strada Comunale Corso 10; d €113-156, tr €141-172; ☉ reception 9am-1pm & 4-7.30pm May-Oct; P ❄ 🛜 ⚊) One of the most peaceful sleeping options on the island, this enchanting villa-turned-upmarket residence is squirrelled away in extraordinary botanical gardens borne out of the island's tufa-quarrying heritage. Guests can while away hours exploring the lush grounds, study dozens of palm tree varieties around the pool and relax beneath the shade-cool gazebo. Kitchen-equipped studios, split between a handful of houses, sleep two or three.

TYRRHENIAN COAST

Castel di Tusa

★ **Casa Migliaca**   AGRITURISMO €€

(⏰0921 33 67 22; www.casamigliaca.com; SP176, Km 7, Pettineo; s/d with half-board €105/170, self-catering apt per day/week €100/600; 🛜) Built around a 17th-century olive-oil mill and surrounded by organic olive and citrus groves, this serene hillside *agriturismo* 9km south of Castel di Tusa offers spacious rooms in a beautiful old stone farmhouse, along with an apartment sleeping up to six. Meals incorporating produce from the farm are served family-style around the historic olive press or in the cosy upstairs kitchen.

Owner Luca invites guests to explore his gorgeous property with the help of an elegant hand-drawn map, and offers a wealth of advice about excursions to secret beaches, hill towns and other local attractions.

Cefalù

★ **B&B Agrodolce**   B&B €

(Map p126; ⏰338 7250863; www.agrodolcebb.it; Via Gioeni 44; d €80-110, tr €100-120; 🛜) Three flights of old stone steps lead up to this lovely upper-floor B&B in the heart of Cefalù's historic centre. Architect Rita Riolo offers four bright and airy rooms with cool tiled floors and bathrooms, along with delicious lemon cake and other home-baked goodies served on a tiny breakfast terrace looking up towards the Duomo.

La Plumeria   HOTEL €€

(Map p126; ⏰0921 92 58 97; www.laplumeriahotel.it; Corso Ruggero 185; d €169-229; P ❄ 🛜) Midway between the Duomo and the waterfront, with free parking a few minutes away, this small hotel offers four-star service in a prime location. Rooms are mostly unexceptional but well appointed; the sweetest of the lot is room 301, a cosy top-floor eyrie with checkerboard tile floors and a small terrace looking up to the Duomo.

Parco Naturale Regionale delle Madonie

★ **Antico Feudo San Giorgio**   AGRITURISMO €

(⏰0921 60 06 90; www.feudosangiorgio.it; SS120, Km 46, Contrada San Giorgio; r per person incl breakfast €40-55, with half-board €55-70, with full board €65-80; ⚊) At the foot of the Madonie, only 7km from the A19, owners Fabiola and Giancorrado have converted this 300-hectare *fattoria* (fortified country estate) into an *agriturismo* producing organic olives, grain, beef and wine. Rooms are simple (no air-con, no TV), encouraging guests to appreciate the divine setting: rolling hills and ancient trees planted with the dowry money of Giancorrado's grandmother.

Castelbuono

Azienda Agrituristica Bergi AGRITURISMO €
(📞0921 67 20 45; www.agriturismobergi.com; SS286, Km 17.6, Contrada Bergi; d €85-109, tr €105-135, q €125-150, half-/full board per person extra €25/40; 🛜🐾) Just south of Castelbuono on the winding SS286, this family-run *agriturismo* has a cluster of modern rooms – including several family-friendly quads – surrounded by olive groves and mountain vistas. Guests have access to a swimming pool and tasty meals featuring the family's home-grown produce, olive oil and award-winning honey.

Relais Santa Anastasia HOTEL €€
(📞 0921 67 22 33; www.abbaziasantanastasia.com; Contrada Santa Anastasia; s €80-119, d €146-206, ste €225-249; 🛜🐾) Set amid the picturesque vineyards of a highly regarded wine estate, this converted 12th-century abbey boasts extremely comfortable rooms, a sensational pool terrace with views of the Aeolian Islands, and the on-site Corte dell'Abate restaurant, serving food and wine from the estate. You'll find it 9km from Castelbuono in the direction of Cefalù.

Petralia Soprana

Locanda di Cadi B&B €€
(📞 338 2890100; www.lalocandadicadi.it; Borgo Cipampini; per person B&B €65, half-board €90; 🛜) The three cosy rooms at this B&B 10km below Petralia Soprana – a double, a triple and a quad – all come with welcoming details: wood stoves, tea kettles, colourful mosaic tiles or a balcony overlooking the surrounding hills. Best of all, sleeping here means you can enjoy a multicourse dinner at the wonderful A Fuoco Lento (p132) restaurant downstairs for only €25 extra.

Petralia Sottana

★**Albergo Il Castello** HOTEL €
(📞0921 64 12 50; www.il-castello.net; Via Generale di Maria 27; s/d €50/70, ste €85-95; 🌬🛜) Tucked into a back street above Petralia Sottana's Duomo, this family-run inn has immaculate rooms and three-star amenities. Its restaurant specialises in pizza (weekends only) and top-notch mountain cuisine featuring local mushrooms and truffles. In chilly weather, consider splurging on the General's Suite, with its wood-burning fireplace. There's parking in the square, half a block beyond the hotel entrance.

Parco Regionale dei Nebrodi

★**Relais Villa Miraglia** HOTEL €€
(📞095 883 48 98; www.relaisvillamiraglia.it; SS289; d €120-160, ste €180) Surrounded by beech forest, this newly restored hunting lodge smack in the heart of the Nebrodi is the perfect base for hiking, mountain biking or horseback riding into the park. The nine rooms and one spiffy suite with freestanding bathtub offer more luxury than you might expect in the middle of nowhere, and the onsite restaurant (p135) serves fine regional cuisine.

San Marco d'Alunzio

B&B La Tela di Penelope B&B €
(📞 0941 79 77 34; www.teladipenelope.it; Via Aluntina 48; s €35-45, d €50-70; 🌬🛜) Attached to a traditional weaving studio, this three-room B&B is perfectly placed in the heart of picturesque San Marco d'Alunzio. Rooms (two with private balconies) enjoy views of the historic centre or the distant Aeolian Islands, and all guests share a small kitchen. Owners can arrange tours of the weaving studio, the town and the nearby Parco Regionale dei Nebrodi.

AEOLIAN ISLANDS

Alicudi

Casa Mulino HOTEL €
(📞090 988 96 81, 368 3351265; www.alicudicasamulino.it; Via Regina Elena; d €70-100; ☺mid-Apr–Oct; 🛜) This peach-and-white honeycomb of rooms is the first thing you'll see when docking at Alicudi...meaning you don't have far to lug your bags! The rooms, many with sea views, include simple doubles, doubles with kitchen and terrace, or two-room, kitchen-equipped suites. Owner Carlo and his brother Italo proudly display their family tree, revealing roots in Alicudi since 1688.

Ericusa HOTEL €€
(📞090 988 99 02; www.alicudihotel.it; Via Regina Elena; d with half-board €150-190, with full board €200-240; ☺Jun-Sep) Alicudi's lone hotel, just south of the port, opens only from June

through September, when its 12 rooms fill up quickly. There's a pleasant terrace restaurant overlooking the sea; half-board is obligatory for hotel guests.

Filicudi

Casa Monti de Luca   B&B €€
(☑328 2404807, 347 1868044; www.casamonti deluca.it; Contrada Rocca di Ciaule 29; d €70-150) Run by Italian-Argentine couple Renzo and Miguel, this three-room B&B has the charm of a small home, with ample outdoor lounging space and an upstairs salon for reading on rainy days. Decor ranges from family heirlooms to modern art from Renzo's years in the fashion industry. Two front rooms share a panoramic terrace; the third (out back) offers greater privacy.

Hotel La Canna   HOTEL €€
(☑ 090 988 99 56; Via Rosa 43; s €60-110, with half-board €85-140, d €100-160, with half-board €150-220; ✳ ☀) Perched high above the port, this long-established, family-run hotel features rooms with beams, terracotta tiles and panoramic terraces boasting a seagull's-eye view of the harbour sparkling below. Delicious traditional meals at its restaurant feature produce from the adjacent gardens.

Lipari

★Diana Brown   B&B €
(Map p146; ☑338 6407572, 090 981 25 84; www. dianabrown.it; Vico Himera 3; s €35-65, d €50-80, tr €65-105; ✳ ☀) Now run by the daughter and son-in-law of longtime Lipari innkeeper Diana Brown, this delightful warren of rooms tucked down a narrow alley sports attractive features including in-room kettles, fridges, clothes-drying racks, satellite TV and a book exchange. Units downstairs are darker but have built-in kitchenettes. Its excellent buffet breakfast is served on the sunny terrace and solarium with deck chairs.

Enzo Il Negro   GUESTHOUSE €
(Map p146; ☑090 981 31 63; www.enzoilnegro.com; Via Garibaldi 29; s €45-50, d €75-90, tr €90-120; ✳☀) Family-run for nearly 40 years, and perfectly placed in the pedestrian zone near picturesque Marina Corta, Enzo and Cettina's down-to-earth guesthouse offers spacious, tiled, pine-furnished rooms with fridges and air-con. Two panoramic terraces overlook the rooftops, the harbour and the castle walls.

★B&B Al Salvatore di Lipari   B&B €
(☑335 8343222; www.facebook.com/bbalsal vatore; Via San Salvatore, Contrada al Salvatore; d €60-120; ☺Apr-Oct; ☀) Once you reach this peaceful hillside oasis 2km south of town, you may never want to leave. Artist Paola and physicist Marcello have transformed their Aeolian villa into a green B&B that works at all levels, from dependable wi-fi to a panoramic terrace where delicious home-grown breakfasts are served, featuring produce from the adjacent garden, fresh-baked cakes and homemade marmalade.

Panarea

B&B Da Luca   B&B €€
(☑333 6753547; www.bed-breakfast-panarea.it; Via Iditella; d €85-240; ✳☀) Offering backstreet tranquility coupled with lovely (if distant) sea views, this whitewashed Aeolian-style hideaway on a dead-end lane in Ditella (15 minutes north of the port) features four rooms with private terraces, a kitchen-equipped four-person apartment, and pretty landscaped grounds. Owner Luca does little to advertise the place; ask someone to point the way once you arrive in Ditella.

Da Francesco   B&B €
(www.dafrancescopanarea.com; s €40-128, d €80-160; ✳☀) These simple, immaculate rooms with pretty tiled floors and bathrooms are the closest thing to budget lodging you'll find in pricey Panarea, Look for them directly above the restaurant of the same name, within paces of the hydrofoil dock.

Hotel Oasi   HOTEL €€
(☑090 98 33 38; www.hoteloasipanarea.com; Via San Pietro; d €87-227; ☀☀) Blue-and-white-clad rooms surround a green oasis of palm trees with a geothermally heated pool and views up to Punta del Corvo at this centrally located San Pietro hotel. Management also rents out several nearby self-catering properties, including the less expensive Dependance La Caletta with its Stromboli-facing patio and the dreamy Zeus apartment, with a waterfront terrace built into sea-sculpted rocks.

Salina

★Hotel Ravesi   HOTEL €€
(☑090 984 43 85; www.hotelravesi.it; Via Roma 66, Malfa; d €90-190, ste €160-290; ☺mid-Apr–mid-Oct; ✳☀☀) Star attractions at this peach

of a family-run hotel beside Malfa's town square include the delightful grassy lounge and bar area and the outdoor deck with infinity pool overlooking Panarea, Stromboli and the Mediterranean. Sea views are especially nice from corner room 12 upstairs and from the two brand-new honeymoon suites with antique furniture, decorative tiles and private terraces.

Hotel Mamma Santina   BOUTIQUE HOTEL €€

(✆090 984 30 54; www.mammasantina.it; Via Sanità 40, Santa Marina Salina; d €110-180; ☻Apr-Oct; ❋@🛜🏊) A labour of love for architect-owner Mario Gullo, this boutique hotel has inviting rooms decorated with pretty tiles in traditional Aeolian designs. Many of the sea-view terraces come equipped with hammocks, and on warm evenings the attached restaurant (meals €30 to €40) has outdoor seating overlooking the glowing blue pool and landscaped garden.

Hotel Signum   BOUTIQUE HOTEL €€€

(✆090 984 42 22; www.hotelsignum.it; Via Scalo 15, Malfa; d €250-700, ste €550-1100; ❋🛜🏊) Hidden in Malfa's hillside lanes is this alluring labyrinth of antique-clad rooms, peach-coloured stucco walls, tall blue windows and vine-covered terraces with full-on views of Stromboli. The attached wellness centre, a stunning pool and one of the island's best-regarded restaurants make this the perfect place to unwind for a few days in utter comfort.

Capofaro   BOUTIQUE HOTEL €€€

(✆090 984 43 30; www.capofaro.it; Via Faro 3; d €260-680, ste €580-1200; ☻May–mid-Oct; ❋@🛜🏊) Immerse yourself in luxury at this five-star boutique resort surrounded by well-tended Malvasia vineyards, halfway between Santa Marina and Malfa. Sharp white decor prevails in the 20 rooms with terraces looking straight out to smoking Stromboli and six brand-new suites in the picturesque 19th-century lighthouse. Tennis courts, poolside massages, wine tasting and vineyard visits complete this perfect vision of island chic.

Stromboli

★ Casa del Sole   GUESTHOUSE €

(Map p161; ✆090 98 63 00; www.casadelsolestromboli.it; Via Cincotta; dm €25-35, s €30-55, d €60-110) This cheerful Aeolian-style guesthouse is only 100m from a sweet black-sand beach

in Piscità, the tranquil neighbourhood at the west end of town. Dorms, private doubles and a guest kitchen all surround a sunny patio, overhung with vines, fragrant with lemon blossoms, and decorated with the masks and stone carvings of sculptor-owner Tano Russo. It's a pleasant 25-minute walk or a €10 taxi ride from the port 2km away.

Pensione Aquilone   GUESTHOUSE €

(Map p161; ✆090 98 60 80; www.aquiloneresidence.it; Via Vittorio Emanuele 29; s €30-50, d €50-70) Convenience and a peaceful location come together at this cheerful, long-established guesthouse tucked away above Stromboli's main drag, just west of the hilltop church square. Guests love the sunny, flowery central garden patio and shared terraces with views to the volcano and Strombolicchio. Three rooms come with cosy cooking nooks; otherwise, friendly owners Adriano and Francesco – both Stromboli natives – provide breakfast.

La Sirenetta Park Hotel   HOTEL €€

(Map p161; ✆090 98 60 25; www.lasirenetta.it; Via Marina 33; s €90-110, d €165-250, half-board per person extra €37; ☻Easter-late Oct; ❋🛜🏊) This whitewashed, terraced complex opposite Ficogrande's black-sand beach was Stromboli's first-ever hotel – the current owner's father counted Ingrid Bergman as an early guest. It's a laid-back place with spacious, summery rooms, a large seawater swimming pool, tennis courts, a cosy lounge with fireplace and grand piano, a first-class restaurant and an amphitheatre used to screen films and stage theatrical performances.

Locanda del Barbablù   B&B €€

(Map p161; ✆090 98 61 18; www.barbablu.it; Via Vittorio Emanuele 17; d €120; ☻Easter-Oct) Just west of Stromboli's hilltop church square, this dusky-pink Aeolian inn under the same ownership since 1985 is a fashionable port of call, with five high-ceilinged rooms done up in rustic-chic decor. There's a two-night minimum stay.

Vulcano

Casa Arcada   B&B €

(✆347 6497633; www.casaarcada.it; Strada Provinciale 178; d €50-80, with kitchenette €60-100; ❋🛜) Conveniently located at the volcano's edge, 20m back from the main road between the port and the crater path, this sweet whitewashed complex offers 10 immaculate tile-floored rooms with air-con and mini-fridges; the best five also have kitchenette-equipped front patios. The communal upstairs sun terrace affords lovely views up to the volcano and across the water to Lipari.

Casa delle Stelle
B&B €

(☑328 4392403; Contrada Gelso; s €30-45, d €50-90; 🅿) This lovely hideaway, high in the hills above the island's south shore, is run by former Gelso lighthouse keeper Sauro and his wife Maria. The two guest rooms share a living room, fully equipped kitchen and panoramic terrace with spectacular views of the Mediterranean and a distant Mt Etna. In summer, local buses will drop you at the gate.

IONIAN COAST

Catania

★ B&B Crociferi
B&B €

(Map p184; ☑095 715 22 66; www.bbcrociferi.it; Via Crociferi 81; d €75-85, tr €100-110, apt €98-110, ste €120-140; ❈🛜) Perfectly positioned on pedestrianised Via Crociferi, this B&B in a beautifully decorated family home affords easy access to Catania's historic centre. Three palatial rooms (each with a private, refurbished bathroom across the hall) feature high ceilings, antique tiles, frescoes and artistic accoutrements from the owners' travels. The B&B also houses two apartments, the largest (called Lilla) has a spectacular, leafy panoramic terrace. Book ahead.

Affable owners Marco and Teresa enhance the B&B's charms with their own personal touches. Teresa (who speaks German, English and Spanish) makes a delicious, varied breakfast in her floral kitchen, while Marco (who speaks French) can organise boat tours of the coastline.

★ Palazzu Stidda
APARTMENT €

(Map p184; ☑338 6505133, 095 34 88 26; www.palazzustiddacatania.com; Vicolo della Lanterna 2-5; d €80-100, q €140-160, main apt €150-300; ❈🛜) Creative hosts Giovanni and Patricia Manidoro have poured their hearts into creating these four family-friendly apartments on a peaceful dead-end alley, with all the comforts of home plus a host of whimsical touches. All are decorated with the owners' artwork, handmade furniture, family heirlooms and upcycled vintage finds. The largest apartment, Ammiraglia, accommodates

up to eight people, with three bedrooms, a kitchen and lounge.

B&B Faro
B&B €

(Map p184; ☑349 4578856; www.bebfaro.it; Via San Michele 26; d/tr €80/100, apt €130-150; 🅿❈🛜) Artist couple Anna and Antonio own this urbane B&B, set in a vibrant quarter dotted with galleries and bohemian bars. Anna's custom-made furniture graces the rooms, which feature double-glazed windows and modern bathroom fixtures. The fabulous apartments offer the convenience of kitchenettes, while the plush communal lounge makes for a wonderful spot to linger. Self check-in and nearby parking (€6) are available.

There's even a studio downstairs at number 30 where visiting artists are invited to come and paint.

Ostello degli Elefanti
HOSTEL €

(Map p184; ☑095 226 56 91; www.ostellodeglielefanti.it; Via Etnea 28; dm €19-26, d €55-70; ❈🛜) Housed in a 17th-century *palazzo* a stone's throw from the *duomo*, this clean, friendly hostel offers incredible location and value. Three dorms (one female-only) and one private room have lofty frescoed ceilings and panoramic balconies, with reading lights and curtains for every bed. The marble-floored former ballroom doubles as a lounge, while the rooftop terrace-bar offers incomparable Etna vistas.

★ Asmundo di Gisira
BOUTIQUE HOTEL €€

(Map p184; ☑095 097 88 94; www.asmundodigisira.com; Via Gisira 40; d from €125; ❈🛜) Not many B&Bs welcome you with a 3m-high pink flamingo at reception, but then this is no ordinary slumber pad. Its six 'Art Rooms' are designed by renowned Italian and international artists, each inspired by local mythological figures. The remaining five rooms find their muse in the 18th-century's Grand Tour era. All are airy, with lofty ceilings, stylish bathrooms and excellent amenities.

Quality extends to the breakfast options, while the location is equally appealing, on the edge of Catania's colourful La Pescheria market and a short walk from Piazza del Duomo.

Habitat
BOUTIQUE HOTEL €€

(Map p184; ☑095 826 67 55; www.habitatboutiquehotel.com; Via Teatro Massimo 29; r €90-150; ❈🛜) 🍃 Rooms at this 19th-century factory turned boutique hotel are sleek, with high-quality bedding, designer lighting, smart TVs and custom-made furniture in timber and steel. The open-plan room design probably makes them best for couples or singles, not so much for friends. The seasonal breakfast buffet is served in a striking communal lounge, lined floor to ceiling with jars filled with Sicilian ingredients.

Messina

B&B del Duomo
B&B €

(Map p172; ☑ 393 9934500, 090 641 32 93; www.bedandbreakfastdelduomo.it; Via I Settembre 156; s €45-60, d €60-80; ✴ 🛜) Just off Piazza del Duomo is this cheerful B&B, run by the young, charming Guendalina. Rooms are simple, clean and functional, with modular furniture and decent, modern bathrooms. In-room TVs include international Sky channels, and breakfast is served either in your room or at a neighbouring bar.

Mount Etna

Rifugio Sapienza
CHALET €

(☑ 095 91 53 21; www.rifugiosapienza.com; Piazzale Funivia; s €46-55, d €70-85; P 🛜) Offering comfortable accommodation with a good restaurant, this place adjacent to the cable car is the closest lodging to Etna's summit.

Shalai
BOUTIQUE HOTEL €€

(☑ 095 64 31 28; www.shalai.it; Via Marconi 25, Linguaglossa; d €162-200, d with frescoed ceiling €247-285; ☉ restaurant 7.30-10.30pm daily, plus 1-2.30pm Sat & Sun; P ✴ 🛜) After a day tackling Etna, retreat to this luxe spa hotel. Softly lit and in muted shades, the hotel's 13 rooms are minimalist and contemporary, with crisp white linen, flowing drapes, designer lighting and (in rooms 101 and 102) original frescoed ceilings. Then there's the stucco-adorned 19th-century lounge, the candlelit spa (for that post-trek massage), bar and fine-dining, Michelin-starred restaurant. Bliss.

★ Monaci delle Terre Nere
BOUTIQUE HOTEL €€€

(☑ 095 708 36 38; www.monacidelleterrenere.it; Via Monaci, Zafferana Etnea; d from €360; P ✴ 🛜 ♨) 🏐 This is one of Sicily's top boutique hotels, set in a winery on Mt Etna's eastern flank, halfway between Catania and Taormina. The 27 rooms and suites – spread between a main villa and outbuildings – impeccably balance rustic architectural elements with contemporary artworks, designer furniture and antiques. Bathroom amenities are

chemical-free, and the fabulous in-house restaurant serves plenty of homegrown and organic produce.

In summer, lounging by the lava-stone pool is sheer bliss. The property is open year-round, with excellent discounted rates in the cooler months.

Taormina

Hotel Condor
HOTEL €

(☑ 0942 2 31 24; www.condorhotel.com; Via Dietro Cappuccini 25; s €50-90, d €60-160; ☉ late Mar-Oct; P ✴ 🛜) Just outside the pedestrianised centre is this cordial, family-run hotel. Its 18 rooms are bright and airy with minimal decor, plain furniture and modern showers. The best have small sea-view terraces (for which you pay slightly more). A buffet breakfast is served on the panoramic rooftop terrace, and parking is available (€15).

Villa Nettuno
PENSION €

(Map p176; ☑ 0942 2 37 97; www.hotelvillanettuno.it; Via Pirandello 33; s €35-44, d €60-78; ✴ 🛜) A throwback to another era, this conveniently located salmon-pink *pensione* has been run by the Sciglio family for seven decades. Its low prices reflect a lack of recent updates, but the inviting lounge, pretty gardens (complete with olive trees and potted geraniums) and the sea views from the breakfast terrace offer a measure of charm you won't find elsewhere at this price. Breakfast costs €4.

Médousa Suites
BOUTIQUE HOTEL €€

(Map p176; ☑ 0942 38 87 38; www.medousa.it; Via Sesto Pompeo 1; junior ste €100-250, ste €150-600; ✴ 🛜) Set above a stylish garden bar-restaurant, these five high-end suites offer an on-point mix of oak panels, linen curtains, Milanese sofas and contemporary takes on Sicily's *cementine* (traditional cement floor tiles). The suites also include coffee machines, SMEG minibars, quality Parisian amenities and handy USB ports by the custom-made beds. Guests also have access to a small garden area dotted with citrus.

Isoco Guest House
GUESTHOUSE €€

(☑ 0942 2 36 79; www.isoco.it; Via Salita Branco 2; r €78-220; ☉ Mar-Nov; P ✴ @ 🛜) Each room at this welcoming, LGBT-friendly guesthouse is dedicated to an artist, from Botticelli to Keith Haring. While the older rooms are highly eclectic, the newer suites are chic and subdued, each with a modern kitchenette.

Breakfast is served around a large table, while a pair of terraces offer stunning sea views and a hot tub. Multinight or prepaid stays earn the best rates.

Hotel Villa Schuler   HOTEL €€

(Map p176; ☑0942 2 34 81; www.hotelvillaschuler. com; Via Roma, Piazzetta Bastione; d €99-200, superior rooms & ste €200-300; ☺mid-Mar–Nov; P❋@☎) ✐ Surrounded by tranquil terraced gardens, the homey 32-room Villa Schuler has been run by the same family for over a century. The retro rooms are comfortable and equipped with orthopaedic mattresses. Standard Vista Mare rooms offer stunning sea views, while the quality a-la-carte breakfast (served on a panoramic terrace) allows guests to order as many items as they please.

★Casa Turchetti   B&B €€€

(Map p176; ☑0942 62 50 13; www.casaturchetti. com; Salita dei Gracchi 18/20; d €220-260, junior ste €360, ste €470; ☺late Mar-Oct; ❋@☎) Every detail is perfect at this painstakingly restored former music school turned luxurious B&B, on a back alley near Piazza IX Aprile. Vintage furniture and fixtures (including a giant four-poster bed in the suite), handcrafted woodwork and fine homespun sheets exude a quiet elegance. Topping it off is a breathtaking rooftop terrace and the warmth of Sicilian hosts Pino and Francesca.

★Hotel Villa Belvedere   HOTEL €€€

(Map p176; ☑0942 2 37 91; www.villabelvedere.it; Via Bagnoli Croce 79; d €120-690, ste €190-890; ☺Mar-late Nov; ❋@☎☀) Built in 1902, the distinguished, supremely comfortable Villa Belvedere was one of Taormina's original grand hotels. Well positioned with fabulous views, luxuriant gardens and wonderful service, its highlights include plush, communal lounge areas and a swimming pool complete with century-old palm. Neutral hues and understated style typify the hotel's 57 rooms, with parking costing an extra €16 per day.

SYRACUSE & THE SOUTHEAST

Modica

★Masseria Quartarella   AGRITURISMO €

(☑360 654829; www.quartarella.com; Contrada Quartarella Passo Cane 1; s €40, d €75-80, tr €85-100, q €90-120; P❋☎☀) Spacious rooms, welcoming hosts and ample breakfasts make this converted farmhouse in the countryside south of Modica an appealing choice for anyone travelling by car. Owners Francesco and Francesca are generous in sharing their love and encyclopaedic knowledge of local history, flora and fauna and can suggest a multitude of driving itineraries in the surrounding area.

Palazzo Failla   HOTEL €

(☑0932 94 10 59; www.palazzofailla.it; Via Blandini 5, Modica Alta; s €55-65, d €69-125; ❋@☎) Smack in the heart of Modica Alta, this four-star, family-run hotel in a nostalgic 18th-century palace has retained much of its historical splendour, with original frescoed ceilings, hand-painted ceramic Caltagirone floor tiles, elegant drapes and heirloom antiques. Start the day with the generous breakfast buffet and end it at the hotel's well-regarded restaurant.

★Casa Gelsomino   APARTMENT €€

(☑335 8087841; www.casedisicilia.com; Via Raccomandata, Modica Bassa; per night €160-200, per week €1000-1260; ❋☎) It's easy to pretend you're a holidaying celebrity in this beautifully restored apartment, its balconies and private terrace serving up commanding views over Modica. Incorporating an airy lounge, fully equipped kitchen, stone-walled bathroom, laundry room, sitting room (with sofa bed) and separate bedroom, its combination of vaulted ceilings, antique floor tiles, original artworks and plush furnishings takes self-catering to sophisticated highs.

Casa Talía   BOUTIQUE HOTEL €€

(☑0932 75 20 75; www.casatalia.it; Via Exaudinos 1/9, Modica Bassa; s €130, d from €160, house from €300; P❋☎) Run by two Milanese architects, this urbane oasis of 10 rooms and five houses occupies a series of converted stone cottages, graced with lush gardens and town views. Rooms – each with a private terrace – are simple and detail-orientated, whether it's worn stone floors, vintage tiles, original bamboo ceilings or artisanal iron bed frames. Quality, seasonal breakfasts are served in a chic communal lounge.

Noto

Ostello Il Castello   HOSTEL €

(Map p215; ☑320 8388869; www.ostellodinoto. it; Via Fratelli Bandiera 1; dm €20, s/d €35/70; P❋☎) Directly uphill from the centre, this renovated hostel offers excellent value for money and is a great option for families or groups. There's one dorm (mixed with 18 beds), with all other rooms private and capable of accommodating up to six people. Some rooms come with a terrace, delivering commanding views over Noto's cathedral and rooftops. Wi-fi in communal areas only. Breakfast included.

★**Nòtia Rooms**   B&B €€

(Map p215; ☑ 366 5007350, 0931 83 88 91; www. notiarooms.com; Vico Frumento 6; d €130-150, tr €150-170; 🛜) In Noto's historic workers' quarter, this sophisticated B&B is owned by the gracious Giorgio and Carla, who gave up the stress of northern Italian life to open this three-room beauty. Crisp white interiors are accented with original artworks, Modernist Italian lamps and upcycled vintage finds. Rooms seduce with sublimely comfortable beds and polished modern bathrooms. Gorgeous breakfasts maintain the high standards.

★**Seven Rooms**
Villadorata   BOUTIQUE HOTEL €€€

(Map p215; ☑ 0931 83 55 75; https://7roomsvilla dorata.it; Via Cavour 53; d from €275; P🌀🛜) This elegantly appointed boutique hotel occupies a wing of the 18th-century Palazzo Nicolaci, one of Noto's most celebrated aristocratic palaces. With their restrained colour palette, rooms are tactile and sophisticated, with artfully distressed furniture, beautiful artworks, alpaca throws, Nespresso machines and luxurious bathrooms stocked with high-quality amenities; the Deluxe Rooms are especially impressive. Quality extends to the breakfast, served at a communal table.

San Carlo Suites   B&B €€€

(Map p215; ☑ 0931 83 69 65; www.sancarlo suites.com; Corso Vittorio Emanuele 127; d from €161, ste from €270; 🌀🛜) Enviably located in a mid-18th-century *palazzo* on Noto's showcase thoroughfare, this thoughtfully designed, seven-room property contrasts historic furniture, maiolica, paintings and stone arches with contemporary perks, from large showers to in-room Bialetti coffee machines. Two suites come with balconies overlooking Corso Vittorio Emanuele and the cathedral, while a third suite comes with a private roof terrace. The Sicilian-accented breakfast includes organic edibles.

Ragusa

L'Orto Sul Tetto   B&B €

(Map p234; ☑ 0932 24 77 85; www.lortosultetto. it; Via Tenente di Stefano 56, Ragusa Ibla; d €75-90; 🌀🛜) This sweet little B&B behind Ragusa's Duomo di San Giorgio offers an intimate experience, with simple, tastefully decorated rooms and a charming, leafy roof terrace where a generous breakfast is served. Service is warm and obliging.

Risveglio Ibleo   B&B €€

(Map p234; ☑ 0932 24 78 11; www.risveglioibleo. com; Largo Camerina 3; d €55-80, q €90-110; P🌀🛜) Housed in an 18th-century Liberty-style villa, this welcoming place has spacious, high-ceilinged rooms, walls hung with family portraits and a flower-flanked terrace overlooking the rooftops. The hosts go out of their way to share local culture, including their own homemade culinary delights.

Tenuta Zannafondo   B&B €

(☑ 0932 183 89 19; www.tenutazannafondo.it; Contrada di Zannafondo; d €79-89; P🌀🛜) Set amid olive-sprinkled hillsides lined with stone walls, this converted 19th-century farmstead sits halfway between Ragusa and the coast (a 15-minute drive from each). Its charm lies in the tranquil cluster of independent stone-walled cottages, each with its own little patio; two rooms in the main house are less appealing. Dinner is available on request.

Locanda Don Serafino   BOUTIQUE HOTEL €€€

(Map p234; ☑ 0932 22 00 65; www.locandadonsera fino.it; Via XI Febbraio 15, Ragusa Ibla; d from €190; 🌀@🛜) Occupying a couple of beautifully restored *palazzi* in the old town, Don Serafino sets a chic scene with its exposed limestone vaults, neutral hues and Michelin-starred restaurant, considered one of Sicily's finest. Most rooms come with rooftop and country views, while three are evocatively set in the grotto-like former stables. Service is refreshingly professional and obliging.

Scicli

★**Scicli Albergo Diffuso**   BOUTIQUE HOTEL €€

(☑ 392 8207857; www.sciclialbergodiffuso.it; Via Francesco Mormina Penna 15; r €77-177; 🌀🛜) This *albergo diffuso* (diffused hotel) offers quality accommodation in numerous locations across Scicli's historic core. Options range from simple rooms in restored *dammusi* (traditional stone abodes) to breathtaking suites in 19th-century palaces. Top of the heap are the frescoed rooms inside the 18th-century Palazzo Favacchio Patanè. Reception is on Via Francesco Mormino Penna, where a buffet breakfast is also served.

Syracuse

B&B Aretusa Vacanze
B&B €

(Map p204; ☑0931 48 34 84; www.aretusavacanze. com; Vicolo Zuccalà 1; d €59-90, tr €70-120, q €105-147; P ✳ ☎) This great, family-run budget option, elbowed into a tiny pedestrian street in a 17th-century building, has large rooms and apartments with comfortable beds, kitchenettes and satellite TV. The recently refurbished bathrooms feature spacious showers and three of the 11 rooms come with small balconies. Parking costs €15 per day.

B&B dei Viaggiatori, Viandanti e Sognatori
B&B €

(Map p204; ☑0931 2 47 81; www.bedandbreakfast sicily.it; Via Roma 156; d €55-70, tr €70-80; ✳ ☎) Enjoying a prime Ortygia location, this relaxed, TV-free B&B exudes an easy, boho vibe. It's a homely place, where books and antiques mingle with the owners' children's toys. Rooms are simple yet imaginatively decorated, and the sunny roof terrace – complete with sweeping sea views – is a fine place for breakfast-time organic bread and marmalade.

Villa dei Papiri
AGRITURISMO €

(☑0931 72 13 21; www.villadeipapiri.it; Traversa Cozzo Pantano Testa Pisima 2c; d €70-110, 2-person ste €90-135, 4-person ste €130-180; P ✳ ☎) Immersed in an Eden of orange groves and papyrus reeds 7km southwest of Syracuse, this lovely *agriturismo* sits next to the Fonte Ciana spring immortalised in Ovid's *Metamorphosis*. Eight suites are housed in a beautifully converted 19th-century farmhouse, with 16 double rooms dotted around the lush grounds. Breakfast is served in a baronial stone-walled hall.

★Hotel Gutkowski
HOTEL €€

(Map p204; ☑0931 46 58 61; www.guthotel.it; Lungomare Vittorini 26; d €90-150, tr €150, q €160; ✳ ☎) Book well in advance for one of the sea-view rooms at this stylish, eclectic hotel on the Ortygia waterfront, at the edge of the Giudecca neighbourhood. Divided between two buildings, its rooms are simple yet chic, with pretty tiled floors, walls in teals, greys, blues and browns, and a sharply curated mix of vintage and industrial details.

There's a fetching sun terrace with sea views, a cosy lounge fit for an *Architectural Digest* spread, as well as an in-house restaurant serving healthy, seasonal dishes with modern accents.

Palazzo Blanco
APARTMENT €€€

(Map p204; ☑342 7672092; www.casedisicilia. com; Via Castello Maniace; small apt per night €210-240, large apt per night €230-260; ✳ ☎) Two elegant apartments await in this *palazzo*, owned by a Milanese art collector. The larger apartment is utterly decadent, with luxurious sofas, king-size bed, dining table, precious artworks and stone, vaulted ceiling. There's a sea-view terrace and bathroom with original stonework and hydro-massage shower. The smaller apartment features floor-to-ceiling artwork and a romantic four-poster bed. Both have kitchenettes and can accommodate up to four.

Algilà Ortigia Charme Hotel
HOTEL €€€

(Map p204; ☑0931 46 51 86; www.algila.it; Via Vittorio Veneto 93; d from €220; P ✳ ☎) This sophisticated property occupies two adjacent baroque *palazzi*, the main one channelling Sicily's Arab heritage with its riad-inspired courtyard, Tunisian tiles and kilims. Although standard doubles are quite small, they're thoughtfully designed, balancing Sicilian antiques with contemporary comforts, including high-quality bedding, free mini-bar (non-alcoholic drinks only) and Bulgari amenities. Beautiful common areas include a lounge inside a 14th-century courtyard.

Henry's House
HOTEL €€€

(Map p204; ☑0931 2 13 61; www.hotelhenryshouse. com; Via del Castello Maniace 68; d €160-300, ste €260-400; ✳ ☎) This waterfront 17th-century *palazzo* was restored by an antique collector. The period lounge is fabulously aristocratic, while the homely rooms blend antiques and modern art. If money isn't an issue, book one of the two upstairs suites (one with terrace, both with water views). The hotel offers free bike use and, for those who book directly through the hotel website, complimentary minibar.

The Noto Coast

Castello Tafuri Charming Suites
BOUTIQUE HOTEL €€

(Via Tonnara 1, Portopalo di Capo Passero; d €100-300, ste €250-450; ✷Mar-Dec; P ✳ ☎ ✸) You'll be slumbering in an eclectic, early-20th-century castle at this 18-room boutique hotel, its restaurant terrace and inviting pool overlooking turquoise Ionian waters, a 17th-century *tonnara* (tuna fishery) and island fortress. Modern, neutrally hued rooms come with contemporary bathrooms and the odd heirloom antique. Sea-view rooms are predictably more expensive.

La Corte del Sole INN €€

(☑0931 82 02 10; www.lacortedelsole.it; Contrada Bucachemi, Eloro, Lido di Noto; d €100-280, q €140-375; P✳❋⑤≋) Ease that stress at La Corte del Sole, an atmospheric hotel housed in a traditional Sicilian *masseria* (working farm). Overlooking the fields of Eloro, it's a delightful place to stay, with a swimming pool and range of activities including cooking lessons (p208) run by the hotel chefs. Rooms are simple but tasteful, many with wrought-iron beds and classic wooden furniture.

CENTRAL SICILY

Caltagirone

★B&B Tre Metri
Sopra Il Cielo B&B €

(☑0933 193 51 06; www.bbtremetrisoprailcielo.it; Via Bongiovanni 72; d €60-80; ❋⑤) Just off Caltagirone's famous staircase, this fantastic B&B is run by a friendly and enthusiastic young couple. The decor varies between the six rooms but is universally tasteful and there can be few finer places to breakfast than on the spectacular balcony overlooking Caltagirone's rooftops and the hills beyond.

★Vecchia Masseria AGRITURISMO €€

(☑333 8735573, 0935 68 40 03; www.vecchiamasseria.com; SS117bis, Km 67.5, Contrada Cutuminello; d €85-140, 2-person apt €100-120, 4-person apt €115-160; P✳≋) It takes some getting to, but once you've found this *agriturismo* 18km west of Caltagirone, you won't want to leave. With elegant, soothing rooms, a highly reputed restaurant, a pair of swimming pools and outdoor spa baths overlooking the olive groves, and a long list of services, it's ideally set up as a rural hideaway. Multicourse dinners cost €28 extra.

Enna

★B&B Centro Sicilia B&B €

(Map p242; ☑393 5438428; https://bb-centro-sicilia-enna-centro.business.site; Via Pentite 6; d from €60; P⑤) Spacious rooms and suites are enlivened with ethnic design touches at this excellent family-owned and centrally located B&B. One of Enna's best breakfast spreads is enjoyed with views of Enna's rooftops and there's a compact top-storey sun terrace. If you're driving, the convenient option of the B&B's secure parking (€5 per day) is recommended. Good cafes and restaurants are nearby.

Baglio Pollicarini AGRITURISMO €

(☑0935 54 19 82; www.bagliopollicarini.it; Contrada Pollicarini; campsite per person/tent €7/9, s/d/ste €50/85/100; P✳❋⑤≋) This splendid *agriturismo* is housed in a 17th-century convent near the Lago di Pergusa. The monks' cells have long since been converted into comfortable guest rooms, but the thick stone walls, vaulted ceilings and fading frescoes leave a historical imprint. There's also a dedicated camping area and an in-house restaurant (meals from €25).

Nicosia

Baglio San Pietro AGRITURISMO €

(☑0935 64 05 29; www.bagliosanpietro.com; Contrada San Pietro; d €60-70; P⑤≋) Near the entrance to Nicosia (on the SS117 to Leonforte), this authentic *agriturismo* incorporates a working farm and offers 10 comfortable, rustic-style rooms and an excellent restaurant (p247) with authentic regional cuisine. Burn those extra restaurant-related calories on horseback (one hour/half-day €18/50) or simply kick back by the pool. Finding it by GPS can be tricky so email ahead for directions.

Piazza Armerina

★Home Hotels APARTMENT €€

(Map p248; ☑0935 68 06 51; www.homehotels.it; Via Garibaldi 26; apt daily/weekly from €95/400; ⑤) An example of the *albergo diffuso* concept growing in popularity throughout southern Italy, Home Hotels has 11 different accommodation options throughout four different buildings in the historic centre of Piazza Armerina. Most have multiple bedrooms and kitchenettes and can accommodate up to four or six people, making them a good option for families. Consistent throughout is stylish and modern decor.

★ Suite d'Autore
HOTEL €€

(Map p248; ☑0935 68 85 53; www.suitedautore.it; Via Monte 1; d €100-140; ❄️🛜) With lime-green polystyrene furniture, 19th-century frescoes and a giant circular bed floating in a floor of liquid tiles, this unique slumber number is one of Piazza Armerina's great sights. Each of its seven rooms is themed after a period in design, and everything you see – and that includes works of contemporary art – is for sale.

The owner, Ettore, is a great source of local information and a guide around the newly restored Villa Romana del Casale.

MEDITERRANEAN COAST

Agrigento

★ PortAtenea
B&B €

(Map p259; ☑349 0937492; www.portatenea.com; Via Atenea, cnr Via Cesare Battisti; s/d/tr €50/75/95; ❄️🛜) This five-room B&B wins plaudits for its panoramic roof terrace overlooking the Valley of the Temples, and its superconvenient location at the entrance to the old town, five minutes' walk from the train and bus stations. Best of all is the generous advice about Agrigento offered by hosts Sandra and Filippo (witness Filippo's amazing Google Earth tour of nearby beaches!).

Terrazze di Montelusa
B&B €

(Map p259; ☑347 7404784, 0922 59 56 90; www.terrazzedimontelusa.it; Piazza Lena 6; s/d/ste €50/75/85; ❄️🛜) Occupying a beautifully preserved *palazzo* (mansion) that's been in the same family since the 1820s, this charming B&B is filled with antique photos, original furniture and period details. As the name implies, it also boasts an inspiring collection of panoramic terraces, the most ample of which is reserved for the upstairs suite (well worth the extra €10).

Camere a Sud
B&B €

(Map p259; ☑349 6384424; www.camereasud.it; Via Ficani 6; s €40, d €50-70, tr €70-100, q €90-120; ❄️@🛜) This lovely B&B in the medieval centre has a variety of guest rooms decorated with style and taste – traditional decor and contemporary textiles are matched with bright colours and modern art. Breakfast is served on the terrace in the warmer months. Two self-contained apartments are a good option for families and groups of friends.

Valley of the Temples

★ Fattoria Mosè
AGRITURISMO €

(☑0922 60 61 15; www.fattoriamose.com; Via Pascal 4a; r per person €55, incl breakfast/half board €65/93, 2-/4-/6-person apt per week €550/850/1100; ❄️) If Agrigento's urban jungle has got you down, head for this authentic organic *agriturismo* 6km east of the Valley of the Temples. Four suites, six self-catering apartments and a pool offer ample space to relax. Guests can opt for reasonably priced dinners (€28 including wine) built around the farm's organic produce, cook for themselves or even enjoy cooking courses on site.

Foresteria Baglio della Luna
HOTEL €€

(☑0922 51 10 61; www.bagliodellaluna.com; Via Guastella 1c, Contrada Maddalusa; d €110-180, ste €205-240; ❄️🛜) This handsome converted *baglio* (manor house) has rooms that are somewhat old and tired, but the garden and the location with views over the Valley of the Temples are magnificent. The Accademia del Buon Gusto (p266), the hotel restaurant, is a romantic spot for a sunset drink or dinner. It is a little tricky to find; check the website for exact directions.

★ Villa Athena
HISTORIC HOTEL €€€

(Map p264; ☑0922 59 62 88; www.hotelvillaathena.it; Via Passeggiata Archeologica 33; d €423-577, ste €505-1165; 🅿️❄️@🛜) With the Tempio della Concordia lit up in the near distance and palm trees lending an exotic *Arabian Nights* feel, this historic five-star hotel in an aristocratic 18th-century villa offers the ultimate luxury experience. The cavernous Villa Suite, floored in antique tiles with a free-standing spa bath and a vast terrace overlooking the temples, might well be Sicily's coolest hotel room.

Caltabellotta

★ B&B Sotto Le Stelle
B&B €

(☑338 2817862, 0925 95 23 27; www.bbsottolestelle.it; Via San Paolo 35; d €79-90, ste €100; ❄️🛜) Owned by the same family that runs Caltabellotta's renowned M.A.T.E.S. restaurant, this B&B is charmingly set in a historic *palazzo* with pretty views down the hillside to the distant sea. The five colourfully decorated rooms and one suite come with vaulted ceilings, antique furniture and gorgeous tile floors, and there's a lovely terrace where breakfast is served in warm weather.

Falconara

Castello di Falconara   B&B €€
(☏091 32 90 82; www.castellodifalconara.it; SS115, Km245; d €150; ☀) For an unforgettable experience, spend the night in this gorgeous 14th-century castle, now converted to an atmospheric beachfront B&B. It sits atop a coastal promontory about 11km east of Licata.

Favara

★ Community Rooms & Wine   B&B €
(☏338 2569029; www.facebook.com/Comunity farm; Cortile Bentivegna 20; d €70-80; ☜) Located within the bohemian laneways of the Farm Cultural Park, Community Rooms & Wine's combination of stylish and spacious accommodation with a good-value restaurant downstairs (meals €20 to €25) reflects Favara's forward-thinking and contemporary outlook. Rooms feature modern bathrooms and heritage tiled floors and are enlivened with striking street art. Best of all, Farm Cultural Park's compelling ambience is just outside.

Sciacca

Fazio Bed & Breakfast   B&B €
(☏338 4186179, 0925 8 59 72; www.faziobb. com; Via Conzo 9; s €50, d €60-85; ☀☜) With all the amenities of a boutique hotel, this classy B&B on the western edge of Sciacca's historic centre is run by friendly father-son team Vincenzo and Aldo. Catering equally to business travellers and casual tourists, it offers spacious, comfortable rooms with good lighting, modern bathrooms, air-con and dependable wi-fi. Don't miss the pistachio cream-filled *cornetti* (croissants) at breakfast time!

★ Domus Maris Relais   BOUTIQUE HOTEL €€
(Map p270; ☏0925 57 52 42; http://domusmaris. it; Corso Vittorio Emanuele 113; d/ste from €70/170; ☜) Enjoying a prime hilltop location with excellent views over Sciacca's fishing port, Domus Maris Relais showcases a relaxed combination of elegance and style. Rooms and suites feature names inspired by Greek mythology. The Scirocco suite is particularly spacious and it's definitely worth paying a little extra for a room with a balcony and ocean views. Bathrooms are modern and extremely comfortable.

Understand
Sicily

Sicily Today

Two decades into the 21st century, Sicily continues to grapple with some age-old challenges, including high unemployment, corruption, rural depopulation and environmental degradation. Two other hot topics of the moment – both reflective of Sicily's long tradition of receiving outsiders – are immigration and tourism. Travellers (both Italian and foreign) seeking Sicily's cultural riches have been arriving in increasing numbers even as Italy's national government tightens restrictions on the flow of refugees to the island.

Best on Film

Stromboli, Terra di Dio (Stromboli, Land of God, 1950) Bergman and Rossellini's explosive tale of romance, with Stromboli's volcanic fireworks as a backdrop.

Nuovo Cinema Paradiso (Cinema Paradiso, 1988) Semi-autobiographical tale of small-town life from Sicilian director Giuseppe Tornatore.

Il Postino (The Postman, 1994) On the gorgeous island of Salina, Pablo Neruda philosophises with a humble Sicilian postman.

Best in Print

The Leopard (Giuseppe Tomasi di Lampedusa; 1958) Sicily's greatest novel, examining the Risorgimento's impact on 19th-century Sicilian culture through the eyes of an ageing aristocrat.

Tears of Salt: A Doctor's Story (Pietro Bartolo & Lidia Tilotta; 2017) Tales from the front lines of Sicily's refugee crisis, told by the long-time director of Lampedusa's only medical clinic.

Sicilian Splendors: Discovering the Secret Places That Speak to the Heart (John Keahey; 2018) Engaging Sicilian travelogue, touching on many aspects of the island's culture and history, by a veteran American journalist.

Immigration Through a Sicilian Lens

With the right-wing Lega Nord's recent ascendance to national power, immigration is a hot topic throughout Italy these days – but nowhere in the country do immigration issues more directly impact daily life than in Sicily. As one of Europe's southernmost gateways, Sicily has always seen a disproportionate share of migrants. The region's long history with immigration, emigration and multiculturalism gives the issue a more nuanced treatment here than in the north, and the prevailing mindset tends to be open to newcomers and those in need.

As Italy has taken an increasingly hard line towards immigrants – shutting down migrant reception centres and stipulating fines of up to €50,000 for NGO rescue boats bringing migrants to Italy without permission – key Sicilian politicians such as Palermo mayor Leoluca Orlando, Sicilian Regional Assembly president Gianfranco Miccichè and Lampedusa mayor Salvatore Martello have vocally defended immigrant rights. Sicilian demonstrators have repeatedly taken to the streets to show their support for a continued 'open door' policy, and many everyday Sicilian citizens have opened their homes to refugees.

Immigration's real-world impact has played out most visibly in places like Palermo, where migrants have arrived in especially large numbers. The city's famous Ballarò market now sports a fascinating mix of Sicilian, Asian and African produce, and lively Via Maqueda is packed with Bangladeshi-owned shops. Even with Sicily's more open mindset, tensions between the newcomers and some old-time Palermitans persist, and despite the largely peaceful integration of immigrants into the community, concerns have arisen about a troubling alliance between a coterie of immigrant gang members and the local Mafia.

Palermo Renaissance

Still glowing from its role as the 2018 Italian Capital of Culture, the long-troubled Sicilian capital continues to improve, with more of the historic centre pedestrianised, a plethora of up-and-coming businesses and cultural venues, and a sense of vibrancy unimaginable 10 years ago.

Since 2017, large swathes of the city centre have been placed off-limits to motorised traffic, including multi-block sections of main arteries Via Vittorio Emanuele and Via Maqueda. Recent studies show that this increased pedestrianisation has been a boon not only to quality of life but also to the local economy, as new businesses move in to take advantage of increased foot traffic.

Benches and flower pots fill spaces where motorbikes once zipped freely about, street musicians play to crowds at the city's central Quattro Canti intersection, and impressive new street art projects have sprung up around the city, for example the Pangrel Murals in La Kalsa, which have turned a row of dull apartment buildings into a veritable alfresco gallery.

Economic Stress & the Double-Edged Sword of Tourism

For all these positive signs in the capital, Sicily continues to face economic challenges. An April 2019 study revealed that even with a shrinking population, Italy's youth unemployment figure has climbed to a staggering 53.6%. Travelling around Sicily, it's hard to ignore signs of economic stress, from crumbling infrastructure to the gradual depopulation of many rural areas.

Some interior towns have been tempted to revive their economies by rolling out the red carpet to outside investors. In 2019, following in the footsteps of the hill town of Gangi, the village of Sambuca held an auction of abandoned homes with initial asking prices as low as €1, with buyers coming from as far afield as Chile.

In general, tourism has seen a recent boom in Sicily. In 2018 Club Med opened an exclusive 'five-trident' resort in Cefalù – its first in Europe. Meanwhile, over Easter week 2019, Palermo logged more visitors than Venice, competing with venerable cities such as Florence and Rome for the title of Italy's top weekend getaway. Many welcome the influx as an economic shot in the arm, but the downsides are also apparent. There's an urgent need to control development in some areas; witness the ugly concrete structures recently built on Favignana's Lido Burrone, previously celebrated as western Sicily's loveliest beach.

Elsewhere, the influx of outsiders has created other challenges. In the Val di Noto, wealthy northern Italians and foreigners have been buying up property from Syracuse to Scicli, restoring buildings and moving in. While this stimulates the economy, some argue that places like Ortygia now risk losing their authentic historical identity and turning into tourist traps.

AREA: **25,832 SQ KM**

GDP: **€87.6 BILLION**

LANGUAGE SPOKEN:
ITALIAN

POPULATION: **5.03 MILLION**

if Sicily were 100 people

96 would be Italian
4 would be foreign citizens

occupation
(% of population)

19   17   11

tourism and commerce   industry   fishing and agriculture

12   6   35

financial and professional services   transport and communications   other

population per sq km

SICILY   ITALY   UK

≈ 195 people

History

Over the millennia, Sicily's strategic position in the middle of the Mediterranean has lured culture after culture to its shores, resulting in one of Europe's richest and most remarkable histories. Disputed for centuries by a steady parade of ancient peoples including the Greeks, Carthaginians and Romans, the island saw subsequent rule by invading forces of Byzantines, Saracens, Normans, Germans, Angevins, Spanish and others before finally claiming its pivotal role within a unified Italy in the early 1860s.

Early Settlement

The first evidence of an organised settlement on Sicily belongs to the Stentinellians, who settled on the island's eastern shores sometime between 5000 and 4500 BC. But it was the settlers from the middle of the second millennium BC who radically defined the island's character and whose early presence helps us understand Sicily's complexities. Thucydides (c 460–404 BC) records three major tribes: the Elymians, of unknown origin, who settled Sicily's northwestern corner; the Sicanians, who originated either in Spain or North Africa and settled a central swathe of the island stretching from the Tyrrhenian Coast south to the Mediterranean Coast; and the Siculians (or Sikels), who came from the Calabrian peninsula and spread out along the Ionian Coast.

Best Prehistoric Sites

....

Necropoli di Pantalica (near Syracuse)

....

Capo Graziano (Filicudi, Aeolian Islands)

....

Punta Milazzese (Panarea, Aeolian Islands)

Greeks & Phoenicians

The acquisition of Sicily was an obvious step for the ever-expanding Greek city-states. The Chalcidians landed on Sicily's Ionian Coast in 735 BC and founded a small settlement at Naxos. They were followed a year later by the Corinthians, who built their colony on the southeastern island of Ortygia, calling it Syracoussai (Syracuse). The Chalcidians went further south from their own fort and founded a second town called Katane (Catania) in 729 BC, and the two carried on stitching towns and settlements together until three-quarters of the island was in Hellenic hands.

The growing Greek power in the south and east created tensions with the Phoenicians, who had settled on the western side of the island

TIMELINE	5000–4000 BC	735–580 BC	480 BC
	Settlers found small colonies at Stentinello and Lipari. They begin the lucrative business of trading obsidian.	Greek cities are founded at Naxos in 735 BC, Syracuse in 734 BC, Catania in 729 BC, Megara Hyblaea in 728 BC, Gela in 689 BC, Selinunte and Messina in 628 BC and Agrigento in 581 BC.	Commanding a vast army of mercenaries, the Carthaginian general Hamilcar seeks to wrest control of Himera from the Greeks, but is soundly defeated by the Greek tyrant Gelon.

around 850 BC; in turn, the Phoenicians' alliance with the powerful city-state of Carthage (in modern-day Tunisia) was of serious concern to the Greeks. By 480 BC the Carthaginians were mustering a huge invading force of some 300,000 mercenaries. Commanded by one of their great generals, Hamilcar, the force landed on Sicily and besieged Himera (near Termini Imerese), but the vast army was defeated by the crafty Greek tyrant Gelon, whose troops breached Hamilcar's lines by pretending to be Carthaginian reinforcements.

A period of peace followed in Sicily. The Greek colonies had lucrative trade deals thanks to the island's rich resources, and the remains of their cities testify to their wealth and sophistication.

With the advent of the Peloponnesian Wars, Syracuse decided to challenge the hegemony of mainland Greece. Athens, infuriated by the Sicilian 'upstart', decided to attack Syracuse in 415 BC, mounting the 'Great Expedition' – the largest fleet ever assembled. Despite the fleet's size and Athens' confidence, Syracuse fought back and the mainland Greek army suffered a humiliating defeat.

Though Syracuse was celebrating its victory, the rest of Sicily was in a constant state of civil war. This provided the perfect opportunity for Carthage to seek its revenge for Himera, and in 409 BC a new army led by Hamilcar's bitter but brilliant nephew Hannibal wreaked havoc in the Sicilian countryside, completely destroying Selinunte, Himera, Agrigento and Gela. The Syracusans were eventually forced to surrender everything except the city of Syracuse itself to Carthage.

Roman Oppression & the Siege of Syracuse

The First Punic War (264–241 BC) saw Rome challenge Carthage for possession of Sicily, and at the end of the war the victorious Romans claimed the island as their first province outside the Italian mainland. Under the Romans, the majority of Sicilians lived in horrifyingly reduced circumstances; native inhabitants were refused the right to citizenship and forced into indentured slavery on *latifondi* – huge landed estates that were to cause so many of the island's woes in later years. Not surprisingly, Rome's less-than-enlightened rule led to two (unsuccessful) revolts by slaves in Sicily: the First Servile War (135–132 BC) and the Second Servile War (104–101 BC).

While the sweetness of victory extended to the First Punic War against the Carthaginians, the Romans would soon suffer a gatecrasher in the form of Hannibal. Breaking into Italy via the Alps, the mighty Carthaginian military commander would lead a number of victories against the Romans, including at the Battle of Cannae (216 BC) in modern-day

Some of Sicily's earliest population centres grew up around Lipari, in the Aeolian Islands. Thanks to Lipari's volcanic origins, it was a prime source of obsidian, valued by pre–Bronze Age peoples as an ideal material for making cutting tools. Obsidian mined in Lipari has been found throughout the Mediterranean.

HISTORY ROMAN OPPRESSION & THE SIEGE OF SYRACUSE

415 BC	409 BC	241 BC	214–212 BC
An emboldened Syracuse seeks to assert its independence from Greece, provoking a massive backlash from Athens. The Great Expedition, an Athenian fleet of unprecedented size, is defeated by Syracusan troops.	Hannibal's army wreaks havoc on Selinunte, Agrigento, Himera and Gela, forcing the Syracusans to surrender their western Sicilian territories to Carthage and retreat to Syracuse.	Sandwiched between the superpowers of Carthage and Rome, Sicily becomes the battleground for the First Punic War, whose outcome is to place it firmly within the Roman Empire.	Ingenious defensive weapons developed by Greek mathematician, philosopher and engineer Archimedes keep Syracuse safe from invading Roman forces for two years. Among these weapons is a boat-capsizing crane.

Sunken ships litter the seafloor around Sicily. Discoveries from these shipwrecks are displayed at museums throughout the region. Three of the most extraordinary are the remains of a Carthaginian warship in Marsala, the statue of a dancing satyr in Mazara del Vallo and the collectión of ancient amphorae in Lipari.

Best Classical Sites

....

Valley of the Temples (Agrigento)

....

Selinunte

....

Segesta

....

Parco Archeologico della Neapolis (Syracuse)

....

Teatro Greco (Taormina)

Puglia. Hannibal's gains soon led many in Sicily to question whether their allegiance to Rome was sensible. Among these doubters was teen tyrant Hieronymos (231–214 BC), who became king of Syracuse in 215 BC aged 15. While some Syracusans supported Hieronymos' courting of the Carthaginians, others did not, and the king's assassination in 214 BC sparked a civil war between the city's pro-Roman and pro-Carthaginian factions. Rome, determined to maintain control of the Mediterranean, was hardly impressed by the pro-Carthaginians' victory in Syracuse, dispatching esteemed Roman General Marcus Claudius Marcellus (268–208 BC) to gain control of the city. Little did they know what a long and arduous task it would be.

The source of their frustration was Greek Syracusan Archimedes (c 287–212/211 BC), considered the most brilliant mathematician and inventor in ancient Greece. Before Hieronymos' rise to power, his predecessor and grandfather Hiero II (died c 216/215 BC) had assigned Archimedes the task of developing weapons to defend Syracuse. Archimedes did not fail, creating a series of ingenious war machines. Among these were catapults capable of hurling objects weighing in excess of 300kg and the extraordinary Claw of Archimedes, a giant wooden crane attached to a grappling hook. Dangling over the city walls of Ortygia (Syracuse's historic centre), the crane would reach down and grab the Roman galleys by the prow, lifting them out of the water and causing them to capsize or sink. While many modern historians doubt it ever existed, legend persists that Archimedes even created a death ray. The invention reputedly used copper or bronze shields to reflect the sun's rays onto approaching Roman vessels, causing the wooden ships to catch fire.

Archimedes' clever contraptions managed to keep the Romans out of the city for two years, until lax defences during a festival in honour of Artemis allowed a small group of Roman soldiers to scale Ortygia's walls and enter the outer city in 212 BC and, eventually, take control of the town. Despite the humiliation that Archimedes' war machines had inflicted on the Romans, Marcus Claudius Marcellus could not help but admire Archimedes and his technical brilliance, so much so that he ordered his men not to harm the mathematician. Alas, it was too honourable an order for one Roman soldier, whose sword cut short Archimedes' life.

Vandals, Byzantines & Saracens

After Rome fell to the Visigoths in AD 470, Sicily was occupied by Vandals from North Africa, but their tenure was relatively brief. In 535 the Byzantine general Belisarius landed an army and was welcomed by a population that, despite over 700 years of Roman occupation, was still largely Greek, both in language and custom. The Byzantines were eager to use Sicily as a launching pad for the retaking of lands owned by the

241 BC–AD 470	535	827–965	1059–72
As Rome's first colony, Sicily suffers the worst of Roman rule: native inhabitants are refused the right of citizenship and forced into indentured slavery.	Keen to use the island as a launching pad for retaking Saracen lands, the Byzantines conquer Sicily; Syracuse temporarily becomes the empire's capital in 663.	The Saracens land at Mazara del Vallo in 827. Sicily is united under Arab rule and Palermo is the second-largest city in the world after Constantinople.	The Norman conquistador Robert Guiscard vows to expel the Saracens from Sicily. With the help of his younger brother, Roger I, he seizes Palermo in 1072.

combined forces of Arabs, Berbers and Spanish Muslims (collectively known as the Saracens), but their dreams were not to be realised.

In 827 the Saracen army landed at Mazara del Vallo. Palermo fell in 831, followed by Syracuse in 878. Under the Arabs, churches were converted to mosques and Arabic was made the common language. At the same time, much-needed land reforms were introduced and trade, agriculture and mining were fostered. New crops were introduced, including citrus trees, date palms and sugar cane, and a system of water supply and irrigation was developed. Palermo became the capital of the new emirate and, over the next 200 years, it became one of the most splendid cities in the Arab world, a haven of culture and commerce rivalled only by Córdoba in Spain.

The Kingdom of the Sun

The Arabs called the Normans 'wolves' because of their barbarous ferocity and the terrifying speed with which they were mopping up territory in mainland Italy. In 1053, after six years of mercenary activity, Robert Guiscard (c 1015–85) of the Norman de Hauteville family joined his brothers in comprehensively defeating the combined forces of the Calabrian Byzantines, the Lombards and the papal forces at the Battle of Civitate.

Having established his supremacy, Robert turned his attentions to expanding the territories under his control. To achieve this, he had to deal

HISTORY THE KINGDOM OF THE SUN

UNCONVENTIONAL HISTORY MUSEUMS

Mixed in with all of Sicily's fabulous archaeological museums and ancient sites are a couple of off-the-beaten-track treasures that shine a light on the island's more recent history.

Palermo's Museo dell'Inquisizione sheds light on the history and impact of the Inquisition on Sicily. Housed in the historic prisons of Palermo's Palazzo Chiaromonte Steri, its series of cells are adorned with the revealing graffiti and artwork of both prisoners and prison staff. Guided tours (in Italian and English) provide fascinating historical context.

CIDMA, south of Palermo in Corleone, brings you face-to-face with the sordid history of the Sicilian Mafia, as well as the powerful resistance movement that's sprung up on the island in recent years. Photos graphically document the Mafia's historical power over Sicilian society, while bilingual tour guides are actively engaged in the museum's anti-Mafia mission.

Southwest of Ragusa, the Castello di Donnafugata houses the Collezione Gabriele Arezzo di Trifiletti, a highly esteemed cache of Sicilian costumes and fashions from the 16th to 20th centuries. Focused mainly on the 1700s and 1800s, it offers a fascinating look at Sicilian style and society through the ages. Rare treasures include mid-18th-century liveries worn by the servants of aristocratic families.

1072–1101	1130–1154	1145	1154-91
Sicily's brightest period in history ensues under Roger I, with a cosmopolitan and multicultural court. Many significant palaces and churches are built during this time.	Roger II builds one of the most efficient civil services in Europe. His court is responsible for the creation of the first written legal code in Sicilian history.	El Idrisi's planisphere (a large, silver global map) – an important medieval geographical work that accurately maps Europe, North Africa and western Asia – is completed for Roger II.	William I inherits the kingdom, triggering a power struggle between church and throne. Walter of the Mill is appointed Palermo's archbishop. The great cathedrals of Monreale and Palermo are built.

with the Vatican. In return for being invested with the titles of duke of Puglia and Calabria in 1059, Robert agreed to chase the Saracens out of Sicily and restore Christianity to the island. He delegated this task – and promised the island – to his younger brother Roger I (1031–1101), who landed his troops at Messina in 1061, capturing the port by surprise. In 1064 the brothers tried to take Palermo but were repulsed by a well-organised Saracen army; it wasn't until 1072, when they mounted a second attack with substantial reinforcements, that the city fell into Norman hands.

Impressed by the island's cultured Arab lifestyle, Roger borrowed from and improved on it, spending vast amounts of money on palaces and churches and encouraging a cosmopolitan atmosphere in his court. He also wisely opted for a policy of reconciliation with the indigenous people; Arabic and Greek continued to be spoken along with French, and Arab engineers, bureaucrats and architects continued to be employed by the court. He was succeeded by his widow, Adelasia (Adelaide), who ruled until 1130 when Roger II (1095–1154) was crowned king.

Roger II was a keen intellectual whose court was unrivalled for its exotic splendour and learning. His rule was remarkable for his patronage of the arts, and also for his achievement in building an efficient and multicultural civil service that was the envy of Europe. He also enlarged the kingdom to include Malta, most of southern Italy and even parts of North Africa.

The Setting Sun

Roger's son and successor, William I (1108–66), inherited the kingdom upon his father's death in 1154. Nicknamed 'William the Bad', he was a vain and corrupt ruler.

The appointment of Walter of the Mill (Gualtiero Offamiglio) as archbishop of Palermo at the connivance of the pope was to create a dangerous power struggle between church and throne for the next 20 years – a challenge that was taken up by William II (1152–89) when he ordered the creation of a second archbishopric at Monreale.

William II's premature death at the age of 36 led to a power tussle, and an assembly of barons elected Roger II's illegitimate grandson Tancred (c 1130–94) to the throne. His accession was immediately contested by the German (or Swabian) king Henry VI (1165–97), head of the House of Hohenstaufen, who laid claim to the throne by virtue of his marriage to Roger II's daughter, Constance.

Tancred died in 1194, and no sooner had his young son, William III, been installed as king than the Hohenstaufen fleet docked in Messina. On Christmas Day of that year Henry VI declared himself king and

1198–1250	1266–82	1282	1487
Under Frederick I, Palermo is considered Europe's most important city and Sicily is a key player in Europe. But Frederick imposes heavy taxes and restrictions on free trade.	Charles of Anjou is crowned king in 1266, leading to a brief and unpopular period of French rule, characterised by high taxes and transfer of land ownership to the Angevin aristocracy.	The Sicilian Vespers, a violent uprising in Palermo, sparks countrywide revolt against the Angevin troops. Peter of Aragon rushes in to fill the vacuum, initiating 500 years of Spanish rule.	The end of religious tolerance is cemented by the expulsion of Jews from all Spanish territories. The Spanish Inquisition terrorises Sicily with nearly three centuries of imprisonment, torture and killings.

young William was imprisoned shortly thereafter, eventually dying in captivity (c 1198).

Wonder of the World

Henry paid scant attention to his Sicilian kingdom and died of malaria in 1197. He was succeeded by his young heir Frederick (1194–1250), known as both Frederick I of Sicily and Frederick II of Hohenstaufen.

Frederick was a keen intellectual with a penchant for political manoeuvring, but he was also a totalitarian despot who fortified the eastern seaboard from Messina to Syracuse and sacked rebellious Catania in 1232. Under his rule, Sicily became a centralised state playing a key commercial and cultural role in European affairs, and Palermo gained a reputation as the continent's most important city. In the latter years of his reign Frederick became known as Stupor Mundi, 'Wonder of the World', in recognition of his successful rule.

When Frederick died in 1250, he was succeeded by his son Conrad IV of Germany (1228–54), but the island was initially ruled by Frederick's younger and illegitimate son, Manfred (1232–66). Conrad arrived in Sicily in 1252 to take control but died of malaria after only two years. Manfred again took the reins, first as regent to Conrad's infant son Conradin and then, after forging an alliance with the Saracens, in his own right in 1258.

Sicilian Vespers, Spanish Inquisition

In 1266 the Angevin army, led by Charles of Anjou, brother of the French King Louis IX, defeated and killed Manfred at Benevento on the Italian mainland. Two years later Manfred's 15-year-old nephew and heir, Conradin, was defeated at Tagliacozzo, captured by the Angevins and publicly beheaded in Naples.

After such a bloody start, the Angevins were hated and feared. Sicily was weighed down by onerous taxes, religious persecution was the order of the day and Norman fiefdoms were removed and awarded to French aristocrats.

On Easter Monday 1282 the city of Palermo exploded in rebellion. Incited by the alleged rape of a local girl by a gang of French troops, peasants lynched every French soldier they could get their hands on. The revolt spread to the countryside and was supported by the barons, who had formed an alliance with Peter of Aragon, who landed at Trapani with a large army and was proclaimed king. For the next 20 years the Aragonese and the Angevins were engaged in the War of the Sicilian Vespers – a war that was eventually won by the Spanish.

Alas, Sicily's prospects did not improve under Spanish rule. By the end of the 14th century the island had been thoroughly marginalised. The

1669	1693	1799–1815	1820–48
The worst eruption in Etna's recorded history levels Catania and other Ionian Coast towns. It's preceded by a three-day earthquake. The eruption lasts four months, flooding the city with rivers of lava.	A devastating earthquake and associated tsunami destroy dozens of communities in southeastern Sicily, leading to the eventual reconstruction of Noto, Ragusa, Modica and several other cities in baroque style.	Napoleon takes control of Naples, leading to a weakening of Bourbon powers and the drafting of an 1812 constitution that establishes a two-chamber parliament and abolishes feudal privileges.	The first uprising against the Bourbons occurs in Palermo. It is followed by others in Syracuse in 1837 and again in Palermo in 1848.

eastern Mediterranean was sealed off by the Ottoman Turks, while the Italian mainland was off-limits on account of Sicily's political ties with Spain. As a result the Renaissance passed the island by, reinforcing the oppressive effects of poverty and ignorance. Even Spain lost interest in its colony, choosing to rule through viceroys.

By the end of the 15th century, the viceroy's court was a den of corruption, and the most influential body on the island became the Catholic Church (whose archbishops and bishops were mostly Spaniards). The church exercised draconian powers through a network of Holy Office tribunals, otherwise known as the Inquisition.

The Wrath of Nature

Punishment of the geological kind hit the island in March 1669, when a fissure on Mt Etna's southern slopes erupted with unprecedented force. Lasting four months and releasing 800 million cubic metres of lava, the eruption would go down as the volcano's most violent in recorded history. The lava submerged a dozen towns in the area, prompting 50 valiant Catanians to dig a trench to reroute the molten rock and save Catania. Reroute it they did, right in the direction of Paternò, a move that sparked clashes between the towns and saw the breach refilled.

Despite the renewed threat, few Catanians fled their hometown, putting their faith instead in the city's ancient defence walls. Alas, the lava proved too much in the end, with part of the wall collapsing and lava entering Catania from the west. Solidified lava is still visible at the Monastero degli Benedettini l'Arena. Thankfully, the hasty erection of walls across city streets managed to halt the flow of lava further into the city centre. By the time Etna had called it a day in mid-July, an estimated 15,000 to 20,000 people had lost their lives in the region and Catania's topography had been dramatically and permanently altered. A case in point is the landlocked Castello Ursino, which originally stood by the sea.

Mother Nature delivered an even crueller blow in January 1693 when two earthquakes shook the Val di Noto in Sicily's southeast. The first – striking on 9 January and measuring an estimated 6.2 on the Richter scale – was a mere precursor to an estimated 7.4 quake two days later. Damaged buildings that had not collapsed in the first tremor toppled like sandcastles in the second. The quake also triggered a tsunami along Sicily's Ionian Coast. Over 60,000 people lost their lives, including two-thirds of Catania's population, and over 45 cities, towns and villages were damaged or completely destroyed.

Yet out of the tragedy came a unique opportunity for the day's great architects – among them Rosario Gagliardi, Andrea Palma and Giovanni Battista Vaccarini – to rebuild the area in an exuberant style that would become the very pinnacle of Sicilian baroque. While Syracuse's historical

1860–61	1860–94	1908	1922–43
Garibaldi lands in Marsala and defeats the Bourbon army, taking Palermo two weeks later. King Victor Emmanuel II becomes the first king of a unified Italy on 17 March 1861.	The emergence of the *mafiosi* (Mafia) fills the vacuum between the people and the state. The need for social reform strengthens the growing trade union, the *fasci*.	A powerful earthquake measuring 7.1 on the Richter scale jolts Messina and southern Calabria on 28 December. The tremor and subsequent tsunami reduce Messina to rubble. Over 80,000 people lose their lives.	Benito Mussolini brings fascism and almost succeeds in stamping out the Mafia. He drags Sicily into WWII by colonising Libya. Sicily suffers greatly from Allied bombing.

core was rebuilt based on the existing town plan, Catania opted to super-impose a completely new plan as part of reconstruction. Other places, such as Noto, were rebuilt in a completely new location. All delivered an abundance of new architectural wonders, including the show-stopping cathedral squares in Catania and Syracuse, the Chiesa di San Giorgio in Modica and the Cattedrale di San Giorgio in Ragusa, not to mention the extraordinary cast of *palazzi* (mansions) and churches flanking Noto's main thoroughfare, Corso Vittorio Emanuele.

Exit Feudalism, Enter Risorgimento

Back on the political front, the weight of state oppression drove ordinary Sicilians to demand reform. But Spanish monarchs were preoccupied by the wars of the Spanish succession and Sicily was subsequently passed around from European power to European power like an unwanted Christmas present. Eventually the Spanish reclaimed the island in 1734, this time under the Bourbon king Charles I of Sicily (1734–59). Under the reign of Charles I's successor, Ferdinand IV, the landed gentry vetoed any attempts at liberalisation. Large exports of grain continued to enrich the aristocracy while normal Sicilians died of starvation.

Although Napoleon never occupied Sicily, the French capture of Naples in 1799 forced Ferdinand to move to Sicily. The Bourbon king's ridiculous tax demands were soon met with open revolt by the peasantry and the more far-sighted nobles, who believed that the only way to maintain the status quo was to usher in limited reforms. After strong pressure, Ferdinand reluctantly agreed in 1812 to the drawing up of a constitution whereby a two-chamber parliament was formed and feudal privileges were abolished.

With the final defeat of Napoleon in 1815, Ferdinand once again united Naples and Sicily as the 'Kingdom of the Two Sicilies', taking the title Ferdinand I. For the next 12 years the island was divided between a minority who sought an independent Sicily, and a majority who believed that the island's survival could only be assured as part of a unified Italy, an ideal being promoted on the mainland as part of the political and social movement known as the Risorgimento (reunification period).

On 4 April 1860 the revolutionary committees of Palermo gave orders for a revolt against the tottering Bourbon state. The news reached Giuseppe Garibaldi, who decided this was the moment to begin his campaign for the unification of Italy. He landed in Marsala on 11 May 1860 with about 1000 soldiers – the famous *mille* – and defeated a Bourbon army of 15,000 at Calatafimi on 15 May, taking Palermo two weeks later.

Despite his revolutionary fervour, Garibaldi was not a reformer in the social sense, and his soldiers blocked every attempt at a land grab on the part of the ordinary worker. On 21 October a referendum was held that

Sicilian History in Print

Sicily: A Short History, from the Greeks to Cosa Nostra – John Julius Norwich

The Leopard – Giuseppe Tomasi di Lampedusa

Seeking Sicily – John Keahey

HISTORY EXIT FEUDALISM, ENTER RISORGIMENTO

1943–44	1950	1951–75	1969
The Mafia collaborates with the Allied forces, assisting in the capture of the island. Sicily is taken in 39 days. Mafia Don Calogero Vizzini is appointed as the island's administrator.	The *Cassa per il Mezzogiorno* is established to help fund public works and infrastructure in southern Italy. Poor management and corruption sees at least one-third of the money squandered.	Sicily's petrochemical, citrus and fishing industries collapse, leading to widespread unemployment. One million Sicilians emigrate to northern Europe.	Caravaggio's painting *The Nativity with St Francis and St Lawrence* is stolen from the Oratorio di San Lorenzo in Palermo. The theft remains one of the FBI's top 10 unsolved art crimes.

saw a staggering 99% of eligible Sicilian voters opt for unification with the Piedmontese House of Savoy, which controlled most of Northern and Central Italy. Its head, King Victor Emmanuel II, aspired to rule a united Italy and had supported Garibaldi's expedition to Sicily. He was to become the first king of a unified Italy on 17 March 1861.

Fascism, Conservatism & WWII

Sicily struggled to adapt to the Savoys. The old aristocracy by and large maintained their privileges, and hopes of social reform soon dwindled.

What the island really needed was a far-reaching policy of agrarian reform, including a redistribution of land. The partial break-up of large estates after the abolition of feudalism still only benefited the *gabellotti* (agricultural middlemen who policed the peasants on behalf of the aristocracy), who leased the land from the owners only to then charge prohibitive ground rents to the peasants who lived and worked on it.

To assist them with their rent collections the bailiffs enlisted the help of local gangs, who acted as intermediaries between the tenant and the owner, sorting out disputes and regulating affairs in the absence of an effective judicial system. These individuals were called *mafiosi* and were organised into small territorial gangs drawn up along family lines. They effectively filled the vacuum that existed between the people and the state, slotting into the role of local power brokers.

In 1922 Benito Mussolini took power in Rome. With the growing influence of the Mafia dons threatening his dominance in Sicily, Mussolini dispatched Cesare Mori to Palermo with orders to crush lawlessness and insurrection in Sicily. Mori did this by ordering the round-up of individuals suspected of involvement in 'illegal organisations'.

By the 1930s Mussolini had bigger fish to fry – his sights were set on the colonisation of Libya as Italy's Fourth Shore, ultimately dragging Sicily into WWII. Chosen as the springboard for the recapture of mainland Italy, Sicily suffered greatly from heavy Allied bombing. Ironically, the war presented the Mafia with the perfect opportunity to get back at Mussolini and it collaborated with the Allied forces, assisting in the capture of the island in 1943.

Postwar Woes & Mani Pulite

The most powerful force in Sicilian politics in the latter half of the 20th century was the Democrazia Cristiana (DC; Christian Democrats), a centre-right Catholic party that appealed to the island's traditional conservatism. Allied closely with the Church, the DC promised wide-ranging reforms while at the same time demanding vigilance against godless communism. It was greatly aided in its efforts by the Mafia, which ensured that the local DC mayor would always top the poll. The Mafia's

Italy's *Mani pulite* (Clean Hands) political scandal became the eponym for an artwork by Geneva-based artist Gianni Motti in 2005. The work, a simple bar of soap, was reputedly made with the body fat of then Italian prime minister Silvio Berlusconi. Motti purchased the fat from a liposuction clinic.

1988	1992	1995–99	2006
Sicilian film director Giuseppe Tornatore releases *Cinema Paradiso*. Shot in Sicilian locations including Bagheria and Cefalù, the film goes on to win Best Foreign Language Film at the 1989 Academy Awards.	Sicilian anti-Mafia magistrates Giovanni Falcone and Paolo Borsellino are murdered within two months of each other. Their deaths provoke widespread outrage and strengthen popular resistance to the Mafia.	Giulio Andreotti, the former Italian prime minister, is charged with Mafia association and goes on trial. He is acquitted due to lack of evidence in 1999.	The Sicilian Godfather, Bernardo Provenzano, is arrested after 40 years on the run. His arrest marks an important milestone in the fight against the Mafia.

reward was *clientelismo* (political patronage) that ensured it was granted favourable contracts.

This constant interference by the Mafia in the island's economy did much to nullify the efforts of Rome to reduce the gap between the prosperous north and the poor south. The well-intentioned Cassa del Mezzogiorno (Southern Italy Development Fund), set up in 1950, was aimed at kick-starting the pitiful economy of the south, and Sicily was one of its main beneficiaries, receiving state and European Communities (EC) money for all kinds of projects. However, the disappearance of large amounts of cash eventually led the central government to scrap the fund in 1992, leaving the island to fend for itself.

In the same year, the huge Tangentopoli (Bribesville) scandal (the institutionalisation of kickbacks and bribes, which had been the country's *modus operandi* since WWII) made headline news. Although it was largely focused on the industrial north of Italy, the repercussions of the widespread investigation into graft (known as *Mani pulite*, or Clean Hands) were inevitably felt in Sicily, a region where politics, business and the Mafia were long-time bedfellows. The scandal eventually brought about the demise of the DC party.

In the meantime, things were changing in regard to how the Sicilians viewed the Mafia, thanks to the investigating magistrates Paolo Borsellino and Giovanni Falcone. They contributed greatly to turning the climate of opinion against the Mafia on both sides of the Atlantic, and made it possible for ordinary Sicilians to speak about and against the Mafia more freely. When the magistrates were tragically murdered in the summer of 1992, it was a great loss for Italy and Sicily, but it was these deaths that finally broke the Mafia's code of *omertà* (silence), which had ruled the island for so long. A series of high-profile arrests have followed in the three decades since, including the apprehensions of legendary Mafia kingpins Salvatore 'Totò' Riina in 1993, Leoluca Bagarella in 1995, Bernardo 'the Tractor' Provenzano in 2006, Salvatore Lo Piccolo in 2007 and Domenico 'the Veterinarian' Raccuglia in 2009, along with Settimio Mineo and other key Palermo-based mobsters in 2018.

HISTORY POSTWAR WOES & MANI PULITE

When half a ton of explosives was detonated to kill anti-Mafia crusader Giovanni Falcone, the bombing registered on local earthquake monitors. The explosives were planted under a stretch of the A29 motorway between Palermo and the airport and ordered by Mafia kingpin Salvatore 'Totò' Riina, who reputedly celebrated the death with champagne.

2012	2013	2015	2016
Rosario Crocetta becomes the first openly gay governor of Sicily. Staunchly and vocally anti-Mafia, the centre-left politician survives several attempts on his life by the Sicilian Mafia.	Sicily continues to struggle economically, with early 2013 figures presenting a harsh reality: overall unemployment at 20.71% and youth unemployment at 52%.	Italian Prime Minister Matteo Renzi revives talk about building a bridge across the Strait of Messina despite the area's high seismic risk and fears of Mafia involvement in the bridge's construction.	The number of illegal migrants reaching Sicily by boat increases by a dramatic 90% in the first three months of the year. Of the 20,000 migrants who enter Italy in the same period, 90% land in Sicily.

Sicilian Table

Sicily boasts one of the finest cuisines in Italy, standing out for its uniqueness and quality even in a nation where food is at the centre of existence and where there are so many delicious regional variations. A huge part of anyone's visit here will be taken up with eating and drinking. Prepare to have your taste buds tantalised!

Land of Timeless Culinary Traditions

Sicily's kitchen is packed with fresh ingredients, unexpected flavours and delectable sweet-and-sour combinations. The island's rich pantry has evolved over a long period, shaped by successive waves of invaders but always finding its roots in Sicily's fertile volcanic soil and surrounding waters. Over the centuries, many traditional recipes have taken hold, surviving to the present day. Fish and shellfish from the Mediterranean form one of the lasting foundations of the island's cuisine. The abundance of fruit and vegetables has also been evident since the times of the ancient Greeks – Homer famously said of the island, 'Here luxuriant trees are always in their prime, pomegranates and pears, and apples glowing red, succulent figs and olives swelling sleek and dark', and wrote about wild fennel and caper bushes growing on the hills.

But it wasn't until the Arabs came to the island that the cuisine really took shape. The Saracens brought the ever-present aubergine (eggplant), as well as citrus fruits, and they are believed to have introduced pasta to the island. They also spiced things up with saffron and sultanas, and contrasted the dishes' delicate flavours with the crunch of almonds and pistachios. Another Arab influence is the seafood couscous still present on many menus in western Sicily. On top of all this, the Saracens brought sugar cane to these shores, helping Sicily develop all those fantastic sweets.

Almost all restaurants in Sicily charge €1 to €3 per person for *pane e coperto* (bread and cover charge). Theoretically this pays for the basket of bread that's brought out while you wait for the rest of your meal to arrive. If the waiter forgets, just ask!

Another fascinating aspect of Sicilian cuisine is that so many of the region's amazing flavours evolved out of poverty and deprivation. The extravagant recipes of the *monsù* (chefs; from the French *monsieur le chef*) employed by the island's aristocrats were adapted to fit the budget and means of the less fortunate, with aubergines substituted for meat, or breadcrumbs taking the place of grated cheese. Ordinary Sicilians applied the aristocratic principles of preserving the freshness of the ingredients and, most importantly, never letting one taste overpower another.

Staples

Ubiquitous, locally grown staples that appear repeatedly in Sicilian cuisine include aubergines, wild fennel, citrus fruits, almonds, pistachios, capers, olives, fresh ricotta, swordfish, tuna, sardines and shellfish. You'll also find loads of traditional regional specialities to sample, many made with products showcased by the Fondazione Slow Food organisation (www.fondazioneslowfood.com).

Bread

Bread has always been a staple food for the Sicilian peasant. Made from durum wheat, Sicilian bread is coarse and golden, fashioned into myriad ritualistic and regional shapes, from braids to rings to flowers, and sometimes finished off with sesame seeds. Baked bread is treated with the greatest respect and in the past only the head of the family had the privilege of slicing the loaf.

Periods of dire poverty and starvation no doubt gave rise to the common use of *mollica* (breadcrumbs), which served to stretch meagre ingredients and fill up hungry stomachs. Such economy lives on in famous dishes such as *involtini,* in which slices of meat or fish are wrapped around a sometimes-spicy breadcrumb stuffing and then pan-fried or grilled. Breadcrumbs (rather than grated cheese) are also sprinkled on some pasta dishes, such as *pasta con le sarde* (pasta with sardines, pine nuts, raisins and wild fennel). Some other popular dishes made with a bread-dough base include *sfincione (*local form of pizza made with tomatoes, onions and sometimes anchovies), *impanata* (bread-dough snacks stuffed with meat, vegetables or cheese) and *scaccie* (pancake-like discs of bread dough spread with a filling and rolled up).

Antipasti

Sicilians' love of strong flavours and unusual combinations lend themselves well to the antipasto (literally 'before the meal', or appetiser) platter. Helping yourself to a selection of antipasti from the buffet is a great way to explore some of Sicily's wonderful flavours, ranging from marinated sardines and slivers of raw herring to fruity cheeses and a whole range of marinated, baked and fresh vegetables, including artichokes, peppers, sun-dried tomatoes, aubergine and the most famous of all – *caponata* (cooked vegetable salad made with tomatoes, aubergines, celery, capers, olives and onions). In mountainous regions, the antipasto

In Palermo, it's not uncommon to compliment a woman by calling her *bella come una cassata* (lovely as a cassata).

SICILIAN TABLE STAPLES

Classic Antipasti

Sarde a beccafico *Rolled, stuffed sardines.*

Arancine *Savoury, fried rice balls.*

Caponata *Sweet-and-sour mix of aubergines, capers and olives.*

SICILIAN IGP & DOP VARIETIES

A number of Sicilian food specialities have earned special recognition under Italy's national DOP (protected origin) program and the European Union's IGP (protected geographical indication) program. These designations help promote and safeguard the reputations of quality agricultural products throughout the island. Some of the most famous DOP and IGP products are listed here, each followed by the name of the region where it's cultivated.

Pistacchi Verdi di Bronte DOP Green pistachios from Bronte, on Mt Etna's western slopes (Ionian Coast).

Pomodori di Pachino IGP Cherry tomatoes from Ragusa and Syracuse (Southeastern Sicily).

Fichidindia dell'Etna DOP Prickly pear cactus fruit from Mt Etna (Ionian Coast).

Limoni di Siracusa IGP Lemons from Syracuse (Southeastern Sicily).

Arance di Ribera DOP Oranges from the Ribera region (Mediterranean Coast).

Arance Rosse di Sicilia IGP Sicilian red oranges (Syracuse and the Southeast, Ionian Coast, Central Sicily).

Pesche di Leonforte IGP Peaches from the Enna region (Central Sicily).

Pecorino Siciliano DOP Sheep's milk cheese, available island-wide.

Ragusano DOP Cow's milk cheese from Ragusa (Southeastern Sicily).

Capperi di Pantelleria IGP Capers from the island of Pantelleria (Southwestern Sicily).

Nocellara del Belice DOP Olives from the Belice Valley (Western Sicily).

Classic First Courses

Pasta alla Norma *Pasta with tomatoes, aubergines and salted ricotta.*

Pasta con le sarde *Pasta with sardines, pine nuts, raisins and wild fennel.*

Couscous alla trapanese *Fish couscous, typical of Western Sicily.*

Pasta all'eoliana *Pasta with olives, capers, cherry tomatoes, olive oil and basil.*

Ever wonder where Sicily's two favourite desserts got their names? *Cassata* comes from the Arabic word *qas'ah,* referring to the terracotta bowl used to shape the cake; *cannolo* comes from *canna* (cane, as in sugar cane).

Classic Second Courses

Scaloppine al marsala *Veal cutlets with Marsala wine.*

Involtini di pesce spada *Swordfish roll-ups with raisins, pine nuts and bread crumbs.*

Frittura mista *Fried squid, shrimp and other seafood.*

selection tends to shift more towards sausages, cheeses, mushrooms or hearty *arancine* or *arancinette* – fried balls of rice stuffed with meat and tomato sauce. If you're lucky, you'll also find rare treats such as delicately breaded and fried sage leaves or squash blossoms.

Pasta

Pasta is possibly Italy's (and Sicily's) most famous export. While fresh pasta *(pasta fresca)* is now common on most Sicilian restaurant menus – with Trapani's hollow corkscrew-shaped *busiate* being one of the most distinctive varieties – it is dry pasta that has always been the staple of Sicily and southern Italy, mainly because dry pasta is more economical.

The most famous of all Sicilian pasta dishes is *pasta con le sarde*: pasta with sardines, wild mountain fennel (unique to Sicily), onions, pine nuts and raisins that combine to create a wonderfully exotic flavour. Other famous dishes include Catania's *pasta alla Norma,* with its rich combination of tomatoes, aubergines and salted ricotta; the Aeolian Islands' *pasta all'eoliana*, made with local olives, capers, cherry tomatoes, olive oil and basil; the ever-popular *spaghetti ai ricci* (with sea urchins); and *pasta al pesce spada e menta*, made with fresh swordfish and mint. In the interior you will often find sauces made from meat and game (including wild boar, rabbit and beef) as well as *pasta alle nocciole*, with a sauce based on the hazelnuts of the Nebrodi and Madonie Mountains. Baroque Modica is where the island's best lasagne *(lasagne cacate)* is made; in this version, two kinds of cheese – ricotta and *pecorino* – are added to minced beef and sausage, and spread between layers of homemade pasta squares.

Seafood

The extensive development of fishing and – until recent years – the widespread presence of fish such as sardines, tuna and mackerel off the island's shores have ensured that fish is a staple food.

A Palermitan favourite is *sarde a beccafico alla Palermitana* (sardines stuffed with anchovies, pine nuts, currants and parsley), served either as an appetiser or a second course. However, the filet mignon of the marine world is the *pesce spada* (swordfish), served either grilled with lemon, olive oil and oregano, or as *involtini* (slices of swordfish rolled around a spicy filling of onions, currants, pine nuts and breadcrumbs).

The best swordfish is caught in Messina, where they serve the classic *agghiotta di pesce spada* (also called *pesce spada alla Messinese*), a mouth-watering dish flavoured with pine nuts, sultanas, garlic, basil and tomatoes. The Egadi Islands are home to two splendid fish dishes: *tonno 'nfurnatu* (oven-baked tuna with tomatoes, capers and green olives) and *alalunga di Favignana al ragù* (fried albacore served in a spicy sauce of tomatoes, red chilli peppers and garlic). It is not uncommon to see the latter sauce also appear as part of your pasta dish.

Shellfish are popular throughout the island, especially calamari or *totani* (squid) and *calamaretti* (baby squid), which are prepared in a variety of ways, including stuffed, fried, roasted or cooked in a tomato sauce. You'll also find plenty of *cozze* (mussels), *vongole* (clams) and *gamberi* (shrimp) – the most famous variety being *gamberi rossi di Mazara* (red shrimp from Mazara del Vallo). Another popular and ubiquitous treat is *frittura mista* (sometimes called *fritto misto*), a blend of lightly breaded and fried shrimp, squid and/or fish.

Meat

Although you can find a limited number of meat dishes along the coast, you won't taste the best until you move further inland. The province of Ragusa is renowned for its imaginative and varied uses of meat, particularly mutton, beef, pork and rabbit. Its most famous dish is *falsomagro,* a stuffed roll of minced beef, sausages, bacon, egg and *pecorino* cheese. Another local speciality is *coniglio all'agrodolce* (sweet-and-sour rabbit), which is marinated in a sauce of red wine flavoured with onions, olive oil, bay leaves and rosemary. The Nebrodi Mountains are famous for a variety of pork products derived from the indigenous *nero dei Nebrodi,* also known as *suino nero* (literally, black pig). In the neighbouring Madonie Mountains, the town of Castelbuono is the home of *capretto in umido* (stewed kid) and *agnello al forno alla Madonita* (Madonie-style roast lamb). Locally caught *cinghiale* (wild boar) is served in stews, sauces and sausages. Don't be put off if goat or kid dishes are described on the menu as *castrato* – it means the goat was castrated, giving the meat a tender quality.

Sweets

Sicily's extraordinary pastries are rich in colour and elaborately designed. The queen of Sicilian desserts, the *cassata,* is made with ricotta, sugar, vanilla, diced chocolate and candied fruits. The equally famous *cannoli,* pastry tubes filled with sweetened ricotta and sometimes finished off with candied fruit, chocolate bits or crumbled hazelnuts or pistachios, are found pretty much everywhere. Another ubiquitous treat is *frutta martorana,* named after the church in Palermo that first began producing them. These marzipan confections, shaped to resemble fruits (or whatever takes the creator's fancy), are part of a Sicilian tradition that dates back to the Middle Ages. In late October they're sold in stalls around Palermo in anticipation of Ognissanti (All Souls' Day), but they're also commonly available year-round in painted souvenir boxes throughout Sicily.

Other Sicilian sweets worth sampling are *paste di mandorla* (almond cookies), *gelo di melone* (something like watermelon jelly), *biscotti regina* (sesame-coated biscuits that originated in Palermo but are now widely available throughout the island), *cassatelle* (pouches of dough stuffed with sweetened ricotta and chocolate, originally from Trapani province), *cuccia* (an Arab cake made with grain, honey and ricotta, sold in western Sicily) and *sfogli polizzani* (a speciality of Polizzi Generosa in the Madonie Mountains, made with chocolate, cinnamon and fresh sheep's milk cheese). While in the Madonie region, also make sure to try the cornucopia of sweets made from *manna,* the edible sap harvested from ash trees around Castelbuono.

Plenty of seasonal treats are prepared in conjunction with religious festivals. These include the cute little *pecorelle di marzapane* (marzipan lambs) that start appearing in pastry shop windows around Easter Week, *pupe* (sugar dolls made to celebrate All Souls' Day on 1 November), *ucchiuzzi* (biscuits shaped like eyes, made for the Festa di Santa Lucia on 13 December) and *buccellati* (dough rings stuffed with minced figs, raisins,

While it's perfectly normal to order 'a *biscotti*' or 'a *cannoli*' back home, note that these are actually plural forms in Italian; use the singular form 'un *biscotto*' or 'un *cannolo*' while in Sicily – unless of course you truly want a pile of them!

SICILIAN TABLE STAPLES

Sweet tooths take note: in Sicily it's perfectly acceptable to eat ice cream first thing in the morning. Two of the island's most popular summertime breakfasts are *gelato e brioche* (a roll filled with ice cream) or *granita con panna* (flavoured crushed ice topped with whipped cream)!

VEGETARIANS & VEGANS

Vegetarianism is not specifically catered to in Sicily but the abundance of excellent local produce means that many *antipasti,* pastas and *contorni* (side dishes) feature veg in some form or other. Salads are common and tasty, though you'll need to watch out for the odd anchovy or slice of ham. Similarly, check that your tomato sauce has not been cooked with meat in it. Vegans will be in for a tough time, with many dishes featuring some sort of animal product (butter, eggs or animal stock), although the situation has improved in recent years. Restaurants catering specifically to vegetarians and/or vegans include Bioesserì (p71) in Palermo, La Cucina dei Colori (p188) and Millefoglie (p188) in Catania, Moon (p208) in Syracuse and Hostaria del Vicolo (p271) in Sciacca.

almonds, candied fruit and/or orange peel, especially popular around Christmas, but also sometimes available out-of-season at the Monastero di Santo Spirito in Agrigento).

Looking for something a little more daring? A good place to start is the southeastern town of Modica, where you can try chocolate laced with spicy peppers (prepared from an Aztec recipe brought here directly from Mexico when Sicily was under Spanish rule) or 'mpanatigghi (Modican pastries stuffed with minced meat, almonds, chocolate, cloves and cinnamon).

Any decent *pasticceria* (pastry shop) will have an enormous spread of freshly made cakes and pastries. It is very common for Sicilians to have their meal in a restaurant and then go to a pastry shop, where they have a coffee and cake while standing at the bar.

> Sicilian restaurants typically open for lunch between noon and 1pm, closing around 2.30pm or 3pm. Places reopen for dinner between 7pm and 8pm, but most Sicilians don't show up until 9pm or later, especially in summertime.

Gelati & Granite

Despite Etna's belly of fire, its peak is a natural freezer, and snow that falls on its slopes lasts well into the searing summer, insulated by a fine blanket of volcanic ash. The Romans and Greeks treasured the snow, using it to chill their wine, but it was the Arabs who first started the Sicilian mania for all things icy – *granita* (flavoured crushed ice), gelato (ice cream) and *semifreddo* (literally 'semi-frozen'; a cold, creamy dessert).

The origins of ice cream lie in the Arab *sarbat* (sherbet), a concoction of sweet fruit syrups chilled with iced water, which was then developed into *granita* (where crushed ice was mixed with fruit juice, coffee, almond milk and so on) and *cremolata* (fruit syrups chilled with iced milk), the forerunner to gelato.

Gelato artigianale (home-made gelato) is sold at cafes and bars across the island, and is truly delicious. You should try it like a Sicilian – first thing in the morning in a brioche!

Granite are sometimes topped with fresh whipped cream, and are often eaten with a brioche. Favourite flavours include coffee and almond, though lemon is great in summer. During July, August and September, try a *granita di gelsi* (mulberry), a delicious seasonal offering.

Wine

Sicily's vineyards cover nearly 120,000 hectares, making it the second-largest wine-producing region in Italy. But while grapes have always been grown here, Sicilian wine is for the most part not well known outside the island.

> Cappuccino and *caffè latte* are served everywhere at breakfast time, but you'll stick out like a sore thumb if you ask for milk in your coffee after noon – at lunch and dinner time, Sicilians only drink it black.

The most common varietal is Nero d'Avola, a robust red similar to syrah or shiraz. Vintages are produced by numerous Sicilian wineries, including Planeta (www.planeta.it), which has various estates around the island; Donnafugata (www.donnafugata.it); Azienda Agricola COS (www.cosvittoria.it); and Azienda Agricola G Milazzo (www.milazzovini.com). Try Planeta's Plumbago and Santa Cecilia labels, Donnafugata's Mille e una Notte, COS' Nero di Lupo and Milazzo's Maria Costanza and Terre della Baronia Rosso.

Local cabernet sauvignons are less common but worth sampling; the version produced by Tasca d'Almerita (www.tascadalmerita.it) at its Regaleali estate in Caltanissetta province is particularly highly regarded (the estate also produces an excellent Nero d'Avola under its Rosso del Conte label).

The sangiovese-like Nerello Mascalese and Nerello Cappuccio are used in the popular Etna Rosso DOC; try the Contrada Porcaria and Contrada Sciaranuova vintages produced by the Passopisciaro estate (www.vinifranchetti.com/passopisciaro) or the Serra della Contessa, Rovittello and Pietramarina produced by Vinicola Benanti (www.vinicolabenanti.it).

Cerasuolo di Vittoria, a blend of Nero d'Avola and Frappato grapes, is Sicily's only DOCG *(denominazione d'origine controllata e garantita)* wine. The more restrictive DOCG classification indicates that Cerasuolo is routinely analysed and tasted by government inspectors before bottling, and sealed with an official label to prevent tampering. Look for Planeta's vintages, which are produced at its estate in Dorilli, and those by COS.

Though the local reds are good, the region is probably best known for its white wines, including those produced at Abbazia Santa Anastasia (p282) near Castelbuono, **Fazio** (✆0923 81 17 00; www.casavinicolafazio.it; Via Capitano Rizzo 39, Fulgatore; tasting per person €20; ◷9.30am-1pm & 2.30-5pm Mon-Fri) near Erice, and by Tasca d'Almerita and Passopisciaro.

Common white varietals include Carricante, chardonnay, Grillo, Inzolia, Cataratto, Inzolia, Grecanico and Corinto. Look out for Tasca d'Almerita's Nozze d'Oro Inzolia blend, Fazio's Catarratto chardonnay, Abbazia Santa Anastasia's chardonnay blends, and Passopisciaro's Guardiola chardonnay.

Most wines are fairly cheap, though (as for any wine) prices vary according to the vintage. In a restaurant a bottle of decent wine should cost you around €15 to €25, with a table wine *(vino da tavola)* at around €10.

Sicilian dessert wines are excellent, and are well worth buying to take home. Top of the list is Marsala's sweet wine; the best (and most widely known) labels are Florio (p113) and Pellegrino (www.carlopellegrino.it). Sweet Malvasia (from the Aeolian island of Salina) is a honey-sweet wine whose best producers include Hauner (p157), Virgona (p157) and Fenech (p157). Italy's most famous Moscato (Muscat), made from *zibibbo* grapes, is the Passito of Pantelleria from the island of the same name; it has a deep-amber colour and an extraordinary taste of apricots and vanilla. Donnafugata (p121) is Pantelleria's most prominent producer, but there are well over a dozen other wineries spread about the island.

The Gambero Rosso Vini d'Italia wine guide (www.gamberorosso.it) is generally considered to be the bible of Italian wines and offers plenty of information about Sicilian wines and wineries.

SICILIAN TABLE WINE

In late afternoon, just before dinnertime, Sicilians go to local bars to socialise over *aperitivi* – glasses of wine and alcohol, often accompanied by free snacks. This ritual is a great way to mingle with Italians, and it can even serve as a light dinner if you're not particularly hungry.

FOOD GLOSSARY

acciughe a•*choo*•geh – anchovies	**aceto** a•*che*•to – vinegar
acqua *a*•kwa – water	**aglio** *a*•lyo – garlic
agnello a•*nye*•lo – lamb	**aragosta** a•ra•*go*•sta – lobster
arancia a•*ran*•cha – orange	**arrosto/a** a•*ros*•*to/a* – roasted
asparagi as•*pa*•ra•jee – asparagus	**bicchiere** bee•*kye*•re – glass
birra *bee*•ra – beer	**bistecca** bi•*ste*•ka – steak
burro *boo*•ro – butter	**caffè** ka•*fe* – coffee
cameriere/a ka•mer•*ye*•re/a – waiter (m/f)	**capretto** kap•*re*•to – kid (goat)
carciofi kar•*chyo*•fee – artichokes	**carota** ka•*ro*•ta – carrot
carta dei vini *kar*•ta dey•*vee*•nee – wine list	**cavolo** ka•*vo*•lo – cabbage
cena *che*•na – dinner	**ciliegia** chee•*lye*•ja – cherry
cipolle chee•*po*•le – onions	**coltello** kol•*te*•lo – knife
coniglio ko•*nee*•lyo – rabbit	**conto** *kon*•to – bill/cheque
cozze *ko*•tse – mussels	**cucchiaio** koo•*kya*•yo – spoon
enoteca e•no•*te*•ka – wine bar	**fagiolini** fa•jo•*lee*•nee – green beans
fegato *fe*•ga•to – liver	**fico** *fee*•ko – fig

finocchio fee·*no*·kyo – fennel

forchetta for·*ke*·ta – fork

formaggio for·*ma*·jo – cheese

fragole *fra*·go·le – strawberries

friggitoria free·jee·to·*ree*·a – fried-food stand

frutti di mare *froo*·tee dee *ma*·re – seafood

funghi *foon*·gee – mushrooms

gamberoni gam·be·*ro*·nee – prawns

granchio *gran*·kyo – crab

insalata een·sa·*la*·ta – salad

lampone lam·*po*·ne – raspberry

latte *la*·te – milk

limone lee·*mo*·ne – lemon

manzo *man*·dzo – beef

mela *me*·la – apple

melanzane me·lan·*dza*·ne – aubergine

melone me·*lo*·ne – cantaloupe; rock melon

merluzzo mer·*loo*·tso – cod

miele *mye*·le – honey

olio *o*·lyo – oil

oliva o·*lee*·va – olive

osteria os·te·*ree*·a – informal restaurant

ostriche os·*tree*·ke – oysters

pane *pa*·ne – bread

panna *pa*·na – cream

pasticceria pas·tee·che·*ree*·a – patisserie/pastry shop

patate pa·*ta*·te – potatoes

pepe *pe*·pe – pepper

peperoncino pe·pe·*ron*·*chee*·no – chilli

peperoni pe·pe·*ro*·nee – capsicum

pera *pe*·ra – pear

pesca *pes*·ka – peach

pesce spada *pe*·she *spa*·da – swordfish

piselli pee·*se*·lee – peas

pollo *po*·lo – chicken

polpo *pol*·po – octopus

pomodori po·mo·*do*·ree – tomatoes

pranzo *pran*·dzo – lunch

prima colazione *pree*·ma ko·la·*tsyo*·ne – breakfast

riso *ree*·so – rice

ristorante ree·sto·*ran*·te – restaurant

rucola *roo*·ko·la – rocket; arugula

sale *sa*·le – salt

salsiccia sal·*see*·cha – sausage

sarde *sar*·de – sardines

sgombro *sgom*·bro – mackerel

spinaci spee·*na*·chee – spinach

spuntino spoon·*tee*·no – snack

tartufo tar·*too*·fo – truffle

tè te – tea

tonno *to*·no – tuna

tovagliolo to·va·*lyo*·lo – napkin/serviette

trattoria tra·to·*ree*·a – informal restaurant

trippa *tree*·pa – tripe

uovo/uova *wo*·vo/*wo*·va – egg/eggs

vegetaliano/a ve·je·ta·*lya*·no/a – vegan (m/f)

vegetariano/a ve·je·ta·*rya*·no/a – vegetarian (m/f)

vino bianco *vee*·no *byan*·ko – white wine

vino rosso *vee*·no *ro*·so – red wine

vitello vee·*te*·lo – veal

vongole *von*·go·le – clams

zucchero *tsoo*·ke·ro – sugar

Sicilian Way of Life

When asked to name their nationality, most locals will say 'Sicilian' rather than 'Italian', reinforcing a generally held Italian belief that the Sicilian culture and character are markedly different to those of the rest of the country. Though sharing many traits with fellow residents of the Mezzogiorno (the part of southern Italy comprising Sicily, Abruzzo, Basilica, Campania, Calabria, Apulia, Molise and Sardinia), Sicilians have a dialect and civil society that are as distinctive as they are fascinating.

Identity

The uniqueness of the Sicilian experience is perhaps summed up best by author Giuseppe Tomasi di Lampedusa in Sicily's most famous novel, *Il Gattopardo* (The Leopard). In one memorable passage, his protagonist the Prince of Salina tries to explain the Sicilian character to a Piedmontese representative of the new Kingdom of Italy as follows: 'This violence of landscape, this cruelty of climate, this continual tension in everything, and even these monuments of the past, magnificent yet incomprehensible because not built by us and yet standing round us like lovely mute ghosts…All these things have formed our character…'

In modern Sicily, the prevailing stereotype is that Palermo and Catania stand at opposite ends of the island's character. Palermitans are commonly viewed as being more traditional, while Catanians are considered more outward looking and better at business. Some ascribe the Palermitans' conservative character to their Arab predecessors, while the Greeks get all the credit for the Catanians' democratic outlook, their sense of commerce and their alleged cunning. Beyond this divide, Sicilians are generally thought of as conservative and suspicious (usually by mainland Italians), stoical and spiritual, confident and gregarious, and as the possessors of a rich and dark sense of humour.

Colonised for centuries, Sicilians have absorbed myriad traits – indeed, writer Gesualdo Bufalino wrote in *Cento Sicilie* (2008) that Sicilians suffered from an 'excess of identity', at the core of which was the islanders' conviction that Sicilian culture stands at the centre of the world. This can make the visitor feel terribly excluded, as there is still an awful lot of Sicily that is beyond the prying eyes of the tourist.

That said, it is difficult to make blanket assertions about Sicilian culture, if only because there are huge differences between the modern city dwellers and those from the conservative countryside. However, modern attitudes are changing conservative traditions. In the larger university cities such as Palermo, Catania, Syracuse and Messina, you will find a vibrant youth culture and a liberal lifestyle.

Agneddu e sucu e finiu u vattiu.
When the lamb's all gone, the baptism is over.
(When the food's all gone, the party's over.)

Cu sparti avi a megghiu parti.
The one who divides things up gets the better share.

SICILIAN PROVERBS

Sicilian culture is big on proverbs. Even as Sicilians embrace many aspects of modern life, their everyday speech is laced with traditional sayings whose roots go back several centuries. Spoken in Sicilian (a language in its own right and quite distinct from Italian), these proverbs often require translation even for other Italians.

Public vs Private

Family is the bedrock of Sicilian life, and loyalty to family and friends is one of the most important qualities you can possess. Maintaining a *bella figura* (beautiful image) is very important to the average Sicilian, and striving to appear better off than you really are (known as *spagnolismo*) is a regional pastime. Though not confined to Sicily, *spagnolismo* on the island has its roots in the excesses of the Spanish-ruled 18th century, when the race for status was so competitive that the king considered outlawing extravagance. In this climate, how you and your family appeared to the outside world was (and still is) a matter of honour, respectability and pride. In a social context, keeping up appearances extends to dressing well, behaving modestly, performing religious and social duties and fulfilling all essential family obligations; in the context of the extended family, where gossip is rife, a good image protects one's privacy.

In this heavily patriarchal society, 'manliness' is a man's prime concern. The main role of the 'head of the family' is to take care of his family, oil the wheels of personal influence and facilitate the upward mobility of family members. Women, on the other hand, are traditionally the repository of the family's honour, and even though unmarried couples commonly live together nowadays, there are still young couples who undertake lengthy engagements for the appearance of respectability.

Traditionally, personal wealth is closely and jealously guarded. Family money can support many individuals, while emigrant remittances have vastly improved the lot of many villagers.

Testa c'un parra si chiama cucuzza. A head that doesn't speak is called a pumpkin. (If something's on your mind, don't keep it to yourself!)

Cu mancia fa muddica. He who eats leaves breadcrumbs. (If you do something wrong, people will find out.)

A Woman's Place

In Francis Ford Coppola's *The Godfather*, Fabrizio (played by Angelo Infanti) describes women as more dangerous than shotguns. Writer Giovanni Verga proclaimed 'A woman at the window is a woman to be shunned' in the 19th century, while a judge faced with a female Mafia suspect in the 1990s declared that women were too stupid to partake in the complexities of finance. As in many places in the Mediterranean, a woman's position in Sicily has always been a difficult one.

A Sicilian mother and wife commands the utmost respect within the home, and is expected to act as the moral and emotional compass for her family. Although, or perhaps because, male sexuality holds an almost mythical status, women's modesty – which includes being quiet and feminine, staying indoors and remaining a virgin until married – has had to be ferociously guarded. To this day the worst insult that can be directed to a Sicilian man is *cornuto,* meaning that his wife has been unfaithful.

Improvements in educational opportunities and changing attitudes mean that the number of women with successful careers is growing. That said, Italy still ranked near the bottom of the list of European nations with regard to women's economic participation and opportunity in the 2018 *Global Gender Gap Index* published by the World Economic Forum.

Saints & Sinners

Religion remains a big deal in Sicily. With the exception of the small Muslim communities of Palermo and the larger Tunisian Muslim community in Mazara del Vallo, the overwhelming majority of Sicilians consider themselves practising Roman Catholics. Even before the 1929 Lateran Treaty between the Vatican and Italy, when Roman Catholicism became the official religion of the country, Sicily was incontrovertibly Catholic, mostly due to 500 years of Spanish domination. In 1985 the treaty was renegotiated, so that Catholicism was no longer the state religion and religious education was no longer compulsory, but this only reflected the

Ogni beni di la campagna veni. All good things come from the countryside.

SPEAKING SICILIAN

One of Sicily's cultural legacies is *sicilianu* (Sicilian). While both modern Italian and *sicilianu* have shared roots in Vulgar Latin (the common language of ancient Rome), Sicilian is considered by many as a distinct language, with 11 regionally based dialects. Indeed, Unesco lists it as a 'minority language'.

Centuries of foreign occupation have helped shape its lexicon, with numerous words rooted in Greek, Arabic, French, Catalan, Spanish and Lombard. Take *cirasa* (cherry), from the Greek *kerási*, *bucceri/vucceri* (butcher) from the Old French *bouchier*, or *azzizzari* (to embellish), which hails from the Arabic *azīz*, meaning 'beautiful' or 'precious'. Arabic is also the root of numerous place names, among them Caltagirone (from *qal'at-al-jarar*, meaning 'castle of pottery jars'), Marsala (port of God), Pantelleria (daughter of the wind) and La Kalsa (from *al Khalesa*, meaning 'the chosen'). The use of written Sicilian has been sporadic over the centuries. In the southeastern town of Scicli, the Chiesa di Santa Teresa is home to a 16th-century fresco with a rare inscription in Sicilianised Latin.

Today, *sicilianu* is mostly spoken in informal situations between friends and family, and more often by Sicily's working class. Decades of mass media has seen a steady influx of Italian words and, according to Unesco, the language is now 'vulnerable'. Interestingly, the overwhelming majority of Sicilian speakers live abroad in countries including the US, Canada, Argentina and Australia, reflecting both the size of the Sicilian diaspora and the endurance of older traditions in many immigrant communities.

reality of mainland Italy north of Rome; in Sicily, the Catholic Church remains strong and extremely popular.

In the small communities of the interior you will find that the mix of faith and superstition that for centuries dictated Sicilian behaviour is still strong. The younger, more cosmopolitan sections of society living in the cities tend to dismiss their elders' deepest expressions of religious devotion, but most people still maintain an air of respect.

Pilgrimages remain a central part of the religious ritual, with thousands of Sicilians travelling to places such as the Santuario della Madonna at Tindari or the Santuario di Gibilmanna in the Madonie Mountains. The depth of religious feeling associated with these sanctuaries is underscored by the large number of *ex votos* (votive offerings) brought to both places by worshippers seeking divine intervention or giving thanks for a miracle attributed to the Madonna.

A megghiu parola e chidda ca unsi rici. The best word is the one that remains unspoken.

Annual feast days of patron saints are also enthusiastically celebrated throughout the island, morphing into massive citywide events in the larger urban areas. Palermo's mid-July Festa di Santa Rosalia spans three solid days, with the patroness paraded down Via Vittorio Emanuele from the cathedral to the waterfront in a grandiose *carro triunfale* (triumphal carriage), flanked by adoring crowds. In Catania, the Festa di Sant'Agata in early February also lasts for three days, with more than a million devotees pouring into the streets to follow a silver reliquary bust of the saint. Syracuse's mid-December Festa di Santa Lucia, while smaller, is celebrated with similar fervour. All three festivals are accompanied by spectacular fireworks.

Sparagna la farina mentre la coffa e' china; quannu lu furnu pari, servi a nenti lu sparagnari. Save flour while the bag is full; when you can see the bottom, there's nothing left to save.

Easter celebrations mark the high point in Sicily's religious calendar. Settimana Santa (Holy Week) is traditionally a time for Sicilians to take time off from work, get together with their families and participate in religious observances. Many places around the island celebrate Holy Week with elaborate processions. The most famous of these is Trapani's I Misteri, a four-day event in which 20 life-sized statues representing different moments in Christ's Passion are carried through the streets by members of the city's traditional guilds. Other cities that have noteworthy Easter processions include Caltanissetta, Lipari and Enna.

Immigration & Emigration

Cu si voli 'imbria-cari, di vino bonu l'avi a fare. He who wants to get drunk should do it with good wine.

Immigration and emigration are among the most pressing contemporary issues, and Sicily is no stranger to the subject. Since the end of the 19th century the island has suffered an enormous drain of human resources through emigration. Between 1880 and 1910, over 1.5 million Sicilians left for the US, and in 1900 the island was the world's main area of emigration. In the 20th century, tens of thousands of Sicilians moved away in search of a better life in Northern Italy, North America, Australia and other countries. Today, huge numbers of young Sicilians – often the most educated – continue to leave the island. This brain-drain epidemic is largely the result of the grim unemployment rate and the entrenched system of patronage and nepotism, which makes it difficult for young people to get well-paid jobs without having the right connections.

Also, the fact that Sicily is one of the favoured ports of call for the thousands of *extracomunitari* (immigrants from outside the EU) who have flooded into Italy, some of them illegally, has led to extra strain being placed on housing and infrastructure as well as increased competition for jobs. It's a pressure that has fuelled a growing frustration among many Sicilians, despite a general hospitality towards these newcomers and an understanding of the difficulties faced by political and economic refugees from neighbouring countries, most notably Libya and Tunisia.

Sicily on Page & Screen

Writers and filmmakers both domestic and foreign have long been inspired by Sicily's harsh landscape, rich history, complex society and wide diversity of cultural influences. They have rarely seen the island through rose-tinted glasses – endemic poverty and corruption are hard to romanticise or whitewash – and their words, images and narratives offer an invaluable insight into the local culture and society.

Sicily in Print

Dogged by centuries of isolation, and divided into an illiterate peasantry and a decadent aristocracy, Sicily prior to the 19th century suffered from an almost complete absence of notable literature – though paradoxically the first official literature in Italian was written in Palermo in the 13th century. Alas, such high-minded works were irrelevant to the peasants, whose main pleasure was the celebration of religious festivals and, later, the popular *opera dei pupi* (Sicilian puppet theatre).

Local Voices

The political upheaval of the 19th and 20th centuries finally broke the long silence of the Sicilian pen, and the literary colossus Giovanni Verga (1840–1922) emerged onto the scene. Living through some of the most intense historical vicissitudes of modern Italy – the unification of Italy, WWI and the rise of Fascism – he had a major impact on Italian literature. His greatest novel, *I Malavoglia* (The Malavoglia Family; 1881), about a family's struggle for survival through desperate times in Sicily, is still a fixture on school reading lists.

Since then Sicilian writers have produced fiction to rival the best contemporary European works. Playwright and novelist Luigi Pirandello (1867–1936) was awarded the Nobel Prize for Literature in 1934 for a substantial body of work, which included the play *Sei personaggi in cerca d'autore* (Six Characters in Search of an Author; 1921). Poet Salvatore Quasimodo (1901–68) won the award in 1959 for his exquisite lyric verse, which included delightful translations of works by Shakespeare and Pablo Neruda. Elio Vittorini (1908–66) captured the essence of the Sicilian migration north in his masterpiece *Conversazione in Sicilia* (1941), the story of a man's return to the roots of his personal, historical and cultural identity.

Sicily's most famous novel was a one-off by an aristocrat whose intent was to chronicle the social upheaval caused by the end of the old regime and the unification of Italy. Giuseppe Tomasi di Lampedusa (1896–1957) published *Il Gattopardo* (The Leopard) in 1958 to immediate critical acclaim. Though a period novel, its enduring relevance lies in the minutely accurate observations of what it means to be Sicilian.

Much of Sicily's more recent literature is more political than literary. None is more so than the work of Danilo Dolci (1924–97), a social activist commonly known as the 'Sicilian Gandhi'. His *Report from Palermo* (1959) and subsequent *Sicilian Lives* (1981), both detailing the squalid

Top Reads

I Malavoglia –
Giovanni Verga

Midnight in Sicily –
Peter Robb

On Persephone's
Island – Mary
Taylor Simeti

The Day of the
Owl – Leonardo
Sciascia

The Silent Duchess
– Dacia Maraini

living conditions of many of Sicily's poorest inhabitants, earned him the enduring animosity of the authorities and the Church. (Cardinal Ernesto Ruffini publicly denounced him for 'defaming' all Sicilians.) He, too, was nominated for the Nobel Prize and was awarded the Lenin Peace Prize in 1958. More recently, Lampedusa-based doctor Pietro Bartolo has gained acclaim for his memoir *Tears of Salt: A Doctor's Story* (2017, co-authored by Lidia Tilotta), which recounts Bartolo's experiences tending to refugees arriving by boat from Africa and the Middle East.

The other great subject for modern Sicilian writers is the Mafia. For a masterful insight into the island's destructive relationship with organised crime, search out the work of Leonardo Sciascia (1921–89), whose novel *Il giorno della civetta* (The Day of the Owl; 1961) was the first Italian novel to take the Mafia as its subject. Throughout his career, Sciascia probed the topic, practically inventing a genre of his own. His protégé Gesualdo Bufalino (1920–96) won the prestigious Strega Prize in 1988 for his novel *Le menzogne della notte* (Night's Lies), the tale of four condemned men who spend the eve of their execution recounting the most memorable moments of their lives. Bufalino went on to become one of Italy's finest writers, mastering a style akin to literary baroque – intense, tortured and surreal. His haunting novel *Diceria dell'untore* (The Plague Sower; 1981), which won Italy's Campiello Prize, is the story of a tuberculosis patient at a Palermo sanatorium in the late 1940s. Guiding the reader through a landscape of doom, Bufalino invokes the horrors of wartime and the hopelessness of the patients who come to know each other 'before our lead-sealed freight car arrives at the depot of its destination'.

Well-known feminist novelist and playwright Dacia Maraini (b 1936) has written a number of novels set in Sicily, including the award-winning historical romance *La lunga vita di Marianna Ucrìa* (The Silent Duchess; 1990), which was made into the film *Marianna Ucrìa* by Italian director Roberto Faenze in 1997.

Through Foreign Eyes

A number of foreigners or expats have also written about Sicily. Enjoyable but lightweight titles include Peter Moore's humorous travelogue *Vroom by the Sea* (2007), which recounts his adventures exploring the island on a Vespa named Donatella (because it's the same shade of lurid orange as Donatella Versace); Brian P Johnston's *Sicilian Summer: A Story of Honour, Religion and the Perfect Cassata* (2007), which is full of village politics and eccentric personalities; and Marlena de Blasi's *That Summer in Sicily* (2008), a Mills and Boon–ish story about a Sicilian woman's relationship with a much-older member of the Sicilian aristocracy.

Mary Taylor Simeti's *On Persephone's Island* (1986), Peter Robb's *Midnight in Sicily* (1996) and John Julius Norwich's *Sicily: An Island at the Crossroads of History* (2015) are much more substantial. Simeti, an American who has been living on the island since 1962, offers fascinating insights into its history, culture and cuisine; and both Robb's and Norwich's portraits of the island's history, culture and struggles are marked by impeccable research and compelling narrative. Norwich's other historical account is the eminently readable *The Normans in Sicily* (2004). American journalist John Keahey has penned a pair of travelogues in this same genre – *Seeking Sicily* (2011) and *Sicilian Splendors: Discovering the Secret Places That Speak to the Heart* (2018) – both delving thoughtfully into Sicily's multi-layered culture and history.

Historical novels of note include Barry Unsworth's *The Ruby in Her Navel* (2006) and Tariq Ali's *A Sultan in Palermo* (2005). Both are set against the backdrop of the Norman court of Roger II (known to his Arabic subjects as Sultan Rujeri).

A collection of short stories by acclaimed postwar Sicilian writer Leonardo Sciascia, entitled *The Wine-Dark Sea*, explores the complicated world of the island's Mafia culture. Sciascia's candid and powerful writings on organised crime played a significant role in changing the way ordinary Italians perceived the Mafia.

Sicily on Film

The rich emotional, psychological and physical landscapes of Sicily have inspired some of the world's best filmmakers. Visconti's two classics, *La terra trema* (The Earth Shook; 1948) and *Il Gattopardo* (The Leopard; 1963), illustrate the breadth of Sicilian tales – the former a story of grinding poverty and misfortune, while the latter oozes the kind of grand decadence that one imagines preceded the French Revolution.

Antonioni's enigmatic mystery *L'avventura* (The Adventure; 1960) focuses on the disappearance of one member of a group of Roman socialites on a cruise around the Aeolian Islands, and though its plot has been described as pretentious, its stunning visuals are universally admired.

In Rossellini's *Stromboli: Terra di Dio* (Stromboli: Land of God; 1950), the explosive love affair between a Lithuanian refugee and a local fisherman is aptly viewed against the backdrop of the erupting volcano, while the hypnotic beauty of Michael Radford's *Il Postino* (The Postman; 1994) seduces viewers into a false sense of security, which is shattered by the film's tragic denouement.

It is, however, Francis Ford Coppola's modern masterpiece, *The Godfather* trilogy (Part I, 1972; Part II, 1974; Part III, 1990), that really succeeds in marrying the psychological landscape of the characters with their physical environment. The varying intensities of light and dark superbly mirror the constant undercurrent of quivering emotion and black betrayal.

Other directors who have worked here include the Taviani brothers, who filmed *Kaos* in 1984, seeking to reproduce the mad logic of Sicilian-born author Luigi Pirandello's universe. The aptly named film is a series of tales about loss, lust, love, emigration and death played out through fantastical story lines. The film's title comes from the village near Agrigento where Pirandello was born (although it is spelled with a 'C').

Sicilians enjoy a good guffaw, and Pietor Germi's *Divorzio all'italiana* (Divorce, Italian Style), set on the island, was a big hit here when it was released in 1961. More recent comedies include Roberto Benigni's *Il piccolo diavolo* (The Little Devil; 1988), *Johnny Stecchino* (Johnny Toothpick; 1991) and satirist Franco Maresco's *Belluscone: Una storia siciliana* (Belluscone: A Sicilian Story; 2014), a wry, quasi documentary about Berlusconi, his rumoured links to the Mafia and the latter's chokehold on Sicilian society.

Other films set in Sicily include Wim Wender's *Palermo Shooting* (2008), lambasted by most critics as pretentious and boring; and *Sicilia!* (1999), a film version of Elio Vittorini's acclaimed novel *Conversazione in Sicilia*, directed by Danièle Huillet and Jean-Marie Straub,

Sicily itself has produced few directors of note, with the best-known exception being Giuseppe Tornatore (b 1956). Tornatore followed up on the incredible success of his semi-autobiographical film *Nuovo Cinema Paradiso* (Cinema Paradiso; 1988) with films including *Malèna* (2000), starring Monica Bellucci in a coming-of-age story set in Sicily in the 1940s; *L'uomo delle stelle* (The Star Maker; 1995), also set in rural Sicily in the 1940s; and *Baarìa – La porta del vento* (Baarìa – Door of the Wind; 2009), the story of three generations of a local family between 1920 and 1980.

Like Tornatore, Roman-born Emanuele Crialese has made Sicily his muse. Two of his films, *Respiro* (2002) and *Nuovomondo* (The Golden Door; 2006), are set here. *Respiro* is about a woman whose unorthodox behaviour challenges her family and islander neighbours, while *Nuovomondo* is a dreamy record of a Sicilian family's emigration to New York at the turn of the 20th century. Crialese's 2011 film *Terraferma* deals with the very contemporary issue of illegal immigration on the island of Linosa through a story of a fisherman's family. Gianfranco Rosi's award-winning 2016 documentary *Fuocoammare* (Fire at Sea; 2016) similarly juxtaposes local island life on Lampedusa against the flood of refugees arriving on the island from North Africa and the Middle East.

See a careful study of 21st-century Sicily in Emanuele Crialese's 2011 film *Terraferma*, dealing with illegal immigration.

SICILY ON PAGE & SCREEN SICILY ON FILM

The Mafia

For many people, Mafia is synonymous with Sicily, thanks to the country's infamous historical relationship with the organisation and the many films made about the Cosa Nostra – namely, and most famously, *The Godfather* trilogy. Starting life all the way back in the 18th century, the Mafia has shaped today's Sicily both through its criminal activities and, more recently, the brave and crucial anti-Mafia movement, which has involved a gradual resistance from all levels of Sicilian society.

Origins

The residents of Corleone once petitioned to change the town's name in order to get away from its criminal connotations.

The word *'mafia'* was in common usage for more than 110 years before it was officially acknowledged as referring to an actual organisation. Although formally recorded in Palermo in 1865, the term was not included in the Italian penal code until 1982.

The origins of the word have been much debated. The author Norman Lewis has suggested that it derives from the Arabic *mu'afah* or 'place of refuge'. Nineteenth-century etymologists proposed *mahjas,* the Arabic word for 'boasting'. Whatever the origin, the term *mafioso* existed long before the organisation known as the Mafia, and was used to describe a character who was elegant and proud, with an independent vitality and spirit.

The concept of the *mafioso* goes all the way back to the late 15th century when commercial opportunities were so restricted that even the overprivileged feudal nobles were forced to make changes in order to survive. They introduced a policy of resettlement that forced thousands of farmers off the land and into new towns; the idea was to streamline crop growth, but it also destroyed the lives of the peasants in the process. Many of the aristocrats moved to big cities such as Palermo and Messina, leaving their estates in the hands of *gabellotti* (bailiffs), who were charged with collecting ground rents. They, in turn, employed the early *mafiosi* – who were small gangs of armed peasants – to help them solve any 'problems' that came up on the way. The *mafiosi* were soon robbing large estates and generally causing mayhem, but the local authorities were inept at dealing with them as they would quickly disappear into the brush.

The bandits struck a mixture of fear and admiration into the peasantry, who were happy to support any efforts to destabilise the feudal system. They became willing accomplices in protecting the outlaws and, although it would be another 400 years before crime became 'organised', the 16th and 17th centuries witnessed a substantial increase in the activities of brigand bands. The bands were referred to as Mafia, while the peasants' loyalty to their own people resulted in the name Cosa Nostra (Our Thing). The early Mafia's way of protecting itself from prosecution was to become the modern Mafia's most important weapon: the code of silence, or *omertà.*

The 'New' Mafia

Up until WWII the Mafia had operated almost exclusively in the countryside, but with the end of the conflict the Cosa Nostra began its expansion into the cities. It took over the construction industry, channelling funds into its bank accounts and creating a network of kickbacks that were factored into every project undertaken. In 1953 a one-off meeting between representatives of the US and Sicilian Mafias resulted in the creation of the first Sicilian Commission, which had representatives of the six main Mafia families (or *cosche,* literally meaning 'artichoke') to efficiently run its next expansion into the extremely lucrative world of narcotics. At the head of the commission was Luciano Liggio from Corleone, whose 'family' had played a vital role in developing US–Sicilian relations.

Throughout the 1960s and '70s the Mafia earned billions of dollars from the drug trade. Inevitably, the raised stakes made the different Mafia families greedy for a greater share and from the late 1960s onwards Sicily was awash with vicious feuds that left hundreds dead.

The most sensational assassination was that of the chief prefect of police, General Carlo Alberto Dalla Chiesa, whom the national government had sent to Sicily to direct anti-Mafia activities. Dalla Chiesa was ambushed in the heart of Palermo in 1982, and his brutal murder led to prosecutors and magistrates being granted wider powers of investigation.

The first real insight into the 'New Mafia' came with the arrest of *mafioso* Tommaso Buscetta, also in 1982. After nearly four years of interrogation, headed by the courageous Palermitan investigating magistrate Giovanni Falcone, Buscetta broke the code of silence. His revelations shocked and fascinated the Italian nation, as he revealed the innermost workings of La Società Onorata (the Honoured Society; the Mafia's chosen name for itself). Tragically, Falcone was assassinated in 1992, as was another courageous anti-Mafia magistrate, Paolo Borsellino.

In 1986, 500 top *mafiosi* were put on trial in the first *maxiprocesso* (maxi-trial) in a specially constructed bunker near Palermo's Ucciardone prison. The trial resulted in 347 convictions, of which 19 were life imprisonments and the others jail terms totalling a staggering 2665 years.

In January 1993 the authorities arrested the infamous *capo di tutti capi* (boss of bosses), Salvatore (Totò) Riina, the most wanted man in Europe. He was charged with a host of murders, including those of

The anti-*pizzo* (protection money) movement was inspired by the defiance of a shopkeeper called Libero Grassi, whose open letter to an extortionist was featured on the front page of a local newspaper in 1991. Grassi was murdered three weeks later.

THE MAFIA ON SCREEN

Il Capo dei Capi (The Boss of all Bosses) Italian TV miniseries (2007) about Salvatore Riina.

Dimenticare Palermo (To Forget Palermo) Italian political thriller (1989) directed by Francesco Rosi and co-written by Gore Vidal.

Excellent Cadavers Alexander Stille's 1995 book about Giovanni Falcone was made into a TV movie directed by Ricky Tognazzi in 1999 and a documentary directed by Marco Turco in 2005.

Il Giorno della Civetta (The Day of the Owl) Damiano Damiani's 1968 film was based on Leonardo Sciascia's novel.

The Godfather Trilogy Francis Ford Coppola's 1972–90 masterwork.

In Nome della Legge (In the Name of the Law) Pietro Germi's 1949 Italian neorealist film was co-written by Federico Fellini.

La Piovra (The Octopus) Hugely popular 1984–2001 Italian TV miniseries.

Salvatore Giuliano Francesco Rosi's 1962 neorealist film.

magistrates Falcone and Borsellino, and sentenced to life imprisonment. Riina died in prison in 2017.

The Anti-Mafia Movement

The anti-Mafia movement is alive and kicking in Sicily, tracing its roots back to the beginning of today's Mafia. According to historians, the movement first appeared in the late 19th century, and lasted in its first incarnation until the 1950s. The movement strove for agrarian reform, targeting the Mafia, conservative political elites and the *latifondisti* (big landowners), but its efforts were shattered when the lack of economic prospects in the postwar era drove thousands of young Sicilians to emigrate in search of work and a better life.

During the 1960s and 1970s, the anti-Mafia movement was headed by political radicals, mainly members of the left-wing groups disenchanted with the Socialist and Communist parties. Giuseppe 'Peppino' Impastato became famous during this period; the son of a *mafioso,* Impastato mocked individual *mafiosi* on his popular underground radio show. He was assassinated in 1978. Things were at their worst for the anti-Mafia movement in the 1980s, when the Mafia was particularly intolerant of anyone perceived as a potential threat. The assassination in 1982 of General Dalla Chiesa is now seen as one of the major elements in sparking a new wave in the anti-Mafia movement, with Sicilians from all sections of society – from educators and students to political activists and parish priests – becoming involved.

The reformist Christian Democrat Leoluca Orlando, who was elected mayor of Palermo during the 1980s, also helped to increase anti-Mafia sentiment. He led an alliance of left-wing movements and parties to create Palermo Spring, which invalidated the public-sector contracts previously given to Mafia families, restored and reopened public buildings, and aided in the arrests of leading *mafiosi*. During the 1990s Orlando left the Christian Democrats and set up the anticorruption movement La Rete (the Network), bringing together a broad collection of anti-Mafia individuals and reform organisations. (The party was eventually absorbed by Romano Prodi's Democrat Party in 1999.)

Civilian efforts saw housewives hanging sheets daubed with anti-Mafia slogans from their windows, shopkeepers and small entrepreneurs forming associations to oppose extortion, and the formation of groups such as Libera (www.libera.it), cofounded in 1994 by Rita Borsellino, the sister of the murdered judge Paolo Borsellino. Libera managed to get the Italian parliament to permit its member organisations to legally acquire properties that had been seized from the Mafia by the government, establishing agricultural cooperatives, *agriturismi* and other legitimate enterprises on these lands (see www.liberaterra.it). Even the Catholic Church, long silent on the Mafia's crimes, finally began to have outspoken anti-Mafia members. The best known was Giuseppe Puglisi, who organised local residents to oppose the Mafia; he was murdered in 1993.

The Mafia Today

Since Salvatore Riina's conviction other top *mafiosi* have followed him behind bars, most notably his successor Leoluca Bagarella, arrested in 1995; the Sicilian 'Godfather', Bernardo Provenzano, caught in 2006 after 20 years on the run; Salvatore Lo Piccolo, Provenzano's successor, arrested in 2007; and Domenico Raccuglia (aka 'the Veterinarian'), number two in the organisation, arrested in 2009 after 15 years on the run. Riina's death in prison in 2017 was another landmark moment in Sicily's anti-Mafia campaign, and was followed in 2018 by the arrests of four-dozen key Sicilian mobsters, including the new Palermo-based *capo* Settimio Mineo.

The arrest of Palermitan Teresa Marino in December 2015 revealed the growing role of women in Sicily's Cosa Nostra. The mother of five became a leading crime figure following the arrest of Marino's *mafioso* husband Tommaso Lo Presti in 2014; her duties included the management of cocaine shipments from South America.

The year 2013 was an eventful one for the anti-Mafia movement. April of that year saw the biggest ever seizure of Mafia-related assets, from businessman Vito Nicastri, who is alleged to have been a front man for the Cosa Nostra. In May more than 50,000 people attended the beatification of Don Giuseppe Puglisi, the Catholic priest shot by a Mafia hitman in 1993. Puglisi was the first Mafia victim to be officially declared a martyr by the Roman Catholic Church, a powerful statement for the anti-Mafia movement. The same month, Italy's former head politicians were on trial alongside Mafia bosses such as Salvatore Riina, for involvement with the Mafia in Sicily. Among the accused politicians was Nicola Mancino, the former interior minister.

No one would be so foolish to suggest that the power of the Mafia is a thing of the past, but these events have meant that the powerful core of the organisation is being weakened and that the silence, which for so many years has made progress difficult, is finally being broken.

Today's Mafia has infiltrated daily life, becoming intertwined with legal society: its collaborators and their children are now 'respectable' and influential citizens. Indeed, the Sicilian Mafia is considered the most bourgeois of Italy's four main crime syndicates, with associates holding significant roles in mainstream politics and business. In late 2015 a police investigation code-named Revenge 5 led to the arrest of 37 suspected clan members in Catania, among them the owners of a funeral home and a nonprofit NGO providing emergency medical care. While the funeral home served as a logistics base for drug trafficking, the NGO's ambulances were used for the transportation of illegal substances.

Despite its involvement in drug trafficking, Cosa Nostra today is upstaged by Calabria's more powerful 'Ndrangheta at an international level. Instead, the Sicilian Mafia mainly busies itself with local criminal activities, in particular the running of extortion rackets and the infiltration of public construction works. It's estimated that around 70% of businesses in Sicily pay *pizzo* (protection money) to the Mafia. In return, businesses receive immunity from theft or vandalism, as well as the help of local *mafiosi* to cut through bureaucratic red tape. In some cases, the *pizzo* is demanded in kind, whether through obligatory transactions with Mafia-run businesses, subcontracting to Mafia-owned companies, or the employment of Mafia-affiliated individuals. Those who refuse to yield are often intimidated with property damage or even physical assault. Critics call this 'the Invisible Mafia'.

Thankfully, not all Sicilians are willing to obey the Mafia's rules. The organisation Addiopizzo (www.addiopizzo.org), which campaigns against these iniquitous payments, urges consumers to support businesses that have said 'no' to paying *pizzo*. Its catchcry that a society subject to extortion is one without dignity seems to have struck a chord across the island and a number of tourism businesses – among others – are actively supporting the campaign by devising tours that support restaurants, shops and hotels that have said no to Mafia extortion (see www. addiopizzotravel.it).

Arts & Architecture

Millennia of foreign domination have left Sicily with a lavish artistic and architectural legacy. Ancient Greek temples litter the long southern coast, blazing mosaics adorn Roman villas and Byzantine churches, and forbidding Norman castles guard remote hilltop towns. Then there are Sicily's one-of-a-kind offerings, from East-meets-West Arab-Norman churches and palaces, to the lavish stuccowork, frescoes and stone-carved flourishes of its bombastic take on baroque.

Prehistoric Art

Prehistoric art enthusiasts will find rock paintings and graffiti all over Sicily. The Museo Archeologico Regionale Eoliano, in Lipari, showcases a fascinating collection of prehistoric and ancient finds from early Mediterranean times; highlights include attractive ceramics and terracotta produced by the first Neolithic indigenous cultures in the region. The Upper Palaeolithic wall paintings and Neolithic incised drawings at the Grotta del Genovese on the offshore island of Levanzo were accidentally discovered in 1949 by the painter Francesca Minellono. Between 6000 and 10,000 years old, the images predominantly portray terrestrial animals, including deer and horses, though you can spot tuna too, a fish traditionally found in the waters off Sicily.

The Greeks & Romans

The Greeks settled in the 8th century BC and left the most enduring architectural legacy on the island. Sicily has some of the most impressive Doric temples in the Western world – the most enchanting are those at the Valley of the Temples in Agrigento. Other magnificent remains are at Selinunte, followed by those at the Parco Archeologico della Neapolis at Syracuse. The remains of the city of Segesta form one of the world's most mesmerising ancient sites with a theatre high on the mountain and a never-completed Doric temple dating from around 430 BC. The Teatro Greco at Syracuse is a masterpiece of classical architecture that could seat 16,000 people, while Taormina's Teatro Greco, built in the 3rd

---

TOP ART GALLERIES

Galleria Regionale della Sicilia (Palermo) Home to works dating from the Middle Ages to the 18th century.

Galleria d'Arte Moderna (Palermo) Sicilian paintings and sculptures from the 19th and 20th centuries.

Museo Regionale Interdisciplinare (Messina) Paintings by Caravaggio and home-town boy Antonello da Messina.

Pinacoteca Villa Zito (Palermo) Four centuries of Sicilian-themed art, housed in an elegant 18th-century villa.

Museo Guttuso (Bagheria) Lesser-known museum devoted to Sicily's foremost 20th-century artist, Renato Guttuso.

century BC overlooking the Ionian Sea and Mt Etna, is the most dramatically situated Greek theatre in the world. It's also the second largest in Sicily, after that of Syracuse.

Sicily's most important Roman sight is the Villa Romana del Casale in Piazza Armerina, an ancient pleasure palace with an extraordinary array of vivid, large-scale floor mosaics dating from the 3rd century. Smaller in scale but nonetheless impressive are the themed floor mosaics at Villa Romana del Tellaro, south of Noto.

The Normans

The Normans collaborated with Byzantine and Arab architects and artisans, transforming Greek temples into basilicas and building innovative new structures that reflect a unique mix of architectural and artistic influences, including mosaics. Norman cathedrals remain some of Sicily's most impressive sights – the Cattedrale di Monreale, the Duomo in Cefalù, and the Cappella Palatina in Palermo are this period's glittering stars – all granted World Heritage status by Unesco in 2015 along with six other Arab-Norman monuments in Palermo.

Palermo's Palazzo dei Normanni was originally constructed by the Arabs in the 9th century and extended by the Normans (namely Roger II) in 1130. At its centre is the Cappella Palatina, Palermo's prime attraction. Hypnotic mosaics aside, the chapel claims one of the finest examples of an Islamic ceiling in the Mediterranean, reputedly created by craftsmen shipped in from Cairo. Other splendid examples from this period are the churches of La Martorana and Chiesa di San Giovanni degli Eremiti, both in Palermo.

The Renaissance: Painting & Sculpture

Although no great architectural heritage remains in Sicily from the Renaissance era, painting and sculpture flourished. The era would also deliver Sicily's best-known painter, Antonello da Messina.

The Gagini family were sculptors and architects who founded Sicily's Gagini school, which flourished until the mid-1600s. Domenico Gagini (1420–92), the school's founder, often worked in conjunction with his son, Antonello Gagini (1478–1536). Antonello's most notable work is the decorated arch in the Cappella della Madonna in Trapani's Santuario dell'Annunziata. He also produced ecclesiastical sculpture in Messina, and a large collection of his works can be seen at Palermo's Galleria Regionale della Sicilia – look out for his statue of the *Madonna del riposo* (1528).

Francesco Laurana (1430–1502), a Dalmatian-born sculptor considered both Italian and Croatian (the Croatian version of his name is Frane Vranjanin), worked in Sicily between 1466 and 1471. Among other works, he produced the tomb of Pietro Speciale in the Chiesa di San Francesco d'Assisi in Palermo, and his bust of Eleanor of Aragon, in the city's Galleria Regionale della Sicilia, is particularly sumptuous.

Baroque Beauties

The Sicilian baroque period was a result of the 1693 earthquake that flattened cities such as Catania and left the space for this highly flamboyant architectural style to flourish. Sicily's brand of baroque combined the Spanish baroque with Sicily's own decorative and structural elements, among them the generous use of *putti* (cherubs) and masks as decorative motifs.

Two architects that dominated the scene were Rosario Gagliardi (1700–70), designer of the magnificent Cattedrale di San Giorgio in Ragusa, and Giovanni Battista Vaccarini (1702–69), who spent 30 years recreating Catania's historical core. Noto's baroque centre is one of Sicily's most powerful examples of this architectural style.

The most important artist from this period was Giacomo Serpotta, born in Palermo in 1656. Working mostly with plaster, Serpotta helped

---

Palermitan architect Ernesto Basile (1857–1932) was one of Italy's most prolific exponents of Liberty (Italian art nouveau) and modernism. His legacies include Palermo's Grand Hotel Villa Igiea, Teatro Massimo and Villino Florio. The term Liberty was inspired by London department store Liberty & Co, which famously sold art nouveau arts and craft.

Palermo's Galleria Regionale della Sicilia is home to the unnerving Trionfo della morte (Triumph of Death), a 15th-century fresco believed to have influenced Pablo Picasso's iconic painting Guernica.

ANTONELLO DA MESSINA

The first great Sicilian painter was Antonello da Messina (1430–79). Originally from Messina, the artist is thought to have painted his first portraits in the late 1460s. They follow a Dutch model, the subject being shown bust-length, against a dark background, full face or in three-quarter view. Most Italian painters had adopted the semi-profile pose for individual portraits up to that point. In *The Portrait in the Renaissance* (1966) John Pope-Hennessy described him as 'the first Italian painter for whom the individual portrait was an art form in its own right'. In *The Lives of the Artists* (1550), Giorgio Vasari described da Messina as 'a man well skilled in his art' and claimed that he was the first Italian painter to use oil paint, a technique Vasari says he had learned in Flanders, though there is no evidence of da Messina having travelled outside Italy.

Sicily remains home to a small number of his luminous paintings. You'll find his graceful *Annunziata* (The Virgin Annunciate, 1474–77) in Palermo's Galleria Regionale della Sicilia and his splendid *Ritratto di un uomo ignoto* (Portrait of an Unknown Man, 1465) – considered to be one of the most distinctive portraits of the Italian Renaissance – in Cefalù's Museo Mandralisca. On the east coast, Syracuse's Galleria Regionale di Palazzo Bellomo claims *L'Annunciazione* (Annunciation, 1474), while Messina's Museo Regionale is home to his *San Gregorio* (St Gregory, 1473) polyptych.

elevate stuccowork in Italy from a craft to a high art, creating a technique for polishing plaster that bestowed his creations with a stone-like lustre. His work adorns numerous churches and oratories in Palermo, among them the Oratorio di Santa Cita, home to his masterpiece, *Battle of Lepanto*. Other places where you can appreciate Serpotta's work include the Cappella di Sant'Anna in Castelbuono's Museo Civico.

Some of the most impressive Doric temples in the Western world are to be found in Sicily – the best are at Agrigento's Valley of the Temples (Valle dei Templi).

Liberty

Palermo flourished in the Liberty (Italian art nouveau) period. The innovation of architects such as Giovan Battista Basile and his son Ernesto, and artists such as Salvatore Gregorietti and Ettore Maria de Begler, who painted the dining room of the Grand Hotel Villa Igiea, marked the epoch. Two kiosks in front of Palermo's Teatro Massimo and one opposite Teatro Politeama Garibaldi are fine examples of Sicilian art nouveau, while Villa Malfitano features some early Liberty elements. Unfortunately, much of the city's Liberty architecture was bulldozed in the Mafia-driven mid-20th-century building boom pejoratively known as the Sacco di Palermo (Sack of Palermo).

Modern & Contemporary Art

Salvatore Fiume (1915–97) and Renato Guttuso (1911–87) remain two of the biggest names in modern Sicilian art. Guttuso's masterful 1974 painting of the Vucciria market is one of Sicily's most impressive recent art works. On display at Palermo's Museo dell'Inquisizione, its vibrant colours are the product of the artist's innovative approach – he used crumbled bricks to produce the reds, and burnt wood and candles for the black strokes.

Among the current crop of prolific creatives are Palermo-based photographer Ferdinando Scianna (b 1943), multimedia artist Ignazio Mortellaro (b 1973) and Catanian illustrators Carlo and Fabio Ingrassia (b 1985). The latter, identical twins, work simultaneously on the same pieces, drawing from the outside of an image towards the centre to create harmonious, obsessively detailed works.

A thought-provoking place for a shot of contemporary Sicilian art is Favara's Farm Cultural Park, where art and social activism go hand in hand and serve art's great purpose – to try to make a real change.

Survival Guide

Directory A–Z

Accessible Travel

Sicily is not an easy island for travellers with disabilities. Narrow cobbled streets, hair-raising traffic, blocked sidewalks, steep curbs and tiny lifts make life very difficult for wheelchair users, and those with sight or hearing difficulties.

Larger hotels in all regions can cater for disabled guests, although many B&Bs and guesthouses cannot due to lack of lifts or steps inside the property. In Palermo, several museums and galleries are wheelchair accessible, while most buses and all trams are wheelchair friendly.

If you have an obvious disability and/or appropriate ID, many museums and galleries offer free admission for yourself and a companion.

Discount Cards

For travellers under 30, the European Youth Card (www.eyca.org) is widely accepted.

At many state museums and archaeological sites, EU citizens under 18 enter free, and those aged between 18 and 25 get a 50% discount. To claim these discounts you officially need a passport, driving licence or ID card as proof of age and nationality; non-EU citizens are technically ineligible for discounts, although some ticket-takers are more lenient than others in enforcing these rules.

The 'reduced' rate in our prices refers to the student discount. Seniors aged 65 or older sometimes (but not always) qualify for similar discounts.

At private museums, children under 18 usually receive some kind of discount, with young children often entering free of charge.

Electricity

Italian plugs have two or three round pins; travellers from countries with a different plug type should bring an adapter.

The current is 230V, 50Hz.

Type F
230V/50Hz

Type L
220V/50Hz

Health

Before You Go
HEALTH INSURANCE

If you're an EU citizen, an EHIC (European Health Insurance Card) covers you for free or reduced-cost public medical care but not for emergency repatriation. It is available from health centres in your home country. Citizens from countries outside the EU should find out if there is a reciprocal arrangement for free medical care between their country and Italy (Australia, for example, has such an agreement; carry your Medicare card with you).

EATING PRICE RANGES

Most restaurants have a *coperto* (cover charge), sometimes called a *pane e coperto* (bread and cover charge), of €1 to €3 per person; some also include a *servizio* (service charge) of 10% to 15%.

The following price ranges refer to a meal consisting of two courses (antipasto or *primo*, plus *secondo*), glass of house wine and *coperto*.

€ less than €25

€€ €25–45

€€€ more than €45

US citizens should check whether their health-insurance plan offers coverage for hospital or medical costs abroad – many don't. The US Medicare service provides no coverage outside the US. If you do need health insurance, make sure you get a policy that covers you for the worst possible scenario, such as an accident requiring an emergency flight home. Find out in advance if your insurance plan will make payments directly to providers or reimburse you later for overseas health expenditures abroad.

VACCINATIONS

No vaccinations are required for travel to Sicily.

In Sicily
AVAILABILITY & COST OF HEALTH CARE

Italy's public-health system is legally bound to provide urgent care to everyone. For emergency treatment go to the *pronto soccorso* (casualty/emergency) section of an *ospedale* (public hospital), where it's also possible to receive emergency dental treatment. For less serious ailments call the local *guardia medica* (duty doctor) – ask at your hotel or nearest tourist office for the number.

Pharmacists will fill prescriptions and can provide basic medical advice. Larger cities generally have a *farmacia di turno* (a designated pharmacy keeping late-night

hours on a rotating basis to ensure round-the-clock emergency service).

TAP WATER

While tap water is reliable and safe throughout the region, most Sicilians prefer to drink *acqua minerale* (bottled mineral water). It will be either *frizzante* (sparkling) or *naturale* (still), and you will be asked in restaurants and bars which you prefer. If you want a glass of tap water, ask for *acqua del rubinetto*.

Insurance

A travel-insurance policy to cover theft, loss and medical problems is highly recommended. It may also cover you for cancellation of, and delays in, your travel arrangements.

Paying for your ticket with a credit card can often provide limited travel accident insurance, and you may be able to reclaim the payment if the operator doesn't deliver.

Note that some policies specifically exclude 'dangerous activities', which can include scuba diving, motorcycling and even trekking.

Worldwide travel insurance is available at www.lonelyplanet.com/travel-insurance. You can buy, extend and claim online anytime – even if you're already on the road.

Internet Access

Public wi-fi hotspots are fairly common in cafes and bars, and most hotels and B&Bs offer free wi-fi. In accommodation listings the internet icon is used to indicate that there is a computer available for guest use, while the wi-fi icon indicates there is wi-fi access. Wi-fi is specifically mentioned in reviews only when charges apply.

Legal Matters

The most likely reason for a brush with the law is if you have to report a theft. If you do have something stolen and you want to claim it on insurance, you must make a statement to the police; insurance companies won't pay up without proof of a crime.

The Italian police is divided into three main bodies: the black-clad *carabinieri;* the *polizia di stato*, who wear navy blue jackets; and the *guardia di finanza*, who fight tax evasion and drug smuggling. If you run into trouble in Italy, you're likely to end up dealing with either the *polizia* or the *carabinieri*. If, however, you land a parking ticket, you'll need to speak to the *vigili urbani* (traffic wardens).

The legal blood-alcohol limit is 0.05% (0.5g/L), and random breath tests do occur. Penalties for driving under the influence of alcohol can be severe.

In general, your embassy should be able to provide a list of local lawyers, interpreters and translators.

PRACTICALITIES

➡ **Smoking** Prohibited in all public spaces, as per EU law.

➡ **Weights & Measures** Sicily uses the metric system.

LGBT+ Travellers

Homosexuality (over the age of 16) is legal in Sicily. The LGBT+ scene is centred on cities including Catania, Taormina, Syracuse and Palermo. In rural areas, attitudes remain largely conservative. In 2016, Italy recognised civil unions for same-sex couples (the last major Western European country to do so, largely due to resistance from Catholic members of parliament).

Large summertime pride parades take place annually in Palermo (www.palermo pride.it) and Catania (www. facebook.com/Cataniagay-pride).

Online resources include the following (all in Italian):

Arcigay (www.arcigay.it) Italy's largest gay organisation, with branches in Catania, Messina, Palermo, Ragusa and Syracuse.

Coordinamento Lesbiche Italiano (CLR; www.clrbp.it) The national organisation for lesbians, holding regular literary meetings, film festivals and other events.

Gay.it (www.gay.it) Website featuring LGBT+ news, feature articles and gossip.

Guida Gay Italia (www.guidagay. it) Details on gay-friendly bars, clubs, beaches and hotels.

Pride (www.prideonline.it) National monthly magazine of art, music, politics and gay culture.

Spartacus World (www.sparta-cus.gayguide.travel/goingout/europe/italy/sicilia) Lists male-only venues in Sicily and elsewhere in Italy.

Maps

Touring Club Italiano (TCI) sells a good 1:200,000 general-purpose Sicily map (€8.50) through its online store (www.touringclubstore. com/it/reparto/sicilia). Arbatus (www.arbatus.com) publishes excellent multilingual trekking maps (€6) for each of the seven Aeolian islands.

For walking in the Mt Etna area, Selca's 1:25,000 *Mt Etna - Carta Escursionistica Altomontana* (€7.20), available from Stella Alpina (www. stella-alpina.com), is a good bet. Maps for other popular trekking areas, including the Monti Madonie and Nebrodi, are available from local park offices.

Money

ATMs

Credit and debit cards can be used in ATMs (which are widespread and known locally as *bancomat*). Most ATMs have multilingual screens, making life easy for English-speakers but, in a pinch, the Italian term for international cash withdrawal is *prelievo internazionale*. Visa and MasterCard are widely recognised, as are cards on the Cirrus and Maestro networks. Remember that every time you withdraw cash there will be fees. Typically you'll be charged a withdrawal fee as well as a conversion charge; if you're using a credit card, you'll also be hit by interest on the cash withdrawn.

If an ATM rejects your card, don't despair. Try a few more ATMs displaying your credit card's logo before assuming the problem lies with your card.

Credit & Debit Cards

Though widely accepted, credit cards are not as ubiquitous in Sicily as they are in the UK or the US, and it's always a good idea to have some cash on hand. Some small guesthouses, trattorias and shops don't take credit cards, and you can't always use them at petrol stations, parking meters or motorway toll booths.

Major cards such as Visa, MasterCard and Eurocard are accepted throughout Sicily. Amex is also recognised but it's less common.

Before leaving home, make sure to advise your credit-card holder of your

travel plans. Otherwise, you risk having your card blocked – as a security measure, banks block cards when they notice out-of-the-ordinary transactions. Check also any charges you'll incur and what the procedure is if you experience problems or have your card stolen. Most card suppliers will give you an emergency number you can call free of charge for help and advice.

Currency

Italy's currency is the euro (€). The euro is divided into 100 cents. Coin denominations are one, two, five, 10, 20 and 50 cents, €1 and €2. The notes are €5, €10, €20, €50, €100, €200 and €500.

Currency Exchange

Money can be exchanged in banks, post offices and exchange offices. Banks generally offer the best rates, but shop around as rates fluctuate considerably.

Opening Hours

Banks 8.30am to 1.30pm and 2.45pm to 4pm Monday to Friday.

Cafes 7am to 8pm (or later if offering bar service at night).

Museums Hours vary, but many close on Monday.

Restaurants Noon to 2.30pm and 7.30pm to 11pm; many close one day per week.

Shops 9.30am to 1.30pm and 4pm to 7.30pm Monday to Saturday.

Post

Sicily's postal system, **Poste Italiane** (☑803 160; www. poste.it), is never going to win any awards for efficiency but sooner or later letters generally arrive. Delivery is guaranteed to Europe within three days and to the rest of the world within four to eight days.

Stamps (*francobolli*) are available at post offices and

authorised tobacconists (look for the official *tabacchi* sign, a big 'T', often white on black), which you'll find in every town and village.

For more important items, use registered mail (*raccomandato*) or insured mail (*assicurato*); the cost depends on the value of the object being sent.

Public Holidays

Most Sicilians take their annual holiday in August, deserting the cities for the cooler seaside or mountains. This means that many businesses and shops close for at least part of the month, especially around the Feast of the Assumption (Ferragosto) on 15 August. Easter is another busy period, with many resort hotels opening for the season the week before Easter.

Italian schools close for three months in summer, from mid-June to mid-September, for two weeks at Christmas and for a week at Easter.

Individual towns have public holidays to celebrate the feasts of their patron saints. National public holidays in Sicily include the following:

Capodanno (New Year's Day) 1 January

Epifania (Epiphany) 6 January

Pasqua (Easter) March/April

Pasquetta (Easter Monday) March/April

Giorno della Liberazione (Liberation Day) 25 April

Festa del Lavoro (Labour Day) 1 May

Festa della Repubblica (Republic Day) 2 June

Ferragosto (Feast of the Assumption) 15 August

Festa di Ognissanti (All Saints' Day) 1 November

Festa della Immacolata Concezione (Feast of the Immaculate Conception) 8 December

Natale (Christmas Day) 25 December

Festa di Santo Stefano (Boxing Day) 26 December

Safe Travel

Despite Mafia notoriety, Sicily is not a dangerous place.

➜ If you experience a theft, always report it to the police within 24 hours, and ask for a statement; otherwise, your travel insurance company won't pay out.

➜ In major cities, roads that appear to be for one-way traffic often have special lanes for buses travelling in the opposite direction, so always look both ways before stepping out.

Telephone

TIM/Telecom Italia (www.tim.it) is Italy's biggest telecommunications company, offering both landline and cellular service.

Mobile Phones

Italian mobile phones operate on the GSM 900/1800 network. If you have an unlocked phone that supports these frequencies, you can purchase a *pre-pagato* (prepaid) SIM card in Italy for as little as €10.

SIM CARDS

As a general rule, local SIM card rates are cheaper than the roaming rates incurred for using your home mobile phone in Italy.

TIM, Wind Tre (www.windtre.it) and Vodafone (www.vodafone.it) all sell a variety of SIM cards offering voice, data and/or international calling, and all have plentiful retail outlets in Sicily. You'll need your passport to open an account. To top up your account, simply pop into the nearest outlet or buy a *ricarica* (recharge) from a tobacconist.

Useful Numbers & Phone Codes

Italian area codes all begin with '0' and consist of up to four digits. The area code is followed by a telephone number of anything from four to eight digits. Area codes are an integral part of all telephone numbers in Italy, even if you are calling within a single zone. For example, any number you ring in Palermo will start with 091, even if it's next door. When making domestic calls you must always dial the full number including the initial zero. Mobile-phone numbers begin with a three-digit prefix such as 333, 347 or 390.

To make an international call from Sicily, dial the international access code (00), then the relevant country and area codes followed by the telephone number.

To dial a Sicilian number from outside Italy, dial your international access code, followed by Italy's country code (39), the relevant area code (including the initial '0') and the number.

International access code	00
Italy country code	39
Directory enquiries	1254

Time

Sicily is one hour ahead of GMT. Daylight-saving time starts on the last Sunday in March, when clocks are put forward one hour. Clocks go back an hour on the last Sunday in October. Italy operates on the 24-hour clock, so rather than 6.30pm, you'll see 18.30 on transport timetables.

Toilets

Public toilets are rare in Sicily except at major tourist sites and archaeological parks. Most people use the facilities in bars and cafes – although you might need to buy a coffee first. In many places public loos are pretty grim; try to go armed with some tissues.

Tourist Information

Sicily's official regional tourist authority is the Assessorato Turismo Sport e Spettacolo (www.visitsicily.info).

You'll find tourist offices located throughout Sicily. Some are more helpful than others but most are able to provide accommodation lists, rudimentary maps and information on local tourist attractions. Most will also respond to telephone and email requests for information, though responses to the latter can be maddeningly slow.

Opening hours vary but as a general rule are 9am to 1pm and from 3pm to 7pm Monday to Friday. Hours are usually extended in summer, when some offices also open on Saturday or Sunday. Some cities have subsidiary information booths at train stations, though these often keep shorter hours or operate only in summer.

Offices in popular destinations such as Palermo, Catania, Taormina, Syracuse, Cefalù and Agrigento are usually well stocked and staffed by employees with a working knowledge of at least one other language, usually English but sometimes also French or German.

Officially, Sicilian tourist offices are known as *Servizi Turistici Regionali* (Regional Tourist Services), but for the sake of simplicity we refer to them as 'tourist offices'.

Visas

For up-to-date information on visa requirements, see www.esteri.it/visti.

EU citizens do not need a visa to enter Italy. Nationals of several other countries, including Australia, Canada, Israel, Japan, New Zealand and the USA, do not need visas for stays of up to 90 days in Italy.

Other people wishing to visit Italy have to apply for a Schengen visa, which allows unlimited travel in Italy and 25 other European countries for a 90-day period. You must apply for a Schengen visa in your country of residence and you can not apply for more than two in any 12-month period. They are not renewable inside Italy.

Technically, all foreign visitors to Italy are supposed to register with the local police within eight days of arrival. However, if you're staying in a hotel or hostel you don't need to bother as the hotel will do it for you – this is why they always take your passport details.

Women Travellers

Sicily in general is a welcoming and safe place for women travellers, including those travelling solo. Cultural stereotypes of Italian men harassing lone foreign women are largely outdated and exaggerated.

That said, eye-to-eye contact remains the norm in Italy's daily flirtatious interplay, and with some men this may segue into overt staring. Usually a simple show of disinterest is enough to nip unwanted attention in the bud. If ignoring such behaviour doesn't work, politely say that you're waiting for your *marito* (husband) or *fidanzato* (boyfriend) and, if necessary, walk away. If you are visibly in distress, people near you or passersby will generally step in to assist.

Transport

GETTING THERE & AWAY

Flights, cars and tours can be booked online at lonelyplanet.com/bookings.

Air

Fares to Sicily fluctuate throughout the year: tickets tend to be cheapest between November and March and most expensive between June and September. Holidays such as Christmas, New Year's and Easter see large price hikes. Flight schedules are also subject to seasonal variations, with the number of flights increasing considerably in summer.

Airports & Airlines

Sicily's two main airports serve the island's two biggest cities: Palermo and Catania.

Named after two assassinated anti-Mafia judges, **Palermo Falcone-Borsellino Airport** (☑800

541880, 091 702 02 73; www.gesap.it) is at Punto Raisi, 30km west of Palermo. Alitalia (www.alitalia.com), Air Italy (www.airitaly.com) and two dozen other airlines operate regular flights to/from major Italian and international destinations, including Frankfurt, London, Madrid, Milan, Munich, New York City and Zürich; Ryanair (www.ryanair.com), easyJet (www.easyjet.com), Volotea (www.volotea.com), Vueling (www.vueling.com) and TUIFly (www.tuifly.com) are among the low-cost carriers serving other cities, including Amsterdam, Barcelona, Bologna, Florence, Paris and Rome.

Just 7km outside Catania, **Catania Fontanarossa Airport** (☑095 723 91 11; www.aeroporto.catania.it; ☎) is served by many national and international airlines, with connections to destinations across Europe, including London, Paris, Zürich, Munich and Berlin.

Sicily's third-busiest airport, **Vincenzo Florio Air-**

port (Trapani-Birgi Vincenzo Florio Airport; ☑0923 61 01 11; www.airgest.it) – also known as Birgi – is 16km south of Trapani. Ryanair and Alitalia serve a handful of destinations, including Rome, Milan, Bologna, Karlsruhe and Prague. DAT (www.dat.dk) flies to the offshore island of Pantelleria.

The much smaller **Comiso Airport** (☑0932 96 14 67; www.aeroportodicomiso.eu; SP5, Comiso; ☎), 27km northwest of Ragusa, is served year-round by Ryanair flights to Italian cities including Rome, Milan and Pisa; a few airlines also offer seasonal flights to other destinations.

Land
Bus

SAIS Trasporti (☑091 617 11 41; www.saistrasporti.it) operates long-distance buses between Sicily and Italian mainland destinations, including Rome and Naples.

CLIMATE CHANGE & TRAVEL

Every form of transport that relies on carbon-based fuel generates CO_2, the main cause of human-induced climate change. Modern travel is dependent on aeroplanes, which might use less fuel per kilometre per person than most cars but travel much greater distances. The altitude at which aircraft emit gases (including CO_2) and particles also contributes to their climate change impact. Many websites offer 'carbon calculators' that allow people to estimate the carbon emissions generated by their journey and, for those who wish to do so, to offset the impact of the greenhouse gases emitted with contributions to portfolios of climate-friendly initiatives throughout the world. Lonely Planet offsets the carbon footprint of all staff and author travel.

DEPARTURE TAX

Departure tax is included in the price of a ticket.

While reservations are not generally necessary on Sicilian buses, they're highly recommended in the high season for long-haul, overnight journeys of this sort.

Car & Motorcycle

Driving to Sicily can be an arduous and expensive proposition. In terms of budget, you'll need to account for the cost of toll roads and the fact that Italian fuel prices are among the highest in Europe. Your journey time will also depend on where you catch the ferry.

The shortest ferry to Sicily is the 20-minute crossing from Villa San Giovanni (on the toe of the Italian mainland) to Messina. It's about a 13-hour drive from the French, Swiss or Austrian border to Villa San Giovanni, but only if you keep to the motorways, go flat out (the speed limit is 130km/h) and avoid traffic, which is something of a vain hope in the summer holiday period (July and August).

A less-demanding option from northern Europe is to drive south to Genoa, Livorno, Civitavecchia, Naples or Salerno and take a ferry from there.

Once in Sicily, a car or motorbike is a major plus, but it is probably easier to hire one than to take your own.

BRINGING YOUR OWN VEHICLE

To bring your own vehicle to Sicily, you will need to have a valid driving licence, proof of vehicle ownership and evidence of third-party insurance. If your vehicle is registered and insured in an EU country, your home-country insurance is sufficient. Ask

your insurer for a European Accident Statement (EAS) form, which can simplify matters in the event of an accident. The form can also be downloaded online at www.cartraveldocs.com/european-accident-statement.

If bringing a motorcycle to Sicily, be aware that a crash helmet and a motorcycle licence (for any vehicle over 125cc) are compulsory.

Every vehicle travelling across an international border should display a nationality plate of its country of registration. A warning triangle (to be used in the event of a breakdown) is compulsory throughout Europe.

Train

If you have the time, getting to Sicily by train is worth considering: it's more environmentally friendly than flying, it's more relaxed and, perhaps best of all, it gives you the option of breaking up your journey, since most north-to-south Italian rail itineraries involve a change of trains in Rome or Naples.

Italy's national rail company, **Trenitalia** (☑892021; www.trenitalia.com), operates direct InterCity trains to Sicily from both Rome and Naples, along with direct night trains (InterCityNotte) from Milan, Rome and Naples; on the latter, you can often book a *cuccetta* (sleeping compartment) for little more than the cost of a normal seat on the day train. Upon arrival at the tip of Italy's boot, Intercity trains are split in two and loaded onto ferries for the crossing of the Straits of Messina to Sicily, with some carriages continuing west to Palermo and others heading south to Catania.

For detailed info on getting to Sicily from London, check out www.seat61.com. Another resource is the *European Rail Timetable*, a Europe-wide compendium of train schedules, available online at www.europeanrailtimetable.co.uk.

Sea

Unless you're flying, arriving in Sicily involves a ferry crossing. Regular car/passenger ferries cross the Strait of Messina (the 3km stretch of water that separates Sicily from the Italian mainland) to Messina from either Villa San Giovanni or Reggio di Calabria. Ferries also sail to Sicily from Genoa, Livorno, Civitavecchia, Naples, Salerno, Cagliari (Sardinia), Malta and Tunisia.

Across the Strait of Messina

Blu Jet (Bluferries; Map p172; ☑340 9848540, 340 1545091; www.blujetlines.it) Hydrofoils to Messina from Reggio di Calabria and Villa San Giovanni.

Caronte & Tourist (☑090 5737; www.carontetourist.it; Viale della Libertà) Car ferries to Messina from Villa San Giovanni.

Liberty Lines (☑0923 02 20 22; www.libertylines.it) Summer-only hydrofoils to Messina from Reggio di Calabria.

From Italy, Tunisia & Malta

During the high season (late June through early September), all routes are busy and you'll need to book several weeks in advance. The helpful search engine **Traghetti Online** (☑010 573 18 00; www.traghettionline.net) provides comprehensive route details and an online booking service.

Note that although you do not need to show your passport on internal routes, you should still keep photo ID handy.

Caronte & Tourist (☑090 5737; www.carontetourist.it; Viale della Libertà) Ferries to Messina from Salerno.

Grandi Navi Veloci (☑010 209 45 91; www.gnv.it) Ferries to Palermo from Civitavecchia, Genoa, Naples and Tunis.

Grimaldi (☑081 49 64 44; www.grimaldi-lines.com) Ferries to Palermo from Livorno, Salerno and Tunis, and to Catania from Salerno.

Siremar (☑090 57 37; www. carontetourist.it/siremar) Ferries to the Aeolian Islands and Milazzo from Naples.

SNAV (☑081 428 55 55; www. snav.it) Summer-only hydrofoils to the Aeolian Islands from Naples.

Tirrenia (☑from abroad 02 7602 8132, within Italy 800 804020; www.tirrenia.it) Ferries to Palermo from Naples and Cagliari.

Virtu Ferries (☑Catania 095 703 12 11; www.virtuferries. com) Ferries to Pozzallo from Malta, with connecting bus service to Catania.

GETTING AROUND

Air

The only commercial flights within Sicily are those connecting the main island with smaller islands offshore. DAT (www.dat.dk) flies daily from Palermo and Catania to Lampedusa, and from Palermo, Catania and Trapani to Pantelleria. **Air Panarea** (☑340 3667214; www.airpanar ea.com) offers helicopter service from Catania, Taormina and elsewhere to the Aeolian Islands.

Bicycle

There are no special road rules for cyclists, but you would be wise to carry a helmet and lights. If cycling during the summer, make sure you have plenty of water and sunblock as the heat can be exhausting.

Bike hire isn't widespread, but it's usually available at coastal resorts and on smaller islands. Some small *pensioni* and *agriturismi* (farm stays) also offer the use of bikes to guests. Bank on around €10 per day for bike hire.

Boat

Sicily's offshore islands are served by *traghetti* (ferries) and *aliscafi* (hydrofoils). To the Aeolian Islands, services run from Milazzo and Messina; to the Egadi Islands, from Trapani and Marsala; to Ustica, from Palermo; and to the Pelagic Islands, from Porto Empedocle (near Agrigento).

Many services run year-round, although they are pared back considerably in winter and can be affected by adverse sea conditions.

On overnight services (for example, to the Pelagic Islands or Pantelleria) travellers can choose between cabin accommodation or a *poltrona*, which is an airline-type armchair. Deck class is available only during the summer and only on some ferries, so ask when making your booking. All ferries carry vehicles.

Operators include the following:

Liberty Lines (☑0923 02 20 22; www.libertylines.it) Runs hydrofoils to Pantelleria from Trapani, to the Egadi Islands from Trapani and Marsala; to the Aeolian Islands from Milazzo and Messina; to the Pelagic Islands from Porto Empedocle; and to Ustica from Palermo. Also offers summer-only service from Palermo to the Aeolians.

Siremar (☑090 57 37; www. carontetourist.it/siremar) Operates ferries from Palermo to Ustica, from Milazzo to the Aeolian Islands, from Trapani to Pantelleria and the Egadi Islands, and from Porto Empedocle to the Pelagic Islands.

NGI (Navigazione Generale Italiana;☑800 250000; www. ngi-spa.it) Runs ferries from Milazzo to the Aeolian Islands.

Traghetti delle Isole (☑0923 2 24 67; www.traghettidelleisole. it) Runs ferries from Trapani to Pantelleria and from Porto Empedocle to the Pelagic Islands.

Bus

Away from the main coastal train routes, buses are generally the best way of getting around Sicily. Buses offer faster, more direct service on certain intercity routes, such as Catania to Agrigento, Syracuse to Palermo or Palermo to Trapani, and they are the only form of public transport serving many interior towns. Note that in rural areas services are sometimes linked to school hours and market opening times, which can mean leaving incredibly early or finding yourself stranded after mid-afternoon. Also watch out for Sundays when services are cut to the bone.

In larger cities, the main intercity bus companies have ticket offices or operate through agencies. In smaller towns and villages, bus tickets are often sold in bars or on the bus.

Sicily's major bus companies cover most destinations:

AST (Azienda Siciliana Trasporti;☑091 620 81 11; www.astsicilia.it)

Interbus (☑091 617 57 94; www.interbus.it)

Lumia (☑0922 2 04 14; www. autolineelumia.it)

SAIS Autolinee (☑800 211020; www.saisautolinee.it)

SAIS Trasporti (☑091 617 11 41; www.saistrasporti.it)

Salemi (☑0923 98 11 20; www. autoservizisalemi.it)

While it is not usually necessary to make reservations on buses, it's best to buy your ticket in advance during peak travel periods or for time-sensitive journeys – for example, if you're returning from Taormina to catch a plane at Catania's Fontanarossa Airport.

Car & Motorcycle

There's no escaping the fact that a car makes getting around Sicily much easier.

That said, driving on the island is not exactly stress-free, particularly in the big cities where traffic congestion, one-way systems and impossible parking can stretch nerves to the limit. But once on the open road, things calm down considerably and the going is generally pretty good.

Roads vary in quality. Some, like the main *autostrade* (motorways), are excellent, but small rural roads can be dodgy, especially after heavy rain, when axle-breaking potholes appear and landslides lead to road closures.

Sicily has a limited network of motorways, which you'll see prefixed by an A on maps and signs on the island. The most convenient east–west link is the A19, which runs from Catania to Palermo. The A18 runs along the Ionian Coast between Messina and Catania, while the A20 runs along the Tyrrhenian Coast from Palermo to Messina. Both the A18 and A20 are toll roads. The toll-free A29, along with its offshoot, the A29D, goes from Palermo to the west coast, linking the capital with Trapani, Marsala and Mazara del Vallo.

After *autostrade*, the best roads are the *strade statali* (state roads), represented on maps as 'SS'. *Strade provinciali* (provincial roads) are sometimes little more than country lanes, but provide access to small towns and villages and some beautiful scenery. They are represented as 'SP' on maps.

Automobile Associations

The Italian automobile association is called the Automobile Club d'Italia (ACI; www.aci.it). Members and nonmembers alike can call ACI for 24-hour roadside assistance (☑803116), though nonmembers will be charged a fee for this service.

Driving Licenses

When driving in Sicily, always carry your driving licence, the vehicle's registration papers and proof of third-party (liability) insurance. All EU member states' driving licences are recognised in Sicily. Licences from the United States and most other major countries are valid in Sicily (including for rental vehicles), but drivers are technically required to provide an International Driving Licence or a certified translation of their home country license if stopped by police.

Fuel

Petrol stations are located on the main *autostrade* (motorways) and state roads, as well as in cities and towns. The bigger ones are often open 24 hours, but smaller stations generally open 7am to 7pm Monday to Saturday with a lunchtime break. Many stations also offer self-service. To use the self-service pumps, you'll need to insert a bill (in denominations of €5, €10, €20 or €50) or an approved credit or debit card into the machine and then press the number of the pump you're using.

The cost of fuel in Sicily is high – at the time of research €1.52 for a litre of unleaded petrol (*benzina senza piombo*) or €1.42 for diesel (*gasolio*).

If you run into mechanical problems, the nearest petrol station should be able to suggest a local mechanic; a few have workshops on-site.

Hire

Several major car-rental firms are represented at Palermo, Catania, Trapani and Comiso airports and in major cities. Agencies in seaside resorts also rent out scooters and motorcycles.

Avis (☑06 452 10 83 91; www.avisautonoleggio.it)

Budget (☑199 307373; www.budgetautonoleggio.it)

Europcar (☑199 307030; www.europcar.it)

Hertz (☑02 6968 2445; www.hertz.it)

Maggiore (☑199 151120; www.maggiore.it)

Sicily by Car (☑800 334440; www.sicilybycar.it)

Sixt (☑02 9475 7979; www.sixt.it)

Rates for advance online reservations made from overseas are often significantly better than those offered on-site. Similarly, airport agencies sometimes charge more than city-centre branches.

To hire a car, you'll need to be over 21 (over 23 for some companies) and have a credit card; for a scooter, the minimum age is generally 18. When hiring, always make sure you understand what's covered in the rental agreement (unlimited mileage, tax, insurance, collision-damage waiver and so on) and what your liabilities are. It is also a good idea to get fully comprehensive insurance to cover any untoward bumps or scrapes that are quite likely to happen.

Reputable car-hire companies will usually give you an emergency number to call in the case of breakdown.

Note that most hire cars have manual transmission.

Parking

Parking in Sicilian towns and cities can be difficult. Blue lines by the side of the road denote pay-and-display parking – buy tickets at the meters or from tobacconists – with rates ranging from €0.50 to €1 per hour. Typically, charges are applied Monday through Saturday between 8am and 1.30pm and then from 3.30pm to 8pm – outside these hours you can leave your car free. You'll also find enclosed car parks in the main cities and ports, charging daily rates of €10 and up. As a general rule, the easiest time to find street parking is the early afternoon between 2pm and 4pm.

Fines for parking violations are applied and your car-rental agency will use your credit card to settle any outstanding charges.

Road Rules

Contrary to appearances there are road rules in Sicily.

➡ Drive on the right and overtake on the left.

➡ Seat belt use (front and rear) is required. Violators are subject to an on-the-spot fine.

➡ Wear a helmet when riding all two-wheeled vehicles.

➡ Carry a warning triangle and fluorescent vest to be worn in the event of an emergency.

➡ Keep your blood-alcohol limit under 0.05% while driving.

➡ Keep your blood-alcohol limit at zero while driving if a new licence holder (those with a licence for less than three years).

➡ Do not use hand-held mobile phones while driving.

➡ Day or night, turn on your headlights while driving on roads outside municipalities.

Toll Roads

Sicily's toll roads are the Messina–Palermo A20 *autostrada* and the Messina–Catania A18. Messina to Palermo costs €10.10, Messina to Catania €3.70. The process is simple: pick up a ticket at the automatic machine as you get on the autostrada, then pay as you exit, either to a toll agent or by cash, coins or credit card at a machine. Make sure you get into the correct lane when you exit – follow the white signs illustrated with a black hand holding bank notes; lanes marked exclusively with the blue-on-yellow 'Telepass' logo are only open to Italian residents who participate in the Telepass prepaid toll program. Credit cards are

SPEED LIMITS
....
Autostrade 130km/h

Main, nonurban highways 110km/h

Secondary, nonurban roads 90km/h

Built-up areas 50km/h

not always accepted, so have cash on hand.

Local Transport

Taxis & Ridesharing

Official taxis are white, metered and expensive. If you need a taxi, you can usually find one in taxi ranks at train and bus stations or by telephoning for one. If you book a taxi by phone, you will be charged for the trip the driver makes to reach you.

Rates vary from city to city, but as a rule the minimum charge is about €4. There's also an array of supplementary charges for night-time/Sunday rides, to/from the airport, extra luggage etc. Reckon on about €10 to €15 for most urban routes.

Uber is practically non-existent in Sicily. The most common app is BlaBlaCar, which is a carpooling service.

Train

Rail travel is reasonably priced and generally reliable, though routes are limited and trains are slow compared to their counterparts in mainland Italy. Services are all operated by **Trenitalia** (☑892021; www.trenitalia.com), except for those that trundle around the base of Mt Etna, which are run by the private **Ferrovia Circumetnea** (☑095 54 11 11; www.circumetnea.it).

There are several types of train: Intercity (IC) or Intercity Night (ICN) trains are the fastest, stopping only at major stations; *espresso* trains stop at all but the most minor stations, while *region-*

ale trains are the slowest of all, halting at every stop on the line.

Note that all tickets must be validated before you board your train. Simply insert them in the yellow machines installed at the entrance to all train platforms. If you don't validate them, you risk a fine. This rule does not apply to tickets purchased outside Italy.

Classes & Costs

There are 1st- and 2nd-class seats on Intercity trains but not on the slower *espresso* and *regionale* trains. Travel on Intercity trains means paying a supplement, which is included in the ticket and determined by the distance you are travelling. If you have a *regionale* ticket and end up hopping on an Intercity train, you'll have to pay the difference on board.

Sample prices for one-way train fares are as follows (return fares are generally double):

From	To	Fare (€)
Catania	Syracuse	7
Catania	Messina	7.50
Palermo	Agrigento	9
Palermo	Catania	13.50
Palermo	Messina	13

Reservations

There's no need to reserve tickets for travel within Sicily, but if you're heading up to the Italian mainland on weekends or during holiday periods, it's probably a good idea. A small booking fee for reserved seats generally applies. Tickets can be booked online, at station ticket booths or at most travel agencies.

Language

Standard Italian is Sicily's official language and is spoken almost universally on the island, although most locals speak Sicilian among themselves. Sicilian is referred to as an Italian dialect, but is sufficiently different for some to consider it a language in its own right. Sicilians will readily revert to standard Italian when speaking to anyone from the mainland or abroad, though with the occasional Sicilian word thrown in.

The sounds used in spoken Italian can all be found in English. If you read our coloured pronunciation guides as if they were English, you'll be understood. The stressed syllables are indicated with italics. Note that ai is pronounced as in 'aisle', ay as in 'say', ow as in 'how', dz as the 'ds' in 'lids', and that r is a strong and rolled sound. Keep in mind that Italian consonants can have a stronger, emphatic pronunciation – if the consonant is written as a double letter, it should be pronounced a little stronger, eg *sonno son·no* (sleep) versus *sono so·no* (I am).

BASICS

In this chapter the polite/informal and masculine/feminine options are included where necessary, indicated with 'pol/inf' and 'm/f' respectively.

Hello.	*Buongiorno.*	bwon·*jor*·no
Goodbye.	*Arrivederci.*	a·ree·ve·*der*·chee
Yes./No.	*Sì./No.*	see/no

WANT MORE?

For in-depth language information and handy phrases, check out Lonely Planet's *Italian Phrasebook*. You'll find it at **shop.lonelyplanet.com**, or you can buy Lonely Planet's iPhone phrasebooks at the Apple App Store.

Excuse me.	*Mi scusi.* (pol)	mee *skoo*·zee
	Scusami. (inf)	*skoo*·za·mee
Sorry.	*Mi dispiace.*	mee dees·*pya*·che
Please.	*Per favore.*	per fa·vo·re
Thank you.	*Grazie.*	*gra*·tsye
You're welcome.	*Prego.*	*pre*·go

How are you?
Come sta/stai? (pol/inf)   *ko*·me sta/stai

Fine. And you?
Bene. E Lei/tu? (pol/inf)   *be*·ne e lay/too

What's your name?
Come si chiama? pol   *ko*·me see *kya*·ma
Come ti chiami? inf   *ko*·me tee *kya*·mee

My name is ...
Mi chiamo ...   mee *kya*·mo ...

Do you speak English?
Parla/Parli   *par*·la/*par*·lee
inglese? (pol/inf)   een·*gle*·ze

I don't understand.
Non capisco.   non ka·*pee*·sko

ACCOMMODATION

Do you have a ... room?	*Avete una camera ...?*	a·ve·te *oo*·na *ka*·me·ra ...
double	*doppia con letto matrimoniale*	*do*·pya kon *le*·to ma·*tree*·mo·*nya*·le
single	*singola*	*seen*·go·la

How much is it per ...?	*Quanto costa per ...?*	*kwan*·to *kos*·ta per ...
night	*una notte*	*oo*·na *no*·te
person	*persona*	per·*so*·na

Is breakfast included?
La colazione è compresa?   la ko·la·*tsyo*·ne e kom·*pre*·sa

air-con	*aria*	*a·*rya
	condizionata	kon·dee·tsyo·*na·*ta
bathroom	*bagno*	*ba·*nyo
campsite	*campeggio*	kam·*pe·*jo
guesthouse	*pensione*	pen·*syo·*ne
hotel	*albergo*	al·*ber·*go
youth hostel	*ostello della*	os·*te·*lo de·la
	gioventù	jo·ven·*too*
window	*finestra*	fee·*nes·*tra

DIRECTIONS

Where's ...?
Dov'è ...? do·ve ...

What's the address?
Qual'è l'indirizzo? kwa·le leen·dee·*ree·*tso

Could you please write it down?
Può scriverlo, pwo *skree·*ver·lo
per favore? per fa·*vo·*re

Can you show me (on the map)?
Può mostrarmi pwo mos·*trar·*mee
(sulla pianta)? (soo·la pyan·ta)

at the corner	*all'angolo*	a·*lan·*go·lo
at the traffic lights	*al semaforo*	al se·*ma·*fo·ro
behind	*dietro*	*dye·*tro
far	*lontano*	lon·*ta·*no
in front of	*davanti a*	da·*van·*tee a
left	*a sinistra*	a see·*nee·*stra
near	*vicino*	vee·*chee·*no
opposite	*di fronte a*	dee *fron·*te a
right	*a destra*	a *de·*stra
straight ahead	*sempre diritto*	*sem·*pre dee·*ree·*to

EATING & DRINKING

What would you recommend?
Cosa mi consiglia? ko·za mee kon·*see·*lya

What's in that dish?
Quali ingredienti kwa·li een·gre·*dyen·*tee
ci sono in chee so·no een
questo piatto? kwe·sto pya·to

What's the local speciality?
Qual'è la specialità kwa·le la spe·cha·lee·*ta*
di questa regione? dee kwe·sta re·*jo·*ne

That was delicious!
Era squisito! e·ra skwee·*zee·*to

Cheers!
Salute! sa·*loo·*te

Please bring the bill.
Mi porta il conto, mee *por·*ta eel *kon·*to
per favore? per fa·*vo·*re

To get by in Italian, mix and match these simple patterns with words of your choice:

When's (the next flight)?
A che ora è a ke o·ra e
(il prossimo volo)? (eel pro·*see·*mo vo·lo)

Where's (the station)?
Dov'è (la stazione)? do·ve (la sta·*tsyo·*ne)

I'm looking for (a hotel).
Sto cercando sto cher·*kan·*do
(un albergo). (oon al·*ber·*go)

Do you have (a map)?
Ha (una pianta)? a (oo·na pyan·ta)

Is there (a toilet)?
C'è (un gabinetto)? che (oon ga·bee·*ne·*to)

I'd like (a coffee).
Vorrei (un caffè). vo·ray (oon ka·fe)

I'd like (to hire a car).
Vorrei (noleggiare vo·ray (no·le·*ja·*re
una macchina)? oo·na ma·*kee·*na)

Can I (enter)?
Posso (entrare)? po·so (en·*tra·*re)

Could you please (help me)?
Può (aiutarmi), pwo (a·yoo·*tar·*mee)
per favore? per fa·*vo·*re

Do I have to (book a seat)?
Devo (prenotare de·vo (pre·no·*ta·*re
un posto)? oon po·sto)

I'd like to reserve a table for ...	*Vorrei prenotare un tavolo per ...*	vo·ray pre·no·*ta·*re oon *ta·*vo·lo per ...
(eight) o'clock	*le (otto)*	le (o·to)
(two) people	*(due) persone*	(doo·e) per·*so·*ne

I don't eat ...	*Non mangio ...*	non *man·*jo ...
eggs	*uova*	*wo·*va
fish	*pesce*	*pe·*she
nuts	*noci*	*no·*chee
(red) meat	*carne (rossa)*	*kar·*ne (ro·sa)

Key Words

| **bar** | *locale* | lo·*ka·*le |
| **bottle** | *bottiglia* | bo·*tee·*lya |

breakfast	prima colazione	pree·ma ko·la·tsyo·ne
cafe	bar	bar
cold	freddo	fre·do
dinner	cena	che·na
drink list	lista delle bevande	lee·sta de·le be·van·de
fork	forchetta	for·ke·ta
glass	bicchiere	bee·kye·re
grocery store	alimentari	a·lee·men·ta·ree
hot	caldo	kal·do
knife	coltello	kol·te·lo
lunch	pranzo	pran·dzo
market	mercato	mer·ka·to
menu	menù	me·noo
plate	piatto	pya·to
restaurant	ristorante	ree·sto·ran·te
spicy	piccante	pee·kan·te
spoon	cucchiaio	koo·kya·yo
vegetarian (food)	vegetariano	ve·je·ta·rya·no
with	con	kon
without	senza	sen·tsa

Meat & Fish

beef	manzo	man·dzo
chicken	pollo	po·lo
duck	anatra	a·na·tra
fish	pesce	pe·she
herring	aringa	a·reen·ga
lamb	agnello	a·nye·lo
lobster	aragosta	a·ra·gos·ta
meat	carne	kar·ne
mussels	cozze	ko·tse
oysters	ostriche	o·stree·ke
pork	maiale	ma·ya·le
prawn	gambero	gam·be·ro
salmon	salmone	sal·mo·ne
scallops	capasante	ka·pa·san·te
seafood	frutti di mare	froo·tee dee ma·re
shrimp	gambero	gam·be·ro
squid	calamari	ka·la·ma·ree
trout	trota	tro·ta
tuna	tonno	to·no
turkey	tacchino	ta·kee·no
veal	vitello	vee·te·lo

Fruit & Vegetables

apple	mela	me·la
beans	fagioli	fa·jo·lee
cabbage	cavolo	ka·vo·lo
capsicum	peperone	pe·pe·ro·ne
carrot	carota	ka·ro·ta
cauliflower	cavolfiore	ka·vol·fyo·re
cucumber	cetriolo	che·tree·o·lo
fruit	frutta	froo·ta
grapes	uva	oo·va
lemon	limone	lee·mo·ne
lentils	lenticchie	len·tee·kye
mushroom	funghi	foon·gee
nuts	noci	no·chee
onions	cipolle	chee·po·le
orange	arancia	a·ran·cha
peach	pesca	pe·ska
peas	piselli	pee·ze·lee
pineapple	ananas	a·na·nas
plum	prugna	proo·nya
potatoes	patate	pa·ta·te
spinach	spinaci	spee·na·chee
tomatoes	pomodori	po·mo·do·ree
vegetables	verdura	ver·doo·ra

Other

bread	pane	pa·ne
butter	burro	boo·ro
cheese	formaggio	for·ma·jo
eggs	uova	wo·va
honey	miele	mye·le
ice	ghiaccio	gya·cho
jam	marmellata	mar·me·la·ta
noodles	pasta	pas·ta
oil	olio	o·lyo

SIGNS

Aperto	Open
Chiuso	Closed
Donne	Women
Entrata/Ingresso	Entrance
Gabinetti/Servizi	Toilets
Informazioni	Information
Proibito/Vietato	Prohibited
Uomini	Men
Uscita	Exit

pepper	pepe	pe·pe
rice	riso	ree·zo
salt	sale	sa·le
soup	minestra	mee·nes·tra
soy sauce	salsa di soia	sal·sa dee so·ya
sugar	zucchero	tsoo·ke·ro
vinegar	aceto	a·che·to

Drinks

beer	birra	bee·ra
coffee	caffè	ka·fe
(orange) juice	succo (d'arancia)	soo·ko (da·ran·cha)
milk	latte	la·te
red wine	vino rosso	vee·no ro·so
soft drink	bibita	bee·bee·ta
tea	tè	te
(mineral) water	acqua (minerale)	a·kwa (mee·ne·ra·le)
white wine	vino bianco	vee·no byan·ko

EMERGENCIES

Help!
Aiuto! — a·yoo·to

Leave me alone!
Lasciami in pace! — la·sha·mee een pa·che

I'm lost.
Mi sono perso/a. (m/f) — mee so·no per·so/a

Call the police!
Chiami la polizia! — kya·mee la po·lee·tsee·a

Call a doctor!
Chiami un medico! — kya·mee oon me·dee·ko

Where are the toilets?
Dove sono i gabinetti? — do·ve so·no ee ga·bee·ne·tee

I'm sick.
Mi sento male. — mee sen·to ma·le

It hurts here.
Mi fa male qui. — mee fa ma·le kwee

I'm allergic to ...
Sono allergico/a a ... (m/f) — so·no a·ler·jee·ko/a a ...

QUESTION WORDS

How?	Come?	ko·me
What?	Che cosa?	ke ko·za
When?	Quando?	kwan·do
Where?	Dove?	do·ve
Who?	Chi?	kee
Why?	Perché?	per·ke

SHOPPING & SERVICES

I'd like to buy ...
Vorrei comprare ... — vo·ray kom·pra·re ...

I'm just looking.
Sto solo guardando. — sto so·lo gwar·dan·do

Can I look at it?
Posso dare un'occhiata? — po·so da·re oo·no·kya·ta

How much is this?
Quanto costa questo? — kwan·to kos·ta kwe·sto

It's too expensive.
È troppo caro. — e tro·po ka·ro

Can you lower the price?
Può farmi lo sconto? — pwo far·mee lo skon·to

There's a mistake in the bill.
C'è un errore nel conto. — che oo·ne·ro·re nel kon·to

ATM	Bancomat	ban·ko·mat
credit card	carta di credito	kar·ta dee kre·dee·to
post office	ufficio postale	oo·fee·cho pos·ta·le
tourist office	ufficio del turismo	oo·fee·cho del too·reez·mo

TIME & DATES

What time is it?
Che ora è? — ke o·ra e

It's one o'clock.
È l'una. — e loo·na

It's (two) o'clock.
Sono le (due). — so·no le (doo·e)

Half past (one).
(L'una) e mezza. — (loo·na) e me·dza

in the morning	di mattina	dee ma·tee·na
in the afternoon	di pomeriggio	dee po·me·ree·jo
in the evening	di sera	dee se·ra

yesterday	ieri	ye·ree
today	oggi	o·jee
tomorrow	domani	do·ma·nee

Monday	lunedì	loo·ne·dee
Tuesday	martedì	mar·te·dee
Wednesday	mercoledì	mer·ko·le·dee
Thursday	giovedì	jo·ve·dee
Friday	venerdì	ve·ner·dee
Saturday	sabato	sa·ba·to
Sunday	domenica	do·me·nee·ka

NUMBERS

1	uno	oo·no
2	due	doo·e
3	tre	tre
4	quattro	kwa·tro
5	cinque	cheen·kwe
6	sei	say
7	sette	se·te
8	otto	o·to
9	nove	no·ve
10	dieci	dye·chee
20	venti	ven·tee
30	trenta	tren·ta
40	quaranta	kwa·ran·ta
50	cinquanta	cheen·kwan·ta
60	sessanta	se·san·ta
70	settanta	se·tan·ta
80	ottanta	o·tan·ta
90	novanta	no·van·ta
100	cento	chen·to
1000	mille	mee·lel

January	gennaio	je·na·yo
February	febbraio	fe·bra·yo
March	marzo	mar·tso
April	aprile	a·pree·le
May	maggio	ma·jo
June	giugno	joo·nyo
July	luglio	loo·lyo
August	agosto	a·gos·to
September	settembre	se·tem·bre
October	ottobre	o·to·bre
November	novembre	no·vem·bre
December	dicembre	dee·chem·bre

TRANSPORT

Public Transport

At what time does the ... leave/arrive?	A che ora parte/ arriva ...?	a ke o·ra par·te/ a·ree·va ...
boat	la nave	la na·ve
bus	l'autobus	low·to·boos
ferry	il traghetto	eel tra·ge·to
plane	l'aereo	la·e·re·o
train	il treno	eel tre·no

... ticket	un biglietto ...	oon bee·lye·to
one-way	di sola andata	dee so·la an·da·ta
return	di andata e ritorno	dee an·da·ta e ree·tor·no

bus stop	fermata dell'autobus	fer·ma·ta del ow·to·boos
platform	binario	bee·na·ryo
ticket office	biglietteria	bee·lye·te·ree·a
timetable	orario	o·ra·ryo
train station	stazione ferroviaria	sta·tsyo·ne fe·ro·vyar·ya

Does it stop at ...?
Si ferma a ...?   see fer·ma a ...

Please tell me when we get to ...
Mi dica per favore   mee dee·ka per fa·vo·re
quando arriviamo a ...   kwan·do a·ree·vya·mo a ...

I want to get off here.
Voglio scendere qui.   vo·lyo shen·de·re kwee

Driving & Cycling

I'd like to hire a/an ...	Vorrei noleggiare un/una ... (m/f)	vo·ray no·le·ja·re oon/oo·na ...
4WD	fuoristrada (m)	fwo·ree·stra·da
bicycle	bicicletta (f)	bee·chee·kle·ta
car	macchina (f)	ma·kee·na
motorbike	moto (f)	mo·to

bicycle pump	pompa della bicicletta	pom·pa de·la bee·chee·kle·ta
child seat	seggiolino	se·jo·lee·no
helmet	casco	kas·ko
mechanic	meccanico	me·ka·nee·ko
petrol/gas	benzina	ben·dzee·na
service station	stazione di servizio	sta·tsyo·ne dee ser·vee·tsyo

Is this the road to ...?
Questa strada porta a ...? kwe·sta stra·da por·ta a ...

(How long) Can I park here?
(Per quanto tempo)   (per kwan·to tem·po)
Posso parcheggiare qui?   po·so par·ke·ja·re kwee

The car/motorbike has broken down (at ...).
La macchina/moto si è   la ma·kee·na/mo·to see e
guastata (a ...).   gwas·ta·ta (a ...)

I have a flat tyre.
Ho una gomma bucata.   o oo·na go·ma boo·ka·ta

I've run out of petrol.
Ho esaurito la   o e·zow·ree·to la
benzina.   ben·dzee·na

GLOSSARY

abbazia – abbey
affi ttacamere – rooms for rent
agora – marketplace, meeting place
agriturismo – farm stay
albergo – hotel
alimentari – grocery shop, delicatessen
anfi teatro – amphitheatre
ara – altar
arco – arch
autostrada – motorway, freeway

badia – abbey
baglio – manor house
bancomat – ATM
belvedere – panoramic viewpoint
benzina – petrol
borgo – ancient town or village; sometimes it's used to mean the equivalent of via

cambio – money exchange
campanile – bell tower
campo – field
cappella – chapel
carabinieri – police with military and civil duties
Carnevale – carnival period between Epiphany and Lent
casa – house
cava – quarry
centro – centre
chiesa – church
città – town, city
clientelismo – system of political patronage
comune – equivalent to municipality or county; town or city council
contrada – district
corso – main street, avenue
cortile – courtyard
Cosa Nostra – Our Thing; alternative name for the Mafia

diretto – direct; slow train
duomo – cathedral

enoteca – wine bar, wine shop

fangho – mud bath
faraglione – rock tower
ferrovia – train station
festa – festival
fiume – river
fontana – fountain
fossa – pit, hole
funivia – cable car

gola – gorge
golfo – gulf
grotta – cave
guardia medica – emergency doctor service

IC – Intercity; fast train
interregionale – long-distance train that stops frequently
isola – island

lago – lake
largo – small square
latomia – small quarry
lido – beach
locale – slow local train; also called *regionale*
locanda – inn, small hotel
lungomare – seafront road, promenade

mare – sea
mercato – market
molo – wharf
monte – mountain
municipio – town hall, municipal offices
museo – museum

Natale – Christmas

oratorio – oratory
ospedale – hospital
osteria – inn

palazzo – palace, mansion
parco – park
Pasqua – Easter
passeggiata – evening stroll
pensione – small hotel
piazza – square
piazzale – large open square
ponte – bridge
porta – gate, door

questura – police station

reale – royal
regionale – slow local train; also called *locale*
rifugio – mountain hut
riserva naturale – nature reserve
rocca – fortress; rock

sagra – festival, generally dedicated to one food item or theme
sala – room
santuario – sanctuary
scalinata – staircase, steps
spiaggia – beach
stazione – station
strada – street, road

teatro – theatre
tempio – temple
tonnara – tuna-processing plant
torre – tower
traghetto – ferry, boat
treno – train

via – street, road
viale – avenue
vicolo – alley, alleyway

Behind the Scenes

SEND US YOUR FEEDBACK

We love to hear from travellers – your comments keep us on our toes and help make our books better. Our well-travelled team reads every word on what you loved or loathed about this book. Although we cannot reply individually to your submissions, we always guarantee that your feedback goes straight to the appropriate authors, in time for the next edition. Each person who sends us information is thanked in the next edition – the most useful submissions are rewarded with a selection of digital PDF chapters.

Visit **lonelyplanet.com/contact** to submit your updates and suggestions or to ask for help. Our award-winning website also features inspirational travel stories, news and discussions.

Note: We may edit, reproduce and incorporate your comments in Lonely Planet products such as guidebooks, websites and digital products, so let us know if you don't want your comments reproduced or your name acknowledged. For a copy of our privacy policy visit lonelyplanet.com/privacy.

OUR READERS

Many thanks to the travellers who used the last edition and wrote to us with helpful hints, useful advice and interesting anecdotes: Stefano Amato, Clare Argent, Charlotte Badarello, Sven, Christina and Alena Behrendt, Rebecca Dangerfield, Carla Fette, Jennifer Garner, Rasmus Holmer, Marieke Martens, Liam McKeevor, Franziska Moll, Thorsten Nieberg, Linn Baalsrud Pradères, David Smallwood, Clare Thrush, Giorgia Tortora

WRITER THANKS

Gregor Clark

Grazie mille to the many dozens of people who shared their love and knowledge of Sicily with me, especially Fausto Ceschi, Angela, Francesco, Fabiana, Micol, Stefano, Mark and Giovanna. Back in Vermont, big hugs to Gaen, Meigan and Chloe, who always make coming home the best part of the trip.

Brett Atkinson

Exploring southern Italy and Sicily with my Lonely Planet hat on was a great experience thanks to Anna Rita in Bari, Luisa in Lecce and Domenico in Reggio Calabria. Thanks also to Amy in Matera for helping me negotiate the town's storied laneways, and to Tony in Vieste for securing me a slow boat to the Isole Tremiti. Special thanks to Anna Tyler for the commission, and to Carol on our gelato- and aperitivi-fuelled reconnaissance trip 12 months earlier.

Cristian Bonetto

Grazie infinite to all those who shared their love and intimate knowledge of the Mezzogiorno. Special thanks to Ornella Tuzzolino, Giorgio Ferravioli and Carla Bellavista, Pierfrancesco Palazzotto, Lorenzo Chiaramonte, Rosario Fillari, Giorgio Puglisi, Gennaro Mattiucci, Ernesto Magri, Giovanni Gurrieri, Joe Brizzi, Giuseppe Savà, Luigi Nifosì, Antonio Adamo, Cesare Setmani, Norma Gritti and Cristina Delli Fiori. .

Nicola Williams

My teeny chunk of Sicily is dedicated to my very own expert, trilingual, family-travel research team – Mischa, Kaya, Mathias (and Niko, vicariously from his desk) – who joined me for a 2000km+ road trip exploring every last nook, cranny, lemon grove and salt pan of the island's wild west. *Grazie mille* to every islander who shared their love and insider knowledge with us, including Gaetana and Giuseppe at Favignana's La Casa del Limoneta, the team at Prokite Alby Rondina, Paolo and Vittorio.

ACKNOWLEDGMENTS

Climate map data adapted from Peel MC, Finlayson BL & McMahon TA (2007) 'Updated World Map of the Köppen-Geiger Climate Classification', *Hydrology and Earth System Sciences*, 11, 1633–44.

Cover photograph: Interior of Chiesa e Monastero di Santa Caterina d'Alessandria, Palermo, Jonathon Stokes/Lonely Planet ©

THIS BOOK

This 8th edition of Lonely Planet's *Sicily* guidebook was curated by Gregor Clark and researched and written by Gregor Clark, Brett Atkinson, Cristian Bonetto and Nicola Williams. The 7th edition was written by Gregor Clark and Cristian Bonetto, and the 6th edition by Gregor Clark and Vesna Maric. This guidebook was produced by the following:

Destination Editor Anna Tyler

Senior Product Editors Elizabeth Jones, Sandie Kestell

Regional Senior Cartographer Anthony Phelan

Product Editor Bruce Evans

Book Designer Jessica Rose

Assisting Editors Kate Daly, Andrea Dobbin, Victoria Harrison, Gabrielle Innes, Kate Morgan, Lauren O'Connell, Fionnuala Twomey, Simon Williamson

Assisting Cartographers Hunor Csutoros, Julie Dodkins

Cover Researcher Naomi Parker

Thanks to Imogen Bannister, Alexandra Bruzzese, Gemma Graham, Martin Heng, Liz Heynes, Kate James, Virginia Moreno, Joe Revill, Wibowo Rusli, Sophia Seymour, Jo-Ann Titmarsh, Brana Vladisavljevic

Index

Map Legend

Sights
- Beach
- Bird Sanctuary
- Buddhist
- Castle/Palace
- Christian
- Confucian
- Hindu
- Islamic
- Jain
- Jewish
- Monument
- Museum/Gallery/Historic Building
- Ruin
- Shinto
- Sikh
- Taoist
- Winery/Vineyard
- Zoo/Wildlife Sanctuary
- Other Sight

Activities, Courses & Tours
- Bodysurfing
- Diving
- Canoeing/Kayaking
- Course/Tour
- Sento Hot Baths/Onsen
- Skiing
- Snorkelling
- Surfing
- Swimming/Pool
- Walking
- Windsurfing
- Other Activity

Sleeping
- Sleeping
- Camping
- Hut/Shelter

Eating
- Eating

Drinking & Nightlife
- Drinking & Nightlife
- Cafe

Entertainment
- Entertainment

Shopping
- Shopping

Information
- Bank
- Embassy/Consulate
- Hospital/Medical
- Internet
- Police
- Post Office
- Telephone
- Toilet
- Tourist Information
- Other Information

Geographic
- Beach
- Gate
- Hut/Shelter
- Lighthouse
- Lookout
- Mountain/Volcano
- Oasis
- Park
- Pass
- Picnic Area
- Waterfall

Population
- Capital (National)
- Capital (State/Province)
- City/Large Town
- Town/Village

Transport
- Airport
- Border crossing
- Bus
- Cable car/Funicular
- Cycling
- Ferry
- Metro station
- Monorail
- Parking
- Petrol station
- S-Bahn/Subway station
- Taxi
- T-bane/Tunnelbana station
- Train station/Railway
- Tram
- U-Bahn/Underground station
- Other Transport

Routes
- Tollway
- Freeway
- Primary
- Secondary
- Tertiary
- Lane
- Unsealed road
- Road under construction
- Plaza/Mall
- Steps
- Tunnel
- Pedestrian overpass
- Walking Tour
- Walking Tour detour
- Path/Walking Trail

Boundaries
- International
- State/Province
- Disputed
- Regional/Suburb
- Marine Park
- Cliff
- Wall

Hydrography
- River, Creek
- Intermittent River
- Canal
- Water
- Dry/Salt/Intermittent Lake
- Reef

Areas
- Airport/Runway
- Beach/Desert
- Cemetery (Christian)
- Cemetery (Other)
- Glacier
- Mudflat
- Park/Forest
- Sight (Building)
- Sportsground
- Swamp/Mangrove

Note: Not all symbols displayed above appear on the maps in this book

OUR STORY

A beat-up old car, a few dollars in the pocket and a sense of adventure. In 1972 that's all Tony and Maureen Wheeler needed for the trip of a lifetime – across Europe and Asia overland to Australia. It took several months, and at the end – broke but inspired – they sat at their kitchen table writing and stapling together their first travel guide, *Across Asia on the Cheap*. Within a week they'd sold 1500 copies. Lonely Planet was born.

Today, Lonely Planet has offices in Franklin, London, Melbourne, Oakland, Dublin, Beijing and Delhi, with more than 600 staff and writers. We share Tony's belief that 'a great guidebook should do three things: inform, educate and amuse'.

OUR WRITERS

Gregor Clark
Aeolian Islands, Lampedusa, Pantelleria, Tyrrhenian Coast

Gregor Clark is a US-based writer whose love of foreign languages and curiosity have taken him to dozens of countries on five continents. Since 2000, Gregor has regularly contributed to Lonely Planet guides, including titles on Italy and France, as well as cycling guides to Italy. Gregor lives with his wife and two daughters in his current home state of Vermont. Gregor also updated the Plan, Understand and Survival Guide sections of this book.

Brett Atkinson
Central Sicily, Mediterranean Coast

Brett Atkinson is based in Auckland, New Zealand, but is frequently on the road for Lonely Planet. He's a full-time travel and food writer specialising in adventure travel, unusual destinations, and surprising angles on more well-known destinations. Since becoming a Lonely Planet author in 2005, Brett has covered areas as diverse as Vietnam, Sri Lanka, the Czech Republic, New Zealand, Morocco, California and the South Pacific.

Cristian Bonetto
Ionian Coast, Palermo Region, Southeastern Sicily

Cristian has contributed to over 30 Lonely Planet guides to date, including *Italy*, *Venice & the Veneto*, and *Naples & the Amalfi Coast*. Lonely Planet work aside, his musings on travel, food, culture and design appear in numerous publications around the world, including *The Telegraph* (UK) and *Corriere del Mezzogiorno* (Italy). When not on the road, you'll find the reformed playwright and TV script-writer slurping espresso in his beloved hometown, Melbourne. Instagram: rexcat75.

Nicola Williams
Western Sicily

Border-hopping is a way of life for British writer, runner, foodie, art aficionado and mum-of-three Nicola Williams, who has authored more than 50 guidebooks on Paris, Provence, Rome, Tuscany, France, Italy and Switzerland for Lonely Planet, and covers France as a destination expert for the *Telegraph*. She also writes for the *Independent, Guardian*, lonelyplanet.com, Lonely Planet Magazine, French Magazine, Cool Camping France and others. Catch her on the road on Twitter and Instagram at @tripalong.

Published by Lonely Planet Global Limited
CRN 554153
8th edition – February 2020
ISBN 978 1 78657 577 7
© Lonely Planet 2020   Photographs © as indicated 2020
10 9 8 7 6 5 4 3 2 1
Printed in China